Praise for the book when it was first published in 1991:

'A large and intricate body of fundamental research on the narrative sources, deployed with clarity and expertise for which many readers will be extremely grateful.'—*The Times Higher Education Supplement*

In this classic textbook history of early medieval Europe, Roger Collins provides a comprehensive account of the centuries during which Europe changed from being an abstract geographical expression to a new culturally coherent, if politically divided, entity. This essential volume:

- examines how the social, economic and cultural structures of Antiquity were replaced by their medieval equivalents
- defines the European context by looking at the external forces which helped to shape it through conflict
- explores key topics such as the fall of the Roman Empire, the rise of both Christianity and Islam, the Vikings, and the expansion of Latin Christian culture into eastern Europe
- features maps, genealogies, a chronology and bibliography to aid understanding and further study.

This third edition has been fully updated, augmented and revised to take account of the latest scholarship and research on all aspects of the period it covers. The text has also been extensively rewritten to make it more accessible for students. Clear and insightful, this is an invaluable guide to an important era in the history of both Europe and the wider world.

Roger Collins is Honorary Fellow in History at the University of Edinburgh, UK.

HISTORY OF EUROPE

PUBLISHED

Early Medieval Europe 300–1000 (3rd edn)
Roger Collins

Sixteenth Century Europe
Richard Mackenney

Seventeenth Century Europe 1598–1700 (2nd edn)
Thomas Munck

Eighteenth Century Europe (2nd edn)
Jeremy Black

Nineteenth Century Europe
Michael Rapport

History of Europe
Series Standing Order
ISBN 978-0-333–71699–1 hardcover
ISBN 978-0-333–69381–0 paperback
(*outside North America only*)

You can receive future titles in this series as they are published by placing a standing order. Please contact your bookseller or, in the case of difficulty, write to us at the address below with your name and address, the title of the series and the ISBN quoted above.

Customer Services Department, Macmillan Distribution Ltd
Houndmills, Basingstoke, Hampshire RG21 6XS, England

Early Medieval Europe 300–1000

Roger Collins

Third Edition

12,284

First edition 1991
Second edition 1999
Third edition 2010

Published by
RED GLOBE PRESS

Red Globe Press in the UK is an imprint of Springer Nature Limited,
registered in England, company number 785998, of 4 Crinan Street,
London, N1 9XW.

Red Globe Press® is a registered trademark in the United States,
the United Kingdom, Europe and other countries.

ISBN 978–0–230–00673–7   ISBN 978–1–137–01428–3 (eBook)

A catalogue record for this book is available from the British Library.

A catalog record for this book is available from the Library of Congress.

For Judith

Contents

List of maps and genealogical tables

Maps

Genealogical tables

Chronology of main events, 238–1000

British Isles	Western Europe	Eastern Europe	North Africa	Near East
	238 Murder of Maximin I	244 Gordian III deposed by Philip	248 Cyprian Bishop of Carthage	241–72 Reign of Shapur I
	253–60 Reign of Valerian		258 Martyrdom of Cyprian of Carthage	260 Shapur I captures Valerian
	253–68 Reign of Gallienus			
	259–73 'Gallic Empire'	282–3 Reign of Carus		283 Carus's invasion of Persia
	285 Diocletian ruling West	284–305 Reign of Diocletian		
286–93 Reign of Carausius	293 Appointment of Caesars			293–303 Reign of Narseh
293–6 Reign of Allectus				296–7 War with Rome
	305–6 Reign of Constantius I in West	303 Beginning of 'Great Persecution'		309–79 Reign of Shapur II
306 Constantine proclaimed at York	306–37 Rule of Constantine in West	305–11 Reign of Galerius	311 Reign of Alexander	
	312 Battle of Milvian Bridge; conversion of Constantine	313 War between Maximin and Licinius	312 Beginning of Donatist schism	
		314 War with Licinius (308–24)		
		324–37 Constantine ruling East		
		324 Founding of Constantinople		

Chronology of main events, 238–1000 (continued)

British Isles	Western Europe	Eastern Europe	North Africa	Near East
		325 Council of Nicaea		
		330 Dedication of Constantinople		
343 Visit of Constans	**337–50** Reign of Constans	**337–61** Reign of Constantius II	**354** Birth of Augustine	
350–3 Britons support Magnentius	**357–9** Julian's campaigns in Gaul	**350–3** Gallus Caesar at Antioch		**360** War between Rome and Persia
367 Raids by Picts, Irish and Saxons; Hadrian's Wall repaired	**360** Julian's revolt	**361–3** Reign of Julian; 'pagan revival'		**363** Julian's invasion of Persia
	364–75 Reign of Valentinian I	**364–78** Reign of Valens		**364** Jovian's treaty
		376 Visigoths admitted into Balkans		
		378 Battle of Adrianople		
	383–8 Reign of Magnus Maximus	**379–95** Reign of Theodosius I		
	392–4 Reign of Eugenius; 'pagan revival'	**391** Closing of pagan temples	**395–430** Augustine Bishop of Hippo	
	395–423 Reign of Honorius	**395–408** Reign of Arcadius		
	395–408 Ascendancy of Stilicho			
			397 'Augustine writes 'Confessions'; Revolt of Gildo	
406 Reigns of Marcus and Gratian	**406** Vandals, Alans, Sueves cross Rhine		**413–27** Augustine writing 'City of God'	

407–11 Reign of Constantine III	**408** Alaric's Visigoths enter Italy	**418** Council of Carthage		
410 Revolt of Britons	**410** Sack of Rome			
	c. **411–21** Ascendancy of Constantius			
c. **425?** Nynia in Galloway and southern Pictland	**425–55** Reign of Valentinian III	**429** Vandal invasion		
431 Palladius sent to Ireland	**430–53** Ascendancy of Aetius	**439** Vandals take Carthage		
	440–61 Leo I Bishop of Rome	**442** Vandal treaty	**440s** Hun raids on Balkans	
c. **446–53** Appeal to Aetius Saxon treaty	**451** Hun invasion of Gaul		**451** Council of Chalcedon	**459–84** Reign of Peroz Persian wars with the Hephthalites
	455–7 Reign of Avitus	**455** Vandal sack of Rome	**453** Death of Attila	
		468 Attack by eastern fleet fails	**454** battle on the Nedao	
	476/80 Formal end of western Empire	**476–84** Reign of Huneric; 'persecution' of Catholics	**474–91** reign of Zeno	**488–97, 499–531** Reign of Kavad I; Mazdakite movement.
480s/490s? Patrick in Ireland	*c.* **481–c. 511** Reign of Clovis in Gaul			

Chronology of main events, 238–1000 (continued)

British Isles	Western Europe	Eastern Europe	North Africa	Near East
490s Battle of Badon	493 Ostrogothic kingdom established in Italy	527–65 reign of Justinian	523–30 Reign of Hilderic	c. 525 Dhu Nuwas in the Yemen
	507 Battle of Vouillé		533 Imperial conquest of Africa	531–79 Reign of Khusro I
	c. 511 Division of Frankish kingdom			
c. 540 Gildas writing 'De Excidio'	535–53 Wars in Italy, leading to imperial conquest	527–33 'Corpus Iuris Civilis'		540 Persian sack of Antioch
		532 Nika Riots	543 Berber revolt	536 Council of Carthage
		550s Beginning of Slav penetration of Balkans	548 Revolt suppressed	
	558–61 Francia united under Chlotar I (c. 511–61)			
	568 Lombard invasion of Italy under Alboin		563 New Berber revolt	570? Birth of Muhammad
c. 560–c. 590 Career of Ceawlin	569–86 Reign of Leovigild in Spain			
563/5 Foundation of Iona	574–84 'Interregnum' in Lombard kingdom			579–90 Reign of Hormizd IV
	589 Third Council of Toledo			
	590–616 Reign of Agilulf in Italy			
597 Arrival of Augustine in Kent and death of Columba	590–604 Gregory the Great, bishop of Rome			591 Maurice installs Khusro II in Iran

604 Death of Augustine	594 Death of Gregory of Tours	590s Campaigns against Slavs		610 Muhammad's revelations begin
	613 Unification of Francia under Chlotar II	602 Overthrow of Maurice		614 Persian capture of Jerusalem
		610 Fall of Phocas	610 Revolt of Heraclius	622 The Hijra
	620s Isidore writing 'History' and 'Chronicle'			628 Murder of Khusro II
c. 626–55 Reign of Penda in Mercia				630 Muhammad conquers Mecca
629–32 Roman mission in Northumbria	623–38 Rule of Dagobert I in Francia	626 Avar siege of Constantinople		632 Succession of Abu Bakr
632 Death of Edwin	636 Death of Isidore of Seville			634 Succession of 'Umar
633–42 Reign of Oswald in Northumbria	636–52 Reign of Rothari in Italy	636 Battle of Yarmuk		636 Arab conquest of Jerusalem
	639 Thuringian revolt	641 Death of Heraclius I		640 Conquest of Egypt
642–70 Reign of Oswy in Northumbria	649–72 Reign of Reccessuinth	649 Arab conquest of Cyprus	646 Revolt of Exarch Gregory	642 Collapse of Persia before Arabs
655–8 Northumbrian rule over Mercia	654 Issue of 'Forum Iudicum'		647 First Arab raid – death of Gregory	651 Death of last shah, Yazdgard III
			656–61 Caliphate of 'Ali	661–80 Mu'awiya first Umayyad Caliph

Chronology of main events, 238–1000 (continued)

British Isles	Western Europe	Eastern Europe	North Africa	Near East
663/4 Synod of Whitby	**657–664/5** Regency of Balthildis			
	c. 660–73, 675–80, Ebroin Mayor of Palace in Neustria			
		668 Murder of Constans at Syracuse	**669** Arab invasion under 'Uqba	
	673 War between Wamba and Paul	**674–7** Arab siege of Constantinople	**670** Foundation of Kairouan	
685 Battle of Dunnichen		**681** Bulgars established in Balkans	**683** Death of 'Uqba ibn Nafi	**680–4** Civil wars
	687 Battle of Tertry		**698** Arab capture of Carthage	
705 Death of Adamnán			**700–12** Governorship of Musa ibn Nusayr	
709 Death of Aldhelm	**711** Arab invasion of Spain	**711** Overthrow of Justinian II		
	712–44 Reign of Liutprand in Italy	**717** Arab siege of Constantinople and accession of Leo III		
	714–19 Charles Martel gains control of Austrasia and most of Neustria			
716–57 Reign of Æthelbald of Mercia	**720s** Charles restores control east of Rhine			**724–43** Caliphate of Hisham

731 Bede finishes his 'History'

735 Death of Bede

733 Battle of Poitiers

735 Charles occupies Aquitaine

737 and 739 campaigns in Provence

741–7 Joint rule of Pippin III and Carloman

726 Leo III's first Iconoclast measures

741–75 Reign of Constantine V; most intense period of Iconoclasm

743–50 Conflicts in Syria

744–55 Rule of Ibn Habib

749 'Abbasid revolt

750 Umayyads replaced as Caliphs by the 'Abbasids

749–56 Reign of Aistulf in Italy

751 Coronation of Pippin III

756 Umayyad Amirate founded in Spain

754 Death of Boniface

757–96 Reign of Offa of Mercia

762 Foundation of Baghdad

761 Restoration of 'Abbasid rule

766 Death of Archbishop Egbert of York – Alcuin's teacher

768–814 Reign of Charlemagne

772–804 Saxon wars

777 Rustamid kingdom in W. Algeria

775–80 Reign of Leo IV the Khazar

774 Frankish conquest of Lombard kingdom

786–809 Reign of Harun ar-Rashid

789 Idrisid kingdom in Morocco

Chronology of main events, 238–1000 (*continued*)

British Isles	Western Europe	Eastern Europe	North Africa	Near East
		787 Second Council of Nicaea		
793 Viking raid on Lindisfarne	790s Frankish Avar wars	796 Blinding of Constantine VI	800 Aghlabid kingdom in Tunisia	
802–39 Reign of Egbert of Wessex	800 Imperial coronation of Charlemagne	802 Deposition of Empress Irene		
804 Death of Alcuin	808–10 Frankish conflict with Godefred	811 Defeat of Nicephorus by Bulgars		
	814–40 Reign of Louis the Pious	813 Iconoclasm revived by Leo V (813–20)		813–19 Civil war in Caliphate
	817 'Ordinatio Imperii'	814 Death of Khan Krum of Bulgars		
829 Compiling of 'Historia Brittonum'	822 Louis's penance at Attigny	815 Byzantine–Bulgar peace treaty	827–78 Aghlabid conquest of Sicily	
835 Beginning of Viking raids on Wessex	830–4 Civil wars in Francia	830, 837 Byzantine victories over Arabs		836 Samarra becomes 'Abbasid capital
	835 Beginning of Danish raids on Francia			
	840–3 Civil wars in Francia			
	843 Treaty of Verdun	847 End of Iconoclasm		
850/1 First Viking wintering in Britain	858 Louis the German invades West Francia	860 Rhos attack Constantinople	861 Murder of caliph Al Mutawakkil: ascendancy of Turks in the 'Abbasid Caliphate until 945	

867 Danish conquest of York

869/70 Conquest of East Anglia

871–99 Reign of Alfred of Wessex

871 Battle of Ashdown

874 Danes expel Burghred from Mercia

878 Danes' winter attack on Alfred, Battle of Edington

886 Alfred captures London

866–910 Reign of Alfonso the Great in Asturias

871 Byzantines recapture Bari

872 Louis II forced to leave south Italy

875 Charles the Bald crowned emperor

877 Death of Charles the Bald

879–92 Resumed Viking raids in N. Francia

881 Imperial coronation of Charles the Fat

882 Death of Hincmar of Reims

885–6 Viking siege of Paris

886–912 Reign of Leo the Wise

864 Conversion of the Bulgars

867 Macedonian dynasty in Byzantium lasts until 1056

870s Byzantine campaigns in Asia Minor under Basil I (867–86)

868 Aghlabids take Malta

Chronology of main events, 238–1000 (*continued*)

British Isles	Western Europe	Eastern Europe	North Africa	Near East
	887 Deposition of Charles the Fat	**889** Abdication of Boris		
892 New Danish invasion under Haesten		**893** Symeon becomes ruler of the Bulgars		**892** Baghdad restored as 'Abbasid capital
894 Dispersal of the invaders				
909 Wessex armies harry Viking kingdom of York	**911** Charles the Simple's treaty with Rollo; Carolingian dynasty in E. Francia extinct		**909** Aghlabids overthrown by Fatimids	
		912–59 Reign of Constantine VII Porphyrogenitos		
918 Death of Æthellaed; Wessex annexes western Mercia	**912–61** Rule of 'Abd ar-Rahman III in Spain			
920 Wessex conquest of East Mercia	**923** Deposition of Charles the Simple	**917–24** Bulgar attacks on Byzantium		
924–39 Reign of Athelstan	**936** Restoration of Carolingian rule in France with Louis IV(d. 954)	**920–44** Romanos Lecapenos co-emperor		
937 Battle of Brunanburh	**939** Battle of Simancas	**927** Death of Tsar Symeon of the Bulgars; peace made with Byzantium		
944 Edmund of Wessex conquers Northumbria				**945** Buyids take Baghdad; 'Abbasid Caliphs under Buyid control until 1055

948 Eadred of Wessex harries Northumbria	**955** Battle on the Lech	**957** Visit of Olga to Constantinople	**969** Fatimids take Cairo
942–50 Hywel Dda 'King of all Wales'	**960** Hugh Capet 'Duke of the Franks'	**c. 962–71** Rule of Svyatoslav in Kiev	**969–76** Reign of John Zimiskes
961–88 Dunstan Archbishop of Canterbury	**962** Imperial coronation of Otto I	**963–9** Reign of Nicephorus Phocas	**972** Zirid kingdom in Tunisia
	972 Otto (II) marries Byzantine princess	**969** Byzantium regains Antioch	
	973 Coronation of Edgar at Bath	**973–83** Reign of Otto II	
		970 Defeat of 'Rhos' invasion of Thrace	
975–8 Reign of Edward the Martyr	**982** Otto II defeated in southern Italy	**980–1025** Rule of Basil the Bulgar-slayer	
978–1016 Reign of Æthelred the Unready		**978** Vladimir becomes ruler of Kiev	
	987 End of Carolingian rule in France; Hugh Capet crowned	**c. 987** Conversion of Vladimir	
980 Viking raids on southern England	**994** Otto III attains his majority		
991 Battle of Maldon			
990s Mounting Viking attacks	**1000** Conversion of Iceland	**995–1000** Olaf Tryggvason King of Norway	
	1002 Death of Otto III		

Preface to the first edition

At an early stage in thinking about the question of its contents it became clear that this was doomed to be a book that nobody could like, or at least that if some of its readers were pleased with some of it, none of them would possibly enjoy all of it. There are too many variables in the topics, themes, events and personalities that have to be considered for inclusion in a work of this (relative!) brevity that has to concern itself with so extended a chronological period. It became increasingly obvious that the real decisions to be made were those concerning what was to be omitted, and for an author temperamentally inclined to squeezing limited and fragmentary evidence as far as it will permit, if not beyond, this has been a particularly hard task.

Wholesale omissions and the reduction of complicated and nuanced arguments to bald assertions are bound to dissatisfy the discerning reader (as much as the author). In consequence, what is attempted here has to be a personal approach that may at times seem wrong-headed in its concentration on some subjects to the exclusion of others, or its occasional descent into detailed argument that seems out of proportion to the scale of the rest of the book. In that sense I can only fall back on the defence of a great, if idiosyncratic, ninth-century bishop, that was recently echoed by a much revered Master: *Scripsi quod sensi*.

It may seem strange to those unfamiliar with these centuries that such an apology is necessary, and that a period of such apparent remoteness and obscurity should not manage to encompass itself totally in a book of even half the length of this one. Only brief acquaintance, however, will reveal how substantial is the corpus of evidence relating to this time, and how numerous and varied the problems involved in interpreting it. Moreover, the proper understanding of this period involves the historian in moving his gaze on occasion from the western fringes of Iran to Iceland, and from Ethiopia and the edge of the Sahara to the steppes of Central Asia. Such breadth of geographical and chronological vision seems to be less necessary – or less demanded – in later periods.

In trying to present, even in outline, this series of interrelated developments, it was clearly necessary to push the chronological limits of this book back to a period earlier than the beginning of the sixth century, which was where it had first been intended to place them. So much of what was to make up the framework of ideas and institutions which shaped subsequent centuries originated in the fourth century that it would have been perverse to start any later than *c*. 300, and, indeed, a lack of Late Roman background has often led to mistaken and misleading interpretations of Early Medieval History. In turn, the decision to start with the fourth century prompted at least some preliminary investigation of the third.

Doubtless such a process could be prolonged indefinitely, recessing ever further back in time, but there is a certain rightness about commencing such a study as this in the mid-third century, when so many of the principal ideas and institutions of Antiquity were undergoing transformation. This period, however little studied and poorly documented, represents the first formative stage of the major changes that were to follow, and it is here that this enquiry begins.

Where to end was to some extent predetermined by the structure of the series in which this volume is to appear, but the disintegration of the Frankish successor empire in the late ninth and early tenth centuries again makes for something of a natural break, at least in some aspects of the history of medieval Europe. Extending the survey slightly further than I might have liked, the symbolic date of the year 1000 makes an aesthetically pleasing, if intellectually not entirely satisfying terminal point. To a certain extent, then, this book could have been given such a subtitle as 'From Constantine the Great to Charles the Simple'! In practice, treatment of the tenth century offered here is less full than for some earlier periods, largely because a number of the major themes that have their origin in this still relatively little-studied time, are best considered in the wider context of their development in the eleventh and twelfth centuries.

Other topics that might have merited inclusion have been omitted partly because of personal style and inclination on the part of the author, and partly because the lack of other general surveys of this period necessitated the provision of a substantial narrative outline of events, taken together with analysis of and comment on the major sources of evidence. In consequence there may be less economic history to be found in this book than some readers might like. This is conditioned on the author's part by a dislike for generalisation based on an insufficiency of evidence, and this is one of several areas for which the Early Middle Ages are poorly equipped in terms of the survival of source material. It is relatively easy to create general models on the basis of limited evidence, but these tend all too often in such circumstances to rest on a priori assumptions as to how societies and their economies should work. Such determinism should be resisted. It is also preferable to ask questions of evidence that its particular nature fits it to answer rather than ones that the historian feels he *ought* to pose.

The first victims of this book – paradoxically, even before it was ever commissioned – were the successive first-year history students in the University of Liverpool, to whom, between the years 1974 and 1980, elements of it were expounded in the form of lectures on this period. The most recent guinea pigs to have suffered in its genesis are those former students at the Royal School, Bath, to whom the first edition is dedicated. I am very grateful to them for their enthusiasm in the discussion of a range of issues and topics that are considered in the chapters below. My especial thanks must go to Ian Wood, who read all of the first draft of this book, and whose comments and suggestions on it enabled me to avoid many errors. The greatest debt of all, though, is that to my wife Judith McClure, with whom so much of it has been shared in all of the phases just mentioned and whose role in it is truly omnipresent.

Bath   ROGER COLLINS
September 1990

Preface to the second edition

Thanks to that miracle of modern publishing, the text of a book on computer disk, it has been both possible and relatively easy to make changes and corrections throughout. Not only has this meant that errors detected since the first publication of this book, including the most delightful of all, the entirely spurious Anskar's *Life of Rimbert*, which eluded detection by both author and first readers alike, have been purged, but it has also been possible to make stylistic improvements throughout. In addition, an entirely new chapter on Spain after the Arab Conquest has been included, while the one dealing with the Ottonian Empire has been expanded significantly.

The early medieval centuries have enjoyed a period of remarkable prosperity and growth in terms of the research that has been carried out and the books and articles published on a wide range of subjects relating to them in the course of the 1990s. This flourishing of scholarship has been taken into account as much as possible in the preparation of this second edition, and has influenced changes to the text throughout. It will also be seen to be reflected in alterations and additions to both the notes to each chapter and to the general bibliography. In some cases it may be too early to see what constitutes genuine advances in our understanding of this complex period and what may prove to be false starts or misleading trails. Only time will tell.

As in the original edition, the selection of subjects for inclusion and the interpretations offered have ultimately to be matters of personal choice and conviction. While trying to take into account the great wealth of current and past scholarship relating to this period, seven hundred years of the history of Europe, North Africa and parts of the Middle East are not easily covered, and fashions in historiography can change rapidly. However, in making revisions I have generally tried to be less judgemental, leaving the reader even greater scope to make her and his decisions as to the merits of the cases argued here.

Edinburgh   ROGER COLLINS
March 1998

Preface to the third edition

The decade of the 2000s has seen continuous growth in scholarly interest in Late Antiquity and the Middle Ages, and with it a great increase in the number of publications relating to these centuries. One purpose of this new edition is to take advantage of this prodigious labour and to revise the content of the book in the light of recent arguments and discoveries. Another intention is to try to improve the literary style of the two previous editions, in an attempt to make the contents more immediately accessible to the reader. This is not to suggest only that a simple style is a good thing in its own right, but is also intended to prove that it is still possible to write history using words that everyone can understand; something that not all practitioners now seem to regard as a virtue. The basic structure of the book is little changed from that of the previous edition, as the nature and distribution of the contents still seem coherent. So, no new chapter has been added, even though each of the existing ones has been extensively revised. Overall, my main concern remains to stress the historian's need always to be asking 'How do we know what we think we know?' With that question permanently in mind, it becomes easier to follow the commandment: 'Take nothing on trust'.

Edinburgh　　　　　　　　　　　　　　　　　　ROGER COLLINS
August 2009

Introduction

When Edward Gibbon surveyed the centuries of 'decline' in the history of the Roman Empire and its Byzantine successor he allowed himself to start with a little mild Utopianism. Of the Antonine period, he commented that 'If a man were called upon to fix the period in the history of the world during which the condition of the human race was most happy and prosperous, he would, without hesitation, name that which elapsed from the death of Domitian to the accession of Commodus' (that is, AD 96–181). Few might nowadays ask themselves such a question, let alone come up with a response that equates 'the world' exclusively with the Mediterranean and 'the human race' with a small economic and social elite. However, for all his enthusiasm for second-century Rome, some of which was intended as implicit criticism of aspects of his own society of which he disapproved, it was not about this period that Gibbon intended to write.

Periods of tranquillity, social harmony and economic stability do not make very exciting history – even if we now would detect more conflict and change in the second century than was apparent to Gibbon. The turbulent centuries that were to follow pose more interesting historiographical problems, not least because they encompassed the most important developments that would take place in the history of the Near East, the Mediterranean and Western Europe between the formation of the Roman Empire in the first century BC and the discovery of the New World in the late fifteenth AD. Even then, much of the way that the society and economy of the Americas were to be developed and exploited was conditioned directly by a body of ideas and through the means of institutions that had come into being in the period of the Late Roman Empire.

In general, the centuries covered by this book constitute a period of the greatest significance for the future development, not only of Europe, but also in the longer term of much of the rest of the world. They saw, not least, the establishment of Christianity as the majority religion of the Roman Empire, and with it an indissoluble fusing of Judaeo-Christian and Romano-Greek thought. Apart from the first brief period of the founding of the religion in the time of the Early Roman Empire, there was to be no time in the whole subsequent history of the Christian Church so fertile in the development of its distinctive ideas and practices as the 'Patristic Age', lasting from roughly the mid-fourth century to the early sixth.

The writings of such men as Athanasius, Basil, Gregory of Nazianzus, Gregory of Nyssa, Ambrose, Jerome, Augustine and their immediate successors provided the intellectual framework of Christian thinking, not only throughout the rest of the Middle Ages but also for the Reformation and more recent centuries. The distinctive Christian emphasis on Virginity and the extraordinary ideological and institutional structures of monasticism were similarly the products of these centuries. They also saw the challenge to and modification of the Romano-Christian tradition with the rise to dominance of Islam over the whole of the Near East and the southern Mediterranean. The direct relevance of this formative period of Islamic thought and institutions to the modern society of these regions, and to various contemporary political and economic issues, hardly needs underlining.

In the West, the Roman Empire dissolved itself as a unitary political entity in the fifth century, but its intellectual and material cultural legacy continued to direct the fragmentary successor states that came into being among its ruins. This was especially true of that extraordinary institution, the papacy, whose own distinctive view of its nature and purpose was formed during this time, together with many of the institutional features that would enable it to play so dominant a role in Western Europe for centuries to come. As a corollary to this, the most substantial (and still unhealed) rift in Christendom – that between the Latin and Greek Churches – came into being at the very end of this period.

This itself was not uninfluenced by political changes in the West, with the emergence of the short-lived Frankish Empire of the Carolingians, which in its territorial expansion both northwards and eastwards further extended the areas of influence of the intellectual culture and some of the material civilisation of Late Antiquity. These would be taken even further to the east in the succeeding centuries, when the German realm that was brought into being under the Ottonian kings and emperors established itself as the dominant force in central Europe. At the same time, a resurgent Byzantine Empire was once more extending its own influence both westwards and northwards, not least into the region that would become Russia, thus creating a long-lasting divide in the cultural traditions of Europe.

To turn once more to the perspective of the historian, it was perhaps easier for Gibbon in an age of relative tranquillity to take a broad, if hardly dispassionate, view of this sequence of events. His approach to it, though, was conditioned by a desire to criticise certain elements in the society of his own day that he found reprehensible, notably its penchant for apparently pointless wars of conquest, and the continuing strength of elements of unreason, above all in religion. At the same time, a much more radical critique, symbolised by the French Revolution, was to lead directly to the subversion of much of the social order of Europe and, perhaps paradoxically, to the proliferation of aggressive warfare on an almost unprecedented scale, together with the emergence of ideologies far more menacing to Liberal individualism and reason than the placid religiosity of the eighteenth century. Flamboyant despots of the succeeding period, from Napoleon to Hitler, also turned to the Roman imperial past and its attempted revival under Charlemagne for some of the imagery and the framework of ideas needed to shape and manifest their regimes.

The revival of scholarly interest in the periods of Late Antiquity and the Early Middle Ages can, as much as the historiography of any period, take on the quality of mere antiquarianism. However, the nature of its subject matter, the scale and significance of so many of its events, and the intellectual force of the thought of so many of its greatest writers should militate against this. History should not necessarily be expected to teach lessons, and certainly is not cyclical, but the study of these apparently remote centuries is as conducive as any to the questioning of received value systems, the evaluation of dogma and the formulation of principles to guide the conduct of states and individuals in complex times.

1 Crisis and change in the Roman Empire, 235–305

Turbulent times, 235–85

In the third century, the Roman Empire came of age. Problems of administration and defence that had been growing for decades or had existed from the very foundation of the empire now made themselves felt so strongly that they had to be confronted and solved. The solutions were not always permanent ones, but at least the search for them was cathartic. Despite the Roman world often being portrayed as only emerging from the period of political and economic problems that marked so much of the century in the reign of Diocletian (284–305), some of his solutions were prefigured in the reforms of his predecessors.

When the young emperor Gordian III was killed in battle with the Persians in 244, many of the features of what is often called 'the crisis of the third century' were already present.[1] Most obvious were the military threats. In the east, the new Sasanian Empire that Gordian had confronted so disastrously was claiming not just the territories lost to Rome earlier in the century by its Parthian predecessor, but also all the lands once owned by the Achaemenid kings of Persia (550–330 BC), whose heirs it claimed to be. On the Danube and Rhine frontiers, pressure was growing, which was to express itself in the movement of peoples – Vandals, Franks and others – into Roman territory when the Empire could no longer defend its borders. Similar threats appeared along the less clearly defined imperial frontiers in North Africa, leading to the permanent loss of Roman rule over all but the coastal areas of the two provinces of Mauretania Caesariensis and Tingitana (the northern parts of modern Algeria and Morocco).

These frontier problems may seem the easiest to understand, as we tend to assume that people outside the Roman Empire, lacking its more developed economic and cultural benefits, dependent on subsistence agriculture, and living in a state of endemic warfare with hostile neighbours would seize any opportunity to invade. Acquiring Rome's fertile lands and relieving its citizens of their treasures would surely come naturally to 'barbarians', as the Romans regarded all those denied the benefits of being part of their civilization. However, raiding and migrating are very different activities. Roman ethnographers – those who wrote about the customs of peoples living beyond the imperial frontiers – were not at all interested in how they actually lived, let alone their motives, and wrote about them primarily in order to make moral or political comments about Roman society. So they were happy with stock descriptions and simplistic explanations for their conduct. In other words, we cannot trust what they have to say about 'the barbarians'. What is certain is that the causes of the collapse of the frontiers in so many parts of the Empire in the mid-third century do not lie in some instinctive rapacity of those living beyond them. Their moving into Roman territory was itself a symptom, but of a process about which we are very ill-informed.

Within the imperial frontiers, problems no less threatening were mounting. For reasons that are almost equally obscure, the economy of the Empire was over-heating, prices were rising fast and the only remedy that was adopted by the central government – reducing the purity of the silver in the coinage – fuelled the inflationary spiral. The impact of this on the army became a prime concern for the emperors, as their survival depended on the continuing loyalty of the military, who by this period were playing the dominant role in both appointing and overthrowing them.

The imperial system had been created through the constitutional fiction of the first emperor, Augustus (27 BC–AD 14), accepting from the Senate a life tenure of a range of key administrative, religious and military offices, which were then similarly conferred *en bloc* on his chosen successor. This concentrated power and central decision-making throughout the Empire in the hands of one individual. The weakness of such a system was that it was only as good as the person controlling it. The incompetence of many of the first emperors was masked by the limited nature of the problems they had to face. As these mounted, the latitude that could be allowed for the eccentricities and ineptitude of emperors who gained power by inheritance or because of their popularity with the imperial guard declined.[2] However, family succession and even some measure of mediocrity could be tolerated in periods in which the emperors did not have to establish their credibility as military leaders.

From an emperor needing to prove himself as a commander in the field, it was a short step to a successful commander in the field becoming a contender for the imperial office. Dynastic sentiment could carry some weight. Because Septimius Severus (193–211) and his son Caracalla (211–17) were militarily successful and paid well, their troops supported their far less competent relatives Elagabalus (218–22) and his cousin Severus

Alexander (222–35). However, when after several peaceful years serious threats developed on both the Persian and the Rhine frontiers, Severus Alexander was eliminated by his own soldiers and the first of a series of professional military emperors emerged in the person of Maximin I (235–238).

This was unacceptable to the aristocracy, although power had often been transferred by decision of the army in the past, as in 68–9, 96, 193–7 and in 217–18. What had changed was the kind of man who commanded the armies, and therefore might be chosen by the troops as their emperor. By traditions stretching back into the time of the Roman Republic, major military commands were entrusted to Senators on a yearly basis. Effective as many of them had proved individually, such amateurism became less tolerable as the threats to the integrity of the Roman frontiers grew, and the Empire took a more defensive stance. The time when office and positions of power had been monopolised by a senatorial aristocracy of exclusively Roman origin was long past, and emperors and senators came from the upper classes of a number of major provinces, notably Spain and Africa, but Maximin I, the army's choice, was a man of lower social origin, and from a frontier province.

He is portrayed by the contemporary Greek historian Herodian as coming 'from one of the semi-barbarous tribes of the interior of Thrace'.[3] This was further exaggerated in the peculiar fourth-century Latin compilation known as the *Scriptores Historiae Augustae*, a set of imperial biographies supposedly written by a variety of authors at the beginning of the century, but most probably the work of a single writer working towards the end of it. Here, Maximin was turned into a complete outsider, the product of the marriage of a Goth and an Alan, and thus a barbarian coming from outside the Empire.[4]

Maximin lacked the cultural sophistication of his predecessors, and his pursuit of the revenues needed to pay his armies intensified the antipathy between emperor and Senate, despite his being an effective military commander. However, he seemed dispensable when the threat on the frontiers temporarily lessened. An unsuccessful revolt in Africa in 238 provided the inspiration for a more serious rebellion in Italy instigated by the Senate, and the emperor was murdered by his own men during a lengthy siege of Aquileia in northern Italy.[5]

The history of the emperors that succeeded him highlights another problem present in the imperial system from at least the murder of Caligula in AD 41. This was the power of the Praetorian Guard, the elite force, normally stationed in Rome, that provided the imperial bodyguard and garrisoned the capital. Control of this unit was exercised by one, sometimes two, Praetorian Prefects, who in certain circumstances could use it to seize power themselves.[6]

The reign of the young emperor Gordian III (238–44) proves the point. He was selected by the Senate as a figurehead because he was the grandson of the elderly proconsul whose short-lived revolt in Africa had precipitated the fall of Maximin, while real military and administrative authority was exercised by two senatorial co-emperors. However, they were murdered within months by the Praetorian Guard, whose Prefect then became the power behind the regime, marrying his daughter to the emperor. After Gordian was killed in battle with the Persians in 244, his next Praetorian Prefect, Philip, was proclaimed emperor by the army.

The growing military threats from the Persians and along the Danube frontier intensified the political instability, as the emperor could not respond to them all in person, and had to delegate command of large armies to generals whose ambitions could exceed their loyalty. In Philip's reign, pressure on the Danube region saw the emperor campaigning successfully along that frontier in 246. However, in 248/9 an incursion across the river into the eastern Balkans by various tribes caused chaos. A local revolt was suppressed, but the victorious general, Trajan Decius, was proclaimed emperor by his army, which he then led into Italy, to confront Philip at Verona.[7]

The death in battle, or more probably at the hands of their own soldiers, of Philip I and his son and co-ruler Philip II gave the empire to Decius. He now faced the problems that had caused his predecessor's downfall. Spiralling inflation and the threats along the frontiers forced the state to raise increasing amounts of money to pay the troops. The massive costs incurred in the celebration of the millennium of Rome in 247 had added a further burden, and substantial increases in taxation in Philip's reign proved counterproductive, as they prompted revolts. The immediate military threat caused by the collapse of the Danube frontier required action, which proved fatal to the new imperial regime. In 251, after some initial success, Decius and his eldest son were killed in battle with the invaders.[8]

The next two decades seem to have been a period of unmitigated crisis. They began with further political instability caused by the events of 249–51. Trebonianus Gallus, the general who extricated the remnants of the Roman army from the Balkans after the death of Decius, was proclaimed emperor, but his regime was weak. A victory in 253 by one of his generals, Aemilian, led to a challenge for the throne, and when Aemilian invaded Italy, Gallus's army would not fight and killed him and his co-ruler, Volusian. Aemilian was then faced by another general, who had been sent to Gaul by Gallus to bring reinforcements. Aemilian was killed by his own troops after a reign of less than four months. His challenger, Valerian, became emperor, with his son Gallienus as co-ruler, and managed to retain power for seven years. For him, disaster took another form.[9]

The Persian threat, held off by the treaty made by Philip I in 244, reasserted itself in 259, and the following year Valerian (253–60 was captured by the Sasanian shah Shapur I (241–72), remaining a prisoner until his death.[10] After this demoralising blow, the central authority of the Roman emperor was not reasserted for a decade, and power was seized by local rulers and a string of aspiring imperial claimants. Most successful were the rulers of the kingdom of Palmyra, who resisted the Persian invasion in 260 and then extended their control to include Syria, Mesopotamia and eventually Egypt. In the Balkans, following the disaster of 251, no effective campaigning was undertaken, leaving several provinces outside imperial rule for the next twenty years.

Military problems on the Rhine frontier also returned in this period, after a time of relative tranquillity. In 259, various tribal groups crossed the river and ravaged their way across Gaul and into Spain unopposed. In the aftermath, one of the military commanders on the Rhine, Cassius Latinius Postumus (259–69), was proclaimed emperor by his troops. He made himself master of Gaul, Britain and parts of Spain. He was murdered by his own men in 269, but three short-lived successors kept this 'Gallic Empire' in being until 273.[11]

In these decades, the debasement of the currency became so severe that the precious metal content of the silver coins known as *antoniniani* was no higher than 5 per cent. The coins themselves were made of bronze, and were dipped in a bath of silver prior to issue. No one seems to have been fooled, and the enormous size of some of the hoards of coins of this period testifies not only to the instability that led to their being hidden – and never recovered – but also to the growing quantities that had to be minted, because of the continuous drop in their exchange value.[12]

While, cumulatively, all of these problems, to which could be added intermittent outbreaks of plague and famine, seem to add up to a picture of political, economic and to some extent social chaos of 'the Years of Anarchy', as they have been called, the impression is to some extent misleading. Many provinces of the Empire were in fact little affected by these difficulties.

For example, between the conclusion of Septimius Severus's campaign against the Caledonians in 210/11 and the revolt of Carausius in 286, Britain appears to have been perfectly tranquil. Similarly, only a few parts of Spain were touched by raids in the middle of the century. This was also a period of considerable prosperity for the cities of Roman Africa, which show fewer symptoms of urban decline that could be detected in many other regions of the Empire.[13] Egypt suffered no external threats, nor did most parts of Asia Minor.

From the point of view of individual provinces, the creation of 'breakaway' regimes such as that of the Gallic emperors Postumus, Marius, Victorinus and Tetricus, was a sensible response. When the legitimate emperor was incapable of defending a province, the creation of a locally based imperial regime ensured effective protection and the exclusive direction of resources to the needs of the region. In these respects, when the western half of the Empire disintegrated in the fifth century, it might have benefited from the kinds of responses to crisis that were seen in the third century.

What is striking is the rapid recovery from the period of military disaster. Despite ruling in the middle of the worst period of crisis, the emperor Gallienus survived for fifteen years, the longest reign between those of Septimius Severus (193–211) and Diocletian (284–305). The cavalry army that Gallenius instituted in the 260s in northern Italy may have been a precedent for the mobile field armies that were to become the standard form of imperial defence from the early fourth century onwards.[14] Unfortunately, the early death of one of his sons and the killing of the other by Postumus left him without heirs. In 268 he was murdered by some of his generals.

This heralded a succession of soldier emperors of great competence but of relatively lowly social origins; similar to Maximin I. But whereas he was unusual as an emperor in the first half of the century, Claudius II (268–70), Aurelian (270–5), Tacitus (275–6), Probus (276–82) and Carus (282–3) represent an unbroken line of such provincial career soldiers.[15] Unlike Philip I, Decius, Gallus and Valerian, they were not senators and did not belong to the cultivated upper class world of the city of Rome. They were, on the other hand, successful in most of the tasks they undertook.

In a brief reign, terminated by illness, Claudius II disposed of the Gothic menace in the Balkans, expelling them from imperial territory. Aurelian put an end to the independent Gallic Empire in 273, even allowing its last ruler to retire to his estates in Italy, and he re-established Roman control in the East the next year. This was made easier by the recent death of the powerful Sasanian shah Shapur I and an ensuing period of internal disorder in Persia. By the time of Carus (282–3), the Romans were taking the offensive, and he launched an invasion that reached as far as the Persian capital of Ctesiphon before he was killed, apparently by lightning.[16]

Aurelian had increased the silver content in the coinage, and gave up the pretence of overvaluing it, by abolishing the residual bronze coin denominations that had existed alongside it. Further economic recovery was gradual, and it must be admitted that the actual causes of it were probably as unclear to the rulers of the Empire at this time as they are to modern historians.

These emperors failed, however, to solve the problem of internal political stability. In succumbing to disease, Claudius II was one of only two emperors in the course of the entire century to die of natural causes. The army often favoured dynastic succession, if a potential candidate from the late emperor's family could be found. This was made clear on the deaths of Claudius II in 270, and of Tacitus in 276, when units of the army attending the deceased emperor proclaimed his brother as his successor. Neither, however, was able to muster enough support to face the challenge of the candidate chosen by other units of the army. In 270, Quintillus, who was proclaimed in northern Italy, survived only seventeen days. In 276, Florian, the brother of Tacitus, was set up by the army in Asia Minor, but was opposed by Probus, the choice of the army in Egypt. Rather than face a war, his own men killed Florian at Tarsus after only a three-month reign.[17]

As well as disputed successions, the period was still marked by occasional military revolts. Probus (276–82) was faced with two: one in Gaul and the other in Syria in 281. It is probable also that his successor, Carus, Praetorian Prefect and commander of the army in the Balkans, was in revolt against him in 282, when he was killed by his own men near Sirmium. It is recorded that the troops did so because he had transferred them to the digging of drainage ditches, but it is more likely that the murder of Probus mirrored the events of 276 and that he was killed because his own men were unwilling to fight for him against Carus.[18]

The basic problem remained the need for the emperor to be in more than one place at the same time, at least in periods of military crisis. He had to command his forces in person, but if more than one frontier was threatened, or if a mixture of internal and external threats needed to be countered, control over a significant body of troops had to be delegated to a subordinate. If the latter proved succesful, his army might proclaim him emperor. But if the rebels then failed to secure broader support for their candidate, they tended to murder him and revert to their previous allegiance. Even with this relative 'safety mechanism', such revolts and contested successions remained frequent in the period 268–85.

The emperor who first tried to end to this instability achieved power in the same way. Carus was the first to attempt to deal with the question of his own succession and to solve the problem of the emperor needing to be in more than one place at a time. On taking power, he nominated his two sons to the rank of Caesar, or junior emperor. When he undertook his Persian campaign in 283 he promoted the elder of them, Carinus, to the superior rank of Augustus or full emperor, leaving him in charge of the West. The younger son, the Caesar Numerian, accompanied him. On Carus's death in Persia, his army then elevated Numerian to the rank of Augustus, but in the course of the army's withdrawal across Asia Minor in the winter of 284 the new emperor was secretly murdered. One of his generals, Diocletian, blamed the Praetorian Prefect, killed him and had himself proclaimed emperor by the troops. In the ensuing civil war, Diocletian suffered an initial defeat, but Carinus was murdered by his own officers. Diocletian was then accepted as sole ruler without further opposition.[19]

The reforms of Diocletian, 285–305

Diocletian's appreciation of the scale of the problems facing the holder of the imperial office, including the need for the emperor to be able to deal personally with any threat involving a military response, was acute and his solution remarkable. None of his immediate predecessors, apart from Carus, had addressed the issue, but the dynastic approach adopted by Carus, following earlier precedents, was only as effective as the emperor's children were competent and popular. Diocletian's answer was more daring and potentially riskier, but initially it proved to be effective.

In 285 he nominated another general, Maximian, as his co-ruler, at first in the junior rank of Caesar, and then, in April 286, in the senior rank of Augustus, making him an equal colleague and entrusting him with the oversight of the West while he returned to the East.[20] This could have produced civil war, if Maximian had ambitions to make himself sole ruler, but he was kept busy with a series of military problems in the West, ranging

from Frankish and Saxon seaborne raiding in the Channel to
a major Berber incursion into the Roman provinces of North
Africa. While this development was probably not envisaged in
286, Diocletian's political solution was taken a stage further in
293, when, with the consent of Maximian, he nominated two
Caesars – Galerius and Constantius – one for the East and one
for the West. These two operated under the authority of the
senior emperor in their half of the Empire, and with particular
oversight of a group of provinces. To further cement the loyalty
of the imperial quartet, each of the Caesars married the daughter of the senior emperor of his half of the Empire.[21] In 305,
the two senior emperors abdicated in favour of their Caesars
and new junior emperors were appointed to bring the imperial
college up to four once again.

The new Tetrarchic ('four ruler') system did not eliminate
the possibility of military revolt, but it reduced the degree to
which a rebel general in a particular province could threaten
the stability of the imperial regime. In 286, Carausius, the commander of the Channel fleet, rebelled. He was proclaimed
emperor by the army in Britain, but while he held out for seven
years he did not extend his power beyond the island, apart from
controlling Boulogne and some other ports on the north Gallic
coast. He was murdered by his finance minister, Allectus, in 293,
and the latter was killed when the Caesar Constantius invaded
Britain in 296.[22] It was principally the difficulty of shipping
an army across the Channel that enabled this rebel regime to
last so long; a prior attempt at invasion in 289 had to be abandoned when the imperial fleet was destroyed in a storm. In contrast, a revolt in Egypt in 296 under Domitius Domitianus was
suppressed within eight months.[23]

The intention of the fully developed Tetrarchic system was
to present the four emperors as working together in the closest harmony and concord. Despite there being a distinction in
status between the two senior Augusti and their junior partners,
otherwise their functions and authorities were equal and inter-
changeable. The ideology was represented in art, above all by
the elimination of elements of individuality in the portraiture
of the rulers. Thus, in the coins of these emperors, only the
inscriptions indicate which of the rulers is being portrayed.
The styles vary from mint to mint, but the individual rulers are
always given identical features.[24] The quintessential imperial
image of this period can be seen in the three-dimensional por-
phyry sculptures of the four emperors, now embedded in the
wall of the Church of San Marco in Venice. Grouped in pairs,
with the senior emperor in each case placing his arm around

the shoulder of his junior, the four men are identical, both in their military costume and in their physiognomy.[25] They form a team, an indivisible unit, and are not separable individuals.

In the official literary depictions of the imperial regime, similar imagery was used. In 291, in the panegyric or speech in praise of the emperor Maximian on his birthday, the Gallic orator Mamertinus imagined the crowd exclaiming as they saw the two emperors together in Milan: 'Do you see Diocletian? Do you see Maximian? There they both are! They are together! How they sit in unity! How they talk together in concord!'[26] This dates from the period before the extension of the numbers in the 'college of emperors' from two to four; something that may have resulted from the failure of Maximian to deal effectively with all the problems besetting the West in the later 280s.[27]

As well as this fundamental change in the imperial office, Diocletian attempted to restructure the administration of the Empire. A reorganisation of provincial boundaries increased their number and reduced their size. At the same time, civil and military authority within the provinces was divided, and parallel army and civil service hierarchies were created within both divisions. The provinces were themselves then grouped into larger units, called dioceses, and these were placed under the direction of a new class of official called *Vicarii*, or Deputy Praetorian Prefects. This process was continued under Diocletian's eventual successor. Constantine I (306–37), who, through disbanding the Praetorian cohorts in 312, turned the Praetorian Prefecture into an essentially civilian and administrative office. Later in his reign, he increased the number of Prefects from two to four and tied them to regional prefectures rather than being attached to the persons of the emperors.[28]

In the reorganisation of the army, as well as the restructuring of the administration, it is difficult to separate the reforms of Diocletian from those of Constantine. What is clear is that by the time of the latter's death in 337, an entirely new organisation had been created, whereby the army was divided into two types of unit. On the one hand, there were the *Limitanei*, garrison groups stationed on the frontiers to provide the first line of defence against incursions, and, on the other, there were the *Comitatenses*, or units of the mobile field armies that were deployed behind the frontiers but which moved rapidly to counter specific threats that were beyond the capacity of the *Limitanei* to contain.[29]

The garrison forces were somewhat less well armed, equipped and trained, and were expected to have only limited mobility. The field armies, on the other hand, contained much larger proportions of cavalry than had existed under the early Empire, when this arm had been considered inferior and its units composed exclusively of the second class Auxiliaries. The army reforms of Diocletian and Constantine led to more flexible responses to the military challenges faced by the empire.[29] At the same time, the frontiers were defended more intensively by the construction of numerous and complex fortifications. This system had certain disadvantages, and the redeployment of field armies to participate in the numerous civil wars within the Empire in the fourth century could leave the frontier provinces open to penetration and destruction.

A reform that can certainly be ascribed to Diocletian is his attempt to curb the inflationary price spiral within the Empire. His approach to the problem was direct, but ultimately ineffectual. It took the form of an edict, issued in the year 301, that stipulated the maximum price that could be charged for a long list of specified items, most of which, not surprisingly, were of direct importance to the army. The penalty for charging more than the decreed prices was execution. In practice, this seems to have had limited effect, in that it ignored the basic mechanisms of supply and demand. Hoarding and 'black market' trading became preferable alternatives to selling on the open market at government-set price levels. The edict had to be repealed.[30] More effective were a series of reforms of the coinage in 296 that reintroduced a bronze denomination and set new ratios of value between bronze, silver and gold. This took up and extended the revaluation tentatively begun under Aurelian.

In general, the whole thrust of the changes introduced around the turn of the century by Diocletian and by Constantine was aimed at the production of a more regimented and rigid society. Laws that required sons to follow the professions of their fathers, laws that fixed prices, laws that established exact hierarchies in the civil and military administration, and laws that forbade an increasing range of opinions and practices all reflect a common social ideal.[31] This was not just a question of the will of an individual ruler, or even of a college of emperors. Many of the elements can be detected earlier in the third century in a less developed and less coherent form, and the transformation that was wrought within the Empire at the end of it must reflect the growth of the public acceptability of so many of the rules that were then introduced or systematised.

In this sense, the culmination of occasional persecution of the Christians in the course of the third century in the so-called Great Persecution initiated by Diocletian in 303 is hardly surprising. This was more thorough, logical and systematic than anything that had gone before, and at the same time developed tendencies within Roman society that had been growing for a century or more. Leaving aside the Neronian persecution, which seems to have been confined to the city of Rome, and was prompted by the need to find scapegoats for the great fire in the city in AD 64, serious state action against the growing Christian communities within the Empire was essentially a third-century phenomenon.[32]

It began with the brief reign of Trajan Decius (249–51), who in 250 issued an edict requiring his provincial governors, urban magxcCd local Commissioners for Sacrifices to obtain certificates from the citizens to establish that they had taken part in the obligatory public sacrifices to the Genius (or guiding spirit) of the emperor on certain specified days. While Christians thought this was aimed exclusively against them, the edict is far more revolutionary, in that this marks the first attempt by the Roman government to force its citizens into performing a public religious act. Both belief and practice in religion were largely regarded as matters of private concern, but, in this case, the emperor was demanding an Empire-wide declaration of political loyalty, expressed through a religious ceremony. Many Christians evaded the edict by bribery, but their reluctance to take part confirmed suspicions of their unreliability. The process was ended by Decius's death in 251.[33]

More sustained and systematic were the measures taken in 258 by the emperor Valerian, who issued a law ordering Christians not to assemble in their own places of worship or to use their own cemeteries, and requiring them again to perform public sacrifices. He also confiscated the property of practising Christians, deprived individuals of their existing legal status, and threatened with death those who persisted in their faith.[34] These laws were repealed in 261 by Valerian's son Gallienus, who also restored their property to Christian individuals and communities. No further state action was taken against them until the time of Diocletian.

The sources of evidence for all of the persecutions are generally later in date than the events themselves, and are written from a Christian point of view. Only the chance survival of an odd document, such as the witnessed certificate of attendance at sacrifices sent to the Commissioners for Sacrifices 'in the Village of Alexander's Island' in Egypt by one Aurelius Diogenes 'son of Satabus ... aged 72; scar on right eyebrow', gives any contemporary and non-Christian perspective on events.[35] Thus it is not easy to determine the real causes of the state-initiated persecutions. From the Christians' perspective, there was no need to try to understand the causes of the actions taken against them, as they expected the pagan Roman world to be antagonistic.

The religious exclusivity of the Christian message meant that no adherent of the faith could participate in any other form of worship. For the Christians, the gods venerated by their fellow Romans were not divinities at all, but evil, demonic forces, whose hold over the minds of their worshippers prevented them from recognising the truth of the Christian revelation. Thus, for a Christian to participate in a pagan sacrifice, even in a passive way, was an act of apostasy, a renunciation of belief. This was unfortunate at a time when the making of sacrifices was the principal way in which acts of public loyalty to the emperor were expressed, but for the Christians, the implicit recognition of a divinity other than the one true God made participation an act of spiritual suicide. In consequence, of course, the Christians could appear to be politically subversive. The successive crises affecting the Empire in the mid-third century and the growth in the number of Christians made the taking of repressive measures against such seeming dissidents increasingly likely.[36]

In general, the growth of Christianity, particularly among the most influential sectors of society, disturbed imperial regimes of a conservative cast. The second rescript of Valerian envisaged the possibilities of Christians being found among the ranks of the Senate, and the second level of nobility, that of the *Equites*. Similarly, there were thought to be many Christians among the members of the imperial household, both at this time and later, in the reign of Diocletian. The emperor Decius, who initiated the series of imperial laws requiring Christian participation in public sacrifices, was particularly anxious to reinforce the imperial cult, not least in the aftermath of his own overthrow of Philip and the spate of revolts in 249. He also issued a series of coins commemorating previous emperors, from Augustus to Severus Alexander, who had been deified or been declared to be gods.[37] That the issue of Christian non-participation in such rites should come to a head at this time is hardly surprising. Imperial attitudes and policy are, however, only half of the story.[38]

While attention normally focuses on the formal measures taken by the state against the Christians in this mid-third-century period, and the later accounts of the martyrdoms of those who refused to abandon their faith often provide vivid images of confrontations with the civil authorities, it is notable that the persecutions also derived from conflicts in local urban contexts. The Christian accounts written in the early fourth century, particularly the *Ecclesiastical History* of bishop Eusebius of Caesarea (d. 339/40), mention some of these. In a letter sent by bishop Dionysius of Alexandria to his colleague Fabius in Antioch, quoted by Eusebius, persecution broke out in his city a year before the promulgation of Decius's edict. This he blamed on 'the nameless prophet and worker of mischief' who incited the populace of Alexandria against the local Christian community, several of whom were lynched.[39]

In the great cities of the eastern half of the Empire, above all in Antioch and Alexandria, the numerical rise of the Christian communities, whose religious practices prevented them from participating in the public festivals of their pagan neighbours, was bound to be a cause of mounting tension in periods of economic hardship and political crisis. It seems that Valerian, who had favoured the Christians to a degree they themselves found surprising at the beginning of his reign, turned against them after he went east and took up residence in Antioch in 256. Bishop Dionysius, in another of his letters, put the blame on one of the emperor's civil servant advisers – later to be an unsuccessful emperor-maker – by the name of Macrianus.[40]

A similar personal influence, but again rooted in sometimes bitter inter-communal hostilities in the eastern cities, may have lain behind the initiation of the Great Persecution under Diocletian. It is surprising that he waited until so late a stage in his reign to begin legislating against the Christians if he had a personal dislike of them. It may be that the initiative really lay with the Caesar Galerius, whose influence was increasing in the final years of Diocletian's reign, and who was to succeed him within two years.[41] However, it is worth noting that it was Galerius himself who in 311 repealed the edict of persecution in the East; in other words, a year before the conversion of Constantine and the formal end to persecution in the West.

Whatever the motives of individual participants, the strength of anti-Christian feeling and the degree to which persecution was actively pursued in the years 303–12 depended largely on local conditions. In the West, where, apart from Africa, Christian communities were neither numerous nor large, the application of Diocletian's legal measures, which were effectively the reimposition of those of Valerian, barely outlasted his reign. Constantius I (305–6) seems to have allowed the penalties against practising Christians to lapse, and Maxentius (306–12) began the process of restoring their property. In the East, however, the Caesar (later Augustus) Maximin II (305–13), who ruled Egypt and Syria, applied the laws in full, not least because of popular anti-Christian agitation within his territories.[42] This prevented him from following Galerius in ending the persecution in 311.

Diocletian's eventual successor, Constantine, who was the heir to so many of his policies, took quite the opposite approach to him in religious matters, and became the first Christian emperor. This was perhaps the logical move. In the more regulated and authoritarian state that had been created in the third century, the hierarchical structures and the Mediterranean-wide organisation of the Church had much to offer the secular rulers of the Empire.

2   The age of Constantine, 305–50

The emperor and his rivals, 305–12

The abdication of Diocletian and Maximian in 305, whether
long-planned or just the product of the senior emperor's recent
ill health, created a second Tetrarchy, in which the dominant
figure should have been Galerius.[1] His succession to Diocletian,
as the Augustus in the East, was matched by the elevation of
Constantius in the West. The two Caesars appointed to assist
them, Severus in the West and Maximin II in the East, are presented in the hostile Christian sources, which provide most of
the political narrative for this period, as both being creatures
of Galerius.[2] Maximin was the new senior emperor's nephew,
and Severus one of his generals. Maximin's appointment seems
the only concession to family relationships in the constitution
of the new Tetrarchy, as neither the sons of Maximian nor of
Constantius were promoted, indicating that dynasticism had no
part to play a part in the new imperial system.

If so, this was a fatal flaw. The death in 306 of Constantius I at
York, where he had gone to campaign against the Picts, led
to the army in Britain proclaiming the dead emperor's son
Constantine as his successor.[3] In the same year, prompted by the
retired emperor Maximian, the army in Rome proclaimed the
latter's son Maxentius as emperor, in opposition to the Caesar
Severus. Galerius attempted to shore up the disintegrating
Tetrarchy by recognising Constantine, but only as a Caesar, while
nominating the beleaguered Severus as the new Augustus for the
West. Maxentius and his father were excluded from his plans.

Galerius's lack of flexibility proved fatal to the entire system.
Severus had little support in Italy and was persuaded, after an
abortive siege of Rome, to surrender himself into the hands
of Maxentius, who soon had him executed. An imperial 'conference' held at Carnuntum on the Danube in 308, between
Galerius and the retired emperors Diocletian and Maximian
(who had just been expelled from Italy by his son) led to a further ill-conceived attempt to force the imperial structure back
into shape. Another Illyrian general, Licinius, who had been
Galerius's candidate to succeed Constantius, was proclaimed
Augustus, in succession to Severus, Maximian was required to
return to retirement, and Maxentius was declared a usurper.[4]

Even so, Maxentius was the de facto ruler of Italy and Africa, and consolidated his position in Rome with a major programme of public works, honouring himself and his dynasty. Furthermore, both Constantine and Maximin, who had been Caesars for the previous two years, refused to accept the elevation of Licinius over their heads. An offer of the title of *Filius Augusti* or 'Son of the Senior Emperor' was rejected, and in 309 they both had to be recognised as *Augusti* in their own right.[5] As a system, the Tetrarchy was dead, replaced by the coexistence of five emperors, four of whom were mutually recognised and the fifth was theoretically a usurper. It was only going to be a matter of time before they fell to fighting among themselves for larger shares of territory and power.

Galerius's failure to prove himself Diocletian's equal was completed by his invasion of Italy in 310. Despite blockading Maxentius in Rome, he was unable to take the city, and his army disintegrated under the twin pressures of military failure and the distribution of bribes by the besieged usurper. Galerius was forced to make a hasty retreat from Italy, returning to his imperial residence at Thessalonica, where he died the following year. Even though he repealed his anti-Christian legislation just prior to his death, his painful terminal illness was subsequently reported with relish and intimate detail in the work *On the Deaths of the Persecutors*, written by the African Christian rhetor, Lactantius.[6]

It is unlikely that conflict between the emperors would have been delayed had Galerius lived longer, as his authority over his colleagues was already lost. The first round was fought in 312, within a year of his death. Constantine marched into Italy, and while Maxentius had successfully sat out two previous such invasions within the walls of Rome, this time he came out to meet Constantine. In the ensuing battle of the Milvian Bridge, just north of the city, Constantine was victorious, and Maxentius drowned while trying to escape across the Tiber.[7] Italy and Africa were joined to Constantine's other provinces of Britain, Gaul and Spain.

Prior to these events, Constantine had already begun distancing himself from the Tetrarchic system. Having been passed over in the redistribution of imperial offices in 305, he had escaped from the eastern court to join his father in the West, ensuring his own proclamation as emperor by the army in Britain when Constantius died there in 306. Subsequently, Constantine started to promote the claim that his family were descended from Claudius II Gothicus (268–70) and thus held the throne by inheritance rather than as a result of Constantius's selection by

Diocletian. A failed attempt to overthrow Constantine in 310 by his own father-in-law, the former emperor Maximian, led to further moves to base his imperial authority on dynastic right and to discredit the Tetrarchic principle of selection. These may have included his first reactions against the Tetrarchic religious system, and the start of his search for a new divine support for his rule, both of which he claimed to have inherited from his father.

Constantine and Christianity

This battle of the Milvian Bridge has long been associated with the conversion of Constantine to Christianity. The earliest accounts of this appear in *Deaths of the Persecutors* (314/15) by Lactantius, who was tutor to the emperor's son, Crispus, and in the Greek *Ecclesiastical History* (completed in 324) and *Life of Constantine* (left unfinished at its author's death in 339), the latter two written by bishop *Eusebius of Caesarea*, one of Constantine's theological advisers in the latter part of his reign.[8]

It used to be suggested that Constantine was cynically self-interested in his conversion to the religion of a minority group subject to state persecution, but such an interpretation is clearly flawed.[9] More Christians lived in the eastern half of the Empire than the western, and it was uncertain how far they would co-operate with the Roman state, even under a Christian emperor. Eusebius wrote his in the 320s for a Christian readership needing to understand what that change meant. Constantine's conversion was not aimed at winning the support of a 'fifth column' of Christians in the provinces ruled by his rivals.

Attempts to understand his conversion cannot come close to the level of personal motivation, though it is clear from some of the documents he issued in 313 and later in his reign, that he had a powerful sense of being divinely guided and of having a mission to restore both good government and true religion. As he himself put it: 'I, beginning from that sea beside the Britons ... have repelled and scattered the horrors that held everything in subjection, so that on the one hand the human race, taught by my obedient service, might restore the religion of the most dread Law, while at the same time the most blessed faith might grow under the guidance of the Supreme.'[10] The language is typical of the convoluted, grandiose but obscure style of most imperial legal and administrative pronouncements of the Late Roman centuries.

That his victory over Maxentius was the first significant confirmation of his new religious adherence, and the particular sense of purpose it gave him, is clear from its central place in the accounts written up by Lactantius around 314/15 and by Eusebius a decade later, which they both claimed were derived from the emperor himself. If only in retrospect, he associated the battle with his conversion. The differences in the narratives of the two authors suggest that he interpreted the circumstances of his conversion rather differently in the course of the years that followed. Constantine was certainly a very different kind of Christian in the 330s from he had been in 312, moving from a more syncretistic view of his faith to a more exclusively monotheistic one.

Devotion to the sun god featured in the political ideology of Constantine's father Constantius I, and Constantine himself used solar imagery for several years after his conversion. Sol/Oriens had in any case already been borrowed for the depiction of Christ in the late third century, as has been suggested on the basis of a damaged mosaic found under the basilica of St Peter's in Rome. This was found on the ceiling of a tomb close to the site of the small shrine erected by Christians in the late second century to mark what was regarded as the burial place of St Peter. Its earlier dating is proved by its location in buildings that were deliberately buried to create a platform on which the basilica dedicated to St Peter was built in the mid-fourth century. The iconography of the mosaic, damaged when excavators smashed their way through the roof of the tomb, combines the traditional imagery of the sun god in his two-horse chariot with Christian symbols, such as the vine.[11]

Constantine used the reverse legend of *Soli Invicto Comiti* – 'To the Unconquered Sun, Companion (of the Emperor)' on his coins until 323.[12] While seen as a compromise between the emperor's newfound faith and the majority pagan traditions of society in the western Empire, this employment of solar imagery by the new Christian could have been a more personal statement. Constantine's views of his new religion became orthodox after his conquest in 324 of the eastern provinces, in which Christianity had a firmer hold.

It would be wrong to assume that the Senate regarded Constantine's new religious enthusiasm with hostility, as the idea of the emperor being under the special protection of a divinity, as the *comes* or companion of the god, was already long-established in the third century. It was a standard feature of the imperial ideology of the Tetrarchy.[13] Constantine's Christianity differed from the sun worship of his father, and of the emperor Aurelian, primarily in the religious exclusivity that it demanded. Most of the other cults in the Mediterranean world in the late Roman period coexisted on the basis of mutual toleration and syncretism, but the Christians, like the Jews, regarded themselves as the possessors of an exclusive religious truth, and as worshippers of the only true God. The Constantinian confusion between Christ and Sol did not last long.

The new Christian emperor is described in a history of the bishops of Rome, a pontificate-by-pontificate narrative known as the *Liber Pontificalis* or 'Pope's Book' first compiled around 540, as having constructed a series of buildings in the city for, and in part at the request of, pope Sylvester (314–35).[14] The relatively late date of this source might make it suspect, particularly as there are other features of its text that can be shown to be unreliable, but in this particular case the account of each building is accompanied by detailed lists of the endowments provided by the emperor for its upkeep. Analysis suggests these date from about a generation after Constantine. So there has been a general acceptance of the wider narrative into which these lists fit, and belief that the emperor constructed a series of large basilicas in and around Rome, which thereby became the first purpose-built places of worship for the city's Christian community and its bishops. These include the Lateran Basilica that became (and remains) the pope's cathedral, or particular episcopal church, St Peter's, built over the presumed site of the burial of the leader of the Apostles, and several others, including those dedicated to Saints Paul, Laurence and Agnes outside the city walls, which mark their tombs.[15]

The basic plan of these buildings was borrowed from that of the secular basilica, a rectangular structure with an apse at one or both ends, normally serving as a law court and to be found in most of the towns and cities of the Empire. Such a basilica, on a monumental scale, and containing space for half a dozen or more courts had been begun by Maxentius in the Roman forum, and was completed by Constantine after 312. The basilican plan had also provided the design for imperial throne halls, in which the increasingly formal state ceremonial of the late Empire could be performed. In such buildings as Constantine's throne room in Trier, later transformed into a church, the rectangular body of the hall provided direction and space for the lesser participants, with the single semicircular apse serving as the location of the imperial throne and the focus of attention.[16] With courtiers and attendants filling the body of the hall, and the emperor enthroned behind curtains in the apse, envoys and others to be received could be led in by the *Silentiarii*, the overseers of court protocol, and brought through the hall. At an appropriate point, the curtain concealing the emperor was drawn back and all present made obeisance to the ruler.[17]

It was this creation of a space suitable for the veneration of the sacred majesty of the emperor that may explain why the basilican form was used for the buildings ascribed to Constantine in Rome, as their purpose in most cases related to the honouring of the martyrs whose bodies were buried below or near to them. Burial rather than worship is also the key to the main function of these constructions. Some of these basilicas, such as the one on the Via Labicana, close to the modern Termini railway station, had attached mausolea, to serve in all probability as imperial burial places. Others, such as the one built beside the catacomb of San Sebastiano, appear to have contained little by way of internal structure, and seem intended instead as enclosed cemeteries. Certainly, they have been found to be full of graves.[18]

It also used to thought that Constantine turned a former imperial palace, close to the basilica originally known as 'the Constantinian' but more widely as the Lateran, into a residence for the bishops of Rome. That a palace attached to the Lateran basilica, which became the papal cathedral, did serve as the main episcopal residence until the late Middle Ages has served to confirm such a belief, but almost as a sleight of hand. The earliest evidence for that papal palace dates to the eighth century, and the fourth century reference is to a quite different building, that was loaned by the emperor to serve as the venue for an episcopal synod in 312. So, the idea that the emperor provided the bishops with a palatial residence is entirely without foundation.[19]

It became clear that a shared religious affiliation was the best route to imperial favour from Constantine, but despite the Senate of Rome marking his second visit to the city and the tenth anniversary of his accession by the erection in 315 of a (still extant) triumphal arch, its members were little in need of the ruler's patronage economically, and the general tendency of emperors in the second half of the third century to exclude senators from government and military office in fact made them less dependent on imperial goodwill than was the case in earlier centuries.[20] However, there were some who, from conviction or convenience, found themselves sharing the ruler's religion and thus his munificence.

Constantine instructed his provincial governors to restore to the Christian communities the property that had been taken from them during the persecution, though this had already been done in Italy and Africa by Maxentius.[21] As the sole ruler of the western half of the Empire, after 312 Constantine was the most powerful of the emperors, with his two eastern colleagues anxious to secure his support in their own disputes. Maximin II, who ruled Egypt, Syria and the provinces of Asia Minor, had previously been an ally of Maxentius, and popular opposition to the Christians was stronger in his territories, especially Egypt, than in the Balkan provinces controlled by Licinius.[22]

Licinius was therefore better situated to reach an accommodation with Constantine, meeting him in Milan soon after his victory over Maxentius, and together they issued the edict in March 313 ending the persecution of Christians throughout the Empire.[23] Even Maximin found it advisable to apply this decree. To some extent, active persecution, which had been at its height in the first two or three years after 303, had then become little more than a formality, and even Galerius, possibly the most ideologically motivated of the tetrarchs, had issued an edict of toleration for the Christians just before his death in 311. From 312 onwards, though, whenever official persecution of Christians revived, it was more of a political gesture, reflecting the persecuting ruler's attitude towards the increasingly dominant Constantine. Thus, Licinius joined Constantine in granting toleration to the Christians in 313, but then reintroduced persecution in the course of his two unsuccessful civil wars with the western emperor.[24] Similarly, Maximin initially accepted toleration when trying to pacify Constantine and Licinius, but reinstated the persecuting edicts when all-out war with Licinius seemed unavoidable.

It could not be said that the emergence of Christianity, as a major force with a growing and socially rising membership, was in itself the cause of the increasing divisiveness in Roman society from the later third century onwards, in that the phenomenon can be detected in areas in which religion had no part to play. However, the exclusivity of Christian religious belief, and its intolerance of other forms of faith, made the intellectual *modus vivendi* of the multitude of different groups, sects and religions of the Roman world no longer tenable, and exacerbated other fissures in the society.[25]

To Constantine, Rome may have seemed a stronghold of opposition to his beliefs. This was because of the conservatism of the Senate, whose tacit opposition to the emperor's religious aims grew stronger the clearer these became, and it has been suggested that his decision to move the centre of his government to the East reflected this hostility. However, apart from the reign of Maxentius, Rome stopped being the traditional imperial residence after the death of Gallienus in 268. Diocletian's precedent would also suggest an eastern capital, and the greater numbers of Christians resident in that part of the Empire might have been at best a secondary consideration.

When Constantine secured control over the whole Empire, the political structures that Diocletian and his colleagues had created were completely eradicated. Despite initial attempts at compromise, the conflict between Licinius and Maximin II for ascendancy in the East was prompted by Constantine's uniting of the West in 312. Early in the spring of 313, while Licinius was still in Italy, Maximin invaded his rival's territory. However, following a hasty return from the West, Licinius routed his opponent in a battle in Thrace on 30 April and drove him back into Asia. Maximin, in flight, died of illness at Tarsus, while Licinius was still busy conquering Asia Minor.[26]

With Licinius as dominant in the East as Constantine was in the West, the restoration of single dynastic rule over the whole Empire became their aim. The first clash occurred in 314. Licinius lost two battles against the western armies in the Balkans and was forced to cede some territory as the price of peace. There followed an uneasy decade of coexistence before the outbreak of the final war in 323. Again, Licinius was defeated in encounters at Adrianople and Chrysopolis, but this time the victories were more decisive and, having been besieged in Byzantium, Licinius was forced to submit. His life, and that of his son, the Caesar Licinius II, were spared at the intervention of his wife, Constantine's sister, but neither was allowed to live for long.[27]

In both of the wars, Licinius had at crucial moments proclaimed co-emperors, Valerius Valens in 314 and Marcus Martinianus in 324. These were probably his candidates for a western emperor to replace Constantine. Both were executed by the man they were intended to supplant.[28] Licinius was still thinking of a college of emperors, created by appointment, rather than sharing the nakedly dynastic aspirations of his rival. Sentiment played little part in Licinius's makeup. He is said to have had the wives and children of both Galerius and Maximin II put to death after they fell into his hands in 313, but in ruthlessness, as in political calculation and military skill, he was far outstripped by Constantine.[29]

It has not been possible for subsequent generations to idealise the first Christian emperor. His treatment of defeated enemies, such as the family of Licinius, was not untypical of his age, but he was also portrayed as being as lethal to his own family as to his foes. His father-in-law, the former emperor Maximian, is said to have been strangled in 310.[30] His eldest son Crispus was supposedly executed in 326 for committing adultery with his stepmother, Constantine's second wife; Fausta, daughter of Maximian, was also put to death soon afterwards, supposedly by being boiled alive in her bath.[31] However, it is more probable that Maximian committed suicide at Marseille following the failure of a coup he tried to lead against Constantine, and the lurid story of the fates of Crispus and Fausta only appears in the *New History* of the sixth-century Greek writer Zosimus, who was a pagan and deeply prejudiced against Constantine and his family.

After 312, Constantine deliberately played down the starkly militaristic images of the imperial office and its incumbents favoured by the Tetrarchy. Instead, a revived classicism manifested itself in the officially sponsored imperial images, to be seen in coin portraits and marble busts. At the same time, the special relationship between the secular ruler and his divine mentor was highlighted by those representations that depict him with his eyes turned upwards towards heaven. The styles selected and adapted by his regime set the pattern for the rest of the century as far as imperial portraiture and the visual propaganda of the imperial government were concerned.[32]

In few ways does the massively self-confident autocracy of Constantine manifest itself so clearly as in his creation of his new capital of Constantinople, begun in 324 and formally consecrated in 330. The political and, in terms of location, military disadvantages of Rome as the centre of imperial government had long been known to the emperors, and under the Tetrarchy four new imperial residences and centres of administration had been selected for the four rulers: Nicomedia, Milan, Thessalonica and Trier. While these cities had been particularly associated with and embellished by one or other of these emperors, the idea of a total re-foundation and renaming of a city, in this case the former port of Byzantium, was an innovation of Constantine's.

Though it is often thought that the emperor's experiences in Rome, particularly in his relations with the predominantly pagan Senate, led him to want to create a new and totally Christian capital, with no pagan places of worship, it also needs to be remembered that no emperor had followed the example of the Hellenistic kings and named his capital with his own name.[33] Nero and Commodus are both accused of having wished to do so in the case of Rome, but even they had not actually done so, and their examples were hardly savoury ones.[34] However, Constantine's decision, taken within months of the overthrow of Licinius, was implemented and the new 'City of Constantine' became his residence for the rest of his reign, and those of his successors in the eastern half of the Empire until 1453.

Conflict and succession, 324–50

The war between Constantine and Maxentius in 312, and the subsequent conflicts between Licinius and Maximin II in 313, and between Constantine and Licinius in 314 and 323–4, mark a change in the way struggles over succession or between rival emperors came to be settled in the Roman world. In the third century, while usurpations and revolts were frequent, in no case were the outcomes decided by a battle between the armed forces of the opposing sides. In such episodes as Decius's revolt against Philip I in 249, Aemilian's revolt against Trebonianus Gallus and Volusian in 253, Valerian's opposition to Aemilian in the same year, Probus's challenge to Florian in 276, and Carus's presumed revolt against Probus in 282, though both sides in each conflict had the support of different units of the army and a military resolution seemed inevitable, in every case the loser fell victim to the swords of his own men before the issue was tested in battle.

In each of these cases, and probably others in which emperors fell to assassination and were smoothly replaced by other members of the army high command, as happened to Gallienus in 268, it looks almost as if the Roman officer corps functioned as a single body, weighing up the merits of rival candidates and then acting to prevent any further unnecessary bloodshed within the forces. There was none of the long and bloody fighting between different legionary armies supporting rival candidates for the imperial office that had been so marked in the years 69 and 193–7. Some elements of this kind of divisive conflict within the army reappeared in the difficult years following Valerian's capture by the Persians in 260, but this was as much a response to as the cause of a breakdown in central authority within the Empire.

On the other hand, in the fourth century very bloody and protracted fighting between units of the Roman army supporting the claims of rival emperors took place on a number of occasions. The imperial civil wars of the time of Constantine may not have caused significant long-term loss, and the rise of Constantine himself to an unchallenged supremacy in the Roman world is regarded as so intrinsically significant that no thought is given to the consequences of the means employed. However, these conflicts were to be the first of a sequence that ultimately proved fatal to the continued existence of the Roman Empire, or at least its western half.

One clear message of the political problems of the third century, and of Diocletian's attempted solutions, was that the

Empire required the presence of more than one emperor when simultaneous military threats co-existed on more than one frontier. The possibility of a successful general being turned by his soldiers into an imperial contender had been demonstrated as a practical reality on numerous occasions between 249 and 282. The alternative 'college of emperors' envisaged by Diocletian had in large measure foundered on the failure to appreciate the popularity of dynastic succession within the army. Even children or candidates of no proven ability could gain the imperial throne with military backing solely on the basis of a family relationship to a venerated predecessor. This occurred in 218 and 222 with the last Severans, in 238 in the case of the young Gordian III, and in 251 with the child co-emperor Hostilian. Equally notable had been the army support for Constantine and Maxentius in 306, which enabled both of them to take and hold imperial titles.

For Constantine, the problem was simpler, in that he had an abundance of sons. The conclusion of the first of his wars with Licinius had been marked by the elevation of two of his sons and his opponent's only legitimate one to the rank of Caesar.[35] All of them were still too young to exercise any practical authority, but their elevation was a clear declaration of intended dynastic succession (see the diagram of the house of Constantine). In practice, Licinius's line was to prove short-lived, and the Caesar Licinius II was executed soon after his father. An illegitimate son of Licinius I was preserved by Constantine, but ended up as an attendant in the women's quarters of the imperial palace at Carthage.[36]

Constantine's younger sons, Constantius and Constans, joined their elder brother Constantine (II) and half-brother Crispus as Caesars in 324 and 333, respectively. Crispus either died or, less probably, was executed in 326, leaving the way clear for the three sons of Constantine's second marriage. The three Caesars received responsibility for different parts of the Empire, though they appear to have remained no more than ciphers during their father's lifetime. Peculiarly, their number was increased by Constantine in 335, when he made his two nephews, Dalmatius and Hannibalianus, a Caesar and king of Armenia, respectively.[37]

This was seen as dividing the cake rather too meanly, and immediately after Constantine's death in 337 both of them, together with most of the other collateral relatives of the late emperor, were massacred by the palace guard in Constantinople.[38] This apparently spontaneous outburst on the part of the military was blamed on Constantius, the only one of

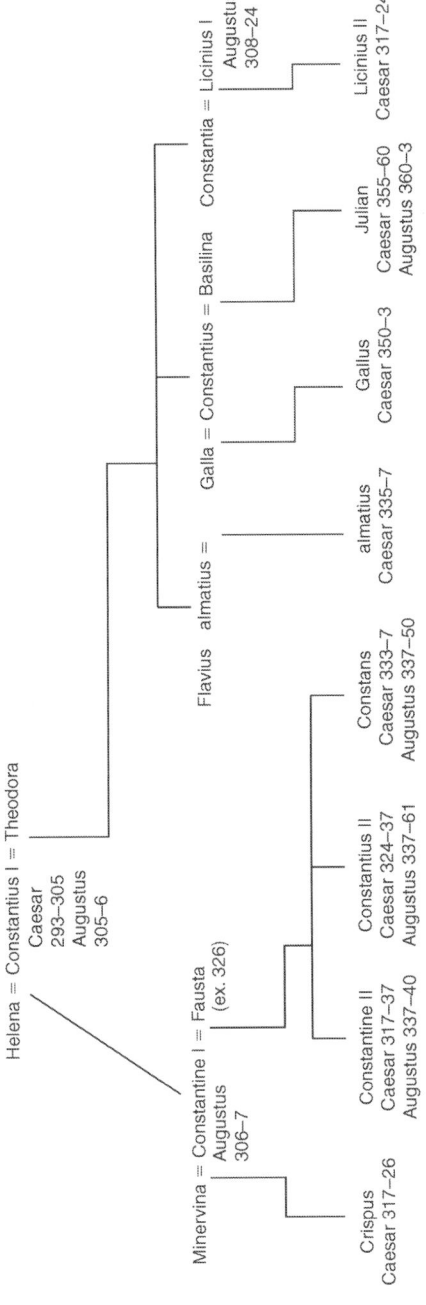

The house of Constantine, 364–533

Constantine's sons present in the capital at the time, and who, together with his two brothers, clearly benefited from this purge of surplus relatives. After a hiatus of three months, perhaps caused by the time taken in negotiation of the ensuing settlement, they were formally proclaimed Augusti or emperors by their armies.

In consequence, the provinces previously subject to the three brothers as Caesars became transformed into their territorial divisions as emperors. Constantine II thus kept Britain, Gaul and Spain; his youngest brother Constans retained Italy, Africa and most of the Balkans; while the middle brother and probable instigator of the purge of the palace obtained control of Constantinople and all the eastern provinces. Such a division was pragmatic in that it represented the existing allocation of armies and provinces, but left the eldest son with the smallest, least economically desirable and militarily most difficult portion. He was not slow to object, and began making territorial demands on his brother Constans to the south. The latter's understandable refusal to compromise led to war in 340, but in attempting to cross the Alps, Constantine's army was defeated and he was killed in a surprise attack.[39]

By this event, Constans found himself master of his late brother's provinces as well, and the Empire was thus effectively divided into eastern and western halves, something that was to become standardised by the end of the fourth century. While Constantius's own propaganda suggests that he graciously consented to his younger brother thus acquiring the lion's share of the Empire, something he must have thought he had achieved himself in 337, there seems no reason to believe that he was anything other than forced to accept a *fait accompli*.[40] The generally acknowledged superiority of the western armies, and the fate of the unfortunate Constantine II, would have made further bickering over boundaries unwise. Moreover, Persian threats to the eastern frontier were growing.

In 298, after an initially poor start, the Roman armies commanded by the Caesar Galerius had achieved a major victory over the Sasanians and had forced the shaky regime of the recently created shah Nerseh (293–302) to make substantial territorial concessions in Mesopotamia as the price of peace – a humiliation that Nerseh's grandson Shapur II (309–79) was anxious to avenge, but was initially too weak to undertake.[41] However, by the last year of Constantine I's life, a war with Persia was imminent. The first Persian attempt to regain the frontier fortress town of Nisibis was launched in 338, and was repeated in 346 and 350.[42] A general state of equilibrium was maintained between the two great empires, at least as long as a Roman ruler was able to devote his constant attention and military resources to the security of his eastern provinces. When, in the 350s, Constantius II was forced to look westward, the tide in the east turned in favour of the Persians.

The lack of substantial literary historical texts makes it very difficult to assess the politics and personalities of this period. The Tetrarchy can at least be viewed from the (admittedly hostile) standpoint of the contemporary Christian authors, and the years from 353 to 378 are described in considerable detail, frequently from an eyewitness's perspective, in the surviving books of the history of Ammianus Marcellinus, often described as being the last of the classical historians and a self-appointed continuator of the work of Tacitus. However, the final years of the reign of Constantine, and most of those of his sons, remain obscure, being described in the briefest of fashions in the diminutive works of some late-fourth-century historical epitomators.[43]

Despite a general tendency to disparage Constantius II, largely as a result of an uncritical acceptance of the attitudes and judgements of the historian Ammianus by his modern counterparts, the success of this emperor in maintaining his eastern frontiers against a renascent Persia should not be minimised. In the West, his brother was apparently equally active in trying to combat growing pressure being exerted on the Rhine frontier by both the Franks and the Alamans. Constans was the last of the Roman emperors to visit Britain (in 343), in response to some military problems of which we know little. Some reorganisation of the defences of the island took place as a consequence, and it has been suggested that the coastal fort erected at Pevensey in Sussex was built on this emperor's orders.[44]

Whatever his other virtues, Constans failed to retain the loyalty of his army, and in 350 was overthrown in a conspiracy hatched by his finance minister or *Comes Rei Privatae*, Marcellinus, and a general of possibly mixed British and Frankish origin called Magnentius, commander of units of the field army, who was hailed as emperor by the armies in Gaul. Constans was captured in flight and executed. There has been conjecture that the rather enigmatic but substantial mausoleum at Centcelles, near Tarragona, whose mosaics seem to date to this period, became his final resting place.[45]

The lack of detailed narrative makes it impossible to understand the underlying causes of Constans's fall, running counter to the sentiment of dynastic loyalty to the house of Constantine which had been strong in the western armies from the beginning of the century. Equally so, the grounds for the alternative popularity of Magnentius remain unclear, though some prior military success may be assumed. This is particularly regrettable in that the consequences of the coup of 350 were in some respects extraordinarily far-reaching, having a permanent and detrimental effect on the military security of the western half of the Empire for the rest of its existence.

3 Protecting the Empire, 350–95

Frontier defence, 350–61

It is a pity that the sections of the historical work of Ammianus Marcellinus that have survived deal only with the events of 353 onwards. There are a number of tantalising references in the extant books to various participants and incidents in the civil war between the eastern and western halves of the Empire of the years 350–3, but the main narrative, which may have been extensive, has been lost. Thus the events of these years can only be reconstructed in outline.[1]

The sudden overthrow of Constans in 350, and with him of the Constantinian dynasty in the West, temporarily shook the political fabric in that half of the Empire. When Magnentius was taking power in Gaul, a relative by marriage of the house of Constantine, called Nepotian, seized power in Rome. A few coins struck in his name have survived, and it looks as if, like Maxentius in 306, he was playing on the Roman Senate's civic patriotism and dissatisfaction at being excluded from real political authority. However, as soon as Magnentius had consolidated his hold in the north, he crushed the ephemeral regime of Nepotian.[2]

More significant was the proclamation of another imperial claimant, an elderly general called Vetranio, who commanded the imperial field armies in the Balkans. Initially, he negotiated with both of his rivals – Constantius II in the East and Magnentius in the West – but he was rapidly persuaded to abdicate in favour of Constantius.[3] Thus his real importance lies in the fact that his brief bid for power prevented Magnentius from gaining control of the western Balkans and the substantial military forces stationed in the region.

Of the ensuing three years of war between Magnentius and Constantius, little detail is known other than the outcome: after some extremely hard-fought and bloody battles in the Balkans and Gaul, the western ruler was decisively defeated, and finally committed suicide in August 353, as did his brother, the Caesar Decentius. This resulted in the reunification of the Empire under the rule of Constantius II, the sole surviving son of Constantine.[4]

However, the longer-term consequences of the war included a significant weakening of the imperial defences along the Rhine.

As the fighting grew in intensity, units of *Limitanei* or frontier troops were transferred to the western field army to assist Magnentius in his increasingly desperate resistance. Certainly, the evidence of Ammianus indicates that in the year 356 virtually all the Roman frontier fortresses north of Mainz had been abandoned, and doubtless in consequence a substantial, if economically not very productive, piece of imperial territory west of the Rhine and north of the Meuse passed into the control of various groups of Franks.[5]

More threatening at the time would have seemed the penetration across the Rhine and into the Gallic provinces further south of large numbers of Alamans, who had defeated a Roman army under Magnentius's brother, Decentius.[6] They were a confederacy of Germanic-speaking peoples, first reported in 213, located south of the river Main and east of the Rhine, and rivals to the Franks, who were their neighbours to the north. Though lacking the siegecraft needed to take walled towns, the Alamans made themselves masters of large stretches of the countryside from the middle Rhine as far west as Troyes, Autun and Sens. This Alamannic penetration of eastern Gaul began in the period of the civil war of 350–3, and was doubtless made possible by it. It continued unchecked until it was reversed in 357.

The elimination, at least temporarily, of this threat from the Alamans was the work of the Caesar Julian. He and a half-brother, Gallus, were the only members of the collateral branches of the house of Constantine to survive the purge of 337, probably because of their youth. When Constantius had to turn his attention to the West to conduct the campaigns against Magnentius, he made Gallus a Caesar, establishing him with a court at Antioch, to provide an imperial presence in the East and oversee the frontier with Persia. However, in 353, after the conclusion of the civil war, he summoned Gallus to come to him at Milan. The Caesar was arrested on his way across the Balkans, and then executed on the emperor's orders.[7]

Although Gallus, by Ammianus's account, had acted as Caesar in a high-handed and tactless way, making himself a number of powerful enemies in the East and in Constantius's entourage, there remains the suspicion that, with the civil war over, his services were no longer required. With his elimination, the surviving male members of the dynasty of Constantine were reduced to two: Constantius II and Gallus's half-brother, Julian. As the emperor had no children, the ranks of the imperial family were becoming dangerously flimsy.

The precedent of Gallus's fate cannot have been forgotten when a similar situation developed in 355. In the East, the threat of a new Persian offensive was growing and pressures were mounting on the Danube. At the same time, Britain had only recently been recovered and the leading adherents of Magnentius on the island purged. In Gaul, the Alamannic threat had not been countered, and the general appointed to meet it had instead been proclaimed emperor by his troops at Cologne. This new usurper, Silvanus, was of Frankish origin and the son of a distinguished general of the time of Constantine I. He seems to have been driven into revolt by a court intrigue directed against him; another sign of the fragility of imperial favour at this time. Like Vetranio in 350, Silvanus was a half-hearted emperor, and immediately opened negotiations with Constantius. The latter's envoys, including the historian Ammianus Marcellinus, then serving as a staff officer, managed to have Silvanus assassinated, and the revolt collapsed.[8]

Whether because this dangerously weakened the city's garrison, or because the murder of Silvanus required avenging by his own people, Cologne was seized and sacked by the Franks from across the Meuse and left abandoned.[9] By this time, the deteriorating conditions in Gaul, together with the existence of equally acute problems elsewhere in the Empire, had led Constantius II to appoint a new Caesar. This was Julian, whom he had recently called from his studies in Athens, and who seems to have had no previous military experience. Proclaimed in Rome in November 355, Julian was dispatched to Gaul, while Constantius prepared to deal with problems on the Danube frontier and in the East.[10]

Julian's campaigning in Gaul in the years 356–9, described in some detail by Ammianus, is particularly revealing, both of the Roman methods of warfare and of the nature of the threat being faced. Julian set out from Rome for Vienne in the Rhône valley and spent the rest of the winter there. At some point in the spring, a force of Alamans attacked the city of Autun, whose walls were apparently in a state of ill-repair. Julian left Vienne to relieve Autun, which he did without any fighting, and then proceeded northwards to Troyes. Here, Ammianus records significantly, the inhabitants were almost too frightened to let him in, which suggests that they could not easily recognise the difference between a Roman army and an Alamannic force. He continued his march to Reims, where the Roman field forces still active in northern Gaul were concentrating. Julian's troops were constantly harassed by Alamannic attack during his march from the south, being particularly vulnerable at road and river crossings. At the same time, the Alamans were raiding in force around the Roman towns and forts on the middle Rhine, from Mainz to as far south as Strasbourg (see map).[11]

However, Julian's priority was the restoration of Cologne, and the whole campaigning season of 356 was devoted to this, and to making treaties with the Frankish kings north of the Meuse.[12] It seems that his intention was to stabilise his rear in preparation for a major assault on the Alamans in 357, and at the same time to regroup and restore the morale of the Roman field forces in Gaul, some of whom had previously supported Magnentius and Silvanus, or had been defeated by the Alamans.

Their threat was renewed later that year, when, after leaving Cologne, Julian dispersed his troops to different winter quarters and he took up residence in Sens. There he was besieged for a month by Alamans, who knew that he had only part of his army with him. The Alamans eventually gave up, as they lacked the ability to take defended towns.[13] However, this incident shows how dependent the Romans were on retaining fortified towns, and also how deeply the Alamans had been able to penetrate the Gallic countryside.

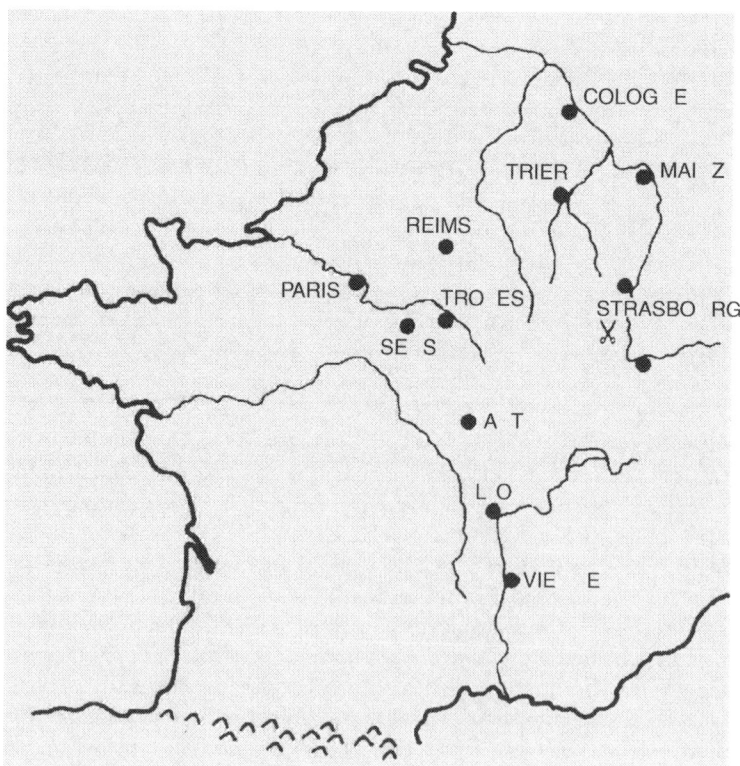

Julian in Gaul, 355–60

Imperial fortunes changed the following year, when a long-planned Roman offensive was launched against the Alamans. This involved a two-pronged pincer attack on their principal concentration in the area of the middle Rhine. Julian and the Gallic field armies, which again concentrated at Reims, marched south-east to reach the Rhine in the region of Strasbourg, while a second and possibly larger army of 25,000 men, under a general of Germanic-speaking origin called Barbatio, marched northwards from Italy to the upper Rhine.

The Alamans seem to have been aware of the threat and concentrated a large army, said to be 35,000 strong, under two supreme war leaders, Chnodomar and Serapio, five other kings and ten 'princes'. They also took the precaution of striking before the two Roman armies could combine in the vicinity of Strasbourg. They intercepted the army commanded by Barbatio and drove it back to the fortress town of *Augusta Raurica* (near Basel in Switzerland), and then turned on the second, probably smaller, Roman army under Julian. Good as their strategy had been, their tactics proved deficient, and in the ensuing battle at Strasbourg the Alamannic army was defeated with the loss of some 6,000 men and the capture of its commander, Chnodomar.[14]

This single battle really turned the tide as far as the Alaman penetration of Gaul was concerned. It broke the Alamannic confederacy of tribes that had largely been built up and held together by the military credibility of Chnodomar, and for the first time enabled the Romans to take the initiative. In the aftermath of the battle, Julian marched to Mainz, and despite some reluctance on the part of his troops, crossed the Rhine. Threatened with a Roman invasion of their own territory, the Alamans sought a truce.[15]

With the Alamannic threat countered, Julian could seek a more effective settlement with the Franks, who had been raiding Roman territory near recently-restored Cologne. He blockaded their strongholds on the Meuse, some of which may well have been abandoned Roman forts, until they were prepared to come to terms.[16] It is notable that Julian made no attempt to penetrate the marshy lands north of the Meuse that the Franks had occupied, and their continuing occupation of this area was tacitly accepted by the Romans. From this small start the subsequent Frankish occupation of all of Gaul would develop. This, it might be said, was 'the birth of France'. In 357/8, however, what was achieved was a treaty of federation: Frankish occupation of Roman territory was accepted in return for their helping to defend the region. In itself this was a good deal, and the Franks remained faithful to the terms of the treaty until the eventual collapse of imperial authority in the area in the fifth century.

In 359, Julian was able to restore seven of the principal Roman fortresses on the lower Rhine, to add to those he had previously rebuilt in the region of Strasbourg and across the Rhine near Mainz.[17] For the first time for nearly a decade, the Roman frontier along the Rhine had been re-established. Alamannic raiding across the middle part of the river had been halted, and though not expelled, Frankish occupation of the west bank of the lower Rhine had been regularised. Thus much of what had been lost in 350–3 had been regained by the end of 359.

Julian the Reactionary, 361–3

Julian was now in a position similar to that of his half-brother, Gallus. He had been made Caesar for a particular purpose, which had now been achieved. His immediate usefulness to Constantius was at an end, and as happened to Gallus in 353/4, he was being subjected to increasing vilification at the emperor's court. While Ammianus Marcellinus was clearly prejudiced against Constantius II and a partisan of Julian, his narrative indicates that suspicion was aroused by those who did well militarily, or who seemed to present a threat to the emperor's security. A recent victim had been the general (*Magister Peditum*) Barbatio, who had masterminded the plot against, and execution of, the Caesar Gallus in 354, and who had commanded the army that was supposed to co-operate with that of Julian on the Rhine in 357. He was executed because of a secret letter written by his wife about an omen that appeared to suggest he might be the next emperor. They were informed on by a maid.[18]

Whether Julian really stood in the same danger as Gallus in 354 is hard to determine. He was now the only other male representative of the line of Constantine, and it is not clear that Constantius was willing to commit dynastic suicide. However, the events of 360 may have given him serious doubts as to his safety. In the East, the war with the Persians had resumed in 359, and was not going well for Rome. The important frontier fortress of Amida fell to Shapur II, and the Persians launched a full scale invasion of Roman Mesopotamia in 360.[19] In the circumstances, Constantius's need of reinforcements was real, and the now pacified state of the West meant that this was the area in which to find them. On the other hand, if Julian was going to be eliminated he would have to be separated from his troops, who had become devoted to him as a result of his highly successful campaigns. The ruse of summoning the Caesar to consult with the emperor, used in 354, might hardly have been expected to work again, and so the dispersal of Julian's armies would be the necessary first step to his elimination.

Whatever the motivation, the order from Constantius to Julian, sent early in 360, to dispatch a number of his units to the East, gave rise to a revolt. Julian, who had deliberately placed himself on the line of march of the soldiers setting out from Gaul, was proclaimed emperor by his armies at Paris, after going through the necessary ritual of refusing the proffered office.[20] This meant yet another civil war, less than ten years after the last one, as it was quickly made clear that Constantius II had no intention of accepting Julian as an equal colleague. However, the war's outbreak was delayed by Julian's need to secure his position in the West, to quell further trouble with the Alamans, and for Constantius to be able to detach himself from the war with Persia. When Constantius was eventually able to make his way back towards Constantinople, he was taken ill and died unexpectedly near Tarsus on 5 October 361.[21]

Although much maligned by Ammianus and some modern historians, Constantius II had proved himself a capable and conscientious emperor, very much after the model of his father, whose ruthlessness and tenacity he had in large measure shared. His tendency to support the bishops opposed to the Trinitarian theology promoted at the Council of Nicea of 325 also meant that the pro-Nicene party in the Church, for whom the standard-bearer was bishop Athanasius of Alexandria, whom Constantius twice exiled, was consistently hostile to him. He may have allowed court politics and the power of the secret agents of the state, such as the notorious Spaniard, Paul 'the Chain', to reach such a point that generals might be driven to revolt rather than face disgrace or even death through factional intrigue, but it was the emperor's favour that they sought, not control over him.[22] He did, however, seem to be willing to see his dynasty become extinct rather than to share power with any of his dwindling band of male relatives.

Julian, on the other hand, in his brief reign (361–3) showed himself to be an emperor of a very different kind. The unforeseen death of his cousin Constantius left him undisputed master of the Empire, and even those units of the army that were making their way west to fight him promptly accepted his imperial authority. He was thus able to turn what had begun as a military campaign into a triumphal progress to Constantinople.

Julian's approach to his new office and the policies he tried to develop through it were in many respects reactionary, in the sense that he wished to undo much of the religious, cultural and

political transformation to which the Empire had been subjected
in the reigns of his predecessors since the time of Constantine I.
This nostalgic and antiquarian tendency in his thinking may
well have been a product of his secluded and scholarly upbringing, which had kept him away from public attention, and had
certainly not been intended to equip him for future imperial
office. Once in Constantinople, he purged the court of a number of the most prominent of the supporters of Constantius,
and had several of his more notorious officials, such as Paul
'the Chain', put on trial. More controversial, however, was the
style of imperial court that Julian tried to create. He dismissed
the eunuchs, who had previously been the personal servants
of the emperor and his family, and tried to revive the image
of the imperial office as no more than the greatest of the civil
magistracies. Thus, although he continued to use a throne, he
rose from it when senators were presented and came forward
to greet them personally, rather than allowing them to perform
the by-now standard acts of obeisance.[23]

In character with this attempt to return imperial protocol,
and the political ideas that underlay it, to something closer to
the standards and practices of the earlier Empire, was Julian's
public revelation of his hitherto private paganism. He had
been initiated into the Eleusinian Mysteries in the course of his
literary studies in Athens, and while maintaining the appearance of being a Christian prince of the House of Constantine
had personally rebelled against the dynastic religion. His accession to power had enabled him to drop the mask, and his reign
marked a period of what is normally called pagan reaction.[24]
In practice, all Julian did was to remove the privileges that had
been granted to the bishops and clergy under the previous
regime, and at the same time redirect the state funding that had
formerly been channelled into the Church into the revival of
classical urban paganism. This meant using imperial resources
to rebuild derelict or neglected temples, and paying stipends
for town priesthoods rather than for the erection and endowment of churches and subsidising of Christian clergy. Ultimately,
Julian took the logical step of forbidding Christians from holding the state-subsidised professorships of rhetoric and grammar
that were to be found in most of the major cities of the Empire,
based on the argument that it was hardly appropriate for them
to teach the literary classics of Antiquity when their writings
showed that they were totally opposed to the religious principles
and cultural ideals expressed in that literature.[25]

For the Christians this constituted persecution, and their hostility to Julian might have become more overt had he reigned

for longer. The brevity of his rule made his reforms a passing threat, and for some time afterwards a troubling memory. The hold of Christianity on ever-increasing numbers and more and more influential sectors of the population as the fourth century progressed might have been reduced by the change in imperial favour, but was unlikely to have been significantly reversed. The reason for this thinking is less the innate strength of the Christian position, though this should not be underestimated, than the moribund nature of much of the classical paganism of the Mediterranean world by this time.

The reason that so many temples were derelict and so many town councils had stopped paying the salaries of the priests who should have serviced the temples, was more a reflection of the lack of public interest than the result of any pressure from the imperial government of the House of Constantine. Indeed, it is notable that the enthusiastic persecutor Maximin II (308–13) had once tried to achieve a similar objective to Julian and to put new life into flagging pagan religious practice at a time when the Christians in his sections of the Empire were a persecuted and harassed minority. The rise of Christianity during the third and early fourth centuries was the other side of the coin to the collapse of public involvement in the religious cults of the towns of the Roman Empire. The upper classes and intellectuals preferred either devotion to the increasingly popular mystery cults or, by no means mutually exclusively, the philosophical reformulation of traditional religious ideas associated with Neoplatonism.[26]

What Julian, who had studied under some of the principal Neoplatonic philosophers of his day in Athens as well as becoming an enthusiast for the performance of the rituals of the old religion, attempted to do was to restore the traditional practices of civic paganism by refurbishing temples, paying for priesthoods, and encouraging the revival of public rites, such as animal sacrifice, and at the same time to give new intellectual life to the religion by disseminating, not least in his own writings, the philosophical interpretations of it that he had learnt from his university masters.[27] Thus he sought single-handedly to unite two increasingly divergent elements in paganism. The result was that he was criticised from both sides. The general non-Christian populations of the towns of the eastern Mediterranean seem to have lost much of their taste for traditional observances, certainly if it meant paying for them, and they also found the philosophical underpinning that Julian was trying to put back into the religion beyond their capacity to understand. The intellectual elite found it ludicrous that one trained

to understand the higher truths that lay behind the old practices should involve himself with the popular level of religion.

What is perhaps most striking about Julian's attempts to
revive old ways, in political life, in religion and in local urban
patriotism, is their lack of success, and the degree of indifference, shading into opposition, with which he was faced. Even his
partisans, such as Ammianus, who valued his military virtues,
thought his expulsion of the court eunuchs was unjustly harsh.[28]
His Republican approach to the imperial office and its ceremonial was condemned as being merely undignified, and his sporting of the philosopher's beard, which he grew after coming to
power, was made into a subject of ridicule by the local populace
during his stay in Antioch in 363.

This city, to which he transferred his court, both to conduct
operations on the eastern frontier and to get away from the
totally Christian environment of Constantinople, was still home
to a large pagan population, and had long been a major intellectual, as well as commercial, centre in the Greek East. Even
here, though, Julian gained little sympathy for his religious and
cultural aspirations. He failed to interest the city council in the
restoration of public buildings and civic religion, and the lam-
pooning of his personal appearance by the populace led him to
write one of his most powerful works, the *Misopogon* or *Beard-
Hater*, in which he struck back at what he considered to be the
Antiochenes' frivolity and lack of purpose. Had he returned
from his Persian expedition in 363, he proposed moving his
seat of government from Antioch to Tarsus.[29]

While the reactions of the urban councils and the ordinary
populations of the cities of the eastern provinces were significant, perhaps even more telling was the attitude of some of
those to whom Julian appealed directly, and who might have
been expected to share many of his aspirations. These were the
pagan philosophers and teachers whose cultural and intellectual
interests the new emperor shared, and who in some cases had
been his own teachers and fellow students. One or two, notably
the Neoplatonist philosopher Maximus, came to join his court,
but many others found excuses to stay away, and wait to see
what happened.[30]

In this they were proved wise, since Julian's regime was
far more short-lived than might have been expected. The
Persians had gained considerable advantage in their war with
Constantius II in 359 and 360, and by the capture of some
strategic towns had effectively redrawn the frontiers in their
favour. In 363, Julian, whose innate if untutored military ability
had been demonstrated in his Gallic campaigns, determined

on launching an invasion of Persia. For this he gathered from Antioch an unusually large army, said to be 65,000 strong, and marched towards the Persian capital of Ctesiphon.

How far Julian imagined that he could recreate the military achievements of Alexander the Great, whose image he some-times used in his propaganda, cannot be known. Certainly, as recent criticism has indicated, his strategic judgement was faulty in both the conception and the execution of this campaign.[31] The Roman army succeeded in making its way by boat down the Euphrates, but lacked both the mobility to force the Persians to give battle and the technical skills to take the well-fortified city of Ctesiphon. Thus Julian was unable to achieve his military and diplomatic objectives by his mighty display of force, and instead had to undertake the demoralising task of withdrawing his troops from an untenable position, and with an enemy still in full strength and enjoying superior mobility. Unable to use the boats they had arrived in to return up the Euphrates, Julian was obliged to burn his flotilla and take his forces overland towards the Tigris in a triangular march back towards Roman territory. The retreat across Mesopotamia was accompanied by frequent attacks from companies of Persian horse archers. In hastening to repel one of these sudden strikes at the army's flanks Julian rushed out from his camp without armour and was mortally wounded in the fray. He died in his tent on 26 June 363, aged only thirty-two.[32]

The argument as to whether Julian and his 'pagan revival' really constituted a threat to the growing hold of Christianity in the Roman Empire is essentially academic in the light of the brevity of his reign. Certainly, one pagan orator later raised the possibility that he had not been struck down by a Persian arrow but had instead been stabbed in the back in the midst of the battle by a Christian member of his own guard.[33] But it is doubt-ful whether a longer reign would have availed Julian much, in the light of the kinds of responses he did evoke from those who should have been his principal supporters. He was also unmar-ried and had no designated successor to pursue his policies and defend his memory.

Civil wars, 363–95

His immediate successor, Jovian, the commander of the corps of imperial guards called the *Domestici*, was selected by the army in the camp following Julian's death, and was faced with the task of extricating the even more demoralised Roman forces from their intolerable position in the middle of Mesopotamia. This he did by immediately making a treaty with Shapur II, effectively giving back to the Persians all that the Empire had gained in the campaigns of the 290s. After this inauspicious start to his reign, he led the army back via Antioch towards Constantinople, only to die on the march on 23 February 364, probably asphyxiated by gas from a heating device in his tent.[34]

Once again, the army command had to choose a new emperor, and after some discussion selected a general called Valentinian. He rapidly decided to associate his brother Valens with him in the imperial office and to divide their respective spheres of activity. He installed Valens in Constantinople and he himself set off for the West. The need for two emperors, for the first time since 350, was made clear by the renewed threats to the Rhine and Danube frontiers from the Alamans and others, who took advantage of the emperor's absence in the East. And in 368, Shapur II abrogated the treaty of 363 on the grounds that he had made it with Jovian and was thus not bound by it to the new imperial regime.[35]

Of the two new emperors, Valentinian I has always enjoyed a good press, from the time of Ammianus Marcellinus onwards, and this is not undeserved. Most of his eleven-year reign (364–75) was devoted to constant and effective campaigning on the western frontiers. His brother Valens (364–78), on the other hand, has generally been seen as inadequate to the tasks he was faced with.[36] This is unfair in some respects, and is largely conditioned by the knowledge from hindsight of his eventual unfortunate fate. Also, his continuing support, like that of Constantius II, for the anti-Nicene faction in the great theological dispute that divided the Church for much of the century, led to his posthumous vilification by the ultimately triumphant orthodox party.[37]

Valens proved competent enough to survive the revolt and seizure of Constantinople by the usurper Procopius (365–6), a former general and relative of the emperor Julian, whom he claimed had promised him the imperial succession.[38] In 367 and 369, Valens led armies across the Danube against the *Theruingi*, who had provided military assistance for Procopius, and in the latter year defeated their principal leader Athanaric, forcing them to sue for peace. Such campaigning outside the frontiers of the Empire was normally considered very risky, and few late Roman emperors ever undertook it. Ammianus, who had left the army early in Valens's reign, makes all too brief mention of it, but this was no mean military achievement.[39]

As well as the purging of the army of the supporters of Julian, another reason for Ammianus Marcellinus's hostility to Valens may have lain in the personal danger he encountered in his native Antioch in 371, when accusations of treason were being bandied about, and imperial agents conducted a series of investigations and trials of prominent citizens suspected of being disaffected towards the regime.[40] Similar inquiries were also carried out in Rome by appointees of Valentinian, and a number of senators were tried and convicted of using magical practices in 372.[41] Several were executed. In the Roman world, secret consultations of oracles and other forms of soothsaying were always regarded with suspicion, as they were assumed to be for political purposes.

With the relative brevity of imperial reigns and the lack of dynastic continuity, the seeking of supernatural information as to how long an emperor would live and what might be the name of his successor was a sign of political dissidence, and the possible first step to conspiracy. As in parts of the third century, friction between the highly cultured civilian aristocracy of the Senate and the less sophisticated provincials who made up the officer class led to hostility and ultimately repressive measures on the part of the emperors. This became particularly marked in the reigns of Valentinian I and Valens, who employed officers of similar background to themselves from their home province of Pannonia in the Balkans in many positions, not least in the city of Rome.

The personal need for dynastic continuity, and the way that the loyalty of the army could be manipulated, is clear in the various succession arrangements of the House of Valentinian. Valentinian himself selected his elder son, Gratian, then aged only eight, to be titular co-emperor of the West with him in 367. In 375, after a highly successful series of campaigns around the lower Rhine, Valentinian transferred his attention again to the Danube, to counter the raids of a people called the Quadi. However, later in the year, he died of a stroke, apparently brought on by a fit of rage in an imperial audience at what he considered the insolence of the excuses offered to him by envoys of the Quadi.[42]

This should clearly have left the way open for Gratian, who was at Trier, but the generals commanding the army on the Danube found it convenient or necessary to proclaim as emperor the four-year-old child Valentinian II, the son of Valentinian I by his second wife. The reason given was that the Gallic contingents could not be trusted not to take the opportunity of setting up a new emperor of their own choosing.[43] When it is remembered that the election of an emperor was always accompanied by the distribution of a cash donation to the troops, it was likely that some attempt would be made, and it was better that it should be in the name of a token representative of the reigning dynasty.

Whatever the causes of the elevation of Valentinian II, authority in the West remained in practice in the hands of Gratian and his advisers. The infant Valentinian was established, together with his mother, in a court at Milan, while Gratian, who was initially much influenced by his former tutor Ausonius, a professor of rhetoric from Bordeaux and a poet of some skill, undertook successful military operations against renewed Alamannic pressure on the upper Rhine.[44] In 378, he and his armies defeated a major incursion by one of these tribes, called the *Lentienses*, killing 35,000 of them, and then crossed into their own territory between the headwaters of the Rhine and Danube to force them to submit.[45]

However, Gratian's popularity with his own soldiers waned. As with so many of these imperial dynasties, the lesser competence of the second generation eroded the initial sense of loyalty to a line founded by a popular commander and emperor. In 383, when a general of Spanish origin called Magnus Maximus was proclaimed emperor by the armies in Britain, the troops in Gaul were defeated by the rebels and rapidly deserted Gratian, who had alienated them by his affection for his barbarian bodyguards, whose national dress he was said sometimes to wear. He tried to flee to the East, but was captured and executed.[46] Among those who quickly joined Maximus was Merobaudes, a leading general under both Valentinian and Gratian.[47]

The regime of Valentinian II in Italy, dominated by his mother Justina, had to look to its defences, but had little military backing. However, the first concern of Magnus Maximus, now master of Britain, Gaul and Spain, was to secure recognition as a colleague by the emperor in the East, Theodosius I (379–95). This and some astute diplomacy on the part of bishop Ambrose of Milan (374–97) prevented Maximus from crossing the undefended Alps to make himself master of Italy as well.[48] Ultimately, Theodosius was willing to tolerate Maximus's rule in the West as long as Valentinian II and his court were left in control of Italy and Africa. Only when Maximus felt strong enough to face an outright breach with Theodosius, in 387, did he finally cross the Alps and make himself master of all the West, following the immediate flight of Valentinian and his mother to Constantinople.[49]

The eastern emperor was not prepared to tolerate this, and there began yet another civil war between the two halves of the Empire, which, though short was, as usual, bloody. Theodosius invaded the West in 388, and in a hard-fought battle in the Julian Alps defeated Maximus, who was captured and executed at Aquileia.[50] The same fate befell his young son and nominal co-emperor, Flavius Victor. Valentinian II was sent to set up his court at Vienne in Gaul, while Theodosius spent a few months in Milan before returning East. Despite reinstating Valentinian II, Theodosius made sure he remained as much of a puppet as he had been throughout his previous reign, by installing one of his own generals, a Frank called Arbogast, as the commander of the western field armies.

Unfortunately, this provoked yet another civil war four years later. In 392, the unfortunate Valentinian II, who enjoyed perhaps the most consistently depressing imperial career of any wearer of the Purple, became so incensed by his powerlessness in the hands of Arbogast that when he failed in an attempt to dismiss the over-powerful general he committed suicide.[51] This was hardly in Arbogast's interests, though he has been accused of murdering Valentinian, and he had to find an alternative emperor to fill the vacancy. He selected a former teacher and civil servant called Eugenius. This was a surprising choice, but his own Germanic origins made him an unacceptable candidate, and he could hardly elevate another military man without losing his own pre-eminence in the army.

Theodosius I began to plan yet another invasion of the West. This materialised in 394, just six years after the previous one. In the meantime, the regime of Eugenius and Arbogast, which had based itself in Gaul, attempted to appeal to all possible interest groups, not least the still largely pagan senatorial aristocracy in Rome. Imperial laws restricting pagan worship were abolished, and some evidence of the restoration of cult sites in Rome itself and elsewhere, including Britain, exists from this brief period. In consequence, some of the most noted non-Christian senators, led by Virius Nicomachus Flavianus, who became Praetorian Prefect, the principal civilian administrator in Italy, threw themselves into active support of Eugenius's regime.[52]

It was of little avail. In 394, Theodosius invaded Italy and, in another and even bloodier battle on the river Frigidus in the Alps in September, the western army, after some initial success, was totally defeated. Eugenius was captured and killed. Arbogast and Nicomachus Flavianus committed suicide.[53] Theodosius I, however, did not long survive. After the battle, he established himself in Milan once more, but died there unexpectedly in January 395, leaving the Empire to his two young sons.[54]

It is not always easy to understand why the emperors of the second half of the fourth century were so unwilling to tolerate the existence of imperial colleagues in other sections of the Empire whom they had not selected themselves. Constantius II could have come to an understanding with Magnentius as the latter wished, despite the loss of his brother: family sentiment was not strong in the House of Constantine. He could also have tolerated Julian, his only living male relative, as a colleague in the West, when he himself was so committed on the Persian frontier. Similarly, Theodosius could have accepted sharing the Empire with Magnus Maximus or with Eugenius. However, in each case, the issue was tested in war, with consequent bloodshed and much damage to the armies.

In the latter respect, whether or not there was a shortage of manpower in the late Roman Empire, as used to be argued, matters less than the fact that these perennial conflicts destroyed the quality of the army, because the losses of highly trained Roman veterans in the ranks of the elite field armies could only be compensated for by the recruitment of either untried civilians or militarily competent, but culturally ambivalent immigrants and mercenaries, from across the frontier. The principal element in Theodosius I's victory over Eugenius on the Frigidus, apart from some luck with the weather, was his large contingent of Gothic troops. How they came to be there requires a look at other features of this turbulent second half of the fourth century.

4 From the battle of Adrianople to the sack of Rome, 378–410

'The coming of the Huns'

Eastern and central Europe beyond the imperial frontiers had been the scene of almost continuous movement of peoples, settling, migrating, fighting, forming and re-forming ethnic identities from long before the founding of the Roman Empire. This period of instability was under way by the middle of the first millennium BC and continued until the end of the first millennium AD. In this context, Rome's wars against its 'barbarian' neighbours form only a part of a longer and more complex whole. Mutually interactive as they were, the chronologies of the great civilisations of the Mediterranean basin and of this 'Age of Migrations' further to the north are by no means synchronous.

In terms of written evidence, at least until the sixth century AD, the only perspective available on the events taking place beyond their frontiers comes from the writings of those Roman historians who included brief accounts of the doings of the 'barbarians' in their descriptions of contemporary events. Even then, not too much reliance can be placed on the detail such authors provide about non-Roman societies. For one thing there was an innate prejudice in their narratives: the Romans divided all the inhabitants of the world into two groups: the citizens of the Empire, who alone enjoyed the benefits of civilisation, and the rest – the 'barbarians' – who did not.[1] The Romans were even less ethnographically minded than the Greeks, and readers expected authors to demonstrate their Antiquarian learning rather than to provide a close observation of contemporary realities when it came to describing the inhabitants of lands outside the Empire.

Thus the Huns, who dominated the northern bank of the Danube during the last quarter of the fourth century and the first half of the fifth, were called Scythians by contemporary Roman authors, because this was the name Herodotus had used for inhabitants of that region nearly a thousand years earlier. In subsequent centuries, long after the collapse of the Hun hegemony in the mid-450s, the peoples who controlled the same region, such as the Avars, were called Huns by eastern Roman authors because this name had become the culturally accepted one to use for its inhabitants.

Even if a classically trained Roman historian had wanted real information about the barbarians across the frontiers, acquiring it would not have been easy. Only one of the historical writers of the fourth and fifth centuries seems to have had first-hand experience of a barbarian society, and this is Priscus, who served as an imperial ambassador to the Huns in the 440s, and who recorded what he saw in much detail, including accounts of conversations in the court of the Hun king, Attila. Unfortunately, only fragments of his work survive as extracts in later texts, principally the *Biblioteca* or 'Library' of Photios, Patriarch of Constantinople (858–67, 877–86).[2]

So, much of the information required for describing the organisation of the societies beyond the imperial frontiers and to explain their actions from their own perspective is missing. Archaeology is of some help here, but the association of particular material cultures with named societies known from the historical record is by no means straightforward. Several populations that are known from literary sources to have been politically distinct shared a common material culture, and thus cannot be distinguished archaeologically. A good case in point is that of the Goths, who, in the first three centuries AD probably formed one component of what the archaeologists label the Wielbark culture, which gradually extended itself from the southern shores of the Baltic to the Carpathians. A far from reliable literary account of their history in this period exists in the *Getica* or 'Gothic History' written in 551 by Jordanes, but there is no way that archaeological research can confirm or deny its claims.[3] Strictly speaking, there is thus no archaeological evidence for the existence of the Goths in this period.

Therefore, it is not surprising that the root causes of the most significant upheaval in the distribution of the peoples to the north of Rome in the imperial period remain largely unknown. This is the phenomenon called conveniently, if too simply, 'the Coming of the Huns', which has often been presented as a Late Roman version of the modern military-political concept of 'the domino effect'. In such an interpretation, the sudden eruption from the steppes of Central Asia of a previously unknown nomadic people called the Huns caused the collapse of the hitherto stable Gothic kingdom of the Greuthungi, located northwest of the Black Sea.[4] This, and the consequent westward flight of the defeated Greuthungi, led to the disintegration of the adjacent confederacy of the Theruingi, who in turn were driven westwards and southwards, arriving in growing numbers as refugees along the north bank of the river Danube, and thus at the frontier of the Roman Empire. The pressure was only relieved by the decision of the emperor Valens in 376 to admit the refugees into imperial territory in the Balkans, but with ultimately disastrous consequences for the Empire.[5]

Even put as simply as that, the flaws in such an account are obvious. It is rather like the argument from 'the first mover': if the Huns pushed the Goths and the Goths pushed the Romans, then who pushed the Huns? Normally, this question is not asked, because there is a tendency to assume that nomads are led almost instinctively to prey on their settled neighbours. In fact, nomadic society is far more fragile than that of agriculturalists, and if anything, even more conservative.[6] Nomads tend to retain long-established patterns of regular migration and pasturing, unless dramatic changes force them to alter their time-honoured procedures. Therefore the unprecedented appearance of the Huns in an area that stretched ultimately from the west of the river Don to the banks of the Danube is itself in need of explanation.

Similarly, the nature of the impact of the Huns on the Goths also demands closer examination. By the middle of the fifth century the Huns had organised themselves into a large and formidable confederacy, dominating several subject peoples, and for the first time with a single leader.[7] However, there is no evidence for such unity in the last quarter of the fourth century, when they first came to the attention of the Romans. The emergence of a single monarch or khan in the time of Attila (died 453) resulted from the Huns' success in establishing control over other peoples, rather than being the cause of it. In late-fourth and early-fifth-century Roman sources, the Huns are perceived as comprising several quite separate groups. In other words, we must not imagine that their conquests in the late fourth century resulted from the leadership of some anonymous Hun equivalent of Genghis Khan. So, if they lacked a unified social and political organisation, operated in relatively small bands, and were not particularly numerous, how were they able to overthrow the seemingly powerful kingdoms of the Greuthungi and the Theruingi, who had dominated the plains north of the Black Sea and the Danube since the third century?

The latter used to be generally regarded as ancestors of, or even identical to, the later confederacies known as the Ostrogoths and the Visigoths. Such a perception has been modified, to the extent that the Greuthungi and the Theruingi are now seen as contributing significant elements of population to the two Gothic confederacies, but by no means exclusively.[8] The Roman sources for the period *c.* 370 to 408 also reveal the existence of other Germanic-speaking groups, several of whom remained

permanently outside Roman territory. One of these, speaking a
Gothic or East-Germanic dialect, survived in the Crimea until at
least the seventeenth century.[9]

The role of the Germanic-speaking elites of the Greuthungi
and Theruingi in the south-Russian steppe from the mid- to
late third century until the 370s was that of a dominant military
aristocracy, ruling over a mixed subject population of very different ethnic and cultural composition. Their own material culture
was almost certainly that named by modern archaeologists after
two of its most significant sites: Cernjachov (in modern Ukraine)
and Sîntana de Mureş (in Romania).[10] This Cernjachov/Sîntana
de Mureş culture shows several striking similarities with the preceding and slightly overlapping Wielbark culture of southern
Poland, whose main sites have been found further to the north
and the west, thus probably implying a phase of south-easterly
migration from one region to the other in the late second to
early third centuries. It can also be demonstrated archaeologically that their subject peoples would have included groups of
Slavs, nomadic Sarmatians, and some of the Hellenised population of the region of Pontus. How their hegemony was established is unknown, but chronologically it must be related to
the period of upheaval and of pressure on the Roman imperial frontiers that took place in the second half of the third
century.[11]

Before the mid-third and from the late fourth century onwards,
hegemonial power in this vast region, extending from the
Danube to the Don, was normally exercised by a steppe nomad
confederacy; previously the Scythians and the Sarmatians, and
subsequently the Huns, the Avars, the Bulgars and the Magyars.
All of these came from the east. Viewed from a long-term perspective, the establishment of Germanic-speaking elites migrating
from the north-west in this region was an aberration, and would
be challenged once a new nomad confederacy formed itself east
of the Don. This may have been assisted by climatic deterioration in northern and eastern Europe in the second half of the
fourth century.[12] The implications of the hypothesis outlined
here would be that the phenomenon to be investigated is not
so much an unexpected and unprovoked invasion of the lands
of the Greuthungi and the Theruingi by the nomadic Huns,
as the rapid re-nomadisation of the Don–Dniester–Danube
region after a brief interval of domination by a sedentary agrar-
ian society. To turn, though, from the causes of the rise of Hun
power to its consequences for the Roman Empire is to enter a
much better-documented area. The events of the years 376–8
form the final section of the historical writing of Ammianus

Marcellinus, and the defeat of the emperor Valens at the Battle of Adrianople was to be the climax of the work.[13]

The Goths and the Empire, 376–95

In 376, as the result of the extraordinary changes taking place to the north of the Black Sea, large numbers of Theruingi and some of the Greuthungi arrived as refugees on the north bank of the Danube, and petitioned the emperor Valens to admit them into the Roman Empire and give them land in return for military service.[14] In itself there was perhaps nothing unwise about his agreeing to their request, which theoretically would have provided the state with new sources of military manpower, and reduced the burden of provincial taxation in the areas in which they were settled. However, it may have been undermined by the greed of the Roman military commanders responsible for overseeing the settlement of the incomers in the eastern Balkans, who are reported to have made them pay for supplies that the emperor had intended them to receive free of charge.[15] However, there may have been other and deeper causes for the ensuing conflict in the way that the incomers had to adjust to a new physical and cultural context, and to a change in the standing and self-esteem of their social elites in relation to Roman imperial and provincial government. The story of their abuse by local officials may be more of a moral explanation to help Roman readers come to terms with the disaster that followed, and to understand it in terms of the failings of a few individuals.

Trouble broke out when Roman commanders began to move the Theruingi and other contingents (whom collectively it would be most convenient to call Goths), under leaders Fritigern and Alavivus, away from the Danube, and south to the city of Marcianople near the Black Sea, which was then the headquarters of the military command in Thrace. There the incident took place that sparked off a revolt. Some of the new settlers sought to force their way into the city to obtain food while the Roman general Lupicinus was entertaining their leaders to a banquet. He panicked and tried to take his guests as hostages, killing their bodyguards. In the confusion, Fritigern at least was able to escape and take command of the various groups of Goths around the city. When Lupicinus marched out against them his army was routed and he was forced to flee for refuge back into Marcianople. Other Gothic detachments further south joined the revolt when the Roman authorities tried to move them on across the Dardanelles into Asia Minor.[16]

Despite some initial successes in restraining the Goths and pinning them down in the Dobrudja, the region between the lower Danube, the Black Sea and the Balkan Mountains, the Roman generals were alternately overcautious and overconfident, and so by the late summer of 378 a campaign had to be mounted by the emperor Valens in person, with an army of some 40,000 men, withdrawn partly from the eastern frontiers. The Gothic commanders concentrated their followers just to the north of Adrianople. In the ensuing battle on 9 August the Roman forces were heavily defeated. Two-thirds of the army was destroyed and the emperor was killed.[17]

In itself, the battle of Adrianople struck a severe, if short-lived, blow at Roman military morale and revived memories of the destruction of the emperor Decius in 251. However, its significance was probably much less than is sometimes claimed. It was the eastern Roman army that suffered the defeat, but that half of the Empire was to survive for more than another thousand years. Its immediate impact, despite the apparently shattering nature of the defeat, was also limited, in that within four years the Goths had been brought to heel by a new emperor, Theodosius I, and were settled by treaty on imperial territory. They then served as vital components in the armies Theodosius used them to invade the western half of the empire in 388 and again in 394.[18]

The Goths' willingness to compromise after what should have been a major victory was the result of their difficulties in feeding themselves. They entered the Empire as refugees, and though promised supplies and settlements, these did not materialise. Within months of crossing the Danube they were at war with the Empire. They were in no position to grow their own food, and had to take whatever they could find. Lacking the necessary military technology to capture towns, and thus the state granaries, they had to obtain what they needed from the countryside. This limited their ability to acquire food to certain seasons, as there was no point in taking harvests that were not ready for consumption or sale. Also, the crops produced in any one district would only be capable of feeding a relatively small number of people. So they could only keep together as a body for military purposes for very restricted periods of time and otherwise had to break up into smaller groups and scatter widely across the countryside. In military terms this was suicidal, as the Roman army was conducting effective mobile operations against them, and could cut off the roaming bands of Goths one at a time.[19]

Although Fritigern proved an able commander in these very difficult circumstances, and at one stage came close to capturing

Theodosius soon after his appointment as emperor by Gratian in January 379, most of the advantages lay with the Romans.[20] Thus it was that the main body of the Theruingi came to terms in 382, and the detachments of the Greuthungi, who had been their allies in the battle of Adrianople, even earlier, in 380.[21] These problems that the Gothic leaders faced in the years 378–82 were to be perennial ones for hostile forces operating within the imperial frontiers during the course of the next century or more, and the military and political triumphs the Empire secured were almost always the result of skilful exploitation of this weakness. On the other hand, direct confrontation, as at the battle of Adrianople, squandered the Romans' primary advantage. The steady wearing down of their opponents, by limiting their freedom of movement and their access to food, paid far better dividends than risking all in a single battle.

On the other hand, the establishment by the treaty of 382 of a large Gothic presence in the eastern Balkans added a new element to all military and political calculations for three decades to come.[22] Theodosius I found this source of manpower so valuable that he cashiered one of his generals who had gone too far in trying to control them, and when in 392 a large band of Goths under the leadership of Alaric broke away from their garrisons on the Danube and started looting civilian areas in Thrace, he prevented his field commander Stilicho from following up an initial victory and eliminating them.[23] It was this predominantly Gothic confederacy, drawn from a variety of different Theruingian and Greuthungic groups which formed around Alaric in the early 390s, that became the group normally known as the Visigoths. (They called themselves the Goths, but to avoid confusion with the other grouping of Goths that developed in the Balkans in the mid- to later fifth century they will be known here as the Visigoths.)

When, after the death of Theodosius I, Stilicho became regent of the western half of the Empire, he failed on three further occasions to take advantage of opportunities to destroy this newly formed Visigothic confederacy. In part, this may have resulted from an understanding of the lesson learnt at Adrianople, that open battle was too risky and that the enemy was at its most dangerous when he stood to lose all. On the other hand, both Theodosius and Stilicho hoped to gain military and political advantages from winning the active involvement of the Goths in the conflicts between the eastern and western halves of the Empire.

While it used to be customary for historians to blame even otherwise traditionally 'good' emperors, such as Theodosius I, for failing to solve the barbarian problem – that is, by expelling or exterminating them – the greater threat to the Empire's continued survival may have been the imperial taste for civil war. Such a conflict could have occurred in 397 and another was imminent in 407.[24] Stilicho's career as regent and virtual military dictator of the West falls between these two dates.

Stilicho or Honorius? Alternative strategies, 395–410

Stilicho had exercised the chief military command under Theodosius I in the West after the fall of Eugenius in 394, and continued to do so after the emperor's premature death early the following year.[25] He claimed that Theodosius on his deathbed had entrusted him with guardianship of both his sons, the emperors Arcadius (395–408) and Honorius (395–423), but this was not accepted by the eastern court. Stilicho's interest thereafter lay in trying to turn his claim to authority in the east into reality or, failing that, to securing the return to the West of the diocese of Illyricum, which the emperor Gratian had ceded to Theodosius I when he proclaimed him his co-ruler in January 379.[26] In this second ambition, Stilicho had to take into account the Visigoths, who now constituted the most powerful military force in the Balkans.

There is no reliable evidence that Alaric 'was of famous stock, and his nobility was second only to that of the Amali', as was claimed by the Ostrogothic historian Jordanes in the middle of the sixth century. His supposed ancestors 'the Balthi, who because of their daring had long ago received their name Baltha, that is, "The Bold"' are nowhere else referred to. Some historians are prepared to follow Jordanes, and see Alaric's heroic descent as the reason for his success in the creation a confederacy of Goths and others from north of the Danube together with elements of the Roman population south of the river; a grouping that would thereafter survive and draw its sense of identity from its loyalty to him and his descendents. Others would prefer to see him as a military leader whose success was itself the attraction that drew a growing body of followers to his side, and whose subsequent movements as a group in the Balkans, Italy and later southern Gaul shaped the resulting Visigothic identity.[27]

Just how the rebel Goths, who had won the battle of Adrianople against Valens in 378, came to be settled in the Balkans after 382 following treaties with Theodosius I is not known. It is sometimes implied that they became farmer-soldiers, receiving land in return for providing detachments for the imperial army. However, recent studies of similar agreements to provide 'hospitality', made between imperial governments and barbarian forces in the fifth century, have suggested that, despite the language of the treaties, what was at issue was not the redistribution of land, but the reallocation of tax revenue.[28] If these arguments are correct for this slightly later period, then they may also be true of the 380s and 390s. There was no clear legal basis by which the imperial government could appropriate its subjects' property at will and redistribute it to barbarian 'guests'. Nor is there any evidence that proves unambiguously that it did so. Had Alaric and his followers possessed a landed base in the Balkans, their situation would have been far less precarious than it appears to have been.

While from one point of view Alaric and his Visigothic confederacy, garrisoning Thrace and Illyricum, were in an ideal situation to exploit the rivalries of Stilicho and his eastern opponents, they had their own particular difficulties to face, such as dependence on the imperial government for supplies of food in return for military service. Alaric's own survival depended on satisfying his followers' immediate practical needs in terms of supplies and security, as well as regular rewards. In practice, what he had to acquire were regular subsidies from the imperial government and a position for himself, and thus his following in the military hierarchy of the Empire.

Thus, throughout the period from 395 to 410, Alaric's persistent demands were for regular supplies of food, annual payments of cash and the office of Master of the Soldiers for himself. This latter, which would have given him the rank, status and salary of commander of one of the imperial field armies, was necessary not only for the material benefits it conveyed and the way it would locate him and his followers in the imperial administrative order, but also to secure Alaric's hold over his own following. Even if Alaric were related to former leading figures in the Theruingian confederacy, such as the 'judge' Athanaric, who died in Constantinople in 381, no permanent central authority had existed among the Theruingi prior to their entry into the Empire in 376, and that their kingship consisted of the temporary war leadership of a section of the people.[29] The political organisation of those Goths who had established themselves in Roman territory in 376 was transformed during the last quarter of the fourth century by the emergence of Alaric as the permanent leader of many of them.[30]

While Alaric could try to play off the rivalries of East and West as far as the Empire was concerned, his own needs were too pressing for him to have much room for manoeuvre. The imperial governments attempted to control him and the Visigoths by focusing on their constant need for supplies. Sometimes Alaric tried to put pressure on one or other half of the Empire by direct action, raiding and looting civil settlements and the countryside of the western Balkans. In 402, for the first time, he led a raiding force into Italy, but was defeated by Stilicho in a battle at Pollentia.[31] Stilicho took steps to contain the Visigoths, but no campaign was decisive. Some damage was inflicted on Alaric's forces, but on every occasion – in 392, 395, 397 and 402 – he and his men were allowed to escape from apparent encirclement by imperial forces.

The Egyptian poet, Claudian, who lived in the western court, which moved from Milan to the more easily defended Ravenna in 402, praised Stilicho (who became his patron) for the greatness of his victories and the mercy he showed to the vanquished. But the speed with which the Visigothic threat reasserted itself suggests the hollowness of his claims.[32] In the first of these episodes, the responsibility for not capitalising on military success lay with Theodosius I, but in 395 and 397 Stilicho had much to gain from winning Alaric over to his side and thus securing western control over Illyricum. However, the invasion of Italy in 402 indicates just how uncontrollable his prospective ally could be. In 407, Stilicho actually came to an agreement with Alaric to obtain for him the regular supplies, subsidies and the title that he demanded, in return for a change of allegiance on the part of the Goths from Constantinople to Ravenna.[33] The eastern half of the Empire closed its ports to westerners, Stilicho was declared a public enemy, and civil war seemed imminent.

In the East, the apparently barbarian-favouring sentiments of the court of Theodosius I were replaced in the year 400 by outright hostility to the domination of the state by Germanic-speaking generals and their soldiers. That year, the inhabitants of Constantinople rioted against the city garrison controlled by a Gothic general, Gainas, who wanted to make himself into the eastern equivalent of Stilicho. Expelled from the city, imperial troops chased them across the Danube, where Gainas was killed by a Hun khan called Uldin, and his head was sent as a gift to the emperor. In the aftermath, a civilian regime, which included prominent literary and cultural figures, came to power in Constantinople. These political groupings did not remain stable, but the eastern court thereafter remained opposed to military domination of the state throughout the first half of the fifth century, and suspicious of the ambitions of army commanders.[34]

A similar attitude developed in the West in the first decade of the century. Legislation was introduced forbidding the wearing of such barbarian (and military) garments as trousers, or the sporting of long hair.[35] The senatorial aristocracy of Rome, who were becoming increasingly opposed to Stilicho's policies, which seemed to be edging them closer to war with the East, initially refused to provide the funding for the implementation of his agreement with Alaric in 407, which would have secured the de facto transfer of much of Illyricum to the West. This senatorial resistance was seen by the emperor and his entourage as a sign that the general had lost the political support he had previously relied on in Rome, and so it marked the end for Stilicho. Dismissed by the emperor Honorius from his offices, he fled to sanctuary in a church, but was coaxed out and then executed on imperial orders. His son and a number of senators who owed their offices to him were similarly put to death. Barbarian soldiers under his command were massacred by regular Roman troops, though many escaped from Italy to join Alaric.[36]

Whether Stilicho was calculatingly self-seeking in his dealings with Alaric, or just militarily cautious, cannot be assessed with certainty, but the consequences of his policies proved damaging to the Empire and to the city of Rome. The Senate now repudiated the agreement of 407 to pay the Visigothic leader 4,000 pounds weight of gold, which they had so been so reluctant to accept. As a result of that, and of imperially sponsored attacks on the Gothic and other barbarian troops in Italy, Alaric led his men in the autumn of 408 into the peninsula to put pressure on the imperial government to honour the treaty, and so marched on Rome.[37]

The sequence of events in Italy over the next two years, which culminated in the Visigothic sack of Rome in August 410, is by no means easy to untangle or to recount in outline. The main players in the drama appear in a variety of locations. First, and most important, there was the imperial court, securely located behind the almost impenetrable marshes that guarded Ravenna. The emperor Honorius and his advisers are often criticised for passivity in these crucial years, but the very immobility of their stance may have been more a matter of policy, and one that, despite the criticisms of historians both ancient and modern, largely paid off. Freed from domination by Stilicho, Honorius had no wish to subject himself or the western half of the Empire to the control of another military dictator. Safe in his capital, the emperor was ideally placed to outface the Visigothic leader and to ignore his demands.[38]

Unable to exercise any direct leverage on Honorius, Alaric went unchallenged militarily in Italy, but was in an increasingly difficult position. He had failed to secure the returns for himself and his people that the agreement of 407 with Stilicho had promised. He had then taken the dramatic step of once more invading Italy to obtain enough of what had been promised to provide for their needs, and to maintain his own credibility. Thus, weak as Honorius's position might seem to be, the pressure was more on Alaric to achieve at least some of the objectives he had publicly set himself.

To achieve this, he depended on the coerced co-operation of the third set of actors in this drama – the Roman senators. Alaric's first move on entering Italy in the autumn of 408 was to blockade Rome, and by the end of the year the Senate had agreed to pay him 5,000 pounds of gold, 30,000 pounds of silver and a large quantity of silk, skins and spices, to lift the siege.[39] They also promised to try to persuade the emperor to make the treaty the Goths wanted. Honorius, however, continued to stand firm, even though some of his advisers supported the Visigoths' demands.

After nearly a year of fruitless negotiation, Alaric marched on Rome again and after a further blockade obtained entry. He had the Senate proclaim a new emperor for him in the person of Priscus Attalus, then the Prefect of the City, or principal magistrate and civil administrator of Rome.[40] Attalus could then invest Alaric with the office of Master of the Soldiers, but the situation was unstable so long as the legitimate emperor remained inviolate in Ravenna. Moreover, the usurper in Rome depended on the protection of his Gothic master.

Thus, in 410, when Alaric decided that the best solution for the Goths was to cross from southern Italy to Africa, long regarded as the granary of the western Empire, to obtain regular supplies of food and, on the other side of the Mediterranean, the security they sought, Attalus was forced to thwart his intentions, as he would otherwise have been left defenceless to face the vengeance of Honorius. So even a puppet emperor proved no solution to the problems that Alaric faced, and he forced Attalus to abdicate in the summer of 410 and tried to renew negotiations with Honorius, perhaps hoping the latter would be grateful to him for removing the usurper he himself had set up.[41] This was fruitless, and Alaric was even attacked by other Goths who had reverted to the imperial allegiance. By now, his position was desperate, above all in relation to his own supporters, and he turned to Rome for a third time. After a further siege of the city, his men broke through the wall on 24 August, and sacked the city for three days.[42]

Despite the undoubted suffering endured by the inhabitants during those few days, and the demoralising blow to an imperial patriotism that still associated itself with the city that had given the Empire its name, the infamous Sack of Rome by the Visigoths has to be seen as the last desperate measure of a leader whose every policy had failed, and whose every ambition had been thwarted. In part, it may have been an insensate act of revenge, though this was hard on the inhabitants of Rome, who had done their best as far as honour and their material resources were concerned to comply with Alaric's demands, but it is probably best seen as a move to stave off the insistent demands of his followers and to provide them with at least short-term satisfaction.

After leaving devastated Rome with their loot and their hostages, the Visigoths turned south, probably intending to cross to Africa. However, within months, and before they reached the coast, Alaric was dead. He was succeeded as leader of the Visigothic confederation by his wife's brother, Ataulf.[43] Under Ataulf's direction they finally gave up all hope of establishing themselves in Italy or of using it as a base for a crossing to the greater security of Africa. Early in 412, Ataulf led the Visigoths over the Alps and out of Italy. Honorius's policy had worked, and Italy was not to be subjected to domination by a Germanic people until after the end of imperial rule in the West.

The lack of evidence relating to both imperial and Visigothic actions and intentions in Italy in the year 411 means we cannot know if the emperor wished Ataulf and his followers to become participants in the complicated affairs of Gaul rather than to see them return east into the Balkans. In Gaul, the years from 406 to 411 had seen considerable upheaval. In 406, the army in Britain, which had thrown up Magnus Maximus in 383, rebelled again and created and murdered two emperors, Marcus and Gratian, in quick succession.[44] A third choice, in the person of a certain Constantine, selected because of the fortunate associations of his name, lasted longer. This he may have achieved by giving his troops something else to think about by leading them across the Channel to make him master of Gaul.

Here he was needed. On the last day of 406, a group from three peoples – the Vandals, the Sueves and the Alans – crossed the Rhine.[45] Here, the Franks were able, at least initially, to show the worth of the agreements they had made with Julian. They took on one branch of the Vandal forces and defeated them, but were then themselves pushed aside by the Alans.[46] Over the course of the next three years, this group of confederated peoples made their way across Gaul, and in September 409 crossed the Pyrenees into Spain.[47] In their wake they left devastation, as they had to loot and forage for their own maintenance.

The effects of their penetration of the frontiers also created a power vacuum in Gaul, which was swiftly filled by the rebel emperor Constantine III from Britain. Landing at Boulogne, his forces restored some semblance of order in the rear of the barbarians' passage, and he made himself master of both Gaul and Spain. From his base at Arles, Constantine III was poised to intervene in events in Italy, and at least one of Honorius's ministers in Ravenna was in treasonable correspondence with him. Constantine tried to secure the legitimate emperor's recognition of him as an imperial colleague, and moved with an army into northern Italy in 410.[48]

However, Constantine's power base was weak and his regime correspondingly ephemeral. One of his generals, a Briton called Gerontius, led a revolt against him in Spain, defeated and executed his son (the recently appointed co-emperor Constans) and besieged the would-be master of the West at Arles. Only the arrival of imperial forces from Italy commanded by a new Master of the Soldiers called Constantius saved Constantine III from death at the hands of his own rebel general. Instead, when Arles capitulated to the imperial army, he was sent as a prisoner to Ravenna, but executed on the journey on the emperor's orders.[49]

Thus, in less than a year after the Sack of Rome, Honorius's forces sent from Italy were restoring imperial control in at least the southern parts of Gaul. Eastern and northern sections still remained to be reinstated, and Britain, which had also rebelled against the luckless Constantine III in 410, had to be left in practice to go its own way, though it would be wrong to assume that Honorius regarded it as subsequently being detached from the Empire.[50] Whatever the psychological reverberations of the Visigothic looting of the Eternal City, the imperial regime in Italy displayed remarkable resilience and activity once the threat of a barbarian domination of the state had been lifted. This would seem to have been the positive outcome of Honorius's policy of passivity in the face of Alaric's threats.

5   A divided city: the Christian Church, 300–460

Conflicts in Church and state

The Sack of Rome in 410 sent a shock around the Latin-speaking half of the Empire, but it aroused little recorded comment in the predominantly Greek East. Equally ambivalent was the attitude towards the disaster and its implications of the leaders of Christian thought. From Bethlehem, in a letter written in 412, the priest Jerome (331–419), who had once been a fashionable spiritual mentor to some aristocratic circles in Rome, and secretary to pope Damasus (366–84), combined the twin literary heritage of Classical and Christian learning in lamenting this disaster, quoting from the Psalms: 'O, God, the heathen have come into thine inheritance; thy holy temple have they defiled; they have made Jerusalem [that is, Rome] an orchard' and following it by a passage from Book Two of the Aeneid: 'The ancient city that for many a hundred years ruled the world comes down in ruins'.[1]

Even so, his feelings for the city of Rome were ambiguous. In this same letter, which describes the spiritual career of the lady Marcella, in whose house in the city his group of disciples used to meet in the early 380s, he also called Rome a 'slander-loving place', in which 'it was the triumph of vice to disparage virtue and to defile all that is pure and clean'.[2] Jerome had close ties to Rome, despite being forced to leave the city in 384 as a result of slanderous allegations, and was someone for whom classical Latin literature never lost its appeal. Other Christians had a less personal involvement with the city and the literary culture with which it was strongly associated. For them, the pagan traditions of Rome's past, and of so many of the aristocratic families who still dominated it, were unpalatable. In 392–4, the 'pagan revival' under the emperor Eugenius had largely been orchestrated by the great Roman families of the Nichomachi and the Symmachi, and even as recently as 408, when the city was threatened by Alaric, it was claimed that pagan sacrifices had been held.[3]

Yet, for Christians, the sack of 410 was an acute embarrassment. Whatever their personal feelings, Rome was, as Jerome called it, 'the city that had taken the world', and which itself had never fallen to invasion in the course of a history that traditionally spanned over 1,100 years. Now, within years of the final triumph of the new Christian dispensation in the Empire of Theodosius I, it had been captured and sacked. The pagan intelligentsia, subjected to increasingly intolerant restrictions under the Christian emperors of the late fourth century, could now claim that this disaster came because of the desertion of the old gods, who had for so long preserved and made prosperous the Roman state.[4]

Whatever literary form these pagan arguments took cannot now be shown, as none have survived, and they may have been fewer and less strident than the Christian replies might seem to suggest. Indeed, it might be asked if the Christian apologists who sprang into action in the aftermath of the sack were really writing to ease the minds of their own co-religionists, to whom these very obvious questions would have been far more unsettling, than to the chivvied and repressed minority of pagan intellectuals.

The first substantial Christian work of justification was by a Spanish priest called Orosius, and appeared in 418.[5] Entitled *Seven Books of History against the Pagans*, it was a survey of the history of Rome and its Empire, whose principal argument was that, however bad contemporary events in the period of Christian rule over the Empire might seem, far worse things had happened in the past under pagan domination. In particular, he stressed how the Goths under Alaric, who had been converted to Christianity, though of the unorthodox Arian form, in the late fourth century, were merciful to the inhabitants of Rome in 410 because they were fellow believers. The main aim of his *History* was to highlight the bloodiness and misery of past events, while playing down such elements in recent times. This was neither intellectually very satisfying nor very credible history, and even fellow Christians, including Augustine, bishop of Hippo (354–430), to whom the work was dedicated, were unconvinced by its tendentious arguments.[6] However, Orosius's *Seven Books* remained very popular throughout the Middle Ages and survived in many manuscripts, largely thanks to the substantial quantity of historical information that it contained.[7]

It was to be Augustine himself who produced the most substantial analysis, in terms both of length and sophistication of argument, of the meaning of these events, and of how they should lead contemporary Christians to view the secular state. This was his magisterial *On the City of God*, written in twenty-two books over the course of twelve years (413–25). In it he rejected the necessary identification of the Roman imperial state with the Christian Church and the need to regard the former as the eternal or divinely chosen vehicle for achieving the aims of the latter.[8] This was not a condemnation of the Roman state, and only implicitly a recognition of its current weakened political and military condition, but instead an explanation of the irrelevance of secular human institutions to the achievement of individual salvation. It also served as a vital step towards the fuller elaboration of Augustine's ideas on divine grace and predestination that absorbed much of his last years.[9]

Though not presented in an explicitly controversial context, these arguments challenged a dominant strand of Christian political thinking in the eastern half of the Empire. Ever since Constantine had established himself in the East, where traditions of absolute monarchy were far stronger than in the West, a series of Christian thinkers had emphasised the unbreakable links between Church and state. The identification had first been articulated by Constantine's adviser and biographer, bishop Eusebius of Caesarea (died 339/40), and the emperor's own personal involvement in internal Church affairs, notably in presiding over the Council of Nicaea in 325 and in using the powers of the state to try to solve theological disputes, established crucial precedents.

In the East, the emperor's role in the Church included powers of appointing bishops, of applying secular punishments to them if they displeased him, of giving force to theological statements by his approval of them, and enjoying such priestly privileges as having a seat in the sanctuary in church, a location otherwise exclusive to the clergy.[10] In general, all of this took place within an intellectual context in which the eternity of the Empire and its role as God's chosen vehicle for the achievement of human salvation was unquestioned. Despite various vicissitudes, such attitudes and such imperial authority survived in the East with little modification up to the final extinction of the Empire in 1453.

This was perhaps all the more surprising in that the emperors had not generally been on the winning side in the many theological arguments that wracked the Church, especially in the East, from the early fourth century onwards. The Arian controversy, which broke out in the Church of Alexandria during the reign of Constantine, exposed something of the problems of imperial involvement in doctrinal arguments. In the years after the Great Persecution, an influential priest in Alexandria called Arius had been teaching that the Son and the Holy Spirit are both neither co-eternal with, nor equal to, the Father, and this doctrine was strongly resisted by Alexander, the bishop of the city (313–26), and by his successor Athanasius (326–73).

The condemnation of Arius by a local Egyptian council in 321 proved ineffective and the controversy led the new Christian emperor to call a council of bishops to meet in Nicaea (modern Iznik in Turkey) in 325. Thus came about the first ecumenical council, representing the whole Church. The bishops, under the presidency of the emperor, condemned Arius's teaching, and Constantine exiled him to Illyria. The Council also issued a formal statement of orthodox faith, which from the start became known as the Nicene Creed. However, Constantine was subsequently persuaded, not least by his sister and by various ecclesiastical advisers, that Arius had been misrepresented and so ordered his restoration in 331.[11]

While the precise theology of Arius himself did not win many adherents, unease was created among some bishops in the East by the arguments used against it and by the doctrinal views accepted by the council. Traditionally, the ensuing conflict, which lasted until 381, is seen as a confrontation between a body of teaching that can be called Arian and another, ultimately triumphant, which may be described as orthodox. In practice there was no monolithic Arian movement or party, and the central issue was primarily the acceptance or not of the theology approved by the Council of Nicaea. Different groups of bishops and others promoted a variety of alternatives to or modifications of the Nicene teaching, with the approval of most of the emperors ruling in the East from 331 to 381. Opposed to them were others, particularly in the West, for whom the decisions of the Council represented the true faith that needed to be defended against all attempts to alter or weaken it. In the East, the standard-bearer and chief spokesman of this Nicene party was bishop Athanasius of Alexandria, who suffered several periods of political exile as a consequence. In the West, his stand was supported by most of the bishops of Rome, despite occasional imperial attempts to pressure them into conforming.

Athanasius was exiled to Trier in Gaul by Constantine I in 336, sent back to Alexandria by Constantine II in 338, and was exiled once again by Constantius II in 340. Constans forced his brother to accept Athanasius back again in 346, with a threat of war over the issue, but Athanasius had to go into hiding with the monks in upper Egypt after Constantius had made himself ruler of the whole Empire in 353 and accused him of treasonable correspondence with the defeated usurper Magnentius. The bishop remained on the run until the death of Constantius in 361, and was then allowed back to Alexandria by the pagan emperor Julian, who was happy to promote divisions within the Christian ranks. Athanasius was very nearly exiled again under Valens, the last of the emperors sympathetic to anti-Nicene views, and in whose reign Christianity was preached to the Goths.[12] The accession of the westerner Theodosius I as ruler of the East in January 379 led to the holding of the First Council of Constantinople in 381, which finally condemned all attempts to modify the theology accepted at Nicaea, which most in the West had long regarded as the only touchstone of orthodoxy.

During this whole period, while some individual bishops, such as Potamius of Lisbon, were opposed, the western Church as a whole remained staunchly pro-Nicene.[13] Western rulers, such as Constantine II, Constans and Valentinian I, were generally less interested in the minutiae of theological arguments than in maintaining order and minimising divisions. The priorities of the two halves of the Empire – the Latin-speaking West and the Greek-speaking East – were fundamentally different. As most of the earliest Christian writing had been in Greek, even in the West until the mid-third century, the Church's learned tradition was accessible primarily to readers of Greek, with the result that the western Church was less able to understand the divisive theological controversies that aroused so much passion in the East.

Only towards the end of the fourth century did a series of great Latin writers appear, who catered for the needs of the growing western Church by translating works written in Greek or who adapted techniques and ways of thought that had been developed in the East.[14] Among the most prominent of these was the priest Jerome, already mentioned, who undertook a new and much improved Latin translation of the Bible, based in part on Hebrew as well as Greek originals, and the writing of a series of large-scale commentaries on many of its books.[15] This exegetical work was greatly influenced by that of the third-century Alexandrian writer Origen (d. 254), a number of whose own works were translated into Latin by Jerome's erstwhile friend, Rufinus of Aquileia. Jerome and Rufinus fell out when, because of certain speculations in some of his writings, Origen was posthumously condemned by various church councils around the year 400. Jerome then vehemently denounced him, while Rufinus remained a defender.[16]

Amongst the principal western beneficiaries and transmitters of eastern theology was Ambrose, bishop of Milan (374–97), who in his life, more than in his writings, articulated an alternative view of Church–state relations in the Empire.[17] The son of Constantine II's Praetorian Prefect, Ambrose was himself on the middle rungs of the ladder of an official career, as civil governor of the province, when he was elected as bishop by the populace and clergy of Milan. By this period, bishops were more than just the spiritual head of a town's Christian community, having taken on a wide range of judicial and administrative responsibilities and enjoying great social eminence. They often contributed generously from their own resources or could call upon useful political connections. So, episcopal elections could determine a town's future prosperity, and there was intense competition to find wealthy and influential candidates for the post. In some cases, they were then forced into accepting election as a bishop, even, as in the case of Ambrose, if they lacked local connections and were not even members of the clergy.[18]

As the principal city of northern Italy, the bishopric of Milan was undoubtedly eminent, but its role was transformed by the death of Valentinian I in 375. The creation of a separate imperial sphere of authority for the infant Valentinian II turned Milan into the seat of an imperial court, for the first time since 305. Ambrose was able to influence and occasionally to dominate the court, not just by strength of personality, but also by a series of carefully stage-managed confrontations.

Valentinian II's mother, the empress Justina, tried to persuade Ambrose to surrender one of the basilicas in the city to serve as a church for the Arian soldiers of the imperial guard. However, this enabled him to mobilise public support by barricading himself and other clergy inside the building. Only by force could the empress get her way, and so she backed down.[19] The discovery, which the bishop claimed was thanks to divine revelation, of the relics of Saints Gervasius and Protasius reinforced Ambrose's position in the city.[20] Despite its secular importance, Milan lacked local patron saints, such as early Christian martyrs, whose celestial protection could be invoked and whose relics would be the focus for Milanese patriotic devotion. This was now provided through Ambrose's public search for, and uncovering of, the buried bodies of these two hitherto unknown martyrs, whose histories the bishop also revealed.

So powerful did Ambrose's influence on the court become that he could intervene in matters concerning the Church outside Milan. Thus when, in 384, Quintus Aurelius Symmachus, the Prefect of the City of Rome, petitioned the emperor Valentinian II to allow the restoration to the Senate House of the Statue of Victory, which the emperor Gratian had had removed as a pagan abomination, Ambrose was able to veto the Senate's appeal by the simple expedient of threatening the thirteen-year-old emperor with excommunication: 'You will come to the church – and your bishop will not be there'.[21] This threat he subsequently put into practice in a confrontation with Theodosius I, who established his court in Milan during his stays in the West in 388–91 and 394–5.

In 388, the Christian community in Callinicum, urged on by its bishop, destroyed both the meeting house of a heretical Christian group and a local synagogue. The emperor ordered the latter to be rebuilt at the bishop's expense and commanded that the perpetrators of the outrage, many of whom were monks, be punished. Ambrose intervened to secure the revoking of these instructions. When a letter he sent to Theodosius failed to achieve his ends, he staged a confrontation with the emperor in church. Having preached on the subject, he came down from the pulpit to face Theodosius directly, and declared that he would not go to the altar to perform the rites of Holy Communion if the emperor did not promise to withdraw his orders.[22]

A similar episode went a stage further in 390. When a riot broke out in Thessalonica over the detention of a popular charioteer arrested as a male prostitute, the garrison commander and other soldiers were killed. Theodosius I ordered a massacre of racing fans in the city in reprisal. Ambrose, when he heard of it, wrote to the emperor, making it clear that he would not celebrate communion in Theodosius's presence until he had purged himself of the guilt through a period of penance. This involved attending church divested of his imperial robes and abstaining from communion until Christmas, thus adopting some of the practices of those entering the formal state of penance.[23]

These confrontations derived from a very different view of the relations between the emperor and the Church to that which Theodosius I would have encountered in the East. Implicitly, Ambrose was demanding that the emperor accept that he was subject to ecclesiastical discipline and in matters pertaining to the Church and to Christian moral conduct must accept the superior authority of his bishop. In practice, Ambrose could only force the emperor into these concessions because of the presence of his court in Milan. This contrasts with Ambrose's inability to oppose the 'pagan revival' – actually more of a return of tolerance – under the emperor Eugenius in 392–4.[24] Because Eugenius was not present in Milan, the bishop was unable to confront him. Influential as Ambrose's example might be, it required an institution rather than an individual to turn his view of Church–state relations into more of a reality.

Authority is given to Peter

The unique standing of the city of Rome in the Empire that took its name from the city, gave the leader of its Christian community a privileged status. However, in the early centuries of the expansion of the Church, Africa may have had a larger population of believers than Italy, and the outstanding Christian Latin authors of the third century were the Africans Tertullian (d. 212?) and bishop Cyprian of Carthage (executed 258). Rome had produced no figures of comparable significance.[25] Even in the later fourth century, the bishops of Rome were eclipsed in political influence by Ambrose of Milan. It was, as we have seen, Ambrose rather than pope Damasus (366–84) who ensured that the Altar of Victory was not returned to the Senate House. In this period, the leaders of lay society in Rome, the members of the great senatorial families, were still predominantly pagan, and the bishops generally avoided conflict with them or with those aspects of the life of the city with which they were intimately involved.[26] Thus, not until the late fifth century would the popes challenge the continuance in Rome of such quasi-pagan festivals as the Lupercalia, in which naked men in wolf masks ran through the streets whipping women, who hoped it would help with conception.

On the other hand, the clergy of Rome were developing an institution that would claim and eventually attain an unrivalled authority over the Church in the West. Rome was fortunate in that it alone of the major Christian centres of the West could claim to have been founded by an Apostle, St Peter, who from the late second century was regarded as the first bishop of the city. According to Christian tradition from at least that same period, both St Peter and St Paul were also executed in Rome, and what were thought to be the sites of the burials were being venerated by the community. No other western Church, and few of the eastern ones, had founding figures even approaching such significance, and this gave Rome a particular Christian prestige to add to its secular one. In the East, the bishopric of Antioch was held to have been established by St Peter, but prior to his moving to Rome, and the bishopric of Alexandria was accepted as being founded by Peter's disciple, the Gospel writer, Mark. So, even the great eastern sees could not match Rome as Petrine foundations, and could not claim the presence of his body. Peter was the acknowledged leader of the Apostles in the Gospel narratives, and, even more significantly, in that of Matthew, where Christ addresses him with the words 'You are Peter and on this rock I will build my Church' (Matthew 16.18).

In the third century, in the writings of Cyprian of Carthage, for example, this saying was interpreted as applying to all bishops, who were thereby invested with the powers 'of binding and loosing' to which the text goes on to refer. However, even in Cyprian's day, his contemporary, bishop Stephen I of Rome (254–7) claimed unique authority as well as precedence for his see, because of its holders being the successors of St Peter. At the time, this view was rejected by many other bishops in Africa and the East in a dispute over whether those who had received baptism from unworthy bishops should have the sacrament read-ministered to them. In both this controversy and in Stephen's claims for his see, the Roman view would eventually emerge triumphant. In part this was greatly assisted by the conversion of Constantine, and the Christianising of the state in the fourth century, with the emperors being increasingly keen to promote ecclesiastical structures that mirrored those of the Empire, and with the Roman Church and its bishop being considered the natural sources of guidance and authority in matters of belief and practice, at least in the West. With imperial backing, the bishops of Rome – or popes as we would now call them, though the title was not used formally by them before the eleventh century – claimed rights of final jurisdiction in all ecclesiastical disputes and the need to confirm all episcopal appointments in the western provinces of the Empire.[27]

While other churches, even in the East, recognised Rome's primacy of honour on the grounds of its apostolic founda-tion, they rejected these institutional demands. However, the fact that these claims were consistently reiterated by successive bishops had the effect of reinforcing their antiquity and of mak-ing them increasingly acceptable. In fact, they offered things that more and more of their fellow bishops in the West came to need. Thus, in a period in which the political and economic importance of bishops in the urban communities was growing, disputed elections and subsequent attempts to eject incumbent bishops became increasingly common.

Therefore, the role of a third party demanding the right to confirm all elections and to act as final arbiter in all local dis-putes, to whom disappointed candidates or deposed occupants of sees could appeal, became ever more important. So the custom grew for bishops in the western provinces to seek papal confirmation of their election. Similarly, Rome's claims offered an opportunity for one party in a theological dispute to secure a more than localised victory. For example, the African Church long resisted Roman claims, but when in 417/18 Augustine and the African bishops wanted to secure the condemnation across the West of the teachings of Pelagius on divine grace and free will, they appealed to the bishops of Rome, thereby implicitly accepting the papal claim to final jurisdiction in disputes and in matters of doctrine.[28]

The late fourth century also saw the growth of the institu-tional complexity of the Roman Church. In particular, this took the form of the establishment of the *tituli*, the principal churches in each of the fourteen ecclesiastical regions into which the city was divided. Each had its own clergy, the senior member of which was also the member of an advisory and administrative body or *curia* around the bishop.[29] Rome also had the advantage, unlike its principal eastern rivals of Antioch and Alexandria, of not being internally divided and wracked by theological disputes, as in the various stages of the Arian controversy. The East was also liable to disputes between its great churches, which included the *parvenu* but politically important Constantinople, established in 330, and the prestigious but less significant see of Jerusalem.

The early fifth century saw the authority of the Church in the city of Rome greatly enhanced. The fall of Eugenius's regime in 394, continuing imperial encouragement and family pressures all combined to hasten the extinction of paganism among the senatorial houses. The sack of the city in 410 also caused the dispersal of some of these families, and in general their wealth declined during the fifth century.[30] By the middle of that century, the secular aristocracy of Rome may have been financially outstripped by the Church, which gradually absorbed the functions of the senators as the principal patrons of the city. The Roman Church took over the charitable work and much of the political patronage of the senatorial families, many of the members of which were entering its ranks or committing themselves to ascetic lifestyles that hastened the demise of their dynasties. As well as material benefits, the Church was also providing new spiritual patronage for the city as a whole, and for each of its fourteen regions.

The growth of the cult of the martyrs who had been executed during the persecutions of Decius and Diocletian's reigns provided new sources of local loyalty. Most urban regions had acquired their own special saint or saints, whose relics, which could be either whole bodies or various limbs, were transported into specially built churches from the cemeteries outside the city.[31] Thus each section of Rome had its special saints and particular churches, in addition to the great patronal figures of Peter and Paul. At the same time, an increasingly elaborate liturgy was being evolved to honour all these saints, and in the form of long and colourful processions from church to church, culminating in the pontifical basilicas of St Peter's or the Lateran, tying them all together into one interrelated whole, and emphasising the special role of the bishop. These processions and the liturgy of the great feast days also provided alternatives to the public festivities of the pagan holidays that the

Church was trying to suppress. A number of these, which their supporters saw as being non-Christian but not actively pagan, survived into the sixth century.[32]

The ideological framework on which claims for the special authority of the Roman bishops rested received further elaboration during the pontificate of Leo I (440–61). Like his predecessors, Leo took as his starting point the Petrine text of the Gospel of Matthew, but he interpreted it in the light of concepts borrowed from Roman law, according to which an heir inherited all the rights but also all the obligations of a testator. In other words, in a legal sense he became that person. Thus Leo argued that Peter had been the bishop of Rome and had passed on his authority to his successor, Clement. (This idea derived from a text known as the Pseudo-Clementine Epistle, thought to have been the work of Clement but was in fact a century or so later in date.) Clement in turn passed on what he had received from Peter to his own successor and thence through an unbroken episcopal succession to all subsequent bishops of the city. Therefore they, uniquely according to Leo, received what Christ had given to Peter – in other words, the powers of 'binding and loosing'. But, more than that, by application of the legal principles mentioned above, they *were* Peter; an identification that Leo made quite explicit in a number of his surviving sermons and letters.[33] From this, Leo claimed that, as Peter's heir, indeed as Peter himself, he alone had the right and the duty of making final and binding decisions on matters of doctrine. This was particularly significant at this time in that the East was once again being wracked by theological divisions.

With the questions of the relationships between the Three Persons of the Trinity more-or-less settled at the Council of Constantinople in 381, it was not long before a fresh controversy arose over the attempt to condemn the total corpus of the writings of Origen (d. 254). This was symptomatic of a wider tendency in the Church at this time to make the definitions of orthodox belief more rigid and to exclude many previously acceptable theological ideas and speculation, as well as those who refused to renounce them. This attack on Origen's teaching caused much controversy in the East, especially in Egypt, around the turn of the fourth century, exacerbated by ecclesiastical politics as much as by theological argument. In particular, this dispute enabled bishop Theophilus of Alexandria (385–412) to present himself as the champion of orthodoxy and an ally of the see of Rome in confronting the bishops of Constantinople.[34] It also enabled the Alexandrian Church to score a moral victory over its other rival, the see of Antioch, whose intellectual tradition owed much to Origen's methods of biblical exegesis – even though he himself had once been the head of the main Christian school in Alexandria.[35]

The rise to prominence of the see of Constantinople, as the result of the city's role as imperial capital, aroused the hostility of the leaders of the other great eastern patriarchal sees, especially Alexandria, whose own authority in Egypt was not always secure. Any political or theological weakness on the part of the incumbent of the see of Constantinople was eagerly seized on by his rivals. Thus the great orator and moralist St John Chrysostom, bishop of Constantinople (398–404), who, as a former cleric of Antioch, was doubly distrusted by the Alexandrian Church, was successfully undermined by his ecclesiastical opponents when he lost the favour of the imperial family.[36] Rome was not entirely easy about this affair, not least as it involved the exile of a bishop by the secular power; something that had only happened in the West under the 'Arian' emperor Constantius II, as well as ignoring Rome's claim to be the final court of appeal in such disputes.

However, the next victim of Alexandrian aggression aroused few such doubts, and his elimination strengthened rather than strained the Rome–Alexandria axis. This was Patriarch Nestorius of Constantinople (428–31). Like John Chrysostom, he was an Antiochene, and he underlined the link by instituting a festival in the Church of Constantinople to commemorate Chrysostom. But, unlike his great predecessor, Nestorius's error was not one of tact but of teaching. On the combining of divine and human elements in Christ, he took a sharply discriminatory line, and argued for the existence of two natures and two persons. As a consequence, he was able to present Mary as the mother of only the human Jesus and to deny her the title of *Theotokos* or 'God-bearer', which was much used in popular devotion, especially in Egypt.[37]

This inevitably lost Nestorius much support and ultimately laid his theology open to condemnation by a general council of the church held at Ephesus in 431. The whole episode was brilliantly orchestrated by bishop Cyril of Alexandria (412–44), the most able ecclesiastical politician of his age. Nestorius himself was exiled to an Egyptian oasis, but his theology subsequently attracted a following among some of the Syriac-speaking Christians across the frontier in Persia. These Nestorians, as they became called, also spread their distinctive theology to various parts of Central Asia and into northern China during the time of the Liao dynasty (907–1125).[38]

In combating Nestorius, Cyril had expounded a strongly opposed theology. For Two Natures in Two Persons he effectively substituted the doctrine of One Nature in One Person: the human and divine in Christ being indistinguishable and inseparable. At the First Council of Ephesus in 431, Cyril and Nestorius and their supporters had excommunicated each other. The emperor Theodosius II had been prepared to see both deposed, and while Nestorius resigned voluntarily, Cyril was forced to retract some of his views because of criticism from Antioch. This was something that his Egyptian followers were determined to see reversed. In the later 440s, the supporters of the extreme One Nature, or Monophysite, theology attempted to have the full version of Cyril's teaching accepted as orthodoxy. In this they had the support of the powerful imperial chamberlain, Chrysaphius, with the result that, at a Second Council of Ephesus in 449, bishop Dioscorus of Alexandria (444–51) was able to gain an extraordinary victory, which included the deposition and exile of bishop Flavian of Constantinople (446–9), and the proclaiming of the One Nature theology as orthodox.[39]

The hour of triumph of its supporters proved short-lived, however, as in 450 a change of emperor led to a reversal of theological emphasis. Marcian (450–7), who had had Chrysaphius executed, was persuaded by bishop Anatolius of Constantinople (449–58) to hold a general council of the whole Church to lay down authoritative teaching on this matter of the Natures and Persons of Christ. This met at Chalcedon in 451, condemned the extreme single nature theology of bishop Dioscorus of Alexandria, and produced what became the orthodox formulation of Two Natures in One Person'.[40]

The procedure followed was not entirely what Rome had wanted. While Leo was convinced that the Single Nature doctrine had to be condemned, for a council to do so was a rejection of the Roman view that only the holder of Peter's chair – Peter himself – could make authoritative pronouncements on doctrine. Leo had produced a theological statement, known as the Tome, which he first sent to the Second Council of Ephesus, but there it was prevented from being read and his representatives were threatened. One of them, his eventual successor, Hilarus (461–6), had to hide in the tomb of St John to escape a mob of 'One Nature' supporters. Leo next sent a copy of his Tome with his envoys to the Council of Chalcedon.[41] His intention was that it should be read out to the assembled bishops and, with Peter having spoken, no further discussion should be required. In practice, this time the document was received and its orthodoxy acclaimed, but not until after the council itself had taken its decisions. The eastern bishops, who conceded to Rome a primacy in prestige but not in authority, accepted the Tome as orthodox because it agreed with the doctrinal statements of earlier ecumenical councils. For Rome, though, it was the authoritative statement of orthodox belief because Leo–Peter had issued it. A fundamental and ultimately irreconcilable divide over the sources of authority in the Church had come into existence.

Leo was also displeased because in the authoritative canons it promulgated by way of stating the conclusions that had been reached, the Council of Chalcedon had accorded special prestige to the see of Constantinople. In Canon 28 it gave Constantinople precedence over both Alexandria and Antioch, as well as augmenting the territory under the ecclesiastical control of the imperial see. While Rome was not affected by this, Leo accused Anatolius of 'self-seeking' and of 'depraved cupidity', because these decisions seemed like an unacceptable novelty.[42] This was another central feature in Rome's view of its responsibilities. Its authority and teaching having derived through the unbroken succession of bishops from St Peter himself meant that this was an unalterable tradition, entrusted to the bishops of Rome alone, capable of being interpreted but not altered by them. Decisions taken by others that conflicted with that tradition, however reasonable they might seem on other grounds, could not be accepted and indeed had firmly to be rejected because they did not derive from that one Apostolic source, which was the sole guarantor of true faith and proper practice. This was to be the start of a series of acrimonious conflicts between Rome and Constantinople which were intensified when the title of 'Ecumenical Patriarch' was adopted by the bishop of Constantinople, possibly as early as the patriarchate of Acacius (472–89).[43]

The controversy over Single Nature theology was far from settled by the decisions at Chalcedon. This merely prevented one side from obtaining outright dominance. Though the power of the secular arm was applied and various eastern bishops who supported Dioscurus were exiled from their sees, Single Nature teaching acquired and retained a majority following among the Christian populations of Syria and Egypt, and at the slightest weakening by the government, the expelled prelates were restored on a wave of popular backing. Violence was frequent and many bishops were killed by the partisans of the other side in this bitter theological controversy, which was still raging when the eastern provinces passed into Arab rule in the seventh century.[44]

Monasticism

Not the least violent of the participants in all the eastern theological disputes were the monks. The rise of the monastic movement is yet another way in which eastern ideas influenced the
West, but came to be transformed and given a very different
institutional character. The origins of monasticism are to be
found in Egypt, and possibly also in Palestine, in the second
half of the third century. Traditionally, the founding figure is
the Egyptian hermit St Anthony, but he is probably best seen
as a representative of the earliest stages of the movement.
Information about him comes from a substantial *Life of Anthony*
written by bishop Athanasius of Alexandria around the year
355, and translated into Latin during his fourth exile in the
West.[45]

According to the *Life*, Anthony (*c.* 250–*c.* 355), then aged
eighteen and following the death of his parents, heard the
Gospel text in which Christ says that those who would be perfect should sell all they possess, give it to the poor, and then
come and follow him. This command Anthony felt obliged to
follow literally. An initial qualm about what provision to make
for his sister was suppressed by his subsequent hearing of the
text 'Take no thought for the morrow'. He retired firstly to a
tomb on the fringes of the desert and then to an abandoned
fort, where he lived a life of renunciation and mortification
for twenty years. After the ending of the persecution under
Maximin II in 313, in which he had gone to Alexandria to try
to achieve martyrdom, he retired deeper into the desert, to
what he called his 'inner mountain', where he remained until
he died, leaving only a cloak, two tunics and a hair shirt.

He had not been alone, and it was the pressure of the attention he attracted that caused him to move in stages into more
remote and ever harsher terrain, deeper in the desert. At the
time of his death he was accompanied by two disciples. The rig-
ours of his self-mortification attracted growing numbers of visitors and would-be followers, impelled by the belief that special
power and holiness were vested in those who gained such mas-
tery over their bodies and the lusts of the flesh. This veneration
for ascetics and belief in their special powers may have had its
roots in earlier and pre-Christian traditions in Egyptian society.

What Anthony and his emulators were doing was undertaking
a geographical flight, away from their homes and families in the
villages and small towns of the Nile valley into the uncultivatable
semi-desert, where they lived in caves and among wild animals.
In other words, they sought out the very conditions most at odds

with their former ways of life. They renounced their possessions and all human ties, living on the minimum possible amounts of food gathered from the land or obtained by manual labour such as basket weaving, the products of which were sold in the villages. The purpose of all of this was the salvation of the soul of the individual, by taking Christ's teaching on renunciation at face value and by the deliberate seeking of conflict with the passions of the mind and body, which were externalised as demons. These were fought against and vanquished by showing that they had no hold over the individual holy man, who aimed to bring his body into total subjection to his will.[46]

Not everyone who shared such ideals could undertake the mortification and the conflicts with the 'demonic' forces in solitude, at least not initially. Thus many aspirants to such an ascetic life wanted first to subject themselves to the guidance of an already established holy man of proven prowess. Some, like Anthony, felt such involvement to be a snare, and escaped further and further away from society. Others, however, were prepared to help aspiring disciples on the spiritual path. Pachomius (*c.* 295–350), having himself become a noted hermit, gathered large numbers of disciples and began to organise them into communities.[47] In these monasteries, or effectively monastic villages, each monk had his own hut and supported himself by his own manual labour, but they all gathered together for the liturgy and were all under the direction and supervision of their spiritual father (*abba* – hence abbot).

These communities could be very large indeed and contain 300 or more members, but there was no sense that the communal life was in itself beneficial.[48] Each monk was there to secure his own spiritual salvation, and the relationship with the abbot was personal. The communal or *coenobite* life was seen only as the first stage, a kind of spiritual primary school, to be followed if possible by the monk going out to lead the solitary life in a remote location, far removed from any other society. In practice, many of the monks never aspired to or failed to be able to advance to this next step and remained in the coenobia. Communities of female ascetics also came into being in this period, though there were fewer of them than of men, and in general the women were never expected to move on to the full solitary life. They remained under the direction of male abbots.[49] Those women who did attempt to lead an individual ascetic life could face misunderstanding, abuse and even violence.

The movement began to attract interest outside Egypt, and similar forms developed in Palestine, where the monastic communities were known as *Lavra*, and also in Syria.[50] In Syria, where the sharp distinction between desert and cultivated land that was characteristic of Egypt was somewhat blurred, a novel form of escape was created with the appearance of the Stylites. These were solitaries who escaped not horizontally but vertically, by establishing themselves on the tops of pillars.

Traditionally, the first of these was St Simeon Stylites (388–460), who began his ascetic career as an ordinary hermit, following the Egyptian model. From 413 to 423 he lived in an enclosed cell near Antioch, but in 423 he began to build himself a pillar, gradually extending it upwards until by 430 it was 60 feet high. The top was said to be only 3 feet in diameter. There he remained with a manacle around his neck until his death, engaged in meditation and conflict with demons. He attracted many visitors who came to him for secular as well as spiritual advice, and was consulted on various political matters by the emperors Theodosius II, Marcian and Leo I. Questioners ascended to him by a ladder, up which also his disciples brought occasional supplies of food.[51]

Mortification, but also the conspicuous display of it, was taken to its extreme by Simeon and other Syrian pillar saints, such as Daniel the Stylite (died *c.* 490), who inherited Simeon's pillar and lived on it for 33 years. His legs were said to be completely atrophied by the time of his death. Unlike Anthony, or even Pachomius, such men as Daniel could exercise considerable influence in secular affairs because of their reputation for outstanding sanctity and their relative accessibility. The opposition to his religious views on the part of Daniel helped to bring about the rapid fall of the usurper Basiliscus (475–6).[52] As the division over Single Nature theology grew in intensity, and the number of such Stylite saints increased, so it apparently became common to encounter pillar saints on adjacent columns shouting theological abuse at each other across the Syrian landscape.[53]

In the West, where Athanasius brought news about the new movement during his exiles, monasticism took on a rather different character. It was initially much more of an urban than a rural phenomenon, and the idea of the superiority of the solitary rapidly gave way to priority being given to the corporate quest of the community. Aristocrats created house-monasteries in their own properties, in which, with selected friends and companions, they lived a life of modified asceticism, following a set of rules of their own devising. Rome was a particular centre for such establishments, and a number of individual spiritual guides became highly fashionable. Jerome was one such popular mentor until he left in 385 for Bethlehem, where, with two of his Roman lady disciples, he established male and female monastic communities.[54] Other westerners, lured also by the growing cult of pilgrimage to the Holy Places, moved to the East, particularly after the sack of Rome and the flight of some of the leading aristocratic families from the city.[55]

At the same time, the theological controversies in the East in the this period led to a migration westwards of a number of monastic teachers. The most influential of these was John Cassian, who left Egypt in the course of the conflict over the teachings of Origen, became a follower of John Chrysostom in Constantinople, and went west to try to gain papal support for the Patriarch in 405. After John's death he moved to Marseille in Gaul, where he set up male and female monastic communities. Around 420, at the request of the local bishop, he wrote a work called the *Institutes*, a collection of monastic rules and regulations, much influenced by the Greek rules and advice of bishop Basil of Caesarea (370–9). He followed this with his books of *Conferences*, recounting the oral spiritual teaching of a series of Egyptian holy men and monastic founders.[56] Both of these works of Cassian remained highly influential in the West and became classics of Latin monastic literature.

In both East and West, the individualism of the monks and their lack of answerability to the established ecclesiastical hierarchy made them difficult to control. The theological divisions and the sheer number of the monks in Egypt made them dangerous partisans in the faction fights within the cities. Monks were responsible for the lynching of the pagan philosopher Hypatia (410), for the sacking of the last great temples, and for the killing of a number of bishops with whose theological views they disagreed.[57] In the West, the more limited and more aristocratic nature of the phenomenon prevented any such developments, but individual monastic teachers could threaten the growing consensus on the nature of orthodox belief being developed by such bishops as Augustine. In trying in 418 to suppress one of these teachers, Pelagius, formerly a fashionable leader of the aristocratic monastic life in Rome, Augustine resorted to seeking the secular aid of the state. For all the arguments of *The City of God*, the Empire still had a role to play in imposing the right beliefs.[58] However, Augustine had been right to doubt the mutual interdependence of church and state: he died in 430 while Hippo was under siege by the Vandals, and the rule of Rome in Africa did not long survive him.[59]

6　The warlords

Gaul or Africa? 410–54

Between the years 395 and 476 Roman armies virtually disappear from the literary sources relating to both the eastern and the western halves of the Empire. While there is a great deal of military activity recorded in these decades, much of it conducted by generals acting for and in the name of a succession of emperors, in most cases their troops are federates or mercenaries. This contrasts with the situation in earlier centuries, in which the formation, deployment and conflicts of clearly Roman armies can be documented in considerable detail. It is thus not surprising to find that many modern historians of the Roman army end their studies around the year 400.[1]

We can be quite precise as to when the presence of Roman field armies is last recorded in many of the provinces of the western half of the Empire. In 407, the usurper Constantine III withdrew the mobile forces from Britain.[2] None were ever returned to the island. After this emperor's fall in 411, and that of the rebel regime of Maximus and Gerontius centred on Barcelona, the field army was withdrawn from Spain.[3] Some garrisons remained in the north-eastern province of Tarraconensis throughout most of the fifth century, but the other Spanish provinces were left without a permanent Roman military presence. Africa, where most of the Spanish field army units were sent in 413, was equally denuded of its troops in 432 when the Master of the Soldiers Boniface took his army to Italy to engage in a civil war with his rival, Aetius.[4] The soldiers were not returned, and, by 439, Carthage and all the North African provinces were in the hands of the Vandals, whose rule was recognised by the imperial government in a treaty made in 442.

The situation in Gaul is less clear cut, in that what occurred there looks like a gradual contraction of the Roman military presence over the course of several decades, accompanied by a growing dependence on mercenary or federate troops to preserve a dwindling area of direct imperial rule. The settlement of the Visigoths in Aquitaine in 418/9 marked the beginning of the process.[5] The last time a Roman general, in the person of Aetius, then Master of the Soldiers in Gaul, appeared in the region of the lower Rhine, once a principal area of imperial

campaigning, was the year 428.[6] Direct control of the area
north of the Loire and west of the Seine seems to have been
maintained at least until the murder of the emperor Majorian
in 461. The Auvergne remained under imperial rule until 475,
but its defence depended exclusively on local resources from
the 450s onwards.

At the same time, the employment of non-Roman forces in
imperial defence in Gaul rose dramatically. The Visigoths were
used against the Burgundians and the usurping emperors
Jovinus and Sebastian in the Rhineland in 413.[7] They were subsequently sent into Spain against the Vandals and Alans from
416 to 418, and were then established by treaty as federates in
the province of Aquitania Secunda in south-west Gaul. When the
kingdom they created around Toulouse, following their treaty
with the Romans in 418/19, began to expand into areas that
the Empire wished to keep under its direct rule, the Visigoths
themselves were attacked by armies of Hun mercenaries in
imperial service. Aetius's deputy in Gaul, Litorius, even threatened Toulouse with a Hun army in 439, but proved to be overconfident and was defeated.[8] Hun units had previously been
used by Litorius between 435 and 437 to suppress Bagaudic
banditry north of the Loire, and were then used against the
small Burgundian kingdom in the middle Rhineland in 437.[9]
In 442, Aetius settled the remnants of the Burgundians in the
region of Savoy to garrison the western Alpine approaches into
Italy.[10]

Unlike the history of the fourth century, many central
events of which are described in the surviving books of the
work of Ammianus Marcellinus, the fifth century has left us
few contemporary historical accounts. Our principal sources
of information take the form of short chronicles, the most
important of which was completed around the year 455 and
was the work of an Aquitanian layman with strong theological
interests, called Prosper. He wrote the final versions of his
chronicle in Rome, where he acted as secretary to Pope Leo
the Great. Another chronicle, written by a Bishop Hydatius of
Chaves (*Iria Flavia*) in Galicia about 469, gives a north-western Spanish perspective on events and is our principal source
for the history of the peninsula in the fifth century.[11] Such
works give an outline of leading events, at least from their
authors' points of view, but tend to offer little or no interpretation of them. Thus, most of the leading actors in these events
remain two-dimensional, and their policies and actions can
only be interpreted on the basis of outcomes, intentional or
otherwise.

What seems clear from such accounts of Roman military activity, and equally significantly from its absence in certain regions, is the diminishing capacity of the imperial government in the West, based in Ravenna from 402 to 450 and then in Rome, to govern and defend its provinces. The authority of central government gradually but irreversibly declined from the crisis period of 406–11 onwards. Up to that point, there are no indications that the emperors might contemplate ignoring the defensive needs of any provinces of the western Empire, or consider delegating their rule over them. Once the process started, in Britain in 410, in Spain in 411 and in Gaul in 418, it accelerated rapidly. Politics at the imperial court was largely focused on deciding on which areas of the western Empire were dispensable and which had to be retained under imperial rule at all costs.

Simply put, the decision made between the 420s and the mid-450s was that Gaul was the main area outside Italy that had to be defended and governed directly. The responsibility for implementing this policy lay with the general, Flavius Aetius, who dominated the western government from 430 to 453. For some historians, Aetius is 'the last of the Romans', the indefatigable defender of a declining Empire. On the other hand, it has also been suggested that 'if Aetius was the last of the Romans, it was because he left nothing to his successors'.[12]

His father, who came from the province of Moesia in the Balkans, made a successful military career for himself in Africa and subsequently in Gaul, where he served as Commander of the Cavalry (*Magister Equitum*) during the ascendancy of Constantius in the years 411–21.[13] Because of his father's military prominence, Aetius himself was sent in the same period as a Roman diplomatic hostage, first to the Visigoths and then to the Huns. The close contacts he made with the Huns in particular led to his being used to recruit an army of Hun mercenaries to fight for the Emperor John (423–5), who had been elevated by the western army after the death of Honorius.

Whether deliberately or otherwise, Aetius returned to Italy with a Hun army too late to save John, who was overthrown by the forces of the eastern emperor Theodosius II in 425, in the last of the succession of civil wars between the two halves of the Empire.[14] Thanks to this personal military following, Aetius was then able to secure a command for himself under the new western regime of Valentinian III and his mother Galla Placidia, the sister of Honorius, being appointed Master of the Soldiers or commander of the army in Gaul. There, he began by relieving Arles, then under siege by the Gothic king Theoderic I (419–51).

In 429, Aetius returned to Italy to take up the post of the junior of the two Masters of the Soldiers 'in the Presence' (that is, of the emperor), in other words, becoming the second most senior general in the West. In 430 he arranged for the murder of Felix, his immediate superior, and assumed his office.[15] In 432, however, he was challenged by Boniface, the military commander in Africa, whose influence at court he had undermined in 427. Boniface was invited to Italy with his army and given the Mastership of the Soldiers by the empress Galla Placidia, then acting as regent for her still infant son. In the ensuing civil war, Boniface was victorious in a battle near Rimini, but died soon afterwards from his wounds.[16] His son-in-law, Sebastian, was appointed to succeed him as Master of the Soldiers, but lacked the support to resist Aetius, who forced his own reinstatement in 433.[17] From that year until his murder at the hands of the emperor Valentinian III in 454, Aetius exercised an unchallenged military, and thus also political, supremacy in the western half of the Empire.

Throughout the 430s and early 440s he used Hun mercenaries to maintain imperial control in Gaul. At the same time, no resources were diverted to aid the defence of other western provinces. An appeal for military assistance against the raids of the Picts and Scots was sent from Britain to Aetius between 446 and 454, but seems to have received no reply.[18] A similar request from the towns of Galicia in 431 had been answered by no more than the despatch of a single officer, sent by Aetius to negotiate with the Sueves, whose kingdom was rapidly engulfing the province.[19] More serious still, was the failure of Aetius to take any action to stem the Vandal seizure of Africa.

From 425 to 432, the North African provinces had been in the hands of Aetius's former rival Boniface, whose supporters still held the major military and administrative appointments in them. So, Aetius may have been less interested in coming to their assistance. On the other hand, the years of the Vandal conquest coincided exactly with those of the most intense conflict in Gaul between Aetius's forces and the Visigoths, and it may be that the resources did not exist to enable war to be waged by the Empire on two fronts simultaneously. Whatever the reason, Aetius clearly prioritised his ultimately unsuccessful attempt to eliminate the Visigothic kingdom in Gaul, and so conceded control of Africa, supposedly the 'granary of the western Empire', to the Vandals. The treaty made in 442 that formalised this recognition included the betrothal of the Emperor Valentinian III's still infant daughter to Huneric, the eldest surviving son of the Vandal King Gaiseric.[20]

Despite the defeat and subsequent execution of Litorius by the Visigoths in 439, Aetius did manage to limit their expansion beyond the areas they had received by treaty in 418/19. He faced a genuine problem, in that the Visigothic kingdom based on Toulouse had become openly aggressive and expansionary after the death of its King Wallia (415–18) and the accession of Theoderic I (418–51). Moreover, Aetius – who had forced himself on the western court in 425, in 430 and again in 433 – was not popular with the empress Galla Placidia and her son Valentinian III.[21]

In consequence, he needed a network of other allies. His principal strength derived from his Hun mercenaries, some of whom had ties of personal loyalty to him. With such military support he won political backing from key elements in the senatorial aristocracy, particularly those with interests in Gaul.[22] Also, the occasional hostility that had shown itself in the later fourth century, and more acutely from 408 onwards, between senators in Rome and the imperial court in Milan and then Ravenna, meant that a commander out of favour with the emperor could expect some support from the Senate.

The 430s, however, saw a major change in Hun society in the plains north of the Danube, the centre of their area of settlement and control. The Huns, who had contributed to the collapse of Gothic power north of the Black Sea in the 370s, lacked a single leader. There was no one 'king of the Huns' at this time. The creation of Hun hegemony over the various earlier inhabitants of the Carpathian basin – which may even have reached across the mountains and as far north as the Baltic, according to one contemporary Roman report – was followed rather than caused by the emergence of a dynasty of khans ruling all or most of the Huns. According to Roman accounts, a certain Rua was leading them by the early 430s. He was succeeded between 433 and 435 by his nephews Bleda and Attila, and the latter secured complete domination by murdering his brother in 444/5.[23]

The emergence of this single authority among the Huns meant that by the mid-440s the continued supply of Hun mercenaries for the armies of the western Empire depended on the continuing goodwill of their ruler or khan. For most of the 430s and 440s, the Huns exploited their dominance on the Danube and Rhine frontiers of the Roman Empire in two ways. They provided increasing amounts of the military manpower used by the western government against the Visigoths, Burgundians and Bagaudae, thus also thereby keeping Aetius in power. They also used the threat, and occasionally the reality, of raids into the

Balkans to extort annual payments of tribute from the eastern half of the Empire, then under the rule of Theodosius II (402–50).[24]

The death of this emperor in 450, following a riding accident, led to a dramatic change of policy in Constantinople. The new ruler Marcian (450–7), a general selected as both emperor and husband by Theodosius's sister Pulcheria, carried out a purge of the imperial court, and refused to continue the annual payments to the Huns. Surprisingly, this did not precipitate a Hun invasion of the Balkans, as had occurred in 441 and 447. Instead, in 451 Attila took his armies into Gaul, thus using against the western empire the very forces that had previously defended it for most of the preceding two decades.

While the intended victims of the Hun assault may have been the Visigoths, contemporary sources record that the Hun army passed through the Rhineland and sacked the city of Metz.[25] A later saint's life also describes the Huns undertaking an unsuccessful siege of Orléans in the Loire valley.[26] Aetius was forced to make a rapid change of policy. Having, since his first campaign in 425, sought to contain or destroy the Visigothic kingdom, he was forced in these new circumstances to ally with Theoderic I against this common threat. In the ensuing battle 'of the Catalaunian plains', in the vicinity of Troyes, the main role was played by the Visigoths. Aetius may not have been present in person, and the limited nature of the Roman involvement again highlights the reduced size of the imperial military establishment at this time.[27] The Visigothic king Theoderic was killed, but the Huns were defeated, and in consequence withdrew from Gaul.

It has been suggested that Aetius deliberately dissuaded the new Visigothic king, Thorismund (451–3), from following up the victory by pursuing the retreating Huns.[28] This story comes from the over-elaborate account of the episode in the mid-sixth-century *Getica* or *Gothic History* of Jordanes, but it could make sense in the light of the previous pattern of Aetius's policy. For him, the principal threat remained that of the Visigoths, and he may have hoped to return to relying on the Huns as mercenaries for the defence of Roman interests in Gaul.

If so, he was quickly disillusioned. In 452, Attila and his Hun army again invaded imperial territory, but this time their target was Italy. They crossed the Danube and broke through the eastern Alpine passes unopposed. What is particularly striking about this campaign is the lack of any Roman military response. The Huns sacked Aquileia and advanced into the Po valley without meeting resistance. The only response offered was the despatch from Rome of an embassy, consisting of two leading senators and pope Leo I. According to the contemporary chronicle of Prosper, himself the pope's secretary, it was their pleas that led Attila to withdraw and retire beyond the Danube once more, but it is possible that the outbreak of an epidemic among the Huns was equally persuasive.[29]

What might have followed can only be a matter of speculation, in that Attila died in 453, and his empire collapsed under the competing claims of his sons and the revolt of most of its subject peoples. A confederacy of these defeated the Hun army in the battle of the Nedao in 454, and in the aftermath the Hun dominion disintegrated even more rapidly than it had first been created.[30] It is hardly coincidental that these events were paralleled by the elimination of Aetius. His principal allies had turned against him in 451. He had failed to defend Italy in 452, and any future hope of using Hun mercenary armies vanished with the collapse of their power in 453–4. Aetius had outlived his usefulness, and he was killed in the palace in Rome in 454, possibly by the emperor's own hand, and with him perished the Praetorian Prefect Boethius, one of his foremost senatorial allies.[31]

Valentinian III's elimination of Aetius led directly to his own murder. Aetius still retained the loyalty of a number of officers who had served under him, and of a force of bodyguards of barbarian origin, who may have been impelled by the traditions of their own society to seek revenge for a murdered leader. Two of these men were suborned by the former Consul and Praetorian Prefect Petronius Maximus to assassinate the emperor during a military parade in Rome on 16 March 455, a mere six months after the death of Aetius.[32]

For the sixth-century chronicler, the count Marcellinus, writing in Constantinople, the western Empire was lost in 454 with the murder of Aetius. Some modern historians have agreed, and have echoed such sixth-century Byzantine views that saw Aetius as 'the last of the Romans'.[33] In fact, the elimination of Valentinian meant the end of the imperial dynasty that had through its branches ruled the West since 364, and the initiation of a period in which the imperial office ceased to carry much weight in the western half of the Empire.

The end of the western Empire, 455–80

The career of Aetius has been followed in some detail, not only because it is crucial to the understanding of the making of Roman imperial policy over a vital three decades that effectively decided the fate of the western Empire, but also because it typifies a wider phenomenon, that of the role of the 'military dictator' in the fifth century. In the West, an almost unbroken succession of generals exercised the real power in all matters relating to the army, military strategy, the making of major political appointments, and the deployment of financial resources from the time of Stilicho right up to the ending of the line of separate western emperors in 476–80.

They can be listed as follows – all of them held the office of *Magister Militum praesentalis* or Master of the Soldiers in the (imperial) presence:

Arbogast	388–394
Stilicho	395–408
Constantius	411–421
Castinus	423–425
Felix	425–430
Aetius	430–432
Boniface	432
Sebastian	432–433
Aetius	433–454
Ricimer	457–472
Gundobad	472–473
Orestes	475–476
Odovacer	476– (became 'King of Italy', 476–93)

Some were short-lived or unsuccessful, as in the cases of Boniface, Sebastian and Castinus (who provided the military backing for the failed regime of the emperor John). Certain periods of particular turmoil, such as the years 408–11 or 454–7, also produced a number of competitors struggling unsuccessfully to gain the ascendancy that men such as Stilicho, Aetius and Ricimer exercised over long periods.

This was not an exclusively western phenomenon. A similar list can be drawn up for the East:

Gainas	399–400
Fravitta	400–401
Aspar	431–471
Zeno	473–474 (became emperor in 474)
Theoderic Strabo	474–475, 475–476, 478–479
Theoderic 'the Amal'	476, 477–478
Vitalian	518–520

However, as this list makes clear, the situation in the East throughout the fifth century is not so clear cut as in the West, largely because the military needs of that half of the Empire were less consistent, and it was often possible to prevent the commanders of the armies from exercising the kind of general control of political life and dominance of the imperial court that was typical of their counterparts in the West. Thus Gainas, one of a number of officers of Gothic origin who rose to prominence in the reign of Theodosius I, tried to control the eastern court in the way Stilicho did the western one, but was driven out of Constantinople in an anti-barbarian riot and was subsequently defeated by another of the Gothic generals, Fravitta. When he fled across the Danube he was killed by one of the Hun rulers and his head sent to Constantinople. Fravitta succeeded to Gainas's post, but within a year he himself had been killed in a coup organised by one of the court factions.[34]

In general, the eastern court was able to present a more consistently civilian image and to prevent its leading generals from acquiring a monopoly of power even in military matters. Aspar, who held the office of Master of the Soldiers for at least forty years, was never able to exercise the dominance over policy-making and appointments long held by his western contemporary Aetius. Under Theodosius II, his influence was limited, and even the succession of Marcian in 450, who had been one of his staff officers, seems neither to have been his choice nor to have specially benefited him. Only with the death of Marcian in 457 did Aspar achieve a real supremacy in the eastern court, when he engineered the succession of Leo I (457–74), another of his military subordinates.[35]

Even so, his supremacy was not secure. By the late 460s, Leo was creating a counterweight to the forces controlled by Aspar by recruiting Isaurians – mountain dwellers from central Asia Minor. He married his daughter to one of their leaders, 'Tarasis the son of Codissa', who then changed his name to Zeno, probably in honour of an earlier Isaurian general. By 471, Leo was strong enough to seize and execute both Aspar and Aspar's eldest son, who had been Master of the Soldiers in the Eastern Provinces.[36] The limitations on Aspar's power and his ultimate failure contrast markedly with the hold over a succession of emperors that was exercised by the principal military commander in the West in the 460s, a general called Ricimer. His rise to power was the product of the period of confusion that followed the killings of Aetius and then of Valentinian III, and was marked by dramatic changes in several areas of western policy. These were initiated by the events of 455.

Having arranged the death of Valentinian III, Petronius Maximus was able to secure his own proclamation as emperor

on the following day, and he linked his family to that of his predecessor by himself marrying the latter's widow and uniting his
son Palladius with the former emperor's daughter, Eudocia.
This, however, broke one of the terms of the treaty made in 442
between Valentinian III and the Vandal king Gaiseric, which
had included the betrothal of Eudocia to Gaiseric's son, Huneric.
Thus, in 455, Gaiseric was not only able to claim that the new
imperial regime had violated this treaty, but could also present himself as the avenger of his son's would-be father-in-law.
A Vandal fleet sailed from Africa and descended on an undefended Rome, giving the city a second sack that was perhaps
more thorough than that of 410. As the Vandals arrived, the
wretched Petronius Maximus tried to flee. An enraged citizen
threw a well-aimed brick at him, bringing his brief reign to a
pathetic end.[37]

The sack of Rome of 455 had the immediate effect of making
the Vandal threat to Italy seem far more menacing than the
more distant danger of Visigothic ambitions in Gaul. Despite
the Vandals immediately returning to Africa with their loot, the
whole episode brought home in a way that seems not to have
been previously appreciated just how vulnerable Italy, and
Rome in particular, was to sea-borne raiding, and how easy it
was for a hostile power in North Africa, in control of the mer-
cantile fleets of the coastal towns of the African provinces, to
carry it out. The Vandal menace and the ambition of regaining control of Africa became the mainspring of imperial policy
throughout the last years left to the western half of the Empire.

The lack of functioning Roman armies in the heartland of the
western Empire, which was apparent from the absence of resistance both to Attila in 452 and to the Vandal sack of Rome in
455, meant that Gaul became the main source of military manpower for the defence of Italy. Petronius Maximus had probably already realised this, as he appointed as his Master of the
Soldiers in the Presence a Gallic aristocrat called Eparchius
Avitus, who had served under Aetius and who also had close personal ties to the Visigothic royal house. This Avitus is reported to
have persuaded Theoderic I to ally with Aetius against the Hun
threat in 451. In 455, he was sent by Maximus to the Visigoths,
this time for aid against the Vandals. While Avitus was still at the
Gothic court in Toulouse, the news of Maximus's death arrived,
and with the support of the new Visigothic king Theoderic II
(453–6) Avitus was proclaimed emperor by the army and an
assembly of Gallic aristocrats at Arles.[38]

The Senate in Rome and the army commanders in Italy
accepted this Gallic seizure of power because of their pressing

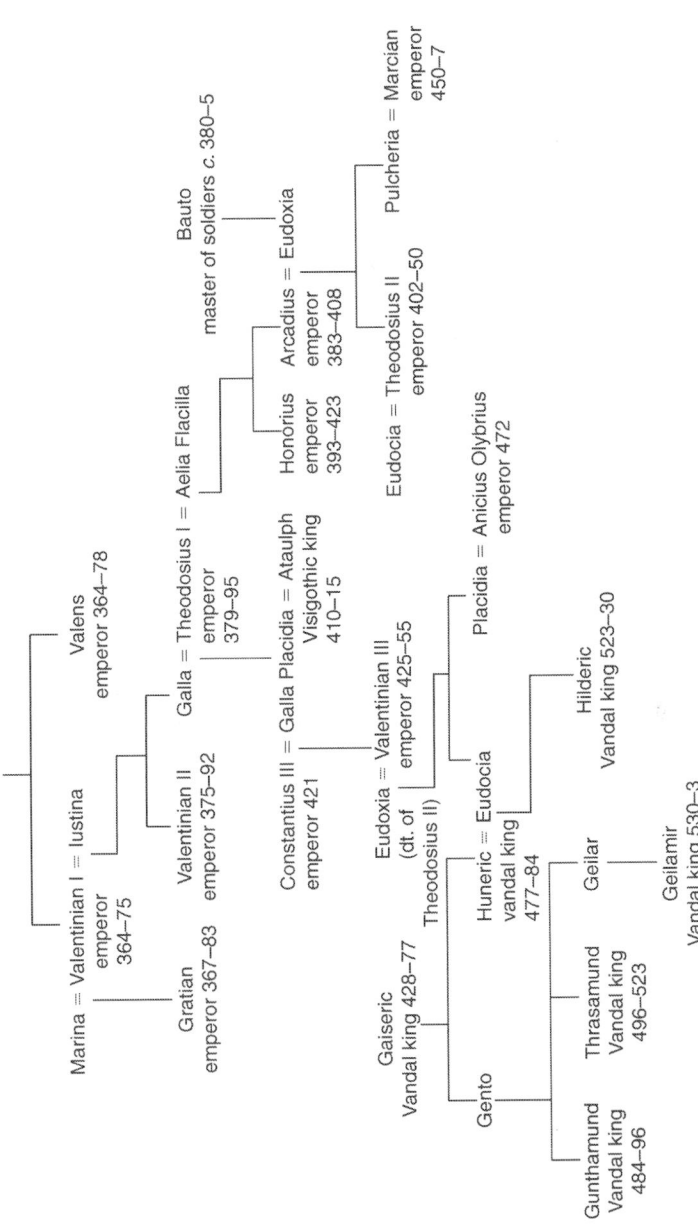

Emperors and kings, 364–533

need for assistance, but clearly resented the necessity. While Avitus came with a largely Visigothic army to Rome, his interests and those of his principal backers lay in Gaul. His close ties to the Visigoths also meant that the threats the latter posed to Roman interests in Gaul were greatly reduced. It is no coincidence that in 456 the Visigothic king Theoderic II led an army into Spain against the Suevic ruler Rechiarius, who was trying to take over the last imperial enclave in the peninsula, the north-eastern province of Tarraconensis.[39] Thus, as under Wallia, the Visigoths came once more to play the role of Roman federate troops, acting in the imperial interests, but at the same time may have expanded their own control over regions that were of secondary concern to Avitus and his Gallic aristocratic supporters. If not fully documented, the Visigothic kingdom may have established authority over much of southern and central Spain following the successful campaign of 456. It is possible too that this move into Spain was also presented to the Italian senators, now obsessively concerned with the Vandal threat, as the necessary preliminary to an invasion of Africa.

If so, the lack of immediate action against the Vandals and the ignominy of accepting provincial emperor-making made Avitus's regime increasingly unpopular in Rome, though he had been accepted as a colleague by the eastern emperor Marcian. In 456, Ricimer, a general of mixed Visigothic and Suevic origin, won a battle at sea against a Vandal fleet. In itself it may not have been militarily significant, but it enabled the Italian high command to feel it could dispense with Avitus. Another of Aetius's former officers, Majorian, who now enjoyed the backing of Ricimer, renounced his allegiance to the Gallic emperor, who then tried to escape from Rome back to his home province. However, Avitus was intercepted and his forces defeated by Majorian and Ricimer at Piacenza (*Pollentia*) in October 456. After the battle, the emperor was promptly ordained as bishop of Piacenza, a manoeuvre to formalise his deposition. His death followed suspiciously soon afterwards.[40]

The determination to regain Africa dominated western imperial policy for the next fifteen years in the same way that the need to contain Visigothic ambitions in Gaul had obsessed it in the time of Aetius. In 457, after an interval probably spent in securing eastern recognition, Majorian was proclaimed emperor.[41] He needed to impose himself on the remaining regions of Gaul still under imperial rule, where the deposition of Avitus had been badly received, but this was as a preliminary to an invasion of Africa, towards which the making of an agreement with the Visigothic king Theoderic II was the second step. With these barriers removed, in 460 Majorian became the last of the Roman emperors to appear in the Iberian Peninsula. He made a formal *adventus*, the ceremony to mark an imperial arrival in a city, into Zaragoza, and then proceeded to the south-eastern coast, where a fleet was being assembled to transfer his army to Africa.[42] Here, however, later that year, disaster struck. The Vandals made a pre-emptive strike on the imperial fleet, destroying or capturing the bulk of it. The campaign had to be called off.

Worse was to follow, in that Majorian then agreed to the Vandal king Gaiseric's request for a treaty. As far as it is now known, this seems to have been an acceptance of the terms of the previous treaty of 442, conceding Vandal control of Africa in return for peace. On his return to Gaul in 461, Majorian disbanded his army, composed mainly of federates, and in the autumn he headed for Rome, only to be intercepted by the forces of Ricimer, deposed and executed.[43] While it is normally attributed to a power struggle between the two men, the unfortunate end of Majorian in truth derived from his failure in the abortive African venture.

Decisive as Ricimer's move had been, it only further fragmented the dwindling territories controlled directly by the western emperor. When, in November 461, two months after the death of Majorian, a senator called Libius Severus was chosen as emperor in Rome, the Master of the Soldiers in Gaul, a general named Aegidius refused to accept him.[44] Roman territory north of the Loire ceased to be ruled from Italy, and Ricimer incited his Visigothic allies to attack Aegidius in return for being given control of Narbonne. Aegidius in turn opened diplomatic negotiations with the Vandal king Gaiseric for joint action against Ricimer and his emperor, Severus III, whose imperial title was not recognised by the eastern emperor Leo I.

The situation improved slightly in 465 with the deaths of both Aegidius and the emperor Severus III; with poison and the hand of Ricimer being suspected in both cases.[45] This did not result in the return of northern Gaul to imperial rule, but it did make possible the restoration of relations between East and West, leading to the acceptance in 467 of an eastern nominee, Anthemius, for the western throne, in return for the eastern Empire launching an invasion against the Vandals in Africa. Leo I benefited from the removal to the West of the dangerously well-connected Anthemius, who was not only a descendant of the emperor Julian, but also a son-in-law of the former emperor Marcian and a former candidate for the imperial office in the East in 457.[46]

In that sense, Leo got the best of the bargain. The eastern expedition to Africa in 468, commanded by his brother-in-law, was a disaster. The fleet suffered a surprise attack by fire ships off the African coast, and the invasion was abandoned.[47] In the West, conflicts between Anthemius and Ricimer reached such a point that civil war broke out. Anthemius, derisively nicknamed 'the little Greek', had little support among the populace or from the Senate. His opponents also accused him of being a pagan, though this may have amounted to no more than a wish on his part for greater religious tolerance. After a short struggle, Ricimer's forces took Rome, and Anthemius was dragged from sanctuary in a church and executed in July 472.[48]

By this time, effective military action against the Vandals was beyond the capacities of either half of the Empire, and so Ricimer himself came to an agreement with Gaiseric. This was symbolised by his choosing as the new western emperor the senator Anicius Olybrius, the husband of the former emperor Valentinian III's second daughter.[49] Her elder sister, pledged to Gaiseric's son by the treaty of 442 and then forcibly married to the son of Petronius Maximus, had been taken to Africa and married to Huneric by the Vandals in 455. Thus, the selection as emperor of this brother-in-law of the Vandal king's heir marked a new stage in relations between the western Empire and the Vandal kingdom, but this had little time in which to demonstrate its worth.

Neither Ricimer nor the emperor Olybrius lived out the year, both dying of natural causes before the end of 472. By this time, the Empire in the West had been reduced to Italy, and the Auvergne and eastern Provence in Gaul. The Visigoths were the masters of everything south of the Loire and west of the Rhône, and added the Auvergne to their territories in 475. The Burgundian kingdom covered Savoy and a large section of the middle Rhône valley. Imperial rule over the Ebro valley and related Catalan coast was ended by the Visigothic king Euric (466–84) in the early 470s.[50] So little did Italy matter, that Ricimer's successor and nephew Gundobad preferred in 473 not to remain to support the regime of the puppet emperor Glycerius that he had set up late the previous year, but to take his forces across the Alps to try to make himself ruler of the Burgundian kingdom in Gaul.[51]

Thus abandoned, Glycerius had no military resources available to resist an eastern imperial nominee, Julius Nepos, the Master of the Soldiers in Dalmatia.[52] Glycerius was deposed and sent as bishop to Salona in Dalmatia. However, like Anthemius, Nepos had little real support in Italy, and after a reign of just over a year he was expelled from Italy back to Dalmatia. His supplanter was his own newly appointed Master of the Soldiers, Orestes, who made his son Romulus emperor in October 475.

In August 476, Orestes himself was overthrown and killed by another and more experienced general of mixed origin, Odovacer, but the young Romulus was allowed to retire into private life on an estate in south Italy, where he may still have been living around the year 510.[53]

Formally, the deposition of Romulus, and the taking of power in Italy by Odovacer under the title of king in 476 did not mark the end of the western Roman Empire. The ejected Julius Nepos still controlled Dalmatia, preventing an eastern recognition of the status quo in Italy. The murder of Nepos in 480, possibly engineered by Bishop Glycerius of Salona, the man he himself had deposed in 474, removed this obstacle, and so technically may mark the end of the Roman Empire in the West.[54]

What is genuinely striking about the process of the 'Fall of the Roman Empire', to which it is essential to add 'in the West', as its eastern half was to survive for another 1,000 years, is the haphazard, almost accidental nature of the process. From 410 onwards, successive western imperial regimes just gave away or lost practical authority over more and more of the territory of the former Empire. Admittedly, in terms of constitutional theory, this was being delegated to imperial appointees in the persons of the various local rulers, whose de facto control of former imperial territories was recognised by treaties.

In this way, the western Empire delegated itself out of existence. It was perfectly logical for Odovacer to set himself up as king of Italy and to declare that there no longer needed to be a division of the Empire.[55] The events of 476 or 480 meant that instead of the Empire being divided, with eastern and western sections, there now existed one indivisible Empire, with the rights of the former western emperor over regional rulers now passing to the sole emperor ruling in Constantinople.

Obviously, in practice, this was not much more than a constitutional fiction, albeit an ideologically powerful one. Direct imperial rule over most of the West had been lost in the course of the fifth century, and was in most areas either only briefly restored or not at all. However much continuity can be detected, and there is an impressive quantity of it, in terms of administrative, fiscal, legal and institutional survivals at the provincial level, the disintegration of direct imperial rule was not to be reversed.

As the exercise of imperial authority in this period related directly to the ability or otherwise of the emperors to defend their territories, the problem is a military one. In that sense, the mysterious disappearance of the Roman army is one of the most significant features of the fifth century. Generals abound and so do barbarian soldiers. The old Roman units do not, even though such archaising texts as the *Notitia Dignitatum* of *c.* 425, appear to prolong their lives. Only the supposed existence of traditional units in Britain and Spain, at a time when other evidence shows they were not there, reveals the unreliability of this as a statement of the actual, as opposed to theoretical, deployment of the Roman army at the end of the first quarter of the fifth century.[56]

As the territories under direct imperial control diminished in size, so too were traditional recruiting grounds lost to the Roman army. From the later fourth century onwards, pressure from the troops themselves had reduced the quantity of armour worn and other long-established features of Roman military practice and equipment. By 425, the surviving units of the Roman army would have been in appearance, including dress and weaponry, little different from the various enemies they were required to fight, most of whom had themselves become increasingly Romanised in terms of material culture over the course of the previous decades. The loss of training and expertise, the expense of maintaining a standing army, and the political difficulties that could result from having one, all combined to make it seem easier, cheaper and safer to use barbarian federates to fight in the emperor's name. In consequence, those who directed them were able to demand more and were being given more by way of control over the government and revenues of the provinces in which they were situated. [57]

At the centre, the prime concern was the protection of Italy and of other regions that were of special interest to the political elite in Ravenna and Rome. Thus, in the time of Aetius, Africa could be dispensed with in order to concentrate on the preservation of parts of Gaul. Under Ricimer there was a change to almost exactly the opposite order of priorities. In consequence, neither Africa nor Gaul was preserved and the Empire itself became in practice no larger than Italy. Odovacer put an end to the fiction and made Italy just another of the several kingdoms into which the West had become divided.

The fall of Rome?

The interpretation outlined here may seem a bit limited as an answer to the perennial question of why the Roman Empire fell. What has just been suggested is that, simply put, it gave itself away: the central administration of the western half of the Empire relinquished day-to-day control over more and more of its provinces as its capacity to defend and administer them directly declined in the face of a growing series of military problems. This, it should be stressed, was seen at the time by the emperors as no more than a temporary expedient, and in no sense did they feel that they were permanently alienating their authority over the western provinces. In practice, however, as we can see with hindsight, direct imperial rule was never to be reimposed on most of these territories, and the central administration of the western Empire succumbed to the process it had itself instigated.

On the other hand, as will be seen in subsequent chapters dealing with the events in the West in the aftermath of the elimination of the last western emperors in 476–80, the intellectual, governmental and artistic traditions of the later Roman Empire continued to exercise influence in the West long after the disappearance of the unitary political structure that had previously supported them. 'The Fall of the Roman Empire in the West' was not the immediate disappearance of a civilisation: it was perhaps no more than the breaking down of a governmental apparatus that could no longer be sustained when faced with certain economic and political realities.

Seen this way, the analysis offered here may support recent revisionist approaches to 'the Fall' that once more emphasise the central role of the 'barbarians' in destroying the military and administrative structures of the Empire in the West, in the process triggering a cultural degradation that took centuries to reverse.[58] Trenchantly expressed, one commentator argues that "The end of the Roman West witnessed horrors and dislocation of a kind I sincerely hope never to live through; and it destroyed a complex civilization, throwing the inhabitants of the West back to a standard of living typical of prehistoric times.' He also argues that 'there is a real danger for the present day in a vision of the past that explicitly sets out to eliminate all crisis and decline'.[59]

This raises important questions, as much current historical scholarship is overly influenced by 'post-modernist' and other literary-theoretical ideas about the problems of knowledge, expressed particularly in an unwillingness to believe that we can understand what a writer is trying to tell us. We can only try to make sense of our personal reception of their work, not of their intention in writing it. One consequence of this has been something of a 'three wise monkeys' approach to literary sources describing violence, destruction, massacre and mayhem, as we are not permitted to place any trust in their authors' ability to provide us with an objective and reliable account. The result is pure intellectual stasis in which nobody is allowed to imply anything, let alone pass any form of judgement. For example, the well documented disappearance of the administrative structures of the Roman Empire in the West and of the trained personnel that maintained them should not be described in terms of decay, as that would be 'to adopt an inappropriate narrative of decline and fall'. Instead, the Roman civil service in the West has to be said to have 'disaggregated and thinned out'.[60]

Faced with such bloodless language and the intellectual approach on which it is based, a new robust revisionism that is willing to regard the loss of a sophisticated social order, and of high levels of intellectual and material cultural achievement, as regrettable is very welcome. That does not mean, however, that the arguments that give priority to the destructiveness of the barbarian attacks on the Empire are necessarily correct. We must at least inquire why it proved impossible for Rome to absorb these invaders and migrants culturally, and thus ultimately politically, as happened to successive waves of nomad conquerors of parts and occasionally all of the Chinese empire across the course of almost 2,000 years.

To some extent this did happen in western Europe, with the absorption of much of the Latin–Christian religious legacy of Rome by the new societies that emerged in the former provinces of the Empire, but much was still lost in the process – not least the complex structures of urban life and trade – and the unitary political-cultural entity that had been the Roman Empire was never revived. For much of the twentieth century, arguments about the 'Fall of the Roman Empire' tended to take more account of this aspect, and to focus on a search for internal causes for Rome's weakness. If the disappearance of the political structures of the western Empire was the product of some kind of decay in Roman civilisation, then the barbarians did little more than walk through an already open door. The popularity of this approach to the problem was for a long time strongly influenced by the dominance of German historical scholarship of the late nineteenth and early twentieth centuries dealing with the *Völkerwanderungzeit* or 'age of the migration of peoples'. This saw the events surrounding the fall of Rome and the emergence of the successor states in the West primarily in terms of a clash of two civilisations: a sophisticated but declining and senescent Roman one against a simple but new and vigorous Germanic one.

Viewed as the conflict of opposed, albeit unequal, cultures, it is not surprising that the issue was seen as a moral one: how could the beneficiaries of a 'higher' civilisation fail to triumph over the representatives of a 'lower' one? Answers to this question have been numerous. However, it has generally been recognised that while the western half of the Roman Empire disappeared in the fifth century, the eastern half survived, despite various modifications, for another thousand years. Thus, any potential explanation has to take into account the very different fates of the two components of the Empire. This effectively undermined the arguments of Edward Gibbon in his famous *Decline and Fall of the Roman Empire* of 1776, who placed the blame squarely on the effects of the adoption of Christianity, which he saw as including a rise in 'other worldliness', manpower shortages from the growth of popularity of monasticism and Christian teachings on virginity, and an ambivalent attitude towards warfare.[61] All these, however would have to have been as true of the eastern half of the Empire as of the western.

So it has long been recognised that for arguments to be credible they must stress differences between the two parts of the late Empire. Most of these have tended to relate to possible differences in the social structure and economic organisation of the Roman world in the fourth and fifth centuries, but have not always been able to provide the evidence needed to prove their case. When it comes to the economy of the late Roman Empire, there is never going to be a sufficiency of evidence to prove *any* generalisations about its nature and functioning.[62] At best, there may be enough material available to establish a picture of localised conditions in a small number of places and at a variety of times. The problem is that the kind of evidence we need to form a proper picture of social interaction and economic activity rarely survives, because it was not intended so to do. Thus, while literary compositions, including collections of letters edited and intended for publication as models of style, were carefully preserved, administrative documents, lists, notes, contracts and many other kinds of document that were far more practical in character have perished. In a few cases, such essentially ephemeral records have survived by chance, thanks to the nature of the materials on which they were written – for example, ones scratched on slate in sixth- and seventh-century Spain (and possibly also Britain) – or because of local conditions – as in the case of some documents written on wood in the Vandal kingdom and preserved by the arid heat of southern Algeria. However, the greatest concentration of such texts is to be found in Egypt, where numerous records written on papyrus have survived in ancient rubbish dumps or in the stuffing of mummified animals. While damaged and fragmentary, very large numbers of these have survived; along with others containing parts of literary works, in some cases otherwise lost.

The preservation of this extraordinarily rich body of material, found primarily in two locations in the north and east and still in the process of being published, has meant that we know far more about the social and economic organisation of Egypt than of any other part of the Roman world. While highly beneficial in itself, and providing the evidence for several important studies of the province, our greater knowledge of Egyptian conditions raises the unanswerable question of how far what we know of its social and economic life can be assumed to be true of other parts of the Empire. Indeed, it has been wondered to what extent the evidence relating to the districts of Oxyrynchos and the Fayum, from which the bulk of these papyri have emerged, can be taken as typical of Egypt more widely. Unsurprisingly, this has generated scholarly debate that can never be fully resolved because of the lack of comparable evidence from other provinces. Some would argue that the Egyptian evidence is generally applicable, while others see it as exceptional and untypical.

A particular issue is the size and prevalence of great aristocratic estates, and their social and economic impact. An important recent study, based on the Egyptian evidence, postulates the Empire-wide existence of really substantial landholdings, and thus limited amounts of free tenure by smaller property owners. This contradicts A. H. M. Jones, who, in his monumental *Later Roman Empire, 284–602* of 1964, claimed that western senators were wealthier than eastern ones, and that there 'were probably more medium landowners in the East, and fairly certainly more peasant proprietors'.[63] Behind this view are the liberal assumptions that free peasant proprietors are economically productive and intrinsically patriotic. Jones valued this productivity and patriotism in the context of the ability of Roman society to support 'idle mouths'. These latter, among whom were included monks and aristocrats, he regarded with the deepest moral indignation as the cause of imperial ruin, and he assumed his readers would share this particular perspective. Here, he is at one with some modern Marxists, who would see such social elites as intrinsically bad morally as well as economically: 'greedy, selfish, hypocritical, and short-sighted, as aristocratic communities generally are'.[64] On the other hand, the Russian historian Rostovtzeff, who was driven into exile by the 1917 Revolution, saw the undermining of the upper class culture of the Mediterranean cities by peasant soldiers as the true cause of Rome's fall.[65] In other words, this is one of those topics that can tell the reader more about a historian's personal prejudices than about the historical reality that he or she seeks to describe.

7 The new kingdoms

Roman generals and barbarian kings

There is a danger when trying to visualise 'the barbarians' of our borrowing images from earlier ages. It would be easy to imagine them as little more than savages – naked, hairy and doubtless garishly painted. In practice, however, by the fourth and fifth centuries, the various Germanic-speaking peoples were, in terms of material culture, little different from the Roman provincials. Their items of dress and personal decoration, including brooches, belt buckles and other fastenings, were mainly of Roman manufacture or were modelled on Roman originals.[1] A major source of inspiration for their designs were the buckles, fastenings and badges of rank used by the Roman army. Trade and the acquisition of loot added to the stock of such items among the peoples living beyond the imperial frontiers, and in general Roman styles of jewellery and practical metalwork became standard in their societies. It is thus possible to find identical objects, dated to the fifth and sixth centuries, among the Anglo-Saxons, Franks and Goths, across an area extending from Britain to southern Spain.[2]

In terms of clothing, the borrowing may have been mutual. In the early imperial period, trousers, worn by both the peoples across the Rhine and the Danube and by the Persians, were regarded by the Romans as being quintessentially barbaric, yet they had become widely accepted except among the social elite of the Empire by the end of the fourth century. In 397, the emperor Honorius issued a law forbidding the wearing of trousers and of a type of Germanic footwear called *tzangae* (boots?) within the city of Rome. That his law had to be reissued in 399 and again in 416, despite the penalty of exile and loss of property, suggests that, even within the limits of Rome, it was impossible to enforce such a decree.[3] In the reissue of this law in 416, the wearing of long hair, another supposedly barbarian trait, was added to the list of offences.

It is possible, however, that it was not so much the barbarian associations of these items and styles that gave offence as their military connotations. In the *Theodosian Code*, the compilation of Roman imperial law issued in 438 and in which the text of these three edicts was preserved, they accompany an earlier law

99

of 382 forbidding senators from wearing military dress within the city.[4] By the later fourth century, it is not possible to distinguish between Roman soldiers and units drawn from peoples beyond the frontiers, on the basis of their dress – as can be seen, for example, in the representations of the imperial bodyguard on such contemporary works of art as the silver *missorium* of Theodosius (388) or the carved obelisk base erected by the same emperor in the Hippodrome in Constantinople (*c.* 390).[5]

Individual soldiers of Frankish, Vandal and other origin were able to rise through military service within the Empire to high commands in the army and admission to the Senate, where, apart from their names, they seem to have been indistinguishable from their Roman civilian counterparts. This process dates back at least to the reign of Constantine I, under whom the Frank Bonitus commanded the Seventh Legion. His son Silvanus was commander of the infantry in Gaul between 352 and 355, and was driven by political intrigue at the court of Constantius II into proclaiming himself emperor at Cologne in the latter year. Only a passing reference in Ammianus Marcellinus reveals his Frankish origin and thus that of his father, as in both cases they had perfectly acceptable Roman names.[6]

Such officers of non-Roman origin were not just found holding commands in the West A Frankish general, Richomer, became Master of the Soldiers in the East in 383, with his headquarters in Antioch. In the following year he was Consul, and from 388 until his death in 393 he was the commander in chief of the eastern armies under the emperor Theodosius I.[7] He was also the first of a veritable dynasty of generals. His nephew Arbogast was the Master of the Soldiers in the West in the same period and was responsible for the suicide of Valentinian II and for the elevation of Eugenius.[8] One of his descendants, also called Arbogast, was Count of Trier around the year 477.[9]

How consciously Frankish such men were, and what kind of contact they maintained with their ancestral people, is impossible to know. When Silvanus was murdered by agents of Constantius II in 355, the Franks sacked Cologne. Was this revenge or just a good excuse for a looting? These prominent soldiers of barbarian descent were rarely illiterate boors. Richomer became a friend of the sophist and orator Libanius in Antioch, and the younger Arbogast was praised by the Gallic author and bishop Sidonius Apollinaris (died *c.* 486) for his literary skill and his knowledge of the classics.[10] Roman contempt for barbarians certainly did not lead to the isolation of such officers in the social elite. The daughter of a Frankish Master of the Soldiers and Consul (385) called Bauto married the emperor Arcadius (383–408), and became the mother of his successor, Theodosius II (402–50).[11]

We might wonder if the rise of such men was a product of their social status in societies in which they were born, but in most cases nothing is known about their earlier lives. However, there are indications that some of them at least were 'self-made'. Arbitio, who was Master of the Cavalry under Constantius II in the years 351(?) to 361 and Consul in 355, began his career as an ordinary soldier in the ranks.[12] On the other hand, a certain Mallobaudes, who held the Roman military rank of *Comes Domesticorum* or commander of a unit of the imperial bodyguard, was also described as being a Frankish king.[13] His Roman appointment may have resulted from his having a ready-made military following, but he had held a junior staff post in the Roman army over twenty years earlier. These examples – and there are many more – indicate how the Roman Empire had been absorbing increasing numbers of soldiers from across its frontiers since the beginning of the fourth century, if not earlier, and how some of them worked their way into the upper echelons of society and into positions of wealth and political power.

Several of the leaders of barbarian confederacies that were invited into, or which formed within, the Empire acquired roles equivalent to those of the imperial Masters of Soldiers, many of whom were themselves of non-Roman origin. This is especially the case in the period that followed the disintegration of the Hun domination north of the Danube in 454. In the aftermath, many of those who had been subject to the Huns made their way into the Empire, where some of them were to prosper. While the history of this period is normally seen in terms of the movements of whole peoples migrating or invading, in practice many of the groups, and the individuals, who rose to prominence in the second half of the fifth century were mixed in their ethnic origins and created new cultural and political entities rather than continuing old ones.

A good example is the case of Odovacer and his brother Onulph. Their father, Edeco, is thought to have been a Hun, and their mother was a member of the probably Germanic-speaking people called the Sciri. Edeco appears in one of the fragmentary contemporary Greek histories of the period as both a bodyguard of Attila and one of his leading advisers.[14] In the 460s, Edeco and Onulph were in the Balkans, leading the Sciri in a war with the Ostrogoths, both independently and in alliance with the Sueves.[15] In the same decade, Odovacer is first recorded, leading an army of Saxons in Gaul. He and his men made themselves masters of Angers, but in 469 lost it to the Frankish king

Childeric and a Roman count, Paul.[16] By 471 he was in Italy, where he supported Ricimer in the civil war with the Emperor Anthemius. In the years after the death of Ricimer he became a leading general of imperial forces in Italy, and when they fell out with their commander-in-chief, Orestes, in 476 it was under Odovacer's lead. After the execution of Orestes and his brother he was made king of Italy by the army.[17]

Despite being less distinguished, the career of his brother Onulph was equally varied. After fighting on behalf of his mother's people against the Ostrogoths in the 460s, he appears in the service of the eastern Empire, holding the officer of Master of the Soldiers in Illyricum from 477 to 479. This was partly the reward for murdering his patron and predecessor at the instigation of the emperor Zeno. In the 480s Onulph moved to Italy, where in 488 he commanded his brother's armies in a victorious campaign against the Rugi on the upper Danube. Immediately after Odovacer's murder in 493, he was dragged from sanctuary and killed.[18]

At the very least, two such careers indicate the geographical range and variety of opportunity open at this time to those with the necessary military talent. A pre-established position in a social hierarchy was not the prerequisite for success, though this could be useful in certain circumstances. Thus, just as Odovacer and his brother rose to positions of command in societies in which they were outsiders, so was it equally possible for those inheriting authority within an established social group to use it to extend their personal power and that of their supporters. The best examples of this phenomenon in the later fifth and early sixth centuries are seen in the cases of the Ostrogothic leader Theoderic and the Frankish king Clovis.

It is misleading to regard the components of the non-Roman armies that were taking control of more and more of the western Empire in the late fifth and sixth centuries as ethnic constants. This is the kind of approach that lies behind those typical maps of the *Völkerwanderungzeit* or 'Age of Migrations', with long lines sprawling across the continent.[19] Each arrowed line has its own colour and each marks the movement of a 'people', starting in their supposed first home, usually located in Scandinavia or the southern shores of the Baltic, and, through the passage of time and several thousands of miles, terminating in their final home. For the Franks, this is France; for the Ostrogoths, Italy; the Visigoths, Spain; and the Vandals, Africa.

Such maps and the rationale behind them ignore elements of the supposed 'tribes' that seem to have got left behind on the way. Thus the Sueves *ought to* be in north-west Spain, where they had arrived soon after 409, but there are Suevic kings and their followers fighting in the Balkans against the Ostrogoths in the 460s. How can Heruli be both making seaborne raids on the northern coast of Spain in 455 and 459 and at the same time be established in southern Moravia?[20] One answer to this is that individuals, families, groups and whole sections of these large-scale ethnic entities had either become detached or had detached themselves from the main body. They remained aware of their particular ethnic origin and this could on occasion colour their actions. For example, it has been suggested that Aspar deliberately sabotaged eastern imperial expeditions against the Vandals in Africa, because the main body of his own people, the Alans, were now a component of the Vandal confederacy.[21]

Many of the older discussions of the history of this period take tribal continuity for granted. However long and tortuous their wanderings, however varied their political fortunes and however powerful the alien cultural influences to which they were subjected, the existence of the people was assumed to remain constant. Yet, how can this be? To take the example of Alaric's Goths: between the middle of the fourth century and the second half of the fifth they had changed their name, moved from the area north-east of the Danube to the south-west of France, via the Balkans, the south of Italy and Spain, converted to Christianity and accepted the rule of a single dynasty of kings for the first time in their history. In other words, their society had undergone an extraordinary range of internal changes. While their case provides one of the best examples of such a broad range of transformations, it is far from unique.

The Gothic kingdom in Italy

The Ostrogoths, like the Visigoths, have a history that is more notable for its discontinuities than its continuities. Not least of these may be a hiatus in the ruling line of kings across the period in which the Ostrogoths, who were then in any case known as the *Greuthungi*, were a subject people of the Huns; that is, from the 370s to the 450s.[22] Relying on the brief *History of the Goths* or *Getica* written in Constantinople by Jordanes around 551, most historians used to accept the claim of Theoderic and his family to be descendants of an earlier line of Gothic kings, known by the dynastic name of the Amals. This continuity in the ruling house is still seen by some as the principal explanation for the long-term survival of the people as a whole. However, it is far more likely that Theoderic's claim to Amal descent was spurious, and was promoted to give legitimacy to his rule.

Perhaps even more convincing are recent arguments that the whole notion of the antiquity of the Amals is little more than propaganda or 'spin' aimed at inventing a distinguished past for the king's ancestors. Theoderic's family may thus have been part of an Amal clan, but this kin-group had no special claim to status amongst the Goths, nor had it ever previously held royal authority over them.

The problem of sorting fact from fiction in the history of the Ostrogoths is essentially, and unsurprisingly, one of evaluating written sources, in particular the *Getica* or *Gothic History* of Jordanes, mentioned above. Little is known of this author other than that he was at least partly of Gothic descent, and that he was almost certainly writing around the year 551, possibly in Constantinople. By his own statement, he intended to produce an abbreviated version of the *Gothic History* in twelve books of his contemporary, the great Roman civil servant Cassiodorus, but as this is entirely lost, his claim cannot be tested. Arguments have been made both for and against it.[23]

Jordanes' own Gothic descent, despite the highly Romanised cultural context within which he lived and worked, has led historians to believe that his short work must contain genuine Gothic traditions. Much weight has also been given to the phrase used in an official letter congratulating Cassiodorus on his *Gothic History*, the model for that of Jordanes, stating that he 'made the Origin of the Goths into Roman History'. In other words, that he took the Goths' own oral legends and turned them into written history. However, the sentence in question continues: 'gathering as if into one crown the flowering shoots that were previously dispersed throughout the fields of books'.[24] In the florid rhetoric of the time, this is saying that he had used literary, in other words Roman, sources for his narrative, not oral 'Germanic' ones.

Most of the texts used to create Jordanes' narrative, and probably therefore also that of Cassiodorus, can be identified. Apart from one royal genealogy there is nothing of genuinely Gothic origin to be found in the work, and even that may be more a reflection of Roman ideas on history than Gothic ones.[25] Studies of the nature, composition and historical reliability of genealogies in other early medieval societies warn us against placing any reliance on the details given in this one. All too often such family trees or king lists represent political manifestos of the period in which they were composed; that is, that of the most recently dated persons to be found in them, and with the limits of their historical trustworthiness extending back no more than four or five generations.[26] Interest in establishing continuity in a royal line was far more the product of Roman presuppositions about the working of Germanic societies than it was something of interest to those societies themselves. In the first half of the sixth century, the Ostrogothic regime in Italy needed a history and a constitutional role for itself that fitted in with the intellectual expectations of the Roman upper classes upon whose goodwill and co-operation it largely depended, and who also liked to imagine great family continuities between themselves and the aristocracies of the Republic and Early Empire.

The reality of Ostrogothic history in the second half of the fifth century was rather different, and in reality more impressive. In the aftermath of the collapse of the Hun supremacy north of the Danube, following the death of Attila and the defeat of his sons by their subject peoples in the battle on the River Nedao in 454, new waves of migrants crossed the Danube into the Empire. Among them were the followers of a certain Valamer, who were settled in Pannonia in the western Balkans by agreement with the emperor Marcian (450–7). Valamer was killed soon afterwards and his role was taken over by Theodemer, who is described as his brother; though this may be yet another piece of later genealogical fiction.

In the same period, a similar group, comprised primarily but not exclusively of those once known as *Greuthungi* and now referred to as Goths, appears in the eastern Balkans under the leadership of Theoderic Strabo ('the Squinter'). This Theoderic was a relative of the wife of the Alan general and imperial Master of the Soldiers Aspar, much of whose military power may have come from this connection.[27] Other prominent Goths had been in imperial service for considerably longer and from before the fall of the Hun empire; for example, Arnegisclus and his son Anagastes held the office of Master of the Soldiers in Thrace in 447 and 469–70, respectively, and had personal followings similar to those of Theodemir and Theoderic Strabo.[28]

Anagastes lost political influence after his abortive revolt in 470, after which the history of the Balkans in the 470s and early 480s focuses on the struggle for supremacy between, on the one hand, Theoderic Strabo and his son Recitach, and on the other Theodemer and his son, another Theoderic, later known as 'the Amal'. The prize was the succession to the power of Aspar as Master of the Soldiers in the imperial presence and as dominant figure in the eastern court. However, the existence of two opposed groups of barbarian soldiery enabled successive emperors to play off their rivalry, until the death of Strabo in 481 and the murder of Recitach in 484 left Theoderic, the son of Theodemer, able to unite both groups.[29] Even then, despite been given the coveted title of Master of the Soldiers, the imperial government denied him real power by cutting off the supplies of food needed to keep his army together. The strength of the defences of Constantinople meant that the capital could resist a siege in 487, as it had in 481 when threatened by Strabo, and in 488 a resolution was reached when Theoderic, abandoning his ambitions in the East, agreed to invade Italy on behalf of the emperor Zeno.[30]

The war between Odovacer and Theoderic, beginning with the latter's invasion of Italy in 489, lasted for almost four years, but much of it consisted of a protracted siege of Ravenna. Theoderic made himself master of Italy fairly rapidly, but Odovacer held out in the former imperial capital until 493, when a power-sharing agreement was reached between the two. However, once admitted into Ravenna, Theoderic quickly murdered Odovacer.[31] Several of the leading Roman supporters of the fallen regime, such as the finance minister Cassiodorus, had already transferred their allegiance to Theoderic. At least one of them, the senator Liberius, refused to take office under the new ruler while their old master still lived.[32] This may have hastened the killing of Odovacer, and Liberius certainly felt no qualms about accepting the office of Praetorian Prefect of Italy in 493 from the hands of his murderer. With Odovacer's military following replaced as the army of Italy by Theoderic's Goths, a new kingdom came into being.

Ostrogothic Italy is normally seen as a forcing ground for, and a highly successful experiment in, Romano-Germanic co-operation and mutual appreciation. To some extent this is true, but we need to recognise that this was not a relationship between two equal, independent partners. While being subject to the political authority of the Gothic king in Ravenna, the upper classes of Roman society, who provided the personnel and expertise to run the administration, and who set the cultural goals for the new regime, were supremely confident of the values of their society and their standing within it. On the other hand, the Gothic element, probably concentrated in garrisons in the area north of the river Po, was still relatively insecure and malleable in both culture and identity.

Their real, as opposed to invented, history extended back no further than the cultural melting pot of the period of the collapse of the Hun empire in the 450s. The ancestors of those who in Italy in the first half of the sixth century would have thought of themselves as (Ostro)Goths will have called themselves Sciri, Rugi, Gepids, and much else besides. It was also in this period that the conversion of many of them to Christianity took place, though we know little of the details of this. Out of the confused conditions that had existed in the Balkans in the 450s, with the combining of soldiers who had served under Aspar, John the Vandal, Arnegisclus and others with newer groups of Goths admitted to the Empire after the battle on the River Nedao, a real fusion was only achieved in the 480s.[33] The Italian conquest of 489–93 further welded together these disparate components, and the resulting kingdom gave them the chance to develop a distinct sense of a common ethnic identity.

The prime movers in these processes, however, were the Romans. From their perspective, the followers of Theoderic were ready-made to fill the role in Italy and regions adjacent to it that had been exercised by Odovacer's forces and previously by the various other mercenary units who had constituted the armies of the last century of the western Empire. At the same time, though, they recognised that their new military defenders were ethnically distinct from themselves, and that their leader was a *rex* or king – that is, the ruler of a *gens* or people. He could not be a new western emperor in name, even if he could be taught to fill most, though not all, of the functions of one.

The *gens* itself had to be given a sense of its past, but a past that fitted Roman expectations. Cassiodorus, son of the former finance minister and himself to be Master of the Offices (head of the civil service) and Praetorian Prefect of Italy, set about providing this in his *Gothic History*.[34] As evidenced in its possible abridgement by Jordanes, this was drawn almost entirely from Greek and Roman literary sources and made to fit a Roman understanding of the past. For the Romans, barbarians had kings: had not Tacitus told them this was the case in his *Germania* of AD 98?[35] So, as well as the people, its ruling dynasty was given a history, not least in a genealogy whose lack of coherence in the pattern of names raises immediate suspicions.

Theoderic himself, though, was no untutored barbarian. He had spent about ten years as a hostage in Constantinople (*c.* 461–71), and had twice succeeded in obtaining the title of Master of the Soldiers (476/7–8 and 483–7).[36] He knew about imperial courts, had received a Roman education, and was well aware of the political power wielded by the commanders of armies. He was thus willing and able to co-operate with his Roman officials, both in fitting his Gothic following into its appointed niche in Italian society, and in fulfilling Roman expectations of continuity.

Odovacer had carried out some restoration of public buildings, not least the making of a new set of named seats for members of the Senate in the Coliseum, the principal amphitheatre and place of public entertainment in Rome.[37] Theoderic's programme of new buildings and the restoration of existing ones was far more extensive, and included the creation or repair of aqueducts, public baths, city walls and palaces – the latter being centres of administration rather than private residences – in a variety of major Italian cities, including Rome, Ravenna, Verona and Pavia.[38]

Other traditional and politically valuable aspects of late Roman imperial government were revived with the re-establishment of the distribution of free supplies of corn to the poor in the city of Rome, and the holding of very expensive but popular circus games. Probably the most magnificent of these were the games held in Rome in 500 to mark Theoderic's visit to the city.[39] So 'bread and circuses' came back, albeit briefly, after an intermission caused by the economic weakness of the last imperial regimes in the West and the Vandal seizure of Africa, the traditional source of grain for the dole.

In his visit to Rome in 500, Theoderic also enjoyed the last western *Adventus*, the formal and elaborate late Roman ceremonial used when an emperor entered a city. A special medal was also issued to commemorate the event.[40] Many of the trappings of the old imperial rule continued in use, and western senators nominated by Theoderic continued to enjoy the honour of the consulship in conjunction with colleagues appointed by the emperor in Constantinople. After the hard times of the years 455–76, the regime of Theoderic offered the upper classes of Roman society a sense of security and of continuity with a much valued past.

This security of Italy was not just imaginary. Odovacer had protected northern Italy with a forward policy beyond the Alps. The defence of the southern part of the province of Noricum had been reorganised, and the Rugi, who had been threatening the area, were effectively destroyed in 488.[41] Theoderic went further, by seizing control in 504/5 of the province of Pannonia, although it was nominally ruled from Constantinople, thereby securing control over access to Italy from the East. He established a similar *cordon sanitaire* in the West by annexing Provence in 508, after the collapse of the Visigothic kingdom in Gaul.[42] Alliances, symbolised by the marriages of one of Theoderic's sisters and of one of his daughters to the Thuringian and Burgundian kings, respectively, preserved the security of the areas north of the Alps, and a similar bond with the Vandal ruler Thrasamund (496–523) helped to ensure good relations with Africa.[43] The annexation of the Visigothic kingdom in Spain in 511 thus turned the western Mediterranean into 'an Ostrogothic lake'.

The image of Italy under the rule of Theoderic differs from that of the Frankish kingdom in Gaul then being created by his contemporary, the Merovingian king Clovis (481?–511?). The latter appears as a violent, rather unsophisticated, but militarily very successful, ruler, under whose rule a small kingdom centred on Tournai in modern Belgium was transformed into a realm extending from the Channel to the Pyrenees and the Rhône Valley. Stories of Clovis burying his axe in the head of one of his soldiers who had once confronted him over the distribution of loot seem to reinforce the presentation of the Frankish king as a 'barbarous' war lord, far removed from the Romanising ruler of Ravenna.[44]

Yet what we have here is essentially a conflict in the nature of the evidence relating to the two kingdoms. Apart from the near-contemporary *Gothic History* of Jordanes, itself probably an abridgement of a work written around the year 519, most of the sources for the reign of Theoderic take the form of contemporary documents: above all, the collections of letters of bishop Ennodius of Pavia (d. 521) and of Cassiodorus.[45] The latter is particularly important in that it contains many of the items of official correspondence that he composed for the Ostrogothic kings while holding the offices of Quaestor (a kind of state secretary) in 507–11 and Master of the Offices in 523–7. The collection of letters was issued in 537. Thus, much of the material is both contemporary and official in character (even allowing for the fact that Cassiodorus took careful and self-interested account of the changed political realities of the later 530s in making his selection of which letters to include and editing their texts).

Clovis and the Franks

In contrast to the quantity and variety of largely contemporary literary evidence for the Ostrogothic kingdom, the principal source for the reign of Clovis (481?–511?) in Gaul is the second of the *Ten Books of History* of bishop Gregory of Tours, a work completed only a short time before his death in 594.[46] It thus dates from almost a century after the time of Clovis himself. It is clear that Gregory's information relating to that period is both slight in quantity and was handled by him in a selective and ideologically motivated way.[47] His Clovis, in other words, had a part to play in the didactic purposes for which Gregory's *Histories* was written. Scholars have long doubted the dating he gives for the baptism of Clovis (497), preferring later ones around 503 or 507/8, and the chronology of other features of the reign, including both its start and finish, may be equally unreliable.[48] More significant still is the suspicion that Gregory's Clovis is in many respects a model figure, representing the image of an ideal Catholic warrior king.

There is a strong probability that Gregory deliberately located the baptism of Clovis before his final conflict with the Arian heretical Visigoths, and also ignored indications that the Frankish king himself had been under considerable Arian influence prior to his finally opting for the Catholic form of Christianity. In fact, it could be argued from contemporary texts, and contradicting Gregory of Tours' version of events, that Clovis, as well as one of his sisters, was a practising Arian Christian rather than a pagan prior to his conversion to Catholicism.[49] So, the greatest care is needed in approaching any aspect of Gregory's account of Clovis.

Unlike the reign of Theoderic, there is very little strictly contemporary evidence for that of Clovis. What there is consists of a small number of letters written by bishops Remigius of Reims and Avitus of Vienne, and one in Clovis's own name.[50] Remigius's letter to Clovis makes it virtually certain that Clovis was a Christian by around the year 486. In fact, once it is appreciated that Gregory's view of Clovis as converting from paganism is unreliable, then there are no grounds for believing that he was *ever* a pagan. Nor does his father Childeric I (d. 481) have to be other than a Christian. The fact that he was buried with treasure and in a funeral mound, discovered and excavated in the seventeenth century, is no proof that he was a pagan, when it is recorded that the assuredly Christian Visigothic king Alaric I also received such a burial.[51]

In fact, all these letters present Clovis in a typical late Roman context. Remigius refers to him as having taken over the administration of the province of Belgica Secunda, and advises him to listen to the advice that he may be given by the bishops under his rule; an injunction that would hardly make sense if not addressed to a Christian.[52] The letter sent in his name to the bishops of southern Gaul in 507/8 is couched in formal rhetoric and uses the administrative terminology of late Roman government. There is little to distinguish this text from the administrative documents being produced at the time in Theoderic's Italy. Its peculiarity resides in it being unique. It is possible to envisage Clovis operating within the traditions of late Roman government, and employing northern Gallic equivalents of those Romans who worked for the Ostrogothic king in Ravenna. They were provincials rather than metropolitan senators, and their administration was less complex for being that of a distant province rather than the vestiges of the imperial central government, but when it is appreciated that a fifth-century Gallic aristocrat such as Sidonius Apollinaris could produce a letter collection as mannered as that of his Italian counterparts and could also become Prefect of the city of Rome (in 469), the distinction between Italy and Gaul should not be pushed too far.[53]

In military matters, Clovis makes most sense when seen in the light of the career of his father Childeric, whose tomb was found near Tournai. Despite being the ruler of one of the groups of the Salian division of the Franks, Childeric differed little from such late imperial commanders in northern Gaul as the Master of the Soldiers Aegidius or count Paul.[54] He could equally well be compared to Odovacer, when the latter was campaigning in the Loire valley with a Saxon army, or to a certain Riotamus, whose services were retained in 469 by the Emperor Anthemius and who commanded an army said to be 12,000 strong, composed of emigrants from Britain recently established in the region around Orléans in the Loire valley.[55]

When to this mix is added the Gothic kingdom south of the Loire and the Burgundians in the Rhône valley, some of whom were ruled by Gundobad, the former Master of the Soldiers in Italy, it can be seen that in the period 461–86 there existed a large number of rivals competing for power in Gaul. No real distinction can be made between competitors whose military backing was largely mono-ethnic – that is, those who would normally be classed as barbarian or Germanic kings – and those who commanded mixed forces of multi-ethnic origin. Indeed, it would be unwise to envisage individuals and groups behaving as if ethnic allegiance was the main influence on their actions. For example, some of those whom from their material culture we would classify as Frisians and Franks appear as settlers in south-eastern Britain at this time, adding to the ethnic and cultural complexity of the kingdom of the *Cantware* or *Cantuarii* in what is modern Kent.[56] Also, at some point, those Franks who followed Childeric transferred their allegiance to Aegidius, forcing their king to take refuge with the Thuringians, probably until the Roman general's death in 464.[57] In other words, not all Franks followed Frankish kings.

Nor were these leaders necessarily just building up local territorial power bases for themselves and their followers. The centre of Childeric's domain was probably Tournai, where he was buried in 481. But in 469 he is recorded as fighting around Angers, and between 476 and 481 he was in negotiation with Odovacer, by then ruler of Italy, over a campaign against the Alamans around the upper Rhine.[58] Neither of these areas was adjacent to his own territories, which were all to the east of the Seine and north of the Aisne.

Clovis was to launch a career that put an end to this period of rival 'warlords' in northern Gaul and transformed the political geography of an even larger area. Following, though with reservations, the chronological structure given by Gregory of Tours' account, it appears that in 486 Clovis, in his early twenties, captured Soissons, then the administrative centre of an area – the province of Belgica Secunda referred to by bishop Remigius of Reims – ruled by Syagrius, the son of Aegidius.[59] In 491, he made himself master (at least temporarily) of some of his mother's people, the Thuringians, and he won a victory over the Alamans, dated by Gregory to 496/7, but possibly identical to one recorded in contemporary sources from Ostrogothic Italy as occurring in 506.[60]

The details of the Frankish-Alaman wars of this period are obscure. Some fighting certainly took place at this time between the Alamans and another group of Franks – those settled in the Rhineland and known as the Ripuarians, who had kings of their own ruling in Cologne.[61] They achieved a victory over the Alamans at the battle of Tolbiac.[62] What part, if any, Clovis played in this is unknown, but the battle in 506, at which he probably was present, led to the absorption of some of the Alamans into his confederacy, while others put themselves under the protection of Theoderic, who used them to defend the northern approaches to Italy against the threat of Frankish aggression. An intervention around the year 500 in a conflict between the Burgundian kings Gundobad and Godegisel was less productive, and led only to the strengthening of the former, who was able to eliminate his brother, despite the latter's Frankish backing.[63]

In 507, a rather better-documented conflict arose with another of the main participants in the earlier wars, the Gothic kingdom still centred on Toulouse, but which by this time also controlled much of Spain, and in the north extended up to the Loire valley, where it threatened the expansionary ambitions of Clovis. He secured the support in this war of the Burgundians, who confronted the Gothic kingdom in the middle Rhône. A battle at Vouillé near Poitiers settled the matter.[64] The Gothic King Alaric II (484–507) was killed and the Aquitanian provinces of his kingdom passed into Clovis's hands in the course of 507 and 508. More might have been taken but for Theoderic's intervention in 508 to secure control of Provence, and in 511 to annexe the whole Visigothic kingdom, then ruled from Narbonne and Barcelona.

No dates are given by Gregory, but the final stage of Clovis's career was devoted to eliminating some of the small Frankish kingdoms based at Cologne, Cambrai, Thérouanne (?) and Le Mans (?).[65] Gregory of Tours implies that Clovis himself died in 511, though a reference in the *Liber Pontificalis*, the official set of papal biographies, to a gift that he sent to Rome would suggest that he was still alive *c*. 513.[66]

Despite being seen, primarily from the perspective of Gregory of Tours, as being the Frankish conquest of Gaul, just as Theoderic's triumph over Odovacer is usually seen as the Ostrogothic capture of Italy, this confuses consequences with causes. Both Clovis and Theoderic emerged from a range of rival rulers of their respective peoples. Theoderic eliminated his fellow contestants at the beginning of his career: but Clovis had to wait until nearly the end of his. Had Theoderic remained in the Balkans he might have inherited Aspar's role within the imperial government, but an autonomous Ostrogothic kingdom would not have emerged.

In the case of Clovis, the issue was not so much emancipation from domination by the Roman state, as a contest between rival claimants – Franks, Saxons, Burgundians, descendants of Roman generals and others – to achieve political authority in Gaul. Clovis's aspirations and achievements were conditioned by pre-existing Roman administrative and military structures in much the same way as were Theoderic's. In his case, though, the distant imperial government in Constantinople could afford to recognise his authority, by the grant of an honorary consulship in 508, while it remained suspicious of the greater and closer power of the Ostrogothic realm in Italy. This difference in imperial attitudes towards them conditioned the subsequent history of the Frankish and Ostrogothic kingdoms in the sixth century.

8 The twilight of the West, 518–68?

Prelude in Constantinople and Rome

The views taken in Constantinople of Clovis's kingdom in Gaul and of Theoderic's in Italy were markedly different. Though Gregory of Tours gives a rather enigmatic account of it, Clovis's victory over the Goths in 507 resulted in imperial diplomatic recognition the following year. According to Gregory, this took the form of Anastasius I granting Clovis an honorary consulship.[1] The Frankish king's baptism and formal renunciation of Arianism may have also taken place at this time. His conversion not only made possible closer diplomatic relations with the Empire, but also indicated his determination to break once and for all with the Arian Goths, hitherto the dominant powers in the West. So it is hardly accidental that Clovis's breach with the Visigoths followed the beginning of hostilities between the Empire and the Ostrogoths, or that it should have resulted in closer ties between Constantinople and the Frankish kingdom.

Anastasius I (491–518) could not easily pose as an upholder of religious orthodoxy as he was himself a Monophysite, and he faced considerable opposition in Constantinople later in his reign, culminating in a riot which nearly overthrew him in 511.[2] However, little of this was known in the West, at least outside Italy. There, the papacy, not least, kept itself informed on the theological shifts taking place in the imperial capital, as it hoped to bring an end, though only on its own terms, to the schism between Rome and Constantinople, resulting from the attempts of the then patriarch of Constantinople, Acacius, to reconcile the opponents of the theology promoted by the Council of Chalcedon – known collectively as the Monophysites.[3]

Disappointingly little evidence survives for the relatively long reign of Anastasius I, but in his religious policies, as in many other areas, he differed from his predecessor, Zeno, who had risen to power thanks to the military backing of his fellow Isaurians, members of a mountain-dwelling people in central Anatolia, whom Leo I had used to break the power in Constantinople of the Germanic troops of Aspar.[4] Unsurprisingly, Anastasius, formally selected in 491 as emperor (and as her new husband) by his predecessor's widow, had to face the hostility of the Isaurians, who now lost the imperial patronage they had enjoyed under

Zeno. Their insurrection in 492, led by Zeno's brother, took five years to crush.[5]

How pleased Zeno had been with the terms of his agreement of 488 with Theoderic cannot be judged, as he died before the Gothic conquest of Italy was completed. Anastasius renegotiated the treaty with the Gothic king around the year 498, though it is not clear exactly what, in eastern eyes, Theoderic's constitutional position in the West really was. This ambiguity may have been a deliberate feature of the treaty of 498. As the inhabitants of the eastern Empire continued to call themselves 'Romans' (*Romaioi*), and would do so right up to 1453, allowing the city of Rome to remain in the hands of a barbarian ruler, whatever his ties to the emperor, was bound to seem dishonourable. But the administrative and political problems, of raising and maintaining armies, limited the emperor's ability to intervene in the West, as did the Isaurian war of 492–7 and then a renewed war with Persia in Mesopotamia, which lasted from 502 to 505.[6]

Although possibly willing to accept Theoderic as a subordinate ruler in Italy in 498, Anastasius was clearly disturbed by the re-extension of Ostrogothic power into the Balkans in 504, when Sirmium was taken from the Gepids, and in 505, when an army of Bulgars, who may have been imperial allies, was defeated by the Goths on the River Morava. Despite being unable to send an army, Anastasius responded by launching an imperial naval raid on the coasts of Italy in 508 and made the first diplomatic contacts with the emergent power in Clovis's Franks.[7] However, Ostrogothic military strength, the death of Clovis and the ensuing division of his kingdom, as well as the emperor's own internal problems, prevented further conflict in the years that followed.

The seizure of power in Constantinople on the death of Anastasius in 518 by Justin, the Commander of the Imperial Guard, led to a further deterioration in relations between the Empire and the Ostrogothic monarchy.[8] In 519, Justin was willing to share the consulship with Theoderic's son-in-law, Eutharic.[9] However, the new emperor, who came from the Balkans and was a native Latin speaker, was far more interested in re-establishing imperial ties with the Roman aristocracy and Church than Anastasius had been. Thus 519 also saw the restoration of normal relations between the papacy in Rome and the patriarchate of Constantinople. Unlike Anastasius, Justin was impeccably orthodox and, at his direction, a council in Constantinople condemned the former patriarch of the city, Acacius, who in 482 had persuaded Zeno to issue the document known as the *Henoticon*. This had been the key element in an attempt to achieve a reconciliation with the supporters of Single Nature theology in the East, but it failed to satisfy them, and its apparent condemnation of the decisions of the Council of Chalcedon served only to infuriate the Roman Church, which broke off communication with Constantinople in 484.[10]

The ending, in 519, of what is known as the Acacian schism raised the possibility of closer political as well as religious ties between Rome and Constantinople, certainly in the minds of some of the western senators who had relatives in the East. A particular case is that of Quintus Aurelius Memmius Symmachus, a descendant of the pagan orator of the late fourth century and himself the author of a lost *Roman History*.[11] Like many of his fellows, he had held high office under Odovacer, as Prefect of the City and Consul (485), but had found no difficulty in coming to an accommodation with the new Gothic regime, from which he received the honorific title of Patrician. Two of his daughters were leaders of the aristocratic ascetic movement in Rome in the early sixth century, and another married the senator Anicius Manlius Severinus Boethius, himself the son of another of the great office holders of the age of Odovacer.[12]

Boethius, like Symmachus, enjoyed the highest social status under the rule of Theoderic, gaining the title of Patrician and holding the consulship in 510.[13] In 522, he and his family were particularly honoured by his two sons being nominated joint consuls. This initiative must have come from the emperor Justin or have been approved by him, but as Boethius himself took over the duties of Master of the Offices, effectively the head of Theoderic's civil service, in the same year, his acceptability to the Ostrogothic government could hardly have been in question. However, in 523 he was accused of treason, tried and executed. A similar fate befell his father-in-law, Symmachus, in 525.

Much debate has been generated by this affair, probably out of proportion to its real importance at the time.[14] In large part this is because of Boethius's intellectual eminence. He had a fine command of Greek, at that time an unusual attainment in the West, had translated a number of the works of Plato and Aristotle into Latin and was engaged in writing a series of commentaries on them at the time of his death.[15] He also wrote some short theological treatises. While in prison, awaiting a painful and slow execution, Boethius composed his most famous and influential work, *On the Consolation of Philosophy*. This used to be seen as evidence that he lapsed into paganism in his final days, but is better understood as demonstrating the powerful hold that classical literary and philosophical culture could still exercise over the Christian intelligentsia in Rome at this time. The work itself and the circumstances under which it was composed combined to immortalise its author and to cast a lasting shadow over the reputation of the government at whose hands he died. Interestingly, though, immediately contemporary comment centred more on the unfairness of the fate of his father-in-law, Symmachus, who may only have been guilty by association.[16]

The fates of Boethius and Symmachus are often presented as evidence of a sudden deterioration in the relations between Theoderic and the Senate, and thus more generally in the previously harmonious co-existence of Romans and Goths in Italy. This is probably an exaggeration, not least as senators continued to serve in the Gothic government. For example, in 523, when Boethius was arrested, Cassiodorus, who claimed family connection with him, promptly succeeded him as Master of the Offices, retaining the position until 527, and later served as Praetorian Prefect of Italy in the 530s.[17]

The accusation of treason made against Boethius came from a fellow senator called Cyprianus, son of Odovacer's finance minister and himself a high official in Theoderic's government. Three other senators testified against Boethius and the trial was conducted by the Prefect of the City of Rome.[18] In his *On the Consolation of Philosophy*, Boethius claimed that his accusers had either been bribed or had joined in the attack on him to obtain a pardon for offences of which they themselves were suspected.[19] This may or may not be true. Senators were always in danger of prejudiced charges being made against them by political rivals. What is important, though, is to appreciate that the legal procedures used were Roman, as were the accusers and judge. Theoderic's involvement consisted only of carrying out the sentence.

A senator's life, while comfortable in material terms, was often politically precarious. For example, the senators Basilius and Praetextatus were accused in 510/11 of engaging in magical practices, a capital crime in late antiquity as it was regarded as a form of treason. Both were tried before the Prefect of the city and condemned. Basilius managed to escape disguised as a monk, but he was hunted down, brought back to Rome and burnt alive.[20] Equally notable is the fact that Boethius's own grandfather was put to death by the emperor Valentinian III without the benefit of any judicial processes at all.[21]

Related to the execution of Boethius, and also interpreted as a sign of the deterioration in Roman–Gothic relations, was the fate of pope John I (523–6). A member of Boethius's social and intellectual circle, and dedicatee of three of his theological tractates, John was one of the Roman clergy who was particularly pleased by the re-establishment of religious orthodoxy in Constantinople in 519, and he may have been much less willing to compromise with the Arianism of the Goths than his immediate papal predecessors.[22] When, by 525, Justin I, advised by his nephew Justinian, began to enforce legal measures against non-orthodox Christians in the Empire, John was sent by Theoderic to try to obtain greater toleration for the Arians in the East, most of whom were of Gothic origin.

The emperor was willing to compromise on most matters, but he would not allow Arians in Constantinople who had recently been forcibly re-baptised to lapse back into Arianism, as this implicitly denigrated their Catholic baptism. Theoderic therefore regarded the embassy, which returned to Italy in 526, as a failure and blamed this unfairly on the pope, who had been greatly feted in Constantinople. John was, in consequence, detained, though not imprisoned, in Ravenna soon after his return to Italy. Unfortunately for Theoderic's later reputation, John died there.[23] However, this did not lead to any apparent breach with the Church in Rome under the next pope, Felix IV (526–30).[24] As with the execution of Boethius, the death of John I produced no immediate effect on relations between the Romans and their Gothic rulers. The consequences of the accession of Justin's successor Justinian (527–65) were of far greater significance for the history of Italy.

Justinian I and Africa, 527–33

The reign of Justin I is sometimes treated as no more than the first phase of that of Justinian, which is how the latter had wished it to be seen.[25] Historical writers of Justinian's time presented him as the obvious and unchallenged heir to his uncle, in the same way that those of the age of Justin II (565–78) suggested that he was the natural successor to Justinian.[26] In neither case should these political myths be credited. In both 527 and 565 other members of the imperial family stood close to the throne and were potential rivals to the emperors who eventually acquired it.

Until officially selected as co-emperor by Justin I in April 527, Justinian had been one of two rival nephews of the old emperor. The other, and ultimately unsuccessful one, Germanus, held the important post of Master of the Soldiers in Thrace throughout Justin's reign, and won a major victory over a Slav confederacy in the course of it.[27] Both nephews were involved in the negotiations to end the Acacian schism and restore links with Rome in 519, and only after this did Justinian gain the advantage over his cousin with his appointment as Master of the Soldiers in the Presence in 520.[28] This gave him a commanding position in the palace and capital. When he died in 565, Justinian himself had not even indicated which of his three nephews he favoured. One of them was Justin, the son of his cousin Germanus, and currently Master of the Soldiers in Illyricum. However, as in 527, a position in Constantinople proved to be a greater asset, and it was another Justin, holding an office in the imperial palace, who was able to seize power on the death of Justinian.[29]

Emperors were now no longer expected to lead their armies in person – a state of affairs that lasted from the reign of Arcadius (395–408) to that of Phocas (602–10) – but being largely resident in the capital left them vulnerable to rioting and popular unrest in Constantinople. Anastasius was nearly overthrown by an urban riot in 511, as was Justinian in 532. The geography of the city, in particular the location of the hippodrome adjacent to the palace, gave the inhabitants of Constantinople access to the emperor that was denied to any other group of his subjects.

In the late imperial period every major city of the Roman Empire had a hippodrome for holding chariot and horse races. These had become the principal forms of public entertainment for all social classes, and had eclipsed the more bloodthirsty games of the amphitheatre under the first Christian emperors. Gladiatorial combats seem to have ended in the fourth century, and wild beast fights were abolished, in theory at least, in 499.[30] However, these buildings were not just places of entertainment: the hippodrome, like the amphitheatre before it, was where governors and governed came face to face. Emperors, provincial governors and urban magistrates all attended the main sporting events in their cities, and their formal entrance into the special boxes reserved for them was greeted with well-orchestrated public acclaim, a long established procedure in Roman society. Such acclamations provided ways of expressing praise of the government and of individual rulers and officials, but also of criticism and making demands, and were the most direct way in which public opinion could make itself felt. The large numbers of spectators involved meant that trenchant criticism and controversial requests could be expressed with virtual impunity.[31]

It is not easy from the evidence available to know how these acclamations were orchestrated in practice. A well-placed claque could get a particular slogan started, which, if it represented a strong current of popular opinion, might then be taken up by more and more of the crowd. Certainly, local administrators and, ultimately, the imperial government ignored these

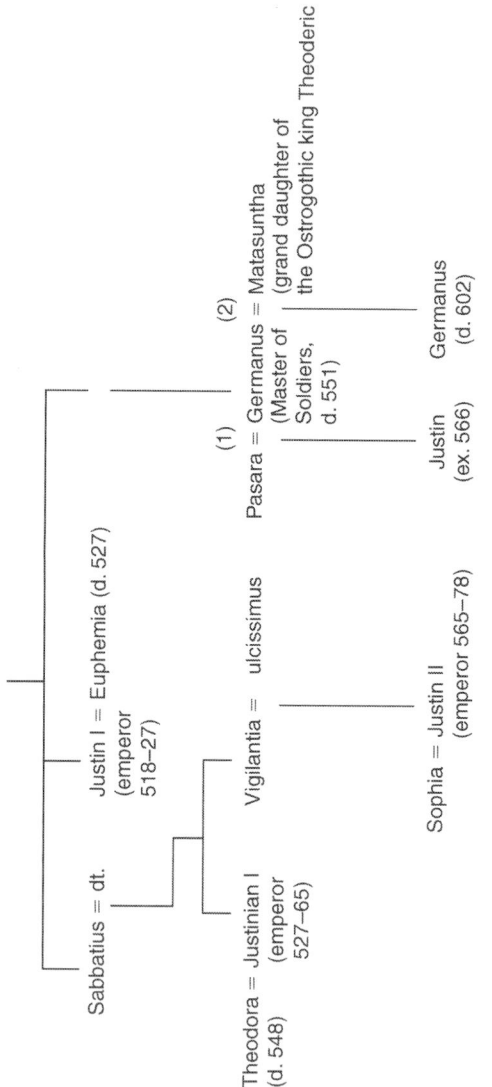

The family of Justin I and Justinian I

demonstrations of public opinion at their peril. For example, the official *relationes* or reports that the Prefect of the City of Rome, Quintus Aurelius Symmachus, sent to the emperors in the year 384 are full of information about such local expressions of popular views and demands. The emperors clearly expected to be told about them, and the Prefect's warning that failure to respond could lead to disturbances was amply justified on various occasions in the late fourth century when riots broke out in Rome, several of which are described by Ammianus Marcellinus.[32]

In Constantinople, the hippodrome, elaborately decorated by Theodosius I, was built next to the imperial palace, and the emperor's box was entered directly from his residence. Thus the centre of the government stood face to face with the main forum for the expression of public opinion. This was formally recognised in the ceremonial of late Roman imperial ordination. After the new emperor had received the regalia from the hand of the patriarch in the principal church in Constantinople, he immediately proceeded to the hippodrome to show himself to, and receive the acclamations of, the city populace.[33]

By the sixth century, the situation had been complicated by the rise of the circus factions. In the major cities of the eastern Empire, racing teams and their supporters had divided into two main groupings or factions, called the Blues and the Greens. Competition and rivalry between the two could on occasion escalate into violence. This created an additional element of instability in late antique urban life.[34] Normally, inter-factional rivalry and mutual hostility were so strong that emperors and provincial governors could try to manipulate them in the interests of preserving local order, but mutual co-operation between the factions could be very threatening.

An example is what occurred in the Nika riots of January 532. After some faction members had been condemned to death for unnamed crimes, the Blues and Greens in Constantinople made a truce with each other and raided the public jail, freeing their supporters and killing some guards and officials. From this first step into lawlessness, which would inevitably lead to punishment, a more overtly political confrontation with the government was the only way forward. The sole account of the episode, given in the *History of the Wars*, written by Procopius in the 550s, glosses over some of the crucial stages.[35] Rioting and destruction of property in the centre of the city intensified, leading Justinian to sack two unpopular ministers, the Praetorian Prefect John and Tribonian the Quaestor (the emperor's speech writer and principal legal adviser) as a sop to the populace.

This was not enough to stop the rioting, and the crowd proceeded to proclaim Hypatius, one of the nephews of Anastasius I, as emperor. He was taken to the hippodrome for a public acclamation, while only the intercession of his wife Theodora prevented Justinian from abandoning the palace and fleeing the city. Some units of the imperial guard appear to have openly supported Hypatius, while others remained neutral. Justinian, however, retained the loyalty of two of his principal generals in the city, Belisarius and Mundus, and a well-timed attack on the rebels in the hippodrome led to the capture and subsequent execution of Hypatius and his brother, and the massacre of large numbers of the rebellious populace, estimated by Procopius as being in the region of 30,000.

It has been argued that it was these riots that led Justinian into undertaking the campaigns to re-establish direct imperial rule over parts of the former western Roman Empire that are a central feature of his reign.[36] Thus, although the emperor successfully suppressed the disturbances in Constantinople, he needed to distract attention in the capital away from the violent suppression of the riots and the underlying tensions that had caused them. For this a military venture, with the prospect of victory and possibly some more tangible economic benefits, would seem to fit the bill.

Tempting as such an argument might be, it should probably be resisted. There are hints from Procopius that the expedition against the Vandal kingdom in Africa was already being planned before the outbreak of the Nika riots. Belisarius, who had been commanding the imperial army in Mesopotamia, was in Constantinople in January 532 because Justinian had just concluded a war with Persia that had been going on since 527. In addition, Procopius, who was attached to Belisarius's staff during both the Persian war and for some of his subsequent campaigns in the West, suggests that Justinian made a treaty with Persia at this point because he wanted to free his hand to launch the expedition against Africa.[37] Admittedly, as he was writing the final version of his work nearly twenty years later, he had the benefit of hindsight in interpreting, or even adjusting, the order and significance of the events he describes.

It also must be admitted that such a venture was potentially extremely risky; something that Justinian's ministers stressed to him at the time. In 442, 468 and 470, eastern emperors had sent similar expeditions against the Vandal kingdom in Africa. All had proved to be expensive failures, and by the reign of Zeno (474–91) some units of the eastern army were agreeing to serve only on condition that they were not sent to

Africa.[38] While it was possible to despatch an army by land from Constantinople to Africa – this was done in the reverse direction in 602 – any element of surprise would be lost, and the problems of communications and logistics would be acute, especially in the final stages when marching through northern Libya. A seaborne operation was the only practical option for Justinian in 533, as it had been for his predecessors.

This raises the question of Vandal naval power and so-called Vandal piracy. Much has been made of this, and at one time it was used as a counter-argument to the thesis of the Belgian historian, Henri Pirenne, who saw the breaking of the cultural and economic unity of the Mediterranean as being the product of the Arab conquests of the seventh and eight centuries. Other historians, notably N. H. Baynes, argued that this process should be dated earlier, and suggested it was caused by the destruction of maritime links between East and West resulting from endemic Vandal piracy.[39]

By their conquest of Roman Africa, the Vandal kings became masters of a large amount of shipping; in particular, the grain fleet that transported wheat, oil and other commodities to Italy. This could be used to ferry Vandal armies to raid selected targets, as in the successful assault on Rome in 455. By such means the Vandals gained control of all of the major islands of the western Mediterranean. But this certainly did not involve a cessation of trade. It is clear, for example, from the wide distribution of the finds of fifth-century North African 'red slip ware' pottery in Italy and southern Gaul, that trading links continued between these areas at this time and beyond.[40]

With the disappearance of a single political authority in the western Mediterranean, in other words the Empire, no overall system of law enforcement existed. Thus, North African ship owners could add to their profits from trade by making occasional raids on isolated or poorly defended coastal settlements. The Vandal kingdom itself, on the other hand, had been at peace with all its Mediterranean neighbours since 472. The impressions that either the Vandal state possessed a specialised war fleet, or that its vessels were lying in wait to prey on commercial shipping on the high seas, are erroneous.

What Justinian's expedition had to fear in 533 was not the prospect of a naval battle – none had been fought since Actium in 31 BC – but the threat of the Vandal land forces being able to oppose their disembarkation and thus catch the imperial forces in their most vulnerable state. Here, secret imperial diplomacy played a vital part. The Vandal viceroy in Sardinia was persuaded into revolt, and, in consequence, part of the main Vandal forces had been despatched to regain control of the island at the very time that Justinian's army of 15,000 men arrived in Africa, in the summer of 533.[41]

The operation, which had been undertaken with considerable trepidation in Constantinople, proved in the outcome to be extraordinarily successful. The landing in the bay of Tunis went unopposed, and the Vandal army was defeated in a battle ten (Roman) miles from Carthage. In the aftermath, Belisarius occupied the city, where the imperial forces were received with great delight by the Roman inhabitants. When the Vandal force that had been sent to Sardinia hastily returned, and was reunited with the remnants of the main body, a second battle took place in the vicinity of Carthage in December 533, with a similar result. The Vandal king Geilamir (530–3) fled inland, was besieged in a stronghold in Numidia and starved into surrender in 534. He and the remainder of his followers were transported to Constantinople. Geilamir himself was given an estate to which he retired, but the remaining Vandals were absorbed into the ranks of the miscellaneous Germanic-speaking federate soldiers in imperial service, and rapidly lost their distinctive ethnic identity. They are never heard of again.[42]

The Vandal war raises obvious questions as to both why it was undertaken, and why the outcome proved so rapidly decisive. The argument based on the Nika riots has already been considered and dismissed. Procopius, who was writing later in the reign and thus still expressing the official view of these events, claimed that Justinian was personally responsible for initiating the plan, despite being opposed by all his advisers. When he seemed on the point of taking their advice, however, a bishop from the eastern provinces told the emperor that he had been instructed by God in a vision to reprimand Justinian for having promised to liberate the inhabitants of Africa from Arian heretical rule and then losing his nerve.[43] This story of divine approval may have been part of the imperial propaganda. Also, as the main opponent of the venture was the Praetorian Prefect, John the Cappadocian, his removal from office in 532 during the Nika riots may have been intended to further the emperor's military plans, as well as to placate the rioters.

Procopius's account emphasises two interrelated motives for the emperor's undertaking of the expedition, and these may have been the interpretations of it that the government wished to present to the citizens of Constantinople and to the army in 533. The first of these was Justinian's sense of his obligation as emperor to free the orthodox Christians of Africa from subjection to the hostile rule of heretics, and the second was his acute awareness of his imperial responsibility to preserve correct legal order in all the territories that had once formed part of the Roman Empire. While these motives fit what else is known of Justinian's high sense of the imperial office, the military realities of the campaign enabled him to draw long-term financial and political rewards from its outcome.

The reasons for the rapidity and completeness of the conquest relate to conditions in Africa prior to 533. Of all the kingdoms established in the provinces of the former western Roman Empire, that of the Vandals was the least stable. Relations between the indigenous inhabitants and the conquerors were consistently poor. In the reign of Gaiseric (428–77), many of the principal Roman landowners of Africa either fled or were expelled, though some families were subsequently permitted to return.[44] A persistent attempt was made to break the entrenched power of the Catholic bishops and priests as the leaders of the local communities, and to replace them with a largely Vandal Arian clergy. This was achieved by exiling Catholic bishops to other parts of the kingdom, not least to Sardinia, where links with their African homeland would be broken. The processes of arrest, detention and expulsion could on occasion be violent, though few lives were actually lost.[45]

The intellectual strength of the African Church was hardly weakened by such treatment, and its leading figure in the century after the death of Augustine, Bishop Fulgentius of Ruspe (d. 532) spent most of his pontificate in exile, not least in composing a series of anti-Arian writings.[46] One of his contemporaries, Bishop Victor of Vita, wrote around the year 500 an intentionally lurid and propagandistic account of the treatment of the African Catholic clergy and Church at the hands of the Vandals, which was almost certainly intended to be circulated in the East.[47] Imperial awareness of the self-proclaimed sufferings of the Catholics in Africa was strong, and particularly appealing to Justinian personally, as he had deeply held theological interests. However, the situation of the Catholic hierarchy in Africa in the sixth century was not as bad as it had been in the fifth. Under Thrasamund (496–523), Arian–Catholic debates had been held, the exile of the bishops had been ended and most of the restrictions on Catholics had then been lifted by his successor, Hilderic (523–30).[48]

The Vandal monarchy employed an unusual system of royal succession, which passed through all the surviving members of one generation before moving on to the next. Thus, while Hilderic was the son of Gaiseric's successor, Huneric (477–84), the latter had had an elder brother, Gento, who died before his father.[49] Following the early death of Huneric, who was a particularly active persecutor of the Catholic establishment, the throne passed to his nephews, the sons of Gento – Gunthamund first (484–96) and then Thrasamund (496–523). Hilderic thus had to wait for forty years before he could succeed his father. He also enjoyed the unusual distinction of being the last heir of the former imperial dynasty of Theodosius I, as his mother was one of the daughters of Valentinian III.[50]

Perhaps as a result of this heritage, or a sense of changing political realities, Hilderic aligned himself closely with the Empire. He also imprisoned his predecessor's widow, the sister of Theoderic the Ostrogoth.[51] The strengthening of ties between Carthage and Constantinople led Theoderic in 526 to construct a fleet to defend Italy against what he saw as the very real threat of an invasion from Africa. In practice, this threat did not materialise, and in 530 Hilderic was overthrown by his cousin and heir, Geilamir.[52] He remained a prisoner until murdered by Geilamir, when the news arrived of the landing of the imperial forces in Africa in 533.[53]

Hilderic's deposition prompted the sending of the imperial letters quoted by Procopius in which Justinian demanded the restoration of the rightful king.[54] The emperor presented himself as the upholder of the will of Gaiseric. So, at the diplomatic level the war was started by Justinian in order to preserve the rules of succession to the Vandal throne laid down by the founder of their African kingdom. As expressed in a letter quoted by Procopius, he was acting 'to avenge Gaiseric'. He may have hoped to win backing from those in the Vandal kingdom who had supported Hilderic, though in the outcome this does not seem to have been forthcoming. Indeed, the murder of Hilderic by Geilamir was more useful to the emperor than to its perpetrator, as Justinian was relieved of the obligation of replacing him on the throne, which had been the stated purpose for starting the war.

The speed and completeness of the military success of the expedition commanded by Belisarius is not hard to explain. Popular resentment against Vandal rule was obviously strong, and there were no reservations in the support given to the invaders by the indigenous population, especially in Carthage. More significant still are the indications in Procopius's narrative that the Vandal presence in Africa was still little more than a military occupation. Though individual Vandals owned estates, the bulk of the people still seem to have lived as garrisoning forces, particularly in Carthage and some of the coastal towns of the Sahel region.

Indicative of this was the speed with which Vandal units were mobilised to meet the unexpected threat, and the fact that the Vandal soldiers were accompanied to battle by their wives and families.[55] They were thus not deeply entrenched in local society and, after the military defeats of 533/4, could be rounded up and shipped off *en masse* without being able to set up a guerrilla resistance. The impression of a lack of an entrenched local Vandal presence is also confirmed by the evidence of a series of land documents written on wood in Numidia during the Vandal period, now known as the Albertini Tablets.[56]

The Italian reconquest, 535–53

Rather different conditions from those encountered in Africa were to be faced by the imperial forces in their next undertaking – the invasion of Italy in 535. However, the reasons given for the intervention were very similar to those of 533. After the death of Theoderic in 526, the throne had passed to his grandson Athalaric, who was still a child, with the regency vested in his mother Amalasuntha, Theoderic's daughter. In practice, the administration continued as before. The indefatigable Cassiodorus carried on as Master of the Offices and subsequently became Praetorian Prefect (533–7). Other senators were equally committed to the regime, and one of them, Flavius Maximus, a descendant of the emperor Petronius Maximus, married a Gothic princess in 535.[57]

The death of Athalaric in 534, however, prompted a political crisis. The Goths had never been ruled by a woman, and so Amalasuntha could not take power in her own right. In consequence, the throne passed to an elderly nephew of Theoderic called Theodehad (534–6). According to Procopius, Amalasuntha persuaded him to take a secret oath that, while he enjoyed the title, she would continue to exercise the real power in the state.[58]

Frankly, this is incredible: secret oaths are just the stuff of rumour. Furthermore, Amalasuntha was in a position of considerable weakness. There was no way that she could have taken the royal title herself, and Theodehad was the senior male representative of the dynasty. At best, this story is a rationalisation of the conflict that obviously did develop between the former regent and the new king.

The *Gothic History* of Jordanes of *c.* 551, which may have been written as a manifesto in favour of Romano-Gothic reconciliation, offers a briefer but essentially similar account.[59] According to Jordanes, who does not mention any oath, Amalasuntha selected Theodehad and called him from retirement to take the

throne. This made her subsequent imprisonment and murder
on his orders all the more heinous. Procopius, however, states
that she was killed not on the orders of Theodehad, but by some
Gothic nobles as an act of vengeance for relatives of theirs whom
she had had executed during the reign of her son; probably the
three military commanders she had ordered to be killed around
527.[60] In general, both Procopius and Jordanes might well be
giving us variants of the official version of events as circulated in
Constantinople. Justinian needed to present himself as avenging Amalasuntha, and this could only be justified if Theodehad's
legitimate claim to the throne was either concealed or made to
be something that was in Amalasuntha's gift.

In 535, following the death of Amalasuntha, Justinian's threat
of military intervention nearly intimidated Theodehad into abdi-
cating voluntarily in the emperor's favour.[61] The Gothic king was
a committed Romanophile and a scholar, and he contemplated
retiring to Constantinople in return for a title and a pension
from the emperor. However, while negotiations were still under
way, the Goths made a pre-emptive strike into Dalmatia, and in
a battle near Salona killed Mundus, the Master of the Soldiers in
Illyricum, and one of the two defenders of Justinian in the Nika
riots.[62] Thus, war became inevitable.

Unlike the conquest of Vandal Africa, the fighting in Italy was
long-lasting, divisive and highly destructive. Procopius provides
a substantial narrative of these wars, which lasted from 535 to
553, though the final phases had to be covered in the much
shorter work of his continuator, Agathias.[63] The conflict falls into
two chronological parts: the first from 535 to 540, and the second from 540 to 553. With recently recovered Africa as a base,
the imperial invasion of Italy could be launched, using some
of the units that Belisarius had commanded in 533. However,
whereas 15,000 men had been sent to Africa, only 7,500 were
sent into Italy, and this was probably too few.[64] Moreover, hardly
had the invasion been launched when Belisarius had to return
to Africa to quell a mutiny among the imperial forces, whose
pay was, as often happened, seriously in arrears.

The opening stages were almost a 'phoney war'. Despite
the trouble in Africa, Belisarius was able to occupy Sicily without resistance and cross to the mainland. Despite the Roman
inhabitants of Naples refusing to admit him and asking him to
pass by, he forced his way into the city, massacred many of the
inhabitants, both Roman and Gothic, and then advanced on
Rome without meeting any military opposition.[65] By this time,
the apparent paralysis of the administration had so incensed
the Gothic elite that they rebelled against Theodehad and

elected as king one of their own number, Wittigis (536–40).[66] Theodehad tried to escape to Ravenna, but was overtaken and killed in another act of private vengeance.

Despite the Gothic garrison initially abandoning Rome, Wittigis subsequently besieged Belisarius and the imperial troops in the city for over a year, starting in the summer of 537. This, however, merely tied the Ostrogothic forces down, while a new imperial army some 5,000-strong landed by sea at Naples and eventually cut Wittigis's lines of communication with Ravenna by taking Rimini.[67] The dispirited Goths had to abandon the siege of Rome, and the whole war moved northwards. By 539 the position had been entirely reversed, with Belisarius preparing to besiege Wittigis in Ravenna. The blockade of the city, which was almost impregnable, began in 540.

At the same time, negotiations were opened for a political settlement with the now thoroughly despondent Gothic regime. Among the diplomatic proposals discussed at this time was the restoration of Italy south of the Po to direct imperial rule, with the main area of Gothic settlement north of the river being turned into a much reduced kingdom under Wittigis.[68] This would have created a valuable military buffer in the north (and may well have constituted the best possible outcome for both sides). In the event, though, a rather different solution emerged. Procopius's account is ambiguous, but it appears that Belisarius refused to accept a Gothic surrender on the terms just mentioned, which had been agreed with the emperor's envoys, but entered instead into secret negotiations of his own. The Gothic leaders, including Wittigis, then agreed to surrender Ravenna to him if he would proclaim himself the new emperor of the West. He refused to take such a step until the city was in his hands, and so they admitted him and his army, expecting he would then make himself emperor.[69]

This, as we know from numerous earlier examples, was typical of the risk to be faced from a military commander winning success in a distant field of action, and may have been behind Justinian's deliberate restrictions on the resources of manpower and money that he put into the western campaigns. It is not clear whether Belisarius used this suggestion of a revolt on his part merely to trick the Goths into surrender, or whether he had intended actually to rebel, but then found that he lacked the support needed among his own officers and men, many of whom were said to be suspicious of him. In any event, the war appeared to have been concluded, with the capture of the Gothic king, the royal treasure and the capital. However, this was nothing like the decisive victory that had been won in Africa in 533–4.

Indeed, though the main royal army had been defeated in the war of 535–40, it was far from a complete conquest. Gothic garrisons and commanders still held most of the principal towns of northern Italy, and other units in Gothic service, such as elements of the Rugi and Gepids, were still active.[70] Something of an impasse followed the cessation of fighting in 540, while a permanent political settlement was considered. However, Justinian was now faced by new problems on the eastern frontiers; partly resulting from the Italian war. In 539–40, facing military defeat, Wittigis had appealed to the Persian shah Khusro I for help: in other words, for the opening of a second front in Mesopotamia.[71] This indeed is what happened, very possibly because the Persians feared that a Roman Empire rejuvenated by the military and economic resources obtained from the western reconquests would soon turn its aggression eastwards.

Thus, in the summer of 540, Khusro broke the 'Endless Peace' signed in 532 and invaded Mesopotamia, marching unopposed as far as Antioch, which he took and sacked. He then carried off the surviving inhabitants into Persia. In consequence, and in dire need of trained military manpower, Justinian ordered Belisarius to return from Italy and to bring Wittigis and the Goths captured in Ravenna with him to reinforce the imperial armies, which in this period were made up almost exclusively of 'barbarian' units. Any idea of a more firmly based political settlement in Italy was thus abandoned. The leaders of the Goths in northern Italy gathered in Pavia, elected as king one of their number called Ildebad (540–1), and after another failed attempt to persuade the departing Belisarius to proclaim himself emperor of the West, renewed the war.[72]

The ensuing struggle, largely fought under the direction of Ildebad's nephew and successor, Baduila (541–52) was protracted and bloody, and required increasing numbers of imperial soldiers to be sent into Italy. Belisarius returned to resume command, but failed to achieve the successes of the 530s. He was eventually superseded by a eunuch and former imperial treasurer, Narses, under whose direction the war was concluded. In 552, Baduila (called Totila in Procopius) died after a major defeat at the battle of *Busta Gallorum*, and his successor, Teias, met the same fate later in the same year in a final confrontation near Mt Vesuvius.[73]

By this stage, the operations in Italy were involving other peoples from north of the Alps, notably the Franks and Lombards, who were drawn into the conflict, and which they exploited in their own interests. The Franks, who first intervened under their king Theudebert I (533–48), looted Milan in 539 and established a hold over Venetia and other regions of northern

Italy, from which they were only dislodged in the reign of his son Theudebald (548–55).[74] In 568, the Lombards, who had been admitted into Pannonia by Justinian during the Gothic wars, invaded Italy and established a kingdom of their own in the north, based on Pavia, which was to last until 774. Other Lombard detachments established semi-independent duchies centred on Spoleto and Benevento in the centre and south of Italy.[75]

The Empire retained control of Rome and Ravenna and a network of other towns and fortresses, but much of what had taken twenty years of warfare to win was lost to the Lombards in less than five. At the same time, the cost and military effort involved in the Italian wars prevented any further expansion of direct imperial rule in the West. An intervention in a civil war in Spain secured for Justinian only a small strip of coast in the south-east of the peninsula, and no further efforts were made to expand this imperial enclave.[76] At best, this created a further defence for the reconquered regions of Africa, and it may be that by 551 the emperor's ambitions extended no further.

For Italy, the costs of the war were incalculable. It is clear enough from various anecdotes in Procopius that many of the Roman aristocracy were less than enthusiastic about their imperial 'liberators'. A number of prominent senators, including Flavius Maximus and pope Silverius, were expelled from Rome by Belisarius prior to the Gothic siege.[77] On the other hand, the Goths became equally suspicious of them as collaborators with the invaders. Wittigis executed all the senators he was holding in Ravenna in 537.[78]

By 552, attitudes had become so extreme that Teias massacred 300 Roman senatorial children he was keeping as hostages, and many Roman adults – including Flavius Maximus, whose life illustrates so many of the changing aspects of mid-sixth-century Italian history – were killed out of hand by the Goths at this time.[79] Though both quantitatively and qualitatively the evidence is less good from this point onwards, the great families of Rome disappear from the historical record with the conclusion of these wars. Archaeological evidence also supports a view of widespread destruction and dislocation of the great villa economy in this period.[80]

The balance sheet on Justinian's western ventures is hard to draw up, even from a purely Constantinopolitan viewpoint. The cost and returns of the African war were very different from those of the Italian war. The turning point was undoubtedly the year 540. Had the terms offered to Wittigis and the Goths by the emperor at that time been implemented, a relatively brief war

with limited involvement of men and money would have produced good material results in terms of re-established imperial
control of most of Italy and its tax revenues, while the problems
of defence against peoples beyond the Alps would have been
solved by the presence of the truncated Gothic kingdom in the
north. However, for whatever reasons, Belisarius prevented that
from occurring, and then failed to take the western imperial
title himself, which might have been the next best thing. The
great Persian raid of the same year entirely altered Justinian's
sense of priorities, and the Italian situation was left without
any sensible solution. Thirteen more years of bitter fighting
merely served to leave an enfeebled Italy liable to have its taxes
drained away to Constantinople in return for a military defence
that was too weak to stop the Lombards from taking most of
what the Empire had spent two decades fighting for.

9 Constantinople, Persia and the Arabs

Rome's eastern neighbours

The disturbed conditions on the Empire's eastern frontiers in the late third and the fourth centuries gave way to a period of greater stability in the fifth. After Julian's disastrous invasion of Persia in 363 and the treaty that Jovian was obliged to accept in order to withdraw his army from Mesopotamia, periods of conflict between the two empires became less frequent and the scale of operations more limited.[1] Persian interests were now concentrated almost exclusively on achieving minor adjustments in the frontiers with Rome, and occasionally using the threat of war to extort regular payments as the price of peace. The most important frontier between the two empires remained the one in Mesopotamia, and the control of certain key fortress towns in this region became the main focus of conflict. More complex were the problems to the north, in the mountainous areas of eastern Anatolia. Here the kingdom of Armenia existed as a buffer state between the two rival powers. The conversion of the Armenians to Christianity at the very beginning of the fourth century – just before Constantine's – brought the kingdom more firmly into the Roman cultural zone. This, in turn, led to the Persians trying to exercise a tighter control over it, and at various times to impose their own Zoroastrian religion on the inhabitants. Armenian revolts in defence of their indigenous Christianity attracted Roman support, and this became a complicating factor in the 'superpower' diplomacy between the two empires.[2]

Except when over-provoked, as in 282–3, 297–8 and 363, Roman responses to Persian aggression tended to be low-key and limited to reinforcing the defence of threatened frontiers. Pitched battles between Roman and Persian armies were rare, and none were in any sense decisive. In general, the Persians' ability to maintain a condition of limited aggression was greater than the Roman interest in combating it militarily. As the economic and political problems of keeping large armies in the field grew, it became cheaper and more sensible for the Roman Empire to buy peace from the Persians.

The Sasanians recognised Rome as a fellow, if lesser, civilised power; in diplomatic exchanges comparing the two empires to the Sun (Persia) and the Moon (Rome) – both eternal and stable, but of different orders of brightness and importance.[3] Roman attitudes were culturally less accommodating, and the Persians seemed to them as barbarous as the German speakers in the West but, even so, the power of Persia induced a grudging respect, and the presence of the Persian empire on the eastern frontiers was felt to be preferable to that of other, more volatile, neighbours.[4] So, when the Persian shah Peroz (459–84) was taken prisoner by the Hephthalite nomads, the emperor Zeno (474–91) paid the ransom for his release.[5]

In the fifth century, both empires had similar problems and a threat in common: the presence on their northern frontiers of powerful nomad confederacies. The difficulties the Romans had with the Huns were matched by those the Persians faced from the Hephthalites.[6] In neither case were the nomads trying to conquer territory, preferring to extort tribute, but, in doing so, they had a considerable impact on the internal politics of the settled states. Under Theodosius II, the eastern Empire was generally willing to accept Hun demands with little resistance, and the western Empire became militarily dependent on them, as we have seen. In Persia, the shah Peroz made two unsuccessful attempts to break the power of the Hephthalites in battle, in the second of which he was killed. The Hephthalites subsequently imposed his son Kavad I (488–97, 499–531), who had been their hostage, as shah in 488, and then restored him in 499 after he had been deposed by his brother.[7]

According to the Syrian chronicler Zachariah of Mitylene, writing in 569, the Persians blamed the Hephthalite menace and the disaster that befell Peroz on the Romans, and this led to renewed war in 502.[8] However, the contemporary *Chronicle of Joshua the Stylite* of 507 makes it clear that the Persians, both under Valkas (484–8) and Kavad I, were trying to get money from Rome in order to pay the tribute they owed to the Hephthalites.[9] The need to create an effective military response to the Hephthalites, finally achieved in the reign of Kavad's son Khusro I, and to ensure Persian control of vulnerable northern frontiers, also produced an escalation in conflict between the two empires in the sixth century.

Minor adjustments in control of the principal fortresses in Mesopotamia continued to occur, but more intensive fighting took place in Armenia under Shah Khusro I (531–79), as the Persians tried to drag this region more firmly into their cultural orbit. Further north, the small region of Lazica, southwest of the Caucasus Mountains, saw the most protracted warfare of all, which continued even when truces had been agreed in other zones of conflict.[10] The reason for this would seem to be the potential strategic significance of this area, which was otherwise relatively unimportant in political and economic terms. The Persians feared that if the Romans controlled it they would allow nomads from the north of the mountains to come through the passes and raid the vital agricultural areas south of the Caspian Sea. On the other hand, control of Lazica would give the Persians access to the Black Sea, and thus create the possibility of naval raids on the north coast of Asia Minor or down the Bosphorus to Constantinople.

Although little contemporary Persian evidence has survived beyond inscriptions, and Roman reports are both biased and limited, it looks as if significant ideological and economic changes were taking place in the Sasanian empire in the course of the sixth century. The reign of Kavad I coincided with the rise of the Mazdakite movement, whose Manichaean-inspired doctrines included the forcible imposition of communal ownership of property. Mazdak and his followers were encouraged by the shah, not least as a means of breaking the power of the great aristocracy, many of whom were descendents of the regional rulers of the preceding Arsacid or Parthian period, whose local authority often far exceeded that of the Sasanian shahs. They were subjected to Mazdakite popular risings and disturbances, with Kavad's support. The Mazdakites were eventually suppressed late in the reign, when their usefulness had declined. Overall, a decisive change in the balance of power between the shahs and the great families was achieved in the reigns of Kavad I and Khusro I.[11]

This was also seen in the greater prominence of a class of lesser nobles called *dihqans,* who were less independent of the shah than the Arsacid great houses. In this same period, the Sasanian administration became increasingly bureaucratic and effective.[12] A new taxation system, modelled on that of the Roman Empire, was introduced under Khusro I, and a substantial programme of town building was begun in Mesopotamia, with the new settlements functioning as centres of royal administration, freed from the control of the old aristocratic families. They also needed a specialised urban population, as the lifestyle and economic activities of towns require particular skills to provide the crafts and markets needed to house and feed their inhabitants and provide employment. In part, this skilled new population was obtained by the wholesale transportation of town dwellers captured in the wars with Rome. For example, the inhabitants of Antioch carried off by Khusro in 540 were resettled by him in a new foundation grandly named 'The Better Antioch of Khusro'.[13]

The problems the Persians faced with the Hephthalites beyond the river Oxus and with other nomads north of the Caucasus, similar to Rome's difficulties with the Huns, were complex and affected the Sasanian regime in several ways. On the one hand, the threat of the Hephthalites and the military support they gave him was valuable for Kavad I in his conflicts with dynastic rivals and with the nobility. They also provided him, in the way the Romans used the Huns as mercenaries in the West, with manpower for his war against Rome, itself intended to extort the money needed to pay the Hephthalites. On the other hand, such allies were neither reliable nor easy to control, and the humiliations suffered under the shah Peroz continued to rankle. The shifts of populations in Central Asia, and the inability of the Sasanian empire to confront the Hephthalites militarily, led to greater Persian diplomatic involvement with other nomad confederacies in Central Asia. Ultimately, they were able to use the Turks to break the power of the Hephthalites.[14] In the same way, the Emperor Justinian manipulated the rivalries between similar confederacies north of the Black Sea to try to prevent a dominant nomad power emerging on the frontiers of the Roman Empire.[15]

Such Great Power involvements in the fragile balances between the various nomad groups to the north of their respective empires bred mutual suspicion. At the same time, the Sasanians were trying to make additional profits out of the Romans by closing their direct access to eastern trade and forcing them to purchase luxuries such as silk and spices from state-controlled Persian intermediaries. One unexpected by-product of this was to be the creation of an imperial silk industry in Syria, when in 552 the emperor Justinian agreed to the proposal of some monks that they smuggle silkworms out of the oases of Sogdia in Central Asia. Hitherto, the Chinese had preserved a monopoly in the manufacture of silk by preventing the export of these essential creatures from their territories and dominions.[16]

Even if the Persian economic blockade, which may also have been aimed at limiting Roman economic and political influence on the peoples of Central Asia, was by-passed, the attempts of the two empires to spread their spheres of cultural domination reached into ever more distant regions. A case in point is south-western Arabia. In the year 525, Dhu Nuwas, the ruler of the Yemen, converted to Judaism and, in consequence, began to persecute the minority Christian population in his kingdom. This, in due course, led the foremost Christian power in the southern Red Sea area, the Axumite kingdom of Ethiopia, to intervene, overthrow Dhu Nuwas and establish a protectorate over the Yemen.[17]

Even when the Ethiopian governor, Abraha, broke away from his allegiance to Axum and created an independent kingdom of his own in the Yemen, he continued to enjoy Roman support. The Yemen was in fact a vital economic entrepôt, receiving a variety of goods by sea and then sending them on by camel caravan up the Red Sea coast. Among the items of trade that were of particular interest to the Romans was incense, produced in the south-east corner of the Arabian peninsula, and used daily in all the churches of Christendom. Spices, precious stones and other luxuries were also traded across the Indian Ocean and up the coast of East Africa. All in all, the Christian kingdom of the Yemen under Abraha (*c.* 535–70) was a vital cultural and economic outpost of the Roman Empire.[18] This made the Sasanians more determined to block this Roman access to the Indian Ocean, and in 575 a Persian expedition conquered the kingdom and installed a governor.

While this struggle for cultural dominance was being played out in the south of Arabia, there was an intensification in Roman and Persian involvement with the tribes of northern Arabia. For several centuries, the two empires had maintained close links with the Arab tribes established in the southern fringes of Mesopotamia. The regular payments of subsidies to the rulers of these tribes made them defenders of the vulnerable desert frontiers of the empires and irregular troops who fought for their masters against the rival empire. The two great Arab confederacies of the Lakhmids and the Ghassanids benefited in particular from this situation and became the principal desert allies of the Persians and the Romans, respectively. Neither, however, was entirely reliable as far as their paymasters were concerned. Some of the Lakhmid allies of the Sasanians were Nestorian Christians and in the mid-sixth century began receiving subsidies from the emperor Justinian. The Romans' allies, the Ghassanids, were predominantly Christian, but were adherents of the 'single nature' or Monophysite theology that was regarded as heretical in Constantinople, and so their loyalty was affected by periodic attempts of the imperial government to persecute their fellow believers in Syria and Egypt.[19]

The intensification of the conflict between the two empires, and their distrust of their Arab allies, led around the turn of the century to ill-judged attempts to force them into closer affiliation with the imperial powers. The Persians tried to impose Zoroastrianism on the Lakhmids, and punitive action taken against the Monophysites in the Roman Empire under the emperors Maurice (582–602) and Heraclius (610–41) led to the detention in Constantinople of successive Ghassanid leaders.[20] In practice, this merely served to alienate the two groups from their traditional paymasters and, in consequence, leave the Mesopotamian frontiers of both empires vulnerable to an unlooked-for threat from the desert.

Before this happened, the military conflict in the Near East reached an intensity unmatched since the third century. In 590, Hormizd IV (579–90), the son of Khusro I, was overthrown by a noble coup and replaced by Vahram VI, the first non-Sasanian ruler, whose military prestige was created by his recent victory over a Turkish raid. Hormizd IV's heir Khusro fled to the emperor Maurice, who invaded Iran in 591, and with the aid of Sasanian loyalists was able to expel Vahram and impose Khusro II (591–628).[21] The price paid for this by the new shah was a considerable readjustment of the frontiers in Armenia and Mesopotamia in Rome's favour.

This brought the endemic warfare between the two empires that had lasted throughout the 570s and 580s to a satisfactory conclusion, from the Roman point of view, and led to an eleven-year period of peace, but the territorial settlement involved a loss of prestige for the regime of the new shah. The overthrow of the emperor Maurice in 602 by a military revolt by the army in the Balkans gave Khusro the excuse to return to war, posing as the avenger of his murdered benefactor.[22] For the first time, the Persians began a systematic campaign of conquest and annexation on the Mesopotamian frontier, taking the key fortress city of Dara after a nine-month siege in 604. By 610, all the main Roman cities beyond the Euphrates had fallen. The same year saw the overthrow of Phocas by an expedition launched by the governor of Africa and his replacement by the latter's son, Heraclius (610–41), but despite Maurice being avenged, as the new emperor pointed out to Khusro, this did not stop the Persian onslaught.

In 610, a Sasanian army reoccupied Armenia, all of which had been ceded to Rome in 591. The Persians were then able to march across Asia Minor to Chalcedon on the opposite shore of the Sea of Marmara from Constantinople. In 611, Caesarea in Cappadocia, the principal city in the centre of Asia Minor, fell to them as well. On the Mesopotamian frontier even greater Sasanian successes were recorded: in 611, they captured Antioch and in 614 took Jerusalem. There exists a short but vivid contemporary account of the siege of Jerusalem, written by Antiochos Strategos, which reports that many Christians were massacred by the local Jewish community, and numerous churches were looted and destroyed. In 616, Egypt was invaded and occupied without significant resistance, and in the same year a Persian army reappeared at Chalcedon, divided from the Roman capital only by the waters of the Sea of Marmora and the Bosphorus. The eastern provinces of the Empire were lost and all of Asia Minor seemingly at the mercy of the Persians.[23]

What caused this dramatic, or, as it was seen by some, apocalyptic collapse of the Roman Empire's eastern defences is hard to tell. Blame has been placed on internal disorder within the main cities of the Empire, each of which was affected by factional violence between 'the Greens' and 'the Blues', the two main groupings (there were also 'Reds' and 'Whites') of chariot-racing teams and their supporters. There is disagreement over whether these divisions also mirrored other political and religious cleavages in the society.[24] Certainly the emperors from Justinian I onwards seem, on occasion, to have given their support to one or other of the two factions, and in turn received some more personal loyalty from their members. Phocas had been given strong backing by the Blues, and, in consequence, the Greens turned out for Heraclius in the coup of 610.[25]

However, attempts to link the factions to the rivalry between Orthodox and single nature or Monophysite Christians are less convincing, and the root causes of these divisions within the major cities, which polarised all classes and sectors of society, have never been explained satisfactorily. Indeed, the search for a single solution may be misplaced, in that the causes supported by and the issues dividing the two factions appear to vary from city to city, though the factional labels remained constant across the Empire.

Despite apparently being unrelated to the circus factions and the intermittent local violence they created, the religious divide in eastern Roman or Byzantine society at this time was another cause of instability and political disaffection. No statistical information exists, but it seems reasonably certain that most people in the eastern provinces of the Roman Empire believed in the various forms of single nature theology. Under Justinian I, whose wife Theodora was a Monophysite, unsuccessful attempts were made to find a compromise theological formula to restore unity, but Maurice resumed what were regarded as persecutory practices.[26] These amounted mainly to the deposition and exile of bishops who supported single nature doctrines, but as such local clergy enjoyed popular support in their dioceses this could turn their followers against the central government. As the majority populations in the eastern provinces also spoke Syriac (Syria and Palestine) or Coptic (Egypt) rather than the Greek of the government and its officials, further cultural alienation existed, though these deeply felt theological distinctions were never a disguise for an anachronistic nationalism.[27]

The military condition of the eastern Roman Empire looked extraordinarily weak for most of the first quarter of the seventh century. The eastern provinces and much of inland Asia Minor had been lost to the Persians. At the same time, the Slavs, who had migrated from north of the Danube into the Balkans during the 540s and 550s, were now over-running most of the countryside of the Empire's remaining Balkan provinces.[28] Behind them, the nomad confederacy of the Avars, which had dominated the Carpathian basin north of the Danube since the 570s, was becoming increasingly menacing. In 626, the two major military threats to the Empire almost combined, quite possibly through Sasanian diplomacy. A large Avar force, with Slav contingents, besieged Constantinople, while a Persian army again crossed Asia Minor to the shores of the Bosphorus with the aim of joining the assault on the capital. In the event, the Roman navy was able to prevent the Persians from crossing and, lacking the technology that the Sasanians could provide, the Avars failed to overcome the defences of the city and eventually had to lift the siege.[29]

It is particularly frustrating that, when so much of the warfare and diplomacy of the sixth century is so well recorded in the works of Procopius and his two continuators, Agathias and Menander Protector, and in the *History* of Theophylact Simocatta (which covers the years 582 to 603), the equally dramatic campaigning of the early seventh century is almost totally hidden from sight. For not only was the original collapse of the Roman position in the East both rapid and far-reaching, but the imperial military recovery was even more extraordinarily speedy. Yet we know frustratingly little of the details of it, and have to rely on just a few hints in the panegyric poems on the emperor Heraclius composed by George of Pisidia, the final sections of the comparatively brief *Paschal Chronicle*, and a handful of Syriac and Armenian texts, mainly devoted to ecclesiastical matters.[30]

From these accounts, it seems that, in the early 620s, Heraclius left his capital to fend for itself, under the direction of its bishop, Sergius. The emperor himself campaigned from 622 in Asia Minor and Armenia, and may have at this time introduced a series of ad hoc reforms in the raising and maintaining of troops that developed into the classic (if historiographically controversial) system of military 'Themes' of the middle period of the Byzantine empire in the eighth to twelfth centuries. The essence of the emperor's success seem to have lain in his ability to use the difficult and mountainous terrain to get his forces behind the Sasanian armies operating in Anatolia, forcing them to abandon their own campaigns in order to defend vulnerable Persian territory. Ultimately, such an operation allowed

Heraclius to bring his army down on Khusro II himself in eastern Mesopotamia, finding Khusro almost defenceless in his palace at Dastagard, and forcing him to flee towards Ctesiphon. This final humiliation prompted a palace coup, in which Khusro II was deposed and executed by one of his sons, who then made a treaty of peace with Heraclius.[31] Thus, while the Persian armies were not defeated directly, the Roman emperor gained the strategic advantage that enabled him to win a crucial victory.

The treaty involved the restoration of the frontiers of the Empire to the positions in which they had been prior to the outbreak of the war. Not surprisingly, the still undefeated Persian armies were not in the mood to tolerate the regime that had accepted this humiliation. The new shah Kavad II was himself murdered in the same year and a period of intense political instability followed in the heart of the Persian empire. At least eight different shahs may have ruled in the years 628 to 632.[32] All met violent ends and the Sasanian dynasty came to an end. One of these ephemeral rulers, previously one of the principal Persian generals in the conquered Roman provinces, concluded the terms of the treaty with Heraclius and returned the relic of the 'True Cross', discovered originally by Helena, the mother of Constantine the Great, and carried off to Ctesiphon after the capture of Jerusalem in 614. It was restored to Jerusalem by Heraclius with great ceremony in 630.[33] Within fifteen years it was gone for ever.

Islam and the Arab conquests

In the Great Power rivalry of Rome and Persia in the sixth and early seventh centuries, to some extent trade may have 'followed the flag', but so to an even greater degree had religion. To a hitherto unprecedented degree, religious affiliation was linked to political allegiance. Theological deviation and unorthodoxy were regarded with distrust. Christian missionary activity was promoted by the emperors to spread Roman cultural influence both northwards into the steppes and southwards down the Nile into Nubia. At the same time, the Persians made repeated efforts to impose Zoroastrianism on Armenia.[34] Subtly, too, it looks as if Khusro II made attempts to portray himself as in sympathy with the Monophysite Christians at a time when they were being oppressed by their own government in Constantinople.[35]

This period saw a religious ferment. Christianity in its various forms and Zoroastrianism were not alone in competing for new believers. As has been mentioned, the Arab king Dhu Nuwas

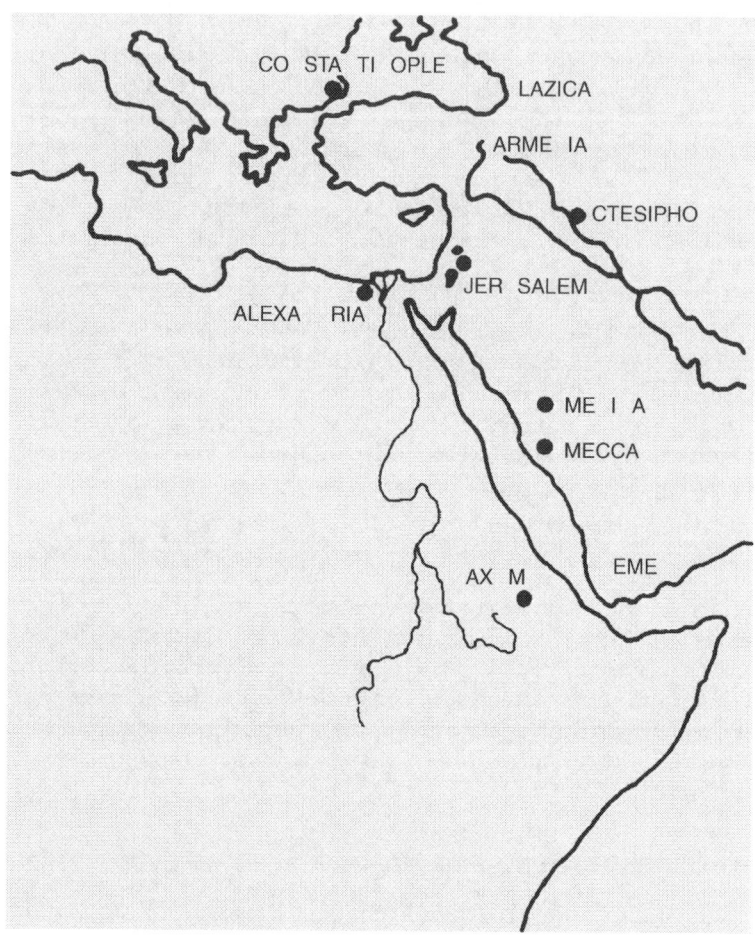

The Near East in the sixth century

converted to Judaism. Other near contemporary references indicate the existence of tribes practising Judaism in Arabia in the course of the sixth century, and the first appearance of the Jewish Falashas in Ethiopia should probably be dated to this period. As with the later conversion of the Khazars in Central Asia, these pieces of evidence suggest proselytising and conversion to Judaism by individuals and groups who were not Jews by descent.[36] The evidence for a considerable expansion in the numbers of adherents of Judaism in Arabia and the horn of Africa at this time cannot be ignored.

This is the background to probably the most dramatic and far-ranging set of changes that were to affect the Near East, the whole Mediterranean basin and much of western Europe in the period between the break up of the Roman Empire in the fifth century and the discovery of the 'New World' in the fifteenth. This was the emergence of Islam and the creation of the Arab Empire that resulted from it.

The evidence for this extraordinary series of events is regrettably limited and its interpretation complex. There are essentially two groups of sources. On the one hand, there are texts in Arabic relating to the life and teaching of the Prophet Muhammad, upon which the orthodox Muslim presentation of these events rests. On the other, there exists a variety of works that are non-Islamic in origin and which relate principally to various stages of the military conquests carried out by the Prophet's followers in the period after his death.[37]

The traditional and long accepted account of the outline of Muhammad's life, and the genesis of his revelation, comes from a genre of biographies of the Prophet that became popular from the eighth century onwards. The most substantial and authoritative of these is the work of Ibn Ishaq (d. 768), which only survives in the expanded version of it prepared by Ibn Hisham (d. 833).[38] It has been argued that this material, dating from 150 years after the death of the Prophet, is contaminated by later pious traditions and the distortions of eighth-century orthodoxy. In other words, the reader should no more expect to find objective biographical reporting in this and comparable works than he would in the Gospels.

For the authoritative teaching of Muhammad, the primary source has to be the compilation of the revelations he received from the Archangel, known as the Qur'an. This, however, is traditionally said to have been given its canonical form in the reign of the Caliph, or Successor to the Prophet, 'Uthman (644–56).[39] The earliest independent testimony to its existence comes from the end of the seventh century. According to the traditional version of its genesis, it was put together from a variety of scraps of writing, inscribed on animal bones and other forms of record. In its present form, the Qur'an consists of a series of individual revelations, grouped together according to their size, with the shortest being placed last. The contents are thus not organised on a chronological basis and are exclusively theological and legal in character. The individual sections or *suras* contain a mixture of different types of material within a single revelation.

Thus, to take as an example the *sura* called 'The Table', it begins with a series of commandments relating to food, listing what is forbidden. There follows a section relating to the ritual procedures necessary before prayer. Then come some lengthy passages that recast biblical texts in order to present the Jewish and Christian messages as partial revelations awaiting their fulfilment in that of Muhammad. This section also contains injunctions as to the treatment of Jews and Christians. The *sura* then returns to laying down legal rules, forbidding Muslims from drinking wine and from 'arrow-shuffling' – a form of divination – and concludes with another long section on the role of Muhammad as the Messenger of God, intertwined with depictions of Jesus as a similar if lesser Messenger. The whole is cast in a diction that could fairly be called poetic, despite the injunctive nature of some of the contents. Modern scholarship, working on clues in the text, has assigned the composition of this *sura* to the final period of Muhammad's life.[40] Some scholars would, as with the biographical texts, warn of the possibility of the text having been interpolated or rewritten to validate teachings and practices that post-dated the time of the Prophet.

The alternative interpretations of the life and message of Muhammad that have been produced largely through ignoring the Arab sources and attempting a reconstruction based upon the other body of evidence that is non-Islamic in origin, have generally failed to convince. This must be partly a result of the equally flawed nature of much of that material. Few of the limited and sometimes fragmentary texts from the Byzantine empire, and elsewhere, that relate to this period are genuinely contemporary, or have not themselves undergone textual transmissions as complex and questionable as those of the Arabic works. For example, the Chronicle written in Greek and/or Coptic around 690 by the Egyptian Bishop John of Nikiu only survives in two seventeenth- and eighteenth-century manuscripts of an Amharic translation made in 1602 of a lost Arabic translation of the equally lost original.[41]

So, it is as necessary to be as cautious about the Arabic traditions as about non-Arabic ones, and vice versa. In such a state of critical impasse, it must suffice for now to give the orthodox account of the Prophet's life and teaching, while drawing attention to some of the evidential problems with which it is surrounded.[42] Thus, the birth of Muhammad is traditionally placed in or close to the year 570. He was a minor member of the Quraysh, the dominant tribe in and around the town of Mecca in the Hijaz, the coastal plain of western Arabia. Mecca was basically a cult site, in which a number of divinities were venerated, especially a sun god in the form of a large meteorite, whose shrine was the rectangular structure known as the Kaaba.

Muhammad's early career was as the manager of the camel caravans of a wealthy widow called Khadija, whom he was, in due course, to marry. Around the year 610, he experienced his first vision and revelation, in which the Archangel Gabriel appeared to him. Despite his initial reservations, he continued to have these experiences and from them developed a coherent body of doctrine and religious practice, with which he began to attract followers. The basic theological tenet of his teaching was the Oneness of God, the affirmation of which became the first and most important of the five 'Pillars of Islam', and to which was tied the acceptance of Muhammad's role as the prophet or Messenger of God. The others were concerned with religious observance and included the requirement to pray five times daily at stipulated times, to fast annually during daylight in the month of Ramadan, to give a fixed proportion of income in alms for the poor and to attempt to make the pilgrimage to Mecca at least once in a lifetime.[43]

This final element was doubtless a sop to the Meccans, and should be dated to the period after Muhammad's conquest of the town, traditionally said to be in the year 630. Initially, however, his new religious message, while attracting a growing body of adherents, was viewed with considerable alarm by the leaders of the Meccan community, who regarded it as a threat to the continued well-being of the town and its dominant tribe. Mecca's position as a cult centre was linked to its economic role as a market and as the centre of the caravan trade that ran up the Red Sea coast from the Yemen to southern Palestine and ultimately Syria. Because of its religious significance, Mecca enjoyed a special role as a neutral point in which, during an annual month of truce, members of tribes in a state of mutual war and feud could meet without a threat of violence. The tribe of Quraysh thus had considerable influence over other neighbouring tribes as middle men in the resolution of feuds and through the wealth they were prepared to distribute to ensure the safe passage of their caravans. Much of this seemed threatened by Muhammad's religious message that looked likely to undermine the special status of the town, and thus of the Quraysh.[44]

In consequence, a plot was hatched in 622 to murder him. As he was himself of the Quraysh, no individual member of the tribe could be responsible for his death, as the others by the strict obligations of bloodfeud would have to avenge it. Thus it is said that a cumbersome scheme had to be hatched in which many of the leading men of the tribe would be involved in a simultaneous attack on him. Muhammad was made aware of this, and having recently received an invitation to establish himself there, was able to remove himself and his followers to the town of Medina before the Meccans could prevent him. This emigration to Medina in the northern Hijaz is known as the Hijra or 'Flight', and from it is dated the first year of the Muslim calendar.[45]

Medina itself had no dominant tribe, but was effectively divided between two rival confederacies, and it was to act as arbitrator in their quarrels that Muhammad was invited to the town. He agreed but was able to require acceptance of his religious reforms as the price of his services. Increasingly, those, including a number of Jewish tribes, who were not willing to do so, were evicted from the town. At the same time, the strategic location of Medina enabled Muhammad to exercise a growing economic stranglehold on Mecca, cutting the caravan routes to the north. Attempts by the Meccans to dislodge him by force were defeated in 624 and 627, and by the end of the decade, gaining control of the town of Taif to the south-east, Muhammad was effectively blockading Mecca. In 630, the Meccans capitulated, putting the town in his hands and accepting his religious reforms.[46]

Within two years the Prophet had died, but, in the meantime, much of Arabia is said to have submitted to his authority and to his religious teaching. This included Persian-ruled Yemen, whose governor is supposed to have embraced Islam in 630.[47] Both the speedy establishment and the wide geographical extent of the Prophet's grip on much of Arabia, secured in no more than the two-year period from 630 to 632, must raise some doubts, though no evidence exists to confirm any alternative to the traditional version. Similarly, it has been plausibly suggested that Arab attacks on the great empires to the north, especially Sasanian Persia, may have begun in the 620s, rather than only commencing around 633. This would make such raids a significant contributory factor in the Sasanian collapse of 628 to 632. Again, the evidence may not be strong enough to prove such a revision of traditional chronology, though the possibility is intriguing.[48] In general, there remain many significant questions to be asked about the career of Muhammad and its impact on both Arabia and neighbouring regions, but few may be answered with certainty.

To move on to the period following the death of the Prophet is to enter a slightly better-documented age, at least as far as the impact of the Arabs on their neighbours is concerned. Traditionally, the death of Muhammad was followed by what is called the *Riddah* or 'Apostasy', when many of the tribes that had so recently accepted his authority and his religion reverted to their previous faiths and broke their political ties to Mecca. A crisis among the inner circle of Muhammad's followers as to how the community was to be led in the absence of the Prophet was resolved with the nomination of the elderly Abu Bakr, traditionally the first to receive his message, as his caliph or successor. The claims to authority of Muhammad's cousin and son-in-law 'Ali on the basis of ties of blood were rejected.[49] Under the rule of Abu Bakr (632–4), the tribes that had defected were forced back into allegiance, and a series of large-scale attacks on the Arabs' northern neighbours, the Great Powers of Persia and Byzantium, was launched. As previously mentioned, it could be that this latter process had started anything up to a decade earlier.

Just before the death of Abu Bakr in 634 and his replacement by 'Umar, another of the inner circle, the Byzantine forces in Syria were defeated by an Arab army at the battle of Al Ajnadan. The Persians also suffered a major defeat in the same year. In 635, Damascus surrendered to an Arab expedition, and faced by this growing threat to the recently recaptured eastern provinces, the emperor Heraclius prepared to intervene in person, but in 636 the imperial army was defeated at the battle of Yarmuk and Heraclius's brother was killed.[50] The emperor evacuated his forces from Syria, and Jerusalem surrendered to the Arabs. The caliph 'Umar (634–44) is said to have made a triumphal entry into the city riding on a donkey.[51] Thus, six years after its recovery from the Persians, the Holy City was lost to the Roman Empire for ever, and the relic of the 'True Cross' fell into Arab hands and was probably destroyed.

For the Persians, the year 637 proved even more fateful. In May or June their army was routed at the battle of Al-Qadisiyah and its commander killed. In the aftermath, the Persian capital of Ctesiphon was captured without further resistance, and most of Persian Mesopotamia passed into Arab rule. The last shah, Yazdgard III (632–51), tried to organise resistance in the western regions of Iran but was forced to flee east after the disastrous battle of Nihavand in 642. He was unable to resist further Arab advances across the Iranian plateau, and in 651 was murdered by some of his own men near Merv.[52]

After the defeat at Yarmuk in 636, Heraclius made no attempts to regain his lost provinces. Reinforcements were sent to Alexandria, which held out until 642, but the rest of Egypt was conquered by the Arab commander Amr during 640 and 641.[53] In the latter year the emperor Heraclius died. In his last years he suffered from an obscure phobia that made it impossible for him to view the sea. Whether this inhibited his military capacities cannot be said, but the victor over the Persians proved no match for the Arabs. A succession crisis developed after his

death, as his elder son Heraclius Constantine was already terminally ill. A subsequent regency for his younger son Heracleonas
under Heraclius's unpopular second wife and niece Martina was
quickly overthrown in favour of his young grandson Constans II
(641–68), son of Heraclius Constantine.[54]

The conquest of the ports of the Syrian coast by the Arabs gave
them a new military arm, and in 649 their fleet took Cyprus. A bid
in 655 by emperor Constans II to check the growth of Arab naval
power ended in his disastrous defeat in a battle in the Aegean,
and imperial control of the sea was lost. In 674, Constantinople
itself was blockaded by the Arab fleet, while an Arab army was
encamped across the Sea of Marmara at Chalcedon. As in 626,
the very existence of the Empire was under threat.[55]

In the same period, the Arab expansion continued westward.
The first incursions into Byzantine-controlled North Africa
occurred in 647. At the time, the governor or exarch was in
revolt against Constantinople and had proclaimed himself
emperor the previous year, only to be defeated and killed by the
Arab invaders near Sbeitla (Sufetula) in southern Tunisia.[56] Arab
occupation of parts of Africa developed more slowly, but in 670
the city of Qayrawan (Kairouan), which became their military
and administrative centre, was founded in the Sahel. From
here, a more determined attempt to conquer North Africa was
launched under a succession of commanders. The indigenous
Berber tribes put up more sustained resistance than had been
encountered in any other region, but by 698 the Arabs had
definitively conquered Carthage.[57] A seaborne expedition in
705/6 secured control of the peninsula around Tangiers, though
the intervening parts of North Africa, largely mountainous and
with few large settlements, would be acquired far more gradually.
By 711, the Arabs were poised to extend their activities to western Europe through an invasion of the Iberian peninsula.

The success of the Arab armies in conquering a swath of territory that in the one hundred years between the death of
Muhammad and the battle of Poitiers had extended itself from
the borders of India to the north of the Pyrenees has often
been commented upon, but never satisfactorily explained.
Some interpretations concentrate particularly on the state,
in terms of morale and of morals, of the various victims of the
Arab expansion. The Persian and Byzantine empires were militarily exhausted after their titanic mutual struggles in the years
602–28. Persia was split by internal social divisions and political
disorder among its governing classes. The Monophysite
majority populations in Syria, Palestine and Egypt may have felt
distanced from the Greek government in Constantinople that

was persecuting their religious leaders. Byzantine rule in Africa has been seen as being no more than the presence of an alien ruling elite holding down an indifferent or hostile indigenous Berber population.

Even if some of these arguments are true, they can, at best, be only partial explanations. To supplement them, attention is sometimes paid to the activities of 'third columns' that may have co-operated with the Arabs. The most prominent of these were the Jews, and some historians have presented the Copts and Jacobite Monophysites of Syria as active collaborators with the invaders. The evidence for such involvement is, in fact, slight. There is no proof at all for any claims that Christians of any persuasion openly sided with the Arabs, and that relating to Jewish involvement is both limited and geographically restricted. While conditions for the Jews in the eastern Roman Empire were far from good, Muhammad had turned against the Jewish tribes in Arabia when they refused to accept his religious message, and thus an Arab and Islamic take-over of the state was not necessarily something they would welcome. More significantly, the magnitude of the events that were taking place, and the scale of violence and disorder that accompanied them, led some Jews to expect the Messianic coming.[58] Thus, apocalyptic expectations, rather than political calculations, determined their actions.

More concrete factors in the explanation for the Arabs' success might include the nature of the warfare and the political geography of the territories affected. In the pursuit of strengthening the defences against Persia, Justinian had devoted much money and material to the rebuilding of town walls and the erection of forts along the east–west frontier in Mesopotamia. However, the eastern fringes of south Syria and of Palestine that fronted on to the desert received no such treatment, as no major military threat was anticipated from that direction, and the allied Arab tribes in these regions were expected to provide sufficient defence against raids by hostile tribes.[59] However, not only did a threat of unprecedented magnitude develop in the 630s, but the previously tractable Arab tribes had been alienated by the treatment they had received from the emperors Maurice and Heraclius. Thus, there were neither fortresses nor allied troops to defend these areas against the unforeseen invasions from Arabia.

As far as we know, the terms and conditions the Arabs offered to the inhabitants of the towns of Syria, Palestine, Egypt and Mesopotamia were intended to eliminate any threat these might pose and to maximise the Arab war effort by freeing them from the necessity of installing manpower-wasteful garrisons in the towns. The choice apparently offered (there being some disagreement about the reliability of such texts) was that, if a town surrendered without resistance, the inhabitants would retain their lives, liberties, local self-government and religious freedom, in return for the payment of land and capitation taxes. If, on the other hand, they fought and the town was taken, their property would be forfeit and they would be enslaved. Lacking the prospect of immediate succour from imperial armies, few towns decided on the second option. If the emperor eventually triumphed, as he had over the Persians, then nothing would be lost, and in the meantime the taxes payable to the Arabs were no greater – and may even have been less – than those owed to the Byzantine government. As the walls of those towns not restored by Justinian were doubtless in a state of poor repair, the decision cannot have been difficult to make.[60]

Persia was peculiarly vulnerable, in that its capital Ctesiphon was situated in Mesopotamia and in the immediate front line of the Arab attack. Its fall was an early and demoralising blow. For the Byzantine empire, however, the location of Constantinople was a strength. The Arab armies, largely of light cavalry, were not suited to mountainous terrain, and it is notable that while they penetrated Asia Minor on numerous occasions, no attempts were made to occupy and hold it. By the time the Arabs were in a position to launch a joint sea and land attack on the city, the Byzantines were able to deploy a 'secret weapon', in the form of Greek Fire, a highly volatile unrefined petroleum from the area around Baku, which ignited on contact with water. Jetted out of hydrants on the Byzantine ships into the sea around the Arab vessels, its effects were devastating, and its use to terminate the great siege of Constantinople in 674–7 in practice marked the limit to the threat the Arabs were able to make against the continued existence of the Empire.[61]

Just as at first the Arabs were disconcerted by the Byzantines' Greek Fire, so, previously, had many of their victims been by the nature and ferocity of Arab tactics. Romans and Persians had long been used to each other's fighting practices and had adapted their own procedures accordingly. Thus, Roman heavy cavalry mirrored Persian. Their armies seemed ill adapted to the military threat of the Arabs, and a series of resounding victories over forces used to set-piece battles was the result. This was to be as true in Spain in 711 as it had been in Mesopotamia in the 630s and 640s.

10 Decadent and do-nothing kings, 511–711

The Gothic kingdom in Spain, *c.* 589–711

One of the most persistent and erroneous views about the end of the Visigothic kingdom in Spain seems at last to have become extinct, and not before time. This is the idea that, by the early eighth century, the Gothic kingdom had become so decadent and its inhabitants so demoralised that the merest hostile push by an alien invader was sufficient to bring about its social and political collapse. This, it is thought, is what happened when the Arabs and their Berber armies entered the Iberian peninsula in 711. Nowadays, we are more inclined to emphasise the strength and sophistication of the Gothic monarchy, with the suggestion that it was actually at its height at the time of its fall.[1] While such a judgement needs some modification, there is no denying the fact that the kings maintained their control of a large, and geographically and culturally diverse realm, despite its difficult internal communications, for well over a century.[2]

The most obvious turning point in the relations between the Goths and the indigenous Hispano-Roman population was the Third Council of Toledo in 589, which formalised the conversion of the kingdom and its ruling elite from Arian to Catholic Christianity. This was made possible by the prior personal conversion of king Reccared (586–601) in 587 and the subsequent acceptance of the need to change by most, though not all, of the Arian bishops.[3] By the time the council was held in May 589, most of the practical problems had been settled. The council spoke as if the conversion of the king and the people was already established, and the assembled bishops went on to legislate for the first time for a unified Church in the Iberian peninsula.

However, the initial impetus towards a closer integration of the majority Roman population with the ruling Visigothic elite may have come from Reccared's father, Leovigild (569–86).[4] Under his immediate predecessors, the Gothic military occupation of most of the peninsula that had been in place since the conquests of the 450s and 470s had disintegrated. Individual towns and regions broke away from Visigothic rule. King Agila (549–54) lost control of Córdoba, and was then overthrown in a civil war with one of his own magnates. One of the two sides in this conflict – the evidence is contradictory as to which it was – had appealed to the emperor Justinian for aid, and the resulting imperial intervention in 551 led to the creation of an imperial enclave all along the south-eastern coast of Spain, from Cartagena to Medina Sidonia, and possibly extending inland as far as Córdoba, which was not finally eliminated until the mid-620s.[5]

Under Leovigild, the fortunes of the Visigothic monarchy revived. In a series of campaigns from 570 to 578, he regained control of northern Spain from the Pyrenees to the borders of the Suevic kingdom in Galicia in the north-west. He also inflicted some defeats on the imperial forces in the south-west and retook Medina Sidonia. In 572, he regained control of Córdoba. Like several of his successors he had problems with the Basques, who frequently raided the upper Ebro valley from their homeland in the western Pyrenees. He undertook a campaign to curb their incursions in 581 and founded a new town, *Victoriacum* (possibly modern Olite in Navarre), to try to force some of them to settle.[6] In 585, the conquest of the Suevic kingdom, where the previous royal dynasty had just been overthrown by a usurper, completed Leovigild's successful imposition of his authority over the whole of the northern half of the peninsula.[7]

In the south, his work remained incomplete. He failed to eliminate the imperial enclave, and in 579 his elder son Hermenigild rebelled and established an independent kingdom centred on Seville. Leovigild seems to have been willing to tolerate this until the rebel ruler's growing rapprochement with Constantinople began to appear threatening. This was the product of Hermenigild's conversion from Arianism to Catholicism: an obvious sign of a shift in political allegiance, which though often dated to the beginning of his revolt probably only occurred in 582.[8] In campaigns in 583 and 584, Leovigild regained control of Mérida and Italica, before finally forcing his son to surrender in Seville. In 585, Hermenigild, initially exiled to Valencia, was killed in Tarragona by a certain Sisbert, but on whose orders is unclear.

The political reunification of most of the peninsula by Leovigild might have had little chance of being permanent if a fundamental divide over religion continued to separate the two main elements in the population. Leovigild had hoped to win over more of the Catholics, who by now included some prominent Goths, by holding a synod in Toledo in 580 which modified Arian doctrine through acceptance of the equality of Father and Son but not of the Holy Spirit, and by removing the need for converts to be rebaptised. However, this generated a Catholic polemical response in works by bishop Leander of Seville and others, and even the military defeat of Hermenigild failed to weaken Catholic intellectual resistance. On the other hand, there are hints that in the last few years of his reign Leovigild was moving closer to Catholicism, and a rumour even spread that he himself converted prior to his death. That his surviving son and heir took such a decision himself within a year of his accession is thus less surprising.

The willingness of the Catholic bishops, who in most cases were the social as well as the spiritual leaders of their communities, to co-operate with the monarchy, once the problem of the Arian heresy was removed, had no parallel in western Europe. It was largely their involvement, which became increasingly institutionalised in a series of kingdom-wide councils held in Toledo from the 630s onwards that knitted the disparate regions of the peninsula together.[9] The lack of military challenge, especially after King Suinthila (621–31) had eliminated the imperial enclave in the south-east around 625, reduced the need for constant military action. The raising of local levies by Romano-Gothic landowners provided the main way of augmenting the *comitatus* that followed the person of the king. So it was not really by the threat of force that the monarchy maintained its authority over the peninsula. In the Church councils held in Toledo, especially in the 630s and 680s, the bishops introduced spiritual sanctions against those who plotted against the monarchs or who conspired against the existing political order. By the 670s, the bishops of Toledo could define a king's legitimacy as depending on his having been anointed in the 'royal city' of Toledo, which had been the administrative centre of the kingdom since Leovigild's time.[10]

On the other hand, the bishops did not apply those spiritual sanctions to rulers, such as Sisenand (631–6) and Chindasuinth (642–53) who successfully overthrew their predecessors. The success of their revolts was seen as proof of divine favour and selection, and so it was against those who tried and failed that the Church directed its condemnation. What was far more important than the bishops' threats of excommunication was the fact that they were willing to meet to discuss such secular matters, and to serve as partisans and propagandists for the monarchy in their sees. For them, the existence of a peninsula-wide kingdom, embracing all five of the ecclesiastical provinces of Spain and Septimania, to the north-east of the Pyrenees, was vital to the well-being of the Church. With a unified Church in a single realm, reform could be imposed in such issues as monastic observance, the conduct of the clergy, and the economic management of dioceses, and uniformity could be achieved in the performance of the liturgy. It also made possible the use of a common body of canon law, much of which was in the process of being created at the sixteen Councils of Toledo that took place between 589 and 702.[11]

Obviously, these objectives had to be acceptable to the majority of Church leaders in the kingdom, but much of the policy-making and direction came from a succession of bishops distinguished for their erudition as well as their political acumen. The most prolific author among them was Isidore, Bishop of Seville (599/600–636), brother of bishop Leander who had been a spiritual mentor to both Hermenigild and Reccared.[12] Isidore's most substantial and best-known work is his *Etymologiae* or *Etymologies*, a vast encyclopaedia in twenty books embracing a wide range of subjects, from grammar (bk I.iii) to God (bk VII.i) and from geometry (bk III.i–iii) to gladiators (bk XVII.vii). The internal organisation of the individual books is generally logical, though after the first five, devoted to Grammar, Rhetoric, Mathematics, Medicine and Law, their overall structure is less so. The guiding principle in Isidore's approach to the topics he selected for inclusion is that of the etymology of names – that is, the origin and inherent meaning of words themselves; as Isidore saw it, 'the investigation of anything is much easier if its etymology is known' (I.xix.2).

As well as providing a corpus of educational texts intended for grammatical and biblical study in this, his largest work, as well as in a range of other, shorter ones, Isidore also wrote two short histories: first, a chronicle giving a synoptic history of the world from its foundation, and second, his *History of the Goths, Vandals and Sueves*.[13] In these two books, each of which has survived in two separate versions differing in length and content, he placed the recent history of Spain, and above all the creation of the Gothic kingdom in the peninsula into the context of both biblical and Roman history. If the ideological contents of these works, especially the *History of the Goths*, make them look like propaganda for the monarchy, at least it was willingly written. As well as presiding over a series of synods in his own metropolitan province, Isidore presided over the Fourth Council of Toledo of 633, which resumed the task initiated by the Third Council of 589 in making the Church the most ardent supporter of the kings.

After Isidore's death, Seville was eclipsed by Toledo. A succession of outstanding bishops – Eugenius II (646–57), Ildefonsus (657–67) and Julian (680–90) – produced a body of work in the form of law, theology, history, grammar, and above all liturgy that was quite unparalleled in Western Europe in the seventh century in both its quantity and in the quality of its writing. They were also all astute politicians, and among other things they created for their own see an unchallenged primacy over the Church of the kingdom. Though formally equal to those of Braga, Mérida, Narbonne, Seville and Tarragona, the metropolitans of Toledo by the time of Julian were able to ordain bishops in the capital to fill sees in the other ecclesiastical provinces.[14] They were also able to impose Toledan liturgy as standard on the Spanish Church. What is more surprising still is that they met no known opposition from their fellow metropolitans, who appear to have co-operated fully in these processes. By 690, contrary to the rules observed throughout the western Church since the Council of Nicaea of 325, a bishop of Seville was translated to the see of Toledo, in itself demonstrating the superior status of the latter.[15]

The principal difficulty in understanding the society and politics of Spain in the Visigothic period lies in the nature of the available evidence. The problem is not simply one of quantity. If the total corpus of the civil and ecclesiastical law produced in the kingdom in the seventh century is added to its liturgical and theological output, then it far exceeds the quantity of written materials produced in any other region of the former Roman Empire in the same period and, indeed, might go a long way towards equalling the entire known literary output of the time. However, it is the particular nature of these texts that limits their usefulness for the modern historian. We know a great deal about what *ought* to have happened in Spain at this time, but very little about what actually *did*.[16] The greater part of the evidence is legal and normative – that is, laying down rules – but there is a serious lack of literary historical writing that, for example, might provide us with detailed information about personalities and events.

No large-scale narrative history was ever written in early medieval Spain. Isidore's two works are extremely brief and after them no historical writing was carried out in the Visigothic period apart from Julian of Toledo's *History of Wamba*, which confines itself to the events of the opening of the reign of king Wamba (672–80), and in particular his campaign in 673 against a rebel count, Paul, who was based in Narbonne.[17] Thus we lack the kind of vivid narrative of events that is available for some of sixth-century Gaul and seventh-century Britain, thanks to the existence of the large-scale historical works of Gregory of Tours (d. 594) and Bede (d. 735). While evidence for the

ideals and aspirations of this society, represented by its civil and
ecclesiastical laws and some of the treatises written by the leading bishops of the kingdom, is unusually strong, that relating
to the interplay of personalities and politics and to the practical
application of the legislators' rules is almost non-existent. Even
administrative texts are extraordinarily scarce and are represented principally by five very mutilated fragments of documents written on parchment.[18]

After the relatively detailed narrative accounts that can be
composed for most periods of the later Roman Empire and of
Frankish Gaul, these evidential problems make the study of
Visigothic Spain seem austere and abstract. However, it is possible to attempt alternative approaches to the subject that can be
both illuminating. In particular, new discoveries and research
have opened up other ways of looking at various aspects of the
period.

The archaeological study of Visigothic Spain is lively, though
the nature of its organisation and in particular its funding
means that certain regions are better served than others, and
so misleadingly seem to be archaeologicially richer than others,
where the money is less readily available or is channelled in
other directions. There is also – and this is a positive feature –
much uncertainty and debate on several topics, with opinions
changing quite rapidly. For example, the rural church of Santa
Maria de Melque near Toledo, which in 1917 had been dated
to the tenth century, was the subject of a detailed excavation in
the 1970s and was studied in comparison with other buildings
of similar plan, leading to its being re-dated to the Visigothic
period.[19] Soon after this, a fresh set of comparisons, this time
with the decoration of some early eighth-century Umayyad palaces in Jordan, led to the suggestion that similar stylistic features could be detected in Santa Maria, and thus it could date
from no earlier than *c.* 750, and might even be from the ninth
century. No allowance was made in this analysis for the Spanish
church and the Near Eastern palaces being the products of
a common, more widely diffused style, rather than one having
to depend on the other. However, recent carbon 14 and thermo-
luminescence dating of items from the site has suggested that
the building was constructed somewhere between the late seventh century and the end of the eighth, thus straddling the
time of the Arab conquest, and leaving open the question of
whether the building – and others whose dating depends on
their sharing similar characteristics – should be classified as
being 'late-Visigothic' or 'early Islamic'. Such problems have
led to the further suggestion that it is unhelpful to try to define

a distinctive 'Visigothic' architecture, and that changes in building and decorative styles are not immediately dependent on
political events.[20]

Current excavations in the city of Mérida in Extremadura
are also producing much new information on the wider context
of changes in town life from the early Roman imperial period,
through that of the Visigothic kingdom and well on into the
centuries of Islamic rule. As well as this important work on new
sites, more critical study of the five extant churches in northern Spain and Portugal that have long been assigned to the
Visigothic period has modified older certainties. These investigations, taken together with the few saints' lives and the writings
of the monastic founder, Fructuosus of Braga (650s and 660s),
and of the hermit Valerius of Bierzo (690s), have, for example,
helped to put much more flesh on the bare bones of the ecclesiastical regulations concerned with monastic life in the canons of
the councils.

Equally valuable, from the way they can share a context
with textual sources, are the recent discoveries and studies of
a series of rock churches and hermits' caves in the upper Ebro
valley. Hitherto, knowledge of this aspect of the ecclesiastical
life of Visigothic Spain had depended on reading the *Life of
St Aemilian*, a late-sixth-century hermit and 'holy man', written
by bishop Braulio of Zaragoza (631–51), a pupil of Isidore of
Seville. The discovery in Alava and the Rioja of large numbers
of these cave churches and associated dwellings, and domestic
rooms – for example, refectories with their dining tables carved
from the bare rock – reveals the extensiveness of the monastic
and hermit communities in this area; a fact entirely concealed
in the *Life*.[21]

One local society in another area of the peninsula can be
extraordinarily well illustrated from the wide range of administrative and other documents that it produced, and which to
our good fortune were written down on sheets of slate rather
than on perishable parchment. The existence of many of these
slate documents, found in relatively large numbers – well over a
hundred – in various sites in the area between Avila and
Salamanca, has been known for a relatively long time. However,
their first transcriber and editor made a large number of mistakes in his copying and, in consequence, many of the texts
appeared to be meaningless. However, new studies and editions have revealed how comprehensible and valuable many of
them are, despite most of them being damaged.[22] The range
of subject matter is impressive, and includes land transactions,
sales, curses and school exercises. In the course of time it will

be possible to present far more precise and detailed accounts of the rural society of this region in the late sixth century and first quarter of the seventh.

Post-Roman archaeology has hitherto had to confine itself largely to the study of cemeteries and grave goods. Even towns which on the basis of documentary evidence can be shown to have been occupied in the early medieval period have failed to show traces of themselves archaeologically, though in Spain, Mérida and Cartagena are significant exceptions. An abandoned town site with Roman, Visigothic and early Islamic phases of occupation, at Tolmo de Minateda, near Hellín in the province of Albacete, is now producing important evidence for all three periods. Recovered from here, as also in Barcelona and Valencia, are many features of not only the cathedral but also of the other ecclesiastical (for example, a baptistery) and residential buildings (the bishop's palace) adjacent to it.[23]

Many more rural settlements of sixth to eighth century date have also been discovered in recent years, especially in the centre of the peninsula.[24] While none of the buildings survive above the level of foundations, the ground plans of several have been uncovered. In most cases they consist of a handful of small dwellings, rarely more than six to eight in each settlement, each of which is associated with what appear to be stock pens and/or grain silos. No churches or other public buildings have been found in these sites, and the settlements themselves have been classified as 'hamlets' rather than villages. Whether they were occupied by free proprietors, or by families of servile, status obliged to provide labour services or pay rents to their lords, is unknown. However, one recent interpretation of the evidence for this period across the whole of Europe argues for these post-Roman centuries to have been something of a 'golden age' for free peasant proprietors, with the economic power of aristocratic landlords greatly curtailed. If so, these could be the kinds of settlements we might expect them to occupy, but we cannot be sure.[25]

On the southern banks of the Rio Segre, about fifteen miles west of Lérida in Catalonia, is the site of El Bovalar. That this centred on a church, probably to be dated to the sixth century, has long been known, and the building itself was excavated in 1967. A more substantial campaign was launched in 1976, and this uncovered a second and more extensive area of construction on the south side of the church, based around two courtyards. This has been identified as a village, though there are problems with such a view, as the buildings seem interconnected. The particular interest of this site lies in the fact that the settlement, whatever its character may have been, was clearly abandoned in haste and at a single point in time. Moreover, this can be dated to the reign of the late Visigothic king Achila (710–13) by the existence of a number of his coins found abandoned in the rooms. The rapid abandonment, associated with destruction by fire, has meant that a wide range of items of everyday use, together with much information relating to diet and the local economy, has been recovered from the site; though it all still awaits publication. The precision in dating and the violent destruction of the location, though not apparently of its inhabitants – no bodies having been found – have led to the plausible suggestion that this should be linked to the Arab conquest of the mid- and lower Ebro valley, which occurred in the years 712/13.[26]

This one site, therefore, seems to take us directly to the final phase of the Gothic kingdom in the peninsula, and helps to confirm the impression given by the *Chronicle of 754* that the Arab campaign in the Ebro was particularly destructive.[27] This is far more useful and reliable information on these events than the much later tales of the conquest in Arabic narratives. Stories of the betrayal of king Roderic (710/11–711) by the sons of his predecessor, Wittiza (693/4–710), and even of their inviting of the Arabs into the peninsula, lack any foundation.[28] Conflict between Roderic in the south and north-west of the peninsula and Achila in the north-east at the time of the Arab invasions can, however, be substantiated, and the first discovery at El Bovalar of a coin of Achila that was struck at the mint of Zaragoza proves that he ruled over the principal city of the mid-Ebro valley as well as over Narbonne, Gerona and Tarragona.

Gothic kings led their own armies. In practice, hereditary succession was the norm, but if a minor or an incompetent succeeded, a challenge from some of the regionally based aristocracy might unseat the leader. Count Paul in Narbonne had attempted to do this to the new king Wamba in 673 but failed. In any case, no royal dynasty lasted longer than three generations, and few even made it to two. The small but wealthy aristocracy of the royal court, from whose ranks the kings were mainly drawn, seem to have been reluctant to allow any of their number to establish a monopoly on the throne. They also proved adept at removing kings through obscure, and usually bloodless, internal coups, as occurred with Wamba in 680 and Ervig in 687, and quite possibly with Wittiza in 710.[29] In 710, Roderic had either been selected to replace Wittiza or had overthrown him in such a coup in Toledo, but he was then faced with a challenge from a regional contender in the North-East, as well possibly as the endemic Basque raiding in the upper

Ebro. It was at this point, and probably not coincidentally, that the Arabs attacked. Following the nearly contemporary *Chronicle of 754* rather than the much later and possibly fanciful Arab accounts, it seems that several incursions were made and that at least two Arab armies were operating in the peninsula when Roderic was defeated and killed at the battle 'in the Transductine Promontories', probably in 711.

With the king dead and his noble following killed or dispersed, the capital fell rapidly to the Arabs, who with the seizure of Toledo gained control of the central administration and of the one place in which the complicated procedures of kingmaking were expected to occur. The possibilities of further centrally organised resistance evaporated, and individual towns and regions submitted on the kind of terms offered to their counterparts in the east. Those that did not submit suffered the consequences. Within a decade, the tide of conquest passed through the peninsula, which broke up into small, localised units now lacking the capacity or the need to resist. By 721, the Arabs were poised for the extension of their conquests beyond the Pyrenees.[30]

Gaul and the Merovingians *c.* 511–687

If the history of the Visigothic kingdom, subjugated by the Arabs between 711 and 720, is difficult to reconstruct and dependent on the teasing out of clues from complex sources, then the earlier history of the next victims of Arab aggression, the Merovingian kingdoms in Gaul, appears deceptively clear. This is because of an almost superabundance of the literary evidence so lamentably lacking in Spain. The *Ten Books of Histories* written by Bishop Gregory of Tours (died 594) and completed around 591, provide a wealth of detailed information on personalities and events, particularly for the period *c.* 550 to 591 (books IV–X).[31]

Gregory's knowledge of episodes affecting his own episcopal city of Tours during his pontificate (571–94) was obviously firsthand in most instances. Moreover, the importance of his city in the Loire valley, its proximity to other major centres such as Orléans and Poitiers, and the relatively frequent shifts in the political boundaries of the Frankish kingdoms, which could affect its political allegiance, all combined to make Gregory peculiarly well-informed about the wider politics of Merovingian Gaul. Furthermore, his upbringing in Clermont and the network of his aristocratic family connections provided additional sources of information for him to draw on in depicting not only the Romano-Frankish society of his own day but also something of its past. Nor were his works confined to history alone. The *Ten Books of Histories* were matched by *Seven Books of Miracles* and one of saints' lives, which, despite being smaller in size and more limited in their content, are also mainly concerned with Gaul and with the fifth and sixth centuries.[32]

The sheer bulk of Gregory's contribution to the study of sixth-century Gaul makes his perspective on events not only accessible but also dangerously persuasive. The problems with his account of the career of Clovis have already been discussed, and so too the difficulty of creating an alternative view.[33] It might be argued that Gregory himself was disadvantaged in writing about some-one, whatever his importance, who was so far removed in time from his own day, and that the information he offers us in so much more detail of periods closer to and including his own lifetime should be more reliable.

In fact, Gregory is seductive. It is simple enough to show, on the basis of comparison with other contemporary sources, that he deliberately distorted his account of the conflicts taking place in Spain in the late 570s and 580s, and that his version of Visigothic history is prejudiced.[34] It is also easy enough to prove that much of his information relating to Italy is erroneous.[35] Unfortunately, there are few such controls to help monitor his treatment of Frankish history, which, unsurprisingly, takes up most of his work. As his very prejudiced account of the Frankish King Chilperic (561–84) shows, Gregory's animosities could be deep and lasting, and his pride in his family and its achieve-ments is, if anything, even more apparent in his hagiographical works than in his historical ones.[36]

If his intense and somewhat masterful personality exercises such a hold over the interpretation of so many aspects of the history of sixth-century Gaul, how can we handle his evidence? It is not easy, in that the author of the principal seventh-century Frankish chronicle, who is known as 'Fredegar' (though that was definitely not his real name – and hence the academic but even more confusing alternative 'Pseudo-Fredegar'), derived much though not all of his sixth-century information from Gregory.[37] The only independent contemporary source is the all-too-brief chronicle written in the 590s by Bishop Marius of Avenches (Roman *Aventicum* in western Switzerland).[38] However, if Gregory's value judgements are treated with caution, his copi-ous materials can be evaluated from the sources that we know, or can assume, he was relying on. A full-scale historical commen-tary on his work would be useful, though it must be admitted that scholars have yet to suggest convincing answers to even such fundamental questions as to what were Gregory's motives in writing his histories, and what was its intended readership.

There is no space here to provide a synoptic version of Gregory's account of the history of the Frankish kingdoms from the death of Clovis up to his time of writing in the early 590s. To some extent it would be irrelevant, and the depiction of sixth-century Gaul, by way of a retelling of Gregory's narrative, is largely responsible for making this society seem so violent, disjointed and savage. It is better for us to try to isolate the salient features of the society, using his materials, but also trying where possible to supplement them from other documentary sources and from archaeological materials.

Frankish settlement in the early sixth century was still limited to northern, and especially north-eastern, Gaul, despite the extent of the territories south of the Loire that Clovis had brought under his control.[39] As we have already seen in an earlier chapter, the administrative strategies available to Clovis were far less sophisticated, especially in northern Gaul, than those of metropolitan Italy. To put it simply, he might fit himself into the role of something like a late Roman provincial Master of the Soldiers, while for the Ostrogothic king Theoderic in Italy there the vacant functions (though not the title) of western emperor were available. Moreover, the political and cultural unity of Italy had not been compromised in the fifth century to anything like the degree of that of Gaul. Until the Lombard invasion of 568, political control of Italy always remained in the hands of one central authority, and the peninsula changed hands as a unit between successive political masters from 476 to 568. The same was largely true of Spain, other than the Suevic-ruled north-west, until the mid-sixth century, and, as we have just seen, unitary rule over virtually the whole Iberian peninsula was re-established in the 570s and 580s.

Thus the Frankish kings who succeeded Clovis were the heirs of the late Roman state to a lesser degree than were the Gothic monarchs in Italy and Spain. They do not seem to have used the powers and resources that this might have offered them, or only attempted to do so selectively and intermittently. One example of this is their almost certain failure to maintain the complex but lucrative system of late Roman taxation. When the innovative and Romanised king Chilperic (561–84) did try to revive the lapsed procedures and introduce new *descriptiones* or tax registers he met with considerable opposition, organised not least by the Church, and bishops such as Gregory told him that the ill-health (and subsequent deaths) of his children resulted directly from this, to their minds impious, intention.[40] In Spain, on the other hand, the bishops seem to have been closely involved in the raising of tax revenue for the monarchs.[41]

This failure to preserve such apparently crucial features of the organisation of the centralised state may seem to imply that the Frankish kings were unsophisticated or more barbarous than their Gothic counterparts, but such an impression would be highly misleading. The problems of continuity really lie in the fifth century rather than in the sixth. Moreover, such a line of argument ignores the structural realities of Gallic society in late antiquity and the early Middle Ages.

From a modern perspective, France is the model of the centralised state, and favourable historical judgements on various phases of its past all too often seem directly related to the degree of political unity and central authority seen to be existing in them. The creation of the unified France is every bit as much product of a 'Whig Interpretation of History' as the development of the British Constitution and parliamentary democracy. In other words, these were long seen by historians as the natural ends to which these particular societies were 'progressing', and that those who assisted in these processes were to be praised as being 'good', 'great' and 'wise', while those who failed to forward them – or worse, whose actions were thought to lead to disunity and disintegration – were described as 'weak' and 'incompetent'.

Thus Clovis has always been highly acclaimed for his military unification of so much of what was to be France, while his successors, especially the so-called *rois fainéants*, or 'do-nothing kings' of the later seventh century were long ignored or belittled.[42] Similarly, Charlemagne's 'achievements' were for a long time contrasted by nineteenth- and twentieth-century historians with his successors' 'failures'. The latter are seen as leading directly to the 'disastrous' tenth century, in which centralised royal authority virtually disappeared. In fact, when the history of France from around the year 400 to the end of the tenth century is surveyed as a whole, the periods of powerful and effective central authority are few in number and all essentially fleeting.[43]

In large part, this was because of the strength of regional differences and of local communities and their leaders. The Romans had imposed their form of political unity on a large number of disparate Celtic tribes, but even they did not achieve a single administrative structure for Gaul. Equally instructive is the political settlement that followed the death of Clovis around the year 511. According to Gregory of Tours, the king's four sons divided the kingdom 'in equal measure between them'. The reality must have been rather different, in that, of the three younger sons (the children of Clovis's marriage to the Burgundian Clothildis), perhaps only Chlodomer (*c.* 511–24), the eldest, had reached the legal age of majority – twelve or possibly fourteen – by this time. Their half-brother, Theuderic, was considerably older and had already been campaigning with their father. So, not all of Clovis's sons could have played a personal role in dividing up his kingdom. Nor were there any intrinsic reasons why the kingdom should have been partitioned between all his heirs.[44] An opportunity to create a single unified Frankish kingdom of Gaul certainly existed but was deliberately rejected in favour of a division. Why?

The nature of this dividing up of Clovis's kingdom is not described by any source, but has to be reconstructed from subsequent references to the territories controlled by the four monarchs. What emerges is that the various component parts of these lands were generally not adjacent to each other; that is, between any two regions of one kingdom there was likely to be a section of another. One explanation for this is that each of the new kings was allotted a portion of the original territory control- led by their father Clovis before 486 and distinct parts of all the other regions he conquered – north-western France, Aquitaine and the Rhineland. Whether or not this was the rationale for such an extraordinary division, unparalleled in the other great kingdoms of the West, it certainly inhibited the growth of an efficient and centralised royal administration.[45]

The details of this crucial process, which provided the prec- edent for a similar division of the briefly reunited kingdom between the sons of Chlotar I in 561, are extremely obscure. That it took place immediately after Clovis's death is uncertain, as there is an almost complete blank in our records of Frankish history between *c.* 511 and 522, but its long-term effects were considerable. The conquest and elimination of the Burgundian kingdom in 534 and the cession of Provence to the Franks by the Ostrogothic king Wittigis in 536 completed Frankish expan- sion within Gaul, other than for Visigothic controlled Septimania along the Mediterranean coast in the south-west.[46] This meant that for any one of the rival Frankish kings who succeeded Clovis – as well as for the sons of Chlotar I after 561 – territorial expansion had to be achieved either at the expense of neigh- bouring non-Frankish kingdoms or be the product of civil war.

In practice, for the first generation after Clovis, sufficient opportunities existed for the kings to co-exist reasonably harmo- niously. The first attempt to conquer the Burgundian kingdom cost the life of Chlodomer in 524, but his kingdom was then divided between his two full brothers Childebert I (*c.* 511–58) and Chlotar I (*c.* 511–61), who murdered his infant sons to enable them to do so.[47] Ten years later, the Burgundian kingdom was dismembered by Childebert, Chlotar and Theudebert I (533–48) (who had just succeeded his father, Theuderic).

Theudebert was undoubtedly the greatest of the Frankish kings of the sixth century.[48] He and his father before him benefited from controlling much of the Rhineland and the long eastern frontiers of the Frankish lands. This gave them the potential for territorial expansion on a very large scale. By the time of Theudebert's death, the Frisians, the Saxons, the Thuringians and a number of lesser peoples east of the Rhine acknowledged his overlordship, and his kingdom had extended itself over the Alps into parts of northern Italy. In the latter stages of the war between the Empire and Justinian, Theudebert may have been presenting himself to the Romans in Italy as a possible new protector. The emperor was also taking seriously the alliance of peoples Theudebert was putting together north-east of the Alps and the resulting threat of a Frankish invasion of the Balkans.[49]

Theudebert's style was deliberately intended to be imperial: he presided in the hippodrome of Arles, and was the first western king to break the imperial monopoly in the minting of gold coins. He issued a series that faithfully copied the designs, weight and fineness of the eastern Roman gold *solidus,* but with his own name and royal title substituted for that of the emperor.[50] Within Gaul, or Francia as it may now be called, he appeared to have deliberately attempted to consolidate a block of territory stretching from the frontiers of Visigothic Septimania and the Mediterranean to the Rhine and beyond.

This domain disintegrated after his death in 548 and that of his son Theudebald in 555, and successful Saxon and Thuringian revolts put an end to this first Frankish extension east of the Rhine soon afterwards.[51] By the time of the death in 561 of Chlotar I, the last of the sons of Clovis, who had for the final three years of his life ruled over all the kingdoms, the possibilities for further Frankish territorial expansion had come to an end. A division between Chlotar's four sons exacerbated the problems of territorial competitiveness, as the kingdom of one of them, Chilperic (561–84), was entirely surrounded by lands belonging to his brothers. By 569, war had broken out between them, which lasted with few interruptions until the murder of Sigebert, the most powerful of the brothers, in 575.[52] Subsequent conflicts or threats of war continued intermittently until 613, when, as in 558–61, all the kingdoms were again united under one ruler, Chlotar II (584–629), the son of Chilperic.[53]

The history of Merovingian Gaul in the seventh century has been relatively neglected, in comparison with the attention devoted to the periods that precede and follow it. The reason is largely related to the evidence. After the vivid and large-scale narratives of Gregory of Tours, the sources available for the 150 years following his death in 594 seem meagre. They consist of the final book of the so-called *Chronicle of Fredegar*, which is far briefer in its treatment than Gregory and which also ends its narrative in the year 642. One or two references in the text indicate that its author was writing no earlier than 658/9, but he did not complete his work up to this point.[54]

For the second half of the seventh century the only narrative sources are very thin indeed. They consist of two eighth-century works. The first of these used to be regarded as little more than a continuation of Fredegar, but it is in fact different in its structure and some of its content, and is better treated as a free-standing historiographical compilation in its own right that is dependent for quite a lot of its subject matter on a manuscript of the seventh-century *Chronicle of Fredegar*, to which it adds, among other things, a narrative covering the years from the 640s to 768. This part of the work also includes a borrowing from a version of our second source from the period, the short, anonymous work known as the *Liber Historiae Francorum* or *Book of the History of the Franks*. This was composed around 726/7, possibly at the monastery of Saint-Denis or possibly in Soissons.[55]

In addition, some historical references appear in a small number of hagiographic texts composed in the seventh century, but some of these have been interpolated with later material, or were rewritten to express views favourable to the later Arnulfing or Carolingian dynasty that replaced the Merovingians in 751. A case in point is that of the *Vita Arnulfi*, a life of bishop Arnulf of Metz (614–627/8), one of the ancestors of the Arnulfing–Pippinid family, which dominated Austrasia, the East Frankish kingdom, for much of the second half of the seventh century, as well as in the eighth. A marked characteristic of this work, as of most other Carolingian-influenced hagiography and historiography, was its hostility to the Merovingian Dagobert I (623–38), probably the most powerful and effective of the Frankish kings of the seventh century.[56]

Equally distorted is the narrative of the events of the late seventh century and early eighth of the chronicle known as the *Annales Mettenses Priores*, or *Earlier Metz Annals*. Although once thought to be the product of a later period, as its contents in its present form extend as far as the year 831, it may originally have been compiled around 805, possibly in the convent of Chelles, of which Charlemagne's sister Gisela was the abbess.[57] Its account of the stages and methods through which the Arnulfings gained power in Neustria (West Francia), is highly tendentious and little more than dynastic propaganda, though this is of considerable interest in its own right.[58]

In the light of the limited quantity and demonstrable bias of the historical narratives, other types of evidence become even more significant. For seventh-century Francia this means charters in particular. Many of these have survived, though few as original documents.[59] Most of the ones that have survived belong to the abbey of Saint-Denis, just north of Paris, which was especially patronised by Dagobert I, under whom the expansion of the abbey church probably took place, and who was buried there.[60] With all early Medieval charters, problems of forgery and interpolation of new material into genuine early texts have to be faced.[61] Even when questions of the reliability of the documents have been answered, the nature of the information that such texts can provide is limited. As evidence for the landholdings of an institution they are invaluable, but as testimony to the political and social processes that lie behind the various gifts, sales and exchanges, they are silent or ambiguous.

Into this evidential vacuum, historians studying this period sometimes try to coax other bits and pieces of information or apply new methodological approaches to try to flesh out the very bare bones of what seventh-century Francia has left of itself. Some of the procedures adopted are of limited use. The occasional reliance on texts written in later centuries in the hope that they may contain orally transmitted information of ultimately seventh-century origin is particularly unsatisfactory. Less uncertain are the arguments of some prosopographers, who use the evidence of personal names and family naming patterns (often in sources of widely different date and reliability) to tease out the genealogical links of aristocratic kin groups.[62] While these can be suggestive, the evidential base for such genealogical research only really becomes strong from the eighth century onwards.

All these evidential difficulties are particularly frustrating in the light of the obvious significance of the period. In the course of the years *c.* 638– *c.* 714, the hitherto dominant Merovingian dynasty lost its grip on power, leading in 751 to its replacement by the Arnulfings, or Carolingians, as they came to be known. Traditionally, its decline was attributed to a variety of personal

factors. In particular, the dynasty was thought to be physiologi-
cally and mentally decadent. This was seen as the product of
a mixture of inherited genetic weaknesses and the effects of a
congenital enjoyment of unhealthy living. These features were
held to make themselves felt through the early deaths of the
kings, and a supposed general decline in their mental powers,
together producing a sequence of long minorities and regencies, in the course of which the aristocracy obtained a firm grip
on royal resources and policy-making.[63]

Admittedly, three of the Merovingian kings – Theudebert II
(596–612), Charibert II (629–32) and Clovis II (638–57) – are
described in our sources as being 'simple-minded' or 'mentally
affected', but this is no more than prejudiced authorial comment on their political decisions and was not a judgement on
their sanity.[64] No evidence exists for mental instability in the
Merovingian family. The other general charges levelled against
them also tend to evaporate on closer inspection. The number
and length of minorities are in practice far fewer than has
often been recognised. Only four reigns began with minorities:
those of Sigebert III (634–56), Clovis II (638–57), Chlotar III
(657–73) and Childeric II (662–75). As, technically, such minorities ended at the age of twelve, the years which they covered
would only have been 634–42, 638–45, 657–65 and 662–*c*. 666,
respectively.

It is also significant that, unlike the period 567–613, most of
the seventh century was not a time of warfare between the various Frankish monarchs. The co-existence of rival Merovingian
kingdoms was actually much rarer at this time, and after the
death of Dagobert II of Austrasia in 678/9, an unbroken unitary kingship over all the component parts of Francia was
maintained until 714.[65] All the kings between these dates
exercised their authority from Neustria. (This in fact allowed
the Arnulfings and their aristocratic allies in Austrasia, where
there was normally no resident royal court, to gain an even
greater grip on the resources and patronage of the monarchy
in this region.) In this same period, it should be noticed, there
were no minorities, and two of the kings reached, at least by
Merovingian standards, ripe old ages: Theuderic III (673, 675–
690/1) was approximately thirty-five at the time of his death, as
was his son Childebert III (695–711).

However, for the late seventh and early eighth centuries, our
sources do not refer explicitly, as they had in the earlier cases
of Chlotar II and of Dagobert I, to the kings taking the lead
in events in person or imposing their own will in decision-
making. While it would be unwise to minimise the role played

by achieving consensus among the leading men of the court and regional aristocracies in any period of Frankish history, the later decades of the Merovingian dynasty see few signs of assertiveness by the kings. From the narrative accounts it appears instead that in both the Neustrian and Austrasian courts from 638 onwards the prime movers were the officials holding the office of mayor of the palace in the former and duke in the latter. These men ran the royal administration and exercised patronage over royal lands and appointments, including those to bishoprics, in the kings' names. Under them, there existed a variety of other officer-holders, including the count of the palace, who controlled the royal household. Again, we must not forget that one family of such office holders, the Arnulfings, would transform themselves into the next Frankish royal house, and thus exercise a strong influence on the way the history of this period was written, but they too would be dependent on the need to achieve high levels of aristocratic consensus to make their rule effective.

Initially, the mayors had been chosen by the kings, but in the minorities caused in Neustria by the deaths of Dagobert I in 638 and of Clovis II in 657, it was the leaders of the Frankish nobility that appointed the wives of the former kings (Nantechildis and Baldechildis) to act as regents for their sons and named the new mayors of the palace (Aega and Ebroin).[66] Nantechildis and Aega co-operated closely in the years 638–42, as initially did Baldechildis and Ebroin, though it is possible that the latter forced the queen to retire into the monastery of Chelles in 664/5 when her son Chlotar III attained his majority.[67] From this point onwards, few of the kings are depicted in our sources as exercising personal authority. Some tried to, such as Childeric II when he became king in Neustria in 673 and ordered the flogging of one of the Neustrian nobility, but this led to his murder and that of his pregnant wife by an aristocratic faction in 675.[68]

Although the older arguments concerning the personal failings and psychological weaknesses of the Merovingian line have little to commend them, it does seem to be the case that the period from 638 to the 660s saw a crucial transformation in royal authority in Francia. In both Neustria and Austrasia the coinciding minorities of Clovis II, Clovis III and Sigebert III during these decades enabled powerful factions to form unchecked among the aristocracy. Some of their leaders, notably the Neustrian mayor of the palace Ebroin, were effective manipulators of factional politics.[69] On occasion, internal conflicts within the ruling elite could erupt into violent division, as when Ebroin and his newly appointed Merovingian king Theuderic III were temporarily overthrown in 673.[70] A similar factional conflict in Neustria in 687 led to one party calling on the Austrasian mayor of the palace, Pippin II, for assistance, resulting in the battle of Tertry between Pippin and his Neustrian allies on the one hand and the Neustrian mayor Berchar and king Theuderic III on the other.

It might be thought that the relative powerlessness of the kings in these decades was a symptom of a wider decline of central authority and in administration in Francia. Paradoxically, the reverse may be true. At a formal level, the central governmental apparatus of the Frankish kingdom, as inherited from the late Roman Empire and modified in the earlier Merovingian period, appears surprisingly well maintained in the seventh century. Frankish royal charters – unlike, for example, those of the Lombard monarchy in Italy – still took the form of mandates from the king to the local count – addressed, in late imperial style, as *magnitudo seu utilitas vestra*.[71] These were royal commands to the count to invest the person or institution named in the document with the property or rights that were described, and were not just records of a title granted verbally. This style of text reflected the continuance of close ties between central authority and its local representatives.

The kings retained their powers of appointment to the principal offices of local authority, those of *dux* and *comes* – 'duke' and 'count'. The titles derived from the late Roman military administration, and the functions of the office-holders did not differ much from those of their imperial prototypes. Identical functionaries could be found in Visigothic Spain in the same period. The dukes commanded regional armies, and the counts were the principal royal officials in the *civitates* (the main towns and their dependent territories) of the Frankish kingdoms, with responsibility for any garrison troops, and for the maintenance of local order, and possibly with oversight of the collection of royal revenues from estates and customs duties (*telonea*). Subsections of the *civitates*, called *pagi*, were under the supervision of the count's deputies, known as *Vicarii*.[72]

As well as through his written mandates, the ruler kept in touch in touch with his representatives and the most powerful elements in local society in other ways. Perhaps most important, in this respect, was the annual assembly of the principal men in the kingdom, held in theory on the Kalends of March (1 March), and in practice at some convenient date during the next two to three months, at a site designated by the king. This gathering was of crucial significance, as it was here that discussion of current problems, grievances and military strategy took place. Legal deliberations were also held between the king and 'the elders and Frankish nobility', and these led to the issue of a number of decrees that recorded the decisions thus reached. A small number of these have survived.[73]

The earliest known Frankish law code, the *Lex Salica*, does not present itself as the product of royal will and, contrary to a widespread belief, the evidence for its being issued by Clovis is slight. The earliest manuscript dates to 770, and the first reference to the existence of such a corpus of Frankish law appears in an edict of King Chilperic (561–84), dated to about 574.[74] However, the legal principle referred to in this edict does not appear in any of the variant forms of the text of *Lex Salica* as we now have them. The earliest known version of one of these written texts of *Lex Salica* is a systematised form of it that was issued by king Childebert II at Cologne on 1 March 596.[75] No mention of Clovis can be found in any version of the code, though an ambiguous claim in a preface written in the mid-eighth century that the first sixty-five sections were the work of 'the first king of the Franks' has all too often been assumed to refer to him.[76] This statement could apply as appropriately to Childeric I as to Clovis, and it is actually better understood as just being a general and unspecific assertion of the antiquity of this section of the text, rather than a precise claim that it was the work of some particular royal legislator.

While it is possible that the earliest form of *Lex Salica* was a systematised collection of the edicts of Clovis (possibly including similar decrees from his father), there is absolutely no certainty that this was put together in his reign. That it did indeed derive from a compilation of royal edicts is a reasonable deduction, and it can be shown from internal references that some of these dated from no earlier than 507/8. As explained above, the collection had to have come into existence in or by 596. On the other hand, this code should not be seen as primarily a propaganda manifesto, designed to enhance the status of a Frankish monarch, and make him look more Romanised or even quasi-imperial. Whatever else may be said about it, it should be seen as being intended to have practical as well as symbolic significance, and it certainly did not derive from any hoary pre-Merovingian past of the Frankish people.

The survival of such procedures of centralised administration and law-making gave the Merovingian monarchy a particular inherent strength, irrespective of the capacity or otherwise of the kings themselves. It thus became far more attractive for those who wished to advance themselves to try to gain control of the apparatus of central government rather than to ignore it and focus instead on building up purely regional power bases. In consequence, regionally based aristocratic factions formed alliances and competed to secure dominance over whole kingdoms – Neustria or Austrasia, and ultimately over both together.[77] The final stages and consequences of this process after the battle of Tertry in 687 will need to be examined in a subsequent chapter.

11 From Britain to the kingdoms of the Angles, 410–874

A 'dark age', 410–597

The history of Britain in the centuries following the end of Roman rule is often seen as very different from that of other parts of the former western Empire. This reflects a degree of insularity in the English historiographical tradition, something that is now starting to change, but it is also a reaction to genuine dissimilarities in the development of Britain and other parts of western Europe. However, these may be fewer and less significant than is usually believed. When British conditions are compared with those of the rest of western Europe in the fifth and sixth centuries we may get a clearer perspective.

The principal problem, as always, is one of evidence. The sources for the history of Britain in the fifth century are exceedingly scanty, even if a bit more substantial than those for some earlier periods, when Britain was generally a sleepy and apparently contented part of the Roman Empire.[1] The main difficulty lies in the interpretation of the evidence, and the weight to be placed on the various parts of it. Some of the relevant texts are much later in date than the period they describe, and their usefulness as evidence can depend on our being willing to believe in the existence of 'missing links'; lost intermediate texts, or information being transmitted orally and without significant distortion over the course of centuries.[2]

A good example of this problem comes from the text known from its manuscript title as the *Historia Brittonum* or *History of the Britons*, and which has also been called 'Nennius', after its supposed compiler. This Nennius, whose name does not appear in all of the manuscripts containing the work, was a disciple of a certain Elvodug, who, it has been argued, is identical to Elfoddw (d. 809) 'archbishop of Venedotia' (probably meaning the see of Bangor in Gwynedd).[3] This is a far from certain identification, as is Nennius's responsibility for the compilation, but the evidence of the earliest manuscript seems to place the date of completion of the work in the year 829–30. No two of the manuscripts of it are identical in their contents, and the 'core text' that was put together by the original compiler has to be reconstructed by deduction.[4]

The *Historia Brittonum*, as it is safer to call it, contains a variety of items relating to the history of the island, not least a section

that includes the first reference to 'Arthur' in a list of twelve battles that he is supposed to have fought against the Saxons as war
leader of the Britons.[5] This has particularly engaged the interest of those who believe a genuine historical Arthur lies behind
the figure of medieval legend, but this is just one of the problems raised by this text.[6] The lack of more closely contemporary
evidence for the period has led historians to rely on several of
the tales in the *Historia Brittonum* in their interpretation of the
fifth and sixth centuries in Britain. Only relatively recently has
such an all-inclusive approach to the sources been challenged,
but the scholarly reaction against acceptance of the testimony
of the *Historia* is now general.[7]

The only issue that still seems contentious in the study of this
text concerns one of the sections, which, unlike any other of the
various parts of the work, is dated by reference to consulships.[8]
This form of dating of historical texts was abandoned by the
last quarter of the sixth century throughout Europe, not least
as a result of the abolition of the consular office by the emperor
Justinian in 551. This might imply that this section of the
Historia, which is very brief and contains no more than a few
chronicle-like entries relating to the fifth century, may be of genuinely early date. However, some historians suspect that later
elements have been interpolated into the original chronological
framework, and that it is, in consequence, impossible to rely on
any of its information. This means, for example, that the precise
date it gives for the arrival of the Anglo-Saxons in Britain – in
the fourth year of the reign of Valentinian III (that is, 428–9) –
cannot be trusted.

Other texts that once were seen as helping to make sense of
the history of this period, but which are now distrusted, include
the collection of apparently interrelated poems known as the
Canu Aneirin (Song of Aneirin'), also as the *Gododdin*.[9] These take
the form of a series of bardic laments over a group of British
warriors, who at the behest of the king of Gododdin, a British
kingdom centred on Dun Eddin (Edinburgh), fought against the
Saxons at Catraeth (Catterick in Co. Durham), perhaps around
the year 600. The text has proved extraordinarily difficult to
understand; so much so that one of its first editors revised and
translated it as if it dealt with a battle fought in 1098 in North
Wales between the Norman Earl of Shrewsbury and king
Magnus III of Norway![10] If more recent scholarship has res-
cued the work from that fate, and shown it to be about a 'Dark
Age' battle instead, it has still not been able to prove the reality of the war described or establish how close the composition
of the poems may have been to the event they describe. Similar

problems affect the rest of the small corpus of early Welsh (in language) poetry relating to historical episodes in this period.[11]

If all the *Historia Brittonum* materials and the Welsh heroic poems must be distrusted, then the quantity of usable evidence for the history of Britain in the period *c.* 410–*c.* 597 is very small indeed. Its most substantial component is the work of the monk Gildas, entitled *De Excidio Brittonum* or *The Ruin of the Britons*. While earlier generations of historians tended to take Gildas's work as an objective narrative of events, it is now seen as a work of moral exhortation that makes some historical references, but in a deliberately tendentious way. It is thus very like the early-fifth-century work, *De Gubernatione Dei* or *On the Governance of God* of the Gallic priest Salvian. This too tended to be rummaged in by historians looking for information about the economic and moral decline of the western Roman Empire, ignoring its author's real purposes and achievement.

It is not possible to be certain when Gildas wrote (probably *c.* 540, but possibly as early as *c.* 520), or be sure where he was working.[12] Later Celtic *Lives* of Gildas offer no reliable information, and little trust is now placed in the idea that he spent his later years in Brittany.[13] A brief penitential for monks is also ascribed to this author. From the details of the penances it imposed – referring to British cheese and Roman units of liquid measurement – it is certainly a British work, but is now thought unlikely to have been written by Gildas.[14]

Possibly the most important thing to understand in making sense of Gildas's *De Excidio* is that the opening historical survey, which is intended to provide the context for his denunciation of British vices, is not chronologically sequential. In the book, the problems the Britons faced in the late fourth and the fifth centuries with the Picts and the Irish appear to precede all their conflicts with the Saxons, but this is because Gildas arranged his materials so that he could describe the wars with the Irish and the Picts first, before turning to those against the Saxons.[15] Ignoring this organisational principle has led, not surprisingly, to chronological problems for historians of the period.

Without delving too deeply into the arguments, it is possible to suggest at least some conclusions that seem to be supported by this limited body of evidence. First, soon after the withdrawal of the units of the Roman field army from Britain by Constantine III in 407, parts of the island were raided by Picts, Irish and Saxons, and in limited areas in the west of the island, such as the Dafyd peninsula, some colonisation by the Irish occurred. Second, from some point in the first half of the fifth century, Saxons, who themselves had been making seaborne raids in the Channel, were hired by the rulers in the southern half of Britain to defend the coasts against the Irish and the Picts. Thus they were introduced into Britain, in a way similar to that by which the Franks and the Visigoths established themselves in northern Francia and Spain, taking on the role that had once been occupied by the Roman army. Increasing numbers of Saxons seem to have been settled at various points in eastern and northern Britain through such agreements. It is possible that the imperial government, then controlled by Aetius, was involved in the making of at least one such treaty of federation around the year 442, but the primary responsibility lay with the various local potentates and oligarchies that came to power in the island after the ending of direct Roman rule, and about whom we know very little.[16]

Now it is normally thought that the most significant feature of the history of the period between 410 and the time when Gildas was writing his *De Excidio* (*c.* 520–40) was the revolt of the Saxons against the Britons, and their ensuing conquest of much of the eastern half of Britain. This used to be thought to involve the Saxons 'pushing' the Britons westwards into the regions of Wales, Cumbria and the south-west. But Gildas's work implies that the problems with the Saxons had been settled, after some heavy fighting, some forty years earlier than the time of his writing, thus in the 480s or around 500. For him, the Saxon menace was a thing of the past.[17]

Taking the period *c.* 410–*c.* 540 as a whole, what was more significant than the occasional problems with the Saxons was the disappearance in Britain of centralised government. In 410, a unitary authority still existed in the island – other than in the regions north of Hadrian's Wall – which had totally disappeared by the mid-sixth century, to be replaced by a series of small-scale and mutually antagonistic kingdoms. Gildas refers to the rulers of a number of these: Constantine of Dumnonia, Aurelius Caninus, Vortipor of the Demetae, Cuneglasus and Maglocunus.[18] Dumnonia is easily located (in the area of Devon) because of the implied relationship with the Celtic tribe of the Dumnonii, and Maglocunus can almost certainly to be identified with a king of Gwynedd known in later vernacular sources as Maelgw(y)n.[19] Attempts have been made to locate the other kingdoms, but these are at best approximate, and because of the later fame of Gildas's work little reliance should be placed on the appearance of some of these names in later Welsh royal genealogies.[20]

Even so, the phenomenon they represent is well attested, not only in the west, but also in the north, and beyond Hadrian's

Wall, where tribal kingdoms had long existed. Moreover, such kingdoms were also coming into existence in the centre and east of the island in the course of the sixth century. That the populations subject to the rulers of these kingdoms were in some cases exclusively Celtic-speaking, and in others both Celtic- and Germanic-speaking, is of rather less importance than has often been assumed. That the Saxons massacred or expelled the British inhabitants of the lowland parts of the island is no longer believed, and even in areas that were, politically speaking, under Saxon rule, there is now no doubt that substantial elements of the former Romano-British population survived.[21] In such regions, intermarriage and mutual cultural assimilation seem to have produced quite homogeneous societies, in which, for example, Old-English-speaking kings could have Celtic names.[22] In some cases, a new socio-political identity was formed that derived from both traditions, as in the case of Kent, an area of major and early settlement by migrants from the Continent, which came to be called the Kingdom of the *Cantuarii* or the *Cantware*, a name derived from the pre-Roman inhabitants, the *Cantiaci*. Its rulers all had Germanic names.

Difficulties come from imposing the perspectives of later centuries on to the realities of the later fifth and the sixth. By the middle of the seventh century, relatively large kingdoms had emerged in Britain that had not existed a hundred years earlier. Subsequently, in at least one of these, the southern kingdom of Wessex, a historiographical tradition developed that created a fictitious past for its royal dynasty. Thus, the compilers of the late-ninth-century first version of the *Anglo-Saxon Chronicle* looked for what they expected to find: a history of their kingdom in a period, the sixth century, in which it had not even existed.[23]

The second half of the sixth century in Britain was a violent but 'entrepreneurial' age, in which numerous individuals and families of mixed Anglian or Saxon and Romano-British origin struggled to secure local power for themselves. The scale of operation of such 'warlords' was generally quite small and geographically limited, but in comparative terms some did very well indeed for themselves. A case in point might be Ceawlin (fl. 556–93), one of those presented by the *Anglo-Saxon Chronicle* as being a king of Wessex, though the area of his recorded activities, in the upper Thames and the Cotswolds, was far removed from the heartlands of the later kingdom, as it also was from the areas in the south of modern Hampshire in which the *Chronicle* locates his supposed relatives and his predecessors.[24]

As the dates for Ceawlin's career come exclusively from the *Anglo-Saxon Chronicle* – the chronological reliability of which is questionable for any period up to the late ninth century – some latitude must be allowed in trying to give a modern account of his career. Taking the *Chronicle* references as approximations (or at worst as guesses), it is in the year 556 that Ceawlin first appears, fighting together with a certain Cynric against the Britons at *Beranburh*. However, as this same Cynric, the son of Cerdic, is also recorded in the *Chronicle* as arriving in Britain in 495, it is hard to believe that he was apparently still going strong over sixty years later.

There is an unbridgeable chronological gulf between the supposed founding period of the notional kingdom of Wessex in the late fifth century and the next period in which those who are said to be members of its ruling house appear, in the second half of the sixth century. Much of the information relating to the early phase is of a distinctly 'folkloric' or rationalising character: for example, Cerdic and Cynric land at a place called *Cerdicesora;* they kill a 'Welsh' king called Natanleod, and subsequently that district is called *Natanleod* (Netley near Southampton), and so on.[25] It must be suspected that the place names preceded the persons referred to, rather than the reverse, and that the history of the latter was concocted to explain the existence of the former.

Genealogical information is equally dubious. Ceawlin's relationship to Cerdic and Cynric is never specified in the *Chronicle*, though he is said in the entry for the year 560 to have succeeded to the kingdom of Wessex that they created.[26] For 568, it is reported that Ceawlin and a certain Cutha fought against Æthelberht of Kent. In 577, he appears fighting alongside someone called Cuthwine against the Britons in the battle of Dyrham (probably the manor of that name close to Bath). To complicate matters further, an otherwise unattested Cuthwulf is reported to have fought the Britons at *Bedcanford* in 571. The continuators of the original version of the *Chronicle* were as confused as are modern historians by all this, and one of them, the scribe of the 'E' or Parker version, added to the text concerning the year 571 a note saying 'That Cutha was the brother of Ceawlin'. As this is not common to all the versions of the *Chronicle* it cannot belong to the core text, and must be a later insertion. Unwisely, some historians, clutching at evidential straws, have believed it.[27]

The battle reported to have taken place at Dyrham in 577 in which Ceawlin and Cuthwine fought against and killed the kings of Bath, Cirencester and Gloucester, is particularly intriguing. It implies, for one thing, the continued occupation of these Roman towns and the existence of various otherwise unattested small kingdoms in the Cotswolds and the Severn valley. Unfortunately, archaeology cannot yet confirm any occupation of Bath between the fourth and seventh centuries; though it is possible that this should be sought in the context of a reoccupied hill fort close by rather than in the former Roman settlement. In the case of Cirencester, however, fairly extensive excavation has revealed that the former Roman amphitheatre, outside the city walls, was converted for occupation in the fifth century.[28] This is something that also happened in a number of towns in the south of France in the seventh and eighth centuries, but so far in the case of Cirencester no evidence of occupation into the sixth century has yet been detected.

If a battle was fought at Dyrham – possibly around another hill fort there – in the late sixth century, and if, as the *Chronicle* records, this led to the conquest of the three small kingdoms by Ceawlin and his allies, this should not be seen in the context of an 'Anglo-Saxon' advance at the expense of the 'Britons', as the later Wessex sources would like to portray it. Certainly, the archaeological evidence from the Severn valley does not confirm a Saxon presence there in cultural terms at this time.[29]

As has been stressed above, it is important to separate the 'Anglianisation' of the culture and language of lowland Britain from the political history of the various kingdoms of mixed Saxon and Celtic origin that were being created – and in many cases also destroyed – in this formative period of the sixth century and the first half of the seventh. Perhaps the nearest the *Anglo-Saxon Chronicle* gets to capturing the reality of this time is in its entry for 597, when it records that Ceolwulf, whom it presents as king of Wessex, 'ever fought and made war either against the Angles, or against the Welsh, or against the Picts, or against the Scots'. Quite how he came to encounter Picts, whose kingdoms were north of the Forth–Clyde valleys at this time, is not explained, and the only people whom the *Chronicle* record him as fighting against were the South Saxons, but as a piece of literary invention this brief entry captures the spirit of this entrepreneurial age.[30]

New Christian kingdoms, 598–685

By the very end of the sixth century, larger, more coherent, kingdoms had emerged in Kent under Æthelberht (565?–616) and in Northumbria under Æthelfrith (*c.* 593–617). The latter evolved from the union of the two smaller kingdoms of Bernicia and Deira, probably divided by the valley of the Tees, which both had Celtic names, testifying again to the fusion of Anglo-Saxon and Romano-British elements in the formation of so many of the societies that developed in the eastern and central parts of Britain in the sixth century.[31]

An obvious question about cultural survivals from the earlier Roman domination of the island is whether there was continuity in the practice of Christianity. Evidence relating to the establishment of Christianity in Britain in the fourth century is itself extremely hard to find, but there are few reasons to doubt that it was present in the three Roman provinces by the time imperial rule had come to an end in 410.[32] What is notable is the strength of Christianity in those areas of Britain which, under the Empire, had been the least Romanised, or where the imperial presence had been predominantly military – that is, in the mountains of Wales and along the northern frontiers.

The penetration of Christianity into these regions may well have been the product of a cultural osmosis between the British kingdoms north of Hadrian's Wall and the Empire to the south. Though it is often suggested that the north of Roman Britain was essentially a military zone, with little civilian settlement and limited Romanisation, the evidence of the impact of Roman material culture north of the Wall might give grounds for doubt. Conflict and resistance in military terms should not necessarily be equated with hostility in cultural ones.

It is possible, however, that the disintegration of the fixed frontier between the Empire and the British tribes to the north of the Wall that came about in the late fourth century accelerated the process of communication and exchange, in which the import of Christianity from the south became a major feature. By the middle of the fifth century, a Christian community certainly existed in Galloway, as is recorded in inscriptions from both Whithorn and Kirkmadrine. The former is usually identified as the church of *Candida Casa* ('the White House') that was founded by the missionary bishop Nynia (popularly known as Ninian) according to the account of him given by the Northumbrian monk Bede in his *Historia Ecclesiastica Gentis Anglorum* (*Ecclesiastical History of the English People*) of 731.[33] The inscriptions record the existence of various named bishops and clerics in this region probably in the later fifth century, and the possible dedication of a church.[34] Nynia, who cannot easily be dated from Bede, may have lived up to half a century earlier or later, and the association of his *Candida Casa* with Whithorn is less secure than is usually believed. Even his name is uncertain, and it has been suggested that he could be the same person as a British monastic founder, Vinniau, who was known to Gildas, and/or a sixth century abbot in Ireland called Finnan, who may be of either Irish or British origin. The latter suggestion has been greeted with hostility by some modern Irish scholars who would not like their Church to have so strong a debt to Britain.

For Bede, what matters about 'Ninian' or Nynia, is his role in spreading Christianity to the kingdom(s) of the Picts. They used to be seen, like the Basques, as one of the oldest and longest established of the peoples of Western Europe, with an origin in the period before the Indo-European migrations into Western Europe in the early Iron Age. Such a view derived primarily from the linguistic analysis of a handful of inscriptions dating from the seventh to ninth centuries, some elements of which were thought to be non-Indo-European. However, this has recently been challenged, and the scanty linguistic evidence relating to Pictish suggests it is in fact a Celtic language of the 'P' family (which includes Welsh, Cornish and Breton, but not Irish and Scots Gaelic, which form the 'Q' family). Despite their own rather bizarre legends of their origins, recorded by Bede, that present the Picts as post-Roman immigrants into Scotland, archaeological evidence suggests continuity in their presence on the Scottish mainland and in the northern isles from at least the Iron Age onwards. While the best known Pictish monuments dating to the period after the end of Roman rule are a series of finely carved free-standing symbol stones, the exact purpose and meaning of which continue to be a source of debate, there is also now secure evidence of their owning and copying books.[35] In particular, excavations at Tarbert in Easter Ross on the site of a monastery of probably eighth century date have uncovered material remains of book production. The contents of the lost manuscripts of Pictland is unknown as none have survived, but some suggestions as to the identity of some of them could be made from Biblical stories that seem to have inspired the more elaborate scenes on a small number of the symbol stones, some features of which imply the influence of late antique exegetical texts. The literacy that all this evidence implies was primarily or entirely confined to the clergy, as in the case of the Anglo-Saxon kingdoms at this time, but reflects the successful spread of Christianity into the Pictish lands.

Conflicting traditions about the routes and timing of this penetration of Christianity, and some of the wider intellectual culture of the Mediterranean Roman world, into their society may have led to the belief that the conversion affected at least two separate groups of Picts, and at different times. Bede, writing in 731, has Nynia converting the 'southern Picts' in the fifth century, while the Irish abbot, Columba (d. 597), the founder of the monastery of Iona off the west coast of the Isle of Mull in the Inner Hebrides, is described in the '*Life*' written about him around 696/7 by his successor, Adamnán, as converting those Picts subject to a King Bruide, who had a royal centre at the northern end of Loch Ness.[36] It has therefore been assumed that Nynia's mission from Galloway was to a southern Pictish kingdom, while that of Columba was to a northern one, with a dividing line between the two lying somewhere in the region of the Mounth, the line of the Grampian mountains that divides eastern Scotland into northern and southern sections. However, serious reservations have rightly been expressed as to the validity of both of these accounts of missionary activity. There are no reasons to believe there were only two Pictish kingdoms in the fifth and sixth centuries.[37] The unique roles claimed for both Nynia and Columba are better understood as reflecting the importance that came to be attached to these two founding figures in the quite separate traditions of Whithorn (even if not the real *Candida Casa*) and of Iona, respectively. They do not constitute reliable evidence of their actual personal involvement in such missionary labours. As in the similar case of Patrick in Ireland (see Chapter 13), it is unwise to place too much emphasis on the work of single individual missionaries, however exalted, rather than focusing on the gradual dissemination of Christianity into new areas through prolonged cultural contact and exchange.

The survival of Christianity in the lowland regions of central and southern Britain, which came under the domination of rulers of Germanic-speaking (that is, Old English-speaking) rulers – even if in some cases with Celtic names – and where the bulk of the new immigrants had settled, is an even more contentious subject of enquiry than its northwards extension beyond Hadrian's Wall. The simple view, derived from the great *Ecclesiastical History* of Bede (d. 735), is that the Anglo-Saxon kingdoms and all their inhabitants were pagan until the arrival of the mission sent to Kent by pope Gregory the Great in 597. Yet even Bede's own account, deriving from information he received from Canterbury, reveals certain anomalies.

The king of Kent, Æthelberht, to whom the mission led by the monk Augustine was sent, had married the daughter of the Frankish king Charibert (561–7). In so doing he had had to agree that she should be permitted to continue the practice of her own religion, and she had been accompanied to Kent by the Frankish bishop Liudhard, who is usually described as her chaplain.[38] However, in this period bishops are never to be found without an episcopal see, and were never sent or consecrated other than to existing Christian communities, therefore the fact that a Frankish bishop was exercising his ministry in Kent in the second half of the sixth century might imply that a body of fellow believers already existed there before his arrival.[39] For them to need a bishop would also suggest that several clergy of lesser rank were already carrying out their ministry. So the presence of Liudhard in Canterbury might imply the existence of a Christian community in Kent prior to Augustine's arrival in 597.

Even so, the appearance of the group of monks sent from Rome by the pope, probably at Æthelberht's request – for that is what Gregory said in a letter to the Frankish rulers – was crucial, in that it led to the baptism of the king and of substantial numbers of his subjects.[40] A new ecclesiastical organisation developed, despite a brief setback caused by the initial apostasy of Æthelberht's son, king Eadbald (616–40). He subsequently came to see the advantages of conversion, and *his* son and successor, Eorcenberht (640–64) became a still more thoroughgoing Christian, even imposing the observance of Lent on his subjects.[41]

The Roman mission to Kent had extended its sphere of influence northwards in 625, when a sister of Eadbald had married king Edwin of Northumbria (616–32), who agreed to accept Christianity as well as a Christian wife. One of the Roman missionaries, Paulinus, who had been sent by pope Gregory to Britain in a second expedition in 601, was consecrated as bishop and accompanied the queen to Northumbria to begin the conversion of the king's followers. However, Edwin's death in 632 in battle against king Cadwallon of Gwynedd and Penda, the king of the Mercians, led to the collapse of his mission. Paulinus, recently appointed as the first archbishop of York, fled south, and was subsequently assigned the see of Rochester in Kent.[42]

In practice, the most significant consequence of these events was that power in Northumbria passed back into the hands of a rival branch of the royal dynasty, whose leader, Oswald, defeated and killed the invading Cadwallon in 633. Oswald (633–42), the son of Æthelfrith, had been converted to Christianity by Irish monks while in exile after Edwin had overthrown his father. (The contentious issues of the origin and nature of Christianity in Ireland will be discussed in Chapter 13.) So, once he was secure on the throne of Northumbria he turned to the Irish monks of Iona to take the place of Paulinus and his southern followers, who had been so closely associated with the rival regime of Edwin and the now much diminished Kingdom of Kent.[43]

The ecclesiastical organisation that had developed in the Mediterranean at the time of the late Roman Empire depended on towns for its structure. Towns were the centres of local administration and fiscal organisation, and the principal local landowners would in most cases also have urban residences. Towns were also the principal market places for the surplus goods of the countryside and the centres in which skilled trades, such as pottery making, could be maintained, depending on a network of exchange relationships with rural as well as urban consumers. Thus, just as civil magistrates, many of whose responsibilities they came to share, administered justice from the towns, so bishops oversaw the ecclesiastical organisation and discipline of their dioceses from an urban centre. Similarly, in pre-Christian Roman times, towns had been the cult centres for the surrounding region, and this was something that the new religion had been able to capitalise on, installing the Christian martyrs as the spiritual patrons of towns and their hinterlands.

This was the pattern that Christian organisation depended on, and which Gregory the Great had obviously envisaged for the Anglo-Saxon kingdoms as conversion spread. He had already devised a blueprint for new episcopal sees and their locations, in which metropolitan (later called archiepiscopal) sees would be established in London and York, with each having twelve suffragan or subordinate dioceses under its jurisdiction.[44] In practice, the realities on the ground were rather different from those understood in Rome. Thus London, the principal administrative centre of late Roman Britain, and probably at that time the largest town in the British provinces, was by the late sixth century part of the territory of the relatively minor kingdom of the East Saxons, and therefore not a suitable headquarters for a Church dependent primarily on the patronage of the kings of Kent. Instead, Canterbury, described by Bede as the *metropolis* of all of Æthelberht's domain, became the see of Augustine and his successors.[45] In the north, while York did become the seat, albeit intermittently, of an archbishop, it long remained the only episcopal see in the kingdom of Deira. Its only suffragans were to be three bishoprics based on monasteries in Bernicia and a fourth, briefly established at Abercorn near Edinburgh during the period of Northumbrian expansion northwards in the mid-seventh century.

It is important to understand something of the state of towns in Anglo-Saxon England in this period if the nature and organisation of the Church are to be understood. The tendency in the past, partly based on views of a thorough 'Germanisation' of lowland Britain, and partly on the negative results of excavations, was to reject the idea of any post-Roman urban survival in the island. More recent excavation, using more sensitive techniques, has uncovered some evidence of continuing, if low-level, occupation of much-reduced town sites in a number of cases, including

Cirencester, Wroxeter and Carlisle, as well as in the former Roman fort of Housesteads. As this last example suggests, such continuities were limited, both in time and extent. Continuing occupation of these and other sites may have amounted to little more than the presence of local potentates and their immediate followers, basing themselves in such largely derelict centres because of their earlier associations with Rome. A flavour of this is given in the Old English poem known as 'The Ruin', thought to refer to the former Roman town of *Aquae Sulis* (now Bath).

Perhaps some Roman towns still functioned as centres of administration, even if their economic roles as markets and centres of population had declined. Canterbury is obviously a case in point, and in Northumbria it seems likely that York remained an important if occasional royal centre, where the king's palace may have been located within the former Roman military headquarters complex. In some cases, strategic or other considerations had led to the relocation of the new centre to a site close to, but no longer within the confines of the previous Roman settlement. This was the case with both Cirencester and *Verulamium*/St Albans. Other 'towns' that feature in the albeit problematic literary sources include Bath, Gloucester, Lincoln, Rochester, Dorchester (Oxon), Edinburgh and Dumbarton.[46]

The number of such survivals was small and in none of these cases, any more than with York or Canterbury, should large-scale occupation be imagined. As previously mentioned, the need for towns as specialised centres of production and as market places for rural produce had declined greatly, not only in Britain but throughout most of the former western Roman Empire from the fifth century onwards. Where towns continued to function it was more as ceremonial and government centres. Because of the previous ecclesiastical organisation and the pre-existing links between urban cult sites and rural worshippers, earlier stone-built church complexes – containing church buildings, baptisteries and episcopal palaces – continued to be occupied and to serve an increasingly ruralised congregation. Thus it is possible to imagine that the major festivals of the Church's year and local patronal festivals would attract country-dwelling Christians to the urban cult sites, doubtless with opportunities for regional market exchange to take place at the same time. Similarly, the rulers, or in larger kingdoms their local representatives, could periodically conduct business in such settings: holding courts and conducting consultations with the leading men of the area or of the kingdom.

It is important also to take into account the role of rural royal residences and administrative sites, such as that excavated at

Yeavering in the Northumbrian kingdom of Bernicia.[47] These would be especially prominent in such kingdoms as Bernicia or East Anglia, which for historical reasons lacked the major Roman towns of some of the other kingdoms, but it is important also to bear in mind that the Merovingian kings similarly appear to have spent most of their time in rural palaces and only occasionally held assemblies and winter courts in towns such as Soissons.

Overall, the nature of the ecclesiastical organisation that developed in lowland Britain in the sixth century was conditioned by such factors as the pre-existence and survival of towns. In a few cases, such as that of Canterbury, where towns were still used as major royal centres, episcopal monasteries of the type that were common in continental Europe (see Chapter 13) could develop. Thus the monks who accompanied Augustine to Kent in 597 were established in the monastery of St Peter, later known as St Augustine's, which became the burial place for the first archbishops and for several of the Kentish kings. In other areas, notably in Northumbria, rural monasteries were the norm.

Monastic establishments very similar to those then to be found in Ireland and on Iona, with wooden buildings and numerous individual cells, were created under Irish inspiration in Northumbria in the mid-seventh century, notably at Lindisfarne, and at both Hartlepool and Whitby, which were ruled by the abbess Hild, a member of the royal family. Others, such as the joint monastery of St Paul at Jarrow and St Peter at Wearmouth, where Bede lived and worked, were partly built in stone, had a more communal organisation, and were generally more strongly influenced by Mediterranean traditions and artistic styles.[48] As the decoration of the famous Lindisfarne Gospels shows (see below), these two cultural and artistic currents were not mutually antagonistic and could coexist both on the page of a manuscript and in the way in which the monasteries were run. But at the Synod of Whitby in 664, debates were held on the respective merits of Irish and Roman customs for the calculation of the date of Easter and the form of the monastic tonsure. With the explicit approval of the Northumbrian king Oswy (642–70), who was present, victory in both arguments went to the supporters of Roman practices, led by the future bishop Wilfrid (d. 709). Those who insisted on retaining the now-condemned Irish customs were forced to leave the kingdom.[49]

Because of the papal inspiration behind the Augustinian mission and the role that Gregory the Great and his successors played in instructing and advising both Augustine and the kings of Kent and Northumbria, very close ties were formed between the Roman Church and that in the Anglo-Saxon kingdoms. It became customary for the archbishops of Canterbury, from Augustine onwards, to receive from the pope after the archbishop's consecration a thin woollen stole called a *pallium*. This was worn around the neck during the performance of the liturgy, as a sign of their special and subordinate relationship. The first account of the life of Gregory the Great was written early in the eighth century in the Northumbrian monastery of Whitby.[50] Thus, despite the largely Irish origins of Christianity in the Anglo-Saxon kingdom of Northumbria, by the later seventh century, kings such as Oswy and aristocratic monastic founders such as Benedict Biscop were looking primarily to Rome for instruction – as were the Irish themselves.

Biscop, the founder of the family monastery of Wearmouth (674) and Jarrow (681), made a number of journeys to Rome to buy books, to obtain the service of specialist craftsmen in such arts as glass making, and to obtain direction on Roman liturgical procedures. For the latter, pope Agatho (678–81) sent the papal arch-cantor John to Wearmouth and Jarrow with Biscop to provide instruction on the spot – and to carry out an investigation into the orthodoxy of the teaching of the English Church.[51] By the early eighth century, the monastery of Wearmouth-Jarrow was able to produce such a masterwork of Mediterranean-style calligraphic and book-painting art as the *Codex Amiatinus* (pre-716), which was to be sent as a present to Rome, that for a long time modern palaeographers were unwilling to accept it as a manuscript of English provenance.[52]

The fusion of Irish and Mediterranean traditions in northern Britain has also left tangible results in the artistic products of Northumbria from the later seventh and the eighth centuries, particularly in the fields of manuscript illumination and sculpture. In both areas, what is most notable is the juxtaposition or co-existence of elements that are either clearly Celtic or Roman in inspiration. In such well-known manuscripts as the Lindisfarne Gospels, written a little before the year 698 by Eadfrith, bishop of Lindisfarne (698–721), the text is decorated in a purely Celtic fashion, while the full-page portraits of the four evangelists are clearly dependent on late antique models from the Mediterranean.[53] Similarly, the earliest works of monumental sculpture produced in the northern Anglo-Saxon kingdoms, principally a series of large free-standing crosses, can display a combination of sophisticated and well understood use of Mediterranean models for figurative art with decorative features that are purely Celtic in inspiration – or they can adhere exclusively to one style or the other.[54]

The Mercian hegemony, 633–874

By the time this artistic and intellectual revival was taking place in the north, the kingdom of Kent had become, politically speaking, a backwater, and had long been overtaken in size and military strength by the more recently developed kingdoms of Wessex and Mercia. The latter, which derived from the amalgamation and conquest of a large number of very small kingdoms (often seen, rather misleadingly, as separate 'tribes' or peoples), only really emerges into historiographical view under its king Penda (626?–55).[55] He was a pagan until his death, though initially the ally, or possibly the subordinate, of the Christian king Cadwallon of Gwynedd (north-west Wales), and this, together with his conflicts with neighbouring kingdoms, has inevitably coloured his presentation in the major narrative sources pertinent to the period: the Northumbrian (and partly Kentish) *Ecclesiastical History* of Bede and the West Saxon *Anglo-Saxon Chronicle*.

In practice, though, Penda may have been the first of the kings of the central part of Britain who, through conquest and diplomacy, was able to put together a powerful confederacy uniting a number of hitherto disparate small kingdoms. Some of these elements may still be seen in an eighth-century document, possibly a tribute list of the Mercian kings of that period, known as the *Tribal Hudeage*.[56] It would be unwise to regard the various 'peoples' listed in this as being separate ethnic entities or survivals of earlier Germanic tribal divisions. They are more likely to represent the small kingdoms in the central parts of the island that came into existence in the fifth and sixth centuries, and were finally swallowed up by the most successful of their number, the Mercian kingdom of Penda, in the first half of the seventh. The most substantial of these conquests at this time was probably another large-scale kingdom, though one in embryo form, that was known as the kingdom of the Middle Angles. Although artificially preserved as an appanage until 656, this then disappeared.[57]

For all his success in subjecting these smaller components of what was to become the kingdom of Mercia, together with his elimination of the rival Middle Anglian kingdom, Penda was not, in the 630s, able to compete with the longer-established, large-scale kingdoms that surrounded his. Hence, when threatened by Northumbrian ambitions, he found it expedient to ally with the dominant British kingdom of the west, that of Gwynedd. This pagan–Christian/Saxon–Celt (distinctions which clearly mattered little in the 630s) confederacy was the product of the threat posed to both by the expanding power of the

Northumbrian king Edwin (617–32), who was defeated and killed by the allies at the battle of Hatfield Chase.[58] As seen through the eyes of Bede, the Northumbrians take centre stage in the complex pattern of events of the middle of the seventh century, but in practice these could be reinterpreted as the successful resistance of the Mercians to this threat of domination from the north, and their consequent rise to overlordship over all the kingdoms of southern and central Britain.

The problems of small-scale Early Medieval warfare are well illustrated by the outcome of the overthrow of Edwin in 632. The two component kingdoms of Northumbria split, each acquiring a new king from the rival branches of the royal line, but both of these monarchs were killed by Cadwallon in 633. However, Oswald, the brother of one of them, Eanfrith of Bernicia, was able to defeat and kill the British king in yet another battle in 633 at *Deniseburn*.[59] The small size of the armies and the difficulties of a king (whose centre of power was in North Wales) in imposing his authority over the region of modern Yorkshire made Cadwallon's attempt to hold on to Northumbria very fragile. Oswald was, thanks to his victory, able to revive his predecessor Edwin's ambitions, which included dominance over the kingdoms of central Britain. It was not until 642 that Penda could mount a renewed resistance to Northumbrian hegemony, defeating and killing Oswald at the battle of *Maserfelth* (probably Oswestry) – possibly, to judge by the location, with British assistance.[60]

This battle was crucial, in that in practice it marked the end of Northumbrian attempts to expand south-westwards. From 642 to 655, Penda and his new Mercian kingdom represented the greatest power among the kingdoms of Britain. One of the sons of the next Northumbrian king, Oswy (642–70), was held hostage at the Mercian court. Cenwalh, the king of Wessex, was briefly expelled from his kingdom by Penda (645/6?) and the East Anglian king Anna was killed by him in 654.[61] It is notable how many kings died in battle in this period, and it is likely that the fate of the commander was crucial in determining the outcome of these inter-kingdom conflicts, fought with small armies with ties of personal loyalty to their leader. Penda himself was killed in an invasion of Northumbria in 655 in a battle fought on the river *Winwaed*, probably near Leeds.

While these events might suggest rapid and dramatic fluctuation, it is clear that Penda's achievements, little as we may now know of them, were permanent ones. In Northumbrian tradition, Oswy emerged as having authority over the kings of the south, but in practice this was short-lived. After the overthrow of Penda, he set up the latter's son, Peada, as king of the southern part of Mercia, keeping the northern territories for himself. But in 658 Peada was murdered by the Mercian nobility, who chose his brother Wulfhere (658–74) as king, and re-established freedom from Northumbrian hegemony.[62] Bede again conceals this process, but it is clear that Wulfhere recovered his father's overlordship of the East Saxon kingdom, and very probably that over the East Angles as well. He also regained control of the northern parts of Mercia, including former dependent territories such as the kingdom of Lindsey (Lincolnshire).[63] His heir, Ethelred (674–704), also ravaged the kingdom of Kent in 676, and reimposed Mercian rule on Lindsey after this region had passed briefly back into Northumbrian control *c.* 674.[64]

Although under Oswy's son Ecgfrith (670–85) the Northumbrian kingdom kept up its hopes of regaining influence in the south, and substantially extended itself northwards, eliminating any remaining British kingdoms between Hadrian's Wall and the Firth of Forth, this expansion was terminated and then rapidly reversed as a result of the king's defeat and death at the hands of the Picts at the battle of Dunnichen (near Aberlemno in Angus), following the revolt of their king Bruide against Northumbrian hegemony. It has been suggested very plausibly that it was Ecgfrith's previous defeat at the hands of the Mercians that emboldened the Pictish king to take this successful stand against his overlord.[65] Thereafter a truncated and confined Northumbria entered a period of internal instability and stagnation.

On the other hand, the Mercian kingdom was able to exploit the achievements of Penda and Wulfhere, and turn its hegemony over the other realms of southern, eastern and central Britain into the norm. There has been a tendency to talk of this period of Mercian ascendancy as being a product of the eighth century, but it is important to see how much of it had already been achieved from the 640s onwards, and the degree to which the eighth-century kings were preserving the state of political affairs that they inherited from their predecessors.[66]

Christianity was introduced into Mercia, first through Irish and Northumbrian influence in the 650s. A single bishopric for the kingdom, including Lindsey, was established around 653 and held by a succession of Irish or Irish-trained bishops.[67] Under bishop Chad (669–71), an episcopal centre was established at Lichfield, which became the principal seat of the Mercian bishops. A second diocese was established in the eastern region of the kingdom around 674.[68]

The close links between the papacy and the Anglo-Saxon kingdoms were emphasised by the growth of the practice of kings of renouncing their thrones to retire into monastic life, either in

Britain or in Rome.[69] The Mercian king Ethelred retired to the
monastery of Bardney in Lindsey in 704. His nephew and successor, Ceonred (704–9) withdrew to Rome; a step so unusual
that it was recorded in the official collection of papal biographies
known as the *Liber Pontificalis*, as well as approvingly in the pages
of Bede's history.[70] In this decision he had, however, been preceded by king Caedwalla of Wessex, who had gone to Rome specially to be baptised by the pope in 688. He had, however, died
there nine days later, so it is not clear whether he had proposed
to make his stay a permanent one as Ceonred had.[71]

The successors of both of these kings – Ine of Wessex (688–
728) and Ceolred of Mercia (709–16) – are reported to have
fought each other at Alton Priors in Wiltshire in 715.[72] The outcome is unknown, but the location would argue that this was an
act of Mercian aggression, very much in line with the style of
kingship practised from the time of Penda onwards. Ceolred's
successor Æthelbald (716–57) appears as a monarch of the same
stamp, anxious to impose Mercian hegemony on his neighbours,
and to obtain material benefits from it.

Evidential shortage is peculiarly frustrating in the case of the
eighth century in Britain, especially in contrast with the relative profusion of the source materials relating to the seventh
century. Bede, who was writing in the 730s, has much less to
say about the early decades of the eighth century, but does at
least confirm that in 731 'all of these kingdoms [Wessex, Essex,
Sussex, East Anglia, Kent and the kingdom of the Hwicce]
and the other southern kingdoms which reach right up to
the Humber, together with their various kings, are subject
to Æthelbald, king of Mercia'.[73] The details of how this was
achieved and precisely how it expressed itself are not revealed.
The whole nature of 'overlordship' is peculiarly difficult and has
been bedevilled by comparisons with artificial Irish legal catego-
risations of the rights of superior kings over their subordinates,
and by the supposed existence of the title of *Bretwalda*.

The blame for the latter really rests with Bede, though he never
used the term himself. In book two of his *Ecclesiastical History* he
listed seven kings who ruled over all the territories of the *gens
Anglorum* south of the river Humber.[74] In the ninth-century West
Saxon vernacular translation of his work this was formalised as
the title of *Bretwalda*, despite Bede not having suggested anything
so precise. Bede's seven were Ælle of the South Saxons, Ceawlin,
Æthelberht of Kent, Raedwald of the East Angles, and three successive Northumbrians: Edwin, Oswald and Oswy.

It has long been recognised that there are some historical
impossibilities here. The evidence relating to Ælle (470s/490s)

is slight and very dubious; that concerning Ceawlin has been examined above and found equally wanting. What is clear is that neither of these exercised much authority over anybody beyond the area of their immediate activities, which were East Sussex and the upper Thames valley, respectively. The case of Æthelberht of Kent is far from conclusive, and Raedwald (d. *c.* 625/7) is almost unknown, despite his being a favoured candidate for the man buried in the greatest and first-excavated of the mounds in the supposedly royal cemetery at Sutton Hoo (near Woodbridge, Suffolk). Only with the three Northumbrians does a stronger case for some form of hegemony over other kingdoms emerge, and in that of Oswy it can have lasted for no more than three years (655–8). Yet, on the other hand, Bede is very specific about Æthelbald of Mercia exercising a supremacy over all the kingdoms south of the Humber in his reference in book five, even though he does not include Æthelbald in his list of such rulers in book two! A slightly less reverential approach to the text of Bede might long ago have convinced historians that he was not attempting to enshrine a fundamental truth about 'the Olde English Constitution' in this clearly partisan Northumbrian reading of history.[75]

More significant than this problem is the practical one of what precisely such overlordship consisted. It is surely probable that it depended above all on the continuing ability of the 'overlord' to be able to back up his demands for tribute or acts of submission with a credible threat of force. Any wavering in this would change the relationship. Thus, it is believed that Æthelbald's successor, Offa (757–96), lost control of Kent during the period 775–85, and that an indigenous dynasty then re-established its independence in that kingdom, as was to happen again in 796.[76]

When the claim to authority could be backed by force, it probably resulted in the annual payment of fixed tributes by the subordinate kings, and providing their overlord with military assistance when required. It may also have expressed itself in the dominant ruler's ability to travel at will through other kingdoms and hold assemblies in them, in which his superior status would have been expressed ritually. Thus, for example, Bede records Oswald of Northumbria as being present in Wessex at the time of the consecration of Birinus as the first bishop of Dorchester (Oxon). Bede states that both kings gave him the *civitas* as the place to establish his episcopal see.[77] As Dorchester was in the Thames valley, on the frontiers between the West Saxon and Mercian kingdoms, and very far from Northumbria, it is usually thought that Oswald, as the superior king, confirmed the grant made by king Cynegisl

(611?–42?) of Wessex. Certainly by the time of Offa a number of the charters or documents recording gifts made by some of the lesser kings of southern England also contain the Mercian ruler's signature, indicating either his presence at the time of the making of the donation or the recipient's subsequent wish to obtain his confirmation of the local ruler's deed.[78] The absence of such confirmatory signatures from Kentish charters in the years 775–85 is one of the major pieces of evidence used to substantiate the independence of this kingdom from Mercian overlordship during the decade.[79]

It must be noted, however, that the number of such charters that have survived in total – virtually all in later cartulary copies – from this period is very limited, and that, statistically, it is unwise to make subtle deductions from so small a sample. Of Offa himself, only forty-three charters are known for his thirty-nine years of rule and, of these, seventeen have been judged to be spurious or interpolated by some or all of the scholars who have commented on them.[80]

In general, the reign of Offa has long vexed historians, who have recognised this king's importance but have been faced with a limited body of evidence with which to interpret it. Thus, for example, Offa's most famous legacy, as seen through modern eyes, must be the great dyke that bears his name, which runs from the River Dee near Chester in the north to the mouth of the Wye at Chepstow in the south. Not a single piece of contemporary evidence in fact connects this impressive piece of engineering and public work to the king. It is only on the basis of a statement in the late-ninth-century Welsh bishop Asser's *Life of Alfred* that the association is made, though few would now deny it.[81] The purpose of the dyke, be it boundary marker or defensive system between Offa's kingdom and those of the Welsh kings to the west, remains contentious and open to alternative interpretations based on archaeology largely because there is no documentary record of its creation.[82]

Offa was one of the few Anglo-Saxon kings whom we know to have had close diplomatic dealings with continental rulers, in his case the Frankish monarch Charlemagne, or Charles the Great (768–814), with whom letters were exchanged dealing with questions relating to English merchants and pilgrims in Francia. These were accompanied by various diplomatic presents. There were also periods of strained relations, as when Offa sought a marriage for his son with one of Charles' daughters (*c.* 790). The diplomatic row this produced led to Frankish ports being closed for a time to traders from Britain. This was finally resolved through the intermediacy of the abbot of Saint-Wandrille in the

Seine valley. Letters from Charles' adviser, the Northumbrian deacon Alcuin, to Offa also hint at the Mercian king's efforts to develop schools for the training of the clergy in his kingdom.[83] This was in line with the kind of programme that the Frankish ruler was trying to foster in his own realm at this same time.

Archaeologically, little is known of the centres of Offa's government. Some traces have been found of what might have been his palace at Tamworth, but little more. From his few charters and the records of assemblies of bishops held in his presence – for example, at the fortified enclosure at Gumley in Leicestershire in 772 and 779 – some idea can be gained of the peripatetic movements of his court and armed following. Under him the Mercian bishopric of Lichfield was patronised substantially by the monarchy, and after the probable difficulties with Kent in 775–85, Offa persuaded the pope (with Frankish support?) to elevate the see to archiepiscopal rank in 786.[84] This would have made the ecclesiastical order correspond with the political, but the promotion was reversed early in the ninth century. The legatine synod of 786, held under the direction of envoys from Rome and also attended by representatives from Francia, was another testimony to both the papal and Frankish ties and the programme of reform within the English Church that Offa was interested in promoting.

To use hindsight it would be possible to argue, anachronistically, that the period of Mercian domination was a cultural 'dead end'. The Viking conquests of the ninth century and the wars of the tenth apparently so effectively destroyed the material and intellectual records of the Mercian kingdom that all that now survive are a handful of charters, a small number of manuscripts (notably the Book of Cerne), some splendid if fragmentary stone carvings in the church of Breedon on the Hill and the great frontier dyke that Offa (almost certainly) built between his realm and those of the Welsh kings.[85] Of the Mercian laws, which did exist, and of the kingdom's historiography, which might have done, few elements survive.[86]

The conflicts of the ninth and tenth centuries were in most respects to prove equally destructive in Northumbria, whose political stability had never been very secure, and in Wessex. However, both of these kingdoms have left more traces of themselves, not least through what they had managed to export, which therefore was not available to be destroyed in the wars with the Vikings and in the long and very destructive conquest of the Anglo-Norse kingdom of York by Wessex in the course of the tenth century. This is not just a matter of the survival of manuscripts, but represents the evidence for a very significant and distinctive contribution to the cultural and artistic development of Western Europe in the seventh and eighth centuries.

After the relative splendour of the period of Mercian supremacy under Offa in the late eighth century, the ninth century in Britain can seem rather more sombre. As is often the case, this is largely a reflection of the character of the evidence. Under the West Saxon king Alfred (871–99) a chronicle was compiled, using various earlier annals, which has become known as the *Anglo-Saxon Chronicle*. Its name is misleading, in that, especially in its ninth-century and earlier sections, it is a predominantly West Saxon work. The indigenous historiography of the two other large kingdoms, of Mercia and of Northumbria, is only represented by brief entries in two much later compilations, those ascribed to 'Florence of Worcester' (actually compiled by John of Worcester) and 'Symeon of Durham' that are held in part to derive from otherwise lost annals composed in these regions. These are neither numerous nor detailed enough to fully compensate for the predominantly West Saxon view of the history of ninth-century England, which also contaminated all the later accounts of the period, including those written in areas that at the time had been hostile to Wessex. The same could also be said of the history of England in the tenth century.

It is worth noting that most of the minor kingdoms that had existed in the later seventh century are still found in the ninth, though they have left us hardly any record of themselves.[87] After the death of Offa, an independent kingdom re-emerged in Kent under a certain Eadbert Praen (796–8?). It may rapidly have been stifled by a still powerful Mercia, but two further indigenous Kentish monarchs were recorded soon afterwards: Cuthred (d. 807) and Baldred, who was expelled by the West Saxons in 825.[88] In the latter year, the kingdom was conquered by the West Saxons, and for several decades it became an appanage, to be held by the eldest son of the West Saxon ruler.

Independent kings continued to exist in East Anglia until its definitive conquest by the Vikings in 870. The names of most of these monarchs remain unknown. Initially still menaced by Mercia, the East Anglians were able to resist its attempts to reimpose overlordship, and two Mercian kings, Beornwulf (823–5) and Ludeca (825–7) were killed in battle by them.[89] Even more shadowy in this period is the kingdom of the East Saxons, but by 839 at the latest it, like Kent, had become a subordinate monarchy being held by the eldest son or heir of the ruler of Wessex.

Northumbria, which had been highly unstable in the eighth century, may have been generally less so in the ninth – at least until the crucial decade of the 860s. Of its kings, all too little may be known beyond their names and probable chronology. One of them, Eanred, held his throne for thirty-three years (*c.* 808–41). His son Æthelred was killed around 850, and power was taken by a king Osbryht, possibly the descendant of an earlier king Osbald (796). In about 863, Osbryht was challenged by a certain Ælla, and expelled from York. These two were still in conflict when the Danish army invaded Northumbria in 866.[90]

Mercia retained some of the pre-eminence it had achieved in the eighth century under Cœnwulf (796–821), a representative from another branch of the ruling house, who took power after the sudden death of Offa's son, Ecgfrith (796). He retained overlordship over Kent and East Anglia for some of his reign, but his death was followed by a period of weakness. Defeats by the West Saxons (825) and the East Angles (825 and 827) were followed by a brief conquest of the kingdom by Egbert of Wessex in 829–30.[91] While the Mercian king Wiglaf (827–41) was able to regain his throne, this decade of the 820s had weakened the kingdom.

The principal beneficiary, and in part also the architect, of Mercia's decline was Egbert of Wessex (802–39), who may well have been of Kentish origin and the son of a short-lived ruler of that kingdom called Eahlmund (*c.* 784–5).[92] Despite the legitimist claims of later Wessex genealogies, it is possible that the line of kings that traced itself back to Cerdic came to an end with the death of Cynewulf in a civil war in 786, and that the next king, Beorhtric (786–802), was a Mercian candidate.[93] On the latter's death in 802, the Kentish adventurer, Egbert, was able to take power. In the 820s, he expelled the Mercian candidate Baldred from Kent (825) and conquered the kingdom and that of Essex permanently, and Mercia temporarily (829–30). He also forced some of the Welsh to submit to him, and made an agreement with the Northumbrian ruler, Eanred.[94] In West Saxon propaganda, Egbert was later presented as a new *Bretwalda*, the first since the Northumbrian Oswy. This was a notion taken directly from Bede and deliberately revived in the interests of promoting the status of the founding figure of the new West Saxon dynasty. It is not surprising that this West Saxon historiography did not bother with a retrospective endowment of this title on the powerful Mercian kings of the late seventh and eighth centuries.

In practice, Egbert's predominance over the Anglo-Saxon kings south of the Humber proved short-lived, though his gains in Kent were not lost. He was confronted by a series of Viking attacks in the south in the 830s as well as war with the British in Cornwall. His successor, Æthelwulf (839–55) faced similar, if less frequent, attacks in the 840s.[95] All this may have made possible a restoration of the Mercian ascendancy. By 851, it is clear that Mercia had regained control of the lands north of the Thames, probably including Essex, and while West Saxon historiography presents it as a plea for help, in 853, contingents were sent from Wessex to serve under king Burghred of Mercia (852–74) in his subjection of the Welsh princes.[96] However, the traditional pattern of the Anglo-Saxon kingdoms and the normal pre-eminence among them of Mercia was finally and irrevocably disrupted by the Viking wars and conquests of the period 865–79, which will be considered in Chapter 19.

12 The Lombards in Italy, c. 540–712

Conquering Italy, 540–72

The name of the conquerors of much of Italy in the late sixth and early seventh centuries was unusual in that it would also have been familiar to readers of classical texts. The Lombards are given a brief mention in the *Germania* of Tacitus (AD 98), and are noted for the smallness of their numbers and their hardiness as fighters.[1] From his account they appear at that time as living along the southern banks of the Elbe.[2]

Despite this apparent evidence of their antiquity, absolute discontinuity exists between the *Longobardi* of Tacitus, and those featuring in the writings of Procopius and his continuators in the mid- to late sixth century, and who made their way from the Danube into Italy. Little is said about them, even in these contemporary sources, and it may seem more sensible for us to search instead for a Lombard view of their own history. For a literary text giving an account of their past, we have to turn to the *History of the Lombards*, written either in the monastery of Monte Cassino by Paul the Deacon in the 790s, and probably intended for presentation to the Beneventan duke Grimoald III (787–806), or composed in the mid-780s in Francia with the aim of informing a Frankish readership about the Lombard past.[3]

This is a work that is full of problems for the historian.[4] Composed in the aftermath of the Frankish conquest of the Lombard kingdom (see Chapter 15), by an author who himself spent some years in Francia in the service of the conquerors, it depends for its information on a variety of sources, not all identifiable, and of uneven worth. Among these is a brief text known as the *Origo Gentis Langobardorum* or *Origin of the Lombard People*. From its own internal references it would seem to belong to the period of the second reign of king Perctarit (672–88), prior to his association of his son Cunincpert as co-ruler in 679.

To the *Origo* and to Paul's *History* can be added another very short, anonymous work, found in only one manuscript, and providing a synoptic account of Lombard history. This was written between the years 806 and 810, but appears to be largely independent of the two earlier works. None of these texts should, however, be treated as purely objective accounts of earlier

Lombard history. Nor should some of the more naïve-seeming narratives in them be treated as survivals of ancient legends of the people.

In all three of these works the span of time regarded as having passed between the first formation of a distinct Lombard people and their entry into Italy in 568 is no more than eleven generations. Some more precise chronological pointers are provided. Thus, for example, the second of the kings of the Lombards, who belongs in the fourth of these generations, a certain 'Lamissio' or 'Laiamicho', is recorded under the entry for AD 423 in an interpolated version of the *Chronicle of Prosper* as ruling for three years at that time.[5] Thus, the history of the Lombards presented in these three texts of the seventh to ninth centuries extends back in real chronological terms no earlier than the late fourth century, getting us nowhere near the time of Tacitus's Lombards.[6]

In practice, all three works, with the interesting variants they contain, represent the views of the Lombard past that were developed in Italy from the seventh century onwards under the influence of contemporary Roman ideas of ethnic formation, and were also affected directly by similarly Romanised accounts of the history of their predecessors in Italy, the Ostrogoths.[7] Thus, as in Jordanes' account of the Goths, the Lombards are represented as a single, homogeneous people moving, partly of their own volition and partly as a consequence of a series of accidents and adventures, from an original homeland in Scandinavia to a new homeland in Italy. Such narratives are the *Genesis* and *Exodus* of the peoples concerned, and their historical reality should be regarded with the same degree of scholarly scepticism as those of the first two books of the Bible.

In the light of such difficulties with the Lombard historiographical tradition it is safer to fall back on the, albeit often hostile but more clearly contemporary, imperial sources and on the evidence of archaeology, to try to establish the nature and causes of the Lombard involvement in Italy in the late sixth century. As will be seen, the information to be found in Procopius in particular can present a different and more complex and more credible version of the history of the Lombards in the preceding eighty years than the one offered by Paul and the *Origo*.

It is clear from Procopius's account that the events of the 480s led to major changes in the location and roles of the principal confederacies in the regions just north of the Danube. Odovacer's elimination of the Rugi in 488, and the removal in the following year into Italy of Theoderic and all his following, left a power vacuum in the northern Balkans and the upper

Danube. The Heruls may have been the first to move into this, but they failed to hold their own against other competitors, notably the Gepids and the Lombards, despite briefly dominating the latter.[8] If Procopius is to be believed, the Lombards were Christians before the accession of Anastasius I in 491, testifying to an already high degree of Roman influence on them.

Though the details of the process are unclear, it seems that in the 540s Justinian relied on all three of these rival groups to defend the Danube frontier in the western Balkans, in the regions between the river and the Illyrian mountains to the south. The Gepids were given control of Sirmium once it was regained from the Ostrogoths, and the Lombards were persuaded to move south of the Danube to establish themselves in the area of what would once have been south-western Norricum and western Pannonia. The Heruls, who provided valuable contingents for the armies fighting in Italy, were by this time located further east, in the area around Singidunum (Belgrade). Their establishment of these forces in adjacent regions secured the Danube frontier and provided defence for the more valued southern parts of the Balkans. However, the degree of imperial control over any of the three confederacies was clearly limited, though individuals and groups were recruited from among them to serve in the imperial forces.[9] As with the rival forces supporting the two Theoderics in the 470s, imperial political influence was maintained primarily by preventing any one confederacy from establishing a clear domination. Throughout the reign of Justinian this seems to have meant providing greater support for the Lombards against the more powerful Gepids.[10]

This policy was completely reversed by Justin II (565–78), who seems almost to have made a principle of turning his predecessor's diplomatic objectives on their heads. From the chronicle of Theophylact Simocatta and the fragments of Menander's continuation of Procopius and Agathias, it seems that the new emperor supported the Gepids against the Lombards, and in consequence the latter appealed for help to the leaders of the nomad confederacy of the Avars, who were in the process of turning themselves into the dominant power to the north of the Danube, in the way the Huns had two centuries earlier.[11] They were already hostile to Justin II because of his refusal to continue paying the annual subsidies to them that had been initiated by Justinian, and may have had their own reasons to wish to end the continuing Gepid occupation of the Carpathian basin.[12]

The outcome was disastrous as far as imperial control was concerned – not only over the western Balkans but also over Italy.

In 567, the Avars and Lombards combined to destroy the Gepid kingdom centred on Sirmium. While in later Lombard tradition their role was implied to be central, there can be little doubt from the contemporary Byzantine sources that the leading participant in these events was the Avar confederacy.[13] The emperor intervened to secure control of Sirmium and gave refuge to the fugitive Gepid king Usdibad, but the rest of the lands occupied by the Gepids passed into Avar control, and the remnants of the people were absorbed into their confederacy or that of the Lombards. Justin II and subsequently Tiberius II (578–82) were able to retain Sirmium, but it was lost to the Avars early in the reign of Maurice (582–602).[14]

The Lombards may not have played the heroic role in these events that they would later claim, but their future was certainly determined by them. The relatively limited threat of the Gepids was replaced by the expansionary power of the Avar confederacy, and it was probably because of this upheaval in the Carpathian basin that in the following year the Lombards abandoned their own fortresses in western Norricum and crossed the passes in the Julian Alps into Italy.[15] According to the Lombard historiographical tradition, they voluntarily gave up their lands to the Avars, on condition that if they ever needed them again they would be returned![16] However, the contemporary chronicler bishop Marius of Avenches indicates that they deliberately devastated their former homeland, thus creating a *cordon sanitaire* between themselves and the Avars.[17]

A story is to be found in Isidore of Seville, writing in Spain in the 620s, and in the probably Burgundian *Chronicle of Fredegar* (later seventh century), as well as in Paul the Deacon's *History*, saying that the Lombards were invited into Italy by the patrician Narses in revenge for his having been dismissed from office by the emperor Justin II.[18] Considerable doubt has been expressed as to the worth of this tradition, not least because Narses apparently retired to the imperially-controlled city of Naples and did not die until the mid-570s, thus remaining available for imperial vengeance.

The issue may turn upon the point at which Narses was replaced as the commander of the imperial armies in Italy. Fighting against remaining groups of Ostrogoths in northern Italy had lasted until 562, when Verona, their last stronghold, fell. In 567, as has been seen, a major upheaval occurred on the Danube, leading to war between the Empire and the Avars over the control of Sirmium and Justin II's refusal to hand over the fugitive Gepid king. It is possible in these circumstances that Narses, who had previously employed Lombard contingents in his campaign against the Ostrogoths, entered into negotiations with them with a view to securing the defence of northern Italy.[19] Such an agreement, if it existed, might well have been repudiated by Justin II when Narses was replaced.

The details of the conquest are to be found in Paul the Deacon. Two of the sources for this part of his *History* have been identified. In addition to sections of the historical work of the less well informed Gregory of Tours, he had access to an otherwise lost *Historiola* or 'Small History' of Bishop Secundus of Trento (d. 612). The latter, devoted to the history of the Lombards and the earliest phases of their rule in Italy, was doubtless extremely valuable, though probably primarily concerned with events affecting Trento.[20] However, it is not possible to determine with certainty which parts of Paul's text derive from this near-contemporary source.

In the years 568 to 572, much of northern Italy was occupied by the Lombards. Milan admitted them with little or no resistance, whereas Pavia required a three-year-long blockade to force it into submission. A number of towns and their territories did continue to hold out, of which the most important by far were Ravenna, the headquarters of the recently re-established exarchate or imperial administration of Italy, and Rome, which, as well as being the papal residence, was also the centre of an imperial duchy. Though much of the land between these two cities passed into Lombard hands, the imperial retention of Perugia preserved a line of communication between them. A number of other enclaves of imperial rule, such as Padua, Mantua and various coastal towns, survived in the north, and more extensive territories were preserved in the south.[21]

The Lombard king, Alboin, established himself at Verona; a significant choice in that it had been the last stronghold of Ostrogothic resistance, only falling to the Empire in 562.[22] His successors, though, were to make first Milan (until at least 616) and then Pavia their preferred city of residence. It was at Verona that Alboin was murdered in 572, apparently at the instigation of his wife, Rosamund, who thereby avenged the killing of her own father, the Gepid king Cunimund. An elaborate account of this episode and its love interest is given by Paul, but this should probably not be taken at face value. The simple affirmation of the *Chronicle of Fredegar* that Alboin was poisoned by his wife, whose father he had killed, may be preferred.[23]

Furthermore, another source that is closer in time to these events suggests other motives, the barest echoes of which appear in Paul. In the early 580s, bishop Marius of Avenches concluded his brief chronicle. Because of his location in the western Alps he was well informed on events in northern Italy, and his work, despite its brevity, has considerable authority. He confirms that Alboin's wife was involved in the murder and that she subsequently married the other leading conspirator, a certain Hilmagis, whom Paul describes as the dead king's foster brother. But whereas Paul has the guilty couple fleeing to Ravenna almost alone, Marius reports that they were accompanied by 'part of the army'. In other words, this episode seems to represent a real divide in the Lombard ranks between those anxious to preserve the independent kingdom Alboin had created, and those who wished to submit to imperial authority, and quite possibly, like the Ostrogoths before them, be relocated within or beyond Italy as part of the emperor's army.[24] Hilmagis and his supporters also took with them to Ravenna the Lombard royal treasure, a vital economic and symbolic resource of the monarchy.

Whatever the nature of previous contacts, imperial reactions to the Lombard presence in Italy were hostile and generally remained so throughout the ensuing period of their kingdom. This has tended to colour both Byzantine and papal sources relating to the Lombards, and until recently much modern historiography.[25] They have been presented as being peculiarly 'barbarous', and their presence in Italy characterised as a disaster. It was in this respect their misfortune that attitudes had clearly been so affected by the horrors of the protracted thirty-year war between the Empire and the Ostrogoths. The replacement of the Ostrogothic presence by a Lombard one offered little attraction to those for whom the achievements of the age of Theoderic were at best a dim memory, overlaid by the years of mutual atrocity and savagery that had intervened.

Dukes and kings, 572–84

It is clear that the imperial government of Justin II had no wish to see the Lombards established as a federate people in Italy, filling the role of the Ostrogoths. As well as the fact that enormous effort had been expended in regaining Italy for direct imperial rule, the Lombards were not necessarily reliable allies, not least because of their links with the Franks. In the 540s, the Frankish king Theudebert I (533–48) had tried to put together an alliance against the Empire with the Lombards and the Gepids, and may even have envisaged a joint invasion of the Balkans and a march on Constantinople. This came to nothing, but in the 550s or 560s a definite Lombard–Frankish alliance was symbolised by the marriage of Alboin to Chlotsuintha, one of the daughters of Chlotar I (d. 561).[26]

It is possible that the relationship involved a subordination of the Lombards, in that sections of other peoples known to be under Frankish hegemony, such as the Saxons, were involved in the Lombard entry into Italy in 568.[27] Moreover, the foremost modern Italian historian of the Lombards has suggested very plausibly that the recorded Lombard invasion of Provence and the lower Rhône valley in 574 was undertaken at the behest of the eastern Frankish King Sigibert I (561–75) as part of his war against his brothers Chilperic and Guntramn.[28] Subsequently, in 582, when Sigibert's successor Childebert II (575–96) received imperial subsidies to undertake a campaign against the Lombards, the latter were obliged to buy his withdrawal from Italy, and the tributary status of their kingdom was reaffirmed in treaties made with the Frankish monarch in 590/1.[29] Only the emergence of a reinvigorated Lombard monarchy under Agilulf (590–616) seems to have resulted in a more active and effective resistance to Frankish military and diplomatic bullying.[30]

Despite the abusive language used about them in such texts as the imperial letters to the Frankish king, the Lombards were by no means the barbarians they have sometimes been made out to be. As we have seen, they were said to be Christians by the late fifth century, and their common adhesion to Catholicism, as opposed to the Arianism of the Gepids, was used as a diplomatic counter in their relations with the Empire in the time of Justinian.[31] Admittedly, this cannot be true of all the people, as in the generation after their invasion of Italy many of them are reported as still being pagans.[32] Furthermore, by the time of Alboin (*c.* 560–72) some of the Christian Lombards seem to have become Arians, possibly in consequence of Gepid influence in the period *c.* 548–67.[33]

In material culture they show themselves no different from the Goths or Franks.[34] Their dress and weapons were, like those of these other peoples, strongly influenced by Roman traditions and above all by the styles favoured by the late imperial army. The period of the conquest itself was doubtless violent and disruptive, as all such phases were. Perhaps, though, the most striking feature of the first phase of the Lombard occupation of northern Italy was the speed with which they were able to establish a new military and administrative order on these regions; one, moreover, that was markedly Roman in its character. In particular, their creation of a system of duchies has most aroused modern historians' interest.

That Paul the Deacon was most probably using the near-contemporary work of bishop Secundus of Trento, and that aspects of his account are confirmed by independent Frankish sources gives credibility to some of his descriptions of the creation of the Lombard duchies. According to Paul, no sooner had Alboin crossed the Alps than he appointed his nephew Gisulf to be the first *dux* or duke, a title of Roman origin, of the region of Friuli. By 573/4, so the historian claimed, there were thirty-five such officials in the kingdom, each centred on a city. It is possible that the actual number is an exaggeration, but several, if not all, of the later duchies did come into existence at this time.[35]

Something of the nature of the office can be deduced from clauses in the law code that was produced by the Lombard king Rothari (636–52).[36] It is clear from these references that the dukes, who were based in the principal cities and towns of Lombard Italy, were – following Roman precedents – responsible for the military and judicial administration of the regions under their authority. Another class of official, the *gastald* (possibly also called *comes* or 'count') acted as something of a counterweight to the duke, being responsible for the overseeing of royal estates and their revenues in the duchy, and for ensuring that the duke administered impartial justice. In certain areas, particularly those not incorporated within the territories of duchies, *gastalds* could exercise the equivalent of ducal functions and were directly responsible to the king.[37]

Rather different conditions existed in the south of Italy, where, for example, in the seventh century the *gastalds* appear to have been responsible to the dukes rather than to the distant monarchs in Pavia. This resulted not only from the greater distances between the southern duchies and the Po valley, but possibly also from the circumstances of their formation. Whereas the north of the country was divided into a large number of territorially quite small duchies, the centre and south of Italy contained only two: those of Spoleto and of Benevento. It has been suggested that these were the products not of Lombard conquests, but, instead were created by the exarchate for groups of Lombards, rather like Hilmagis in 572, who wanted to enter imperial service rather than accept the authority of their own kings.[38] If so, their initial purpose may have been to resist the expansion of the Lombard kingdom, but with the decline in imperial control in the late sixth century, the new dukes effectively went their own way as regional powers, answering neither to exarch nor king.

This is not as paradoxical as it may seem, in that, as previously mentioned, detachments of Lombards had been used by the Empire in the later stages of the war with the Ostrogoths. Political cohesion among the Lombards was far from strong, and numerous other ethnic groups, including Gepids, Sueves, Saxons, and Utigur and Kutrigur Bulgars, were involved in the movement into Italy in 568. Paul the Deacon provides examples of Lombard dukes in Italy who were prepared to ally with the emperor and his representative in Ravenna, the exarch, against the Lombard kings. A certain duke Droctulf, of Suevic origin, is particularly singled out as a collaborator with the Empire, and his obituary inscription in Ravenna was recorded by Paul.[39] Also, as has been seen, a major division of opinion may have existed among the Lombards over the question of co-operation with or resistance to the Empire.

Intriguing and even plausible as this theory is, it has no definite evidence to support it. Indeed, the first appearance of a duke of Spoleto in Paul's *History* is in the context of an attack on the exarchate of Ravenna. Faroald is reported to have taken and looted Classis, the port of Ravenna, probably around the year 579.[40] Whether the duchy of Spoleto actually existed at this time is uncertain, and it is possible that the entrepreneurial Faroald went on to be established as the first duke in the next phase of his career, and possibly by a treaty with the Empire. The origins of Benevento are equally obscure. What is clear is that both duchies existed by the time of king Authari (584–90) and that he was able, perhaps briefly, to impose royal authority over both of them.[41] This could not always be maintained effectively by his successors.

A dating of the formation of the great duchies of Spoleto and Benevento in the early 580s makes particular sense in the light of the conditions then existing. Following Alboin's murder – which brought to an end his dynasty, which itself had only lasted for two generations – one of his dukes, Cleph, was chosen by the Lombard army to succeed him.[42] He survived for little more than a year before being murdered by 'his boy'; a rather enigmatic fate that neither Paul the Deacon nor Marius of Avenches further illuminates.[43] There followed a ten-year interregnum in which no king was chosen, and authority was exercised by the dukes alone, each in his own duchy.[44]

This has been frequently held against the Lombards as proof of their lack of sophistication. More recent interpretations have, rightly, been far less critical.[45] Even so, some have tended to assume that such a phenomenon must represent an aberration, explicable only as a manifestation of hostile and external influences working on Lombard society. Byzantine gold has been seen as the particular motive for and instrument of the 'crime'.[46]

However, other historians have argued that Paul the Deacon was indicating that this was just a ten-year-long regency for Cleph's son, Authari, and that his investiture as king was merely delayed until he was of suitable age.[47] This solution has the virtue of simplicity, but a further modification will be suggested below.

The period of the interregnum and of the succeeding reign of Authari (584–90) also mark the point at which a military occupation of certain Italian towns and cities began to be transformed into a more permanent Lombard settlement. As with the Gothic kingdoms in Spain and Italy, the first step towards this had to be a fiscal one: the establishment of a mechanism whereby the Lombard soldiery could receive regular pay and supplies, and not have to rely on the profits of war or random extortions. As in the case of the other and earlier-established post-Roman societies in the West, this meant a system of *hospitalitas*.

What is involved in this remains as controversial as when an alternative to the traditional view of this as a redistribution of property was first suggested.[48] Even those who believe the mechanism was a purely fiscal one, rather than involving actual transfers of ownership of land, have found it hard to believe this could also be true of Lombard Italy.[49] This is largely because too much weight has been given to the negative image of the Lombard presence in Italy, itself almost totally the product of prejudice, ancient and modern.[50]

Two passages in Paul's *History* are of particular relevance. After recording the arrangements made following the murder of Cleph, he reports that: 'In these days many of the noble Romans were killed from love of gain, and the remainder were divided among their "guests" and made tributaries, that they should pay the third part of their products to the Lombards.'[51] For some this has meant that after a fairly thorough slaughter of the surviving Roman upper classes, the remainder of the subject population were divided up, effectively as serfs for the conquerors, bound to the land and obliged to render up a fixed proportion of the produce of their labours to their Lombard overlords.[52] Once again, this is primarily a reflection of the predisposition to expect the worst of the Lombards, and to accept the verdict on them of their enemies.

It is not unreasonable, instead, to translate the word *tributarii* in this passage as in its more natural meaning of 'taxpayer'.[53] Moreover, it is clear enough from the construction of the phrase that the 'remainder' referred to represents the Roman upper classes and not the whole non-Lombard population. The passage, if anything, is proof of the survival rather than the elimination of elements of the Roman landowning class in the territories under Lombard rule. This is also what might be expected from the strong imprint of Roman ideas and institutions on Lombard government and administration.[54]

The second pertinent passage in Paul's *History* is to be found in his account of the elevation of Cleph's son, Authari, to the kingship (584).[55] In this single sentence certain ambiguous words hold the key to the meaning, and these are likely to be interpreted in the light of how the previous passage has been understood, and more generally in accordance with a priori expectations of Lombard society.[56] In Foulke's classic translation of Paul, the sentence is rendered as: 'The oppressed people, however, were parcelled out among their Langobard guests.' It is quite possible, though, to translate this passage as meaning that there took place in 584 a redistribution of 'those under a fiscal obligation'.[57]

In earlier instances of the application of *hospitalitas*, the receipts due from taxpayers under obligation to provide fixed proportions of their produce (be it in cash or in kind) were assigned directly and personally to the intended recipients, the military 'guests', thus eliminating the role of the state in collecting and redistributing this revenue.[58] There are no good grounds for doubting that such a system could have been reapplied for the benefit of the Lombards in 573 and again in 584.

The second of these was caused by the decision of the dukes in that year, to surrender half of their *substantiae* to the new king in order to provide him, his court and his officials with a sound financial basis on which to maintain themselves. In that the royal administration had been in abeyance since 573, and that the presumed allocation of taxpayers to recipients had occurred during that time, it was inevitable that the re-establishment of a royal household would involve an adjustment in the allocation of taxpayers. In 573, those obliged to pay had been assigned to the dukes and their followers, as there was no king and court to take a share. Thus the *substantiae* referred to, already understood to mean 'productive resources from which public revenues flowed', need to be seen as including rights to a proportion of the taxes due from Roman landowners.[59]

If this is accepted, it throws a different light on the period of the interregnum. It is surely significant that the first major effort to set up a new administrative and fiscal system took place immediately after the monarchy had effectively been suspended. Not Byzantine gold, but the opportunity for the dukes to acquire the resources of the monarchy may have been behind the decision not to replace Cleph. The preceding loss of the royal treasure in 572 also meant that the monarchy would have required considerable financial underwriting if its economic position was to be restored, and this may not have been felt to be worthwhile at this time. The dukes were able in 573 to take control of those resources that would otherwise have been those of the king, and to establish fiscal arrangements that directly benefited themselves and their own followers, whose needs were catered for without the need for royal patronage, as happened in Francia.

By 584, the growing belligerence of the Frankish king Childebert II and the threatening moves of the Empire against the Lombard kingdom made a return to a central authority desirable, and so a new king was installed. As was mentioned earlier, as a consequence the dukes had to relinquish some of the resources they had accumulated during the previous decade. But what is perhaps more striking is that they were able to retain half of these. This in practice gave them an independence *vis-à-vis* the king that was unmatched on the part of the greater nobility in both Visigothic Spain and the Frankish kingdoms. So, it is not surprising that the duchies became hereditary offices, and that the kings often had great difficulty in imposing their will on the dukes.

We might also suspect that the rather unusual nature of the office of *Gastald* sprang from these circumstances. In each duchy, certain revenue-producing estates as well as rights to proportions of taxation were conceded to the crown in 584. It was clearly necessary for a royal official, in theory independent of the local duke, to be appointed in each duchy to oversee the management of the royal lands and the collection of dues owed to the crown. Hence the Lombard administrative pattern, which otherwise has many generic resemblances to those found in the other kingdoms in the West, developed its distinctive characteristics. Whereas in Francia and Spain both the urban magistrates and governors (the counts) and the military commanders (the dukes) were royal appointees working together, at least in theory, in a unified administrative structure, the peculiar conditions and events of the early period of the Lombard settlement in Italy led to the creation of more powerful, often autonomous duchies, which frequently inhibited the exercise of royal power.[60]

The kingdom of the Lombards, 584–712

From the arrangements made in 584 there emerged a much revitalised monarchy. Not least this was because of the personality of the new king, Authari, who was much admired by Paul the Deacon and so most probably also by his principal source, bishop Secundus of Trento. Militarily, Authari's short reign was vital to the survival of the Lombard kingdom. He won a major victory over Byzantine forces in 586, though was defeated by them in renewed conflict the following year.[61]

More significant still were relations with the Franks. Having received hefty Byzantine subsidies the previous year, Childebert II sent an expedition into Italy in 585, but this may have been mainly to impress the emperor Maurice. In 588, to end the threat of further invasion, Authari tried to negotiate a treaty with Childebert II of Austrasia, doubtless involving some tribute paying, which was also to be symbolised by his marriage to the Frankish king's sister. This plan fell through, though, as Childebert preferred to betroth her to the newly converted Visigothic king Reccared (586–601), and instead decided to honour the undertakings made to the emperor, by launching another invasion of Italy. This proved to be a disaster.[62]

In 590, another large-scale Frankish invasion took place. The Lombards survived by holding the principal cities, notably Pavia and Milan, against Frankish sieges until the latter were forced to withdraw as a result of the rising incidence of disease. Various fortresses were taken, and it seems probable that the primary purpose of the invasion was to force the Lombards into accepting Frankish suzerainty and the regular payment of tribute. After the withdrawal of the Frankish forces, said to have been commanded by twenty dukes, Authari opened negotiations with Childebert II, also trying to secure the good offices of the latter's uncle, Guntramn, the Frankish king of Burgundy. Negotiations were still in train when the news came of Authari's death.[63]

Prior to his death he had contracted a marriage that was to be of considerable importance for the future of the Lombard monarchy. Deprived of Childebert's sister (her betrothal to Reccared proved equally short-lived) he turned instead to the Bavarian ducal house of the Agilolfings and married Theodelinda, daughter of Duke Garibald (d. 592). Theodelinda's mother, Garibald's wife, was the daughter of an earlier Lombard king, Waco (d. *c.* 540), whose dynasty, at least according to later tradition, had ruled over the people for the previous seven generations.[64] His line in the male descent died out soon after, and the kingship passed to the short-lived dynasties of Audoin and of Cleph.

But as a Frankish marriage had seemed more desirable in 588, Authari may not have made this match out of an urgent need for dynastic legitimation. The Bavarians, a people whose origins have been a matter of much debate, were potentially valuable allies for the Lombards because of their location immediately to the north of Italy.[65] However, on the premature death of Authari in 590, marrying Theodelinda became the best means by which a new king could be grafted on to the stock of the former royal line. That she was given a free choice between all of the dukes, as Paul would have us believe, is not entirely easy to credit.[66] Hard political bargaining or even naked force must have underlain the ritual acts.

Dynastic continuity and legitimacy became increasingly important for the Lombards, and while Theodelinda's own male descent died out with her son Adaloald (616–26), marriage to her daughter Gundiperga legitimised two further kings, and, when even these lines failed, the descendants of Theodelinda's brother Gundoald (d. 616) provided most of the Lombard monarchs up to the year 712. The only alternative royal dynasty, that of Audoin and Alboin, was able to impose a representative in the person of Grimoald (662–71), a descendant of Alboin's nephew duke Gisulf of Friuli, but even he found it expedient to marry into the 'Bavarian' royal line (see the genealogical table below). While the Lombards have been criticised for the number of coups and conspiracies that convulsed their monarchy in the seventh century, what is striking is their fidelity to dynastic continuity, which may represent another example of strong Roman influence on their political institutions.

The new king, symbolically 'chosen' by Theodelinda, was Agilulf, partly of Thuringian origin and previously duke of Turin. His reign (590–616) saw the achievement of a much greater degree of internal stability and external security for the kingdom. He brought the negotiations for peace with the Franks, initiated by Authari, to a successful conclusion. The removal of the threat of Frankish intervention freed the king's hands to take a more active role in Italy. It also enabled him to impose much greater royal control over the dukes, at least in the north. A number of them are recorded by Paul the Deacon as having conspired against the king, who had originally been one of their own number, and several of them were executed. In some cases he used the royal army to break their power.[67] He replaced them with men expected to be more faithful to him, but he did not alter the basic administrative structures.

The increasing military problems of the Empire, first with the Slavs and Avars in the Balkans and then with the Persians and the Arabs on the eastern frontiers, meant that fewer and fewer resources could be spared for the defence of imperial interests in Italy, let alone for major campaigns against the Lombards. Agilulf, on occasion, made use of an alliance with the Avars in his wars against the Byzantine forces in Italy, and was even able, late in his reign, to use them as a threat against the Franks.[68]

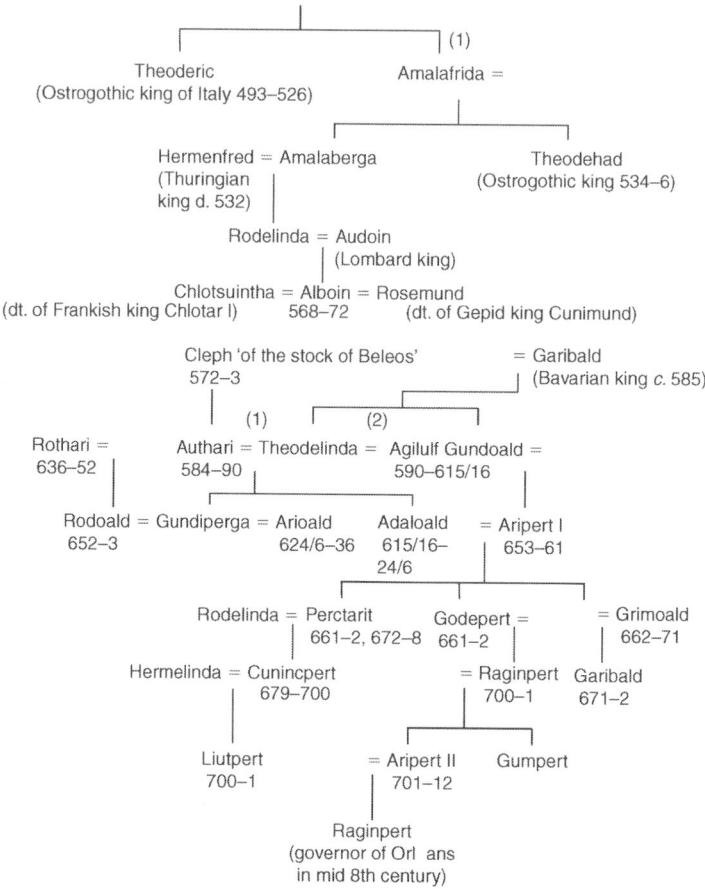

A simplified genealogy of the Lombard royal dynasties *c.* 568–712

(*Note: Regnal dates of the Lombard kings are enclosed in square brackets.*)

In such circumstances, Agilulf was able to renew the expansion of the kingdom. He may also have been spurred on in this by the need to curb the growing territorial power of the dukes of Spoleto and of Benevento. The first major Lombard attempt to take Rome was made by duke Faroald of Spoleto in 579, and his successor duke Ariulf (591–601) tried again in 592. He was also able briefly to make himself master of the crucial fortress town of Perugia, breaking Rome's communications with Ravenna. Agilulf's own, more protracted, siege of Rome in 593 may well have been a response to the fear of the city falling into the hands of these overly independent dukes.[69] In all cases,

Rome held out, but it was Agilulf who had become master of Perugia by the end of these campaigns.

It must be wondered, if Agilulf had been able to take Rome, whether the position of the Lombards in Italy might have been strengthened, and whether a genuinely united Italian kingdom, on the lines of the one that had existed under the Ostrogoths, would have emerged. It is impossible to say if the papacy, which remained implacably hostile to the idea of Lombard political control of Rome throughout the whole existence of the kingdom, might not have proved more pliable if this had actually been imposed, and if it had become necessary to work out a *modus vivendi* with the conquerors. But, while the city and territories of the duchy of Rome remained an imperial enclave, the popes had at least a political obligation to remain opposed to the Lombards. This was initially accentuated by religious divisions.

Despite the deliberately heightened language with which they were described in Byzantine and papal documents, in which their supposed 'frightfulness', 'abominableness' and 'savagery' are referred to constantly, there was little about the Lombards that should have made them any less acceptable to the civilian population of Italy than their Ostrogothic predecessors.[70] Like the latter, they were, in the early stages of their settlement south of the Alps, Arian Christians, but in that the popes had collaborated easily enough with Theoderic and his successors this should not have been an insuperable bar to good relations with the Church of Rome.

In fact, the religious history of the Lombards is far from easy to understand.[71] Alboin appears to have been an Arian in the 560s, if the letter of bishop Nicetius of Trier to the king's then Frankish wife is to be believed, despite the Lombards having portrayed themselves to the emperor Justinian as fellow Catholics only a decade and a half earlier. Authari also seems to have been an Arian, and at Easter 590 is said to have forbidden Lombards to receive Catholic baptism.[72] Agilulf's position is not known for sure, though Theodelinda was certainly a Catholic, as was their son Adaloald (616–26). The next two kings, Arioald (626–36) and Rothari (636–52), were Arians. Only with Aripert I (653–61) did these fluctuations cease, though some historians have seen Grimoald (662–71) as the last Arian king.

This is quite unlike anything to be found in any of the other kingdoms in which the kings and the people passed through an Arian phase before becoming irrevocably Catholic. In the cases of the Burgundians and the Goths in Spain (and possibly the Franks), periods of conflict and debate preceded the decision of the king to convert, but once the decision was made the issue ceased to be a live one. In Spain, in the brief period between the announcement of Reccared's conversion in 587 and the formalising of the conversion of the kingdom through the holding of the Third Council of Toledo in May 589 virtually all the contentious issues concerning the dismantling of the institutions of the Arian church and the redeployment of its personnel had been resolved.[73] After 590, Arianism was a dead issue in the Visigothic kingdom; there were no more Arians.

The constant shifts in religious affiliation on the part of the Lombard monarchy thus require explanation. For some historians this is no more than proof that religion, uniquely in Early Medieval Europe, was not a matter of real concern at anything above the personal level in the Lombard kingdom. Others would like to see these fluctuations as representing the shifting ascendancies of rival groups: one forward-looking and willing to compromise with Roman cultural norms; and the other conservative and wedded to the ancestral Germanic traditions of the people.[74] Neither of these approaches is satisfying.

What must be clear, from comparison with the Spanish case, is that whatever the fluctuations in the religious affiliations of the monarchy, this did not have any direct effect on the existence and functioning of an Arian Church within the kingdom. Very little is known of this institution, but certain casual references prove its existence. Arian Lombard bishops certainly functioned, and a number of churches consecrated by earlier generations of Arians in Italy still existed in the 580s, even in Rome.[75] Slight as this information is, it seems to suggest that initially the Arian bishops and clergy were attached to the Lombard garrisons, rather than having a fixed urban base. The Arian bishop referred to in Gregory the Great's *Dialogues* comes into Spoleto to try to obtain a church for Arian use, but does not, as was the case in Spain prior to 589, appear to be the Arian bishop *of* Spoleto; that is, part of a parallel and rival hierarchy. His miraculous discomfiture is said to have dismayed the Lombards garrisoning the region. On the other hand, if Paul the Deacon is to be believed, such parallel Arian and Catholic hierarchies existed in a number of cities, including Pavia, by the time of Rothari (636–52).[76]

In general, it would seem reasonable to suggest that support for and maintenance of an Arian clergy and church depended on the religious affiliation of the local de facto rulers, which in the Lombard state meant that an Arian duke could set up or preserve an Arian establishment in his duchy, even when the king was a Catholic. The kings lacked the strength to impose religious uniformity on the duchies, particularly those in the south. This also meant, in the light of the way that the monarchy passed through the hands of a number of ducal families in the period 572–672, that it was quite possible for a duke, chosen for whatever political reasons, or who managed to take the crown, to be an Arian or a Catholic king, according to his previous religious affiliation.

This was doubtless facilitated by the existence of a division within the Catholic Church in Italy, which was only finally healed in 612, known as the Istrian schism. A number of the north Italian bishops had felt that the popes had fallen into heresy by compromising with the emperor Justinian's attempt at reconciliation with the Monophysites. His denunciation of some of the works of three earlier and strongly pro-Chalcedonian theologians had generated what came to be called 'The Three Chapters Controversy'. The opposition to this on the part of Pope Vigilius had led to his arrest and considerable ill-treatment in Constantinople before he submitted to the imperial will. His successor, Pelagius I (556–61), who had supported Vigilius's resistance, had himself eventually accepted the condemnation of the three theologians, and had in consequence been anathematised by some other Church leaders in Italy and Africa. While most of them returned quickly to communion with Rome, continuing alienation from Rome of several bishoprics in the north-east of Italy, centred on Aquileia, meant that the Catholic Church in Italy took a much less unified stand on the matter of Lombard Arianism.[77]

Nor, apart from Authari's attempt to prevent Lombards receiving Catholic baptism, does the division between Arians and Catholics in the kingdom seem very contentious.[78] There are no accounts of theological debates or of confrontations over the ownership of churches. Though some bishoprics remained vacant, there is no evidence to suggest that the Catholic establishment was downtrodden or incapable of maintaining itself.[79] Arian rulers such as Agilulf were probably willing to patronise Catholic shrines, and even Catholic monks. Agilulf donated a votive crown to his wife's foundation of the Basilica of St. John the Baptist at Monza, and the earliest extant Lombard royal charter is the king's grant of 613 to the newly established monastery of Bobbio, founded with Agilulf's support by the Irish abbot Columbanus after his expulsion from Burgundy.[80] Last, and not least, Agilulf was prepared to have his son and heir baptised as a Catholic, doubtless at the behest of his wife Theodelinda (c. 604). In such general circumstances, it is perhaps less surprising that Lombard Arianism should expire gradually and without notice, rather than for the issue to require a single authoritative but contentious resolution.

With the death of bishop Secundus of Trent in 612, Paul the Deacon's primary source of information came to an end. His account of the rest of the seventh century is in consequence extremely brief, and whole reigns received the barest mention. Thus, of Arioald (626–36), who replaced the young Adaloald when the latter apparently went mad, Paul can only say 'Concerning the acts of this king hardly anything has come to our knowledge.'[81] His successor, Rothari (636–52) has left more trace of himself, not just in Paul's report of his conquest of various imperial fortresses on the Ligurian coast, but most substantially in the law code that he promulgated in the eighth year of his reign (643/4).[82]

Paul the Deacon's statement on the nature of the law contained in Rothari's code, or Edict, as it should more properly be known, has generally been taken at face value. According to Paul, the king 'collected in a series of writings the laws of the Lombards which they were keeping in memory only and custom'. This appears to be a reflection of the statement on the procedures followed in collecting the laws, which is to be found in the Edict itself.[83] It is important to appreciate, however, how marked is the impression of Roman ideas on the formation and character of the code.

In his preface, the king declared: 'The collection which follows makes evident how great was and is our care and solicitude for the welfare of our subjects ...' as '... we have perceived it necessary to improve and to reaffirm the present law, amending all earlier laws by adding that which is lacking and eliminating that which is superfluous.' Such a statement corresponds remarkably closely to the declarations of purpose that preface such Roman legal collections as Justinian's Code and Institutes, and the earlier Theodosian Code. Similarly, the title given to the code is a direct reflection of the interpretative and emendatory Edict that the late Roman Praetorian Prefect was empowered to issue, in order to modify or make pertinent the application of imperial law. It was also the title given to the similar but briefer compilation of Rothari's Italian predecessor, the Ostrogothic king Theoderic.[84]

Certain items in the Edict can in no sense represent ancestral custom. Thus, a law punishing the forging of charters by the loss of a hand is thoroughly Roman, both in the importance implicitly ascribed to written titles to property, and in the jurisprudential principles underlying the penalty to be inflicted.[85] Similarly, all tariffs of compensation for injuries – and this is what most of the Edict is concerned with – are calculated in the

Roman unit of value, the *solidus*. Perhaps most significant of all
is the fact that the laws of the Edict, whatever their supposed
traditional origins, were intended to be applied to all subjects
of the monarch, whether they were Lombards or not. This is
stated explicitly, both in a concluding section of the Edict and in
one of the laws that states that all foreigners entering the kingdom shall be subject to these rules of law unless the king agrees
otherwise.[86] This was, in other words, intended to be a fully
territorial code, applicable to all living within the geographical
regions subject to the authority of the king of the Lombards.

Some of the laws have been ridiculed as representing quaint
survivals of primitive Germanic superstition and savagery. For
the great English historian of Early Medieval Italy, Thomas
Hodgkin, writing in the late nineteenth century, 'the Code of
Rothari, promulgated on the sacred soil of Italy ... is like the
black tent of the Bedouin pitched amid the colonnades of some
stately Syrian temple, whose ruined glories touch no respon-
sive chord in the soul of the swart barbarian'.[87] Such laws as
those forbidding the killing of someone else's female slave on
the suspicion that she is a vampire would be used to support
such a contention.[88] However, other texts, such as the *Dialogues*
of Gregory the Great, provide proof, if it be needed, that such
'irrational' beliefs were to be encountered widely in Italy, as
indeed elsewhere and at all periods of antiquity and the Middle
Ages, and were in no sense a Lombard contribution to the society of the peninsula. Nor should the concentration in the Edict
on rural contexts and the legal problems to be encountered
in them make us ignore the importance of urban survival in
Lombard Italy.

What is so impressive about the Lombards is that they took
over, not without difficulty, a society in which towns were still
the administrative and economic centres of their regions, even if
the size of their populations and the state of their former public
buildings were in serious decline. The Lombards adapted effectively to this situation. Indeed, as has been seen, this is what
saved the kingdom during the great Frankish invasion of 590,
when the Lombards held the cities against them. Their royal
and ducal centres of government were town-based.[89] What is
more, certain types of public works continued to be carried out
in the towns under Lombard rule. These included repair to fortifications, and in one case at least this may have been paid for
by the royal or ducal administration.[90] Urban church building
and monastic foundation on the part of several of the seventh-
century kings and dukes is well recorded in Paul the Deacon.[91]
This continued to be a marked feature of the Lombard kingdom

in the eighth century, as is testified to by such surviving monuments as the monastic church of San Salvatore in Brescia.

Certain aspects of late Roman ceremonial and protocol were also preserved in the Lombard kingdom. In 604, Agilulf held a great ceremony in the amphitheatre in Milan, in the presence of envoys of the Frankish king Theodebert II, in which his infant son, Adaloald, was associated with him as king. Similarly, in the 670s, king Perctarit (661–2, 672–88) had a special ceremonial gate built in the palace at Pavia.[92] Indeed, war and victory remained central both to the formal role and to the practical functioning of the Lombard monarchy. The continuing pressures from both beyond the Alps and the surviving imperial enclaves in Italy placed a premium on military competence, so, despite such moves as that of Agilulf in 604 and a similar association of his son Cunincpert by Perctarit in 679, proven ability in war remained the primary quality required for the survival of a Lombard king.

Thus when Godepert and Perctarit, the sons of Aripert I (653–61), began fighting among themselves in 661/2 they were quickly overthrown by the experienced duke Grimoald of Benevento (662–71), at the behest of at least one of his northern ducal colleagues. His reign, coincidentally, was to see the most serious military threats posed to the continued existence of the kingdom since the 580s. He faced a Frankish invasion from Provence and a major Avar incursion into Friuli, while the most serious threat of all developed in the south, directed against his duchy of Benevento, which he had delegated to his son Romuald (duke 662–87). The Byzantine emperor Constans II (641–68) transferred his capital to Syracuse in Sicily in 663, and launched a campaign of conquest against the Lombard holdings in the south of Italy. All three of these invasions were met and ultimately defeated, and the murder of Constans II in 668 led to the return of the imperial government to Constantinople.[93]

If external threats decreased after the reign of Grimoald, the problem of the entrenched power of the dukes remained as a permanent challenge to royal authority.[94] The death of Grimoald in 671, leaving a minor as heir to the kingdom in the person of Garipald (671–2), led to the rapid restoration of Perctarit, who had passed an adventurous exile among the Avars and Franks, before crossing to England. A trace of this may be found in the fact that his son Cunincpert (679–700) married an Anglo-Saxon.[95] Both of these kings faced serious threats to their authority from Alahis, duke of Trento and additionally of Brescia, who early in the sole reign of Cunincpert was able to expel the latter from Pavia and briefly seize the crown.[96]

The 'Bavarian' dynasty was to be irrevocably displaced by a similar coup in 712, though its own internal divisions may have played a part in this. When the inevitable crisis of credibility was created by the succession of a minor, Cunincpert's son Liutpert (700–1), power was seized violently by a rival branch of the family, represented by Raginpert (701), duke of Turin and son of the king Godepert (661–2), who had been killed by Grimoald. The new king died in the same year, and was succeeded by *his* son, Aripert II (701–12). He in turn had to struggle against a rival aspirant in the person of duke Rothari of Bergamo, who briefly proclaimed himself king.

Among those displaced by the coup of 701 was a certain Ansprand, whose origins are never revealed by Paul but who was obviously a figure of considerable importance in the following of Cunincpert, as he was appointed *tutor* (guardian?) to the latter's heir. It was this Ansprand who in 712 invaded the kingdom with an army provided by Theotpert, the duke of the Bavarians. Paul's account of the outcome is highly obscure, in that he states that Aripert II defeated the invading army, but then felt he ought to flee to Francia, only to be drowned swimming across the River Ticino.[97] His brother Gumpert did manage to escape to the Frankish kingdoms, and his descendants were still living there and holding offices of some importance when Paul the Deacon was at the court of Charlemagne.

The crown fell into the hands of Ansprand in 712 but he died in the same year, and was succeeded by his son, Liutprand (712–44). Under this monarch, a revival of both royal power and the territorial expansion of the Lombard state took place. At the same time, though, changing conditions in the Empire, in Francia and in Rome were to lead to a combination of circumstances that would ultimately prove fatal to the continuing existence of the independent Lombard kingdom.[98] But in looking back over the period of the ascendancy of the 'Bavarian' dynasty (590–712), it is hard not to be impressed by the Lombard achievements, especially in the light of unremitting hostility on the part of so many of their neighbours and the political difficulties caused by their resulting inability to recreate a single unified Italian kingdom.

13 The parting of East and West

An end to cultural unity

The Arab conquest of North Africa in the late seventh century completed the collapse of what had once been the intellectual powerhouse of Latin Christianity. Ever since the third century, the African Church had produced the majority of the outstanding thinkers in the western tradition. Even after the death of Augustine in 430 and the Vandal conquest, Africa had continued to produce writers of high intellectual stature. Nor had they been of purely local significance: from exile in Sardinia, bishop Fulgentius of Ruspe (d. 532) had exercised considerable influence through his contacts with aristocratic and ecclesiastical circles in both southern Gaul and Rome, and which made itself felt in his letters and theological treatises.[1] In the seventh century, his writings also came to be much read in Spain.

The restoration of imperial rule over Africa in 533 by Justinian had proved to be a mixed blessing as far as the Church was concerned, even if it did put an end to the intermittent persecutions by Arian kings. Militarily, the imperial armies took over the struggle against the raids of the Berber tribes in the south, which the Vandals had been losing for the last three or four decades of their rule in Africa, and after some hard fighting reestablished stable, if reduced, southern and western frontiers.[2] However, the theological preoccupations of Justinian proved as unwelcome to the African bishops as had the Arianism of their former rulers. The emperor's condemnation of some of the works of three fifth-century theologians was resisted in various parts of the Empire and beyond because it was regarded as a denial of the authority of the Council of Chalcedon of 451, which had defined orthodoxy as far as the West was concerned, and this generated a new division in the Church known as the dispute over the 'Three Chapters'.[3]

Some of the Africans, who disputed the emperor's right to change theological orthodoxy by imperial will, led the resistance and wrote works in defence of the views of the condemned authors and challenging Justinian. They suffered exile for their pains, and attempts to impose the imperial policy by force led to a migration of African clerics and monks into Spain. They and the books they took with them made a vital contribution to the intellectual renaissance of the Spanish Church in the last quarter of the sixth century. Subsequent Spanish manuscript transmission saved a number of African writings that would otherwise have been entirely lost.[4]

Other Africans travelled, willingly or as exiles, to Constantinople in the course of the sixth century, and it is from the extant writings of the grammarian Priscian, the poet Corippus and the chronicler bishop Victor of Tunnunna (Tunis) that we can appreciate the continuing vitality of African learning in the later sixth century. Another indicator from the next century is the influence in Britain of the African abbot Hadrian, who was appointed in 668 by pope Vitalian to accompany the new archbishop of Canterbury, Theodore of Tarsus, and who soon became abbot of St Peter's monastery (better known as St Augustine's) in the Kentish capital. Among his pupils was the poet and grammarian Aldhelm, later bishop of Sherborne (705/6–9), who as a poet and letter-writer became the leading intellectual figure in the Church in southern Britain in his day.

That an African-born monk could end his life as an abbot in south-eastern Britain, and quite possibly also be exchanging letters with a bishop of Toledo (Julian) in Spain, gives an impression of the continuing network of contacts and the possibilities for travel still existing between the former territories of the Roman Empire, even as late as the middle of the seventh century.[5] A Spanish cleric from the north-west of the peninsula in the same period, bishop Fructuosus of Braga (c. 655–75), planned (though he was prevented from carrying out) a visit to the eastern Mediterranean, and his contemporary bishop Eugenius II of Toledo (646–57) wrote a (now lost) work on the Trinity to send to Africa and the East as a contribution to the contemporary theological dispute over the One or Two Wills (or Energies) of Christ, known as the Monothelete Controversy.[6] Even more striking may be the remark in the work of the Irish abbot of Iona, Adamnán (679–704) *On the Holy Places*, that his informant, a Frankish bishop, Arculf, had travelled to Arab-ruled Jerusalem, probably in the 680s, and had spent nine months there.[7]

The controversy that Bishop Eugenius II of Toledo had wanted to take part in had resulted from yet another failed attempt to settle the dispute within the eastern Church between the supporters and opponents of the theology of the Council of Chalcedon – or the Orthodox and the Monophysites as they are more succinctly called. This began with the emperor Heraclius and patriarch Sergius of Constantinople issuing in 639 a document called the *Ekthesis*, which stated that Christ had two

Natures and two Persons but only a single Will or 'Energy'. It was hoped that this formula would provide the basis for reconciliation, but it failed to attract support from most of the different groups of Monophysites and was strongly condemned both in Africa and in Rome, where uncompromising adherence to the theology of Chalcedon was the touchstone of orthodoxy. An imperial edict of the emperor Constans II in 648, known as the *Type* or 'Rule' forbade any further discussion of the issue, but instead this only served to intensify opposition, which even savage punitive measures against pope Martin I (649–53) and others failed to quell.[8]

Much more acceptable in the West were the canonical decisions of the Third Council of Constantinople of 680–1, finally condemning Monothelete theology – and pope Honorius I (625–38), the only major western Church leader to have sympathised with it. Ahead of the main Council, a synod was held in Rome in 680 under pope Agatho (678–81) to co-ordinate western theological views and condemn Monothelete teaching. Various provincial councils were also held under papal inspiration, of which that of the church in the Anglo-Saxon kingdoms, held at Hatfield in 679/80 under the direction of archbishop Theodore of Canterbury (669–90), is the best recorded.[9] Subsequently, the Fourteenth Council of Toledo was specially called in November 684 to accept the acts of the meeting in Constantinople.[10] So, the tradition of Ecumenical Councils, of which III Constantinople had been the sixth, representing all the orthodox components of Christendom, was still a living one in the late seventh century.

Trade is the topic through which most attention has been paid to the problems of continuities and discontinuities in contact and communication within the Mediterranean and beyond. Examples of exchange are not hard to find in the case of some items, such as Egyptian papyrus, which was used as a writing material for both lay and ecclesiastical documents, not only in Rome and Ravenna, but also in the Merovingian kingdoms – as evidenced by the survival of several examples from all three locations.[11] But in general, evidence for long-distance trade is slight, but that is true for almost any aspect of the economic life of antiquity and the Early Middle Ages. Miracle stories in saints' lives can be called on to compensate for the lack of harder data, as in the case of an episode in the seventh century *Life* of the patriarch of Alexandria, John the Almsgiver (610–19). In this, a trading ship, funded by the Alexandrian Church, returned from Britain with a cargo of tin. That the tin was found on arrival to have transmuted itself miraculously into silver would suggest a less than objective record. At the very least, though, it shows that the author of the *Life*, Leontius of Byzantium, both knew of Britain and was correct in referring to tin, a relatively rare metal, as a product of the island. More supportive of arguments in favour of continuing contacts with Britain in the seventh century are the finds of Mediterranean products, notably various kinds of pottery, in several trading and residential sites, particularly in the western parts of the island, from Galloway to Cornwall. The precise nature of several of these sites has been subject to debate, as in the case of Tintagel in Cornwall, which was once thought to be a royal fortress and was then reinterpreted as being a monastery. New excavations have undermined the arguments for ecclesiastical use and present it again as a secular settlement. Interestingly, an inscribed slate discovered in the course of the recently published excavations may be a document similar in character to those found in much larger numbers in Spain, and dating to the same period. The presence of a name on this slate that may be 'Artos' has, unfortunately, led to far more attention been given to the supposedly 'Arthurian' connotations, at the expense of its more interesting and real significance as evidence for the survival of Roman documentary and legal practices in parts of post-Roman Britain.[12]

All these examples of the movement of individuals, ideas and goods need to be seen against a background of growing linguistic incomprehension. St Augustine did not learn Greek at school and only seems to have mastered it later in life. After his death in 430, few of the leading figures of the western Church can be said with certainty to have learnt Greek. The layman Boethius, who translated works of both Plato and Aristotle, was certainly fluent in the language, but he was exceptional. Neither Isidore of Seville nor pope Gregory the Great (590–604), the principal Latin authors of the early seventh century, seem to have been able to read much, if any, Greek, or to have felt that this was a lack on their part. This, in Gregory's case, was despite a five-year stay in Constantinople as papal representative at the imperial court.[13]

In Constantinople, Latin came increasingly to be associated with the 'barbarians' who were the political masters of most parts of the former western Empire, and its use declined accordingly. It had been the language of the law in both parts of the Empire, and when in 528 Justinian set up a commission to codify the imperial edicts, systematise and excerpt the writings of the jurists, and produce a new introductory textbook for legal studies, all these were issued in Latin.[14] The textbook, known as the *Institutes*, which was published in 533 and was to be used by students in the two principal legal schools of the Empire, those of Beirut and of Constantinople, presupposed the continuing use of Latin in the learning and the practice of law in the East. Yet, before the end of the reign, all new imperial legislation was being issued exclusively in Greek.

On the other hand, it is important not to overemphasise the significance of this phenomenon. In the past, the level of learning in the West was measured primarily on the basis of individual authors' knowledge of, or more often lack of knowledge of, Greek.[15] But this is limited as a yardstick for the measurement of cultural attainments. The ignorance of Latin in the East is not seen as equally regrettable, besides which, numerous exceptions can be found. The African Latin poet, Flavius Cresconius Corippus, expected to be understood when he wrote a verse panegyric in Latin in Constantinople to celebrate the accession of emperor Justin II in 565. Nor did the Latin-speaking Gregory have problems in engaging in a public debate with the patriarch Eutychius in 582, during his stay in Constantinople.[16] Equally striking is the fact that a number of his seventh-century successors as pope were native Greek speakers, mainly from Sicily, and that it was possible for two native Syrians, Theodore (642–9) and John V (685–6), to become bishops of Rome in the same period.

The first serious divide within the fabric of the Mediterranean world was between north and south, and was caused by the Arab conquests. However, reactions to the rise of Islam and the extraordinary military success of the Arabs also helped to fracture the cultural cohesion of the Christian-ruled northern shores of the Mediterranean. As will be seen, the succession of demoralising military defeats and the theological challenge that Islam seemed to present caused a series of dramatic reassessments within the eastern Roman Empire, not only of strategy and administration, but also of the nature of the relationship between God and Man. The effects of this, together with the decline in the Empire's ability to play a significant military role in the defence of the West against a still expanding Arab empire, led to a breaking down of the ties that bound together the Christian world. Within the former Christian-ruled territories to the south of the Mediterranean and in Spain, the changes in political control produced equally profound intellectual change.

Christian communities survived and Latin remained in use in some eastern parts of North Africa until at least the eleventh century, but it was by then no more than the second language of a dwindling minority of the population.[17] Unlike Egypt, however, where sizeable numbers of Christians continued to dominate the villages of the Nile valley, the tribal organisation of the Berbers of

North Africa led to more rapid and extensive mass conversions to Islam; in what is now Morocco this took place primarily in the eleventh century. In such a society, conversion was less a matter of individual choice than the decision of whole communities, who elected their own leaders. Muslim holy men, whose tombs or *marabouts* dot the North African landscape, also played an important part in this process, similar to that of their earlier Christian counterparts in the evangelisation of the Syrian countryside.[18]

The Arab conquest of Spain, completed militarily in the decade after 711, increased the detachment of the African Church from western Christendom. As in Egypt, the speed of conversion from Christianity to Islam was far from rapid in Arab-ruled Spain, known as *al-Andalus,* and it is quite possible that the majority of the population in the south of the peninsula were still Christians in the early eleventh century. This was certainly what one Arab traveller said was the case in the countryside in 948. Despite the changed circumstances, the Church of Toledo retained some authority over other Christian communities in the peninsula throughout the eighth century, but a controversy that erupted in the 780s over bishop Elipandus of Toledo referring to Christ *adopting* his human nature led to the isolation of the Christian communities in the south from the rest of the Latin Church.[19]

Other theological disputes, allied to a real divide in religious sensibilities, had by this time also produced a fundamental rift between East and West elsewhere in the Christian Mediterranean. Overall, the first three-quarters of the eighth century was marked by an ultimately irrevocable fragmentation in the cultural and religious inheritance of Rome. To understand this process requires us to look at the political changes in the eastern Mediterranean in the early eighth century.

The role of Iconoclasm

In the eastern Roman or Byzantine empire, the dynasty of Heraclius came to an end in 711 with the overthrow of the flamboyant, if unstable, Justinian II (685–95, 705–11). Despite being by no means an incompetent ruler during his first reign, his single-minded pursuit of revenge on those who had opposed him or who had failed to help him during his ten-year exile led to another army revolt, and his murder and that of his only son.[20] The period of political turmoil that began with Justinian II's deposition in 695 now intensified, and three emperors ruled between 711 and 717, each in turn being overthrown, while a fourth seized power in yet another military coup in the latter year.

The new ruler, Leo III (717–41) might have been as short-lived as his predecessors, not least as the year of his accession saw another sustained effort by the Arabs to capture Constantinople. However, the 'Greek Fire' proved as effective against the Arab fleet as it had in the siege of 674–7, and so the Arab army was prevented from establishing itself on the European shores of the Bosphorus. After a year, the last major attempt by the Arabs to take the imperial capital was abandoned, and not until after the accession of the Umayyad Caliph Hisham (724–43) were their land-based attacks on the imperial territories in Asia Minor renewed.[21]

The removal of the immediate military problem gave Leo III an opportunity to create a more firmly-based regime than those of his predecessors, and the dynasty that he founded lasted for eighty-five years. Sources relating to it are very sparse, and are found principally in the entries in the *Chronicle* attributed to abbot Theophanes of Megas Agros in north-west Asia Minor (d. 818). Until recently, accounts of the reign of Leo and his son Constantine V (741–75) have been simply paraphrases of the chronicler's words.[22] However, Theophanes is by no means a friendly witness. Though close in time, his annalistic account is brief, and more importantly, he was deeply hostile to the religious policies of Leo and his successors. Thus, for example, he recorded the story of the infant Constantine V defecating into the font in the course of his baptism.[23] This was not vulgar abuse: it was intended to symbolise the damage that Theophanes thought that Constantine had inflicted on the Church in his reign.

The cause of his hostility was the imposition of Iconoclasm by Leo III and his son. Simply put, this was the prohibition of the depiction of human figures in religious art and it required the removal of all images of Christ, the Saints and Old Testament scenes from places of worship. The process began in 726, when an imperial edict was issued condemning the veneration of icons, and one of the principal sacred pictures in the city of Constantinople, the portrait of Christ that adorned the Chalke or Bronze Gate into the Palace, was destroyed on the emperor's orders.[24] More extensive measures were delayed until 730, but popular hostility to the imperial attack on religious art had already been begun. An insurrection in Constantinople was crushed in 727, and a revolt by the imperial armies in the southern Balkans and the Aegean islands was defeated, again largely through the use of 'Greek Fire'.[25]

The roots of this attack on the veneration of holy pictures are not easy to untangle. A strand in Christian thinking had long treated any attempt to depict Christ in art as a breaking of the second commandment. This had been a view expressed very forcefully by the Cypriot bishop Epiphanius of Salamis (d. 403), among others, in the late fourth century. His had also been the period in which a distinctively Christian art emerged, and the traditional iconography of Christ, angels, the leading Apostles and the representation of many biblical scenes that is still familiar today took shape. Images of Christ with long, brown hair and beard, and angels with the wings of classical Victories and wearing the robes of silentiaries of the Roman imperial court, were all created at this time, and they became fixtures by the middle of the fifth century. However, minority opposition to the whole notion of representing the sacred in human art continued to make itself felt.

Particular impetus may have been given to the re-emergence of Iconoclast, or image-hating, theology by the rise in the popularity and intensity of image veneration in the late sixth and seventh centuries. Images of Christ and the Saints were treated by worshippers as routes of privileged access to the objects of their veneration. Icons were not just pictures but were spiritually linked to their prototypes, that is to say Christ, or the Virgin Mary, or the saint who was depicted in the image. Some icons were thought to be particularly powerful. The saint worked miraculous power more effectively, or more willingly, through some images rather than others. Thus one particular icon of the Virgin Mary, known as the Hodegetria, was regarded as a very special and powerful defence for the city of Constantinople, and to its strength was attributed the lifting of the Arab siege of the city in 718, as well as its preservation from the Avars in 626. When Theophanes and other Iconodules (image venerators) had to explain such military successes on the part of the hated and heretical regime of Leo III, it was by attributing the victories to the continuing veneration of icons throughout the Empire, despite the attempts of the imperial government to destroy them.[26]

Certainly, the rising tide of popular veneration of religious images must have stirred up the counter-current of unease about such devotion and the fear of idolatry, but it is often suggested, not least by Theophanes himself, that the real catalyst for the triumph of Iconoclasm at this time was a decree of the Umayyad caliph Yazid II (720–4) forbidding the Christian veneration of religious images in the Arab-ruled territories.[27] Doubt has been cast on the reality of this edict, however, and it may be that the whole purpose of the story was to portray the Christian Iconoclasts as being no better than Muslims, whose religion was seen at this time as just a particularly heretical form of Christianity.

Even so, the frequency with which the Iconodules accused the Iconoclast emperors and their supporters of being influenced by both Muslim and Jewish doctrines suggests that the critiques that both of these religions directed against Christian religious art and the ideas that underlay it had made some impact at this time. In particular, the great territorial losses in both East and West suffered by the Empire since 634, and the succession of military humiliations at the hands of the Arabs, could easily have led to a sense that divine chastisement was being inflicted on the Christians because they had deviated in some way from true belief or right conduct. The identification of this error as the recent growth in the veneration of images makes sense in a context in which Old Testament and Apocalyptic strands in Christian thinking were again coming to the fore.

For the modern student of this period, the lack of evidence for a better understanding of the conflicting ideas and mentalities of the participants is peculiarly frustrating. The Iconoclasts under Leo III and Constantine V destroyed much of the religious art of the much reduced Byzantine empire, with the result that the mosaics of the churches that Justinian I had erected in Constantinople are all lost. In turn, the aniconic or image-less art created by the Iconoclasts was destroyed after the final restoration of icon veneration and the formal condemnation of Iconoclasm in 843.[28]

Similarly, the theological treatises and conciliar pronouncements of the Iconoclasts were almost all destroyed after the end of the period in which they had dominated the Byzantine Church. So it is very difficult to recapture much of their thinking, which now survives mainly as supposed quotations in some of the attacks made on them by their enemies. These cannot be relied on to present an objective picture of the Iconoclast position. Moderation was not the fashion in such theological conflicts. For Theophanes, the enthusiastic Iconoclast Constantine V was 'a totally destructive bloodsucking wild beast ... deceived by wizardry, licentiousness, blood sacrifices of horses, dung and urine'.[29] Thus, many problems remain insoluble in the interpretation of these issues.

What is clear is that, despite some intense initial opposition in the capital and the remaining western regions of the Empire, emperor Leo III enjoyed sufficient support from the armies in the eastern provinces in Asia Minor to be able to impose his theological policy. Indeed, the pressure to do so may have come from the eastern units, and that the emperor adopted his Iconoclast stance because this assured him of the backing of the most numerous and powerful elements in his regional armies.[30] This support proved vital for his son and successor, Constantine V, as the units of the Anatolic and Thrakesian Themes supported him against the usurper Artavasdos in 742–3, when the rebel general claimed that the restoration of Orthodoxy, implying icon veneration, was the main purpose of his revolt.[31]

By this period, the Empire had been split up into a small number of military commands, known as Themes, which were based geographically on previous Roman administrative divisions. The nature of the organisation of the army within these areas is by no means clear. It used to be thought that the Themes emerged in their fully developed form as early as the first quarter of the seventh century, and that the troops attached to each Theme were remunerated by being settled on state-owned lands within each region. They were thus farmer-soldiers, whose loyalty and commitment to the defence of their particular Theme were ensured by their being given a physical stake in it in the form of the lands allotted to them.[32]

Such a view links with older interpretations of the nature of the accommodations made with the peoples in the West by the imperial regimes in the fifth century. Traditionally, the Roman system of *hospitalitas* (hospitality) that was employed in making such arrangements with the Goths, Burgundians and others, was seen as involving the state expropriation of a third, or in some cases two-thirds, of the estates of the principal Roman landowners (the 'hosts') in the regions in which the troops were being established, in order to give the lands, together with fixed percentages of the unfree population attached to them, to the occupying forces or 'guests'.

However, it has been suggested that what was distributed was a fixed proportion of tax assessments.[33] In other words, the taxpayers – the Roman landowners, were linked directly to the beneficiaries – the soldiers who were due to receive the assigned revenues. This reduced the intermediary role of the state and its cumbersome apparatus for the centralised collection and redistribution of tax. While the evidence does not fully substantiate it, such an interpretation is perhaps more convincing than the older view. If so, this may help us to a better understanding of the nature and organisation of the Themes in the period before the tenth century.[34]

The origin of this system in the time of Heraclius has also been questioned, and it is more helpful to see the reorganisation of the army as a product of the very changed military and geographical state of the Empire after the rapid period of

Arab expansion in the 630s and 640s rather than of anything earlier. The reign of Constans II (641–68) is the one in which such changes could be expected to have started, but so limited is the evidence that all that can be said is that by the end of the reign of his son, Constantine IV (668–85), the four principal Themes of Asia Minor – the Anatolic, Armenian, Opsikian and Thrakesian – were in existence, together with another in Thrace. To these, Justinian II added Themes in Greece (Hellas) and Sicily, and Leo III created the Kibyrreot Theme in southwest Asia Minor, which was an exclusively naval force.[35]

The greatest concentration of troops was thus in the east, in Asia Minor, facing the ever-present threat of attack from the Arab caliphate. Under Hisham (724–43) this took the form of almost annual raids into the Byzantine territory in Asia Minor. To the west the Empire, apart from Sicily and the various enclaves in Italy, had been reduced to little more than the area of modern Greece and the plains of Thrace. Former Roman territories to the west and north in the Balkans were now in the hands of the Slavs and the Bulgars. The latter, a steppe confederacy, had crossed the Danube around the year 680 and established themselves south of the river under their khan Asparuch after a decisive victory over the emperor Constantine IV.[36]

Under Constantine V (741–75) the religious reforms prompted by the territorial decline and military defeats of the Empire, were taken considerably further than under his father, and embraced a wholehearted attack on monasticism and on the veneration of relics. As usual, our evidence comes only from the deliberately distorted accounts of the ultimately victorious opponents of Iconoclasm, but the references in Theophanes to the emperor forcing monks to shave off their distinctive beards and to marry are precise enough to be credible.[37] This process seems to have started in the year 765 with the execution of a famous monastic teacher and ascetic called Stephen, and probably reflects the role played by monks in leading the opposition to Iconoclasm. The *Life* of this martyr for the Iconodule cause is one of the few contemporary, if partisan, sources for this period of Byzantine history.[38]

Rome between Constantinople and Francia

The effects of the developments in the Empire on the West were considerable. In the late seventh century the emperors dominated the Church in the imperial territories, and could depose and appoint the patriarchs of Constantinople at will.

The formulation of doctrine, however, remained something that could only be done in the context of a council representing all the orthodox churches of Christendom. These were only held in the East and were all called under the authority of the rulers of Constantinople: in 680–1, the sixth in the series of Ecumenical councils was held in Constantinople by command of emperor Constantine IV to condemn the Monothelete theology, which taught, as noted above, that Christ might have Two Natures and Persons but only had one Will or Energy. Under popes Leo II (682–3), who had its acts translated into Latin, and Benedict II (684–5) the Roman Church co-operated actively in securing the acceptance of the decrees of this council throughout the West.

The next such general council was, for the westerners at least, much less successful. In 692, under Justinian II, another council was called to meet in Constantinople, and was intended to supplement the work of the previous Fifth and Sixth Ecumenical Councils of 553 and 680–681. From this it got its name of the 'Quinisext' (or 'Fifth-Sixth') Council. Doctrinally there was nothing in this council's agenda that should have caused difficulties. However, because it included in its acts regulations that for the first time formalised certain divergences in practice between the Greek and Latin Churches, it proved to be extremely divisive. The principal problem concerned clerical marriage.[39]

From the time of pope Leo the Great (440–61) firm regulations existed in the West on the subject of clerical marriage. Those already married could be admitted to the clergy, as long as it was not a second marriage. Married clergy were encouraged but not required to be celibate. Those already in clerical orders were forbidden to marry. A similar view was taken in the East, but this did not change while the western position did, moving across the centuries towards an absolute opposition to married clergy and an ambition to impose complete celibacy. The decision of the 'Quinisext' Council to include the eastern rules in its acts, which were then sent to the western Churches for ratification, forced an open debate on this issue.

Pope Sergius I (687–701), a member of a Syrian family resident in Sicily, refused to accept the decisions of the Council, though the acts had been signed by his representatives at the meeting. He took his stand not only on the issue of clerical celibacy, but also on the renewed precedence given to the see of Constantinople over the older Churches of Jerusalem, Antioch and Alexandria, an issue that had caused contention between Rome and Constantinople for nearly three centuries.

Justinian II's attempt at coercing Pope Sergius into accepting the decrees of the 'Quinisext' Council in 692 only served to show the limitations on imperial authority in Italy by the late seventh century. In 649, when pope Martin I had convened a synod in Rome that opposed Constans II over his Monothelete *Type*, the emperor had promptly ordered his arrest. The exarch, or imperial governor, in trying to carry out these orders, had found the support in Rome for the pope so strong that he manipulated it for his own purposes, and rebelled against the emperor, thus probably receiving papal recognition. However, in 653, following the rebel's death, a new exarch seized pope Martin and sent him to Constantinople for trial. He was sentenced to death, later to be reprieved but flogged and exiled, before dying in captivity.[40] In 692, when Justinian II wanted to apply the same tactics against Sergius I, not only was support for the pope's stand overwhelming in Rome but also the army in Ravenna mutinied and marched south to defend him. The commander of the emperor's bodyguard, who had been sent to Rome to arrest Sergius, was thus forced to take refuge under the pope's bed, and had to appeal to his intended victim for protection against his own soldiers.[41]

Not only had the position of the popes within the city of Rome become almost invulnerable as far as the emperor was concerned, but the possibility of imperial military intervention in Italy became ever less realistic after the collapse of the regime of Justinian II in 695 and the ensuing quarter century of military and political instability. However, the popes continued to see themselves as subject to the emperor and acted to defend his interests. Pope John VI (701–5) protected the exarch Theophylact from murder at the hands of mutinous militia, and John VII (705–7) was willing to try to compromise with Justinian II over the acts of the 'Quinisext' Council. He did, however, embellish the church of Santa Maria Antiqua in the Forum in Rome with frescoes in which his predecessor, Martin I, who had suffered at the hands of Constans II, was depicted as a saint.[42] Pope Constantine (708–15) was persuaded to visit Constantinople in 711 and was extraordinarily well received by Justinian II.[43]

The popes' willingness to co-operate with the emperors was put under considerable but not fatal strain by Leo III's Iconoclast decrees of 726. In the seventh century, imperial involvement in theological arguments had been behind all the major disputes with Rome, though the popes were normally able to blame the patriarchs of Constantinople for misleading their imperial masters. However, emperor Philippicus (711–13), who overthrew Justinian II, reintroduced Monotheletism by his own decree, and the fiction of imperial innocence could hardly be sustained any further.[44] In 726, pope Gregory II (715–31) strongly condemned not only the Iconoclast doctrine favoured by Leo III but also the whole principle of the emperor being involved in making doctrinal pronouncements.[45]

The stand taken by Gregory II was far stronger than those of Martin I in 649 and Sergius I in 692, but the emperor's ability to take action against him was very limited. Instead, between 726 and 730, he tried without success to persuade the pope to accept the Iconoclast doctrine. Leo also faced revolts in parts of northern Italy still under imperial control, which had suffered from severe increases in taxation after 717.[46] The dispatch of an imperial fleet to Italy in 732 proved disastrous, in that much of it was destroyed in a storm, with the loss of men and materials that the Empire could not easily afford, and so no further attempts were made to impose a solution by force.[47]

Despite the strain in relations at this time, what is most striking is the survival of political loyalty towards Constantinople on the part of all the popes of the early eighth century. Neither Gregory II nor his successor Gregory III (731–41), another of the numerous popes of this period of Syrian origin, wavered in their allegiance to the Empire. Gregory II dissuaded the rebels in northern Italy from setting up an emperor of their own. The tenacity of the Roman imperial traditions that underpinned the papal world view was remarkable in a period marked by the popes' consistent resistance to Leo III's religious policies. They were certainly not aiming to create a 'papal state'.

On the other hand, circumstances in Italy forced them, from the time of Gregory the Great (590–604) onwards, to play an increasingly independent political hand. Thus Gregory, faced in 593 by a Lombard siege of Rome and with no prospect of a military intervention by the exarch in Ravenna, made a separate treaty with king Agilulf. For this, he was criticised by both the exarch and the emperor Maurice, but it was their inability to defend the city that had prompted his action.[48] For similar reasons, pope Zacharias (741–52) made a twenty-year truce for Rome with the Lombards in 742.[49]

Increasingly, as the military problems facing the Empire in the East grew, the defence of Italy came to be neglected or left dependent on such local resources as the exarchs could gather. In these circumstances, the popes came to play the leading role in organising and paying for the defence of Rome. For example, a repair of the city walls was carried out by Gregory II.[50] They also began to represent wider Italian interests, and to act as spokesmen in confrontations between the provincials and the imperial government, represented by the exarch. The ecclesiastical importance of the popes gave them access to the emperor that was denied to other Italians, and enabled them to go over the heads of the exarchs if necessary. For example, pope Gregory II led the resistance to the increased rates of taxation that Leo III demanded from imperial territories in Italy.

In the circumstances of the seventh and early eighth centuries, the popes also came to play a vital role as diplomatic intermediaries between the exarchs and the Lombard rulers. The importance of this function intensified as the military situation in northern Italy turned further and further to the disadvantage of the Byzantines. In 743, pope Zacharias persuaded king Liutprand (712–44) to halt his attack on the almost defenceless exarchate, and he repeated this in negotiations with king Ratchis (744–9) in 749.[51] However, the latter's successor, Aistulf (749–56), was less easily persuaded – not least as Ratchis had been deposed by the Lombards for agreeing to the pope's request not to take Perugia – and in 751 he captured Ravenna and so eliminated the Byzantine exarchate.[52] Apart from Sicily, Apulia and Calabria in the far south, only two tiny enclaves in Venetia and Istra remained of the former imperial territories in Italy.

King Liutprand had brought Spoleto and Benevento, the two great and hitherto largely independent Lombard duchies of central and southern Italy, firmly under his control, and Aistulf had continued this. He had then gone on to capture Ravenna. A Lombard reunification of Italy seemed possible. Apart from the few surviving Byzantine enclaves in the south, the duchy of Rome, controlled for the emperor by the pope, was all that remained to be conquered.

However, it is possible that the Lombard rulers were in two minds about adding the city of Rome to their kingdom. The popes had, largely through the imperial inability to defend the central Italian duchy and the city, made themselves into the de facto secular rulers of the region, though still acknowledging the suzerainty of the emperor. They had also taken on a wider role in Italian politics and could, as did pope Gregory III, ally themselves with the neighbouring Lombard dukes of Spoleto in resisting the expansion of Lombard royal power. So, there was much to be gained in annexing the Roman duchy and eliminating it as a potential military and political threat.

On the other hand, the popes' influence extended far beyond the confines of the duchy and even of Italy, and as the foremost bishops in the West they could hardly be treated in the same way as, for example, the recalcitrant dukes of Spoleto or Benevento. Nor could the Lombard rulers openly dictate the election of popes in the way they could, from the time of Liutprand onwards, control the succession to the other duchies. So it may be that the kings of the Lombards were reluctant to try to incorporate Rome into their kingdom.[53] It seems likely that, in the early 750s, the Lombard rulers were more anxious to neutralise Rome than to annexe it. This must explain the fact that when, in the spring of 752, Aistulf invaded the duchy of Rome, he was ready to make a forty-year treaty of peace with the pope, rather than press his undoubted military advantage and take the city.[54]

From the point of view of the pope, now Stephen II (752–7), the integration of the Roman duchy into the Lombard kingdom offered no attraction, and within months of making the treaty with Aistulf in June 752 he had appealed to Constantine V for military aid. This was not forthcoming, as the emperor was busy taking advantage of the chaos following the overthrow of the Umayyad caliphate in 750 and recapturing Theodosiopolis (Erzurum) and Melitene in eastern Asia Minor.[55] In Italy, Aistulf, who had been warned that the pope was already attempting to undermine the treaty made in the summer, prepared to launch a major assault on Rome in the spring of 753. Stephen II turned for aid to the greatest Christian power in the West, the Arnulfing or Carolingian kingdom of Francia, whose ruler already stood in debt to the papacy for support in replacing the previous Merovingian dynasty in 751. The Frankish king Pippin III's subsequent intervention in Italy proved decisive in bringing about the final detachment of the papacy from Byzantine political allegiance and the creation of a new western Empire.

14 Monks and missionaries

The changes that took place in the seventh and eighth centuries were by no means all negative. One of the most striking features of this period was the way in which the former cultural boundaries of the Roman world expanded beyond the line of the former imperial frontiers, which had once represented the limits of the civilised world as far as its inhabitants were concerned. Those who lived beyond the borders had been of little or no interest to the Empire's citizens, beyond being an occasional threat to their security. It was never thought necessary to try to export the benefits of Roman civilisation to such 'barbarians'.

Inevitably, bits of Roman material and intellectual culture did seep across the borders, which became in the process increasingly attractive in the literal sense to those who lived beyond them, and population just across the frontiers grew as a result of the economic and other opportunities that proximity to the Empire offered. In due course, this contributed directly to the collapse of those frontiers and the disintegration of the old political order. In the formative centuries that followed what is customarily called 'the Fall of the Roman Empire', the large-scale political structures of late antiquity vanished in the West, and would never be restored in anything like the same way. But equally significantly, the static political and intellectual boundaries of the older order were replaced by an expanding cultural frontier. Geographical areas such as Ireland, central Europe east of the Rhine, the steppes of southern Russia, Scandinavia and Iceland, which had scarcely been touched by Rome, were brought gradually into a single cultural continuum as the result of the spread of Christianity.

In the East, from the sixth century onwards, the imperial government saw the value of exporting Christianity through missionary activity as a means of bringing hostile peoples beyond the frontiers into the political and cultural orbit of the Empire. Both in the final stages of the wars with the Zoroastrian rulers of Sasanian Persia and in the following period of conflicts with Islam, religion played a crucial role. Similarly, too, in the Balkans the threats presented to the Empire by such peoples as the Slavs and the Bulgars were ultimately contained not so much by military means, which proved only occasionally and temporarily successful, but through a cultural realignment that turned the Balkan kingdoms and khanates into what has been termed 'the Byzantine Commonwealth'.[1]

In the fourth and fifth centuries, a number of what we think must have been large-scale conversions to Christianity had taken place among the peoples entering the Empire. This was almost a 'rite of passage'. Participating in the benefits offered by Rome also meant, for the Goths, Franks and others, the acceptance of its religious values and beliefs. Extraordinarily little information exists about the mechanics of this process, as contemporaries did not regard them as being sufficiently interesting to record. On the other hand, an extensive literature of conversion came into being from the late seventh and the eighth century onwards, which provides considerable, if usually ambiguous, evidence for the conversion of the Anglo-Saxons, and of the various Germanic-speaking peoples east of the Rhine, and in Scandinavia.

In these processes, it is not easy to distinguish the religious dimension from the wider cultural context. Conversion was attractive to those who accepted it because it brought with it a range of other benefits. Thus, to take a simple example, because Christianity was a religion based on a book, which depended on a knowledge of reading and writing to understand its message, the introduction of these skills always accompanied Christianity in those societies in which literacy was not yet present. This could also, in the case of the Slavs in the Balkans, result in the creation of a new and distinctive script, reflecting the special characteristics of the spoken language.[2]

In the West, the principal architect of the movement to expand the frontiers of Christianity has often been seen as being the papacy, and a starting point has sometimes been assigned to the process in Gregory I's sending of the Roman mission to the Anglo-Saxons in 596. But papal interest in evangelism was, in fact, a relatively late phenomenon, and was largely the outcome of that particular pope's highly developed sense of his personal pastoral responsibility. This too was not so much an aspect of the ideology of the nature of papal authority that had been developing in Rome since at least the late fourth century, as a product of the growth of monastic ideas and institutions.[3]

The growth of western monasticism

When Augustine became Bishop of Hippo in 395 he established a house-monastery for his episcopal household and as a base from which he would carry out the pastoral and administrative duties of his office. He may have been one of the first western provincial bishops to do this, but he was adopting a tradition already well established in the East. Noted bishops and theologians, such as the three 'Cappadocian Fathers' – Basil, bishop of Caesarea (370–9), his brother Gregory of Nyssa (372–95), and their friend Gregory of Nazianzus (Bishop of Constantinople 379–81) – had set up 'private' monastic institutions on their own property and had tried to combine office in the Church with continuing personal commitment to an ascetic life.[4] Under their inspiration, a number of laymen created similar monastic households.

From the late fourth century, this was also the way in which many monastic institutions developed in the West. Wealthy individuals or families, inspired by the ideal of gaining personal salvation through renunciation and a disciplined and regulated life of prayer, meditation and good works, decided to turn their houses into monasteries in which to live with selected companions, following a pattern of ascetic life of their own devising. The founders of such establishments were almost always wealthy, as they depended on their own financial resources to create and maintain them.

A number of bishops, especially in Gaul, founded and endowed monastic houses, over which they themselves did not preside. Instead, they appointed abbots to govern them. Such institutions were intended to be permanent, in a way that aristocratic household monasteries might not be. It would be unwise, however, to draw too firm a distinction between such establishments. In some cases, founders of 'private' monastic houses were subsequently persuaded into accepting episcopal office, and then turned their private foundations into regular permanent monasteries. For example, Martin, Bishop of Tours (d. 397) created a private monastery at Ligugé, south of Poitiers, before his episcopal election, and after his ordination set up another one at Marmoutier on the Loire, from which to direct his diocese.[5]

A similar case is that of the famous island monastery of Lérins, near Cannes on the Côte d'Azur.[6] This was founded by Honoratus (d. 430), a member of a Gallic aristocratic family. He attracted a growing number of followers, and when he was persuaded to become bishop of Arles in 427 he appointed one of them, Maximus, to succeed him as head of the community. In turn, Maximus became bishop of Riez in 433, and his successor as abbot of Lérins, Faustus, eventually became his successor in his diocese as well.[7] By this time, Lérins had established itself as the most influential monastic house in the Rhône basin and

Provence. Others of its members, and not just its abbots, were sought after for episcopal appointments throughout the region. One of them, Caesarius, bishop of Arles (502–42) founded a major monastic house for women in his diocesan city, and wrote rules for it.[8]

Such monasteries were frequently in urban locations, but a number were also established on rural estates. Cassiodorus (d. *c.* 580) retired to his country property at Vivarium in the south of Italy after the fall of the Ostrogothic kingdom, and set up such a monastery there. For the monks he permitted to live in it under his direction, he wrote his *Institutes,* providing advice on what they should read and how they should copy books, checking their doctrinal orthodoxy and textual accuracy.[9] Many monasteries did not survive the death of their founders, but from the sixth century onwards, it became increasingly common for founders to try to ensure their continuance by putting into writing the rules of life to be followed in them. In some cases, these were just Latin translations of earlier Greek monastic rules of Basil of Caesarea (d. 379) and others.

Fuller and more comprehensive sets of regulations did, however, start to appear in the West by the sixth century. Among the earliest of these is the anonymous work known as *The Rule of the Master,* written around the year 525, possibly somewhere near Rome. Slightly later in date (*c.* 540) and in part dependent on *The Rule of the Master* is the more famous *Rule of Benedict.*[10] This is the first of the major western Rules whose author is known by name, thanks to the testimony of some of the manuscripts containing it. Biographical information on Benedict comes from the account of him in Book II of Pope Gregory the Great's *Dialogues,* a series of stories concerning the lives and miracles of recent Italian holy men, written in 593.[11]

We should not expect all the details of Gregory's stories about Benedict to be accurate, as they were primarily intended to be edifying, and in any case only the barest outline of his life can be reconstructed. Benedict (*c.* 480–547) is said to have been educated in Rome, but to have retired into a spiritual retreat in a cave at Subiaco around the age of twenty. He founded twelve monastic communities in the area over the next few years, and received the children of a number of senators from Rome for education. He subsequently moved further south and established his most famous monastic community on the site of a former pagan temple on Monte Cassino, in the Apennines north-west of Capua around the year 529.[12]

The *Rule,* composed by Benedict, has long been the best known example of such a set of instructions for leading the monastic life, as a result of attempts in the early ninth century Carolingian empire to establish uniformity in monastic, canonical and liturgical observances on the basis of a model text. Though less severe in its discipline than the majority of early medieval Irish monastic rules, the twelve 'degrees of humility' propounded by *The Rule of Benedict* show the extent of the abbot's authority over his monks. A monk was required to be obedient to his abbot in all things, to have no will of his own, not to complain about any injuries or ill-treatment to which he might be subjected when under obedience, to 'be content with the meanest and worst of everything', to call himself and think of himself as being the lowest of the low, to take no independent action, not to speak except in reply to a superior, and to avoid laughter.[13]

Benedict's *Rule*, like that of 'the Master', was unusual in its time for being so all-embracing in what it wanted to regulate. The other rules, mainly anonymous or wrongly ascribed to famous authors, that were followed in the monasteries of southern Gaul in the fifth to eighth centuries, remained closer to eastern originals, in that they were concerned more with the nature of the spiritual instruction to be provided and less with the details of communal life. That the *Rule of Benedict* emerged as the most widely used of all western monastic rules was certainly a product of its intrinsic merits, but its spread was also a reflection of the influence of pope Gregory the Great, and in particular of his popular *Dialogues*.

Of the popes of the early Middle Ages, Gregory I (590–604) – known as 'the Great' – is the most outstanding, as well as the best known. The survival of 850 of his official letters (though only a small proportion of the total that once existed) provides an extraordinary insight into the working of his mind and the practical problems he faced during his pontificate.[14] To this letter collection can be added the substantial corpus of his exegetical writings, composed mainly during his period as papal representative in Constantinople (*c.* 580–5) and in the opening years of his pontificate.[15]

Almost all of these were written for monastic audiences and readers. For where Gregory was most original was in being the first pope who was also a monk. He belonged to the tradition of the founders of aristocratic 'house-monasteries', having turned his family house on the Caelian Hill in Rome into a monastery. Like a number of other bishops, he also maintained a monastic lifestyle during his pontificate.[16] It was from his community on the Caelian that he chose the group of monks whom he sent under Augustine to evangelise the Anglo-Saxon kingdom of Kent in 596.

The subsequent history of missionary ventures has often been seen as a symbiosis between Irish monasticism (which will be discussed below) and the Roman traditions that lie behind Gregory's mission to Kent. The Anglo-Saxon Church's involvement from the later seventh century onwards in missions to spread the Gospel to the pagans east of the Rhine (not least their own continental Saxon 'relatives') developed from these two elements in its own genesis. In turn, the special ties between the Anglo-Saxons and the papacy provided a route through which the Frankish rulers, under whose political aegis the missionaries had to work, renewed their contacts with Rome. From these derived the papal support for the replacement of the Merovingian dynasty by the Carolingians in 751, and ultimately the coronation of the second king of this line as the new Roman emperor in the year 800.[17]

This reconstruction has at least the virtue of neatness. However, the reality of the past is rarely as tidy as we might like, and these events present a case in point. While both Irish monasticism and the papacy had roles to play in the expansion of Latin Christianity, and in the political and cultural realignments of eighth-century Francia, we should not emphasise these to such an extent that other elements are hidden. In this chapter, the first parts of these processes, the missionary ventures, will be examined, while the political developments in Francia will be considered in Chapters 15 and 16.

The Irish Church

Ireland was the first territory beyond the Roman imperial frontiers in the West that was converted to Christianity by missionary activity. In turn, the Irish Church was to play a crucial role, both in the promotion of monasticism elsewhere in Western Europe and in the further geographical expansion of the Christian message, and thus also some of the intellectual culture of late antiquity. So the origins and distinguishing characteristics of Irish Christianity need to be considered here. However, these topics remain controversial. The problems are, not surprisingly, evidential ones, but they are intensified by a further linguistic dimension.[18]

Much of the source material is written in Old Irish ('archaic' and 'classical') and in Middle Irish, both of which are sufficiently far removed from the modern language for genuine difficulties of interpretation to occur.[19] In particular, there have been problems in trying to assign dates to many of the vernacular texts by using linguistic criteria. Dating is, of course, central to the question of

what weight to allow to the witness of particular sources, especially when, as in the case of many of the Irish texts, the extant
manuscripts are all relatively modern (for example, as recent as
the seventeenth century), and are thus no guide in themselves.[20]

The dating of the numerous law tracts has proved to be
among the most contentious of issues, but that of the various
sets of annals upon whose testimony the chronological framework of early Medieval Ireland must hang has been scarcely
less so.[21] The generally accepted view, though, is that the contemporary recording of events in the extant sets of annals cannot have begun earlier than *c.* 730.[22] Some annals and narrative
histories have been shown to be both much later in date and containing a good deal of literary invention – in other words fiction –
than was once thought.[23] Other quasi-historical texts, such as
saints' lives, which also used to be treated as having considerable value as evidence, have also been subjected to new critical
scrutiny. While such works are of intrinsic interest, their value
as genuine records of the early Medieval centuries has in most
cases been reduced.[24]

The limited quantity of pertinent evidence relating to many
subjects of interest, and the presence of much unhistorical leg-
endary material in so many texts, makes the study of this period
peculiarly difficult. Not the least controversial topic is that of the
arrival of Christianity in Ireland. In the indigenous tradition,
the primary role has always been ascribed to Patrick. However,
there is still no agreement on whether his activities should be
dated to the first or second half (the more likely option) of
the fifth century, and that is just the start of the problems to
be faced in trying to make sense of him.[25]

To sidestep what would otherwise have to be a lengthy historiographical discussion, it is fair to say that the only sources concerning Patrick that should be taken into account in studying
his life, as opposed to the growth of his legend, are the works
he himself wrote. Two subsequent *Lives* (or rather a *Life* and a
Memorandum) by Muirchú (*c.* 690) and Tírechán (*c.* 670), provide no route to the realities of the fifth century.[26] Similarly, the
substantial *Tripartite Life* of *c.* 895/900 is a marvellous guide to
the ambitions at that time of the monastery of Armagh, which
claimed to have been founded by him. It was on the strength of
that supposed but highly improbable foundation, that Armagh
began claiming an absolute pre-eminence in the Irish Church.
So, the *Tripartite Life* is even further removed from the real
Patrick than the works of Muirchú and Tírechán.[27]

Patrick's own writings, though, are tantalisingly obscure.
They consist of a *Confessio*, which seems to be a defence against

slanders that were being circulated about him, and a letter directed to the soldiers of a certain Coroticus.[28] In the former, Patrick referred to various events in his life: how at the age of sixteen he had been taken from Britain to be sold as a slave by an Irish raiding party, and how he had escaped six years later. Then, after he had returned to Britain (the chronology at this point becomes extremely vague), he had experienced a vision in which he received letters from Ireland via a certain Victoricus, appealing to him to come back.[29] In consequence, he devoted the rest of his life to missionary activity in Ireland, becoming a bishop in the course of it. There may have been doubts at the time as to the validity of his episcopal ordination, which may have been performed irregularly – it would have had to be carried out, for example, by three other bishops; possibly a difficult requirement in Britain at the time. It has also been suggested that his ministry in Ireland was directed mainly at groups of fellow Britons, who, like himself, had been carried off in Irish slave raids.[30] If this view is correct, then we cannot know precisely when, how and by whom the Irish themselves were converted to Christianity.[31]

While the authors of later *Lives*, who shared with the modern historian the problem of developing a coherent account from Patrick's own obscure writings, explicitly attribute the introduction of Christianity into Ireland and the conversion of the most powerful kingdoms to his missionary activity, this is almost certainly an exaggeration. Both from independent sources and from the logic of Patrick's own words, it is clear that there were Christians in Ireland before he began his work there.

Despite never being politically a part of the Roman Empire, and in consequence retaining elements of a pre-Roman Iron Age social order for much longer than most other parts of Western Europe, Ireland was influenced by the culture of its dominant neighbour from the first century onwards, especially via Britain.[32] That this involved the gradual penetration of Christianity, either through Britain or northern Gaul, is proved not least by the reference in the contemporary *Chronicle of Prosper* to pope Celestine in 430 sending 'the Irish believing in Christ' a certain Palladius, probably a deacon of the Roman Church, to be their 'first bishop'.[33] In his *Life of Patrick*, Muirchú, who knew Prosper's work, had to kill off Palladius after an abortive visit to Ireland, to safeguard Patrick's status as the true founding father of the Irish Church.[34]

In view of this evidential obscurity, it is hard to say more than that it looks as if Christianity was establishing itself in Ireland in the course of the fifth century, as it was also doing at this time in Roman Britain and among some of the independent Celtic kingdoms north of Hadrian's Wall.[35] It is not certain how soon monastic communities began to appear in either Britain or Ireland, though some certainly existed in the former by the time of Gildas (fl. 520/40). The Irish evidence is even less clear, in that the subsequent centuries saw a proliferation of monasteries anxious to claim an early and distinguished origin for themselves. For such reasons, a large body of highly inventive but unhistorical saints' lives came to be written in these monasteries, mainly intended to endow their founders with miraculous powers and deeds. The evidence of most of these texts has to be discarded in trying to get back to the real origins of Irish monasticism. From what little can be used in such a quest, it seems that by the end of the sixth century a small number of monastic communities had come into being in Ireland. The same can be said of western Scotland, where cultural contacts with Ireland extended back for centuries, if not millennia. Between the two, and the islands in between, there has been a constant movement of population since prehistoric times.

Such early monastic establishments should not be imagined as being like later medieval monasteries. Nor were they similar to the aristocratic 'house-monasteries' of the south of Gaul, Rome and North Africa, which constituted the principal form of monastic institution before the spread of the Irish monks. We can get the best impression of what the earliest Irish monastic communities were like from some of the extant monastic sites in Ireland and the Hebrides, such as Glendalough, Clonmacnois, Monasterboice and Iona, while recognising that most of their more visible features, such as their stone churches and round towers, date from the tenth to twelfth centuries. Such monasteries are reminiscent of the earliest communities of Egypt and Syria, in that within the compound wall each monk had his own individual hut or cell. They contained several small and architecturally very simple churches, each dedicated to a different saint and, at this period, built like the monastic cells, entirely in wood rather than stone. These churches were places of pilgrimage and meditation rather than settings for communal worship.[36]

Those Irish monasteries that are known to have existed by the late sixth century include Bangor (Co. Down), founded by Comgall; probably Ciaran's foundation at Clonmacnoise; and certainly the three linked communities of Derry, Durrow and Iona (in the Inner Hebrides) that were created by Columba (d. 597).[37] It is possible that others were equally firmly established by this time, but the nature of the relevant evidence is too unreliable for certainty in most cases. The foundation of Iona in 565 represents the first establishment of an Irish monastery outside the island.[38] It is also the earliest reasonably securely dated (an important qualification) Irish monastery. Monasteries certainly existed in Britain, from at least the early sixth century, and it is possible that the current of influence, normally seen as flowing from Ireland eastwards into Argyll, in fact, ran more strongly in the opposite direction, and that Iona helped to spread the British monastic tradition westwards into Ireland.

Before considering the nature and effects of the Irish impact on Europe, it is necessary to look briefly for the answers to two questions: why did monastic communities start to play a dynamic role in Irish society so quickly; and why were they such useful vehicles for the transmission of a learned, but only recently received, intellectual culture to other regions outside Ireland? A lack of towns, at least before the tenth century, and the peculiarities of the political structures of Irish society made the creation of episcopal dioceses similar to those of the Roman Empire a practical impossibility in Ireland. However, monasteries that resembled those of Egypt, in terms of their size and organisation, provided an alternative. While the evidence is not impressive either in quantity or clarity, it is possible that by the seventh century the greater monastic communities had become the principal ecclesiastical landowners in the island, and that their abbots were by then the main source of authority in its Church. It is often pointed out that a monastery might in consequence include a bishop in its community, who performed the liturgical functions that were particular to his office, but who remained subordinate to the abbot.[39] This system may, however, have been peculiar to the monastic confederacy created by Columba.[40]

Attempts have been made to explain such developments, which were quite out of step with the organisation of the Church elsewhere in Europe. Most would relate them to the lack of large-scale political structure in Ireland at this time, when the island was divided into many small and not very stable kingdoms, perhaps between eighty and a hundred in number.[41]

We must avoid the rigid categorisation beloved by the creators and subsequent glossators of the Old Irish legal texts that offer a pattern of different types of kingdom, neatly and hierarchically arranged, with the rights of 'over-kings' in relation to their 'sub-kings' precisely tabulated.[42] The reality was altogether messier, with dramatic shifts in local and regional power depending on the competence as war leaders and providers of reward (treasure, cattle and beer) of individual kings. It was on such grounds that a small kingdom could grow to become a big one, or just as easily be overrun by a neighbour. The king of a *tuath*, the basic small tribal–political unit, might find himself obliged to pay tribute to a more powerful local ruler, but only for as long as the latter had the power to enforce it. We have already seen something similar in Britain, in the case of Ecgfrith of Northumbria in 685 facing a successful revolt by his Pictish sub-king, following his defeat by the previously equally subservient ruler of Mercia.

In such circumstances, monasteries, given lands and herds by local rulers, and in many cases with the royal house also appointing the abbots from its own ranks, proved easier to establish than episcopal dioceses, whose boundaries could rarely correspond to fluctuating political frontiers. The lack of centralised authority in Ireland also meant that there was no secular power that could guarantee the protection of the ecclesiastical organisation in the way that was standard elsewhere in Western Europe.[43]

Monks were also more able than secular clergy to fit into the slots in Irish society recently vacated by the pagan learned and priestly classes. Rigorous asceticism and mortification seem to have formed part of the initial training and subsequent lifestyle of the *druid* and the *filid* or 'seers' – who may for convenience be called the poets and the magicians. The former in particular were of vital importance in pre-literate Irish society, for their memorising of laws, genealogies and heroic poems provided the only means of preserving the records of the kingdoms, and thus the historical dimension of their separate identities.[44]

With the introduction of writing, the monasteries, many of which were established close to the main royal centres, took over most of these functions. The monks also acquired the legal status and immunities once enjoyed by the pagan learned classes. A number of the monasteries, such as Clonmacnoise and Kildare, became intellectual centres to which aspiring monks were drawn, as much by their reputation for learning as for the ascetic sanctity of their abbots, who exercised an authority very reminiscent of the Egyptian founding fathers of coenobitic monasticism.

Because Ireland had never formed a part of the Empire, the Latin language and the literary culture of Rome and of Christianity were alien. This is not to say that the Irish were unaware of their powerful neighbour, but it meant that the conversion of the Irish involved not just a change in religious allegiance but also a major cultural transformation.[45] Irish clerics became avid to obtain whatever they could of the literary records of their new faith. They were also, because they had had to learn Latin to master the texts they needed to read, uniquely well qualified to instruct others who were similarly placed, such as the Germanic-speaking Anglo-Saxons.[46]

In a way that is again most reminiscent of the traditions of Egyptian and Syrian monasticism, the Irish monks took very literally the injunctions concerning self-negation and renunciation. Since a desert could hardly be found in Ireland, this could instead take the form of physical withdrawal to rocks and small islands off the coast, illustrated most dramatically by such a site as Skelig Michael in the south-west. But withdrawal could also be achieved by self-imposed exile away from the local society, which guaranteed the individual his freedom and status, and where his strong family and tribal ties were located. In consequence, there developed the tradition of what later became known as the greater and the lesser *Peregrinatio*, or pilgrimage. In both forms, the ascetic withdrew from the protection that came from his own family and *tuath*. In the lesser form he removed himself from the boundaries of his own kingdom, in which his security had been guaranteed by his family and his ruler. In the greater form he withdrew entirely from Ireland, under a self-imposed vow not to return.[47]

It has often been assumed that this tradition of *Peregrinatio* was what led Irish monks to cross the seas to Britain and to the Continent, there to found or join existing monastic communities. This would make it the motivating force for the impetus given by the Irish to Western European monastic reform and expansion, and thus the mainspring of the whole movement of missionary activity. Yet, as with so many of the traditional certainties of the scholarly consensus on early Irish history, it starts to crumble in the hand the more closely it is examined. The evidence, inevitably, post-dates the supposed early stages of the phenomenon, and in the classifications of *Peregrinatio* we may once again be encountering the love of artificial systematising that is typical of so many of the normative texts, both secular and ecclesiastical, produced in early medieval Ireland. It is clear that Columba, who according to the rules should never have returned to Ireland after the foundation of Iona in 563 or 565, frequently went back there in later years.[48]

Certainly, Irish monks in their self-imposed (if reversible) exile took themselves to the Continent, following long-established trade routes, and founded communities in what were intended to be remote locations in Gaul and northern Italy. The best known of the continental Irish monastic founders is Columbanus (d. 615), whose rule for the ordering of the daily life and discipline of his monks has survived, together with a small collection of his letters. He was also the author of a penitential, which, in three sections devoted to monks, the secular clergy and the laity, respectively, laid down the penances to be imposed as expiation for a large number of offences.[49] This work shows traces of borrowings from an earlier British or Irish penitential ascribed to a certain Vinniau, who might be identified with a correspondent of Gildas of the same name, or indeed be Bede's 'Ninian'.[50] All these works were written in a distinctively florid Latin. At some point before *c.* 660, an Italian disciple and monk of Bobbio, Jonas of Susa, wrote a *Life of Columbanus*, which is the principal source for our knowledge of him.

From Jonas's work, it seems that Columbanus arrived in Francia around the year 590 and established two monastic communities in the Vosges – at Annegray and at Luxeuil. His relations with the Gallic episcopate were not good, largely because of the liturgical and other differences between Irish practices (not least concerning the dating of Easter) and those more generally followed in the Latin Church.[51] Despite this, he enjoyed royal protection, until he offended king Theuderic II (596–613) by refusing to bless his illegitimate children. This led to his expulsion from the Frankish kingdom of Burgundy and his eventual removal into Lombard Italy, where, with the backing of King Agilulf, he established the last of his foundations, at Bobbio, prior to his death in 615.[52]

Such monasteries on the Continent attracted other Irishmen to them, either to join or to visit in the course of pilgrimages. In consequence, they became channels through which more Christian Latin texts were passed to Ireland. For example, a number of the works of Isidore of Seville reached Ireland soon after their author's death in 636, probably by transmission via Bobbio.[53] These Irish monasteries also began to interest the local inhabitants of the regions in which they were established, and several entered them as monks. Thus, Columbanus's successors as abbots of Bobbio were not of Irish origin.[54] In general, this should warn us not to overemphasise the Irishness of these monasteries, particularly after the first generation. If non-Irish speakers were attracted into them it was because the Irish linguistic element in them was not strong. The language of the liturgy, the works of exegesis and scriptural study, and of the monastic and penitential rules, was Latin. The language used by the monks in general to communicate with each other must have been one that was mutually comprehensible – so this could not have been Irish.

As such foundations proliferated they started to attract the attention of members of the local Frankish aristocracy, some of whom themselves considered becoming monks or establishing settlements of monks on their own estates.[55] For example, the Frank, Wandregisel, founded the monastery of Fontanelle in the Seine valley in 648, apparently in consequence of a dream in which he saw the life of the monks of Bobbio, an at least implicit indication of a debt to Columbanus's work.[56] The neighbouring monastery of Jumièges was founded around 655 by another Frankish aristocrat called Philibert, apparently also under some Irish influence. It was largely, though not exclusively, via this Irish-inspired movement that such monastic houses began to proliferate in certain parts of Francia.

It is important, though, to recognise first that what may be called indigenous Gallic monastic traditions were already long established and, second, that some regions of the Frankish kingdoms were more rapidly and more intensely influenced by the Irish than others. The sites for most of the Irish or Irish-inspired monastic foundations in Francia in the seventh century are to be found in the area between the Seine and the lower Meuse, or in parts of central Burgundy between Besançon and Strasbourg. Very few of the new houses were located outside these regions.[57] Thus, while Irish traditions such as the *Peregrinatio* and Irish monks played a significant part in the expansion of the frontiers of Latin Christianity, we must not forget the existence of alternative sources of inspiration. Over 200 new monasteries are known to have been founded in Gaul in the seventh century, and only a limited number of these can be linked to Irish connections or influence. Indeed, in view of the slight nature of the evidence, it is possible to speculate that the growth of Irish monasticism in this same period may have been stimulated by these continental developments.

There has been a fashion for attributing virtually every development in the intellectual and spiritual life of Western Europe in the later seventh and the eighth centuries to Irish influence. Extraordinary claims were made for the learning of the Irish scholars, which in some cases was supposed to include a fluent knowledge of Greek.[58] In practice, though, the number of texts that can be found in Ireland itself, compared to continental monasteries that had some Irish links, is both small and of limited character. By and large, such works consisted of biblical exegesis and other aids to scriptural study, computus (necessary for liturgical calculations), and relatively simple grammars.[59]

These were also the kinds of texts that were produced by Irish writers. The more enthusiastic Irish scholars went to the Continent, not just for pilgrimage and monastic retreat, but also to uncover its store of learning. In consequence, they did blow the dust off some books that may have ceased to be read, and may also have awoken some of their Western European contemporaries to the treasures among them. Even so, what they were looking for was not a revival of the secular literature of antiquity, but works of exegesis, grammar, and monastic spirituality and Rules. The Irish appreciated the *Rule of Benedict* almost before anyone else, and a number of the monasteries they founded or influenced lived under a mixed Rule, combining Benedict's work with that of Columbanus.[60] This also influenced the hold that the *Rule of Benedict* had on the monasteries of Northumbria, though here the special reverence of the Anglo-Saxons for Gregory the Great, who had mentioned this rule in his *Dialogues*, may also have played a part.

The rigorousness of monasticism in Ireland, the reputation for sanctity of many of its leading ascetics, and the new impetus it gave to scriptural studies began to attract visitors to the island from the Continent by the middle of the seventh century. Among these was the Frankish aristocrat Agilbert, who was in due course to become bishop of Wessex (650s) and later of Paris (667/8–*c*. 680).[61] Ireland, in these respects, began to offer something of the spiritual appeal of the desert monasteries and ascetic teachers of Egypt and Palestine, access to which was now reduced because of the Arab conquest. From this milieu of Franco-Irish monastic development was to spring much of the impetus behind the great missionary ventures of the seventh and eighth centuries.

Spreading the word

The roots of the processes that led to the spread of Christianity, and with it elements of the intellectual culture of late antiquity, into regions beyond the former frontiers of the Roman Empire are complex. The primary means of its achievement has long been recognised as monasticism. Monks were ideally suited for missionary ventures, in that not only were they tightly disciplined and under obedience to their superiors, but the monastic ideal of renunciation, involving physical relocation, and the endurance of bodily privation, made them ready to move into potentially hostile territories and to put up with considerable hardship.

They were also better able to operate in lands in which there were few, if any, functioning towns, around which non-monastic ecclesiastical structures would normally expect to organise themselves. As shown by Augustine of Hippo and others in the fifth century, it was quite possible for bishops to perform their administrative, pastoral and liturgical functions whiles living within a monastic household.[62] Thus, in due course, it proved relatively easy for the diocesan administration of territories that had no towns to be centred on monasteries. Additionally, monasteries were also able to serve as schools, a facet of their functioning that was particularly important in societies in which town life, around which the older Roman secular educational system had evolved, was absent.[63]

However much monasticism seems the obvious instrument for the physical expansion of Christianity in these centuries, though, there were features of it that militated against such a development. For example, particularly in the West, there was a considerable emphasis placed on stability. Individual monks and ascetics not under the authority of recognised superiors or resident in fixed locations were distrusted. Several regional churches legislated against 'vagrant monks' in the acts of their provincial synods.[64] Moreover, the whole tenor of monastic spirituality was directed towards the inner, contemplative life, rather than the cultivation of active programmes of 'good works'. It was to escape the distractions of the *Saeculum* that monks gathered together in withdrawn communities and devoted themselves to regular observance.

However, especially in Gaul, there had long existed traditions of monastic evangelisation. These stretched back to the time of Martin of Tours (d. 397), the founder of Ligugé and Marmoutier, who, according to the *Life* written by his aristocratic disciple Sulpicius Severus, had devoted much effort during his episcopate to the extirpation of paganism in the rural parts of his diocese.[65] The spread of the cult of Martin after his death is also closely associated with evangelism. In north-west Spain, the conversion of the Suevi from Arianism to Catholicism is associated by Gregory of Tours with the arrival of relics of Martin from Tours.[66] Similarly, the church of *Candida Casa* that may have been a centre of the preaching of Christianity to the southern Picts in the fifth century was subsequently dedicated to St Martin, relics of whom may have been deposited there.[67]

It is important also to note that the Frankish Church was well aware of the existence of pagans living on the fringes of the Merovingian kingdoms. When Pope Gregory was preparing the dispatch of his monks to the kingdom of Kent in 596, he wrote to the bishops of the various Frankish dioceses through which they would pass, soliciting assistance for the missionaries.[68] Even more significantly, in some of the Anglo-Saxon kingdoms Frankish clergy played a crucial role in the early stages of the establishment of Christianity. The second bishop in the kingdom of Wessex (*c.* 650) was the Frank, Agilbert, whose nephew Leuthere was later to be bishop of Winchester (670–6). Similarly, the first bishop of the East Angles (*c.* 630) was a Burgundian called Felix, who established his see at *Dummoc* (Dunwich?).[69] At the same time, the degree of Frankish political involvement in Britain should not be exaggerated. There is no evidence for a Frankish hegemony over any of the southern Anglo-Saxon kingdoms. The latter is a good case of an idea that is first advanced as a speculation, but which turns itself into dogma through constant repetition.[70]

It is notable that Frankish royal support for missionary ventures on the frontiers of their realms pre-dates the beginning of the Roman and Irish inspired Anglo-Saxon missions to the Continent, which got under way in the late seventh century. In particular, Dagobert I (623–38) may have inspired and certainly backed the activities of the Frankish evangelist and monastic founder, Amandus. As with so many of the leading figures of the Gallic Church in the sixth to ninth centuries, information about Amandus comes principally from a *Life*. Unfortunately, many of these hagiographical compositions, whose authors are usually anonymous, are either hard to date or have been shown to have been written at periods long after the lifetime of their subject. There was clearly a more developed tradition of such writing in Francia, related to liturgical commemoration of particular founders, patron saints and bishops of special note in their own dioceses.[71] In the ninth century, numerous such *Lives* of the luminaries of the Gallic Church were composed and existing ones rewritten to make them better suited to contemporary needs. Thus, in the great five-volume edition of Merovingian saints' lives produced in the late nineteenth century by the *Monumenta Germaniae Historica,* very few of the texts they contain are genuinely early. The editor, Bruno Krusch, attributed the greater part of them to the Carolingian period. This view has been revised somewhat in recent decades, and a handful of the works that Krusch distrusted are now seen as being of Merovingian date. Also more allowance is now made for the existence of earlier elements being preserved within a Carolingian rewriting.[72]

The *Vita Amandi* is less problematic than some of these texts, but its history is by no means straightforward. As one of its stories was vouched for by a named monk known to the anonymous author, the work may have been written soon after Amandus's death, around 675.[73] However, arguments exist for placing the actual date of composition somewhere in the middle of the eighth century, and it is clear that the chronological structure of the *Life* is by no means fully reliable.[74] While this must affect the assessment made of the work and the weight to be assigned to the individual features of its account, it is at least useful testimony to what the monks of Elnone, among whom was probably numbered the author, believed they knew of their founder at that time.

Particularly significant is the association between Amandus's vow of perpetual exile and his entry into the clergy, with a visit to the tomb of St Martin at Tours. He was an Aquitanian and, though the cult of Martin was by this time widespread, it was particularly powerful in the Loire valley and northern Aquitaine. Amandus's roots would thus appear to be located in the Martinian tradition, and not in Irish monasticism, which had made little impact on Aquitaine.[75] Even the reference to 'exile' is no indicator of Hibernian influence, in that Martin, who came from Pannonia, had undertaken all his monastic and episcopal activities in regions far from his native land.

The second element that the author of the *Life* wished to underline in Amandus's motivation was Roman. After a period of ascetic preparation in the vicinity of Bourges, lasting for fifteen years, Amandus went to Rome to visit the shrines of the saints. In the basilica of St Peter, where he passed the nights, he experienced a vision of the Apostle, who instructed him to undertake the task of 'preaching' (*praedicatio*). This term was one much used by, and given special significance by, Gregory the Great. It did not mean 'sermonising', but rather the undertaking of a duty of spiritual responsibility and guidance.[76] It is clear also from the author's words that this charge, though presented in a visionary context, was essentially a papal one. Amandus received the blessing of the pope (unnamed) and was given relics, the prerequisite for the foundation of churches. The pope in question was almost certainly Honorius I (625–38), the first since Gregory the Great, whom he greatly revered, to maintain a monastic lifestyle during his pontificate, and who had turned his family mansion in Rome into a monastery.[77] He was, therefore, a conscious emulator of Gregory, and his support for Amandus's missionary plans should be treated as a dimension of this.

Amandus's missionary activities covered a wide geographical range. The first and ultimately most important of his areas of operation was the region to the east of the river Scheldt, which, though under Frankish rule, was still predominantly pagan. In his missionary work here, Amandus operated with the backing of Bishop Acharius of Noyon (d. 640), and through him with that of king Dagobert, who was probably the donor of the royal estates on which the monastery of Elnone (later called St Amand) was founded.[78] The *Life* speaks generally of Amandus's success in this area, though he encountered difficulties with at least one of its Frankish counts. He is also reported to have travelled and preached 'across the Danube' to the Slavs.[79] This is vague but must indicate another missionary venture further to the south: possibly in the old Roman provinces of Norricum and Pannonia.

Amandus was not just the evangelist and wonder worker that the author of the *Life* is so keen to depict. He was also a figure of considerable political importance. Certainly in the 640s, he was closely allied to the powerful family of the Austrasian mayor of the palace, Grimoald (d. 657), and it is possible this was equally true in the time of the latter's father, Pippin I (d. 640). Moreover, he was chosen by Dagobert I to be the 'co-father' (*compater*) of his son Sigebert. This is significant in that, first, the relationship of compaternity – between the father and the god-father of a child – was a very close one; so Dagobert must have wanted to forge special ties with Amandus.[80]

Second, and this may lie behind Dagobert's decision, Sigebert was illegitimate. Columbanus had refused even to bless the illegitimate sons of Theuderic II, and none of them had managed to maintain themselves in the kingdom of Austrasia after their father's death in 613. Whether this was the precedent that worried Dagobert is not clear. However, Amandus's influence in Austrasia was clearly significant, and it is possible that his Roman connections were also important. His acceptance of the role of godfather may thus have made possible Dagobert's nomination of the infant Sigebert (III) as king of Austrasia in 634.[81] For Amandus, this act gained him the immediate support of the most powerful Merovingian king of the seventh century, and the prospect of future backing from his new godson. It is notable that he did not take the kind of stand that Columbanus had and, while it is hard to generalise from one example, it is possible that the greater rigidity of Irish adherence to the rules of canon law and emphasis on public penance made them less compromising and thus less effective in their dealings with the secular powers on the Continent.

The interests of the ruler may also have influenced Amandus's next choice of mission field. This was to be among the Basques south of the Garonne, the future Gascony. It is notable that this coincided with Dagobert's acquisition of the kingdom in Aquitaine previously held by his half-brother, Charibert II (629–32), and with a large-scale campaign to subjugate the Basques of the western Pyrenees in 635. While no mention is made of this in the *Life*, the timing suggests that Amandus was attempting with royal support to put the Basques more firmly under Frankish lordship through conversion, which meant the adopting of the value systems of the conquerors. As in later complaints about the Vikings, the Basques are frequently denounced in the Frankish sources for 'perfidy'; that is, the breaking of oaths. But if the value systems of the two parties to an agreement are different, what is sacred to one side is no more than expedient to the other. In practice, Amandus does not appear to have been successful, and the division of the kingdom on Dagobert's death, with the legitimate Clovis II acquiring Aquitaine, put an end his efforts in this area and led to his return to Austrasia.[82]

Here, at the behest of Grimoald, the mayor of the palace, he became bishop of Maastricht in 648/9, but was faced with considerable opposition from his clergy towards his programme of spiritual regeneration, leading him to resign the see in 650/1.[83] However, the strength of the cult of St Martin of Tours in the Scheldt valley in the seventh century may be the product of his influence. His continuing links with Rome at this time are demonstrated by the chance survival of the text of the letter sent to him in 650 by pope Martin I (649–53), dealing with the recent papal condemnation of Monotheletism.[84] He was also closely involved with the family of the mayor of the palace in the creation in 648/9 of the monastery of Nivelles on their estates and the installation of Grimoald's sister, Geretrudis (d. 659), as its first abbess. Two other monasteries may have been founded by the Arnulfing family with Amandus's aid at this time: those of Fossès (651?) and of Moustier-sur-Sambre (650?).[85]

Paradoxically, the longer-term beneficiaries of this campaign of monastic foundation were to be Irish monks. When in *c.* 651 the Irish abbot Foíllán and his followers were expelled from Péronne by the Neustrian mayor of the palace, Erchinoald, they were given refuge at Fossès, and Nivelles, which had begun as a single monastery for women, and was then transformed into a double monastery, a peculiarity of the Irish tradition.[86] Amandus, on the other hand, seems to have lost wider influence after his retirement from Maastricht, possibly affected by the temporary eclipse of the Arnulfing family in the period 657–*c.* 675. It is likely that he continued his evangelising ventures from his monastery of Elnone, but apart from an attempt, resisted by the local bishop, to found a monastery in the diocese of Uzès in the south of the kingdom of Burgundy, little is reported of him until his death in 674/5. Even so, the fact that his southern venture enjoyed the backing of Childeric II, and that it coincided with that king's short-lived extension of his authority from Austrasia into Neustria and Burgundy in the years 673–5 suggests that once again Amandus was playing a role that was as much political as spiritual.[87]

The case of Amandus is particularly important, in that it highlights the contributions made by indigenous Gallic monastic and missionary traditions, and the links between Amandus, the Frankish rulers and Rome in the mid-seventh century closely parallel the kind of ties that were to develop between the Anglo-Saxon missionaries, the papacy and the Carolingian dynasty in the middle of the eighth. In the case of Nivelles, it is also important to note that a monastery that has long been thought of as a product of the Irish revival of continental monasticism, actually owed its creation to the indigenous tradition.

We must not make too much of a dichotomy between the insular (Irish and Anglo-Saxon) and continental traditions. For one thing, the Gallic impact on Ireland and on the Irish Church should never be underestimated. Nor was there a conflict between the two strands, though there could be between their patrons. The Neustrian mayor of the palace, Erchinoald, had founded the monastery of Péronne in the valley of the Somme, burying in it the body of the recently deceased Irish hermit Fursa, who had previously lived in the ruined Roman fort of Burgh Castle in East Anglia. But soon afterwards (*c.* 650/1), Erchinoald expelled his Irish monks from Péronne, who were given refuge by the Arnulfings in their foundations in the valley of the Maas.[88] This was indeed a frontier area between the two kingdoms, and it is possible, though not vouched for in the sources, that Erchinoald's unexplained turning against his former Irish protégés was caused by their openness to Arnulfing influence.

The Irish were no less willing than the indigenous monks to become involved in the increasingly turbulent politics of Francia in the middle of the seventh century. When Sigebert III died in 656, Grimoald the mayor of the palace had the king's young son Dagobert tonsured and sent off to Ireland, and put on the throne instead of a certain Childebert (656–62?), whom hostile sources claim was in fact his own son.[89] The patronage extended to the Irish monks in the Arnulfing monasteries of the Maas may well explain the Irish dimension in this conspiracy. It did Grimoald himself little good, in that he fell into the hands of the Neustrian Clovis II later in 656 or 657 and was executed. Childebert, however, continued as king in Austrasia until around 662; which may argue that he was a genuine Merovingian.

The political turbulence of Francia in the period of the 670s and 680s seems to have limited the ability of the indigenous Frankish monastic founders and missionaries to pursue the example set by Amandus, and it was to the Irish-inspired and frequently Irish-trained Anglo-Saxons that the Arnulfings were to turn in the very late seventh century, when they wanted to ally the extension of Christianity to that of the frontiers of the Frankish kingdom. The region they targeted was Frisia, the flat, marshy land between the Rhine and the North Sea, whose inhabitants were noted for their maritime and trading activities and who had contributed a distinctive element to the Germanic settlement of Britain in the post-Roman period, but who had so far resisted both Frankish political overlordship and conversion to Christianity.[90] The extension of missionary activity into this area was a natural development from that of the adjacent regions of the Scheldt and the Maas, which had been undertaken by Amandus and others in the mid-seventh century. In the 690s, however, it also coincided with the efforts of Pippin II to restore Frankish control of Frisia.

The origins of the evangelisation of Frisia lay in the visit of bishop Wilfred of York (d. 709) in the winter of 678/9 and his attempt, while delayed there on his journey southwards, to convert the Frisians and their king, Aldgisl.[91] Wilfred is often seen as the most Romanised of the Northumbrian clergy, and he had been the victorious spokesman at the Synod of Whitby of the party in the Church that wanted to introduce the customs of Rome in such matters as the dating of Easter and the style of clerical tonsure. However, he also enjoyed close ties with Ireland. Thus, in 676 when on his way to Rome, Wilfred had been asked by leading men in Austrasia to engineer the return of Dagobert from monastic exile in Ireland. This, Wilfred was able to achieve, and Dagobert II (676–8) had duly been installed as king of Austrasia.[92]

In 678/9, Wilfred was on his way to Rome again, to appeal to Pope Agatho against the ultimately successful attempt of archbishop Theodore of Canterbury to split the enormous diocese of York into four new, smaller sees.[93] While Stephanus, the author of *The Life of Wilfred*, presents his patron's work in Frisia as being highly successful, it is clear that at best only a small beginning had been made. The next effort originated in Ireland in the 680s, where a Frisian mission was one of the plans drawn up, but not carried out, by a Northumbrian, Egbert, who had gone to study in the monastery of *Rath Melsigi* (probably to be identified with Clonmelsh in County Carlow).[94] He was later to establish himself in Iona, after the Columban confederacy had finally accepted the Roman customs on Easter observance. His frustrated intention of undertaking a mission to the Frisians was subsequently taken up by another Anglo-Saxon, Willibrord, who had come to *Rath Melsigi* to study under Egbert. It is notable that Willibrord had previously been a monk in the monastery of Ripon founded by Wilfred, and of which he remained abbot.[95] Though no textual source links Egbert and Wilfred directly, the common theme of the Frisian mission suggests close ties between them, and it may be assumed that Willibrord went to *Rath Melsigi* and from there to Frisia under Wilfred's aegis.

In the 690s, Willibrord and a group of companions sailed from Ireland and established themselves in the ruined Roman fort of Utrecht. Willibrord's efforts at converting the Frisians, now under a king Radbod (d. 719) were supported by the dominant aristocratic figure in Francia at this time, Pippin II, who in the 690s was trying to bring Frisia back under the Frankish control to which it had been subject in the sixth century and earlier in the seventh. Frankish protection secured the safety of the missionaries, but the clear association of Willibrord and Pippin linked conversion to Frankish overlordship, and not surprisingly Radbod refused to accept Christianity. But some success was achieved, as the Christian community became sufficiently large to require its own bishop.

Bede, writing in the early 730s, records that when Willibrord was given permission by the Frisian king to preach to his people, he decided first to go to Rome to receive papal approval and to try to obtain some relics for the churches he hoped to found in Frisia. His companions in the mission field selected another of their number, a certain Swithberht, to serve as bishop, and he returned to Britain in order to receive his ordination – significantly enough, from the hands of Wilfred.[96] He subsequently went on to preach outside Frisia. By 695, the situation of the Church in Frisia looked sufficiently well-established for Pippin II to send Willibrord back to Rome with the request that he be consecrated archbishop of the Frisians, giving him supreme ecclesiastical authority in the region.[97] Pope Sergius (687–701) complied, and Willibrord established his archiepiscopal seat in the former Roman fortress of Utrecht (*Traiectum*).

The death of Pippin II in 714 led to a five-year period of political upheaval in Francia, and to the Frisians breaking free of Frankish control. This also halted Willibrord's missionary activities in Frisia, and he may have withdrawn to a settlement in Antwerp, founded in the mid-seventh century by Amandus. This again is a reminder of the crucial role played by the latter and his followers in these north-eastern frontier regions of the Frankish kingdoms.

Willibrord was able to re-establish the Church in the south-western parts of Frisia after the death of Radbod in 719, but made little further progress. In the years preceding his death in 739, he was devoting his attention to the evangelisation of Thuringia from his base in the monastery he founded at Echternach (in Luxembourg).[98] The Thuringian duke, Hedeno, appears to have backed him and, from the evidence of charters, it is clear that he, as well as the Carolingians, endowed Willibrord with land for the foundation and material support of his monasteries.[99]

Willibrord's intended heir in the Frisian mission field was another Anglo-Saxon monk, Wynfrith. Unlike his predecessors, he came from Wessex, which under the leadership of Aldhelm, abbot of a monastic community at Malmesbury and later bishop of Sherborne (705/6–9), had developed its own intellectual tradition, which like that of Northumbria fused elements obtained from Ireland with increasing debts to Rome and to Francia.[100] Wynfrith, whose name was later changed by the pope to Boniface, had been educated in monasteries at Exeter and at Nursling (near the later port of Southampton), before undertaking a brief voyage to Frisia in 716. He arrived there to find the mission in a state of collapse, because of the current state of war. His next visit to the Continent came in 718 and this took him directly to Rome, where he told the pope of his commitment to undertake some form of missionary activity and was in consequence, in May 719, commissioned by Gregory II (715–31) to carry out just such work and to report to Rome on its progress.

Boniface spent three years (719–22) with Willibrord, assisting in the revival of the Frisian mission, before moving south to establish his own field of operations in the region of Hesse. He devoted most of the next thirty years to working in Hesse and Thuringia, though in 753 he was to undertake a missionary journey into the hitherto neglected area of northern Frisia, where on 5 June 754 he and his companions were attacked and murdered by a band of pirates.[101] One of three extant manuscripts that are thought to have been his personal property is marked with cuts that might validate the story in his *Life* that presents him as defending his head with a book in this savage and fatal encounter. However, as none of these impinge on the text of the manuscript but are all rather neatly and improbably orderly in their placing, it seems more likely that they were added at a later date, to give a greater appearance of authenticity to this treasured relic.[102]

Much of Boniface's missionary career, like that of Willibrord, was passed in regions that had once enjoyed exposure both to Christianity and to Roman civilisation as mediated through Francia. These elements had diminished or had been lost in the period of the political decline of the Frankish kingdoms in the second half of the seventh century. The new rulers of Francia, therefore, had considerable interest in promoting missionary activities that went hand in hand with their own restoration of political influence, and ultimately of control over these regions east of the Rhine. Pippin II's son, Charles Martel (d. 741), may have been slightly less helpful than his father, but much of his attention was devoted to the securing of his power in Aquitaine and Burgundy. His sons were more active allies, especially Carloman (741–7), who had secured the eastern frontier regions in the division of territories in 742. The missionaries, for their part, depended on the Frankish rulers not just for protection, but also as a counterbalance to the distrust and hostility of the bishops of many of the major Rhineland sees, close to whose dioceses they were often working but from whose authority they were free. These men, normally members of the great aristocratic families of Austrasia, had little reason to like the missionaries, who were not only outsiders and not under their episcopal authority, but were also noted for their reforming zeal and were in direct contact with the see of Rome.[103]

Unlike the Augustinian mission to Britain in 596/7, the papacy had not initiated the continental ventures of the Anglo-Saxon and Irish monks, but it rapidly came to see their value, not just in terms of evangelisation but also in the spread of Roman doctrinal views and liturgical practices. In his mandate to Boniface of 15 May 719, Gregory II had required the new missionary to 'insist upon using the sacramental discipline prescribed by the official ritual formulary of Our Holy Apostolic See'.[104] In its sponsorship of the Anglo-Saxon missionary ventures on the Continent, the papacy hoped to outflank the entrenched Frankish episcopate, whose resistance to self-reform on the model envisaged by Rome went back to the time of Gregory I, if not earlier.

With the support of the mayors of the palace of the family of Pippin II, who were pleased to establish links to Rome, and who had much to gain from fostering alternatives to the independent and powerful Austrasian episcopal dynasties, the popes found themselves able to appoint to bishoprics within the political sphere of Francia. Willibrord, as archbishop of the Frisians, should have been able to create a network of subordinate episcopal sees, though this was limited by the effective stagnation of this missionary field after 714. Boniface was given an archiepiscopal *pallium* by Gregory III (731–41) in 732, and in 738, deflecting him from an interest in pushing on from Thuringia into the lands of the Saxons, the pope gave him instead some new responsibilities further to the south in Bavaria.[105]

This region had close ties to the Lombard kingdom in Italy, and a line of dukes of its own who were anxious to resist Frankish political domination.[106] Boniface, as a representative of Rome, was more welcome, and under his direction four episcopal dioceses were said to have had their boundaries established, to provide the basic structure of ecclesiastical organisation within the duchy. Boniface returned northwards in 741, and the dominant role in evangelisation in Bavaria was afterwards played by the Irish bishop, Virgil of Salzburg, with whom Boniface notoriously failed to agree.[107] Back in Thuringia, Boniface created new dioceses to which he appointed fellow Anglo-Saxons, and in 744 in Hesse he founded the monastery of Fulda, as his own spiritual retreat and as the centre of planned missionary expansion into Saxony. This, together with his monastery at Fritzlar in Saxony, was placed under direct papal authority, thus exempting it from the jurisdiction of local bishops.[108]

In a territory that was rapidly taking on an ordered ecclesiastical structure, Boniface was in the anomalous position of being an archbishop without a fixed see. In 746, a vacancy in the great Rhineland archbishopric of Mainz, following the deposition of the previous incumbent, was used to give him the needed institutional setting, and this see, once the preserve of Frankish aristocrats, passed after his death to his fellow Anglo-Saxon and missionary disciple, Lullus.[109] It is claimed in the Frankish annals compiled roughly forty years later, that Boniface in 751 was the consecrator of the former mayor of the palace, Pippin III, as the first king of the new ruling house of Francia, but this is unlikely.[110]

For all Boniface's undoubted importance, testified to by the collecting of his letters after his death and the composing of lives both of him and of some of his foremost disciples and associates, it is important not to overlook the work of other bishops and monastic founders on the eastern frontiers of Francia and its dependencies, both at this time and earlier. In particular, the areas to the south-east of the Frankish kingdoms, around the upper Rhine and upper Danube, owed most to the activities of men of very similar background to Amandus.

One of these was Emmeram, a fellow Aquitanian from the area around Poitiers, who planned a mission to the Avars in the plains around the Danube. He was persuaded at Regensburg by duke Theoto (d. 717) to work among the Bavarians instead, because of the current state of warfare between them and the Avars. After an apparently successful period of missionary labour in Bavaria in the area of Regensburg, he was savagely murdered, the victim of a conflict within the ruling ducal house (*c.* 690).[111] Another outsider, persuaded around 693 by duke Theoto to work among the Bavarians, was Hrodbert, later known as St Rupert, who established a bishopric in the former Roman settlement of Salzburg, where he also re-founded the monastery of St Peter, as well as creating a new house for nuns.[112] In the early eighth century, a Frank from Melun, south of Paris, Corbinian (d. 730), created another monastic bishopric in Bavaria at the natural fortress of Freising. His church was dedicated to St Martin, as were several others in the duchy.[113] With both Salzburg and Freising in existence and the cult of a founding saint well established at Regensburg, it may be wondered whether the importance of Boniface's activities in Bavaria in the years 738–41, discussed above, have not been exaggerated in the texts written by his followers. Similarly, his return northwards in 741 may be more a result of the well-entrenched opposition that he faced from already firmly established ecclesiastical bodies in Bavaria than to any sense of the fulfilment of his aims.

In Bavaria, as also in some of the regions east of the Rhine, the missionaries and monastic founders were working in regions that had once been influenced by Christianity, or in which Christian and non-Christian practices co-existed. In part, this was the product of the weakening of the Frankish empire after the death of Dagobert I. Territories and peoples once subject to Frankish political and cultural sway (or, in the case of Bavaria, with Christian traditions stretching back to the late Roman Empire) lost the ecclesiastical infrastructure of Church organisation that had once existed. On the other hand, we should not always accept reformers' views of themselves. Monasticism was still a relatively new departure in the West, especially in its more intense Franco-Irish forms, and it is possible that what monastic authors saw as the sweeping away of paganism or of pagan contaminations of Christianity was instead the elimination of older, more easy-going late Roman attitudes to religious belief and practice.

15 Francia revived, 714–68

Charles 'the Hammer' and the recovery of Francia, 714–41

The change of dynasty in Francia, in 751, inevitably coloured the outlook on the past of all historical works composed subsequently. There is very little contemporary evidence for the last century of the rule of the Merovingians, and most of what we know about it reaches us reflected by the distorting mirror of the Carolingian historiographical tradition. Even a work that is as firmly Merovingian in date of composition as the so-called *Chronicle of Fredegar* was largely replaced by an alternative version of itself in the Carolingian period. The original text, completed around 660, or certainly before 713/4, was revised, restructured and extended to create an entirely new compilation, known as the *Historia vel Gesta Francorum* (*History and Deeds of the Franks*). This revision was carried out in the middle of the eighth century on the orders of count Childebrand, the half-brother of Charles Martel, the mayor of the palace and father of the first Carolingian king, and was extended by a final section covering the years 751 to 768 for his son, count Nibelung.[1]

A number of sets of brief annals that were composed in the eighth century exist, but virtually all of these were written under Carolingian rule or when the family's control of Francia was already assured. While there are usually some earlier materials preceding the eighth-century sections, none of these sets of annals were put together before the 730s, and the strong Carolingian influence on them is clear – for example, from the way that several of them choose the death in 708 of the elder son of Pippin II, Drogo duke of Champagne, as the starting point for their narratives.[2]

The only significant historical text that may be said to be even partly free of Carolingian political bias is another anonymous work, known now as the *Liber Historiae Francorum* (*Book of the History of the Franks*), composed around the year 727 somewhere north of Paris. Arguments about a more precise location have centred on the royal monastery of Saint-Denis and, less probably, on Rouen, while a strong, though not decisive, case has been made for Soissons.[3] The Neustrian or West Frankish perspective of the author is beyond doubt, but he was writing when the political authority of the Carolingian mayor of the palace, Charles Martel, was firmly established. His account is also extremely brief, and its accuracy on various issues can be questioned. Various hagiographical texts can reveal aspects of their, usually anonymous, authors' views on contemporary Frankish events, but it is difficult to separate them too rigidly into 'pro-' or 'anti-Carolingian' categories.

So it is not easy to assess the final stages of the Merovingian period in Frankish history. The image of the late-seventh-century kings as *rois fainéants*, or 'do-nothing kings', has already been examined briefly and found in several respects to be misleading and the product of a Carolingian historiographical perspective. However, it is equally clear that, in the first quarter of the eighth century, the kings ceased to exercise real authority, and became little better than puppets in the hands of rival aristocratic factions, among which the faction led by the Arnulfings, later to be known as Carolingians, who were dominant in Austrasia or East Francia, was the most powerful.

The Arnulfings themselves had passed through a period in which they suffered from some similar problems to those of the kings in whose name they exercised power. In 710 or 711, Childebert III died and was succeeded by his young son Dagobert III (710/1–15). Pippin II had made arrangements for the succession by appointing his surviving legitimate son, Grimoald, as the mayor of the palace in Neustria, only for him to be murdered at Liège, for reasons that were never explained. In consequence, Pippin designated Grimoald's infant son, Theudoald, as the new mayor in Neustria.[4] To be able to appoint a child to such a post is a sign of Pippin's power at this time, but it was hardly a compliment to the Neustrians. Unsurprisingly, on Pippin's death in December 714 the flawed structure he had created for his succession collapsed.

Pippin's widow, Plectrudis, assumed control in Austrasia, but several leading Neustrian families, waiting for the chance to break free of domination by the Arnulfings and their allies among the Neustrian aristocracy, revolted against the rule of Theudoald, and defeated his supporters in battle. They appointed one of their own number, Raganfred, as mayor, and in 715 invaded Austrasia. On the death of Dagobert III in the same year, they chose as king another Merovingian, Chilperic II, who had previously been confined to a monastery. At the same time, they allied with the pagan Frisians, whom Pippin II had been trying to conquer during the later years of his ascendancy.[5]

According to the author of the *Liber Historiae Francorum*, who admittedly was writing a decade later under his rule, it was only the decisive action of Pippin II's illegitimate son Charles, known from the ninth century onwards as Charles Martel, or 'Hammer', that saved the day for the Arnulfings. It did, however, take him some time to do so. He had been imprisoned by Plectrudis during the sensitive period following his father's death, but was able 'by God's help' to get free.[6] As the only male member of his line of fighting age, he was better able to rally support than the infant Theudoald.

His first efforts were not impressive. He led his forces against the Frisians, who were invading Austrasia under their king Radbod as the allies of the Neustrians. However, after heavy fighting he was forced to retreat, and the Frisians united with the Neustrian army that was approaching from the west. The allies then advanced on Plectrudis's base at Cologne, and she had to come to terms with them, surrendering 'much treasure', which may well have included that taken from Neustria by Pippin II in 687. The Neustrian army was ambushed on its way

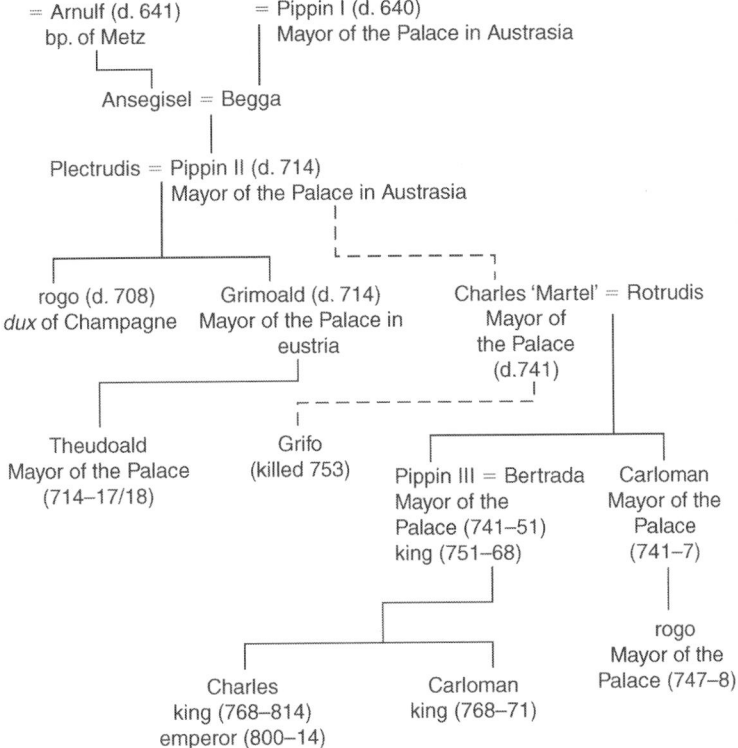

The early Carolingians

home by Charles at Amblève in April 716, but while our author speaks of it suffering 'heavy losses', this was hardly decisive, as the fighting continued unabated the following year.[7]

Renewed war in the spring of 717 proved decisive. The Neustrians tried to crush Charles, and despite his offer of a peace treaty, forced him to give battle at Vinchy, where on 21 March Charles was victorious, driving king Chilperic and Raganfred back to Paris. Charles was then able to turn on Plectrudis, defeat her supporters and force her to surrender Cologne and the remainder of the Arnulfing treasure. Charles then appointed a Merovingian of his own, Chlotar IV (d. 719), as King of Austrasia, and, in 718, secured the eastern frontiers of the kingdom with a victory over Radbod and the Frisians.[8]

Though Neustria and Austrasia were once more divided, with separate kings and mayors of the palace, this was no more than a temporary solution. Looking around for new allies, the Neustrians had asked for assistance from the effectively independent duke Eudo of Aquitaine, who could provide them with an army of Basque mercenaries. However, when war resumed, Charles and his now united Austrasian forces overran eastern Neustria.[9] Eudo may in any case have been more concerned about the growing threat to southern Aquitaine from the Arabs, who first crossed the Pyrenees in 720. He came to an agreement with Charles, handing over the Neustrian king Chilperic, who then reigned briefly over a nominally reunited kingdom until his death in 721 or 722. Even so, Raganfred and his followers continued to hold out in western Neustria, probably based at Angers, until 730.

In comparison with the crucial years of 714–21, the rest of Charles' ascendancy is particularly badly documented. The *Liber Historiae Francorum* ends its account with the death of Chilperic, and in the *Historia vel Gesta Francorum* almost nothing is recorded for the years between 721 and 733.[10] However, it seems clear from the minor annals that in the early 720s Charles controlled most of the region between the Seine and the Rhine under the nominal rule of another Merovingian king, Theuderic IV (721/2–37), but little more than that. Large areas of Francia, notably Aquitaine, Burgundy and Provence, remained under independent dynasties of dukes, descendants of office-holders appointed by the seventh-century Merovingian kings. Nor was Charles' hold over Neustria necessarily secure, as he faced similar problems there to those encountered by his father, Pippin II.

While it is often assumed that the battle of Tertry in 687 made Pippin II the undisputed master of both Austrasia and Neustria, this is a gross oversimplification. In Neustria, the previous mayor

Berchar and his supporters had been overthrown soon after the battle, and they were replaced in the court and elsewhere by those who had opposed them, several of whom had previously been political refugees in Austrasia or had appealed to Pippin to help them against Berchar. These included bishop Reolus of Reims, and count Audramnus.[11] So, in 687, Pippin's victory led to the installation of a new ruling group in the Neustrian court, composed of his allies such as the new mayor Norbert, and Audramnus, who became count of the palace by *c.* 693. Some of the Neustrian nobility also found it expedient to form even closer ties with the powerful Austrasian duke: the widow of Berchar was married by her family to Pippin's eldest son, Drogo.[12]

Pippin turned his attention elsewhere, not least in the 690s, to campaigns to regain Austrasian hegemony over Frisia, but his influence in Neustria was at best vicarious, and depended on the alliances he had made with prominent Neustrian aristocrats. It is clear, too, that the prominence he and his family achieved in Neustria was increasingly resented, as evidenced by the events following his death.

Some historians have turned to the charters, and above all the records of the *placita*, or legal hearings, conducted by some of the late-seventh-century Merovingians, for indications of rising political tensions of this kind. In particular, Childebert III (695–710/1) has been singled out as a ruler able to take an unusually independent line for a late Merovingian king, and one that was, moreover, markedly anti-Pippinid.[13] The evidence offered in support of this view consists of three of these *placita* documents, recording cases heard before the king in which the losing parties were the sons of Pippin.[14]

Unfortunately, this evidence will not bear the full weight of the interpretation placed on it. Even if the legal decisions were deliberately intended to inflict pinpricks of humiliation on the Arnulfings, this would not prove that the king, rather than the Neustrian nobility, was orchestrating them. However, it is equally possible that such apparently confrontational legal disputes were in fact a formal device through which a secure title to property could be obtained, with a documentary record being created to preserve it.[15] But whatever position is taken on these arguments, it is certain that Pippin's influence in Neustria depended on his maintaining a network of aristocratic allies within the kingdom, and after 719 his son Charles had to do the same.

Through longer and more bitter warfare in the years 714–19, Charles won a far more decisive military victory over Neustria than his father had in 687, and he was not so beholden to a powerful faction of the Neustrian aristocracy as Pippin had been. Even so, it is clear that as he did not wish to remain permanently at the royal court, which continued to be resident in Neustria, he had to establish a body of supporters in that kingdom to run it for him. Narrative history being almost non-existent at this time, and with few royal charters surviving, it is not easy to identify this group.

One of those who almost certainly was a member of it was Charles' nephew, Hugh. By 724, when he became abbot of Fontanelle (Saint-Wandrille), he already held the archbishopric of Rouen, and the bishoprics of Bayeux and Paris. He also became abbot of Jumièges, where he was to be buried in 732/3.[16] This gave him control of virtually all the major churches of the lower Seine valley and the area of the future Normandy. Some indication of his personal landholdings may be gained from the brief references to the gifts he made to his abbey of Fontanelle. The estates in question, which he inherited from his parents, were located in the valleys of the Oise and the Somme. Since these were previously owned by his grandfather, the Neustrian mayor of the palace, Waratto (680s), it is possible to see Hugh as a representative both of the dominant Austrasian line of the Arnulfings and of the greater aristocracy of Neustria.

It has been argued, against older views, that Hugh should not be assumed to be an automatic supporter of Charles, and that he might even have opposed him.[17] Hugh was a grandson of Pippin II by his wife Plectrudis, whereas Charles was the product of Pippin's probably unsacramental relationship with Alpaida. That Charles had replaced the legitimate and older line as a result of the events of 715–19 could have left that branch of the family hostile towards him. However, there are signs that another and possibly more crucial division had taken place within the Arnulfing line at an earlier point. Hugh's father, Drogo, had been Pippin II's eldest son, and Hugh himself, born *c.* 695, had been both an adult and still a layman at the time of Pippin's death. Yet, in the arrangements made by Pippin after the death of his son Grimoald, which were then preserved by Plectrudis, Hugh and at least one other adult brother of his were passed over in favour of appointing Grimoald's infant son, Theudoald (d. 741) to the office of mayor of the Neustrian palace; with disastrous consequences. The fact that Hugh had already been passed over in 714 may have made him more willing to co-operate with Charles in controlling Neustria after 719, especially when the rewards he received were so many and so valuable.

Another of the likely partisans of Charles in Neustria was Godobald, who was made abbot of the great monastery and royal pantheon of Saint-Denis by *c*. 726/7. He had been a supporter of Dodo, probably a brother of Charles' mother, Alpaida, and at his instigation had been involved in the murder of bishop Lambert of Maastricht (*c*. 705).[18] According to later Saint-Denis tradition, he undertook a penitential pilgrimage to Rome and benefited from a miraculous cure, but it is hard not to suspect that he received this important abbacy as a tried and trusted friend of Charles' family.[19] It was with the support of such men that Charles was able to keep Neustria loyal to himself and to free his own hands for expeditions east of the Rhine.

There he had to face a problem that was to occupy his successors throughout the century: the gradual southward movement of the Saxons into the lands across the Rhine that the Franks controlled directly – the future Franconia, centred on the River Main. The continental Saxons had previously lived in the low-lying and marshy lands around the Rivers Weser and Aller, but by the early eighth century were edging themselves south-westwards on to the high ground south of the river Lippe.[20] It was in this area that many of the Frankish–Saxon wars were fought throughout the century, and what was at stake was control of this region. The Frankish chroniclers always speak of the Saxons as being 'in revolt', but this was referring to the first half of the seventh century, in which they had paid tribute to the Franks. Charles Martel's first encounter with the Saxons occurred around 720, and another and more hard-fought campaign was launched in 738.[21]

In 725, Charles led a major expedition east of the Rhine against the Alamans, Thuringians and Bavarians, all of whom had been subject to the Franks during the heyday of the Merovingian dynasty, but who, since the mid-seventh century, had largely gone their own way under ducal dynasties of Frankish origin. They were, as the compiler of the *Historia vel Gesta Francorum* puts it, 'punished' and 'subjugated'. The wife and daughter of the former Bavarian duke Grimoald (717–25) were taken as hostages.[22] In practice, Charles could not impose his authority directly on these peoples, but they had been brought firmly back within the sphere of Frankish political influence. Closer integration had to await the time of his grandson, in the 770s and 780s.

The next extension of Charles' power was primarily the result of luck. The duchy of Aquitaine had retained its independence throughout the 720s, until Charles launched a series of attacks on it around 730, following his acquiring of control over western Neustria after the death of Raganfred. At the same time, the

Aquitanian duke Eudo, threatened since 720/1 by Arab attacks in the south of his territories, had allied himself with the leader of the Berber army that the Arabs had installed in the western Pyrenees. When the Berbers' revolt was crushed by the forces of the Arab governor of Spain, a punitive campaign was also planned against the Aquitanians, which was launched in 732 or 733. Duke Eudo was defeated by the Arab army on the River Garonne and had to appeal to his northern enemy, Charles Martel, for assistance against this greater threat from the south. The Frankish army met the Arab forces under the governor 'Abd al-Rahman ibn Gafiqi as they were moving northwards towards Tours after sacking Poitiers.[23]

The ensuing battle of Poitiers in October(?) 732 or 733, in which the Arabs were defeated and forced to retreat to Spain, may not have saved Christendom from imminent Islamic conquest, as is sometimes asserted, but it certainly left Aquitaine open to the re-imposition of control from the north. When duke Eudo died in 735, Charles returned to Aquitaine, occupied Bordeaux and installed his own garrisons in the principal fortresses and towns of the duchy.[24] As in the duchies to the east of the Rhine, a once closely integrated component of the Merovingian kingdom had been restored, albeit temporarily, to Frankish control.

In the meantime, in 734, with the duchies east of the Rhine cowed and Aquitaine neutralised, it became possible for Charles to impose his authority on the former Frankish kingdom of Burgundy. He appointed new officials and, according to the *Historia vel Gesta Francorum*, he carried out an extensive redistribution of lands in favour of his own supporters. This was clearly resented locally, and in 736 he had to invade the region again, and take Lyon by force. With Burgundy cowed into accepting his suzerainty, the way lay open for penetration further down the Rhône valley into Provence.[25] An expedition was sent there in 737, initially under his brother, count Childebrand, and then under Charles himself. It was prompted by the recent Arab conquest of Avignon, which had effectively cut off the Rhône valley from the Mediterranean, but the chronicler implies that the ultimate target for the Franks was duke Maurontus of Marseille, whom he calls 'base', 'craven' and 'heretical'.[26]

Maurontus was also accused of having allied himself with the Arabs. It is just possible that this was true, as they were the only possible counterweight to the growing power of the Frankish mayor, but it is worth noting that the same author also accuses duke Eudo of Aquitaine of being allied to the Arabs at the very time they were invading his duchy, defeating his army and sacking his cities.[27] In fact, the events in Provence in 737 and 739 are almost a carbon copy of those that occurred in Aquitaine in 733 and 735.

It could well be that Charles' campaign of 737 was actually launched in response to an appeal for help from duke Maurontus against the rapidly developing Arab conquest of Provence. The Frankish army retook Avignon, but failed to capture Narbonne, which was the main Arab fortress in south-west France. Charles did, however, sack and burn Nîmes, Agde, Béziers, and probably Maguelonne as well.[28]

In 739, Charles was back in Provence again. This time his target was explicitly duke Maurontus. Avignon, which may have been returned to Maurontus in 737, was retaken, and the duke was forced to flee from Marseille to take refuge on an island off the coast. His eventual fate is unknown.[29] It looks, as in Aquitaine in 735, as if an initial intervention by Charles and his Frankish forces against an Arab threat led to a subsequent annexation of the region, following some careful distribution of patronage, in the form of both lands and offices, to some of the leading local families to win them over to the Carolingians and turn them against the regional dukes.

Thus, in a series of campaigns lasting from 732/3 to 739 Charles, from his base in north-east Francia, made himself master of virtually all of the south and the west. His methods were generally ruthless. His treatment of those who turned to him for help was cynical, to say the least. On the other hand, those elements in local society upon whom he relied benefited considerably from his favours. A century later, he was castigated by the Church for his treatment of monasteries, particularly in forcing them to make precarial grants of property to those on whom he depended for military support. Such grants were in effect leases for life in return for fixed annual renders. In themselves they were not intrinsically harmful to the grantor, in that a regular income was thus guaranteed. They were only detrimental in periods of escalating prices or land values, in which higher returns could be guaranteed by shorter or more flexible leases. There are no reasons to suspect that the 730s were such a period, and it is likely that this particular accusation owes much more to the political and economic circumstances of the 830s than to those of the 730s.[30]

What Charles achieved by such practices was the creation of networks of local supporters, controlling the principal offices and with a powerful landed base, who could transform what were military conquests into the longer-term re-imposition of centralised authority, exercised still in the name of Merovingian kings by the Pippinid dynasty. As well as lay magnates, institutions of the Church gained from the patronage that Charles exercised on an increasing scale. In return, he looked to those whom he rewarded for political loyalty and other signs of gratitude, spiritual as well as material. Thus the monastery of Saint-Denis to the north of Paris, burial place of the kings of Neustria since Dagobert I, benefited particularly from a grant by Charles of the former royal villa and estate of Clichy, and it was in Saint-Denis that he was to be buried, following his death on 22 October 741.

Regaining the periphery: Pippin 'the Short', 741–68

The legacy of Charles Martel, from the point of view of the Pippinid or Arnulfing house and its northern Frankish aristocratic allies, was inherited by his two eldest sons, Pippin III (known in the French historiographical tradition as 'the Short') and Carloman. A third son, Grifo, the product of a liaison with the daughter of Duke Grimoald of Bavaria, may also have been intended to inherit a share in power, and was established as duke in Thuringia immediately after his father's death, but his half-brothers lured him into a trap at Laon and imprisoned him in a monastery until 747. Another victim of this period was the former mayor of Neustria, Theudoald, who was killed in 741, possibly because he represented a threat from the rival line of the dynasty. His survival to that date is evidence of the kind of political compromises and alliances that Charles Martel had had to make, even at the height of his power.[31]

Though Pippin III and, more briefly, Carloman, were to be able to consolidate and increase the conquests of their father in the last years of his life, this was only after reacting to their almost complete collapse. On the death of Charles, Aquitaine regained its independence under duke Hunald, the son of Eudo; the Alaman duke Godefred threw off his subservience to the Arnulfing mayors; and Odilo, the duke of the Bavarians, backed Grifo. Needless to say, the compiler of the *Historia vel Gesta Francorum* presents Pippin III and Carloman's reactions to these threats as being decisive and almost immediately successful. Thus in 742 they invaded Aquitaine, and are said by the chronicler to have 'stood as victors around'. The reality of what he describes is rather less impressive: they burnt the suburbs of Bourges, but did not take the city, and otherwise only captured the fortress of Loches, just south of the Loire.[32] In practice, duke Hunald was able to maintain himself without serious challenge, and the brothers were obliged to accept the re-emergence of the duchy in a treaty made in 745.[33]

With the Alamans, an autumn campaign in 742 led to the submission of some of them, but they were not finally defeated until after further campaigning in 744 and 746.[34] At this point, the independent ducal line was terminated. Similarly, the Bavarians under duke Odilo (737–48) continued to reject the authority of the two joint mayors, despite what the chronicler records as a defeat in the year 743. Only after Odilo's death in January 748, when the Bavarians refused to accept the rule of his infant son, Tassilo, whose mother was the sister of Pippin III and Carloman, were the Franks able to make a decisive intervention in Bavaria. Grifo, who had escaped from monastic incarceration in 747, briefly seized the duchy thanks to his part-Bavarian descent, but was quickly driven out by Pippin. Their nephew Tassilo was then imposed as duke, holding office as a normally loyal subordinate of successive Frankish rulers for the next forty years.[35]

It thus took eight years for the influence exercised by Charles Martel over the duchies east of the Rhine to be recovered by his sons, and it was another twenty years of hard fighting before the independence of the duchy of Aquitaine was extinguished. The process of the restoration of Arnulfing power may have been aided when, in 747, Carloman decided that he wished to enter a monastery, and left for Rome.[36] It is possible that he did so in the expectation that his son Drogo would eventually succeed to authority over all the Frankish lands, as Pippin at this time was probably still unmarried and certainly had no children. In the meantime, Drogo succeeded his father as mayor of the palace in Austrasia. However, Pippin then married a lady called Bertrada and their first son, Charles, was born in 748. Soon afterwards, and perhaps in consequence, Drogo was deprived of his office in a coup led by his uncle, and supported among others by archbishop Boniface of Mainz. Even so, Drogo and his supporters continued to resist Pippin in regions across the Rhine until as late as 753.[37] So too did Pippin's half-brother, Grifo, who was finally killed in a battle in the Alps in the same year, while on his way to request Lombard aid against Pippin, who by this time had made himself king of the Franks.

The achievements of Charles Martel and Pippin III in reimposing centralised authority, on the primary components of the Frankish realm and over most of its peripheral duchies raise a number of questions. It is easy to imagine the duchies east of the Rhine, the Frisian kingdom, and the great southern and western duchies of Francia – Aquitaine, Burgundy, and Provence – as being naturally inclined to breaking away from Frankish overlordship. In most of these cases, the inhabitants were not Frankish in origin and had their own distinct cultural traditions and long, independent histories. Even to the west of the Rhine, modern historians have seen continuities in Burgundian and Aquitanian ethnic identities which, taken together with limited Frankish settlement, should have made them favour independence.

However, research has also emphasised the Frankish origin of many of the dominant families in all these regions. Moreover, there are indications that even in times of relative political and military weakness in the late seventh century, some of these men still travelled to Neustria to attend the royal court.[38] Other arguments also cast doubt on the reality of the genuine survival of separate Aquitanian and Burgundian identities.[39] This all leads to the suggestion that it was the rising power of the Arnulfings, and their attempt to take over the still considerable authority of the kings, that drove the regional potentates into trying to build up their own independent local power bases. At the same time, the existence of long-term feuds between the principal aristocratic families within the regions enabled the Pippinids to find allies in local society, who would serve their interests both in the military subjugation and in the subsequent government of these great duchies. The best-documented case of this is probably that of a certain Abbo, member of a long-established and powerful southern Burgundian aristocratic kinship, who supported Charles Martel against Maurontus, and was rewarded with the office of patrician (*Patricius*) of Provence after 737.[40]

While there is no evidence of Burgundian, Provençal or Aquitanian revolts against the Merovingians in the seventh century, this is not true of the eastern regions. The Saxons had freed themselves from paying regular tribute to the Franks during the time of the otherwise powerful Dagobert I (623–38). This may have been a consequence of the latter's hard-fought war against the Wends, a Slavic people who were forged into an aggressive confederacy by a Frankish adventurer called Samo. The Alamans won a significant victory over the Wends at the same time as the Franks suffered a humiliating defeat, and this may have led the Alamans then to throw off Merovingian tutelage. The other major ethnic group in the area of the central Rhine, the Thuringians, broke into open rebellion after the death of Dagobert and defeated his heir, Sigebert III (634–56) in 639. The *Chronicle of Fredegar* records that the revolt was also a direct consequence of a victory they had won over the Wends.[41] So, Frankish military failure against the Wends led to the wider collapse of their hegemony east of the Rhine. In the same period, the Bavarians also broke free of Frankish tutelage under a ducal family of Frankish origin known as the Agilolfings.

Though little is known of these ducal families of the various peoples east of the Rhine, and substantial gaps exist in their genealogies, they were all of Frankish origin.[42] This is almost certainly also the case with the Aquitanian ducal line that emerges with Eudo, and probably also with the line of the counts of *Vasconia*, the region of Basque settlement between the Garonne and the eastern Pyrenees.[43] As would happen on a larger scale in the ninth century, such dynasties of Frankish 'viceroys', installed by the Merovingians to keep the various tributary and subject peoples under control, came, over time, to identify with the interests of the inhabitants of the territories they ruled. This process, that had begun across the Rhine in the mid-seventh century, extended itself west of the river in the early eighth century, and genuine regional powers began to develop in Aquitaine, Burgundy and Provence, which the military and political activities of Charles Martel and Pippin III cut short.

It could be asked how they succeeded in doing so when the previous half century or more had favoured the secessionist tendencies of the duchies. The answer lies in the nature of military power in Francia. Control of the eastern duchies had been an important resource for the Merovingians, and the rulers of Austrasia in particular had called upon the levies of Saxons, Thuringians and others to assist them in their wars, not least in the conflicts between the kingdoms in the period 567–613. Sigibert I had used such forces against his brother Chilperic in 574, as did Theudebert II against *his* brother Theuderic II in 612.[44] It is possible, therefore, that Charles Martel's greater military strength in the 730s derived from renewed access to such sources of manpower from east of the Rhine.

This itself can only be a partial answer, as a further explanation is needed as to how Charles, following his father's precedent in Frisia, gained a military advantage over the various eastern duchies. Here, the answer must lie within Francia, for none of the other major kingdoms in the West in the aftermath of the disintegration of the Roman Empire was as effectively and continuously organised for warfare as was that of the Franks.

The primary institution, which was also a vital instrument of political control, was that of the annual assembly or 'Marchfield' (which could in fact be held between March and May).[45] The leading territorial magnates of the kingdom(s) were summoned to this. At the assembly various issues were discussed, disputes settled and new laws promulgated. Also, the military campaign for the year was agreed and planned. The nobles in turn could call on the services of those who were dependent on them, and who formed the basis of the fighting forces they then contributed to the royal army, which later in the year gathered at a location and date agreed at the Marchfield. So these assemblies guaranteed a large measure of consensus for royal decisions and laws, and could generate a powerful military force to direct against internal or external foes.

With such a system, the power of the Merovingian state should hardly have suffered the prolonged decline it faced in the period from the late 630s to the 690s. However, there were other factors to consider. Above all, the effective functioning of the Frankish monarchy rested on the role of the kings as war leaders. In the generation after Dagobert I, a real crisis of credibility arose. While the Merovingian dynasty suffered from fewer and less prolonged minorities than is sometimes assumed, the most protracted of these occurred in the crucial period of the very late 630s and 640s, when the consequences of Frankish defeats by the Wends were making themselves felt in the break-up of their hegemony east of the Rhine. Well may it have been recorded that Sigebert III 'wept unrestrainedly' after his defeat at the hands of the Thuringians; he was, after all, only ten years old.

In the decades that followed, rival aristocratic factions took control of the two kingdoms of Neustria and Austrasia, with the kings able to play only an occasional part. In the circumstances of factional conflicts within the kingdoms, combined with periods of tension between them, it is not surprising that expeditions to re-impose Frankish domination east of the Rhine were not undertaken. It is also understandable that the end of conflict between Neustria and Austrasia following Pippin's victory at Tertry, and the political settlement that he and his allies imposed, opened the way for the resumption of more aggressive warfare on the frontiers and the beginnings of the process of re-establishing Frankish power in the east. This was threatened again by the internal conflicts of 714–19, but was resumed more fully and effectively in consequence of the more thorough-going resolution of the political problems achieved by Charles Martel. Though some ground was lost again in the 740s, his sons were thereafter able to consolidate their father's work.

The establishment of his authority east of the Rhine, and the recognition that Aquitaine for the time being had to be allowed its independence, freed Pippin's hands to turn to other matters. In 743, he and his brother had set up another Merovingian king, Childeric III, possibly a son of Chilperic II (715–21).[46] This had followed a six-year gap in which no king had held office. The fact that they needed a Merovingian to legitimise their regime is indicative of the relative weakness of their position in 743, but may also suggest that their own relations with each other were not so good that they could co-operate outside of such a structure. By 749, Pippin III felt that he could dispense with the king he had thought to be so necessary in 743.

In 750, he sent bishop Burchard of Würzburg and the royal chaplain, Fulrad, abbot of Saint-Denis, to Rome. As recorded in the *Annales Regni Francorum*, or *Annals of the Kingdom of the Franks*, which began being compiled somewhere between the years 787 and 793, they were to ask pope Zacharias if it was right for the kings of the Franks to rule but without wielding power. The pope's reply was that 'it was better to call king the one who had the royal power'. In consequence, on his 'Apostolic authority' he commanded that Pippin be made king. Doubt has rightly been cast on the reliability of this report, which reflects a later need to justify Pippin's actions on grounds other than mere expediency.[47]

The compiler of the *Historia vel Gesta Francorum* is rather more circumspect. He records that a mission was sent to Rome, and that what followed was done with papal consent, but makes the constituting of Pippin as king the product of 'the election by all of the Franks ... consecration by the bishops and the acknowledgement of the princes' (that is, the dukes).[48] The account in the *Annales Regni Francorum* seems to betray the contamination of the ideological preoccupations of a slightly later period, and greater weight should probably be placed on the *Historia vel Gesta*'s version of events, even allowing for its author's partiality for the Carolingian house. Papal consent may have been needed primarily to persuade the Frankish bishops of the legitimacy of the deposition of the existing king and the replacement of his dynasty.

In political terms, what was crucial was clearly the agreement of the Franks, probably obtained at one of the annual 'Marchfield' assemblies, and the acknowledgement of the new ruler's status by his former peers, the other leading Frankish nobles, and those of the other areas subject to Frankish overlordship. The liturgical procedure adopted for the ceremony in 751, in which Pippin was made king, may have involved anointing with chrism, following the Old Testament parallel of Samuel's pouring oil on the heads of Saul and David.[49] However, this is by no means as certain as is often made out. There is no reference to such a procedure in the contemporary sources, and it first appears in the later *Annales Regni Francorum*.

What is undeniable is that this anointing ritual was used in 754 when Pippin was re-consecrated, together with his two sons, by Pope Stephen II.[50] This strengthens the arguments of those who see the introduction of this particular practice into Frankish royal consecration as the product of papal influence. It had never previously been employed in Francia. Though used by the Visigothic kings, at least from 672 onwards, it is unlikely that this was the precedent for its adoption in 754 (or 751). Others have argued that the influence came from Ireland via Iona, but no evidence exists for any actual Irish royal unction or anointing.[51]

The pope had come to Francia in the winter of 753/4 to seek Pippin's aid in restraining the Lombard king Aistulf, whose advances into Roman territory in the summer were bringing him ever closer to Rome. Aistulf obviously felt that no serious threat was to be expected from Francia, as he had made no effort to prevent Stephen from passing through the Lombard kingdom on his way north, and he disregarded Pippin's request that he desist from further attacks on Roman territory.[52]

In this he proved unwise. Pippin's position in Francia may not have been very secure, but the papal request for assistance gave him the opportunity to cut a figure on a wider stage; also, the chance of an expedition into Italy, which might prove financially lucrative, had obvious attractions as far as welding together some of the supporters of the new Frankish royal regime was concerned. Thus, in the spring of 755, Pippin led an army across the Alps. He was able to besiege Aistulf in Pavia and force him to agree to terms. These consisted of a guarantee of inviolability for Roman territory, and the giving of hostages and 'rich presents' to Pippin and the Frankish magnates.[53]

The papal source, the *Liber Pontificalis* or *Pontifical Book*, a series of generally contemporary biographical records of the popes, gives a rather more elaborate and ideologically slanted version of these events. In the '*Life*' of Pope Stephen II, Pippin is said to have been consecrated by the pope only after he had promised to obey his instructions, and an elaborate account is given of the initial reception of Stephen at Ponthion in January 754 at which Pippin prostrated himself before the pope and kissed his stirrup.[54] Contemporary Frankish sources make no mention of these features. By 754, the pope probably had more to gain from Pippin than the reverse. The title of 'patrician of the Romans' that he gave to Pippin at his anointing was intended to commit the Frankish king to the continuing defence of Rome and the papacy.

Aistulf certainly did not expect any further Frankish interference after his defeat in 755, and not only failed to carry out the territorial restorations he had promised, but also renewed his threats to the independence of the Roman duchy. Pippin led a second expedition into Italy in 756 and, paralleling the events of the previous year, besieged Aistulf in Pavia once more. The treaty was renewed, though it seems that the Lombard king was on the point of breaking it yet again when he died later in the year in a hunting accident.[55]

After his two successive interventions in Italy, and despite subsequent papal pleas, Pippin then stopped involving himself in events south of the Alps. The latter part of his reign was devoted to checking the Saxons and to trying to conquer Aquitaine. In 758, he defeated some of the Saxons, destroyed various forts they had built on the Lippe, and forced them to pay an annual tribute of 300 horses.[56] In 760, he turned his attentions to Aquitaine, now ruled by duke Waiofar (745–68), a son of duke Hunald (742–5). In a series of annual campaigns between the spring of that year and his death in 768, Pippin plundered and slaughtered his way across Aquitaine.[57] Much destruction is recorded: perhaps more than was to be inflicted by the Vikings on the region in the ninth century. Though Waiofar had been made a fugitive and then murdered, and armed Aquitanian resistance apparently crushed, the conquest was still not complete when Pippin died in Paris on 9 October 768.

16   Charlemagne, 768–814

The route to the imperial throne, 768–800

Just before he died, at Saint-Denis in September 768, and with the consent of the Frankish nobles and bishops, Pippin divided up his kingdom between his two sons. To Charles, later known as Charles 'the Great' or Charlemagne, he gave the primary Frankish territories of Austrasia and a rather reduced Neustria. To his younger son, Carloman, he entrusted the rest of Neustria and most of the territories that he and Charles Martel before him had subdued: Burgundy, Alamannia, Provence and Septimania.

The co-existence of the two new kings in the years 768 to 771 was uneasy. One cause of friction was the control of Aquitaine, which the compiler of the *Historia vel Gesta Francorum* described as being intended to be divided between the two brothers, but which the later *Annals of the Kingdom of the Franks* claim to have been given entirely to Charles.[1] Certainly, when in 769 Charles invaded Aquitaine to suppress ongoing local resistance, now led by Hunald II, son of duke Waiofar, a confrontation occurred between the brothers at Moncontour, north of Poitiers, and Carloman withdrew from Aquitaine.

In 770, a series of alliances was created to encircle Carloman. The diplomacy for this appears to have been led by his own mother, Pippin's widow, Bertrada, and the parties allied against him were his brother Charles, duke Tassilo III of Bavaria, and the Lombard king, Desiderius (756–74). Pope Stephen III was initially uneasy at the prospect of some of his Frankish protectors allying themselves with his Lombard enemies, but he was won over by the violent elimination of a group of powerful clerics in Rome, linked to the family of his predecessor, Paul I, and which dominated the papal court. However, the death of Carloman in December 771 and that of the pope the following month, both from natural causes, led to the dissolution of this confederacy.[2] Charles sent his Lombard wife back to her father, with whom the widow and infant children of Carloman also took refuge when the leading men in his kingdom decided to accept the rule of his brother.[3] So, in 771, Charles gained control of all the kingdom that his father had once ruled. Without this, the succeeding period of military conquest and expansion could never have occurred.

As well as everything he had acquired from his two predecessors, Charles also inherited their problems. Of these, the greatest, certainly in terms of the time and effort involved in solving it, was that of the Saxons. Individual campaigns by Charles Martel and Pippin had checked the Saxon pressure along the Lippe, but had not turned Frankish rule into a reality in the area, let alone over Saxony more generally. In 772, Charles was determined to subjugate the southern group of Saxons. This involved not just a military conquest, but also their integration into the Frankish cultural orbit through their forcible conversion to Christianity.[4] Whether this was his intention from the start is not clear, but it had certainly become so by 775.

The campaign of 772 was aimed at the capture of a Saxon fortress on the river Lippe at Eresburg and the destruction of the shrine of the cult object known as the Irminsul. The exact nature of this object is uncertain, but its location in recently acquired territory on the expanding southern frontier of Saxon territory suggests that it was more than an item of traditional reverence and was directly associated with military victory and conquest. Thus its destruction was not only financially lucrative, because of the capture of the treasury of offerings in the shrine, but also intended as a blow to Saxon morale.[5] This shrine was still remembered by Saxon chroniclers in the tenth century.

The Saxons retaliated in 774, when they overran and destroyed Eresburg and tried to take the Frankish fort of Syburg in the valley of the Ruhr. They also attacked the monastery of Fritzlar on the upper Weser, which had been created by Boniface as a centre for evangelising the region. This was vengeance for the destruction of their sacred Irminsul in 772. The *Annals of the Kingdom of the Franks* are vague about the Frankish riposte ordered by Charles after his return from Italy later that year. It was certainly left to a major expedition that he commanded in person in 775 to regain the forts lost in 774. This campaign was one of the most extensive conducted in Saxony, and took the Frankish forces through the disputed lands around the Lippe, the Ruhr and the Diemel, then across the Weser, where a Saxon army was defeated, to the River Oker.[6]

On the Oker, the Eastphalian Saxons came to terms with the Frankish king, giving hostages and promising loyalty. Charles received a similar submission from the southernmost Saxon confederacy of the Angrarii, while returning west to rejoin the detachment of his forces he had sent against the Westphalians. The distorted narrative of the main Frankish source, the *Annals of the Kingdom of the Franks* is tellingly exposed by its account of this army, which was recorded as having won a great victory in which many Saxons were killed. The anonymous author of the revised version, probably produced after Charles' death, reveals a different story, in which the overconfident Franks had their camp overrun by the Saxons when taken by surprise. It was only when Charles arrived with the main body of the army that the Westphalian Saxons were defeated and forced, like the Eastphalians and Angrarii, to come to terms with the Frankish king.[7] Such humiliating submissions were effective only as long as Charles and the main Frankish army were present to enforce them. In 776, when Charles had to go to Italy once again, the southern Saxons attacked and destroyed Eresburg and threatened Syburg. Another large-scale expedition had to be launched by Charles in the autumn, which recovered the lost territory and the Saxons again submitted to him. This they did at the source of the River Lippe, a place of particular significance for them. They promised to become subjects of the king and of the Franks, and to accept Christianity. A number of them appeared before Charles in 777 at his new settlement of Paderborn, built deliberately close to the source of the Lippe, to receive Christian baptism.[8] These agreements, however, proved as fragile as those made in 775.

In part, the problem in subduing the Saxons was the difficulty of the marshy terrain in and around the edges of which the fighting took place. This was a region that had baffled Roman efforts at conquest in the time of Augustus. But, perhaps more significant still, was the nature of the Saxons' social and political organisation. They had no kings or permanent central institutions. Nor, apart from such forts as Eresburg, did they have any large settlements. The basic Saxon social units were the extended families, and these occupied fortified farmsteads, rather like small villages. A good example of these types of settlement can be seen in the one excavated at Warendorf.[9]

Thus, the Saxons could not be incapacitated by the defeat of a single leader, nor would the seizure or destruction of key settlements lead to a rapid conquest. It is only when they banded together to fight, either offensively or defensively, that they were brought to battle as a group. And only in the aftermath of such encounters do the annals record the different Saxon confederacies submitting or making agreements with the Franks. In comparison with the Franks, the Saxons were relatively few in number and poorly organised for conducting offensive warfare against their powerful neighbour, so in most respects this was a most unequal struggle. Otherwise, in their material culture, not least in terms of weapons, the Saxons and the Franks were very similar.

The social structure and political organisation of Charles' other target in the 770s, the Lombard kingdom of Pavia, were the very opposite of those of the Saxons, and this explains the difference in the speed and decisiveness of the two conflicts. As seen in 755 and 756, the Lombard kingdom in northern Italy could be incapacitated by a single military defeat, and by a threat to its centre of administration and the principal royal residence at Pavia. What the events of those years had also shown was that it was difficult for Frankish rulers to impose on the Lombards a permanent political settlement if they were going to withdraw from Italy at the end of the current year's campaigning season. To force the Lombard kings to make treaties under duress was not the same as ensuring that they would adhere to the terms of the agreements.

In 773, Charles received an appeal for help from the new pope, Hadrian I (772–95) against renewed Lombard threats to Rome. He had his own reasons to be interested in a show of force in Italy at this time, in that the widow and children of his brother Carloman and other political exiles from Francia had taken refuge with the Lombard king Desiderius. According to the *Liber Pontificalis*, Desiderius was hoping to use them against Charles.[10] This may have been true – or it may have been a piece of papal disinformation aimed at securing the Frankish king's intervention against the Lombards. Whatever the cause, Charles invaded Italy with a large army in 773. One detachment of his forces outflanked the Lombard attempt to hold the Alps, and Desiderius was rapidly besieged at Pavia, like his predecessor, Aistulf, in the 750s.

Unlike the sieges of 755 and 756, this one was protracted and lasted on into 774. After six months, Charles himself, who had been joined outside Pavia by his new wife Hildegard (d. 783) and their son, proceeded to Rome, where he met pope Hadrian. On his return after Easter 774, the siege of Pavia finally came to an end. Unlike the submissions of 755 and 756, on this occasion the Lombard king had to surrender himself, his family and the royal treasure.[11] The Lombards were obliged to submit to Frankish rule, and Charles himself took the title of king of the Lombards. In the late summer he returned to Francia, where fighting with the Saxons had now resumed, leaving a garrison in Pavia.

What or who had prompted Charles to take the unforeseen step of annexing the Lombard kingdom is unknown. It was quite unprecedented for a ruler of one ethnic group to style himself as king of another. In the fifth and sixth centuries, such a conquest would normally have been followed by the elimination of the defeated people's separate ethnic identity, as happened to the Vandals, Sueves, Ostrogoths and others. Similarly, in seventh-century Britain, where in a number of cases kings of more powerful peoples defeated and killed the rulers of the smaller neighbouring kingdoms, in no case did this lead to, for example, the ruler of Mercia proclaiming himself to be king of the East Angles. It is possible that pope Hadrian played a key role during Charles' Easter visit to Rome, persuading him that a final solution to the Lombard kingdom was required. The limited usefulness of earlier Frankish interventions from the papal point of view was obvious, and it is unlikely that Charles had long-term ambitions of annexing the Lombard kingdom. But for the *Rex Francorum* to proclaim himself to be *Rex Langobardorum* was a more extraordinary act than is generally appreciated. Charles had taken this title by September 774 and he used it consistently, and not just in documents relating exclusively to Italy, even after both his royal titles were supplemented by his imperial one.[12] The most likely explanation, and the possible constitutional justification, for Charles' action lay in the much earlier tributary relations between the Franks and the Lombards, which, according to Frankish sources at least, had also led to Pippin III being consulted over the choice of Desiderius as king in 756. So his deposition in 774 could be explained in terms of disloyalty to his Frankish overlord.

While the centralised nature of its royal government was so well developed that the occupation of Pavia and the exile of Desiderius to a monastery in Francia established Frankish control over the Lombard kingdom, the great duchies of Spoleto and Benevento had in practice to be left in the hands of their local rulers. The newly installed duke Hildeprand of Spoleto, a papal ally, acknowledged Charles' overlordship, in 774 or 775, but Benevento, under its duke Arichis, only came to terms with him in 787.[13] Even in the north, the return of the new king of the Lombards to Francia led, in 775, to a revolt by duke Hrodgaud of Friuli, which forced Charles to undertake an expedition into Italy early the following year to eliminate him.[14]

The simple truth was that, if the king was in Francia there would be trouble in Italy, and if he was in Italy the Saxons would resume fighting. Faced by such a dilemma, it is then perhaps surprising to find Charles undertaking a campaign in Spain, as he did in 778. The foundation of Paderborn and the mass conversion of some of the Saxons may have convinced him that the Saxon problem had been dealt with. At the Paderborn assembly in 777, he received envoys from the de facto independent Arab rulers of Barcelona and Zaragoza, who were threatened by the rising power of the Umayyad amir of Córdoba, 'Abd al-Rahman I (756–88), who had gradually made himself master of most of the south and centre of the Iberian peninsula in the course of the previous twenty years.[15] For Charles, a Spanish venture represented yet another way in which, as in Aquitaine, Italy and across the Rhine, he could pursue some of the traditional Frankish aims of his Merovingian and Carolingian predecessors. Since the sixth century, Frankish kings had been interested in the possibilities of loot or even conquest offered by the great Roman towns of the Ebro valley and the area of modern Catalonia, and Charles' father Pippin III had succeeded in conquering all the remaining Arab-ruled areas in south-western Gaul, culminating in his capture of Narbonne in 759.

Traditional as may have been the motives, and unexpected as was the opportunity suddenly offered by the appeal from the Arab regional potentates, the expedition that Charles led into the Ebro valley in 778 was probably ill-conceived, and it turned out to be the nearest that any of his undertakings came to disaster.[16] As in his Italian campaign of 774, he divided his forces into two columns, to cross the Pyrenees in different places: one in the east to approach Zaragoza via Barcelona and the other, led by him in person, to cross the western end of the mountains and descend the Ebro. However, one of his two erstwhile Arab allies had by now murdered the other. The Frankish forces were refused admission to Barcelona and found Zaragoza held against them. As an Umayyad army approached the Ebro from the south, Charles was obliged to withdraw his army back up the valley and into Francia, dismantling the fortifications of Pamplona, which he had occupied. In the retreat across the Pyrenees, the rearguard of his army was set upon and annihilated by the Basques, and a number of prominent officers of his court were killed.

Even ignoring this humiliation, which the *Annals of the Kingdom of the Franks* omit entirely from the account of this year, the whole expedition had failed to achieve any of its objectives, and in the meantime the Saxons had risen up against the Franks in the king's absence. They penetrated as far as the east bank of the Rhine at Deutz, opposite Cologne, and destroyed the new Frankish settlement on the Lippe, which Charles had rather unwisely named after himself as *Carlopolis*. In response, a retaliatory expedition in 779 defeated the Westphalians and induced other Saxons east of the Weser to send hostages for their future good conduct. This was reinforced by a major progress through Saxony, as far as the Elbe, that Charles conducted in 780, and a large number of Saxons submitted to mass baptism on the River Oker.[17]

Even after these displays of force, the submission of the Saxons was still far from secure, and the Frankish chronicle sources, notably the *Annals of the Kingdom of the Franks*, cannot conceal this fact, despite repeated assurances of great Frankish victories and the slaughter of numerous Saxons. Charles had to go to Italy in 781, not least for the papal coronation of two of his young sons: Pippin as king of the Lombards, and Louis as king of the Aquitanians. The substantial campaigns that then had to be launched against the Saxons in 782, 783, 784 and 785 show that not only had their resistance still not been broken, but also that, as in 774 and 778, the king's absence in other parts led to major Saxon revolts.[18]

The compiler of the *Annals of the Kingdom of the Franks* in the 790s was keen to present an unremittingly triumphalist image of the king, and of the Franks. Thus, while forced to record that two leading Frankish nobles were killed, he presents the 782 campaign against the Saxons, which was not directed by the king in person, as yet another military success. Fortunately, the author of the revised version of these annals admits that the Frankish forces were severely defeated, and two of the king's principal officials and four other counts were killed. Charles reacted to this reverse with a massive show of force and the sub-sequent massacre at Verden of 4,500 Saxons – though this num-ber is disputed – who had been surrendered to him.[19]

The protracted campaigns of the first half of the 780s were ultimately to bring the Saxons to heel in 785, when, as the Annalist put it, Charles was able 'to march through all of Saxony, wherever he wanted, on open roads and with no one resisting him'. Widukind, the leader of Saxon resistance since 777 and possibly the descendent of a former ducal dynasty, was forced to submit and to receive baptism.[20] In practice, this was to be only a temporary pacification, in that Saxon resistance revived in the later 790s, but it was at least sufficient at the time for Charles to feel that his grip on Saxony was secure, and therefore that he was able to turn his attentions to Italy once more.

He spent Christmas of 786 at Florence and proceeded south to Rome in the spring of 787. Faced with the prospect of royal intervention in the south, duke Arichis of Benevento offered a token submission, but pope Hadrian persuaded Charles to invade the duchy, and force him into a more abject surrender. The first manifestation of Frankish power in southern Italy in 781 had encouraged the imperial government in Constantinople to try to make an alliance with Charles, who had received a pro-posal from the empress Irene, then acting as regent, that one of his daughters be betrothed to her son, the emperor Constantine VI (780–97). The reappearance of the Frankish king in south-ern Italy in 787 now led the Empire to push for the implemen-tation of this agreement.[21]

However the Franks viewed this invitation, for the Byzantine court such a marriage of a member of the imperial family to someone who was regarded as a 'barbarian' was a useful diplomatic act. Constantine VI's father, Leo IV (775–80) had been the son of a Khazar princess, whom Constantine V had married when it was helpful to look for allies north of the Black Sea.[22] In 787, it was advisable for the imperial government to neutralise any threat that Charles presented to their surviving enclaves of territory in southern Italy, and at the same time the empress may have been looking for wider support at a time when she was alienating some of the units of her own army by reversing her predecessors' religious policies. A first effort to put an end to imperially sponsored Iconoclasm had foundered in 786 when soldiers had broken up a council in Constantinople. A second attempt to hold such a meeting was successful in Nicaea in 787, where Iconoclast theology had been formally condemned.[23]

With both Italy and Saxony more firmly under royal control, Charles' next aim was the elimination of the principal power in the region lying between them, the duchy of Bavaria. As a duke, Tassilo III of Bavaria was subject to the Frankish king, to whom he was also related, but the regional independence such a local ruler could enjoy had been amply demonstrated in Aquitaine. Tassilo is accused in the Frankish sources of having conspired with the Saxon leader, Widukind, in the period before 785, and with the Avars and Slavs in the year 788.[24] However, Frankish chroniclers' accusations of treachery are rather debased coinage, and little trust should be placed in this one.

Tassilo failed to attend the assembly held by Charles at Worms in 787 after his return from Italy, and in consequence his duchy was invaded. When obliged to submit by an overwhelming display of force, he was reinvested with his office, but the following year at the assembly at Ingelheim, which he was obliged to attend, he was accused of treachery and condemned to death. During his attendance at the assembly, Frankish troops entered Bavaria and took his family hostage. In the circumstances, there was little he could do but confess his guilt, real or otherwise, and he was imprisoned in a monastery. His deposition and that of his dynasty was later confirmed by the council held at Frankfurt in 794.[25]

Significantly, the allies with whom Tassilo was said to have been conspiring, the confederacy of the Avars who controlled the plains of Hungary, twice invaded Bavaria in 788, and met with stiff resistance from the inhabitants.[26] As with the Arab raid into Aquitaine in 733 and their capture of Avignon in 737, it is surprising to find those whom the Frankish chronicles describe as allies actually engaged in desperate struggles with each other. There are reasons for doubting the truth of the charges made against Tassilo III, and for suspecting that his confession, repeated in the Council of Frankfurt in 794, was as untrue as those of the victims of Stalin's 'show trials' of the 1930s.

Frankish military expansion in the course of the first two decades of the reign of Charles created its own problems. In all areas it seriously worried those living just beyond the initial targets of Frankish aggression. The wars in Saxony led to problems with the Slavs, and then with the Danes; the Italian conquest alarmed the Byzantine empire and led to difficulties with the Slavs in the western Balkans; while the intervention in the duchy of Bavaria contributed directly to a confrontation with the Avars. This latter conflict, which began in 788, continued intermittently throughout the early years of the 790s.

In 788, the Avars had twice raided Bavaria and sent an army into the March of Friuli in the north-east of Italy, but in all cases had been repulsed by local forces. Charles himself came into Bavaria later in the year to establish frontier defences against further Avar attacks. In 790, an attempt was made to settle the disagreements over boundaries by negotiations held at Worms, but to no avail. In 791, at a Marchfield held at Regensburg, it was decided that a campaign should be launched against the Avars because of 'the excessive and intolerable outrage committed by the Avars against the Holy Church and the Christian people'. What exactly was implied is not clear, but the expedition, which was clearly planned long before Charles came to Regensburg, was given a strongly religious justification.

The ensuing war is not easy to understand. Our only accounts of it come from the Frankish annals, augmented by such chance survivals as a letter from Charles to his wife Fastrada (d. 794) written at the end of the 791 campaign. The most perplexing features are the nature and causes of the Avar collapse. In 791, a Frankish army sent from Italy under Charles' son, Pippin, defeated an Avar force, while Charles himself proceeded along both banks of the Danube with another army without meeting any significant resistance. The explanation for, or possibly the consequence of, this Frankish triumphal progress in 791 was a civil war among the Avars and the rapid break-up and disappearance of their confederacy. Frankish armies from Italy marched unopposed into Avar territory north of the Danube in both 795 and 796 and there looted and ultimately destroyed a great ceremonial centre known as the Ring.[27]

By this time, Charles, nearly fifty years old, was campaigning in person less frequently, and from 794 his court came most often to spend the winter months in the newly developed palace complex at Aachen.[28] Later still, he would remain at, or in the vicinity of, Aachen throughout the summer months as well. In 794, he also convoked a general council of the Frankish church to meet at Frankfurt on the Main, which some Italian and British bishops also attended. Its purposes included discussing the Byzantine restoration of image-veneration at the Second Council of Nicaea in 787. One of the king's principal theological advisers, a Goth called Theodulf, who was later made bishop of Orléans, had been preparing a substantial critique of what were seen as the heretical views of the Greek bishops. This work was presented as being Charles' own, and in consequence it later became known to scholars as the *Libri Carolini* or *Caroline Books*. Both Theodulf and the bishops attending the council of Frankfurt in 794 were critical of Byzantine image-veneration, which they suspected of verging on idolatry.[29] Pope Hadrian I, however, had welcomed the restoration of what he accepted as orthodoxy in Constantinople, with considerable enthusiasm, and the papal espousal of the decisions of II Nicaea resulted in the suppression of the probably still unfinished *Libri Carolini*, which were not presented as planned to the bishops assembled at Frankfurt.

Ideological ties linking the Church of Rome and its bishop to the Empire were still very strong, despite the practical need of the papacy for Frankish military assistance. An eastern imperial attack in 788 on the duchy of Benevento, recently subdued by Charles, may have been intended to break up the new political alignments in the West before they became too firmly fixed. However, the Byzantine forces were defeated by the armies commanded by the appointees of the Frankish king.[30] It must have been clear in Rome that the Empire was in no position to re-impose its control on Italy, and that at least in the short term the future lay with the Franks.

Indeed, developments in Constantinople in the 790s would have reinforced such a view. Constantine VI took power into his own hands in 790 when a military revolt overthrew his mother, the regent Irene. However, he allowed her to return to Constantinople in 792, where she began to conspire against him.[31] A scandal over his sudden divorce and remarriage in 796 undermined his popularity with the Church, and fears were growing that he was thinking of restoring Iconoclasm. In July 797, the empress was able to seize power in a coup backed by the imperial guard, and the emperor was blinded, to render him formally incapable of holding the imperial office. Whether intentionally or not, this was done so brutally that he died as a consequence of it.[32]

Even the chronicler, Theophanes, for whom, as a committed Iconodule, Irene, the restorer of image-veneration, was the 'wise and God-loving' empress, 'who had struggled for the true faith in a martyr's fashion', found this act incapable of justification. On Constantine's deposition and death, his mother took the throne in person. However, no woman had ever ruled the Empire in her own right, and, while she used the male form of the imperial title, her opponents regarded the office as vacant. Her increasingly unstable regime survived until she was deposed in 802 in a coup led by her finance minister. In the meantime, she had had to look for allies and, rather than renewing war against the Franks in Italy, she may even have proposed a marriage between herself and Charles. The theoretical vacancy of the imperial throne also proved opportune in the context of a rapid and unforeseen series of developments in the West.[33]

There, another blinding was to have rather different consequences, leading directly to the creation rather than to the death of an emperor. On Christmas Day 795, pope Hadrian I died. In his pontificate, formal ties with the eastern Empire ended, when in 781 Roman documents stopped being dated by imperial years and the emperor's coinage was replaced by one bearing the image of St Peter and the name of the pope. Since early in the century, holders of the papal office had been controlling not only the city of Rome but also the whole former imperial duchy and other substantial territories in central Italy, and now they did so without an imperial overlord. So the election of a new pope was a very significant event, with important consequences for those who had benefited under the previous pontiff, and who might lose their access to power and wealth under his successor. As dynastic succession was rare, the nephews of Hadrian I secured the choice of Leo III (795–816), who was not of noble origin and whom they expected to control.[34] He quickly proved himself less amenable than expected, and they plotted to replace him. Though there were no legal means of doing so, they anticipated that, as in the case of the emperors, serious physical mutilation would render him incapable of ruling.

They had, however, overlooked the Frankish involvement in Roman affairs. Leo III had announced his election to Charles, a procedure normally reserved for the emperor in Constantinople.[35] He was the first pope to do so. On 25 April 799, the conspirators struck, ambushing Leo in the course of a procession. He was seized, blinded and an attempt was made to cut out his tongue, before he was imprisoned in a monastery. However, aided by supporters in the city, Leo was able to escape from the monastery and from Rome, and make his way north to

Charles, who was then at Paderborn.[36] Even worse for his enemies, the blinding and mutilation had been so ineffectual that the fugitive pope regained the use of all his senses and his supporters were able to claim these as miraculous healings.[37]

Agents of those who had overthrown Leo III came after him to appear before Charles in Saxony and present accusations of fornication and perjury against the pope. The Frankish king's position was not an easy one, in that serious accusations had been made against the pope by relatives of his predecessor, whom Charles had long regarded as a friend.[38] On the other hand, Leo had been anxious to present himself as Charles' reliable ally from the very start of his pontificate. To complicate matters, a number of the king's ecclesiastical advisers, notably the Northumbrian deacon Alcuin (d. 804), on the basis of arguments developed during the Laurentian schism in the time of the Ostrogothic king Theoderic, urged on Charles the need to accept that the Bishop of Rome could neither be judged in a secular tribunal nor, because of the Petrine foundation of his see, could he be answerable to any of his ecclesiastical inferiors, even in a council.[39]

After discussions almost totally concealed from us, Leo was restored to Rome with Frankish backing in the summer of 800, and in November Charles himself arrived in the city, in theory to preside over a council that would enquire into the accusations against the pope. This body, meeting at the beginning of December, shared Alcuin's view and declared itself to be incompetent to carry out such a role, and instead Leo was permitted on 23 December to take a public oath that he was innocent of all the charges levelled against him. Two days later, in the course of the celebration of the Mass of Christmas, he crowned Charles as emperor.[40] What Belisarius had been unable or unwilling to do in 539 was thus achieved, and three and a quarter centuries after the deposition of Romulus in 476 a new emperor was created in the West.

Though often seen as the natural culmination of the military conquests of Charles and his Frankish kingdom, the imperial title and coronation at the hands of the pope were the products of particular and limited circumstances, and were by no means the natural ends towards which the king and his advisers had long been working.[41] At best, the coronation was brought about by purely Italian or even Roman circumstances, and was the outcome of the particular events of the years 799–800, helped by the peculiar constitutional position of the current ruler in Constantinople. If anything, the imperial title was to be more of a hindrance than a help to its recipient, and was to be the most ambiguous of the legacies that he would pass on to his successors.

The meaning of Empire, 800–14

It is doubtful whether any of the participants in the dramatic imperial coronation in St Peter's on Christmas Day in the year 800 knew for certain what they were doing, or precisely where it was intended to lead.[42] This is true even in the literal sense, since there had been no imperial ordination in the West since the fifth century, and the liturgical procedures followed were entirely new and not borrowed from the Byzantine empire. The use of a crown was unprecedented and was not to be a feature of imperial investitures in Constantinople before the tenth century. Thus, the Roman Church invented its own rites for the occasion.[43]

According to Einhard, a former member of Charles' court, who wrote a *Vita Karoli* or *Life of Charles*, probably in the mid-820s, the king declared that if he had known what was going to happen he would never have entered the church that day.[44] This is no more than a reflection of the tradition, current since antiquity, of the refusal of power. Prospective emperors, like holders of high office in the Church, were expected to resist attempts to elevate them to their new status. It may be that the idea of creating a new western emperor was first raised in the discussions between Charles and pope Leo III in Saxony in the winter of 799/800, and it may well have been discussed openly in Charles' presence at the assembly of bishops from both Francia and Italy that was waiting to meet following his arrival in Rome in late November of 800.[45] But this is not something our sources can be expected to tell us, as that would suggest the act was premeditated, and thus a deliberate seeking of power, which was the mark of a tyrant.

The rapid expansion of the Frankish kingdom under Charles, and his conquest of other peoples, had led to the use of the terminology of *imperium* or Empire in the correspondence of his court, but this was conventional in such circumstances, and had been used, for example, by Bede in writing about some of the seventh-century kings of Northumbria who had exercised overlordship of other kingdoms.[46] Such usage did not imply an actual imperial title or the ambition for one. In the Roman imperial tradition, the Empire was in any case single and indivisible. Two emperors could co-exist, but only as colleagues ruling a single Empire. Frequent civil wars had been fought in the fourth century over the refusal of an emperor to accept a self-proclaimed imperial colleague. In 800, it was only the theoretical vacancy in Constantinople resulting from *femineum imperium* or 'a woman's rule', which gave the Roman Church its excuse to elevate Charles.

The nearest that the king's advisers in Francia came to expressing the view that the extent of his power required an enhancement of his status were references in letters of Alcuin (d. 804) to an *Imperium Christianorum* or *Empire of the Christians*. It is important to grasp that previously the whole notion of an Empire had been tied to Rome, not so much the city, though this was the symbol of it, as the civilisation. If a Frankish king could not, or did not wish to, claim to be a Roman emperor, an entirely new ideological base had to be found for such a change in his status.

How far the kind of ideas that lay behind Alcuin's term could have been developed cannot be said. Certainly the conquest of the Saxons had been turned into an armed evangelisation, the Spanish expedition of 778 was transmuted in retrospect into a bid to succour the Christians under Islamic rule, and the Avar campaign of 791 was seen by the king at the time as an act of Christian vengeance accompanied by litanies and fasting on the part of his army.[47] But whether the notion of a Christian citizenship could have provided a new ideological cement for the disparate peoples under Charles' rule, or could have transformed the Roman overtones of the imperial office and thus also Frankish suspicions of it is unclear, as the still incoherent process was given a new direction and impetus by pope Leo III and his advisers.

It may be that just as the popes of the mid-eighth century had been anxious to bind the rulers of the Franks to Rome as their defenders against the Lombards, so Leo III wanted to ensure his personal protection from his factional enemies within the city. The events of 799 had shown that, without Charles' support, his own survival was in jeopardy, and just as Stephen II had tried to institutionalise the relationship between the Frankish ruler and the City of Rome by investing Pippin and his sons with the title of 'Patrician of the Romans', so Leo needed to go a step further and make Charles into the *Imperator Romanorum* or *Emperor of the Romans*.[48]

Even if the pope's motivation was not as self-interested as that, it is likely that the impetus for a re-creation of a western emperor was largely Italian in origin and direction. In part the problem was one of authority. Since 774, Charles had been *Rex Langobardorum*, but the extent of the former Lombard kingdom within Italy was limited, and the constitutional relationship between the monarchy that had been centred on Pavia and the two great central and southern duchies of Spoleto and Benevento was by no means certain; all the more so since the Beneventan rulers had taken the title of prince in the aftermath of the Frankish conquest.

Leaving the problems of the loosely structured Lombard kingdom to one side, there remained difficulties to face in virtually every other area of Italy as far as Charles' right to rule, as opposed to his power to do so, was concerned. The area of the former exarchate of Ravenna and its related region of the Pentapolis had been taken from imperial control by the Lombards in 751, but this had never been recognised by Constantinople. The status of these territories and the right by which Charles ruled them remained unclear. This was also true of the city of Rome and the lands of its duchy.

Some scholars have argued that the popes in this period were gradually and consciously working towards the creation of a fully independent territorial state, a 'Republic of St Peter'. However, there is no definite evidence for this. There would seem instead to have existed a situation of pragmatic uncertainty about the relationships between Empire, papacy and Frankish kingdom for most of the last quarter of the eighth century. Leo III's decision to send formal notification of his election to Charles instead of to Constantine VI is the first real sign that this was breaking down, and that one of the parties, the Roman Church, was seeking a clear and unambiguous realignment of its relationship to the other two. In other words, the creation of a new western emperor would resolve the lingering constitutional difficulties faced by the popes in terms of their secular allegiance. At the same time, it could provide a new and more satisfactory framework for the exercise of authority by the Frankish ruler over all parts of Italy (and all and any other parts of the former Roman Empire in the West).

This may have suited the interests of the pope and to some extent those of Charles himself, but it was totally unacceptable in Constantinople, the capital of a much diminished state but one that still saw itself as the one and only Roman Empire. War was unavoidable once the regime of the empress Irene was swept aside, but under her successor, Nicephorus I (802–11), the Empire was too weak to make any impression and merely lost more of its remaining territory in Istria to the Franks. At the same time, the growing power in the Balkans of the Bulgars under their khan Krum (805–14) presented a far more serious threat to Byzantium than the coronation of Charles. In 811, Nicephorus was defeated and killed by the Bulgars, and his skull was turned into a drinking vessel for the khan. In 812 the new emperor, Michael I (811–13), made a treaty recognising the imperial status of the Frankish ruler, though only as *Imperator Francorum* or *Emperor of the Franks*.[49]

By this time, however, Charles' own view of his new office and its title had changed significantly. He seems personally never to have warmed to Leo III in the way he had to Hadrian I, whose epitaph he had had specially composed, carved and sent to Rome for the pope's tomb. Following his return to Francia in 801, Charles and his advisers quickly turned to working out what his new status might mean in a Frankish context. By the middle of that year, the imperial title, as it appeared in documents, had been changed from *Imperator Romanorum* to the rather more abstract *Imperator Imperium Romanum gubernans* or 'Emperor governing the Roman Empire'. This style had antecedents going back to the time of Justinian I, but may have been particularly attractive in divorcing the imperial office from what to the Franks would appear to be the ethnically qualifying element 'of the Romans'.[50] This, for the Franks, meant the inhabitants of the City of Rome and its territories. The form of the title used in Rome by Leo III at the coronation, which subsequently appeared in the *Liber Pontificalis*, was thus far too limiting, and also seemed to tie the office to the City of Rome and to the papacy.

Einhard, in his *Vita Karoli*, specifically links the reform of the two primary codes of law under which the Franks lived and the writing down of the laws of their subject peoples to the aftermath of the imperial coronation.[51] He presents these as tasks that could only be carried out after Charles had attained the status of emperor. As in the classic 'refusal of power' attributed to Charles in his words about the ceremony at St Peter's, this looks like a reminiscence of Roman constitutional ideas. Only an emperor was permitted to make new legislation, though certain of his subordinates could 'interpret' existing laws in such a way as to give them new application and meaning. Thus Procopius had specifically praised the Ostrogothic king Theoderic for not making law, though in fact a set of regulations, known as the 'Edict of Theoderic' has long been ascribed to him.[52]

The existence of a version of the law code used by the main body of the Franks, the *Lex Salica*, that can be attributed to the revision of the year 802/3 mentioned by Einhard has been identified by modern scholarship.[53] There are more problems with the second element in Einhard's description of Charles' legal activity: the writing down of the laws of the subject peoples. A number of collections, many of which are very brief, that purport to be the codes of the laws of the Thuringians, the Saxons, the Alamans, the Bavarians, the Chamavian Franks and others, have survived in numerous manuscripts and have received modern editions. That the redaction of most of these should be associated with the programme described by Einhard has rightly been accepted.[54] But it needs to be asked if these texts really do represent the written form of the customary laws of the peoples to whom they are ascribed.

Many of them, for example the *Leges Saxonum* (*Laws of the Saxons*) or *Lex Thuringorum* (*Law of the Thuringians*), are very brief indeed and comprise little more than lists of compensations for injury and homicide, moderated by the legal status of the victim. All these compensations, however, are assessed in terms of *solidi*, which were in origin the principal denomination of gold coin used in the later Roman Empire but which became theoretical units of valuation in the Frankish and Visigothic kingdoms. Whatever else they were, *solidi* were not used by the Saxons and Thuringians. Similarly, there exist in these codes regulations concerning the punishment of those who commit murder or other offences in churches or of those who plot against the king of the Franks or his sons. As Christianity was first imposed on the Saxons from the mid-eighth century, and as they became subject to the Franks only from the 780s, there is no way of seeing these as ancestral customs or traditional laws. In other words, these are Frankish rules that the Saxons were required to abide by.[55]

This is by no means an isolated phenomenon. A number of other indications exist that show the Franks of the late eighth century trying to 'tidy up' their neighbours, to impose firm ethnic identities on them and give them distinct customs and laws. They seem to have been, from our perspective, strangely anxious to think of their neighbours and non-Frankish groups within their own territories as being distinct *gentes* or peoples. It is in looking at the treatment of Aquitaine and Burgundy that this emerges most clearly, but the implications are significant for weighing up the value of Frankish information relating to those peoples beyond their frontiers whom they subjected in the time of the first Carolingians.

It is, thus, notable that the contemporary sources referring to the Frankish wars in Aquitaine in the period 733–69 do not treat the inhabitants of that region as a distinct ethnic group and refer to their leaders only as dukes or princes of Aquitaine. However, slightly later Frankish sources, such as the *Annals of the Kingdom of the Franks*, always call them dukes *of the Aquitanians*, and imply a common ethnic identity for all the inhabitants of the duchy.

In so doing, they are deliberately altering the earlier historical sources upon which they rely.[56] In fact, to put it simply, there is no evidence whatever for the existence of a common Aquitanian 'national' or ethnic identity before the period in which this Frankish annalist was writing – that is, in the 780s.[57] This is also the decade in which Charles set up his youngest son, then aged only three, as 'king of the Aquitanians' in 781. This kingdom was in fact an almost wholly artificial creation that fell apart when first subjected to serious strain in the 830s and 840s.[58]

Similarly, it has been shown how unreal is the supposed Burgundian identity that is also emphasised in the Carolingian historical and legal texts of the later eighth and the ninth centuries.[59] While there had once been a Burgundian people and kingdom, centred on the middle Rhône and western Alps in the period 442–533, total discontinuity exists between it and the notional Burgundians of the Carolingian texts. These people were supposed to be legally distinct from the Franks, in that they lived under the norms of the code known as the *Lex Gundobada* or *Law of Gundobad*, named after the Burgundian king (d. 518) who was held responsible for the first version of it.[60] However, it may rather be the case that the Carolingian rulers required them to be distinct and to use a code of law supposedly representing their national tradition. In the same way, the Aquitanians were required to use Roman law, because the Franks regarded them as a distinct people of Roman origin.

If this is accepted, the whole notion of the 'personality of the law', whereby an individual would be judged only according to the legal rules of his or her own ethnic group, becomes a Carolingian Frankish invention and not something that should be expected to be found in earlier periods.[61] Much earlier legislation makes more sense when seen as applying territorially – in other words, to all the inhabitants of a kingdom, irrespective of their particular ethnic origin.[62]

What does all this mean in terms of the objectives the Carolingian rulers and their advisers were trying to achieve? How conscious a process this was cannot be gauged, but it does look as if the Franks were trying to define their own identity against those of all surrounding groups, who were forced by their Frankish conquerors into accepting far more rigid and formal definitions of their customs, history and ethnicity that were in many respects anachronistic. At the same time, the older divisions within the Frankish body politic, notably the division between Neustrian and Austrasian kingdoms, virtually disappear.

All this in turn has important consequences for the strength and stability of the political structure created by Charles and his immediate predecessors. The Roman Empire had achieved the extraordinary feat of turning a large and disparate number of subject peoples, most of whom had been forcibly submitted to Roman rule, into a single, long-lasting and more-or-less culturally coherent political entity. For many of the Celtic-speaking peoples in the West, Rome had represented an intellectually and materially superior culture that had much to offer, at least to the elite elements in their societies. In the Greek East the situation was almost reversed, but in both cases the concept of a common Roman citizenship and a shared set of values and cultural ideas provided the ideological cement to hold together the upper classes of the Roman Empire, from Hadrian's Wall to the Mesopotamian frontiers with Persia, and from the Danube to the fringes of the Sahara.[63]

In comparison with this, the task facing the Franks was simpler, in that their empire was geographically more limited, and they did have the advantage over some of the ethnic groups under their rule of having definite intellectual and material inducements to offer, largely in things they had themselves inherited from Rome. However, there had to be some overarching sense of community if a viable single political entity was to be created, to hold together all the ethnically diverse components of the new Frankish empire. Here, the kind of 'empire of the Christians' idea that Alcuin was articulating around the year 800 might have served the purpose. An ideological unity might have been able to outweigh the linguistic, historical and material cultural divisions between the different ethnic components of the Empire. This is what to a large extent Islam had done for the Arabs and was in due course to do for many of the large numbers of non-Arabs subject to their rule.[64]

However, it is important to note that, in the case of the Arab empire, the ability of the Arab tribes to absorb ethnically different elements into themselves by means of bonds of clientage was central to their creating a cultural unity among the ruling classes. In other words, within a century, there were a relatively large number of non-Arabs, in terms of their ancestral ethnic origins, who were thinking of themselves and their forebears as being Arabs. Similarly, the exact identity of the regions of Arab political control, and of the practice of the Islamic religion, strengthened the mutual identification of the two.

The Franks, on the other hand, were trying at the very time of their greatest territorial expansion to be ethnically exclusive and to force the peoples subject to them to recognise that not only were they not Franks but also that they were very decisively Saxons, Thuringians, Lombards or whatever else, with strong cultural traditions of their own. It was also impossible to present the frontiers of Christendom and of the Frankish empire as being conterminous.[65] Thus, whatever the Franks had to offer to some of their subject peoples by way of enhanced material and intellectual culture – and this was by no means negligible – it was not backed by the inducements needed to create a new ethnic or cultural identity, which in turn might have ensured the survival of their empire.

17 The Carolingian regime

The apparatus of government

The efficient working of Carolingian government depended above all on the personal capacity of the ruler.[1] The dynasty hardly suffered from the purely accidental but debilitating problem of long royal minorities that had afflicted the Merovingians at crucial times in the seventh century. While some of the monarchs of the new line came to the throne when young, the first case of one being under the age of majority did not occur until 899, with the accession of the East Frankish king Louis, later known as 'the Child' (899–911). Significantly, he was chosen because of the lack of any other legitimate heir – this, as we shall see, is a crucial distinction – and his early death put an end to the rule of the Carolingian dynasty in that part of Francia.

Competent royal leadership was not so much a reflection of the need for a king to display martial prowess and lead his armies in person, though this remained standard practice, as a requirement for him to be able exercise personal control over the decision-making processes. It used to be taken for granted that 'strong' kings, such as Charlemagne, could impose their unchallenged authority on their kingdoms, appointing and dismissing at will such significant office holders as the regional counts, and ensuring the uninterrupted flow of revenues from the royal estates and customs duties for which such officials were responsible. 'Weak' rulers, on the other hand, and this included Charles' son Louis the Pious, were ineffectual, appointing the wrong men to regional office and failing to prevent them from diverting local patronage and resources to themselves and their cronies, with the result that, over time, central authority became weak, and more active and far-sighted monarchs were later unable to undo the damage done by their feebler predecessors. The bottom of this downward spiral would be reached in the tenth century, when the Frankish kings in practice controlled no more than a small part of their kingdoms, and then only with the consent of their leading magnates, while the rest was in the hands of regional potentates whose power was so great that they have been called 'princes'.

As we shall see in subsequent chapters, such a view of the ninth and tenth centuries in the West has recently been modified, and the tenth in particular is no longer characterised as 'the iron century', as it once was. We now think we have a better understanding of the problems that had to be faced, and are more appreciative of the more localised solutions – not dissimilar to the Roman Empire in the third century – that enabled these societies to cope with them most effectively. Strong central government was not always an option, and in any case should not automatically be thought to be something that is good in own right or offering the greatest benefit to the greatest number of people.

Modern critics have rightly pointed out how much traditional twentieth-century and earlier European and American historiography focused on the theme of the rise of the nation state – that is, 'How we got to be who we are today' – and how as a result some historians, however unintentionally, distorted their narrative of earlier periods by highlighting and praising those features that seemed to be heading in the direction of 'the now', while ignoring or deriding others that did not.[1] Unfortunately, the reaction has been so strong that recently almost any narrative of events over time has begun to be regarded with suspicion, as inevitably being misleadingly selective and dependent on hindsight. Many practitioners of the historical art now feel obliged to protest in their writings against the wickedness of narrative, and to apologise for indulging in it when forced so to do for lack of any better way of expressing themselves. While some of these concerns are legitimate, so too is the assumption that it is in fact possible, and even desirable, to work out how and why particular features of the past came into being. If that is the case, then that is a task that a historian can properly undertake. Those who would question the very possibility of understanding causation in the past have to retreat into a philosophical position of 'knowing nothing', whereby no source of evidence is thought capable of being open to anything other than a purely subjective interpretation, which, while valid for the author, is not necessarily so for his or her readers. For those who have driven themselves into such an intellectual dead-end, a change of discipline may be the only escape.

The main reason why a competent monarch was essential for the smooth running of the Carolingian empire – and for any one of its component kingdoms once it began to be divided – was that decision-making, including the making of appointments, depended on consensus and on the maintenance of balance. There was no standing army or any other military resource permanently at the disposal of the monarch beyond his own personal retinue. The armed forces of the kingdom consisted primarily of the contingents provided by the great landowners for expeditions, whose purpose and timing were discussed and agreed at the annual assemblies. These could as easily be directed against a regional rebel as at a target outside the kingdom, but the assembled magnates would need to agree on the objective. In the case of regional revolt by a local count or others claiming to have been driven to act by being denied justice, for example, the great landowners might be reluctant to agree to immediate military action rather than negotiation if they felt the king was in the wrong and the rebels had legitimate claims for redress. On the other hand, at the annual assemblies, the personality of the ruler could play a critical role in winning over wavering opinion. Trusted leaders can persuade even those who may have reasons not to agree into accepting the leaders' decisions because of the confidence they inspire and their track record of success. This was something eminently true of Charlemagne, but seemingly lacking in his heir, Louis the Pious.

As well as in the relatively brief encounters with large numbers of their leading subjects, as at the annual 'Marchfields', a successful early Medieval monarch also had to have a deft touch in local politics.[2] Success in this area could also guarantee a more enthusiastic body of support at the assemblies, and smoother-decision making there too. The key issue was the successful exercise of patronage. As previously mentioned, the kings had offices to bestow as well as material rewards to distribute in the form of lands and treasure, especially in periods of territorial expansion. In most regions there existed several great landowning families, some possibly very long-established and others more recently arrived in status or residence. All such families had their own social-political networks, consisting both of other members of the wider clan claiming descent from a common ancestor, and of unrelated client families. In both cases their loyalty was not unconditional. Both the relatives and the clients supported their patrons in the expectation of favour and material reward. So, when a king had an appointment to make or some land to give in a particular region, he would be faced with choosing between the competing claims of several such clientage networks, though not necessarily of equal size and local standing.

To appoint as count the head of the most powerful regional confederacy might guarantee a loyal supporter for the monarch in the assemblies, who would also be able to impose order on his county without resistance. On the other hand, it could merely serve to entrench an already overmighty magnate, allowing him to strengthen his grip on the territory at the king's expense, by giving him responsibility for all the royal estates in the county, with little by way of audit and oversight. On the other hand, in such a situation, to appoint the leading representative of a less powerful local clientage network might just result in the greater one going into a state of permanent opposition, and doing its best to make the county ungovernable. A third option, of appointing an outsider with no previous landed stake in the county and no existing ties to its major landholders, could work if he was able to put together a coalition of local allies – perhaps as a counterweight to an overly dominant family, but could also result in all the regional magnates uniting against him as an unwelcome outsider. So, any such decision had to be made with the greatest care, weighing the factors involved, and in many cases sweetening the pill for disappointed candidates by giving them other patronage, and the promise of more to come in return for their co-operation. Too great a partiality for particular aristocratic networks and alliances could drive their disappointed rivals into the arms of the king's enemies, both within and outside his kingdom.

It is clear that if a king, aided by his court advisers, was not competent and made significantly unwise choices in the exercise of patronage, a great deal of resentment would be created. Worse still, if the monarch was incapable for whatever reason of keeping personal control over the key decisions on patronage and allowed others to do so for him, they could use the opportunity to further their own clientage networks – as the local ones had links of kinship and political alliance with others in other regions and at court. Thus factions could be created that became almost kingdom-wide, and might exploit such opportunities of power to advance their own interests and belittle their rivals, to such an extent that the latter would to tempted to support any rebel or a neighbouring monarch who was prepared to challenge theirs. Examples of how this worked out in practice, not least in the reign of Louis the Pious (814–40), will be seen below.

While considerable astuteness was clearly required, along with good local knowledge, in the decisions that kings and their advisers had to make, it should not be assumed that all the factors involved were purely rational. A feeling of offended honour, in particular, could wreck the most careful and sensible of schemes. Patronage was often requested from the king by influential bishops and aristocrats to advance their own interests and benefit their allies, and refusal could give offence. Those who were denied it in favour of local rivals might also be alienated and become rebellious, even in defiance of their own greater self-interest. So, personal factors, on which we are often generally poorly informed, could cut across all other considerations. In trying to make sense of the conduct of individuals and of family and other wider groups in these post-Roman centuries in the West, we have to take into account both the nature of the system, briefly outlined here, which made government dependent on the achieving of consensus and balance in both local and kingdom-wide politics, and the unpredictable factors that could upset the most carefully devised plans. Examples of both will be seen in the chapters that follow.

Despite the Carolingian monarchs receiving revenue via officials whom they appointed from all parts of their realms, the administrative network on which this depended was so rudimentary as to make it questionable whether we should regard the Frankish empire of Charlemagne as a state in any meaningful way. Such a suspicion is strengthened by the means, to be discussed below, that were employed to create political cohesion within it. The concept of citizenship died with the Roman Empire and, as we have seen, other ways in which Charles' subjects could have been given a sense of common identity were rejected or went unexplored, in favour of a paradoxical emphasis on the legal and ethnic differences that divided them. An apparatus of government, such as the vast civil service that was already long-established and flourishing in the Chinese empire by this time would not emerge in the West for many centuries. A much smaller but professional lay bureaucracy still functioned in the Byzantine empire, where a continuing sense of Roman identity and Christian orthodoxy sustained its citizens throughout a long period of intense military crisis.[3] In the West, though, whatever had survived of the apparatus of imperial government into the time of the Ostrogothic kingdom was disrupted by wars of reconquest under Justinian, followed by the division of Italy after the Lombard invasion. In Gaul, the breakdown of central authority in the fifth century had meant that the Frankish kings inherited little of the governmental apparatus of the Roman Empire, and the problems they faced from this have already been considered.

What the earlier Merovingians had, but their Carolingian successors seem entirely to have lacked, were instruments of local urban self-government. The survival of such Roman institutions as the municipal archives appears reasonably certain into the early seventh century, and a number of major urban centres were clearly still flourishing in Aquitaine, Burgundy and Provence at the beginning of the eighth.[4] These, however, were in many cases damaged or destroyed by the campaigns of Charles Martel and Pippin III.

Under Charlemagne, as in the time of his father and grandfather, the administrative apparatus of the Frankish kingdom was minimal.[5] Counts still functioned as the principal royal local officials, but assisted by no more than an officially stipulated minimum of one notary to write the documents they needed to produce. Deputies or viscounts they might have, at least from the early ninth century onwards, but in practice they depended on the goodwill of local landowners and their clientage networks for any effective imposition of justice. The only sanction that lay behind them other than their own personal military followings was the power of the king, as represented by the army that could be assembled annually after discussions at the 'Marchfield'. As suggested above, its deployment depended on the achievement of a high level of consensus among the lay and ecclesiastical magnates participating, and for minor conflicts this was a clumsy weapon to wield, whose usefulness in any case was greatly reduced in periods of military crisis or political turmoil, when agreement might not be reached or assemblies held.

The best inducement that a king such as Charles could offer, to secure the loyalty of the leading families of Francia and the other territories under his rule, was military success and the rewards that came from it.[6] Those who served in his campaigns could expect to profit from them, as their predecessors had in the time of Clovis and his sons. When, however, expansion stopped, as it did under Charles' son, the emperor Louis the Pious (814–40), and campaigning became defensive in nature, the interest of those who turned out to fight was blunted by the lack of expectation of profits and office, and they became increasingly aware that better opportunities might be offered in exploiting internal divisions within Francia or in promoting their own purely local concerns, especially when royal patronage also began to be mishandled, as occurred in the 820s.[7]

Like Clovis, Charles established his reputation as a leader by an almost continuous process of expanding the frontiers and rewarding his Frankish following with the loot obtained in war and the new offices for the governing of conquered territories. On the other hand, both Clovis and Charles left impossible legacies to their successors. No state, even Rome, could support itself on a basis of indefinite expansion. New structures and institutions had to be created to provide a proper administration of the conquered territories and to absorb the energies of those who had previously depended on the profits of war for their sustenance and that of their own followers.

Whatever else his achievements, Charles made no significant improvements to the governmental apparatus of the greatly expanded kingdom that he himself had created. The actual central administration remained minimal, and consisted of no more than the ruler's immediate entourage. Those documents that were not left to their beneficiaries to produce were written for the king by the clerics of the royal chapel, which thus doubled as the government's writing office.[8] Policies were agreed, and most military, legal and administrative decisions were still made at the annual assemblies, and the king was able to oversee his local officials, notably the counts, only by means of special emissaries or *missi*, dispatched from the court to carry out enquiries and to report back on the functioning of the local administration. Decisions taken at the annual assemblies were also communicated to the peripheral counties through the *missi*. Such decisions and sets of instructions were not necessarily written, or could be recorded only by a series of headings rather than in full.[9]

It would be unfair to suggest that Charles was unaware of these problems, or that he did not have a well-developed sense of his royal and subsequently imperial obligations. Indeed, what is most impressive about the Carolingian regime at this time is the very high-minded nature of its declarations of principles. Putting them into practical effect was not so easy, but the frequent failure to do so was not for want of the will to try.[10] More frequent and more extensive use of *missi* was a sensible expedient in the light of the very real limitations that the restricted nature of existing administration forced on the king.

A bureaucracy could not be created overnight by royal will. It depended, not least, on the existence of a sufficiently well-educated class of men able to understand the needs of an administrative system that depended on writing. In Francia in this period, knowledge of even the basic requirements of reading and writing was to be found only among the ranks of the clergy, and even there it seems that much ignorance and illiteracy existed. According to Einhard, Charles himself only began to learn to write late in his life, and made only limited progress with it.[11]

At the same time, as is well evidenced in some of the capitularies – royal administrative orders to the *missi*, records of councils and so on – Charles felt a strong sense of responsibility for the good order of the Church in his kingdom, and of how much the secular fortune of the ruler and his subjects depended on it. So, for a combination of reasons, relating both to his sense of the duties of his royal office and the more practical needs of developing a learned class, capable of undertaking the administrative tasks that the growing size and complexity of the Frankish kingdom demanded, the king and his advisers devoted themselves to ecclesiastical reform and a revival of learning.

The ideological programme

From such beginnings grew what is generally called 'the Carolingian Renaissance'. The title is not unfair. Just as in the late Medieval Renaissance, what the scholars of this period attempted, with varying degrees of success, was to recover and employ some of the learning and arts of antiquity. That they succeeded to a significant degree can be seen from the fact that most of the works of classical Latin authors that are known today have only survived because they were copied and preserved in manuscripts of Carolingian date.[12] However, the primary impetus was Christian and its motivation practical. The pagan content of much of the art and literature of the Roman past could still arouse unease in Charles and many of his advisers in the way that it had in pope Gregory the Great.[13]

It must also be recognised that the level of literacy that Charles and his advisers aimed for was little more than the equivalent of that of the primary level of education in the time of the Roman Empire, and was focused principally on elevating the attainments of the clergy rather than of lay society.[14] Even so, such aspirations and the degree of success in achieving them should be measured against the base from which they started.

Charles was interested first of all in attracting to his court a selection of scholars to advise him, and perhaps to invest his regime with the aura of intellectual sophistication associated with late Roman and even some of the earlier Merovingian courts.[15] The conquest of the Lombard kingdom gave him access to the resources of learning in northern Italy, and the first major luminary of the court was the deacon Peter of Pisa, who is reported to have instructed the king in (Latin) grammar.[16] Other notable Italians included Paul the Deacon, who had written a *Roman History* prior to the overthrow of the Lombard kingdom, and who was persuaded to stay for four years in Francia when he came in 782 to seek the release of his brother, who had been taken hostage after the revolt of duke Hrodgaud of Friuli. During his stay in Francia he composed an account of the lives of the bishops of the see of Metz, including the important Carolingian ancestor St Arnulf, and he later prepared an edition of the *On the Meaning of Words* of Sextus Pompeius Festus, which he dedicated to Charles. His most famous work, the *History of the Lombards* was probably written after his return to Italy in 786 and his entry into the monastery of Monte Cassino, though an alternative interpretation suggests that it was written during his time in Francia, with the aim of telling the Franks something about the Lombard past.[17]

The same period of the early 780s saw the arrival in Charles' entourage of two other foreign scholars: Theodulf, who was to become Bishop of Orléans (798–818) and Alcuin (d. 804). The precise origin of Theodulf is uncertain. It used to be thought that he came from the former Visigothic region of Septimania in south-west Gaul, but it is possible that he arrived in Francia in the aftermath of Charles' failed intervention in the Ebro valley in 778 and was a native of the western Pyrenean region.[18] His most significant intellectual contribution was his almost certain authorship of much of the initial draft of the *Libri Carolini* (794).[19] He was also a skilled poet, with the rare distinction for his time of knowing the works of Ovid. He was implicated, perhaps falsely, in a conspiracy in 818 and died in disgrace in 821.

Alcuin is the best known of the scholars who surrounded the Frankish king.[20] He was a Northumbrian, educated at York, who became head of its archiepiscopal school, though in the ecclesiastical hierarchy never rising above the rank of deacon. It is possible that the survival of so many of his writings, especially his letters, has distorted his significance in the Frankish context, and he might have been less frequently at court than was formerly believed. While he may have met Charles in Italy in 781, he does not seem to have joined his court before 786 at the earliest. He was back in Northumbria again between 790 and 793, and after 796 he passed most of his time in the monastery of St Martin at Tours, of which he had just been appointed the lay abbot. He died there in 804.

A poet, theologian and teacher, Alcuin's influence has been detected in a number of the key texts produced at the Carolingian court, notably some of the most important of the capitularies. Some of his poetic and epistolary writings also illuminate aspects of the life of that court, even in such minor details as the nicknames Alcuin gave to his colleagues. He most frequently addressed Charles himself in such works as 'David', referring to the Biblical monarch who was the effective founder of the kingdom of Israel and was, as the supposed author of the Psalms, also a poet and scholar. The image of a Frankish king as a new David had in fact already been used in the Merovingian period, and was thus not original to Alcuin, but he gave it new and more elaborate expression.

The preservation of a large corpus of Alcuin's letters, over 300 in number, has made available an illuminating source of information on a wide range of aspects of the central period of Charles' reign, in particular during the years when he was not at court after 796. He may also have had a minor role in the compiling of the *Libri Carolini*, and he was the principal spokesman in the dispute with bishop Elipandus of Toledo over the latter's use of a heterodox terminology in writing of Christ's adoption of his human nature.[21] His Northumbrian origin made him the natural spokesman in Charles' relations with the principal Anglo-Saxon kings of the period, notably Offa of Mercia (758–96).[22] He also became the principal teacher of the members of the noble families who were attached to the king's immediate following. It has been suggested that his work *De Orthographia* was intended to initiate or assist in a revision of the spelling and pronunciation of Latin throughout the Carolingian empire.[23]

While each of these men offered different skills and individual expertise in such matters as the devising and expressing of the king's official theological views, the writing of textbooks to promote simple literacy amongst the clergy and so on, overall, the aim of the reforms was to impose standardised norms in grammatical education, liturgy, canon law and, at a later stage, in monastic observance. The models used were in several cases ones that came from Rome. Thus the current version of the Gregorian Sacramentary, the papal Mass book of the Roman Church, was obtained from pope Hadrian I, as was the collection of ecclesiastical laws known as the 'Dionysio-Hadriana'.[24]

While it is customary to speak of this group of scholars in the service of Charles as 'a court school', it is hard to understand what in practice might be meant by this term, particularly in the period prior to the establishment in 794 of Aachen as the king's favourite, though by no means exclusive, residence. Much of the king's time was spent on campaign, and normally he and his entourage were peripatetic. However, a fairly extensive winter stay was passed each year at one or other of the royal seats – mainly rural palaces – and it is probable that these were the occasions for Charles' meetings with his court scholars and other ecclesiastical advisers. It is clear, too, that they were a far from homogeneous group and were frequently given to mutual jealousy and academic 'cattiness'.[25]

The achievements of Charles' advisers are perhaps most impressively displayed in the formulation of the objectives and the ideological underpinning of his regime. These are expounded most clearly in the royal capitularies, particularly those issued between the years 789 and 806.[26] The authors and inspirers of these various sets of instructions and decrees are nowhere named. Nor is it possible to build up a picture of

Charles's entourage from the signatures appended to royal documents (unlike other comparable cases in the medieval West), since attestations by witnesses were not included in Frankish royal charters. Indeed, from the court annals, themselves also entirely anonymous, it is clear that the officially sponsored impression was that all major decisions were taken by the king alone. It is possible to speculate, though, that significant advisory roles were taken in practice by such figures as Archbishop Hildebald of Cologne (785–819), the arch-chaplain, and the abbots Fardulf of Saint-Denis (792–806) and Angilbert of St Riquier (d. 814), and that in the last years of the reign the most significant influence may have been that of the emperor's relatives, abbot Adalhard of Corbie and his brother, count Wala.[27]

The capitularies are not an easy body of documents to define, largely because their role as written texts is entirely secondary to the purposes for which their contents were originally intended.[28] That is, they are written records, full, partial or merely in note form, of administrative decisions and decrees that had first been delivered orally, and whose authority lay in their spoken rather than their written form. They could deal with a variety of subjects and might range from records of gatherings that were largely or almost exclusively ecclesiastical in composition, to sets of legal regulations that were promulgated to add to or modify the rules to be found in the various legal codes of the Frankish empire. Such capitularies of laws 'added to the codes' concerned themselves exclusively with the two Frankish codes, the Salic and the Ripuarian, and in theory the Frankish ruler did not seek to alter the supposedly traditional laws of his other subjects. Other capitularies represent sets of instructions given to the *missi,* the royal officials sent to oversee and report on the working of the local administration of the empire.

Because the authority behind the various rules and instructions lay in the spoken word of the king, their recording was haphazard, and the subsequent preservation of the written versions depended on individual initiatives. Abbot Ansegisis of Saint-Wandrille made one collection of capitularies of various kinds in the late 820s, in the time of the second Carolingian emperor, Louis the Pious.[29] It is possible that this was carried out at the request of the emperor and his advisers, who certainly made use of it on occasion, as no other mechanism existed whereby oral decrees made under previous rulers could be preserved for the use of future governments.

This lack of an established procedure for the written recording of the administrative and legal pronouncements of the

Frankish rulers has nothing to do with supposedly Germanic traditions of oral law, but reflects identical problems to be encountered in the late Roman Empire, in which no mechanisms existed to ensure the preservation and distribution of the imperial legal decisions made in the emperor's court, despite their enjoying the force of law.[30]

The capitulary known as the *Admonitio Generalis* or *General Encouragement* represents the records of a primarily ecclesiastical assembly held, probably at Aachen, in 789. The document consists of a collection of eighty-two canons drawn from the acts of many of the earlier ecumenical councils of the Church (fourth to sixth centuries), which were here recast as royal decrees. Probably at the same time and place, another set of injunctions were issued relating mainly to aspects of monastic life.[31] What is so striking about this process is that it involved the secular power using its own procedures to issue what would previously have been regarded as purely ecclesiastical laws. For Charles and his advisers, it seems that the need for monasteries to ensure that the right sort of monk was appointed to the office of cellarer had become a matter directly related to the good working of the entire kingdom.

In their own minds, the distinction made here between the secular interests of government and the discipline and order of the church would be incomprehensible. As Charles declared in the preamble to his *Admonitio Generalis*:

> Considering with the salutary judgement of a pious mind, together with our bishops and counsellors, the abundant clemency of Christ the King toward us and our people, and how necessary it is not only to render unceasing thanks to his goodness with all our heart and voice but also to devote ourselves to His praise by the continuous practice of good works, that He who has conferred such great honours on our realm may vouchsafe always to preserve us and it by His protection.[32]

Such a view had precedents that stretch back to the earliest days of the Christian Roman Empire, but never before had the well-being of the state been so closely related to the proper observance of the minutiae of ecclesiastical regulations and discipline. The moral health of the Church in his territories was seen by Charles to be indissolubly linked to the material prosperity of his empire.

In 792, the failure of a conspiracy against Charles at Regensburg by his illegitimate son, Pippin (known as 'the Hunchback'), led to a new and significant burst of legislative activity.[33] The conspirators, when accused of treason, claimed that they had not taken an oath of loyalty to Charles, and were therefore not guilty of the crime of *perfidia* or 'breaking faith' in plotting against him. In consequence, in 793 Charles sent out panels of *missi*, normally consisting of an abbot or bishop and a count, to require all of the bishops, abbots, counts, principal landholders and other lesser officials, both secular and ecclesiastical, of his kingdom to take such an oath of loyalty.[34]

While their not having sworn loyalty did not protect the conspirators of 792 from punishment – 'Some were hanged, some beheaded, some flogged and exiled' (*Chronicle of Moissac*) – it was felt that the lack of direct personal ties between the ruler and his principal subjects could lead to the hatching of plots that threatened the stability and material well-being of the kingdom. It was not just that such actions were politically unsettling, but, as the contemporary Lorsch annalist saw it, for a king to achieve power through the murder (as had been planned in 792) of his own father and brothers was bound to provoke divine vengeance on the whole realm.[35]

The bishops who gathered with Charles at Regensburg also decreed, as recorded in another capitulary of the spring of 793, that they would all say three special masses: one for the king, one for the army, and one for help in this 'present tribulation'.[36] They further ordered the holding of a two-day fast by all the clergy and landowners, and drew up a graduated table of alms to be given by all bishops, abbots, abbesses, counts and royal vassals. These kingdom-wide acts of reparation and penance seemed the only way of atoning for the threat to the divine ordering of society created by the conspiracy of Pippin the Hunchback.

Similar ideas influenced another burst of capitulary-producing after Charles' return from Italy in late 801, and may hint at his reflections on the significance of his new imperial title. In 802, following a great assembly at Aachen, he sent out panels of *missi* with instructions to investigate and rectify any cases of injustice. The *missi* were also to impose a new oath, similar to the one that had been made to him as king in 793, but this time in his new status of emperor. While we do not have the wording of the oath of 793, the text of the one of 802 has fortunately been preserved in an abbreviated text of the capitulary prepared for the panels of *missi*. The full version of this capitulary is known as the 'Programmatic Capitulary', because it contains a new ideological framework for the relations between ruler and ruled'.[37] The oath of 793 had only to be taken by major office-holders and landowners, but the oath of 802 was to be sworn by all men in the kingdom aged twelve and above, though whether this happened in practice is not known. A subsequent capitulary, issued at Thionville in 805, forbade the taking of oaths of loyalty to anyone other than the monarch.[38]

The implications of the oath of loyalty were interpreted by Charles and his advisers as being far more extensive than just a promise not to conspire against the ruler's person or against the security of his kingdom, together with an obligation not to conceal any knowledge of proposed infidelity on the part of others. In the capitulary of 802, the *missi* were instructed to explain the wider implications of the oath to all those to whom they administered it. Each oath-taker was to be regarded as having promised 'to strive to the best of his understanding and ability to maintain himself fully in God's holy service', and that he would refrain from a whole series of acts that were seen to be detrimental to the material welfare of the ruler.[39] For example, by the interpretation of the new oath contained in the 'Programmatic Capitulary', it became an act of disloyalty to move a boundary marker on lands owned by the emperor, to disregard any imperial order, or to fail to pay any rent owed to him.[40] It also became an act of disloyalty and the breaking of faith not to turn out for the required period of military service.

What might seem like relatively harmless offences thus became acts of high treason, and liable to capital punishment, because they were now seen as being breaches in the compact made between ruler and ruled that was created by the taking of the oath. Even more striking is the way that any malpractice in the administration of justice was similarly taken as an act of infidelity. This could involve trying to argue on behalf of someone you knew to be guilty or failing to testify to the best of your ability for someone you believed to be innocent. The particular responsibilities of judges were reaffirmed strongly and frequently.[41] It is clear that, in the minds of Charles and his advisers, divine support for the emperor was dependent on his provision of justice for all his subjects.

The implications of these ideas were worked out in considerable detail, and in a number of areas. Thus, in a document normally classified as a capitulary but which generically takes the form of a letter, addressed to abbot Baugulf of Fulda, and probably dating to the later 790s, Charles worries about the effects of monks not being able to express themselves in a grammatically correct fashion – 'those who seek to please God by right living may not neglect to please Him also by right speaking'. More serious consequences still could result from such mistakes, as the king had found in a large number of letters that he had recently received from monasteries: 'Wherefore it came about that we began to fear lest, as skill in writing was deficient, so also wisdom for understanding the holy scriptures might perchance be less than it ought properly to be. [42] From this, in turn, could spring doctrinal error – heresy – which would inevitably incur divine displeasure, and thus disaster for ruler and kingdom alike.

It was such a belief that made Charles and his ecclesiastical advisers so anxious to act against the perceived threat of heresy in the acceptance by one bishop in the Frankish-ruled eastern Pyrenees of the Adoptionist theology of Elipandus of Toledo. There was, in practice, little prospect that Felix of Urgel would win over more supporters in Francia, but the existence of a single dissentient mind in the episcopate threatened the doctrinal uniformity of the Church in Charles' territories. So the bishops assembled for the council held at Frankfurt in 794 'rejected and unanimously denied adoption and decreed that this heresy must be wholly eradicated from the holy church'.[43]

This ideological thoroughness is one of the most striking features of the reign of Charles. In part, it may be seen as the nearest that the Carolingian rulers ever came to trying to work out a system of public obligation that would compensate for the inadequacy of the governmental structures of their empire. They could not rely on the notions of citizenship and legal obligations that had helped to underpin the Roman Empire. Nor did they even try to establish a political consensus around a reformed common cultural identity. Instead, they tried to create ties of personal loyalty on the part of subjects towards their ruler, based on the sanctity of oaths, using a set of ideas that can be traced back to Rome and to the Christian writers of the fourth century. In practice, though, this was not going to be sufficient to hold together the heterogeneous group of territories and peoples forced into political unity in consequence of Charles' campaigns of the 770s–790s.

Chroniclers of a warlike society

In comparison with the eighth century, the ninth century in Francia has left us a fairly detailed account of itself through several large-scale chronicles and annals. The most substantial of these is the text known, from the monastic library that housed the best known of the manuscripts containing it, as *The Annals of St Bertin*.[44] These were a continuation of the substantial set of annals called by modern scholars the *Annales Regni Francorum* or *Annals of the Kingdom of the Franks*. While some sections of those earlier annals were probably drawn up annually by anonymous scribes, possibly working in the royal court and under the supervision of the archchaplain, the head of the royal chapel and writing office, after 835 the continuation was essentially a private one and represents the views of two successive and identifiable authors. The first of these was the Spaniard Galindo (probably originally from Aragón), who was also known as Prudentius, and who became bishop of Troyes (843–61). After his death, his work was carried on by archbishop Hincmar of Reims (845–82), under whose direction the annual entries became even more substantial, but also more idiosyncratic.[45] Because of the locations (Troyes and Reims) and particular concerns of its compilers, this chronicle is clearly most concerned with the events in the independent West Frankish kingdom that came into being in the early 840s.

The principal collection of annals relating to the history of the eastern Frankish kingdom in the ninth century is one traditionally associated with the monastery of Fulda. The compositional history of this work, known as the *Annales Fuldenses* or *Fulda Annals*, remains controversial because of the lack of a modern critical edition.[46] Three different versions of the text survive, the third of which includes a continuation covering the years 882–901 that was probably written in Bavaria. The second version shows a distinctive partiality towards the ill-fated emperor Charles the Fat (d. 888), but the primary version is associated with archbishop Liutbert of Mainz (863–89), who twice held the office of imperial chancellor. Among earlier items incorporated into these annals is a version of the *Annales Regni Francorum*, and it has been suggested that the section of the text covering the years 838–63 was the work of a monk and author of saints' lives from Fulda called Rudolf (d. 865). It was the presence of a marginal reference to him in one of the manuscripts of the first class that led to the whole compilation being linked to Fulda.

The *Annals of St Bertin* and the *Annals of Fulda* are the most substantial and informative of these ninth-century compilations, but they can sometimes be supplemented by other, shorter and chronologically or geographically more restricted texts. For example, the *Annals of St Vaast* provide much independent information about the northern regions of the Frankish kingdoms in the years 874–900, as to some extent do the *Annals of Xanten* (probably written in Ghent), despite their compiler's apparently greater interest in natural phenomena and unusual weather than in the doings of men.[47] More substantial than these, and the work of another identifiable author, is the chronicle of the monk Regino of Prüm, covering the period from 813–906, but which is principally valuable for its account of the period from the 860s onwards.[48]

From such chronicles and annals, a consistent view of the period emerges, according to which 'pagans', represented by heathen Vikings from Scandinavia in the north and west, and Muslim Arabs in the south, pillage, burn and enslave with apparent impunity, while growing numbers of Carolingian kings squabble over fragile and declining kingdoms. It should be noted that most of these literary sources were written or compiled during the last three decades of the ninth century, when the Viking depredations were at their height, and when the Carolingian monarchs were most frequently in conflict with each other, not least because of the high rate of mortality among them at this time. So, it is fair to say that the dominant historiographical perspective on the century as a whole is one that is in fact conditioned by the events of a much shorter period.

Even so, we might wonder if certain fundamental flaws existed in the administrative and ideological structures of the Carolingian empire from the time of its founder, Charlemagne, onwards, and if these contributed to the rapid disintegration of the political unity that had been achieved so arduously by him in the late eighth century. Similarly, we must consider what role personality played in bringing about the conditions that so disturbed the late-ninth-century annalists, as they tended to express strong views about many of the rulers whose reigns they recorded. Inevitably, these were coloured by the chroniclers' own personal prejudices, and the particular concerns of the monasteries in which they wrote, but conditioned by the need for self-preservation. Thus few of the annals offer open criticism of the ruler in whose territory they were being written. So, for adverse comment on Charles the Bald (840–77) in his conflicts with the Vikings, it is necessary to turn to annals written in the kingdom of his half-brother, Louis the German (817–76).[49] Inevitably this leaves us wondering if this was an objective criticism, shared by Charles' own subjects, or just a propagandistic accusation against an ambitious rival of the annalist's own monarch?

Historiography was (and still is) hardly ever neutral. In Francia it had contained a high degree of ideological content ever since the mid-eighth century. Supporters of the rising Carolingian house rewrote the history of the late Merovingian period in their own interest. Under Charlemagne the *Annals of the Kingdom of the Franks* had deliberately suppressed and minimised Frankish reverses, while extolling or even exaggerating his triumphs. In the troubled reign of his successor, Louis, partisan historiography took on even greater importance. This extended itself to the new (or revived) genre of imperial biography. Einhard's *Life of Charles* which was partly modelled on Suetonius's *Life of Augustus*, was the first such work.[50] Despite following its main literary exemplar, providing details of the emperor's appearance, tastes and character that would otherwise be entirely lost, its idealised portrait of Charles was probably intended to serve as a role model for his successor.

Louis the Pious was himself to be the subject of two 'Lives', both written by his supporters.[51] One of these was Thegan, an auxiliary bishop in the diocese of Trier. His work, which unlike that of Einhard is a chronologically organised record of the events of the new emperor's reign, ends abruptly in the year 836 and omits any discussion of Louis's personal habits and tastes. A similar structure was selected by the anonymous author of the other, and longer, *Vita Hludovici Imperatoris*, or *Life of the Emperor Louis*. The writer of this work is often called 'The Astronomer', because of his interest in astronomical phenomena. This was a taste he shared with several other annalists of the period. His book is more substantial than that of Thegan, which, however, retains its independent value, and it extends up to the emperor's death in 840. Partisan as are both of these *Lives*, as are also the final section of the *Annals of the Kingdom of the Franks* and its continuation in *The Annals of St Bertin*, it is on their testimony that Louis the Pious is often condemned. His reign still needs more intensive scholarly study, not least as the *dissensio regum* that is so strong a theme in the history of later ninth-century Francia can be traced back into this period, and the political divisions within the previously united empire are the products of it.

18 'The dissension of kings', 814–911

Louis the Pious, 814–40

The publication in 1948 of an article by the Belgian historian François-Louis Ganshof prompted a debate among historians of the Carolingian period as to whether the last years of the reign of Charlemagne represent a period of decline.[1] However they are regarded, the events of the years 800–14 do hint at several of the major problems that were to afflict the Carolingian empire through the rest of the ninth century. These included questions of succession and of the division of territory between the ruler's heirs; the nature of the imperial title and the way in which it should be transmitted; and the responses required to military threats posed by Viking and Arab raids. To these could also be added the difficulty, discussed in the previous chapter, of preserving an empire whose internal governmental structures were as attentuated, and whose cultural, linguistic and political cohesion was as fragile, as that of the Carolingians.

Charles delayed unveiling a plan for the division of his empire among his three legitimate sons until the year 806.[2] By the capitulary issued at Thionville in February of that year, known as the *Divisio Regnorum*, all his realm was to be divided on his death into three more-or-less equal parts. In practice, this was based on the already existing arrangements of 781, in which Pippin had been made king of the Lombards, and Louis king of the Aquitanians. Their future share of the empire as envisaged in 806 added additional sections of territory to these, while allotting to Charles, the eldest brother, the Frankish heartlands of Neustria and Austrasia, together with the territories conquered or subjected east of the Rhine and north of the Danube.

The *Divisio* also laid down instructions as to how these three kingdoms were to be subdivided between the survivors in the event of any of the brothers dying before their father and not leaving an heir. No mention was made of the imperial title, and it has been suggested that Charlemagne at this time regarded that as a personal honour, not to be transmitted to the next generation.[3] On the other hand, a very persuasive interpretation of the document makes the wording imply a rather sophisticated political concept: that the proposed three kingdoms, while separate, were to be seen as also constituting a single greater

Regnum. It is suggested that this three kingdoms/one kingdom idea was influenced by the theology of the Trinity, to which some particular attention was being given in the Carolingian Church at this time.[4]

Whatever Charlemagne's views in 806, the events of the next few years led him to a simpler solution. His son Pippin died in 810, though leaving a son of his own, Bernard, and in 811 Charles, the eldest of the brothers, also died, aged thirty-nine. The despatch of the young Bernard to rule Italy in 812 may have been a sign that a new division was under consideration, and other members of Charles' close family, including his cousins and even the illegitimate children of his daughters might have been eligible for a share in the Frankish territories.[5] While this remained uncertain, the emperor resolved the problem of the imperial title. In September 813, after a great assembly of bishops, abbots and secular magnates, he summoned Louis from Aquitaine, and in a ceremony at Aachen the latter crowned himself emperor at his father's command.[6] He was, however, then sent back to Aquitaine. On 28 January 814 Charles died at Aachen, where he was to be buried. Louis, worried that one of his relatives would attempt to stage a coup, hastened to Aachen and rapidly consigned most of his family to house arrest in monasteries throughout Francia.

Louis, later known to the French as le Débonnaire and to the rest of the world as 'the Pious', was fortunate in his brothers' premature deaths.[7] The empire may have been less so. Despite the oath to his father in 813 to follow his precedents, Louis does not seem to have learned from that shrewd and intimidating man many of the real secrets of political management. Some of the criticisms that have been made against Louis are probably unfair, but as will be suggested, at certain crucial points in his reign his own weaknesses exacerbated political difficulties that could have been alleviated by a more flexible or conciliatory approach. However, we can doubt the value of some of the older accusations levelled against him.

Two of what historians have in the past regarded as his greatest mistakes were made early in the reign, even though this was a time when he had advisers of the highest calibre. The first of these supposed errors was the decision to have himself re-crowned as emperor by pope Stephen IV (816–17). The initiative for this appears to have come from Louis himself, who took advantage of the new pope's desire to travel to Francia for a personal meeting to discuss problems concerned with Rome, to include a papal anointing and re-coronation, which took place at Reims in October 816.[8] However much Louis felt this had strengthened his title, the precedent set by this ceremony restored the pope to the central role in the ritual of emperor-making. In practice, all future imperial coronations followed the precedent of the papal investiture and anointing of Charles and Louis in 800 and 816, and not the purely Frankish secular coronation of 813. After 823, no legitimate emperor was to be crowned without papal participation, and this in due course could come to mean without papal approval – at least until the time of Napoleon, who reverted to Charlemagne's precedent of 813.

Louis's second supposed mistake was to be too quick to make arrangements for the succession. Charles had ruled for nearly forty years before issuing his *Divisio Regnorum*, while Louis was on the throne for less than four before producing his equivalent, known as the *Ordinatio Imperii*. In themselves, the plans that were unveiled at an assembly in Aachen in 817 were very different from those of his father, though he, like Charles, had three sons to accommodate, and in many respects they were strikingly innovative. The two younger sons, Pippin and Louis, were invested with relatively small kingdoms in Aquitaine and Bavaria, respectively, while the lion's share of territory was promised to their elder brother, Lothar. He was also to receive the imperial title immediately, and with it a specified future authority over his brothers, even within their own realms.[9] Louis invested Lothar as co-emperor, a process confirmed when the latter received a papal re-coronation and anointing in Rome in 823 at the hands of pope Paschal I (817–24).

Whatever his subsequent errors of judgement, criticisms levelled against Louis over these decisions are not well founded. In the circumstances of 816, a papal anointing presented a confirmation rather than a threat to his imperial authority, and Louis was not responsible for later developments in papal ideology, and the political circumstances of later decades, that made the imperial office something the popes could use to lure Carolingian and other rulers to the defence of Rome. And Louis was not averse to repeating the purely Frankish ceremony of 813 when he made his son Lothar co-emperor in 817. Only when the latter was sent to govern Italy in 823 were the arrangements made for the further papal anointing.

In the opening period of his reign, as during most of that of his father, the secular relationship of emperor and pope was essentially that of master and servant. Rome remained a political dependency of Francia.[10] In 823, when it was reported that pope Paschal I (817–24) had ordered the execution of two of his own leading officials, the emperor sent two of his *missi* to investigate, and the pope found it expedient at the same time to send an embassy to Louis to present his version of these events. In 824, Lothar, on his father's orders, carried out an inspection and reform of the workings of the city of Rome and its territory, which according to the *Annals of the Kingdom of the Franks* had 'been ruined by the perversity of recent popes'.[11] One consequence of this was even closer supervision of papal elections. Thus in 827, Gregory IV (827–44) was unable to be ordained until an imperial *missus* had come to Rome to make sure the papal election had been carried out properly.[12]

Equally unjust is criticism of Louis, for the speed with which he made plans for his succession. The early deaths of his own brothers and a potentially fatal accident that befell him just before Easter in 817, made Louis sensitive to his own mortality and the danger of dying without such arrangements being in place.[13] This would also have been an issue pressed on him by his court advisers and the lay and ecclesiastical magnates of the empire, who at this time had nothing to gain and much to fear from a contentious succession. On the other hand, the precise arrangements of the *Ordinatio Imperii* of 817 led to immediate problems, which the emperor and his advisers proved increasingly less capable of handling. It is only fair, though, to note that many of these difficulties were not products of the particular scheme devised in 817, but represent fundamental structural problems in the fabric of the Carolingian Empire and were part of the legacy of unsolved problems that Louis inherited from his father.

The ambiguity over the nature and precise verbal form of the imperial title was one of these. Louis, whose long residence and upbringing in Aquitaine (781–814) may have made him less careful of traditional Frankish susceptibilities, used an exclusive title, that of *Imperator Augustus*, which was that of the early Roman emperors.[14] He did not, unlike his father, employ the subsidiary titles of *Rex Francorum* and *Rex Langobardorum*. As revealed not least by the *Ordinatio*, Louis and his advisers, most of whom had served him in Aquitaine, held views on the nature of the imperial office that were ideologically more sophisticated than those of their predecessors.[15]

Unfortunately, the realities of Carolingian society were more complex. As previously discussed, the problems of turning a set of disparate peoples with separate histories, traditions, laws and in some cases languages into a viable unitary political entity had never been solved, or even been adequately regarded as an ideal, in the time of Charles. Frankish ethnic separateness had instead been strengthened. Neither the adoption of an imperial title by the ruler nor the concept of a common Christian culture had been used to provide ideological 'cement' shaping a new common identity for the population of the empire. The administrative structures were tenuous, and even the establishment of Frankish aristocratic dynasties in the principal offices and lands of the conquered territories failed to guarantee loyalty, as, like their predecessors under the Merovingians, such families quickly identified themselves with regional interests.

Greater emphasis on the unity of the empire, expressed in Louis' imperial title and in the scheme he devised in 817 for the succession, failed to solve these fundamental problems. In fact, the animosities within the imperial family that were to be raised by the *Ordinatio* gave greater scope for regional conflicts and the growth of the inherent divisiveness of the society of the empire. In this respect, the weaknesses of the *Ordinatio* of 817 were twofold. First, the scheme left no room for the possibility of additional heirs, however unlikely this might have seemed at the time. However, Louis's wife, Ermengard, died in October 818 and his remarriage four months later to Judith, daughter of the Bavarian count Welf, contributed directly to his subsequent political problems.[16] Charles, known as 'the Bald', the son of this second marriage, was born in 823, and the need to revise the provisions of the *Ordinatio* to create an additional kingdom for him was a constant element in the politics of the rest of the reign.

The second weakness of the *Ordinatio* lay in the fact that it assumed the future harmony of unequally treated beneficiaries. Thus, while it gave Lothar a power and status that he was able to use against his father, at the same time it created the grounds for future resentments on the part of his less well endowed and supposedly subservient younger brothers. These personal animosities and conflicting ambitions in the ranks of the Carolingian house were fanned by regional aristocracies whose hopes for power and status were improved by the emergence of smaller rival provincial monarchies, in which their influence would be significantly greater. Marriages among the Carolingian regional rulers to members of their leading local aristocracies only furthered these tendencies. Such considerations may have inspired one immediate result of the issue of the *Ordinatio* – the revolt of Louis's nephew, Bernard, who had been formally established as king of Italy in 813. On the other hand, Bernard may in fact have been the victim of a pre-emptive strike on the part of the emperor, anxious to put an end to the autonomy Bernard had been granted by Charlemagne.

Care is needed in assessing this episode, as even the *Annals of the Kingdom of the Franks*, then being produced under the direction of the arch-chaplain, abbot Hilduin of Saint-Denis, admit that the report that Bernard was planning to make an independent kingdom for himself in Italy was 'partly true and partly false'.[17] Bernard enjoyed the loyalty of a group of Frankish counts in his service in Italy, together, apparently, with the support of three bishops, including the veteran adviser of Charlemagne, bishop Theodulf of Orléans. No other connection with the Italian court exists in his case, and it has been suggested that he was the victim of a false accusation made by his political opponents, such as his local rival, count Matfrid of Orléans.[18]

It is possible, though, that this was not the only piece of cynical political manipulation in this murky episode. Late in 817, Louis had raised a large army with which to force his way into Italy, but Bernard appears to have given up even before the emperor and his troops were within sight of the Alps: he crossed into Francia and submitted to Louis at Châlon-sur-Saone in December 817.[19] In the ensuing trial, Bernard and his associates were condemned to be blinded. As in the case of Constantine VI in Byzantium, this was done in such a way that Bernard died early in 818. Just as with Charles' treatment of Tassilo of Bavaria, the outcome of this judicial action on the part of the supposedly threatened and betrayed Frankish ruler was politically expedient. With the elimination of Bernard, of whom no mention had been made in the *Ordinatio Imperii*, the whole empire could now be divided between Louis's sons, and the anomalous Italian kingdom of his nephew was from 822 put into the hands of Lothar, to be his particular sphere of activity.[20] As will be seen, the devising of the *Ordinatio*, the elimination of Bernard and the elevation of Lothar, both to imperial office alongside his father and to a special role in Italy, were all the products of the policies suggested to the emperor by a powerful group of advisers.

On succeeding his father in 814, Louis had purged the court of his relatives and his father's courtiers, and he installed a new group of advisers, drawn from the ranks of those who had previously been in his service when he was king of Aquitaine.[21] A dominant figure among these was the Gothic abbot and monastic founder Wittiza, better known as Benedict of Aniane, under whose direction a series of reforming ecclesiastical councils were held at Aachen in 816 and 817. Among other things, these were intended to impose the *Rule of Benedict* as the norm for monastic observance throughout the Frankish empire.[22]

The death of this powerful personality in 821, appears to have coincided with changes in the court. To members of the group who had been dominant in the years 814–21, who had included the former chancellor Helisachar and his successor Hilduin of Saint-Denis, were now added a small number of those who had previously been influential in the last years of Charles, such as Adalhard of Corbie and his brother Wala, cousins of the late emperor who had been relegated to monasteries by Louis in 817.[23] Louis's own half-brothers, Drogo and Hugh, illegitimate sons of Charles, were freed in 822 from similar detention and permitted to take active roles in the Church, but did not become members of the court inner circle.[24] The most extraordinary of these events was the public confession made by the emperor at the assembly held at Attigny in August 822, in which Louis undertook a penance to atone for what he had done to his nephew Bernard, and for his treatment of the other members of his family.[25]

Traditionally, this episode has been seen as a humiliation for the emperor, forced on him by the newly reconstructed faction that dominated the court, but such an interpretation has rightly been challenged. The explicit comparison made in the anonymous *Life* of Louis with the penance of Theodosius I suggests that the image intended to be conveyed by the emperor's penance was far more positive.[26] His act was also followed by a similar confession of failings on the part of the assembled bishops. What was being symbolised was a new relationship between church and state, in which the secular ruler publicly acknowledged the special authority in all spiritual matters, even over himself, of the episcopate. This went beyond anything that Charles had been willing to concede to his clergy, and may also have been matched by Louis's removing the discussion of ecclesiastical issues from the annual assemblies, and giving the decision-making on such questions exclusively to the bishops and abbots.

While doubts have often been expressed about Louis's own political judgement, it must be conceded that, for the first half of his reign, the empire was governed firmly and effectively. The ideological programmes of the last period of Charlemagne's reign were preserved and extended in such documents as the capitularies issued as a result of the councils held at Aachen in 816/17. Other capitularies maintained the pressure for effective administration of justice on the part of the counts, while yet others included modifications to the Frankish law codes, both *Lex Salica* and *Lex Ribuaria*. In Italy, where members of the same group of advisers that had emerged in Aachen in 821 dominated the court of Lothar at Pavia, similar capitularies were issued for the Lombard kingdom.[27]

Militarily, the empire had become defensive rather than expansive.[28] This is hardly surprising in view of the rapid growth in its territories under the rule of Charlemagne. While it would be hard to say that all the empire's frontiers were 'natural' ones, in many cases their locations made strategic sense.[29] It is notable, for example, that the collapse of the Avar hegemony out on the Danubian plains after 796 had not tempted the Franks into an imperial extension in that direction. In any case, in an empire with such limited administrative capacity and with such problems of communication, further expansion became less and less of a possibility. On the other hand, in the period 814–29, external threats to the existing frontiers were always dealt with vigorously, and generally effectively. This included problems with the Slavs beyond the Elbe and in the north-west of the Balkans, with the Lombard duchies in the south of Italy, with the Bretons, with the Bulgars and with the Arabs on the recently created Marches south of the Pyrenees.[30]

While successful in retaining what had been gained in the preceding reign, such frontier warfare was inevitably less profitable than that conducted for aggressive expansionary purposes. Those who under Charlemagne had acquired status and wealth through war may under Louis have been forced to look for such opportunities through internal conflicts. The presence of several royal heirs with established regional interests provided the context for these, as it had in the sixth century. At the same time the grip on central authority throughout the period 814–29 of a single dominant faction, and the growing frustration of others denied access to such power, made a violent resolution increasingly likely, especially once the emperor allowed himself to become involved in a partisan way.

In the later 820s Louis was falling under the influence of another faction forming in his court. By this time, the empress Judith, whom he had married in 819, and her two brothers were seeking to secure a share in the imperial inheritance for her son Charles (born in 823) and to dislodge the dominant group of advisers and office-holders around the emperor. These included Hilduin of Saint Denis, Helisachar, Wala, who had now succeeded his brother Adalhard (d. 826) as Abbot of Corbie, and such secular magnates as Counts Matfrid of Orléans and Hugh of Tours. The latter was father-in-law of the co-emperor Lothar, who also had close ties to Wala, who had been his principal adviser in Italy since 822. The catalyst for factional confrontation emerged, surprisingly, not in Aachen but on the frontier between the Frankish empire and the Arab rulers of Spain.

The Umayyad amir of al-Andalus, 'Abd ar-Rahman I (756–88) had made himself master of much of southern Spain from 756 onwards, expanding his rule into the centre of the peninsula in the 760s and into the Ebro valley in the aftermath of Charlemagne's failed attempt to take Zaragoza and Barcelona in 778.[31] On the other hand, to the north-east of the Ebro Valley the Franks had been welcomed into Gerona by the local populace in 785, and a renewed attempt to expand this frontier march had been undertaken in 801 when Louis, then King of Aquitaine and acting under his father's orders, had captured Barcelona.[32] His subsequent attempts to extend the new Frankish enclave further south to Tarragona failed, but a marcher administration was created, centred on Barcelona. As the most substantial and much lauded achievement of a ruler who otherwise took very little personal part in the military activity of his reign, the preservation of this city was dear to Louis's heart. In 827 its safety was threatened.

A local revolt, stirred up by the descendant of one of the former rulers of the region, provided the opportunity for an intervention on the part of the Umayyad Amir of Córdoba, 'Abd ar-Rahman II (822–52). An army sent from the south menaced Barcelona, then held for Louis by its count Bernard, son of one of the original conquerors of the city and a distant relative of the emperor. Louis ordered an Aquitanian army under counts Hugh and Matfrid to go to the assistance of Bernard, but it did not arrive before the Arabs, who, having ravaged the countryside around Barcelona and Gerona but otherwise achieving little, returned to Zaragoza.[33] At an assembly held at Aachen in February 828, Hugh and Matfrid were accused of deliberately delaying the arrival of the army on the March the previous year, and were dismissed from their offices. This was an extraordinary reaction in the light of the limited nature of what had happened in 827, and of the close ties of at least one of the accused to the co-emperor Lothar. From their point of view and that of their allies, worse was to come in 829, when Bernard of Septimania, the count of Barcelona, who must have been their principal accuser the previous year, was given the important court office of chamberlain or head of the imperial household.[34]

This provoked a confrontation on a scale that the evidence relating to the earlier years of the reign hardly prepares us for, but which must represent the surfacing of resentments and conflicts that had been growing in preceding years.[35] In the spring of 830, after Louis had held an assembly at Aachen to plan a campaign against the Bretons, the mobilisation of the army in Neustria was used as the cover for an armed conspiracy.

In April, the assembled forces, led by Louis's son Pippin, the king of Aquitaine, marched instead to seize the emperor at Compiègne. His wife Judith was sent to the monastery of Sainte-Croix in Poitiers, and the hated Bernard only avoided the death that the rebels planned for him by precipitate flight to the Spanish March. His brother, though, was captured and blinded. Lothar, who did not arrive from Italy until May but must have been involved in the conspiracy from the start, had his father confined in a monastery and assumed his role as emperor. The *Ordinatio Imperii* of 817 was thus put into effect prematurely.

The consequences of that may have contributed to the equally sudden and rapid reversal of the coup of the spring of 830. The sources say little, but by October of the same year Louis had been released from custody and had regained his authority. It seems from the brief account in the *Four Books of Histories* of Nithard (d. 844) that the two younger sons, Pippin and Louis, known as 'the German', relegated to their kingdoms by their brother Lothar, soon began to resent his overbearing manner, and were persuaded by supporters of their father to join in a plot to reinstate him.[36] Thus by the late autumn of 830, Lothar found himself in the humiliating position of sitting beside his father at Noyon in judgement on his own supporters from the revolt of April.[37] These included such previous props of Louis's own regime as his former chancellors, Hilduin of Saint-Denis and Helisachar, as well as abbot Fridugis of St Martin's, Tours. They were all sentenced to death, but this was commuted to perpetual confinement in specified monasteries. That such men, several of whom had served him from before his imperial accession, should have turned against him earlier in 830 is testimony to how poorly Louis had handled the growth of factionalism among his advisers in the preceding years.

The empress was permitted to return to court, but this was delayed until the following year, and Bernard was not reinstated. A liaison between the two of them in the winter of 829/30 is claimed in hostile sources, but the truth of this can not be established.[38] Louis himself may have learnt few lessons from the events of 830, and soon alienated the two sons who, whatever they may have done in the spring of that year, had been crucial to his restoration in the autumn. In the winter of 832, Pippin of Aquitaine fled from his father's Christmas court in apparent fear for his safety, and when deprived of his royal title in 833 he joined forces once again with his brother Lothar, who had been relegated to Italy by Louis in 831. Their other brother, Louis the German, who had been threatened with the loss of some of his kingdom to create a realm for his half-brother Charles, was not slow to join the revolt, which also gained the initial backing of pope Gregory IV (827–44).[39] In the midsummer of 833 Louis was confronted by the forces of his three sons at a site thereafter called the 'Field of Lies' in Alsace. His own supporters melted away without striking a blow and he was taken into custody once more by Lothar, and imprisoned in the monastery of Saint-Denis.[40]

This episode is characteristic of the role played by consensus in Frankish politics. The various narrative sources, notably the two *Lives* of Louis and the *Annales Regni Francorum* with their continuation in the form of the *Annals of St Bertin*, also indicate the crucial role of the assemblies, at this time held at least twice a year on dates set from one meeting to the next, in the expression of the opinions of the lay and clerical magnates of the empire. That all-important opinion could be worked on in the intervening periods, especially in the case of those invited to attend the court over the winter or during its spring and autumn hunting seasons. However, it was only at the assemblies that its real direction would become clear. In 830, the coup against Louis earlier in the year was undone by the swing in majority support that was only able to reveal itself clearly in the October assembly. Similarly, at the 'Field of Lies' the issue was resolved by the coalescing of magnate consensus around the claims and complaints of Louis's sons, and this was then expressed in the draining away of the emperor's following.

Within a year of these events, Louis was once again free, liberated by the forces of his two younger sons, who seem to have preferred his occasional malice to the more thorough-going dominance of their elder brother. Lothar's lack of political finesse, to say the least, must have been considerable to have twice alienated crucial support for a regime whose legitimacy was far from self-evident. Magnate opinion though this time may have been more divided, in that the issue was not decided as cleanly as at the 'Field of Lies' and recourse was made to violence. After a brief civil war in the summer of 834 against the forces of his father and brothers, Lothar was once more relegated to Italy with his principal lay supporters.[41] Those bishops who had backed him in 833 and had provided the canonical justification for the deposition of his father, such as Ebbo of Reims and Agobard of Lyon, were deposed.

The last phase of the reign of Louis saw the emperor more firmly in control of events, though he showed no signs of trying to effect a real reconciliation among all his heirs or between them and himself.[42] The death of his second son Pippin, in 838, provided him with the long-sought-for opportunity of investing his youngest son, Charles, who had already been given territory between the Loire and Seine, with a more substantial kingdom. This meant, however, dispossessing Pippin I's son, also called Pippin, whose supporters in the south of Aquitaine continued vigorously to resist this process until eventually Pippin II was captured and imprisoned as a monk in the monastery of St Médard in Soissons in 852.[43]

Louis's relations with his son, Louis the German, also remained strained. The emperor, anxious to secure at least one potential ally for the young Charles, decided to make a compact with Lothar, whose prospects at this point were of inheriting nothing more than Italy, and offered a new division of the empire into two equal parts, in return for a promise of support for his half-brother. This agreement was sealed at an assembly at Worms in May 839.[44] Understandably, Louis the German, who by this new division was to be left with no more than Bavaria, resorted once more to military action, and tried to make himself master of all the lands east of the Rhine. It was in the midst of a new campaign against this son that the old emperor died, on an island in the Rhine, on 20 June 840.[45]

Those who have devoted themselves to the study of the reign of Louis the Pious have long wanted to find deeper underlying explanations for the apparently suicidal behaviour of the Frankish empire under his direction. Some have tried to invest the participants with more abstract and perhaps too rarefied motives. The opposition of 830 has been seen as the work of what has been called the *Einheitspartei*, or 'Unity Party', consisting of those, such as the emperor's former advisers, for whom the ideal of defending the unity of the empire, as envisaged in the *Ordinatio* of 817, was more important than continuing political loyalty to their master. Some such construction could be made out of the writings of bishop Agobard of Lyon, but as a motive for the wider participation of lay and clerical magnates in the events of 830–40, this fails to convince.[46]

The problem is that there is no simple structural explanation. The various divisions, actual or theoretical, conceived of by Louis and his advisers from 817 onwards do not correspond easily with underlying ethnic or other divisions within the empire. The coherence of some of the smaller units, such as Bavaria, clearly had a part to play in shaping the politics of the period, while the artificial nature of some larger constructions, such as the kingdom of Aquitaine, is revealed by the fissures that emerged within them in the course of these years. The latter region split into northern and southern halves in their respective support for Charles and Pippin II.

As has been mentioned already, the reign of Louis did correspond to a period of passivity and even defensiveness as far as the frontiers of the empire was concerned. There were no longer the kinds of profits to be gained from war that had existed in the time of Charlemagne, and indeed, as the case of the condemnation of Hugh and Matfrid showed, it now became an area with a high degree of political risk attached. In such circumstances, material and political rewards could be gained from factional conflict within the empire and not from fighting on its borders. Families, such as that of Bernard of Septimania, who wanted to establish themselves either locally or on a wider stage, could best do so by exploiting the divisions within the Carolingian dynasty.

The lesson to be learnt from the reign of Louis may be that, as a functioning political entity, the Carolingian empire had become an irrelevancy. It was a matter of almost total indifference to its leaders as to how it could be split up. The imperial title had failed to acquire any true significance – though it was to be much coveted by individual Carolingians, primarily because it had once belonged to Charlemagne, their supreme exemplar. The failure of the ideological aspirations of the age of the first emperor to be felt beyond the bounds of a narrow circle of ecclesiastics, and the structural inadequacies of the central administration of the empire were thus fully highlighted in the difficult second period of the reign of his son.

Kings and emperors in the West, 840–911

In such circumstances, the succession arrangements made by Louis had little hope of working. Accepting the plan drawn up in 839, whereby the empire would be divided into equal halves between Lothar and Charles, with Louis the German retaining only Bavaria, had only been a temporary expedient as far as Lothar was concerned. His ambitions always seem to have exceeded his capacity to attract loyalty. He crossed the Alps immediately on hearing of the death of his father, proclaiming his rights as emperor and demanding that oaths of loyalty to him should be taken by all principal landholders, lay and clerical throughout the empire. Lacking the military strength to confront Louis the German directly, he set about trying to dispossess the young Charles, who by the agreement of 839 should have been his ally, of some or all of his kingdom.[49]

The result, unsurprisingly, was an alliance between Charles and Louis the German, and in due course their victory over Lothar at the battle of Fontenoy in June 841.[50] What is striking about this quick resort to war between the brothers was that it marked the end of the kind of consensual politics that had typified the reign of their father. In the 830s, realignments of support among the aristocracy had caused Louis to lose power in 830 and 833, and Lothar to do the same in 830 and 834, without a blow having to be struck. The battle of Fontenoy in 841 was thus the exact opposite of the Field of Lies of 833.

While open warfare between rival Carolingians never became standard practice, and after Fontenoy there would be no other battle in which leading members of the family fought out their differences face to face, it clearly marked a watershed. There was no hope of restoring the system envisaged by Louis the Pious, in which one dominant ruler held superior authority over all the territories of the Frankish empire, accepted by the consensus of magnate support. Division of the empire into separate and rival states became the only practical alternative.

In itself, the battle of Fontenoy was not militarily decisive, but the alliance between the two kings against the emperor was cemented by a meeting and the taking of mutual oaths at Strasbourg in February 842. The text of the oaths was recorded in Nithard's *Histories*, and this is important for thus preserving the earliest known examples of French Romance and Old High German languages.[51]

By the end of 842, Lothar had to accept the need for compromise, and in 843 an agreement was finally reached at Verdun, whereby the territory of the empire was divided into three roughly equal portions.[52] Pippin II of Aquitaine, who had supported Lothar, was disregarded, and continued to fight Charles until 849, when he was forced to take refuge with the Basques. Adjustments were made in the proposed frontiers that as far as possible took into account the distribution of the scattered landholdings of the principal followers of the various monarchs, but in some cases these had to be ignored, and this caused some resentment. It has been suggested that Charles' relative and historian, Nithard, lay abbot of St Riquier, failed to regain, or even be compensated for, the lands he owned within Lothar's territories that the emperor had redistributed to his own supporters. For this failure to look after his interests, Nithard's enthusiasm for Charles seems to have declined by the time he wrote the fourth book of his *Histories*.[53]

Lothar kept his imperial title, and his allocation of lands in 843 was arranged to include the former imperial capital of Aachen as well as Rome. The emperor never really accepted the division made at Verdun as final, and attempted until 849 to subvert his brothers' kingdoms from within, not least by winning over their supporters among the aristocracy. His attempts had little success, however, and the idea that the office of emperor conveyed superior authority and oversight of the other kings of the Frankish-ruled territories died with the treaty of Verdun. In this way, both Charlemagne and Louis the Pious's conceptions of it were lost, and it became possible within another half century for it to become little more than a title awarded to the ruler of northern and central Italy.

The division of the empire into a series of kingdoms may in some respects have been beneficial, because of the many geographically widespread military problems that had to be faced from the 840s onwards. A single ruler would have needed to concentrate military resources on too many widely scattered frontiers to be fully effective. As in the Roman Empire of the third century, a multiplicity of monarchs was needed in Francia. As will be seen, this process was to develop further, with power and authority increasingly being devolved to localised de facto rulers: the counts and territorial *principes* or 'princes' of the late ninth and the tenth centuries.

The inherent danger, as in the third century, was that the various kings would spend as much time fighting each other as combating the external threats to their kingdoms. Indeed, such internal conflicts could result in one Carolingian king in allying with the enemies of another. The history of the period *c.* 840–82 is so complex and detailed that it is only possible here to give some examples of this phenomenon. The conflicts in Aquitaine are, perhaps, particularly revealing.

Despite ignoring his interests in the treaty of Verdun, Lothar I continued to give at least moral backing to Pippin II of Aquitaine, whose resistance was centred in the south of the kingdom, especially around Toulouse. Charles besieged the city in 844, but one of his armies was dramatically defeated by Pippin near Angoulême. Among those killed in the battle were the historian Nithard and Charlemagne's illegitimate son, Hugh.[54] It was not until 848 that Charles was able to make himself master of southern Aquitaine, assisted by the Viking raids on the region and their sack of Bordeaux in that year.[55] Pippin II remained in exile in the Basque duchy of Gascony south of the Garonne, until betrayed to Charles by its duke in 852. This, however, was to be only the first phase of the conflicts affecting the former kingdom of Aquitaine.

In 853, an aristocratic faction in northern Aquitaine and the Loire valley, whose leader had been executed by Charles the Bald for unknown reasons, appealed to Louis the German to intervene in the region, and Louis sent his son to try to make

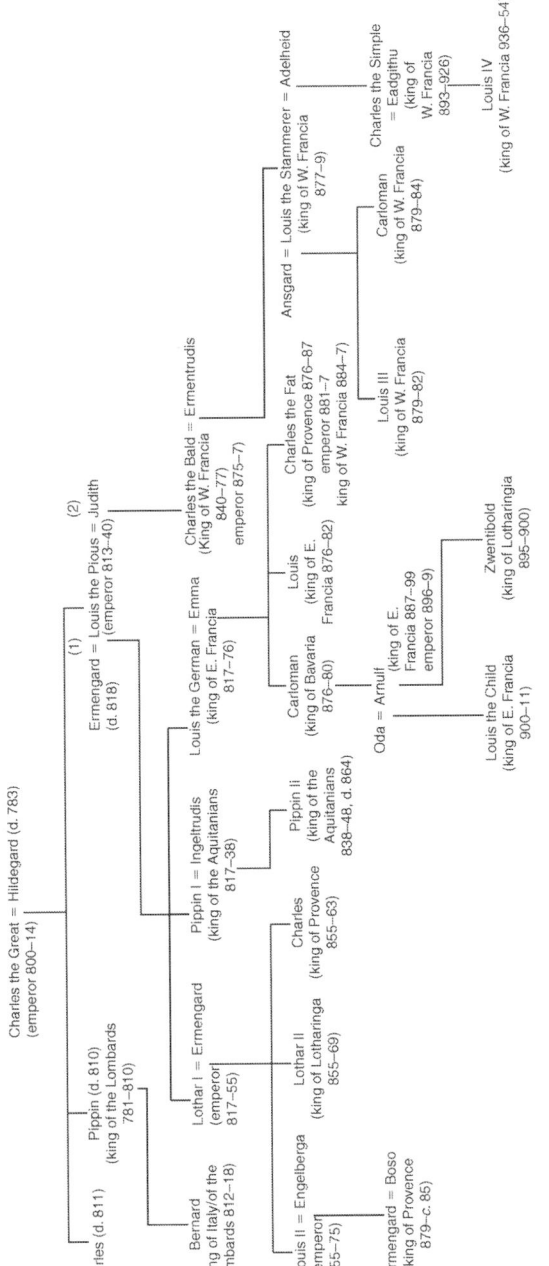

The later Carolingians (a simplified genealogy)

himself king of Aquitaine. Charles responded by sending envoys to the Bulgars, who had replaced the Avars as the dominant confederacy in the northern Balkans and the plains north of the Danube, to persuade them to attack Louis on the eastern frontiers of his kingdom.[56] While Louis the German's son, the later king Louis the Younger, failed to achieve much support in Aquitaine and was expelled by Charles in 854, in the same year Pippin II escaped from monastic imprisonment and renewed his claim to his kingdom.[57] In the ensuing conflicts he allied with the Bretons (859) and subsequently (864) with the Vikings in the Loire, and was accused by the, admittedly hostile, *Annals of St Bertin* of renouncing Christianity and becoming a pagan.

In the same period, the disaffected aristocracy of northern Aquitaine and the Loire valley appealed twice more to Louis the German to invade his brother Charles' territories. He rejected the request in 856, having already committed himself to a series of campaigns against the Slavs on his eastern borders, but in 858, when the count of Anjou rebelled, Louis seized his chance.[58] His invasion was militarily successful, as far as the northern parts of the West Frankish kingdom were concerned, but the refusal of its bishops, led by Hincmar of Reims, to accept him as king undermined his position, and he was obliged to withdraw eastwards in 859.[59] In 860, a reconciliation was negotiated between the two brothers at Coblenz, largely through the intermediacy of their nephew, Lothar II.[60] In the 860s the tide turned the other way, with Charles increasingly starting to interfere in the politics of Louis's kingdom.

There are numerous such episodes of rivalry and conflict between the various Carolingian monarchs in this period, and it is possible to isolate a number of causes that are common to all or most of them. At the simplest level, the acquisition of another kingdom or additional territory could help to solve problems of inheritance. For example, if a ruler left three legitimate heirs, his realm, like that of Lothar I in 855 and of Louis the German in 876, might have to be broken up into yet smaller sections in order to provide separate kingdoms. Had Louis been able to instal his son in Aquitaine in 853/4, part of this process would have been avoided.

A major factor in virtually all cases of conflict between the kings was aristocratic factionalism. Rival landowning families struggled to dominate the regions in which they were established, and possession of the office of count, which at this time was in the king's gift, was a route to local supremacy, with opportunities for further enrichment through responsibility for the lands belonging to the fisc (that is, the monarchy) within the county.[61] Families that had once enjoyed such office but had lost it to their rivals might hope to regain it through a change of royal regime. Even those who were loyal followers of a particular king might be alienated by a change of policy that seemed to threaten their local interests. Thus, for example, Charles the Bald had tried to provide subordinate kingdoms for his two sons, installing one, Charles, as king of the Aquitanians in 855, and the other, Louis the Stammerer, as duke of Maine in 856. This also involved a settlement of the long-running conflict with the Bretons, and the young Louis was betrothed to the daughter of their king Erispoë (851–7). In turn, this threw count Robert of Anjou (d. 866), who had previously dominated the Breton March, into opposition to the king and into adding his name to the appeals to Louis the German in 856 and 858.[62]

The continuing attraction of the imperial title, and thus the strongest claim to the inheritance of Charlemagne, was another factor that caused inter-Carolingian conflict, particularly in the late 870s. The existence of a multiplicity of Frankish rulers made the transmission of the practically valueless but very prestigious imperial title a more complex matter than one of simple inheritance within the dynasty. After 875, the papal role in consecration enabled successive popes to choose between rival claimants from among the rapidly proliferating royal branches of the Carolingian dynasty, but they themselves were constrained by the need to find an effective military protector as quickly as possible for a city increasingly threatened by Arab raids and the ambitions of rival local potentates. Therefore, in practice, the choice always fell on whoever seemed best able or willing to serve the material needs of Rome, above all in ensuring the protection of the city and its bishop.

The linking of the imperial tide to that of 'the king of the Lombards' was made explicit by Lothar I (817–55), who entrusted northern Italy to his eldest son, Louis, in 844, and then had him crowned as co-emperor by pope Leo IV in 850.[63] On Louis II's death without male heirs in 875, there followed a scramble among the surviving Carolingians to gain the papal gift of the title of emperor. Charles the Bald – some of whose military and other problems within his own kingdom at this time will be examined in the next chapter – launched an expedition into Italy in 875 to obtain the imperial office by posing as a credible protector of the papacy. In deliberate imitation of his grandfather, he was crowned emperor by pope John VIII (872–82) on Christmas Day 875. An assembly of Italian Frankish nobles and bishops at Pavia then 'elected' him king of the Lombards in February 876.[64]

The family compact that had agreed to his new status and his role in Italy was ruptured in 876, when, on the death of his half-brother Louis the German, Charles tried to annex some of his kingdom, and in particular to make himself master of the imperial seat of Aachen, a necessary adjunct to his new title. However, he was resoundingly defeated by Louis's son, Louis the Younger (876–82), in a battle at Andernach. Summoned to Italy in 877 by pope John VIII, to make good the oath he had taken at his imperial coronation to defend the see of Rome, Charles found himself threatened by the forces of another nephew, Carloman king of Bavaria (876–80), and the new emperor was forced to retreat precipitately back across the Alps, only to die just north of the mountains in October 877.[65]

It was to be only a brief time before the next aspirant to the universal authority exercised by Charlemagne appeared. This was another Charles, later to be known as 'the Fat'. Like his predecessor, Charles the Bald, this new Charles was not able to claim the imperial title because of an unchallenged authority in Francia north of the Alps, but he acquired it instead through securing of power in northern Italy and then from papal approval. The papacy was itself subject to mounting external pressures that made the finding of a suitable candidate for the imperial office a matter of urgency. For pope John VIII, the growing designs on Rome on the part of count Lambert of Spoleto made the presence of a new imperial defender of the city ever more vital.[66] In 877, there were more potential contenders than in 875: in the persons of three sons of Louis the German and one of Charles the Bald. However, not all of them were prepared to bid for the vacant title, being faced by military problems within their own kingdoms, and the prospect of having to take on commitments in Italy was not necessarily attractive. Nor, in practice, were all of them physically in a condition to undertake such a task.

By this time, the Carolingian dynasty was suffering, through no identifiable fault of its own, something of the problem of lack of longevity that had afflicted its Merovingian predecessor. Of the four kings at whom John VIII was looking for the new emperor in 877, only one would still be alive by the end of 882.[67] In western Francia, even the subsequent generation of Carolingians would be almost extinct by that time. Charles the Bald's son, Louis the Stammerer (877–9), who was the only monarch prepared to receive John VIII in 879, died the same year, aged thirty-three. His two sons, Louis III and Carloman, who succeeded him jointly as the result of a political compromise among the West Frankish aristocracy, followed him into the tomb from accidental deaths in 882 and 884, respectively, neither having attained the age of twenty. A posthumous son by a second wife, known as Charles the Simple, survived to reappear as king in 893.[68]

In the realm created for Lothar by the treaty of Verdun in 843, and later known as Lotharingia, a partition between his three sons in 855 had been followed by the extinction of the male line by 875. The emperor Louis II left only two daughters. Of his two brothers, Charles, king of Provence (855–63), left no heirs, and Lothar II (855–69) engaged in a long and ultimately fruitless struggle with the papacy to obtain the annulment of his marriage, which had proved barren.[69] The immediate beneficiaries of the extinction of this branch of the dynasty were these monarchs' uncles, Louis the German and Charles the Bald, who dismembered Lothar II's kingdom on his death.

Louis the German's heirs proved equally prone to die young and without heirs. Louis the Younger died in 882 and Carloman, who had seemed to John VIII to be the most promising candidate for the vacant imperial throne in 878, became terminally ill the same year, dying in 880. Only their younger brother, Charles the Fat, survived this dynastic mass extinction of the early 880s, and in consequence was able to reap, albeit briefly, the rewards.[70]

He had inherited the small kingdom of Alamannia in southern Germany from his father in 876. The protracted illness of his brother Carloman (d. 880) led the latter to cede him his rights in northern Italy in 879, and he was formally elected as king of the Lombards at Pavia in November that year. His unwillingness to give the pope the guarantees he wanted for the defence of Rome led to a delay in his selection as emperor, but by the year 881 there were no alternative candidates left, and when Charles presented himself in Rome in February he was crowned.[71] The death the next year of his only surviving brother, Louis the Younger, made him master of all the eastern Carolingian territories, and the demise in 884 of the young west Frankish ruler Carloman left Charles the Fat as the first member of the dynasty since 817 to exercise authority over the whole of the empire created by Charlemagne. However, each of the kingdoms remained politically and administratively separate. This was not a complete re-unification of the Carolingian empire; it was instead the chance accumulation of its various components by one individual.

Around 884, Charles commissioned a new work about his great-grandfather, Charlemagne. It is called the *Gesta Karoli* or *Deeds of Charles*, and was composed by the monk Notker the

Stammerer (d. 912) of St Gallen. Though very different from
the biographical work of Einhard, as it concentrates on retelling
a series of anecdotes, it is testimony not only to the new emper-
or's interest in his ancestor, but also to the very real fear of his
subjects that the dynasty was in danger of extinction. Twice in
the short work Notker uses the excuse of proposing the Charles
and Louis as names suitable for his patron's future sons, to
emphasise that Charles the Fat still lacked legitimate heirs.[72]

Despite the appearance of a re-unification of the Carolingian
empire by Charles the Fat in 884, the substance was lacking. In
November 885, the Vikings besieged Paris.[73] The failure of initial efforts to lift the siege meant that the emperor had to go
in person to deal with the problem in October 886. Contrary
to expectations, and his self-image as the new Charlemagne,
Charles the Fat bought off the Vikings without serious fighting,
and made a hurried return to Alsace early the next month. By
February 887 his health was in decline.[74]

The events of this year are poorly recorded, and the contemporary sources are very partisan. Factional conflict seems
to have developed within the ranks of Charles' supporters, as
he was forced at an assembly held in Alamannia around June
887 to dismiss his chancellor, bishop Liutward of Vercelli, and
to give the office instead to archbishop Liutbert of Mainz.[75] The
latter had previously served as chancellor to Charles' brother,
Louis the Younger (d. 882), and this may represent the successful political re-emergence of some of the former courtiers
of that monarch. Those, such as bishop Liutward, who had
long been Charles' own personal followers, may not have for-
given him for his apparent weakness and lack of loyalty. As both
Liutward and Liutbert were originally from Alamannia, this episode also marks a major division in the heart of the royal entourage, which also occurred at a peculiarly sensitive time.[76]

Over the winter of 886/7 the emperor's health showed signs
of breaking down. He is reported to have suffered from a
severe, if not easily identifiable illness. Even after an initial
recovery, he had to be bled to relieve the pain in his head.[77] In
these circumstances, the politically charged issue of his succession took on a critical importance. Charles now separated from
his wife, accusing her of adultery with bishop Liutward, and it
must have seemed impossible that he would produce a legitimate heir. Having previously failed to secure noble support
for the succession of his own illegitimate son, he now adopted
Louis of Provence, the son of the former usurper Boso, king of
Provence, as his heir. This was probably the cause of a revolt
that then broke out under the leadership of Arnulf, count of

Carinthia and illegitimate son of Charles' brother, Carloman. Arnulf might otherwise have expected to succeed his uncle, the ailing emperor, and his position was clearly threatened by the adoption of the young and only half-Carolingian Louis.

Serious conflict was prevented when Charles was prostrated at an assembly near Mainz in November 887, probably by a stroke. The magnates present then called on Arnulf to assume the crown, and Charles, who was probably totally incapacitated, was sent home to his family estates in Alamannia. He died in the Black Forest on 13 January 888.[78] The *Annals of St Vaast* state that he was murdered by his own men, but no other source corroborates this.[79]

Despite the apparent lack of lasting achievements during his brief reign as emperor, Charles the Fat was seen by some of his contemporaries as a figure of almost saintly character. This probably testifies at least to a lack of unanimity over his deposition, heightened by doubts arising from his rapid and mysterious death. According to the *Annals of Fulda*, when he was buried in the monastery of Reichenau 'Heaven was seen to open by many of the bystanders, thus clearly demonstrating that he who died rejected from his earthly office by men was deemed worthy by God to deserve joyfully to become a servant of the heavenly fatherland.'[80] Writing in the early tenth century, Regino of Prüm recorded of Charles that:

> he was a most Christian prince, fearing God and keeping his commandments with all his heart ... who, it was seen, ought to possess easily and in a brief space of time, without conflict and with none gainsaying it, all of the kingdoms of the Franks, which his predecessors had acquired not without effusion of blood and with great labour. But when near the end of his life, he was stripped of his dignities and deprived of all his goods, the suffering was, we believe, not only to be a purification but also, and which is better, a testing ... which he bore most patiently, giving thanks in adversity as in prosperity, and thereby he received or doubtless has deserved to receive the crown of life that God has promised to those who delight him. [81]

The events of this period suggest that the importance once attached to the survival of the Carolingian dynasty had greatly diminished in most parts of their empire. The career, described below, of Boso of Provence (879–87) had shown that it was possible for a non-Carolingian to aspire to a throne. The difficulties placed in the way of Lothar II (855–69) over his divorce, and of

Charles the Fat and of Arnulf in their attempts to secure the succession of illegitimate sons indicate that survival of the Carolingian dynasty was not the main priority for the lay and clerical elite of the empire.[82]

While the attraction of Carolingian legitimacy continued to make itself felt well into the tenth century, other factors could be given greater weight when a royal succession was being decided. In western Francia, on the death of Charles the Fat the nobility passed over the last member of their branch of the dynasty, the nine-year-old posthumous son of Louis the Stammerer, and instead elected as king one of their own number, count Odo of Paris. The choice was probably a result of the important role he had played during the Viking siege of that city in 885–6, and the need for an active and adult king of proven military ability. But the special status of the Carolingian line continued to be acknowledged, as Odo recognised the superior authority of the East Frankish Carolingian, Arnulf, who provided him with regalia for his coronation at Reims.

In Italy, duke Guido of Spoleto was elected king by the nobility of the former Carolingian kingdom in 889. His family had been trying to make themselves masters of Rome for several years, and his father, Lambert, had been the particular enemy of pope John VIII (872–82). Even so, faced with the need to find a real protector for the city and see of Rome, and with the new ruler of eastern Francia clearly unable to involve himself in Italy at the time, pope Stephen V(VI) (885–91) crowned Guido as emperor in February 891.[83]

Guido (d. 894) had himself recrowned by the next pope, Formosus (891–6), together with his son Lambert (d. 898), but at the same time Formosus began a secret correspondence with Arnulf, to try to induce him to intervene in Italy and reassert the Carolingian rights to the imperial title. This he finally did in 896 and expelled the emperor Lambert's troops from Rome. Formosus then transferred the imperial title to Arnulf by coronation in February, only for the new emperor to be paralysed by a stroke and have to be carried back to Germany, where he was to die in 899.[84]

Formosus himself was probably lucky to die in April 896, before Lambert regained Rome. His successor, Boniface VI, lasted only fifteen days before dying himself, but the next pope, Stephen VI (VII), found it expedient to be an active partisan of Lambert. Under his direction, the body of Formosus was dug up, decked in pontifical robes and put on trial in what is known as 'the cadaver synod' of January 897. Found guilty of perjury and of violations of canon law, the body was then thrown into the Tiber. However, reports of miracles being performed by the washed-up corpse led to a popular revolt against Stephen, who was deposed, imprisoned and strangled in August 897. The decrees of the 'cadaver synod' were overturned and Formosus was reburied by pope Theodore II during his twenty-day pontificate in November of the same year. Picaresque as the story of the 'cadaver synod' might seem, it at least testifies to an almost obsessive concern in Rome with legal forms and procedure in such matters as the transfer of both papal and imperial authority. Behind it, however, also lies the reality that the papacy, like the imperial office, had become a prize in an increasingly localised game of central Italian politics.[85]

In Germany, as it is probably easiest now to call the eastern Frankish lands, the Carolingian dynasty was entering its terminal phase. Arnulf had managed to hold together the various regions east of the Rhine in the aftermath of the overthrow of Charles the Fat. However, his stroke in 896 weakened his personal authority, and he, like Charles before him, faced succession problems. He could not secure acceptance of his illegitimate son Zwentibold (d. 900), whom he had created king of Lotharingia in 895, as his heir in the rest of his realm, and his only legitimate son was not born until 893. On Arnulf's death in 899, this infant, known as Louis the Child, succeeded, but he died at a young age in 911. With him, the Carolingian line in the East was extinguished.[86]

In the West, the dynasty was to enjoy two brief revivals following the death of king Odo in 898. Charles the Simple (d. 929), the posthumous son of Louis the Stammerer, was put up against Odo in 893 with the backing of archbishop Fulk of Reims (883–900) and count Heribert of Vermandois. Supporters of Carolingian legitimacy assisted him, and Odo lost control of most of his kingdom before his death in 898. Thereafter, Charles maintained himself in office, if not always in real power, until he was deposed in 923. His attempts to maintain control over Lotharingia at all costs led to a revolt among the West Frankish nobility in 922, in the course of which they proclaimed a new king, Robert I (922–3), the brother of Odo.[87] Though Robert was killed in battle the next year, Charles was captured by his opponents and held prisoner until his death in 929.

He was replaced by another non-Carolingian, duke Rudolf of Burgundy, a son-in-law of Robert I. On Rudolf's death in 936, Charles' son Louis IV was recalled from exile in Wessex by the West Frankish nobility, but he and his son Lothar (954–86) were to spend most of their reigns in conflict with different sections of it. Lothar's son, Louis V (986–7), died at the age of twenty without issue, and though he had younger brothers and an uncle still living, the magnates elected Hugh Capet, a grandson of Robert I, as king. This replacement of the Carolingians, unlike that of 888, proved permanent.

Apart from the last of them, who lacked the time to demonstrate his qualities for good or ill, none of these final West Frankish Carolingian rulers were lacking in the skill and determination needed to maintain themselves in the very difficult and changed circumstances of this period.[88] The disintegration of central authority within the already fragmented Carolingian domains can be dated to the last phase of the reign of Charles the Bald and the chaotic decade of the 880s. As will be seen in the next chapter, the military problems facing the various kingdoms were acute at this time. This was also the period in which dynasties of hereditary office-holding nobles appear to have established themselves throughout the Carolingian lands.

In part, this process was accelerated by such royal initiatives as the transferring of fiscal estates that had previously been administered for the crown by its local agents, the counts, into the ownership of those officials. This may not have happened all at once or in all regions, but it can certainly be documented in parts of the West Frankish kingdom in the 870s.[89] That hereditary succession to comital offices can also be shown to have begun in a number of cases in this same period is hardly coincidental.[90] In practice, the king was recognising his inability to control local society. The system of *missi*, employed by Charlemagne and his successors, had in the last resort been based on the threat of force. In the circumstances of the later ninth century when, as will be seen, the military problems facing the crown were rapidly becoming insuperable, this became little more than a bluff.

Even against flagrant political disloyalty it was difficult for the monarchy to act decisively. After the death of Louis the Stammerer in 879, Boso, the count of Provence, who had been the brother of Charles the Bald's second wife, made himself king of a substantial region in the south-east of France centred on Vienne, without the West Frankish kings being able to take military action against him. It was only in 881, by turning his brother Richard against him, that Vienne was retaken.[91] Even afterwards Boso maintained some shadowy hold in the region until his death, around 887.

In practice, such attempts to usurp a royal title were rare, and tended only to occur in regions that had once had their own monarchy. What was really at issue was the power that was built up from the late ninth century onwards by local dynasties of counts and dukes, who turned themselves into what have been

seen as territorial 'princes'.[92] Though by the nature of their
titles and the origin of their offices they were formally subject to
kings in western or eastern Francia, in practice they were independent masters of their own territories, taking oaths of fealty
from lesser landowners, controlling the administration of justice, and taking what profits were to be gained from it and from
other rights, such as tolls, that would have previously been due
to the monarchy.

Political life in tenth-century western and eastern Francia was
largely determined by a monarch's skill, or lack of it, in building
and maintaining alliances among the firmly entrenched local
'princely' or ducal families. In eastern Francia or Germany, the
situation was made easier by the concentration of power into
the hands of a small number of dukes, whose territories cor-
responded to the older ethnic divisions of Thuringia, Saxony,
Bavaria, Suabia (Alamannia) and Franconia. In western Francia
many more such units existed, derived mainly from the long-
established Carolingian administrative divisions, which added to
its greater fragmentation and to the more severe political problems faced by the west Frankish kings.

The importance of institutions of central authority became
greatly reduced in many parts of western Europe in the later
ninth and the tenth centuries. Their principal value was in
the co-ordination of military action to be taken against such
large-scale threats as the Viking raids and the incursions of
the Magyars from the plains across the Danube. This was the
testing ground that determined whether strong monarchies
re-emerged in the various realms of the former Carolingian
empire and adjacent areas.

In some cases, as in tenth-century England, successful military action against such a threat could lead to a rebuilding of
a relatively powerful, centralised monarchy, able to impose its
will on all levels of society and to develop more complex and
sophisticated forms of administration.[93] Also in Germany, in the
same period, the role of the kings of the new Ottonian dynasty
from Saxony in the wars against the Magyars was crucial in the
development of their power over the dukes of the component
regions of the eastern Frankish kingdom, whose equals they
had originally been. On the other hand, failure, as in Charles
the Fat's role during the Viking siege of Paris, could further discredit a monarchy and render it less and less necessary. In this
way, the 'new participants' in the history of western Europe –
the Scandinavian Vikings, the Magyars, and even the Arabs –
served as a vital catalyst to change in the political order of the
older societies.

19 'The desolation of the pagans'

Raiders and traders

On 8 June 793, the island monastery of Lindisfarne off the Northumbrian coast of Britain was sacked by raiders coming from the sea.[1] This is the first recorded of a series of such attacks on settlements and monasteries in Britain, Ireland, and the Channel and Atlantic coasts of France that grew in intensity and at times became an annual occurrence. The raids themselves were the forerunners of waves of migration out of Scandinavia. Those who took part in both the raids and the subsequent settlements are generally known as 'Vikings', a rather misleading name, as it probably only applies properly to the inhabitants of the region of Vik in the south-west of modern Norway. It also obscures the differences between the various Scandinavian ethnic and political groups. However, for convenience, it will be used here as a general term for the raiders, traders and settlers from the Scandinavian peninsula and Denmark found outside their homelands in these centuries, but only when it is not possible to specify more clearly where they came from – that is, if they were Danes, Norwegians (Norse) or Swedes.

While the divisions mentioned above correspond closely to modern political geography and the three Scandinavian states we are familiar with today, we must not imagine that anything very similar existed in the early Middle Ages. A single 'kingdom of the Danes' had come into existence by time of the Frankish emperor Charlemagne, but this disintegrated early in the ninth century, and the few references we have in Frankish sources of the time suggest that it was followed by a period of rival dynasties and much internal warfare. A kingdom covering the south of modern Norway did not emerge until the very end of the tenth century, and in Sweden a much longer-established monarchy, centred on Uppsala, just north of Stockholm, controlled only the eastern parts of the modern country. As in the case of Denmark, the more developed nature of this Vendel kingdom in Sweden may have resulted from the presence of trading centres such as Birka, from which the kings were able to extract tolls.

The destructiveness of the Viking period in the history of Western Europe, which extended from the end of the eighth century to the early eleventh, has long been recognised, despite

344

recent attempts by some historians to minimise it.[2] The slogan that has been applied to the Vikings – 'traders not raiders' – is misleading in implying that the same people could not be both. On the other hand, in some of the regions in which they settled, the economic and cultural contributions made by the Scandinavians in the ninth to eleventh centuries did make real advances on what had gone before.[3]

The Viking phenomenon is not an easy one to explain, in that Scandinavian literary historical sources are all much later in date than this period. Doubts exist about the reliability of almost everything they have to say about individuals and events before the mid-eleventh century.[4] Before then, runic inscriptions carved on stones are the only form of contemporary written evidence, and as most of these are memorials to otherwise unknown individuals they do not tell us very much.[5] There has been a good deal of material culture uncovered archaeologically, especially from southern Scandinavia, but this is not easy to put into a historical context without written sources. One particular type of artefact – the large, decorated medallions known as bracteates – has been interpreted in the light of later texts relating to the pre-Christian beliefs of Norse societies, and figures and scenes engraved on them have been taken as representations of heroic and mythical tales. Unfortunately, most of the literary evidence for these stories of gods and heroes is itself late, much of it coming from works written in thirteenth-century Iceland, and the attempts to apply them to the decoration of the bracteates has generally failed to convince.

While we may have little easily usable evidence from within Scandinavian societies of the eighth to eleventh centuries, more-or-less contemporary ninth- and tenth-century West Frankish and Anglo-Saxon annalists provide us with a narrative of the Norse raids on their lands. However, these authors, who were all clerics, were not interested in their enemies' motives, seeing the raids instead as evidence of divine displeasure at the failings of their own societies.

In consequence of these evidential problems, there is still no agreement on what caused the sudden appearance of long-distance seaborne raiding among the Scandinavians in the late eighth century. We do not know if the Viking raids and migrations were or were not the products of overpopulation, climatic deterioration, or other ecological changes affecting Scandinavia.[7] Similarly, it has been suggested that advances in boat-building techniques could explain the timing and character of the Viking raids, but the evidence from the excavation of several ships seems to indicate that Scandinavian ships had had the capability to undertake long sea voyages for some time prior to the first records of their presence in England and western Francia.[8] Other interpretations concentrate on social change and particularly on the growth of more powerful monarchies within Scandinavia, which, it is suggested, drove unruly elements in their kingdoms overseas, but this explanation may be confusing cause with effect.[9]

Arguments that stress external causes are easier to support from written evidence, but can at best be only partial, as they have to ignore the role of internal changes within Scandinavian society. As will be seen, the growth of Danish assaults on the Frankish kingdoms and southern England may be a response to the earlier expansion of Frankish power into Saxony and across the Elbe, but this does not easily explain the growth of raiding by the Norwegians across the North Sea and the creation of their settlements in Ireland and the Northern Isles. In any case, the first Viking raids – by Norwegians on Lindisfarne and by Danes on Wessex – preceded the establishment of a Frankish presence on the Elbe by about ten to fifteen years.

It is probably best not to look for a single explanation, nor to try to reduce the Viking period contacts between Scandinavia and western Europe to too simple a pattern. Problems of evidence aside, what is most remarkable about the Viking phenomenon is its complexity. Simply put, different groups of Scandinavians were doing different things at different times in different places for different reasons. Thus, for example, it is likely that various families from coastal regions of south-west Norway were founding settlements in the Orkneys and the Hebrides even before the first raid on Ireland (795), and thus over half a century before the start of the largely Danish settlements in northern and eastern England.

What is clear is that when the Viking raids were first recorded in contemporary annals they represented, in their violence and destructiveness, something unexpected and unprecedented.[10] When Danes first appeared in Wessex, in 789, the royal official who went out to meet them (and got killed for his pains) 'did not know what they were'.[11] He probably thought they were traders. Those who experienced the Viking attacks looked for the explanation for this new and violent threat to their lives and property in the ills of their own society, and saw in it an element of divine retribution. Thus, Alcuin, writing to the community of Lindisfarne in the aftermath of the raid on the monastery, interpreted it as a divine chastisement: 'Truly it has not happened by chance, but is a sign that it was well merited by someone.'[12]

The unexpected nature of the first raids did not imply, as other remarks in this letter of Alcuin's have been taken to suggest, that the raiders of Lindisfarne belonged to a people unknown to all their victims. Contacts between Scandinavia and continental and insular western Europe had been prolonged and continuous during preceding centuries.[13] Economic exchange between the Roman Empire and the Baltic extended back to at least the first century AD, and appears to have intensified in the fourth century.[14] In the fifth century, large quantities of gold, that analysis has shown came from Roman coins, was turned into high-status jewellery in southern Sweden and other Baltic regions. In material culture and in the dynastic legends of the ruling house, evidence exists of links between the East Anglian kingdom in Britain and parts of Scandinavia in the sixth century. In particular, the helmet found in the largest of the burial mounds at Sutton Hoo in East Anglia, which has been dated to the 620s, shows very close parallels with a series of slightly later ones found in the cemeteries at Vendel in Sweden.[15]

The seventh and eighth centuries saw extensive new trading connections formed along the southern shores of the North Sea and the eastern end of the Channel. These involved the import, among other things, of goods such as furs, walrus ivory and amber from Scandinavia and the Baltic, and intensified existing economic links with these regions. The port of Quentovic, whose precise location close to Etaples has only recently been confirmed, was developed by the Franks near the former Roman naval base of Boulogne, and Dorestad on the junction of the river Lek with the Rhine became the main market for this whole region by early in the eighth century.[16] To the north of the Channel, two other significant entrepôts came into being – at Hamwih (just to the east of the medieval site of Southampton) and at Ipswich in East Anglia (the '-wic/h' endings identifying them as *vici* or trading centres).[17] Similarly, the growth of a number of trading settlements in Scandinavia, notably at Birka, Hedeby and Kaupang, were clearly related to these developments to the west.

A relatively powerful kingship may have emerged in Jutland – the mainland part of Denmark – during the eighth century, in reaction to Slavic pressure from the south-east and the growing Frankish involvement in Saxony, alongside the economic opportunities created by the growth of new markets and ports in northern Francia and southern England. One of the most impressive large-scale archaeological features in early Medieval Denmark is a series of interrelated defensive earthworks that link the Schleifjord and the Schwansen peninsula with the valley of the River Rheide. Because of the marshy character of the land further west, this system of earthworks, known collectively as the Danevirke, controlled all land routes from the south into the Danish kingdom of Jutland.[18]

The *Annales Regni Francorum* attribute responsibility for this work to king Godofred, dating it to 808.[19] However, archaeologists have established by dendrochronology (dating by tree rings) that the real date of building of the Danevirke was around the year 737; at least, that is the date when the trees used in its construction were cut down. Like Offa's Dyke in Britain, the scale and purpose of the undertaking suggest it required considerable mobilisation of labour. Otherwise undocumented, this large-scale defensive system suggests the existence of a centralised authority in Jutland at this time; one that was perhaps able to impose an obligation on its subjects to take part in public works.

During the eighth century, paralleling the rise of the ports of northern Francia, a number of trading settlements came into being in Scandinavia. One of the most important of these was Hedeby (Haithabu), at the southern end of the Schleifjord. This was related to the Danevirke system of defences. By the time of Godofred (d. 810), Danish kings were taking tolls on the merchandise brought through such ports and trading stations, providing the monarchy with a lucrative source of revenue. King Godofred destroyed a Slavic trading station at an unknown Baltic site called Reric, and transplanted its merchants to his own kingdom, to remove competition and increase his own takings.[20]

After the growth in political and economic complexity in Denmark in the course of the eighth century, there are signs that much of it was lost in the ninth. Following the murder of Godofred in 810, Frankish sources record civil wars among the Danes, and the greater level of turbulence throughout northern Europe reduced the economic gains from peaceful trading. This helps to explain the period of predatory raiding that followed. As with the Vandals in the fifth century and English pirates in the Caribbean in the sixteenth, possession of suitable ships enabled people to indulge simultaneously in trade and piracy, depending on the opportunities offered.

It has been questioned whether a single kingdom could have existed in Denmark at this time, but the Frankish chronicles do not refer to rival territorial kingdoms in Jutland and the islands, but rather to civil wars between members of an extended royal dynasty. Such conflicts are recorded in 812, 813, 814, 817,

819, 823, 827, 828, 850 and 854, and there may have been others.[21]

From 811/12 onwards, the Frankish chroniclers imply that Danish kingship could be shared between all available members of a particular branch of the ruling family. Thus, for example, all the sons of Godofred are described as being kings in the period c. 813 to 827 and beyond. They were not always in concord, and the heirs of former kings from collateral branches of the dynasty frequently challenged the power of the ruling group. So there were numerous actual and potential monarchs and leaders among the Danish royal house, whose political and other fortunes depended on their ability to maintain their personal followings.

Failure in the clearly bloody struggles in Denmark drove the leaders of a defeated faction into exile, together with their supporters, who themselves could have been the losers in struggles with local rivals. Such exiles could either try to impose themselves as the rulers of territories outside Denmark – among the Slavs, for example – or re-establish their reputation and wealth (and thus their chance of building up a new following) through profitable raiding in Britain, Ireland and Francia. In such competitive circumstances, rival Danish kings and lesser war leaders also found it useful to turn to raiding to maintain themselves and their followers. Unfortunately, the Frankish and Anglo-Saxon sources do not tell us about the origins of the principal Viking leaders overseas in the ninth century. In some cases they are called *reges* or kings, but it is not clear whether this reflects their leadership of a raiding army or their inherited status in Scandinavian society.[22]

Norway, on the other hand, shows no evidence of the growth of more powerful or territorially larger monarchies at this time. This only happened in the tenth century and is associated, at least in later tradition, particularly with the reign of king Harald Hárfagri (d. 936?), who began to extend a kingdom centred on Vestfold into the western fjords and northwards into the Trøndelag.[23] In the eighth and ninth centuries, it is probable that all these regions were parcelled up between a series of petty local rulers. The same would seem to be equally true of Sweden.[24]

It was from parts of Norway and Sweden that the first ventures overseas were undertaken, both westwards and eastwards.[25] As has been mentioned, it is suspected that the Norwegian settlements in the Orkneys and the Hebrides were already underway at the time that the first raids on Northumbria and Ireland took place in the 790s, and it was probably from these northern islands that the raiders came, rather than directly across the North Sea. These are areas located on the periphery of the zone of accelerating commercial activity in the Channel and the southern shores of the North Sea, and lacking resources of their own that would enable their inhabitants to participate in the wealth-generation to the south of them. So the new settlers may have begun to prey on their southern neighbours to secure resources they were not able to acquire through trade; thus becoming 'raiders because they could not be traders'.

While saga material, almost all of which was composed in the twelfth and thirteenth centuries, is an unreliable source for the history of Scandinavian societies in the Viking period, it offers imaginative impressions of how raiding could fit into a pattern of life otherwise centred on farming. A good example can be found in the *Orkneyinga Saga*. Here, Norse freemen in the Orkneys take to their ships in the spring (which arrives late in those latitudes), after sowing their crops, leaving their farms to be maintained by slaves, large numbers of whom were to be found in Scandinavian society.[26] Raids either along the east coast of England or in Ireland provided loot that would be divided up after they returned home in the autumn to take part in the harvest. Winter was passed almost in hibernation (assisted by quite a lot of drink) in their farmsteads.[27] This is a pattern that is not unlike the structure of warfare to be found in the same period in Francia. The scale is different, as there was no royal direction, but the integration of campaigning into a seasonal pattern that accommodated the needs of farming is identical.

The initial plundering of the island monasteries around the British, Irish and French coasts – Lindisfarne in 793, Iona, Inisbofin and Inismurray in 795, and St Philibert's monastery on Noirmoutier in 799 – shocked the societies that suffered these attacks because of the lack of a shared value system between raiders and victims. Other than in Ireland, where church burning was relatively common in the endemic warfare between the numerous rival kingdoms struggling for regional hegemony, attacks on monasteries were almost inconceivable in war between Christians.[28] From the pagan raiders' point of view, such easily accessible and wealthy establishments, housing large quantities of easily portable treasure in the form of precious metal reliquaries, book covers and liturgical ornaments, were endlessly attractive, and they returned repeatedly to attack them. Iona was looted in 795, 802 and 806, and in consequence, in 807 most of the community moved to Ireland to a newly established monastery in the inland site of Kells.[29]

Greater wariness on the part of coastal settlements might have been sufficient to counter the relatively small-scale, if occasionally bloody, raids of this first period. However, the limited threats of the Norwegians were to be followed by much larger-scale warfare and migration on the part of the Danes, affecting regions untouched by the earlier phase of Scandinavian raiding. Whatever the causes of the Norwegian migrations across the North Sea that produced the raids in Britain and Ireland, the Danish attacks on their neighbours were products of different circumstances, and reflect external economic and cultural pressures on their own society.

The Vikings and Francia

The campaigns of Charlemagne against the Saxons clearly made themselves felt on the peoples further to the north and east, particularly on the Slavs living along the southern shores of the Baltic, and on the Danes.[30] Diplomatic contacts between the Frankish ruler and a Danish king Sigefred go back to at least 782, but Charles' tampering with the balance of power east of the Elbe in 804 may have been the prime cause of the ensuing problems. Facing continuing resistance from the Saxons living north of the Elbe, the Frankish emperor had them rounded up and removed to exile in Francia, destroying their society in an act of 'ethnic cleansing'. Their lands were then given to the Slavic Abodrites, who had been allies of the Franks since at least 789.[31] The resulting rise in Abodrite power in the region prompted a Danish attack on them in 808, and in response the sending of a Frankish army to defend the Elbe. In 809, the Abodrites retaliated against other lesser Slavic tribes who had supported the Danes the previous year.

Conflict between the Slav allies of the Franks and of the Danes escalated into direct confrontation between the two kingdoms.[32] In 810, the Danish king Godofred sent a fleet to raid Frisia, which had been under Frankish control since the time of Charles Martel. However, in the period of internal disturbance that followed Godofred's murder in the same year, competing kings of the Danes found a new use for the Franks as allies in their civil wars. One of the competitors, called Harald Klak (812–13, 819–27), who had been ousted temporarily, felt it expedient to receive Christian baptism in a great ceremony at the royal palace at Ingelheim in 826, in which the emperor Louis stood as his godfather.[33] Though he was then able to return to his kingdom with Frankish backing, in practice this did not do him much good, and may have contributed directly to his renewed expulsion from Denmark the following year.

As with Rome in the fourth to seventh centuries, the growth of closer and more complex cultural and economic interchange across the frontiers between an empire and its less-developed neighbours made the latter all the more ready to exploit any signs of military weakness. So, it is no coincidence that the first large-scale Danish raids on imperial territory started in 834, when the civil war between Louis the Pious and his son Lothar was at its height. From 834 to 836, annual raids were made on the trading settlement of Dorestad in Frisia.[34] Louis, who generally responded better to military than to political problems, ordered the building of a series of coastal forts in 837, though the one on the island of Walcheren was captured almost immediately.[35]

Danish assaults on Francia proper began in 841, when the sons of Louis the Pious were engaged in civil war. In that year, Rouen on the Seine was sacked, and in 842 so too was the port of Quentovic, near Boulogne.[36] In 843, a Danish fleet raided Nantes, killing the bishop, and then wintered on an island near the mouth of the Loire. In 844, this force sailed up the Garonne, before proceeding by land to sack Toulouse. Returning to the sea, they sailed along the north coast of Spain, and made an unsuccessful descent on Galicia, then part of the small Christian kingdom of the Asturias. From there they sailed south and looted the Arab-ruled towns of Seville and Lisbon. Spanish sources report that this fleet consisted of fifty-four ships.[37] In 845, a fleet that was said to consist of 120 ships sailed up the Seine to threaten Paris, but was bought off by Charles the Bald, now the undisputed master of most of western Francia, for the sum of 7,000 pounds of silver.[38]

Criticism has been levelled at some of the figures given in the annals for the numbers of ships said to be involved in some of the Viking raids. Accepting that they are unlikely to be precise, it has to be asked how realistic is such a figure as that of the 120 ships given for the fleet on the Seine in 845? On the one hand, taking the reasonably conservative figure of thirty men to a ship this would indicate that the Danish fighting force numbered some 3,600. This may seem at least minimal in view of the scale of the threat presented, and the king's unwillingness to take on the raiders in battle. On the other hand, if this figure for the manpower involved is approximately correct, then the bribe they received from Charles would have netted them less than two pounds of silver per man, which is hardly impressive. The issue, like so many in Viking studies, remains inconclusive.

From the entry for 845 in the *Annals of St Bertin*, it is clear that at least three separate Viking forces were operating independently at this time. There was one in the Seine. The fleet that had devastated Toulouse and southern Aquitaine in 844 returned from its expedition to Spain, and was then raiding Saintonge; and another, reported improbably to consist of 600 ships, and which had been sent by the Danish king Horic (d. 854), sacked Hamburg and sailed up the Elbe, before being defeated by the Saxon forces of Louis the German.

This was one of the few military successes recorded on the part of royal armies operating against the Scandinavian raiders in this period. In 847, the Danes in Aquitaine began a blockade of Bordeaux, and Charles the Bald, then engaged in crushing the last resistance of Pippin II and his supporters, is said to have defeated them in 848; but it can hardly have been of much consequence, as they proceeded to take and sack Bordeaux later in the year.[39]

Overall, what is striking about the fairly full accounts of events given in the *Annals of St Bertin* for the period 830–82 is the lack of effective action taken by the Frankish kings to check this growing series of raids, particularly in the period from the death of Louis the Pious in 840 to the early 860s. Even the one concerted military effort that was made, involving not just the army of Charles the Bald but also that of his half-brother, Lothar, proved ineffectual. In 852, a Danish fleet was blockaded in the Seine by these combined Frankish armies, but in the end Charles the Bald made a treaty with its leaders, which permitted them to stay until March 853. Thus refreshed, these Vikings sailed into the Loire, where in the years to follow they were to sack Nantes, Tours, Blois, Angers, Orléans and Poitiers.[40] The causes of these failures on the part of the Carolingian rulers reflect not only the difficult nature of the military problem the Vikings posed but also the serious political difficulties they were facing within Francia, discussed in the previous chapter.

Large-scale as some of these Viking operations were, few if any of them seem to have been directed by Danish kings of the type represented by Godofred. The kings ruling in Denmark generally appear amenable to diplomacy, but the leaders of the great expeditions overseas, such as those in Aquitaine in the 840s, in the Loire in the 850s, and in the Seine from 856 to 862, enjoyed a mobility and lack of need to defend their own land that made them very hard to contain. The Viking raiders tended to base themselves on islands, such as Thanet and Sheppey in southern England, Batavia off Frisia, and a variety of isles in the rivers Seine and Loire, which gave them both secure bases that the Franks seemed unable to attack – the Anglo-Saxons were more successful – and places in which to store their loot.[41] While they were very keen to get their hands on treasure and precious objects, such as books with bejewelled and ivory covers, the greater part of the proceeds of their raids was probably of the two-legged kind.

From the attack on Dorestad and Frisia in 836 onwards, the annals record the Danes 'depopulating' monasteries, towns and districts. What they were doing was carrying off slaves. In some cases their captives were of sufficient worth to be able to command large ransoms from their families. When, in April 858, Charles the Bald's cousin and chancellor, Louis, abbot of Saint-Denis, was captured together with his brother by Vikings operating in the Seine valley, the king had to raise a ransom of 688 pounds of gold and 3,250 pounds of silver to buy their release.[42] Those for whom no ransoms could be expected were sold as slaves.

The slave trade had long existed in western Europe, but, while statistics do not exist, it had probably declined considerably in importance in the period after the fall of Rome. The existence of servile status, of families tied to the land and under fixed obligations to their lords, made the need for the expensive buying of slaves unnecessary. When land was sold, the unfree families attached to it were normally included in the price. However, from the later eighth century onwards, an enormous new market for slaves brought from other parts of Europe opened up in the Islamic world. Slave armies were replacing the previous use of Arab tribal forces in Spain, North Africa and the Near East.[43] There was a considerable demand for household slaves throughout these regions. It is also conceivable that a certain percentage of those enslaved were destined for the home market back in Scandinavia, where servile labour appears to have been used on the land.

In the same period, new Scandinavian settlements were developing overseas, for which, again, locally captured and imported slaves were needed. In the 830s, the Norwegian Vikings began raiding more intensively in Ireland, taking numerous captives for the slave market, as well as looting monasteries. A number of prominent ecclesiastics were also taken prisoner, and like their counterparts in Francia, released in return for ransoms. Thus Forannán, abbot of Armagh (835–48), head of the foremost monastic federation in Ireland, was held captive in 845–6.[44] In a similar paralleling of developments in Francia, the Vikings began to winter in Ireland, as first recorded in 840/1, when they established temporary strongholds in which to lay up their ships. At least one of these, Dublin, turned into a permanent settlement and market. Paradoxically, this made the Vikings more vulnerable, in that a fixed base of this sort needed to be defended, and its own growing wealth made it attractive to the Irish rulers. Dublin was sacked for the first time in 849 by a confederacy led by the Uí Néill king of Mide, Máel Sechnaill (843–62).[45] The Vikings also became increasingly embroiled in the inter-kingdom conflicts within Ireland, which they could sometimes exploit to their advantage, but which could also lead to military disaster.[46]

Just as the Norwegians in Ireland began to lose some of the advantages of mobility, so did the Danish groups in Francia. By the late 850s, the Vikings were so numerous and so well-established in the main river valleys of northern France that it became easier for the western Franks to contain them. The need for the individual leaders to maintain their followings by providing them with profits meant that one group was quite willing to fight against another for the Frankish king, as long as he was able to pay them. The fact that by this time their depredations had been going on for twenty years may also have reduced the quantity of loot accessible to them: some monasteries and larger settlements in the vulnerable areas appear to have been abandoned, and Viking slaving and ransom-seeking techniques were by now all too well known.[47] Thus, in 858, one group of Vikings established in the Seine agreed to fight for Charles the Bald, and in 862 he was able to use others then controlling the River Somme to attack the main base of those in the Seine. By such manoeuvres and by the employment of new defensive tactics, such as the establishment of fortified bridges across the vulnerable rivers, the Franks began to make the Viking operations less profitable and more risky. It is thus hardly coincidental that from 865 onwards their attacks on the Anglo-Saxon kingdoms intensified, while those on western Francia decreased. At the same time, Danish groups, who had hitherto largely concerned themselves with Francia, began to operate in Ireland, and in consequence to come into conflict with the longer-established Norwegians, and in due course they made themselves masters of Dublin.[48]

The period of relief was short-lived, however. In the last years of Charles the Bald, Viking activity in western Francia revived. Some historians believe that it was primarily the Frankish king's defensive measures that had led the raiders to turn their attention elsewhere in the period 865–76, but when the attacks on Francia resumed, the kingdom was unprepared and royal military action was largely ineffectual. As the *Annals of St Vaast* record, in 876 an army was sent against the Vikings in the Seine but 'it did nothing useful'. In these circumstances, Charles' involvement in Italy and his quest for the imperial title might appear, as they did to archbishop Hincmar of Reims, to be a dereliction of duty. From the last year of the new emperor's life (877) comes a capitulary stipulating the sums to be paid by all bishops, abbots, counts and royal vassals as a tribute to the Vikings in the Seine, 'so that they would withdraw from the kingdom'.[49]

Following the premature death of Charles' son, Louis the Stammerer, in 879, Viking activity in the north of Francia intensified. A dispute broke out between the principal West Frankish magnates over the succession. Some supported Louis's young sons, and others wanted the East Frankish king Louis the Younger (876–82) to take over the kingdom.[50] Possibly prompted by these divisions, a large Viking force crossed from England to sack Thérouanne and loot Brabant and the valley of the Scheldt. From 879 to 892 their depredations in northern France continued unchecked. In 881, they looted the famous monasteries of St Vaast, St Riquier (Centula) and Corbie, while in 882 they sacked Reims, and its aged archbishop Hincmar died a fugitive from his see.[51]

The young West Frankish king Louis III (879–82) won a victory over one Viking contingent at Saucy in 881, but as in the case of all the other reported military successes in this period, this had no significant consequences.[52] In every case, the victory was not or could not be followed up, and the Vikings, having withdrawn from the area they had been ravaging, turned their attention to another one instead. Ultimately, their highly profitable siege of Paris in 885/6 contributed directly to the replacement of the Carolingian dynasty in western Francia.

According to the *Annals of St Vaast*, the Viking army left Francia in 892 because of the famine that was then afflicting much of the land. They did not return until the winter of 896/7. From this point onwards, however, things went somewhat better for the Franks. The removal of the Vikings in 892 had been followed by, and may well have made possible by, the outbreak of war between the adherents of king Odo and the supporters of the only surviving heir of the West Frankish branch of the Carolingian dynasty, Louis the Stammerer's posthumously born son, Charles (later known as 'the Simple' – in the sense of 'direct and uncomplicated', not of 'simple-minded'). Despite various swings of fortune, this was finally resolved (not least through the death of Odo in January 898) in favour of Charles.[53] In the latter's reign, a generally more vigorous resistance was offered to renewed (but possibly smaller-scale) Viking threats, and this was allied to a new policy of settling the invaders in vulnerable frontier regions.

The first success was secured in 897 when Vikings in the valley of the Maas retreated to their ships, fearing the size of an approaching royal army. Later in the year, their leader made an agreement with Charles the Simple, accepting Christian baptism, with the king as his godfather. In 898, one of the most powerful of the territorial magnates of the West Frankish kingdom, count Richard of Autun, defeated a Viking force raiding overland into northern Burgundy.[54] Despite these more aggressive and effective reactions, though, the lower valley of the Seine remained an irreducible Viking stronghold, something that came to be accepted and regularised in 911.

By this period the hitherto plentiful chronicle sources have become much rarer. The *Annals of St Bertin* end in 882, and those of St Vaast in 900. No major West Frankish historiography was written until Flodoard, a canon of the Church of Reims, composed a set of annals covering the years 919–66. This became the main source for the monk Richer of Saint-Remi in Reims, who wrote (*c.* 996) an account of the period 888–995. He generally added fictitious embroideries to his predecessor's brief accounts, and his work has no independent authority for the period before the 970s.[55] This has meant that one of the most significant developments in the history of Frankish–Viking relations remains obscure. This was the agreement made in 911 between Charles the Simple and the Viking leader, Rollo, who thereby became in practice though not in title, count of Rouen.[56]

A second settlement, based on Nantes and the frontiers of Brittany, was made in 921 after a large force of Viking marauders was besieged in the Loire valley and forced to surrender by duke Robert of Neustria, brother of the former king Odo.[57] This also involved the baptism of the Viking leaders at Paris. Such conversions were, as in parallel cases in England, normal practice after a Viking defeat and submission. In many cases, such baptised Vikings reverted to paganism once they were ready to break the agreements made with their Christian conquerors. This seems like cynicism, but it is probably better to see them feeling that, for the moment, Christ was in the ascendancy, but that in due course Odin and Thor would reassert themselves. In other words, by professing themselves followers of Christ they were not necessarily denying the existence of their other gods.

What is significant, though, in the better-documented instance of 921, is that the conversion and grant followed a military defeat and formal submission on the part of the Vikings. It is therefore possible that Rollo in 911 accepted baptism and the responsibility for protecting western Francia from attack by other Vikings coming up the Seine because of a previous defeat by the king. In practice, Rollo remained a useful ally of Charles the Simple, and opposed his two non-Carolingian successors, Robert (922–3), the brother of Odo, and his son-in-law, Rudolf (923–36). Admittedly, this also served his own interests, in that his main territorial rivals, the counts of Flanders and Vermandois, were on the opposing side. Despite occasional setbacks, Rollo and his successors expanded their territory into what around the end of the century became the duchy of Normandy.[58]

The practice of giving Vikings territory in return for military assistance was not new. As early as 827 the exiled Danish king Harald Klak had been granted land around Walcheren by Louis the Pious, as part of the Franks' defensive measures against raids, and a similar agreement had been made between the emperor Lothar and the Danish leader Godofred, son of Heriold – which Godofred broke in 852.[59] The nearest parallel to the West Frankish treaties with the Vikings was the one made by the emperor Charles the Fat with the Danish leader Godofred in 882.[60] By this, Godofred and his followers were settled in Frisia, and the Viking leader was adopted into the Carolingian family through marriage to Gisela, daughter of Lothar II. The intention of this treaty, like those of 911 and 921, was to fit the invaders permanently into the Frankish administrative and military structures. Thus, in 911, Rollo seems to have been granted all royal rights over the county of Rouen, other than that of nominating its bishop.

While Viking occupation was geographically and chronologically more limited in Francia (other than Normandy and the Breton marches) than in England, the effects of their activities were equally dramatic. In England, the elimination of the Anglo-Saxon kingdoms of Northumbria, Mercia and East Anglia in the 860s and the survival under Alfred of Wessex enabled his successors to unite all these territories into a new kingdom of the English in the tenth century. In Francia, the Viking threat and the limited royal response to it led to the growth of greater regional independence. The dukes and counts raised their own forces and built their own fortresses to resist Viking and Arab raiding. Royal estates and regalian rights were ceded to them to help them maintain local order.

Frankish evidence for the Carolingian rulers' responses to Viking activities gives the impression that many of them did not regard this as a problem that required urgent attention. Unlike their Anglo-Saxon counterparts, they appear to have treated the activities of the Vikings more as problems of local order than as threats to the continued existence of their kingdoms. In a sense they were right. At no point were Viking armies poised to conquer a Frankish kingdom in the way they did in England. At their worst, Viking depredations affected only certain parts of the Frankish kingdoms and did not threaten their integrity as a whole.

Even so, it is strange to see how militarily restrained Frankish reactions were, at least before the 880s. Direct confrontations between Vikings and Frankish forces, led either by kings or by their local representatives, were very rare. This changed in the 880s and 890s, but the battles of those decades fought by Louis III (879–82), Carloman (879–84) and Odo (888–98) were generally limited in their military and political effects. However, by the early tenth century, the more aggressive and reactive responses on the part of the Frankish leaders when allied to a new policy of accepting Viking settlement in certain regions and integrating them into existing administrative structures was surprisingly successful.

It would only be fair to add that, by the time of Charles the Simple, the number of Vikings active within West Francia was fewer than had been the case in the 850s/860s and in the years 879–92. Many of their number had been absorbed into the substantial settlements in northern and eastern England. It was the presence of these that may also have made the Vikings in the Seine ultimately more ready to accept something similar for themselves.

The Vikings and the Anglo-Saxon kingdoms

While the presence of Norwegian settlements in the northern islands of Britain and in Ireland had resulted in occasional raids on vulnerable coastal sites, especially in Northumbria, large-scale attacks on the Anglo-Saxon kingdoms did not begin until the 830s. Conditions on one side of the Channel affected those on the other, and it is no surprise to find that the start of Danish raids on the Frankish ports in Frisia was matched by attacks on England, particularly on the more southerly coasts. Thus, the Isle of Sheppey was devastated in 835, and Romney Marsh and other parts of Kent as well as the Lincolnshire coast suffered in 841. London and Rochester were attacked in 842.[61] These parallel the intensified raids on northern Francia in the early 840s.

Other Viking attacks occurred further to the west, and it is possible that these were in fact the work of Norwegian raiders from Ireland and the northern isles. As they demonstrated in Francia, the Vikings were adept at taking advantage of their enemies' weaknesses and in exploiting divisions among them. Thus, in 838, a group of them, possibly from Ireland, allied with the Britons of Cornwall in an attack on Wessex.[62] They were, however, defeated by the West Saxon king Egbert.

In general, the Anglo-Saxon rulers and their local subordinates, the ealdormen, the equivalents of the Frankish counts, actively resisted Viking incursions, and shire (county) levies were quickly raised to meet their threats. Thus, in 840, an ealdorman, Wulfheard, defeated thirty-three ships' companies of Vikings in the vicinity of Hamwih. Eanwulf, ealdorman of Somerset, won a victory at the mouth of the River Parrett in 848, and his colleague Ceorl, ealdorman of Devon, was equally successful at an unidentified *Wicgeanbeorg* in 850. In the same year, Athelstan, the West Saxon king of Kent and his ealdorman Ealhere defeated a Viking force at Sandwich, capturing nine ships.[63]

Not all such encounters went the same way, and a number of defeats are recorded in the same period.[64] Even so, the reports of Viking attacks on towns and monasteries are far fewer than those in the Frankish sources for the 840s and 850s. Canterbury, for example, which would have been a major target, was attacked only once, in 851.[65] In part this may reflect the more limited nature of urban settlement and the relatively small number of wealthy monasteries to be found in England, particularly in the south and west. It is not surprising, in view of the limited returns and the more spirited nature of the defence put up by the West Saxons in particular, that the Vikings devoted more attention to northern Francia in these decades.

The situation changed in the mid-860s, possibly because of the more effective resistance that the Franks were then beginning to offer.[66] For 865, the *Anglo-Saxon Chronicle* records the arrival in East Anglia of 'a great host of the heathens'. Though no such movement is reported in the contemporary Frankish sources, it is notable that Viking activities in West Francia eased off quite dramatically from 866 onwards, especially in the Seine valley. They were to resume again in the very late 870s, however, when increasing settlement and the victories of the West Saxon king Alfred brought to an end the expansion of Danish power in England.

The outline of the movements of the Viking 'Great Army' is recorded in the *Anglo-Saxon Chronicle,* lthough its information concerning events outside the West Saxon kingdom is very limited. The invaders descended on the kingdom of East Anglia, which made peace with them, maintained them over the winter of 865–6, and provided horses for their campaign in the following spring. Thus equipped, in 866 they invaded Northumbria, which was then torn by the war between the rival kings Ælla and Osbryht, and occupied York. In consequence, the two kings joined forces to try to regain the city in March 867. They were both killed in the ensuing assault, and the Viking leaders set up a new king of Northumbria of their own choosing, called Egbert (867–72), who concluded a formal peace with them.[67]

In the same year, the Viking army moved south into Mercia, and established itself in Nottingham for the winter. Here, in the spring of 868, the Vikings were confronted by a combined Mercian and West Saxon army, but no battle ensued. Instead, the Mercian king Burghred concluded a peace treaty with them, and they then returned to York. In 869, they crossed Mercian territory unopposed to invade East Anglia again, and to establish themselves for the winter at Thetford. Here they were attacked by the East Anglian king Edmund, who was defeated and killed.[68] In 870/1 it was to be the turn of Wessex. The Viking army came up the Thames valley, and a series of battles followed between them and the West Saxon kings Ethelred (865–71) and Alfred (871–99) at Reading, Ashdown, Wilton and other unnamed locations. After a series of defeats, the West Saxons made peace with the invaders, as did the Mercians when they occupied London for the winter of 871/2.[69] The 'peace' (*frith*) that the various Anglo-Saxon kingdoms are recorded as making with the Viking army must be assumed to have had a monetary side to it, even though the *Chronicle* makes no reference to any payments. Thus, when Mercia is found 'making peace' both in 871 and 872, it is reasonable to believe that this was purchased on both occasions. In other words, the Vikings were operating a highly lucrative 'protection racket' as far as the Anglo-Saxon kingdoms were concerned, and keeping themselves safe over the winters by occupying defendable towns.

For this to be effective they had to maintain the central authority in each kingdom, so that treasure with which to pay them could continue to be collected. This was the reason for their setting up Egbert in Northumbria when his two predecessors perished in the battle at York. When he proved unsatisfactory in some way, they replaced him with another king, Ricsig (872–3/4). Similarly, when in 874 Burghred of Mercia was either forced or decided to relinquish his royal office and go as a pilgrim to Rome, the Vikings chose a new king, Ceolwulf, to replace him.[70]

By the mid-870s, significant changes began to occur in Viking strategy and objectives. One of the leaders of the 'Great Army', called Halfdan, split off from the rest in 874 in order to raid northwards into the kingdom of the Picts and that of the Britons of Strathclyde. In 876, he seems to have made himself king of Northumbria, and to have distributed land to his followers. In the meantime, the other leaders of the host carried on as before, descending on East Anglia again in 874 and then on Wessex in 875/6.[71] Once again, Alfred had to buy 'peace' (876). The *Anglo-Saxon Chronicle* perhaps exaggerates in referring to the Vikings as having to 'evade' the West Saxon armies in order to make themselves masters of Wareham. It also mentions their swearing a unique and especially sacred oath to the West Saxon king Alfred, but it seems probable that, in the end, Wessex, like the other kingdoms, found it more expedient to come to terms with the raiders and to buy their withdrawal.

What may have changed the situation on this occasion was a disaster that befell the Danes at sea. Part of the fleet they had used to convey themselves to Wareham was destroyed by a storm off Swanage, leaving the land forces, which had moved on to Exeter, cut off in the south-west peninsula.[72] Alfred blockaded them in their fortress there, but was unable to take it. An agreement was eventually reached whereby the Vikings returned to Mercia. Here in 877, following the lead given in the north, they partitioned the kingdom with its ruler Ceolwulf and distributed land among themselves in the eastern part of it.[73]

At least one of their leaders appears to have determined to do something similar in Wessex, and a part of the host made a sudden attack on Alfred's winter court at Chippenham in January 878. The king, whose military following at that time of year was minimal, managed to escape south into the Somerset marshes, and to hold out in Athelney until the coming of spring made it possible for the shire levies to be gathered. In the ensuing battle at Edington, the invaders were defeated and then besieged in their fortified camp. In due course their leader Guthrum was forced to submit, and to accept Christian baptism as part of the agreement.[74] In 879, Guthrum led his followers into East Anglia and settled them on the land.

The traditional view of Alfred as saving 'England' hardly needs airing here. But it is worth considering his role in preserving Wessex from being turned into a kingdom ruled by a Viking dynasty. The interpretation offered here implies that when the full force of the 'Great Army' was directed against Wessex, Alfred and his kingdom had to purchase peace in the way that the Northumbrian, Mercian and East Anglian rulers already had. This was equally the case after the division of the Viking host in 874. However, the settlements in the north in 876 and in Mercia in 877 meant that when an attempt was made to eliminate Alfred and overrun his kingdom in January 878, it was by a greatly reduced part of the original host, under only one of its initial four leaders.

There is no question that the shire levies of the West Saxon kingdom fought hard against the invaders in 870/1 and 875/6, but despite a number of tactical successes they achieved no real victory, in the sense of securing their strategic aims of eliminating or expelling the Vikings. Nor, in the light of its limited and partisan character, should we assume that the lack of mention on the part of the *Anglo-Saxon Chronicle* of similar intensive conflicts in Northumbria and Mercia means that such resistance was an exclusively West Saxon phenomenon. Ultimately, Alfred was lucky that his kingdom was, for geographical reasons, the last of the invaders' targets, and even more so that he was warned in time at Chippenham in January 878.

By 879, Viking dynasties had replaced native Anglo-Saxon ones in Northumbria, East Anglia and the eastern section of Mercia. Some distribution of land had also taken place among the followers of the Danish leaders. The nature of this and the procedures employed in it are obscure, though its subsequent effects can be discerned more easily.[75] It is not at all clear how far and in what ways existing landholdings were affected. The presence of Scandinavian-influenced place names in the regions under Danish political control are not necessarily an accurate guide to settlement, in that they are not chronologically precise. Moreover, they are often found in economically marginal areas that were first exploited in the period of the late ninth to eleventh centuries, and would thus have lacked earlier pre-Viking names.[76]

It is important to realise that, as in earlier periods of migration and conquest, the invaders represented a small minority of the total population in the territories they occupied. A degree of cultural assimilation between conquerors and conquered was necessary if a military occupation was to turn itself into a real settlement. This does seem to have occurred quite rapidly in the case of the Danes in England, especially in Northumbria.

By 900, the Vikings in Northumbria were prepared to put themselves under the leadership of a fugitive West Saxon prince, Alfred's nephew, Æthelwold (d. 904), and to support his unsuccessful bid to oust his cousin Edward from Wessex.[77] The rapid fusion of interests in Northumbria meant that no 'English' anti-Danish sentiment can be detected in the north in the course of the tenth century.[78] Equally instructive is the text of an agreement made around 886 between Alfred and Guthrum, the Danish king of East Anglia. No distinction is made between Danes and Angles in referring to 'the people who are in East Anglia', and the final clause envisages – and prohibits – freemen from Wessex wanting to cross the frontier to join the Viking host.[79] If such a movement could be imagined in Wessex, how much more likely is it to have already occurred within the existing Anglo-Norse kingdoms in Northumbria, East Anglia and eastern Mercia?

Where Alfred showed his capacity as ruler and military commander was in preparing his kingdom against the possibility of another Viking invasion from the Continent.[80] In 879, the year that Guthrum established himself in East Anglia, a large host that had been assembling in the Thames valley crossed into Francia where, as has been seen, it terrorised the northern lowland regions of the West Frankish kingdom continuously until 892. It has been suggested this was another body of Vikings that only crossed into England in 878 and then found that Alfred had made conditions too difficult for them to remain, but this is not what the *Chronicle* says.[81] It is perhaps better to imagine that those members of the original 'Great Army' who did not become involved in the land divisions and settlements carried out in 876–8 by their original leaders, then gathered together in the Thames valley to put themselves under new commanders and resume their careers as mobile raiders.

In 892, this Viking army, originally formed in southern England, and which had been operating in northern Francia since 879, returned from the Continent because of a widespread famine.[82] It crossed via Boulogne to southern Kent and established a fortified base at Appledore. Soon afterwards, a second Viking fleet, under a certain Haesten, sailed into the Thames. It is likely that this is the same man as the 'Hasting', who is reported in 866 and 874 as the leader of the Vikings in the Loire.[83] If so, it would seem that the Loire Vikings, who had not formed part of the 'Great Army' that had invaded the Anglo-Saxon kingdoms in 865, were dislodged from Francia at this time, also possibly by the famine.

In a series of campaigns between 893 and 896, the now united Danish forces pushed through the Thames valley, up the length of western Mercia as far as the deserted Roman fortress of Chester and then into North Wales.[84] In the process, they were harried continuously by the Anglo-Saxon levies of Alfred, and of his son-in-law Æthelred (d. 911). The latter was, in West

Saxon eyes, the ealdorman of west Mercia from *c.* 883, and he may have acknowledged himself as such during Alfred's lifetime, but there are indications that he was recognised as king of Mercia, and may have been a member of the former royal dynasty.[85] The Vikings were prevented from occupying or looting any of the major settlements by the continuous harrying, and by the success of Alfred's policy of fortifying such *burhs*. In the light of what must have been a disappointing series of campaigns, the Viking confederacy broke up in 896. Some of its components went off to the Danish kingdoms of Northumbria and East Anglia, and others returned to the Continent, where they were to be defeated in the Seine valley the following year by the forces of Charles the Simple. As has been seen, the reign of this West Frankish monarch saw the establishment of major Viking settlements in what would later become Normandy.

The last quarter of the ninth century and the opening decades of the tenth thus saw a diminution in Viking activity, in the sense of large-scale raiding by mobile groups of Danes without fixed settlements or lands. Such bodies had existed as loose confederacies of individuals or ships' companies taking service under leaders of established reputation, whom they could leave at will. They based themselves each winter in fortified camps, normally moving on in the spring. There is evidence that in such circumstances a distribution of loot and the profits of ransoms and slave trading occurred at the beginning of each winter season. The greater the success of any given 'host', the larger it would become as others were attracted to it by the expectations of profit. These, certainly in parts of England, might well include elements of the local population.

In place of these dangerous but volatile confederacies, from 876 onwards – and earlier in Ireland – a series of permanent settlements developed. As has been seen, in England these took the form of Viking domination of existing kingdoms. In Francia they were brought about by integrating Viking leaders and their followers into the local administrative structures of the Carolingian empire. In Ireland, fortified coastal settlements, above all Dublin and Limerick, became the centres of territorially small but powerful local kingdoms, that drew their wealth from trade, as well as involvement in the interminable wars of the indigenous Irish realms.[86] In all cases, the emergence of such Viking states was matched by growing integration with elements of the indigenous population and its culture. Not least did this involve fairly rapid conversion to Christianity.

Conversion and expansion

The origins of the evangelisation of Scandinavia are, inevitably, obscure. It is not unreasonable to suspect that increasing political and economic contact between the Frankish empire and the Baltic and Danish kingdoms was accompanied by cultural influence of the former on the latter, and that this would have included a growing awareness of Christianity. It is possible that some of the mid-ninth-century Danish kings at least hinted at a willingness to convert, and this could well be linked to periods of co-operation between them and some of the Carolingian rulers.

The first known missionary venture intended to propagate Christianity among the Scandinavians was that initiated in the early ninth century by archbishop Ebbo of Reims (817–35), with the support of pope Paschal I.[87] This expedition has been dated to around 823, and may have led to the conversion and baptism of the Danish king Harald Klak at Ingelheim in 826. However, after Harald's expulsion from Denmark in the following year no other Danish ruler repeated this experiment until king Harald Bluetooth (*c.* 940–*c.* 985) was converted around the year 965. On the other hand, this did not prevent some Danish kings from occasionally allowing Christian Frankish missionaries to operate within their territories or to pass through on the way to Sweden.

The Swedish kingdom was to be a further target for the next major Frankish evangelising ventures, those conducted by the monk Anskar, who re-established the episcopal see at Hamburg, first founded in the time of Charlemagne, and worked for some years among the Danes. An account of his career has been preserved in a *Vita Anskari* written by his disciple, Rimbert (d. 865).[88] The first mission to the Swedes is dated to 829/30 and this was followed by another in 845. The trading settlement of Birka on Lake Måleren, close to modern Stockholm, was the intended centre for the missions, but they proved short-lived and abortive. Both of them correspond in time with short periods of temporary stability in Frankish–Danish relations, and the Danish ruler Horic I is said to have specifically supported the re-establishment of the mission to the Swedes in 845. However, internal upheavals within Denmark and periods of Carolingian weakness undermined both ventures, and in 845 the mission centre of Hamburg was sacked. The archdiocese of Hamburg may briefly have resumed its interest in Sweden *c.* 936, but it was not before the reign of Olof Skötkonung (*c.* 995–1021/2) that a Swedish king was definitely converted.[89]

In both Norway and Sweden, conversion is associated with the appearance of more powerful and geographically more extensive monarchies in the second half of the tenth century. As previously mentioned, the emergence of a dominant kingdom, absorbing other smaller ones, is dated in Norway to the time of Harald Hárfagri (d. 936?). His great-grandson, Olaf Tryggvason (995–1000), was the first of this line of monarchs to accept Christianity, and to try to impose it in his kingdom. His actions may also have influenced the decision of the free Norwegian settlers of Iceland to accept the new religion in the year 1000. The process was resumed more forcefully in Norway itself by his eventual successor, (St) Olaf II (1016–30). While Norwegian tradition emphasises the role of these two monarchs, an earlier ruler, Håkon (d. 960), son of Harald Hárfagri, who had been educated in the court of Athelstan of Wessex (924–39), is reported to have favoured Christianity, but not finally accepting baptism. Another direction from which Christian influence made itself felt on Norway was from Denmark, after the conversion of Harald Bluetooth. In 970–5, as also from 1030 to 1035, the Norwegian kingdom became an (unwilling) dependency of the Danish realm.[90]

In turn, the Danish monarchy, which had rather vanished into a historiographical mist in the second half of the ninth century, was only beginning to reassert itself over all of Jutland in the time of Harald Bluetooth's father, Gorm the Old (d. c. 936). Thus in the cases of Denmark, Sweden and Norway, the final acceptance of Christianity by the ruling dynasty, and within a relatively short time the imposition of it on the kingdoms, was directly related to the emergence or revival of strong unitary kingship. Such monarchies were much more susceptible to outside political and cultural influences, such as those exerted by the Ottonian kingdom/empire in Germany, and the kingdom of Wessex, which was making itself master of most of the Scandinavian settlements in England in the period 917–54.

The conversion of their Scandinavian homeland in fact lagged considerably behind the growth of the acceptance of Christianity on the part of the Vikings settled in Western Europe. In the case of the settlements in West Francia, it has been seen how such conversions were related directly to military defeats at the hands of the Frankish monarchs or their deputies, and how these were followed by the baptism of the Viking leaders. Thus the military triumph of Christ made acceptance of the religion of the conquerors tolerable, though it is unlikely that the converts understood the exclusivity of the Christian message.

In England, the situation was rather different, in that, apart from the agreement between Alfred and Guthrum in 878, baptism was generally not the product of Viking military defeat. Indeed, the success of the invaders in taking over the long-established Anglo-Saxon kingdoms in the north and the east might have been expected to confirm them in their traditional beliefs. Even so, in both England and Ireland the conversion of the Vikings proceeded rapidly, and was achieved long before a similar process got under way in Scandinavia. This may be seen as an example of the attraction exercised on an alien conquering elite, of the more sophisticated culture of their larger subject population.

In particular, it is quite clear that the Vikings in England, as in Ireland, rapidly became involved in the dynastic politics and traditional conflicts of these societies. Thus, for example, the alliance of the Vikings of Northumbria and East Anglia against Edward the Elder of Wessex (899–925) in 903–4 involved not only the fugitive West Saxon pretender Æthelwold, but also a certain 'Beorhtsige, son of prince Beorhtnoth'. The similarity of name, together with the title, would suggest that this was a representative of the Mercian royal line of Beornwulf (823–5) and Beorhtwulf (841–52), themselves possibly related to the Mercian appointee to the throne of Wessex, king Beorhtric (786–802).[91] Much of the warfare in England in the first half of the tenth century makes more sense in terms of such traditional antagonisms and feuds than in terms of a conflict between Anglo-Saxons and Scandinavians or between Christians and pagans.

In the wars that led to the eventual conquest of Northumbria by Wessex in 954, religion played no part. The army of the West Saxon king Eadred (946–54) sacked and burnt the Northumbrian monastery of Ripon that had been founded by Wilfred, and the see of York was kept so impoverished after the conquest that it was frequently linked to that of Worcester to provide revenue for its incumbent.[92] This manoeuvre also tied the primatial see of the north firmly to West Mercia. The north and the east remained conquered and subordinate territories, never visited by the southern kings.

The growth of Christianity among the Vikings, either by assimilation from the broader cultural context in which the new settlers in Western Europe had established themselves or through imposition by the new Scandinavian monarchies of the second half of the tenth century, inevitably affected other regions into which they had been moving from the ninth century onwards. Such areas were of two kinds: north-western lands in which the Vikings found themselves effectively the first settlers, and territories to the south-east of Scandinavia on which they preyed as slave raiders or in which they arrived to found trading stations and other settlements. Into the first category fall the Faroe Islands, Iceland (except for the possible presence of a handful of Irish monks and hermits) and Greenland; and into the second come the Slav lands south of the Baltic and the overland routes via Lake Ladoga and the Volga to the Black Sea.

In the eastern expansion it was, not surprisingly, the Swedes who played the leading part. Slave raids on the Slav territories served as an additional source for the human commodity so avidly sought by the Arab societies of the Mediterranean from the early ninth century onwards. Some of the captives were traded either by sea or overland westwards, but as the Scandinavians began exploring the routes southwards, down the great Russian river systems, so in due course they came in contact with the Muslim powers of the near East, and with the longer established trading routes from Constantinople into the steppes of south Russia. In typical fashion, such commercial possibilities combined perfectly with obtaining profit by violence. The Vikings first became known to the inhabitants of the truncated Eastern Roman or Byzantine empire in the late 830s.[93] However, after they had displaced the Khazars in control of Kiev in the middle of the century, the scale of their contacts with Byzantium grew, and in 860 they tried to make a surprise raid on Constantinople.[94] Another and larger-scale attack was made in 907 by one of the first Viking 'princes' of Kiev, Oleg (c. 882–c.912/13).

This is a controversial topic in some quarters. The brief Byzantine chronicle references to the activities of people who were known as the *Rhos* do not confirm that they were Vikings, who at this period seem to have been founding trading stations on the middle Volga, notably on the site of the later city of Kiev. As the society of the south Russian steppes was still preliterate, no indigenous texts exist from this period to provide information. Not surprisingly, therefore, Russian historians have denied the association, preferring to see the *Rhos* as a predominantly or exclusively Slavic people. Inasmuch as in England and Ireland the existence of mixed marriages and a measure of cultural assimilation between invaders and subject populations is well established, there is no reason to doubt that the same processes occurred in the Viking settlements on the Volga, where a militarily dominant Scandinavian elite ruled over a more numerous Slavonic subject population. In this, they were replacing the latter's previous rulers, the Khazars.[95]

The growth of such commercial contacts, together with recruitment by the empire of mercenary soldiers from this south Russian society, inevitably opened it up to increasing Byzantine cultural influence, which had already been making itself felt there since the time of the Khazar domination and earlier.[96] Some form of Christian organisation existed on the Volga by the later 860s, and in 874 an archbishop was sent from Constantinople.[97] The first member of the ruling family of the Viking–Slavic Kievan state to be baptised was the regent Olga, who accepted Christianity, probably for political reasons, during a visit to Constantinople in 957. A definitive conversion of the dynasty, and with it the imposition of Christianity on the kingdom, did not follow until 986 in the reign of her grandson, Vladimir (*c.* 980–*c.* 1015).[98]

This was the period in which the principal ruling dynasties of Scandinavia also converted, and began to force their subjects to follow suit. It is not clear how far such developments around the Baltic were known to have affected attitudes in the increasingly Slavicised principality of Kiev, though it is reported in 959 that Olga (under her baptised name of Helena) made contact with the East Frankish ruler Otto I, and requested him to send a missionary bishop and priests.[99]

Otto was at this time exerting diplomatic pressure on Denmark, whose king Harald Bluetooth converted soon afterwards (*c.* 965), under the influence of the German priest Poppo.[100] Thus, by around the year 1000, all the major areas of Scandinavian settlement, from Iceland to Kiev, had at least formally accepted Christianity. This was a symbol of the degree to which these peoples had come to see the value of integration into a cultural tradition that extended back to the Mediterranean world of the fourth century.

20 The western frontiers of Christendom: Spain, 711–1037

The Christians of al-Andalus

The Arab and Berber conquest of the Iberian Peninsula that began in 711, was rapid. By 714, the conquerors were in the Ebro valley, sacking Zaragoza, its principal city, and in 720 they crossed the Pyrenees and destroyed a vestigial Gothic kingdom centred on Narbonne. The lack of any sustained resistance before their first attacks on Aquitaine, in 721, was a reflection of the previously peaceful and also relatively centralised nature of the Spanish Visigothic kingdom, which had not had to face the external threats in the seventh century that had existed in the sixth. With few opportunities for territorial expansion, and only a limited land frontier across the Pyrenees, and no apparent danger to be expected from the south, its society, unlike that of Francia, did not need to be one that was primarily organised for war.

In these circumstances, some of the kings had had difficulty in mobilising forces even for small-scale campaigning, primarily in response to Basque raids and during disputed royal successions.[1] There were thus only limited or slowly mobilised military resources to call on against invaders. At the same time, the special status of the *urbs regia* of Toledo, the only site in which the rituals of royal inauguration could be carried out for a king to be considered legitimate, made the rapid fall of the city to the invaders a fatal blow to any hope of centralised opposition.[2]

The Arab accounts of the conquest come from sources of much later date, and while some of these make use of the work of earlier writers, whose accounts might otherwise have been lost, none of the these date from earlier than the later ninth century. Nor, from what is known of the general development of historiography among the Arabs, should we be surprised that this is the case.[3] There are real problems, some barely recognised as yet, in the transmission of some of these works, and interpolation and distortion of some of the contents have been found in a number of them, including several of the earliest.[4] While accounts of the later tenth and eleventh centuries are generally far more reliable, this still leaves us seriously deficient in information on the eighth and ninth centuries in Spain.

There is one contemporary Latin account that covers some of the history of the peninsula in the first half of the eighth century. This is the text known as the *Mozarabic Chronicle* or *Chronicle of 754*, which was probably composed in Toledo by an anonymous cleric some time soon after the year 754, which is the date of the last event that the work records. From this text it has been possible to deduce something of the events of the four decades following the conquest.[5]

The rule of the governors that lasted until the Umayyad *coup d'état* in 756 that established an independent Arab monarchy in al-Andalus, falls into distinct periods. The earliest of these, covering the years 711 to 721, saw almost continuous fighting in different parts of the peninsula, as the conquest was extended up to and then across the Pyrenees. At this time, Berber garrisons were established in a small number of major towns in Spain, but most areas were allowed to retain a high degree of autonomy under local leadership in return for political submission and the payment of a regular tribute. The latter was probably fixed by the terms of a treaty of capitulation made between the conquerors and local officials.[6] The texts of some of these treaties, including one from Spain, have been preserved in later works, but doubt has been cast on how reliable a guide these are to the actual agreements made in the first century of Islamic expansion.

Within ten years of the invasion, governors, who were appointed either directly by the Umayyad caliphs in Damascus or, under his authority, by the *wali* or governor of North Africa (*Ifriqiya*) to whom they were subordinate, had begun to establish new administrative and judicial processes in Spain, or *al-Andalus*, as it was called. The origin of the name remains uncertain. In 731/2 the first Berber revolt broke out, among garrisons in the eastern Pyrenees, fuelled by accounts of conflicts that were intensifying in North Africa. The outbreak of a major revolt among the Berbers in Africa in 739/40 led to a parallel rising in Spain, which was crushed after some hard fighting, thanks to the arrival of a relief force sent from Syria. This consisted of a detachment of an army sent to North Africa by the caliph against the Berbers. The main body had been defeated, which meant that this detached force, sent to the Tangiers peninsula, had been unable to return home via Tunisia. So, its leaders had arranged to bring their troops across the straits into al-Andalus to help crush the Berber revolt there. Once this had been achieved, however, the Syrians refused to leave, and friction developed between them and the longer-established Arabs. This was exacerbated by news of factional conflicts – articulated through tribal rivalries – in the Near East in the mid-740s.[7] These contributed directly to the 'Abbasid revolt of 749, which led the following year to the overthrow of the Umayyad caliphate.[8]

In Spain, family ties between the first generation of Arab settlers and their counterparts in North Africa, together with a virtual breakdown in communications with Egypt and Syria because of the civil wars that had broken out there, led to the creation of a de facto independent government in 746. This lasted until it was overthrown ten years later by a combination of opposition groups who rallied together around the person of 'Abd al-Rahman ibn Mu'awiya, a fugitive member of the former Umayyad dynasty, who had escaped the massacre of his family in Syria in 750. Though able to overthrow the last of the independent governors and make himself amir or king in Córdoba, it took him over twenty years to extend his authority over all the regions of the peninsula that were still under Arab and Berber occupation.[9]

The hold of the Umayyad rulers over al-Andalus fluctuated greatly during the next two centuries. In some periods it shrank to little more than control over the Guadalquivir valley and its principal cities of Córdoba and Seville. The former remained the capital, and enjoyed the patronage of the amirs, who built numerous palaces and mosques in or close to the city. The most famous of these is the mosque known as the Mezquita, now the cathedral of Córdoba, whose gradual enlargement in stages extending from its foundation by 'Abd al-Rahman in 786 up to the dictatorship of the *hajib* or grand vizier Al-Mansur (d. 1002) testifies to the growth of the Muslim population of the city.

The questions of to what extent and how quickly the Romano-Gothic population converted to Islam are not easy to answer, in that there is little hard evidence available. One useful and influential attempt to solve these problems was based on a study of the changing patterns of names in the families of those Muslims of non-Arab descent who were included in the great medieval biographical encyclopaedias. In most cases, the names of several generations of ancestors are included, and so by noting the point in such genealogies at which the names first became distinctively Muslim, it is possible to deduce approximately when conversion occurred in each family line. From the various cases thus detected, the author, Richard Bulliett, was then able to prepare graphs relating numbers of conversions to dates, thus giving an indication of the peak periods of religious change in the major regions of the Islamic world. Not surprisingly, as this is what our literary texts would lead us to expect, in al-Andalus the sharpest rise in conversion is located in the later tenth and the eleventh centuries.[10] However, this can only be used as a means of measuring the rate of conversion for those families that actually changed their religion. It is quite incapable of showing what percentage of the total non-Arab population of al-Andalus converted at this or any other time. So, even if there was a steep rise in conversions in the tenth and eleventh centuries, there could still have been a Christian majority among the population as a whole.

Indeed, when the Arab traveller and geographical writer, Ibn Hawqal, visited al-Andalus in 948, he reported that the population of the countryside was still predominantly Christian.[11] There is no evidence to contradict his claim, which is in any case perfectly credible and reasonable. The greatest pressure or incentive to convert was likely to be felt in the towns, above all in Córdoba, the permanent residence of the court. This was especially true of the educated classes, members of which could earn their living in Umayyad government service. It is clear from the accounts of the Arab historians that educated Christians did reach the upper levels of the bureaucracy, as well as serving in specialised but highly prestigious posts such as those of the ruler's doctor.[12] On the other hand, in certain periods, especially when there were too many non-Muslims in government service or some of them became overly influential, the *ulama*, the Islamic jurists and religious teachers, could put pressure on the amirs either not to take so many Christians and Jews into their service or to require them to convert in order to retain their jobs, which indeed some did.

This was particularly true in the reign of Muhammad I (852–86), in the aftermath of the 'Martyr Movement'. This had been a short-lived period of confrontation in the 840s and 850s, confined almost entirely to Córdoba, in which a group of Christians had deliberately sought judicial execution by publicly reviling the prophet Muhammad and Islam. They tried to emulate the sufferings of the early Christian martyrs, and the accounts of their deaths were written up in conscious imitation of the late Roman martyr acts. Among the leaders of this movement were the priest (and later titular bishop of Toledo) Eulogius and the layman Paul Alvar. They were responsible for composing most of the descriptions of the martyrdoms, and Alvar wrote a *Life of Eulogius* after his friend's execution in 859.[13]

The causes of this outbreak of religious conflict are varied, but may reflect conditions that were peculiar to Córdoba.[14] Among these were the pressures within families of mixed religion. While under Islamic law it was forbidden for a Christian to take a Muslim wife, the opposite was tolerated, but the children of such a union had to be brought up as Muslims. As several of the martyr acts reveal, in such cases the children of a Christian mother could, as a result of closer contact with her than with their father, prefer her faith to his, but were forbidden from expressing this openly. Among the others who publicly defied Islam in this period were members of the still numerous monastic communities that existed in and around Córdoba, not least in the mountainous region immediately to the north of the city.

Such monasteries were also the principal repositories of Christian Latin culture in Al-Andalus. A remark in one of the works of Alvar in which he criticises the way in which the Christian community of Córdoba had become Arabised in language and literary taste has often been interpreted as indicating a marked decline in the use of Latin.[15] This in turn might imply loss of access to the Christian Latin literary heritage of late antiquity. The Martyr Movement and a less confrontational attempt by Eulogius to foster a Latin poetic revival in Córdoba in the early 850s have been seen as reactions to this threat to the survival of Christian Latin culture in southern Spain.[16]

This interpretation underestimates the extent to which Latin remained in use in Christian circles long after the period of the Martyr Movement. Beautifully inscribed and linguistically complex Latin funerary inscriptions continued to be carved in many parts of al-Andalus even as late as the first quarter of the twelfth century – with only the very latest ones being bilingual in Latin and Arabic. Latin manuscripts continued to be copied, and even a handful of new works were composed in the language in the same period.[17] There is increasing evidence of bilingualism, but Latin remained central to Christian culture and identity in the south, up to the time of the deportation of the surviving Christian communities to Morocco by the Almoravids in 1126.[18] This is hardly surprising, as Christian communities in the area of modern Tunisia were still in existence and were using Latin in communication with the papacy at least up to the pontificate of pope Gregory VII (1073–85).[19]

By this time, however, a major movement of population had already taken place in Spain. As the result of inter-communal tension and the reprisals following the end of the Martyr Movement, involving the destruction of several of the monasteries in the hills above Córdoba, a migration of Christians began. Whole monastic communities moved to the Christian realms in the north of the Iberian peninsula. It is impossible to quantify this movement, which is best documented by the spread of the distinctive style of building and of manuscript illumination, much influenced by contemporary developments in Islamic art, that the refugees took with them. This can be seen in a series of churches and chapels they built in the tenth and eleventh centuries in an area extending from Galicia to the eastern Pyrenees, as well as in a small but significant body of manuscripts.[20]

These Christian refugees are generally known as the Mozarabs (and their art and architecture as Mozarabic), a name taken from an Arabic word for non-Arab Muslims who had absorbed the culture of their conquerors. It is thus not technically correct to apply it to the southern Christians who had absorbed much Arab culture but had not changed their religion, but it has become accepted usage.[21]

It is by no means clear if those Mozarabs who migrated north were predominantly clerics and monks, or whether the unsettled conditions in the south, which were marked by increasing inter-communal conflict, also prompted significant numbers of the urban and rural Christian laity to flee northwards as well. Of those that remained, the descendants of some would later come under the rule of Christian kings as the Castillian and Aragonese kingdoms extended themselves into the middle and south of the peninsula from the mid-eleventh century onwards.

Those in the Guadalquivir valley and related areas were deported *en masse* to Morocco by the Almoravids in 1126. This was an event that put an end to the continuity both of Christian traditions in southern Spain and to the occupation of a wide range of settlement sites all across the region. The Mozarabs who had fled north in the earlier period had by the twelfth century begun to lose their distinctive identity and were being absorbed into the societies that had formed on the frontiers between al-Andalus and the Christian realms.

The kingdoms of northern Spain, *c.* 718–910

It is clear from the course of events in the first half of the eighth century that the Muslims were not much concerned with the north-west of the peninsula. Their initial route of conquest was from the south-west to the north-east. They took advantage of clearly defined lines of communication created by the mountainous geography of Spain that had previously been used by the Romans in creating their extensive system of roads. The Roman road that linked Seville to Mérida, Salamanca, León and the Asturias may also have been used earlier to impose a rapid subjection of the north-west, but this region was a dead-end, providing no opportunities for further expansion. Although once famed for its gold mines, the area now offered relatively few economic inducements to the conquerors to make them invest their relatively limited resources of manpower in retaining control of it.

With the advantage of hindsight it may be said that the Arabs' lack of concern to secure this region was the fatal mistake that nearly eight hundred years later would lead to the complete elimination of a Muslim presence in the peninsula. This is not to endorse older views of the *Reconquista* that saw it as a sustained Hispano-Christian resistance to an alien Islamic rule, that was initiated in the Asturias, developed in León and brought to triumphant conclusion by the rulers and people of Castille, who thereby earned a right to political and cultural hegemony over the whole peninsula.[22] Even so, the failure of the Arab conquerors to retain their hold over the whole of the former Visigothic kingdom created centres of opposition that began to exploit periods of weakness and division among the rulers of the south, with ultimately fatal consequences.

The first of these Christian states to come into existence was a small kingdom based in the west of the Asturias, the mountainous region in the centre of the northern coast of the peninsula. The history of its creation became the stuff of legend in subsequent centuries, and no extant sources for these events date from before the late ninth century. These take the form of very brief chronicles composed in the 880s, which were subject to revision and expansion in the next century.[23] The earliest of these is the *Chronicle of Albelda,* which, from references in the text, seems to have been written in or very soon after the year 883. Though this was not where the original version was compiled, the work received its name from the Riojan monastery in which a brief continuation of it was added in 976.

A second, slightly more substantial chronicle was composed in the Asturias, probably not long after the first version of the *Chronicle of Albelda* in 883. This is the work called the *Chronicle of Alfonso III.* It survives in two rather different forms, generally known as the *ad Sebastianum* and the Roda versions. The former probably achieved its present shape in the reign of Alfonso's son, García I (910–13/14), but there is no early manuscript tradition for it. In this *ad Sebastianum* version, the text is prefaced by a letter from Alfonso III (866–910) to a bishop Sebastian, which, if authentic, establishes the king's authorship of it. The other version, which is preserved in more numerous and earlier manuscripts than its rival, takes its name from the oldest of them, which once belonged to the cathedral of the Pyrenean see of Roda de Isábena. This is probably the closer of the two versions to the lost original form of the chronicle.[24]

By the time these chronicles were being composed in the Asturias in the 880s, the crucial victory that secured the kingdom's independence from Arab rule had become firmly associated with a miraculous intervention. This would receive further elaboration in twelfth-century and later texts. Even the two versions of the *Chronicle of Alfonso III* contain lengthy passages of dialogue between the Christian leader and a treacherous bishop, Oppa, who was in collusion with the Arabs, that are quite out of keeping with the extreme brevity and markedly un-literary character of the rest of the work.[25] So it is not easy to uncover the true sequence of events in the revolt in the Asturias.

According to tradition, this uprising was led by a certain Pelagius, a Gothic noble who had taken refuge in the north and who, according to the *ad Sebastianum* version of the *Chronicle of Alfonso III*, was of royal descent. What prompted his revolt is not clear. The Albelda chronicler sees his objective as restoring freedom to the Christians of the Asturias, while the Roda version of the Alfonso III chronicle spins a tale involving the lecherous designs by a governor of Gijón called Munnuzza on Pelagius's sister.[26] However, all the chronicles agree in reporting Pelagius's victory over Munnuzza, who from his name must have been a Berber. The location of the battle at Covadonga, later the site of a major Marian shrine, is stated explicitly in both versions of the *Chronicle of Alfonso III*.

Just how seriously the Arabs took this uprising is hard to gauge, as no mention is made of it in their records of this period. A Berber garrison at Gijón on the Biscay coast was isolated and distant, and of no real military significance. It is not even easy to date the revolt, and the traditional chronology, which would place it in the year 718, derives entirely from deductions made from later Asturian regnal lists. An alternative case has been made out for the year 722, but no certainty can be attached to either date.[27]

Largely because no response was made to the revolt, probably because the Muslims were involved in campaigns in the Pyrenean region, Pelagius created a small kingdom in the Asturias in the aftermath of his victory. His first capital was at Cangas de Onis, but hardly anything else is recorded of his reign before his death in 737. After his son Fafila (737–39) was killed by a bear, the Asturian nobles chose Pelagius's son-in-law Alfonso I (739–57) as king. Nothing more is known about the origins, number or wealth of the Asturian aristocracy in this period.[28]

The accession of the new king resulted in the expansion of the still diminutive Asturian kingdom. Alfonso's father, Peter, is described as being duke of Cantabria, the region to the east of the Asturias. Whether this title was a vestige of the Visigothic administrative system or refers to an independent territorial authority is unknown, but the uniting of the Asturias and Cantabria strengthened the fledgling kingdom.

Under Alfonso I and his son Fruela I 'the Cruel' (757–68), the frontiers of the Asturian monarchy were also extended westwards into Galicia and eastwards into the Basque regions between the upper Ebro and the Biscay coast. In neither case did this involve a liberation from Islamic rule.[29] The Basques, other than those living in a few towns of Roman origin in the western Pyrenees, had not been conquered, and Berber garrisons in Galicia had already been withdrawn, probably as a result of the Berber revolts in North Africa, southern Spain and the eastern Pyrenees.

During the period of turmoil in the south in the 730s and 740s, Alfonso I of the Asturias is said to have captured many of the towns of the Meseta, the high plateau that fills most of the inland area of the north-western quarter of the Iberian peninsula.[30] This was bounded to the south by the mountains of the Sierra de Guadarrama, beyond which lay Toledo, Talavera and Mérida, which housed significant Berber garrisons. Several formerly important Roman towns were situated on the Meseta itself, such as León and Astorga in the north and Avila, Segovia and Salamanca towards its southern edge.

According to the Asturian historiographical tradition of the late ninth century, Alfonso, and Fruela after him, were able to capture and depopulate virtually all the major settlements of the Meseta. The towns themselves were abandoned and their inhabitants taken back into the Asturias to help repopulate the kingdom, leaving their old territory as a deserted *cordon sanitaire* between the Christian north and Muslim south. This area would only be reoccupied from the late ninth century onwards, as the frontiers of the Asturian kingdom were finally pushed southwards. The difficulty with this once widely accepted view of events is that it does not make sense, and the evidence for it looks as if it may have been conditioned by the particular circumstances of a later period.

Other interpretations cast doubt on the reality of the mid-eighth-century depopulation of the Meseta, and no proof has been found of a significant repopulation of the Asturias.[31] The impression given by the chronicles that the region had been conquered by the Asturian monarchy in the mid-eighth century served the interests of Alfonso I's late-ninth and early-tenth-century successors, at a time when they were establishing control over much of it and redistributing it to favoured families and religious institutions. In other words, this tale of conquest and depopulation established the legal right of the later kings to impose their authority over these lands and dispose of them as they saw fit.

It is likely that Asturian campaigns in the time of Alfonso I and Fruela I were less wide-ranging, less frequent and probably less successful than the later chroniclers claimed, particularly as far as the southern sections of the Meseta were concerned. Here, the best archaeological evidence for continuity of occupation during this supposed period of depopulation has been found in settlements such as Avila and Segovia.[32]

The end of the reign of Alfonso I also saw major changes taking place in Al-Andalus. In 756, the Umayyad refugee'Abd al-Rahman crossed from Africa and overthrew the regime of Yusuf al-Fikri. However, it took him nearly twenty years to establish control over the centre of the peninsula and to begin extending it into the Ebro valley, while still ignoring the northwest. This continuing lack military response allowed the Asturian kingdom to develop territorially and institutionally in relative tranquillity throughout most of the century. It did, however, suffer from internal conflicts, which are all too briefly recorded in the chronicles. Fruela I earned his nickname 'the Cruel' by murdering his brother, Vimara, for reasons that were never explained. This led to his own assassination in 768, and the passing over of his infant son in favour of another adult member of the dynasty, the late king's nephew, Aurelius (768–73), in whose reign a servile revolt was suppressed.[33]

A series of short reigns followed that of Aurelius, with Fruela's son Alfonso still being denied the succession, probably because of his age. The most notable feature of this period, lasting into the late 780s, was the transfer of the capital from Cangas to Santianes de Pravía in the reign of Silo (774–83). The same king issued the first extant Asturian royal charter, giving property to a newly founded monastery.[34] This is also one of the earliest of any of the Spanish documentary records of the post-Visigothic period. Such texts start to become more numerous in the second half of the ninth century, but many present problems of authenticity. Of the eighty charters of all kinds purporting to date from before the reign of Alfonso III (866–910), a high percentage are either forgeries from later periods or may have been interpolated.[35]

On the death of Silo, his widow Adosinda had hoped to secure the long-delayed succession of the young Alfonso, but she was thwarted by a noble faction that gave the throne instead to an illegitimate son of Alfonso I called Mauregatus. On his death in 788, the same or a similar group installed yet another member of the family, Vermudo, later to be known as 'the Monk'.

The death, in 788, of the Umayyad amir 'Abd al-Rahman I opened the way to Alfonso finally gaining the Asturian throne. A succession crisis developed in al-Andalus, with some of 'Abd al-Rahman's brothers challenging the designated successor, his son Hisham I (788–96). When the latter had finally secured his position after two years of civil war, he launched the first of series of annual expeditions against the Christian states in the north – both the Asturian kingdom and the Frankish enclave around Gerona on the eastern fringes of the Pyrenees.[36]

These do not seem to have been systematic campaigns of conquest, unlike those of the earlier eighth century. Instead they were intended to inflict damage, take captives and carry off loot from the Christian territories. One of the first of these great raids achieved all three objectives when it penetrated the Asturias in 791. Vermudo I tried to resist and was heavily defeated. In the aftermath, he abdicated, or may even have been compelled so to do, and the throne was given instead to Alfonso II (791–842).

The latter's long reign is often seen as marking a fundamental change in the Asturian kingdom, symbolised by the move to yet another new capital, Oviedo. Here, Alfonso is said to have commanded that 'the whole order of the Goths, as it had been in Toledo' should be established 'as much in the church as in the palace'.[37] This statement concludes the Albelda chronicler's description of the churches of San Salvador, Santa María and San Tirso which Alfonso II built in Oviedo, and it could just be a reference to artistic style. In other words, the king had his new buildings decorated in the ways that had been fashionable in Visigothic Toledo.

On the other hand, it has often been argued that the phrases referring to 'the order of the Goths' are not about Alfonso's artistic taste but are a statement of constitutional principles.[38] In other words, what the chronicler was trying to say was that Alfonso II imposed not just the aesthetics of Visigothic Toledo on his new capital, but also its character, traditions and ethos. Thus, what may be said about the Visigothic kingdom in terms of its law, the structure of government, the organisation of palatine administration, and the nature and functioning of ecclesiastical institutions, might also be taken to be true of the Asturian kingdom from the time of Alfonso II onwards.

This would seem also to imply that such Visigothic institutions and procedures had not previously existed in the Asturias under Alfonso's predecessors. This important change, it has been argued, must mark the influence of exiles and fugitives from the south, bringing with them the ideas and practices of the Visigothic past. By this once authoritative line of reasoning, the Asturians were assumed to have resisted cultural absorption in the preceding Roman and Visigothic periods and to have retained exclusively indigenous social and political traditions of their own. Thus not until the time of Alfonso II, and thanks to southern incomers, was the Visigothic imprint finally imposed on these independent northerners.[39]

In fact, no corroborative evidence exists to support the idea that Alfonso II's reign saw any change, let alone marked a watershed, in the political or administrative organisation of the Asturian kingdom. The greater probability must lie with the view outlined above, that what the chronicler was referring to in speaking of the *Ordo Gothorum* was metropolitan artistic taste rather than administrative and legal reform.

New cultural currents may indeed have been making themselves felt in the Asturias at this time, but they came from the north rather than from the south. In 797, Alfonso II is known to have made diplomatic contact with Charlemagne, sending the Frankish ruler some spoils from a successful raid on Lisbon.[40]

While Frankish cultural influences continued to be felt, the diplomatic links were short-lived. When Charles established a significant Frankish presence in the eastern Pyrenees with the conquest of Barcelona in 801, there is no reference at this time to exchanges of envoys with Oviedo or any coordination of military activity, as had occurred in 797. This may be because Alfonso was driven briefly from his throne in a coup at some point that can not be precisely dated, but was certainly around 801. Alfonso took refuge with Basque relatives of his mother, but was soon recalled to Oviedo when an aristocratic faction loyal to him murdered the unnamed usurper and seized the palace.[41]

The latter part of the long reign of Alfonso II has left little record of itself, even in the Asturian chronicles, but at this time another, much smaller, Christian state came into being in the north of Spain. This was the kingdom of Pamplona, or of Navarre as it later became known. Like that of the Asturias, this kingdom emerged in consequence of a revolt. In this case, though, it was directed against the Franks rather than the Arabs.

Left defenceless by Charlemagne on his retreat from the Ebro valley in 778, Pamplona had soon reverted to Arab control, but was captured again by the king Louis of Aquitaine in 806.

Following earlier unsuccessful risings, a local rebellion in 824 put an end to Frankish rule. This was confirmed by the second battle of Roncesvalles later that year, when a Frankish punitive expedition was defeated, and the two counts who led it were captured. The independent kingdom of Pamplona that emerged was ruled by a local Basque dynasty, founded by Iñigo Arista, until it was replaced by another ruling family in 905.[42] Relatively little is known of the history of the kingdom in the ninth century, as it produced no chronicles or annals.

The same is equally true as far as tenth-century Navarrese history is concerned, but occasional mentions in Arab sources and in the records of the neighbouring Leonese kingdom, successor to that of the Asturias, provide us with some illumination. It is clear that, in both the ninth and the tenth centuries, the rulers of Pamplona were willing to enter into close relations with the Muslims, particularly the often autonomous local rulers of the upper Ebro valley.[43] Iñigo Arista made a marriage alliance with the most powerful of these, the Banu Qasi, and the two dynasties supported each other, both against the Umayyads and against the Christian Franks and Asturians.[44] In particular, the Asturian kings were trying to expand eastwards into the Basque-speaking regions of the upper Ebro, with which at least one of their kings, Alfonso II, had family ties.

Alfonso II of the Asturias has long been known in the Spanish historiographical tradition as 'Alfonso the Chaste', because he never married or produced children. This is mentioned with approval by the later-ninth-century Asturian chroniclers, but it was never used to suggest that he was particularly pious, let alone a saint. It is impossible to know what his personal motives might have been, but it has been suggested that, as in the case of the sons of Edward the Elder who succeeded each other on the throne of Wessex in the first half of the tenth century, Alfonso secured the throne in 791 in return for an agreement not to produce heirs of his own.[45] It is also possible, though the sources give no hint of this, that he had been forced into clerical orders at some point during the long period in which he was prevented from succeeding his father. Vermudo I was said to have been a deacon or a monk prior to his accession in 788, and his supposed desire to return to the clerical state was used as the justification for his abdication in 791.

It is notable that, on Alfonso's death in 842, it was a son of Vermudo I by the name of Ramiro who thought that he had a prescriptive right to succeed. He was, however, absent from Oviedo at the time, embarking on a second marriage on his estates in Galicia, and the throne was taken by a nephew of

Alfonso II, Nepotian.[46] He may indeed have been his uncle's preferred heir, but the greater weight of noble support lay behind Ramiro, who rapidly defeated and blinded his rival.

Already elderly, Ramiro I (842–50) enjoyed only a short reign, but his success ensured the possession of the throne by his branch of the royal house for nearly two centuries. He built a palace complex on the slopes of Monte Naranco, immediately to the north of Oviedo. Some of this can still be seen, in the form of a barrel-vaulted hall (later converted into the church of Santa María de Naranco) and the western end of the palace chapel (now known as San Miguel de Lillo).[47] He was also called a 'rod of justice' by the Albelda chronicler for the penalties he imposed on wrongdoers, including the blinding of thieves and the burning of magicians. If this implies that he produced new laws, no trace of these has survived. The Visigothic code, known as the *Forum Iudicum*, continued to be enforced, and despite several manuscripts of it having survived that date from the ninth and tenth centuries, none contains any new enactments by the Asturian and Leonese kings.

Ramiro faced an attempted usurpation in the course of his reign, but his son, Ordoño I (850–66), succeeded without opposition. In Ordoño's reign, the Asturian kingdom, which had hitherto expanded almost exclusively westwards and eastwards into Galicia and the Basque regions, took its first tentative steps towards the occupation of the northern fringes of the Meseta. This meant the re-establishment of settlements, such as the old Roman legionary fortresses of León and Astorga, which were located in much more militarily exposed sites to the south of the Asturian and Cantabrian mountains. Raids were also made across the Meseta and through the passes of the Guadarrama.

Such an expansion in the territorial extent and power of the Asturian kingdom was facilitated by the increasingly disturbed condition of Al-Andalus. Under Muhammad I (852–86), al-Mundhir (886–8) and 'Abdallah (888–912), the authority of the amirs of Córdoba declined rapidly in the face of revolts, banditry, and the establishment of local potentates across most parts of the south and centre of the peninsula.[48]

One of the earliest and most powerful of the regional rulers who emerged at this time was Musa ibn Musa, a member of the Banu Qasi, a family of indigenous origin that had converted to Islam, which had long dominated the upper Ebro valley. From initial deference to the Umayyads, in whose name he had originally governed Tudela, Musa moved to outright defiance and the building up of a territorial state in virtue of which he came to be described as 'the third king of Spain'.[49]

Lying on the south-eastern fringes of Ordoño's kingdom, Musa's realm was a closer and more powerful threat to the Asturias than the weakened amirate of Córdoba. This was represented not least by Musa's creation of a fortress at Albelda. In 859, Ordoño attacked and destroyed Albelda, and defeated Musa. The latter's death in 862 led to a temporary weakening of his dynasty's regional power.

Surprisingly little is known about the long reign of Ordoño's son and successor, Alfonso III (866–910). This is in part because the Asturian chronicles, first compiled in the 880s, only extend their accounts up to the death of Ordoño I, and were not continued for nearly a century and a half. By the time the next historical work was written in northern Spain, the reign of Alfonso III was a distant memory. Even the events with which it ended, when it seems that the elderly king was overthrown in a bloodless coup led by one or more of his own sons, are briefly and ambiguously described, and contradictory traditions exist as to his eventual fate.[50]

The kingdom of León and the county of Castille, 910–1037

For the history of the last phase of the Asturian kingdom and for its continuation after 910 in a new capital at León, the evidence of narrative sources becomes even less substantial than for the preceding period. After the composition of the various sets of Asturian chronicles in the 880s, there follows a gap of well over a century before another indigenous historian began to write a very short account of the period extending from the accession of Alfonso III in 866 up to the death of Vermudo II 'the Gouty' in 999. This author, Sampiro, has been identified with a bishop of Astorga of the same name, who held the see in the mid-eleventh century (*c.* 1034–*c.* 1042), as well as with a royal notary responsible for the drafting of a handful of extant charters.[51] The latter extend in time over the years 977–1018, and while not totally improbable, the chances that they were all the work of a single individual who twenty years later would become a bishop is stretching the bounds of probability. So, little if anything is known for certain about Sampiro.

His work, which takes the form of short accounts of the successive kings, has also not survived in its original form. It is only preserved in two later versions, which are different in length and in some of the information they contain. Both of these versions, written in the twelfth century, re-use Sampiro's narrative as part of more extensive histories.

The longer and apparently more informative of the two versions is that found in the history written by bishop Pelagius (or Pelayo) of Oviedo, who enjoys a well-deserved reputation as a forger and fabricator of documents. His intentions of furthering the power and wealth of his own diocese are not hard to detect, and in his use of the material of Sampiro's chronicle, his additions are easily recognised when his text is compared with that of the anonymous *Historia Silense* or 'Silos History'. This work, which was probably compiled in León rather than in the monastery of Silos, after which it is named, made more scrupulous use of Sampiro, though the lack of an independent version of his text means even the *Historia*'s treatment of it cannot be checked, and some degree of textual corruption or interpolation may have occured.[52]

If the narrative sources for the tenth century become briefer and more problematic, then at least the documentary evidence grows in abundance. This, however, has only limited value. Apart from one or two references to contemporary events and the chronological information of the regnal dates given in most of these charters, the significance of these texts lies more in what they can reveal of legal and economic practices and procedures in this period.[53]

The continuing weakness of the Umayyad regime in the south, which only began to recover its former strength in the 920s, contributed directly to the greater security of the Asturian kingdom. The more localised threat on the eastern fringes of the kingdom presented by the Banu Qasi in the upper Ebro valley was also eliminated with the death of the last member of this family in 907. By this time, the Asturian kings had been occupying and granting out lands in the Duero valley for several decades. New settlements, such as Zamora and Burgos (884) were founded.

With the deposition of Alfonso III in 910, a move from the traditional but distant capital of Oviedo to a new location in the northern Meseta became viable. Zamora may have served this function in the short reign of Alfonso's eldest son, García I (910–13/14). The latter's brother and successor, Ordoño II (914–24), who had previously been sub-king in Galicia, established himself in León, which afterwards remained the principal royal centre.[54]

Colonisation and settlement was taking place in three distinct but adjacent areas. In the west, the extension of the Asturian kingdom to the River Miño in Galicia took place more or less in a single phase in the mid-eighth century, and was followed by a more gradual expansion into the area between the Miño and the Atlantic coast. With that achieved, the local nobility turned their attention southwards to the area between the lower Miño and the Duero valley.[55] In the east, the area between the Cantabrian mountains and the upper Duero, which became known from its numerous small fortresses as Castille, had begun being settled in the last quarter of the ninth century. Here, a major contribution to the new population came from the Basque regions to the north east, as demonstrated by the presence of numerous Basque personal and place names in the extant charter collections from the region.[56]

While in Galicia (which now included the northernmost part of what would in the twelfth century become the kingdom of Portugal) a number of rival aristocratic families can be detected from the charters, one dominant house emerged in Castille.[57] This is not to say that there had been no conflict between noble factions competing for land and power, but these eventually resolved themselves in favour of the family of Fernán González (d. 970), who held the office of count of Castille for most of the middle years of the tenth century, and transmitted it as a hereditary possession to his descendants.[58]

Unfortunately, though his later heroic status in Castillian legend led to extravagant claims being made for Fernán González's origins, deeds and legacy, the actual evidence relating to his career is meagre, and it is not easy to see precisely how he and his family acquired their almost unchallenged control over this large and important frontier region.

That this was achieved initially with royal support is likely, but it is notable that the kings of León found it expedient to maintain Fernán González in office even when he had been personally disloyal to several of them. This can only indicate the degree to which he had made himself indispensable. This is reflected in the contemporary charters, which differ from those of Galicia and León not least in the way most significant legal and administrative powers appear to be exercised by the count, without reference to higher royal authority.[59] The kings are frequently not mentioned in dating clauses, which refer instead to the counts.

The central section of the frontier, between southern Galicia and Castille, was that of the Leonese kingdom proper. To the north of it, the former heartland of the Asturias seems to have gradually declined into political and economic obscurity, as its leading families were denied access to the opportunities offered on the frontiers. It could, however, still serve as a refuge for the kings in times of trouble.

As well as the infrequent larger-scale royal campaigns into Arab-ruled territory as far to the south as Mérida, Lisbon and

Coimbra, there was more frequent, virtually endemic smaller-scale raiding of Muslim territories being conducted by the frontier lords and their followers. Umayyad responses were primarily directed against these frontier magnates and their small fortresses, which is why so many expeditions from Córdoba are recorded as ravaging parts of Castille.

The threat of major Umayyad reprisals was probably lifted as a result of the battle of Simancas in 939. By the late 920s, 'Abd al-Rahman III (912–61) had largely restored the fortunes of his dynasty in the south and centre of the peninsula by means of a series of campaigns against the various local potentates and rebels who had carved out independent territories for themselves over much of al-Andalus.[60] Only once this had been achieved was it possible for him to resume expeditions into the north of the kind that had been commonplace in the later eighth century. This in 939 proved a disaster, in that his army was defeated as it attempted to force its way across the valley of the Duero.[61] The caliph never led an expedition in person again, and large-scale confrontations between the Umayyad caliphate and the Leonese kingdom were not to resume until the mid-970s. However, there was constant local raiding across the frontier in both directions.

The great period of expansion, settlement and re-population of the northern Meseta that began in the middle of the ninth century and lasted for a hundred years or more transformed the political and economic alignments of the original Asturian kingdom almost out of recognition. The southern frontier became the main area for expansion, with a marcher aristocracy emerging to defend and to exploit it. The processes involved are clearest in the case of monastic houses, whose records have survived to a much greater extent than those of secular land-holders. However, because of the great weight placed on written evidence and documentary proofs in the legal systems of all the Christian realms of northern Spain, their charter collections usually contain several items relating to preceding periods of secular possession of estates that subsequently were gifted or sold into monastic ownership.

The small number of contemporary charters and the problems of authenticity previously mentioned particularly affect the study of the early period of the history of Castille and the other frontier regions. Another type of document that is potentially very significant in the study of these processes is the *fuero* or charter of privileges, in which a founding lord concedes various rights to those whom he has persuaded to occupy a new settlement that he has founded or revived.[62] These were increased over the course of time, as circumstances changed, more concessions were made, or greater precision became necessary in defining the inhabitants' rights. It is thus not surprising that many of the earliest sets of these *fueros* granted to individual settlements only survive as the opening sections of later, more complex texts. Also, in several cases these documents can be shown to have been altered or interpolated at periods later than their supposed date.[63]

The initiative for settlement was largely taken by the frontier nobility, which conquered territories that then needed to be populated with new settlers, drawn from the mountainous regions to the north or the Basque territories to the east. These settlers would need, with the lord's support, to establish fortified centres to defend their land from raids coming from the Arab frontier zones to the south as well as from bandits. The *fueros* specified duties expected as well as exemptions from taxes, tolls and other burdens that a founder was prepared to offer the settlers. These could include modifications to the use of the existing law, as contained in the still authoritative Visigothic code.[64]

As well as those escaping from the burden of more restrictive and oppressive lordship in the Asturian and Galician heartlands, the new settlers on the Meseta included groups of Mozarabic refugees from the Arab lands in the south. Many of these were Christian clerics and monks, who established new monastic houses in several of the abandoned and ruined churches in this region, whose existence is abundantly testified to in the documentary records. There may also have been large numbers of lay Christians migrating from the south, but they are not as easily found in the texts as their clerical counterparts. It used to be believed that the opposite was true, and that the presence of lay Mozarabs could be proved from the large number of Arab names in the northern charter collections. Such names were thought to be exclusively those of refugees from the south and their descendants. However, recent study has shown that naming patterns are more complex than this view allowed, and that these names might be used almost indiscriminately in families whose origins can be proved to lie in the north.[65]

Marcher societies have always been notoriously independent. Central authority usually required the services of some of those families who had already established their own power bases in such regions to try to control the rest. Political skill consisted in building up the strength of these representatives of distant central authority against local rivals, but at the same time not letting them become so dominant that they could ignore or defy their royal masters.

This was a danger in periods when the kings were weak – for example, because of uncontrolled factional conflicts at court, which were particularly prevalent during royal minorities. Such court rivalries could be manipulated by ambitious marcher lords, through allying with one side or another and switching allegiance when it suited them, just as their own local conflicts were similarly exploited by the kings in times in which central authority was more effective.

Thus the reign of Ramiro II of Léon (931–51), victor over the Umayyad caliph in 939, saw royal power generally in the ascendant, and the frontier zones remained quiescent.[66] His death ushered in a period of instability, lasting with few interruptions until the end of the century. This was the product of disputed royal successions and the attempts of members of the dynasty to acquire regional power. A sub-kingdom had come into being in Galicia following the deposition of Alfonso III in 910, either as an appanage for the heir apparent or as a dependency to be given to a close relative of the reigning monarch. In the reign of García I (910–13/14), his brother Ordoño held Galicia, before succeeding to the Leonese throne itself. On Ordoño's death in 924 the kingdom passed to another of the brothers, Fruela II (924–25), despite the existence of at least three sons of Ordoño II.[67]

It was not Ordoño II's sons who seem to have presented the most immediate threat to Fruela II: this came from the sons of a brother of Alfonso III called Olmund. This implies that, as in the preceding Asturian period, almost any adult male member of the royal house, extending to at least the second generation, could be considered a potential candidate for the throne. In this case, Fruela took pre-emptive action, executing the three of them and thus ending that branch of the dynasty. This was obviously regarded as unjust and, according to Sampiro, Fruela was struck down with leprosy, from which he died in 925 as a divine punishment.[68]

His death precipitated a brief struggle for the throne between the sons of the former king Ordoño II, which is only recorded in one of the fragments of the work of the Arab historian Ibn Hayyan (d. 1076).[69] The eldest of them, Sancho, took León, but was dislodged by his brother Alfonso, who had the backing of the Navarrese king Sancho I Garcés (905–25). However, Sancho maintained himself independently in Galicia until his death in 929, at which point he was succeeded by the third brother, Ramiro.

In 930 or 931, Ramiro reunited Galicia with the rest of the Leonese kingdom when he succeeded Alfonso IV. The latter is said, like their ancestor Vermudo I, to have abdicated in order to enter monastic life.[70] It seems more probable that he was the victim of a coup, backed by the military force of the Galician aristocracy, as within a few weeks of his supposedly voluntary renunciation of the crown, Alfonso escaped from his monastery and seized the city of León, when Ramiro was absent on campaign. Alfonso's attempt to regain the throne failed as he was unable to mobilise enough support. On Ramiro II's rapid return to León, Alfonso was returned to monastic seclusion and several other members of the royal house were blinded.

It is notable that in this period of conflict between the sons of Ordoño II, two of them enjoyed strong backing in Galicia, and were able to maintain themselves in that region even when one of their rivals ruled in León, while the third one had Navarrese aid. The subsequent failure of Alfonso IV to maintain himself against Ramiro II or then to recover his throne may well reflect the contemporary weakness of the kingdom of Navarre, then under the regency of queen Toda. This pattern of the rival polarities of Galicia and Navarre, exerting fluctuating degrees of influence over León, remained a constant in the politics of the kingdom for the next hundred years.

The particular involvement of the royal dynasty with Galicia rather than with Castille – thereby allowing the house of Fernán González to secure its pre-eminence, and the creation of a Galician sub-kingship – may have resulted from the presence of substantial royal estates in that region. As previously mentioned, Galicia had provided the support for Ramiro I's seizure of power in 842, the year in which he had married a major Galician heiress.

While Galician aristocratic factions played a dominant role in the politics of the Leonese court in the earlier part of the tenth century, by its middle years the leading role had been taken by the count of Castille. Fernán González had tried to gain autonomy for himself and his territory during the latter part of the reign of Ramiro II, and that of the latter's elder son and successor, Ordoño III (951–6), even rebelling when thwarted.[71] His revolts had been crushed, but he and his dynasty remained indispensable to the Leonese monarchs and he could not be replaced.

The early death of Ordoño III opened up new opportunities, as the regime of his half-brother, Sancho I the Fat, was weak. This was partly because of the new king's obesity, which prevented him from mounting a horse and thus exercising the military leadership upon which royal credibility depended. He became vulnerable to a coup, which was not long in coming. This was fomented by one of the alternative lines of the still extensive royal family, in the person of a son of Alfonso IV, who seized the Leonese throne in 958.[72] The new king Ordoño IV (958–9) was in later tradition given the sobriquet of 'the Bad', though it has to be admitted that no particular acts of ill-renown can be laid at his door.

Sancho the Fat fled eastwards to his maternal uncle, the king of Navarre, who in turn sent him south to the Umayyad court. Here, he was provided with both the medical treatment necessary to slim him down and the military assistance that enabled him to regain his throne the following year. Ordoño IV continued to hold out briefly in the Asturias, but by 960 he too had to make his way to Córdoba, to petition the caliph for aid. In his case, aid was refused, and he died in exile.[73]

The role played in these events by Fernán González of Castille is noteworthy. He seems to have been involved in the conspiracy that led to the overthrow of Sancho I in 958 and he married his daughter Urraca, already the widow of Ordoño III, to the new king Ordoño IV, indicating his backing for the latter's regime. However, the support for the deposed Sancho from the Navarrese, who were the Castillians' eastern neighbours, and by the Umayyad court led to a change of allegiance on the part of Fernán González. He switched back to the cause of Sancho, and prevented his daughter from accompanying Ordoño IV on his fruitless visit to Córdoba. For all this, he was well rewarded by the restored monarch, whom he had betrayed only the previous year. Following the subsequent death in exile of Ordoño the Bad, Urraca was married to her cousin Sancho II Abarca ('Slipper') of Navarre (970–94), cementing the new alliance between the counts of Castille and the Navarrese royal house.[74]

In line with a policy already adopted by the court of Navarre during the long regency of queen Toda, the Leonese monarchy became markedly more subservient in its diplomatic dealings with the Umayyads over the next decade and a half. It also came increasingly under the influence of the kings of Navarre and their Castillian allies. Castillian and Navarrese nobles frequently attended the court of Sancho I and his son Ramiro III (966–85), and there seem to have been very close relations between León, Burgos and Pamplona at this time.[75]

In consequence, Galicia, whose aristocracy had been favoured under Ramiro II and Ordoño III moved from being the main source of support for the Leonese monarchy to becoming the principal focus of rebellion. In 966, Sancho I was forced to mobilise his forces against a revolt led by the leading noble house in the area south of the Miño. Unable to resist the king militarily, count Gonzalo Muñoz opened negotiations, in the course of which he was able to poison Sancho with a gift of apples.[76]

During the reigns of Sancho's sister, the regent Elvira Ramirez (967–75) and that of his son, Ramiro III, royal authority hardly extended into Galicia. Vermudo, an illegitimate son of Ordoño III, the last monarch the Galician nobles had openly supported, was proclaimed king in opposition to Ramiro III in 982. The latter's regime in the period of his personal rule, which began in 975, seems to have been riven by factional conflicts, and in 984 he was ousted from León with relative ease by Vermudo II (982–99) and his Galician forces. Ramiro retained his support in Castille, but disappears from record in 985, when he may be assumed to have died.[77]

The politics of the Leonese kingdom, which lurched from periods of Galician predominance to ones of Navarrese and Castillian ascendancy, followed the same pattern into the eleventh century. Vermudo II, his son Alfonso V (999–1027) and grandson Vermudo III (1027–37) all enjoyed significant support from the leading families of Galicia, while relations with Navarre deteriorated as the ambitions and power of its royal house grew.[78] Sancho III the Great of Navarre (1004–35) built up a political hegemony that embraced the county of Barcelona in the east and the duchy of Gascony to the north, both of whom had hitherto been subject to the West Frankish kings. He also followed his predecessors in extending the territories of the Navarrese kingdom southwards, deeper into the Ebro valley. To the south-west, the county of Castille passed into direct Navarrese control after the murder of the last descendant of Fernán González in León in 1029, when it was inherited by Sancho the Great's son, Fernando.

Having thus gained control of Castille, it was a small step for Sancho to try to annexe the Leonese kingdom itself. In 1031, a Navarrese invasion of León overran the capital and the territory around it without encountering much resistance. Vermudo III was able to retain control of Galicia and the Asturias, the traditional strongholds of his branch of the Leonese dynasty. The death of Sancho the Great in October 1035 enabled Vermudo to regain León, but he faced a renewed challenge two years later from two of his old adversary's sons, Fernando, count of Castille, and king García IV of Navarre (1035–54). In a battle at Tamarón, Vermudo was defeated and killed. With him died the direct line of the Asturian royal house, and his kingdom passed into the hands of the count of Castille, who took the throne as Fernando I (1037–65) of León-Castille.

21 The Empire revived, 875–1002

Italy, 875–961

While the threat of a major Arab incursion into Western Europe never revived after the early eighth century, seaborne raids, not least linked to slave trading, were a serious problem in the Mediterranean regions. Spanish Arab and Berber raids on the Balearic Islands in 798 led to the islands putting themselves under Frankish protection in 799, but by the middle of the ninth century they were under Arab rule.[1] Charlemagne is reported to have had to taken defensive measures against Arab raids along the southern coast of France in the latter part of his reign. By the middle of the ninth century, just as Viking raids were intensifying in the north, so in the south Arab pirates were employing equivalent tactics. In 840, 850 and 869 they conducted large-scale raids up the Rhône, in search of slaves or those, such as the bishop of Arles, whom they could hold to ransom.[2] Similar problems had already been encountered in Italy. In 806, raids were launched against Corsica, then part of the Italian kingdom ruled by Charles' son, Pippin, and these soon extended to Sardinia and the Italian mainland. These raids, unlike those on the Balearics, came from Africa.

After the overthrow of the Umayyad caliphs in Syria in 750, North Africa had come under the rule of their successors, the 'Abbasid dynasty, who made their capital in Baghdad, in Iraq. However, the political break-up of the previously monolithic Arab empire had soon followed. Spain had gone its own way in 756 under a fugitive Umayyad prince, and other smaller, independent amirates came into existence in the regions now known as Morocco and western Algeria in 789 and 777, respectively. In 800, the province of *Ifriqiya* (modern Tunisia) was ceded to its principal general as an Amirate, in return for the promise of an annual tribute to the caliph. It was under the direction of this Aghlabid dynasty in *Ifriqiya* that the raids on Italy were organised, and so too from 827 was the conquest of Sicily.[3]

Sicily had remained the most substantial Byzantine holding in the West after the fall of the exarchate of Ravenna to the Lombards in 751. Its conquest by the Arabs took over half a century to complete, but the maritime raids on the Italian mainland grew in frequency and seriousness throughout this period. Moreover, Arab forces also crossed to mainland Italy, took Reggio, Bari and Taranto, and by 840 were penetrating as far as the southern frontier of the papal territories. Pope Gregory IV (827–44) built a fortress called Gregoriopolis at Ostia, but its garrison fled in 846 when an Arab fleet sailed up the Tiber. The defences of Rome itself held, but the two great basilicas of St Peter's and St Paul's, which lay outside the walls, were looted. Pope Leo IV (847–55) subsequently fortified the area between St Peter's and the mausoleum of Hadrian, now the Castel Sant'Angelo.[4] Known as the Leonine City, this walled area west of the Tiber also became a place of refuge for the popes if they lost control of Rome itself.

This continuing Arab threat provides a background to the conduct of papal relations with the various rival Carolingian rulers throughout the ninth century, and explains the popes' attempts to use the imperial title as a lure to commit the rulers to defend Rome. Pope John VIII (872–82) built a small papal fleet, but as the help the Carolingian emperors were able to provide was limited and he failed to win much support from the Lombard princes of southern Italy, he was soon reduced to buying immunity from the raiders.[5] The emperor Louis II (850–75) had been active, if not ultimately successful, in trying to stem the Arab advance in the south, but his successors proved less effective from the papal point of view. Their own internecine conflicts in the period 875–81 and the priority given by Charles the Fat to the Viking threat in the North meant that the chances of Carolingian military intervention in Italy rapidly receded. The expedition of the emperor Arnulf (887–99) to Rome in 896 was ended by a stroke that paralysed him and was followed by his early death.

By this time, however, a new actor had begun to play a role in these complicated events in southern Italy – or to be more accurate, to resume one previously abandoned. Since the time of the emperor Leo III (717–41), the Byzantine empire had been prevented by threats to its existence in the eastern Balkans and in Asia Minor from attempting to restore its position in Italy. By the mid-ninth century the towns of Naples, Amalfi and Gaeta still belonged in name to the empire, but effectively conducted their own affairs under the rule of local dynasts. The other former Byzantine possessions of Bari and Otranto fell to the Arabs in the 840s. On the other hand, the rival Lombard duchies of Benevento and Salerno belonged formally to the Frankish empire, but were willing to co-operate with the Byzantines when it suited them.

Under Basil I (867–86) the empire began to take a more active interest in protecting its Italian interests. Initially he was prepared to co-operate with the western emperor Louis II in a joint campaign against Bari in 869, but it proved impossible to co-ordinate the efforts of the two allies. At the same time, following the breakdown of negotiations for a marriage between Louis's daughter and Basil's eldest son, Constantine (d. 879), the latent problem of the imperial title re-emerged. In 812, Byzantium had recognised Charlemagne as 'emperor of the Franks', seeing his title as a purely ethnic one quite different from the true imperial authority of the ruler of Constantinople. In 869, however, Basil I seems to have been unwilling to call Louis II, who after all controlled no more than certain parts of northern and central Italy, anything more than king of the Franks. Particular offence had been given by the western ruler's revival of the style 'emperor of the Romans', a title that had been abandoned by Charlemagne soon after his imperial coronation.[6]

Louis's response, our main evidence for this disagreement, came in a lengthy letter to Basil, probably drafted for him by Anastasius, the papal librarian, who served as the western emperor's envoy to Constantinople. In this letter are found arguments identical to those contained in the forged text known as the 'Constitution of Constantine'. This was written in Francia in the early ninth century, but the ideas it expressed were older in date and may have been developed in papal circles in the mid- to late eighth century. These concern the 'donation of Constantine' (the distinction between the ideas about the supposed donation and the versions of the written text that claimed to be the imperial constitution that gave legal force to that donation is an important one), the concessions it was believed that Constantine had made to the pope when he left Rome to rule from Constantinople. It should be stressed that, while the existence of this donation was widely accepted, possibly from as early as the sixth century, it has no historical foundation.

According to the 'donation', Constantine I, when he left for the East, invested pope Sylvester and his successors with wide-ranging privileges, including the right to appoint an emperor in the West should the need arise.[7] One consequence of this was that it became possible for the emperor in the East to be seen as just the ruler 'of the Greeks', also denying the Byzantines self-identification as the *Romaioi* or Romans. It was in this fashion that Louis II, in the summer of 871, addressed Basil I and his subjects, writing that: 'It is the Greeks who, in their blindness and heretical spirit, have lost the faith, abandoned the city, and the seat of empire, the Roman nation and the very tongue of Rome, and migrated to distant parts.'[8]

Any chance of co-operation between the two emperors in southern Italy was thereby lost. Louis had initially seemed to be all the papacy needed by way of an effective defender of the city and its territory against the Arab menace. In 871, he took Bari in Apulia, which had been captured by Arab raiders in 847 and turned into a small kingdom or amirate. However, Louis's long stay in southern Italy, which had begun in 866, became a burden to his principal host, Adelchis (854–78), the Lombard duke of Benevento, who had to maintain the emperor and his following. With the backing of the rulers of both Naples and Salerno, Adelchis seized the poorly guarded emperor in August 872, holding him prisoner in Benevento for a month. To gain his release, Louis had to swear an oath to leave the duchy and never to return. Later, southern Italian tradition blamed the arrogance of Louis's wife, the empress Engelberga, for alienating the Beneventan court, while Frankish sources accused the Byzantines of being involved, but the main responsibility would seem to lie with the south Italian princes. After this humiliation, the 'emperor of the Romans' was forced to withdraw northwards to Ravenna.[9] He was persuaded to intervene briefly in the south once more, to protect Capua from an Arab attack, and it was there that he died in 875, leaving no male heir.

The loss of the only Carolingian ruler exclusively concerned with Italy weakened the ties between the dynasty and the papacy that had been forged a century earlier by Charlemagne and Hadrian I. After the brief and politically damaging tenure of the imperial office by Charles the Bald (875–7), other Carolingian rulers to the north of the Alps began to doubt whether it was worth getting involved with Italian problems just to obtain the title of emperor, despite its direct association with the legacy of Charlemagne. Thus, despite his deep distrust of the Lombard dukes in the south, pope John VIII found himself forced to look to the papacy's former political master, the Byzantine emperor, for the military assistance the Frankish rulers were unwilling or unable to provide.[10]

Despite being reconciled theologically after the death of the last Iconoclast emperor, Theophilus (829–42), the churches of Rome and Constantinople had broken off relations over the deposition in 858 of the patriarch Ignatius and the election of a layman, Photios, as his successor.[11] Pope Nicholas I (858–67) had protested that no council could be held nor could any bishop be deposed without the prior consent of the see of Peter. In a synod held in the Lateran in 863, he ordered the reinstatement of Ignatius, the return of Photius to his previous lay status, and the excommunication of the archbishop of Syracuse, who had consecrated him. This annoyed the Byzantine bishops, who had consistently denied the validity of papal claims to such far-reaching authority.

In 867, the murder of the emperor Michael III (842–67) had been followed rapidly by the deposition of patriarch Photius of Constantinople, enabling good relations to be restored with Rome. In return, pope Hadrian II (867–72) was even prepared to concede something that his predecessors had resisted since the late fourth century, which was the placing of Constantinople as second to Rome and ahead of Alexandria and Antioch in the order of precedence of the patriarchal sees.[12]

Unfortunately, by the time John VIII was looking for military aid from the emperor, the situation had changed yet again. After the restored patriarch Ignatius had died in 877, Basil I re-appointed Photius. Despite the latter's condemnation by two previous popes, John VIII's secular needs were so great as to make it necessary for him to co-operate.[13] He revoked pope Hadrian II's excommunication of the patriarch, and sent representatives to the Eighth Ecumenical Council, which was held under Photius's presidency. The pope subsequently accepted the acts of this council, even though this seems to have involved an implicit recognition of an equality of status between the sees of Rome and of Constantinople. In return, a Byzantine fleet was sent to the west coast of Italy in 879.

Basil's intervention in southern Italy was generally successful, though nothing could be done to reverse the loss of Sicily that had been completed by the fall of Syracuse to the Arabs in 878. On the mainland, however, maritime expeditions had already begun to achieve results that would compensate for the losses in Sicily. Otranto was regained in 873 and Bari fell to the Byzantines in 876. In 883, a major war of conquest was launched under the command of Basil's general, Nicephorus Phocas, which imposed imperial rule over much of southern Italy for the first time since the seventh century. In consequence, in 892 two new military themes were created in southern Italy, those of Calabria and Langobardia.[14] The latter briefly extended itself to include Benevento (892–95), although this soon returned to Lombard princely rule. Even if truncated Lombard states survived in Salerno and Benevento, Byzantine rule was re-established over most of Apulia, Calabria and Basilicata, though the frontiers continued to fluctuate. The Lombard duchies regained some of what they had lost in a series of wars in the 920s–40s, and the Arab threat from Sicily grew in intensity in the same period. Subsequently, the revival of a somewhat stronger and more extensive western empire than had existed in the period *c.* 899–960 led to a period of competition and rivalry in southern Italy between the rulers of the old and the new Romes during the second half of the tenth century.

Germany: the kingdom and the duchies, 911–62

The extinction of the eastern branch of the Carolingian dynasty in 911, with the death of the eighteen-year-old Louis the Child, the only legitimate son of Arnulf, left a political vacuum in Germany. Unlike the 880s, when Charles the Fat effectively had the whole of the empire fall piecemeal into his lap thanks to the deaths of his relatives, there was in 911 no prospect that the sole surviving adult Carolingian, Charles the Simple, would be able to take over the vacant eastern kingdom. He did, however, have hopes of acquiring Lotharingia – the region located between Eastern and Western Francia.

This kingdom, which formed the northern part of the realm that had been given to Lothar I in the Treaty of Verdun in 843, had lost its last independent Carolingian ruler with the death of Arnulf's illegitimate son, Zwentibold, in 900, and had reverted to the nominal rule of its imperial overlord, Louis the Child. On the latter's death in 911, the Lotharingian nobility preferred to put the kingdom into the hands of the Western Frankish ruler Charles the Simple rather than those of the king who had just been selected by the eastern Frankish dukes.[15] Charles, whose first wife was a member of a Lotharingian noble house, was deeply committed to his new acquisition, to the extent that his over-involvement in its affairs at the expense of theirs led to a revolt against him by a significant part of the West Frankish aristocracy in 922.

In East Francia, the growth of multiple military threats on the frontiers, and the weakening and ultimately the extinction of the branch of the Carolingian dynasty descended from Louis the German saw the apparent re-emergence of earlier structures of political organisation. In the first decade of the tenth century the title of 'duke [*dux*] of the Bavarians' reappears for the first time since the deposition of Tassilo III in 788. The first holder of the revived office was probably the duke Liutpold, who was killed in a battle against the Magyars near Bratislava in 907. He had been appointed to the lesser office of *marchio* or march warden by the emperor Arnulf in 895 and was subsequently count of the palace, and we are not certain that he actually used the title of duke. His son Arnulf, later known as 'the Bad' (d. 937), certainly did, and in a charter confirming an exchange of lands dated to 908 he appears to be exercising royal authority in all but name.[16]

A similar development had already taken place in Saxony, which may have had a ducal dynasty up to the time of Charlemagne. In the late ninth century, responsibility for Saxony, now an important marcher territory confronting the northern Slavs, had been given to the family known as the Liudolfings or the Ottonians. Liudolf (d. 866), whose origins are uncertain, was the first of a new line of Saxon dukes, whose position was consolidated by his son Otto (d. 912).

Interestingly, the Saxon leader Widukind, who in the Frankish sources of the late eighth century is given no title at all, appears in tenth- and eleventh-century Saxon texts as 'duke' or even 'king' Widukind, and the Ottonians stressed their descent from him through Matilda, the wife of Henry I (919–936). For example, in the first *Life of Queen Matilda*, written for her grandson, the emperor Otto II (973–83), her descent from Widukind is strongly emphasised.[17] This legitimising claim may also have contributed to Henry's decision to bypass the son of his earlier marriage and bequeath the crown to his eldest son by Matilda, the future emperor Otto I (936–73).

In Alamannia, which also came to be known as Suabia, the rivalry of two powerful families made the issue less clear cut. The holder of the office of count under Louis the Child was a man called Burchard, who had already begun to call himself 'prince of the Alamans', until he was overthrown and executed in the course of the confused events that followed the death of the young king Louis in 911. Burchard's successor was from the rival family, and he adopted a ducal title in 915, only to be condemned for rebellion and executed in 917. Burchard (II) emerged from the fall of his rival as the uncontested duke of Suabia from 917 to 926.

Similarly, in the original heartlands of eastern Frankish settlement across the Rhine, the area that came to be called Franconia, centred on the valley of the Main, feuds between the leading families made the emergence of a single dominant dynasty less easy, but the issue was finally resolved in favour of the Conradines in 906. At the beginning of the tenth century, Thuringia was in the hands of another duke of the name of Burchard, until his death in 908, but then, or soon afterwards, it disappears as a separate entity, merging with Franconia. To the west, in Lotharingia, the death of the emperor Arnulf's illegitimate son, Zwentibold, early in 900 ended the brief period (895–900) in which this region formed a separate kingdom, and power passed into the hands of a duke Gebhard, and then after his death in battle against the Magyars in 910 to members of another family.[18]

While German scholars have labelled these revived quasi-ethnic political entities 'stem-duchies', not all of them equated to the pre-Carolingian duchies that had been used by the Frankish rulers to control the various peoples living beyond their eastern frontiers. Lotharingia in particular was an entirely artificial creation resulting from the treaty of 843. However, the sense of the cultural and historic distinctions between the various Germanic peoples was still clearly a major factor in the social and political articulation of the eastern Frankish realm, and claims to dynastic links with the original ducal houses was an asset to be exploited. As well as trying to justify their status by appeals to the past, the new ducal houses made sure that they secured the means of expressing it and the resources upon which it depended. They openly exercised several of the functions that would once have been exclusively royal prerogatives, and in particular were able to appropriate the revenues and resources in their own regions of the former Carolingian fisc. Two of them, Burchard II of Suabia and Arnulf of Bavaria, even exercised the royal right of appointing to bishoprics in their duchies.

What they could not do, however, was to stand alone against the attacks of the Magyars (on whom more will be said below), especially when other threats, notably from some of the Slav peoples on the eastern frontiers of Saxony, were also making themselves felt strongly. Military co-operation between the duchies required acceptance of a superior authority, in the person of a king. At no point either was it thought that the duchies should break with historical precedent and transform themselves into separate small kingdoms. So, following the early death of Louis the Child, the dukes and other leading magnates of his realm, other than those of Lotharingia, had met and rapidly selected the Franconian duke Conrad to be their new king.

It has been argued that that Conrad had close family ties to the Carolingians, but this seems unlikely.[19] Nor did his recently acquired position as duke of Franconia, the traditional Frankish heartland in the region east of the Rhine, gave him any special claim to the vacant royal authority. He is not known to have been an outstanding military leader, but for whatever reasons he emerged as the most acceptable of all the candidates. That a matter as contentious and divisive as the choice of a non-Carolingian to take over the vacant throne was settled with such apparent ease and speed was largely a result of the serious military problems the kingdom was then facing.[20]

The Avar confederacy that had long dominated the plains around the upper Danube, to the east of Bavaria, disintegrated rapidly as a result of internal conflicts and its defeats at the hands of Charlemagne's commanders in the 790s. Its place was soon taken by the Slav kingdom of 'Greater Moravia', the location of whose main centres has generated much scholarly controversy. The traditional view that associated it with the valley of the River Morava in the modern Czech Republic has been challenged by rival interpretations of the limited literary evidence that favour either an area south of the Danube around the former Roman city of Sirmium, or the Hungarian Alföld.[21] This debate remains to be resolved, and probably cannot be on the basis of the archaeological evidence any more than the literary.

Wherever the location of its heartland, the Moravian kingdom, which was the most powerful eastern neighbour of the East Frankish realm, collapsed surprisingly rapidly at the very end of the ninth century under pressure from a new steppe nomad confederation, that of the Magyars, or as they were known in the East Frankish chronicles, the *Ungari* or Hungarians (probably deriving from a conflation of the name of the Magyars with that of the archaic Huns). The first appearance of the Magyars in these Frankish texts is in an entry for the year 889, but from Byzantine accounts it seems clear that they had been pushed west towards the upper Danube by the growing power of the Petchenegs in the south Russian steppes.[22] By 892, they were being used as mercenaries by king Arnulf in his campaigns against the Moravian kingdom.[23] In the same decade they were also employed by the Byzantines in their wars against the Bulgars.

As with their predecessors, the Huns and the Avars, such contact with the more sophisticated sedentary societies to the south and the west led to greater social cohesiveness among the nomads, and in consequence a more formidable and predatory military organisation. In 899, the Magyars launched a raid across the Julian Alps into northern Italy 'killing many bishops', and this was followed by a devastating attack on Bavaria. Their raids grew in range and scale. Another attack on the Bavarians in 907 led to the death of their duke Liutpold. In 908, the Magyars were ravaging the duchies of Thuringia and Saxony; in 909 they were in the duchy of Alamannia; and in 910 they defeated a Franconian army, killing its duke Gebhard.[24] Thus by 911 all the major duchies had suffered at the hands of the Magyars, and further raids could be expected.

The short reign of Conrad I (911–18) saw little relief. Despite a victory over them on the River Inn in 913, the Magyars are reported in 915 as devastating the whole of Alamannia (Suabia) and raiding through Thuringia and Saxony as far as the monastery of Fulda.[25] This monastery, founded by Boniface, was to be Conrad's burial place in 919. His death the previous December resulted from injuries received in an unsuccessful expedition against duke Arnulf of Bavaria earlier in 918, testifying to the real problems the kings faced in trying to impose their authority over the duchies if the dukes were not willing to concede it. On his deathbed, and seeking to avoid a contentious election, Conrad is said in later Saxon sources to have commended duke Henry of Saxony to the East Frankish nobles as the best choice for his successor.[26] In practice, only the Franconian and Saxon magnates were present at the assembly at Fritzlar in May 919 that gave the crown to Henry, and he had to face down an immediate challenge from Arnulf of Bavaria before his new status was recognised by all the dukes. Despite this shaky start, it was to be under this new king, the founder of the Ottonian dynasty, which took its name from Henry's father, duke Otto of Saxony (d. 912), that the first effective action was to be taken against the Magyars.

Henry I (919–36), or Henry the Fowler as he was later known, was lucky that the Magyar onslaughts were suspended during the opening years of his reign, but they resumed in 924, when they 'devastated eastern Francia'.[27] Henry was forced to take refuge in the fortress of Werla. However, the chance capture of a Magyar leader enabled him to obtain a nine-year peace, in return for his paying them an annual tribute. Henry used this time both to develop new fortified settlements and to rebuild his army, largely through a series of campaigns against the Slavs. So, when the truce ended and the Magyars resumed their attacks in 933, he was able to inflict a major defeat on them at the battle of Riade.[28] When they turned eastwards the following year, they were defeated again, this time by the forces of the Byzantine emperor, Romanus I Lecapenos (920–44).[29]

This by no means put an end to the Magyar menace in the West. In 937, one of their expeditions penetrated as far as western Francia, obliging its king Louis IV (936–54) to endure a siege in Laon, and it returned to the Danube by way of northern Italy, causing havoc as it went. This or another Magyar force also penetrated as far south as the duchies of Benevento and Salerno in the same year. However, the tide had certainly turned. A Magyar attack in 938, early in the reign of Henry's son, Otto I (936–73), resulted in another victory over them. The Bavarians, who had suffered perhaps more than any from these raids, gained their particular revenge in 943, when duke

Arnulf the Bad's brother inflicted another major defeat on them. By 950, the eastern Franks were themselves able to take the offensive, and the king's brother Henry led a successful raid on the Magyars. The culmination of this series of victories was to be the battle won on the River Lech by Otto I in 955.[30]

The decline of the Magyar threat, from the early 930s onwards, released the kingdom from its most pressing problem, but also opened up new, internal ones. While military activity was so constant there was less opportunity for the kings to impose themselves on the powerful dukes. As a territorial duke prior to his election in 919, Henry I was no more than one of several, and his royal title did not greatly enhance his power in practice, which tended to remain confined to his own duchy of Saxony. His authority was at least sufficient to enable him to appoint a duke of his own choosing in Suabia in 926, when that position became vacant, and he and his son Otto I gradually extended their influence through such appointments of supporters and members of their own family to the other great duchies, sometimes through to marriages to key heiresses. However, the traditions of regional independence were so strong and the lack of institutions of central government so absolute that the appointees did not afterwards see themselves as dependents of the monarchy. Indeed, the greatest internal threats to the monarchy came from members of the Ottonian family who had been entrusted with such duchies.

Otto I faced a rebellion in 938 led by duke Eberhard of Franconia, brother of the former king Conrad, in which both his own elder half-brother, Thankmar, and his full brother, Henry, took part against him. The fighting escalated the following year, when the Duke of Lotharingia, which had reverted to eastern Frankish rule after the revolt against Charles the Simple in 922, joined the rebels, and Louis IV (936–54) of western Francia invaded the kingdom.[31] However, the west Frankish realm itself was so wracked by internal divisions by this time that many of its leading noble houses promptly offered their support to Otto, who made an effective counter-invasion of Louis's territories, forcing him to withdraw. The deaths in this war in 939 of both the rebel dukes of Franconia and Lotharingia then gave Otto the chance to replace them with his own appointees. He was also able to instal his younger brother, Henry, despite the latter's hostility towards him in 938 and 941, as duke of Bavaria, through a marriage to the daughter and heiress of Arnulf the Bad (d. 937). A similar marriage made Otto's son Liudolf duke of Suabia.[32]

It was in the ensuing period of relative stability both within the East Frankish kingdom and on its eastern borders that Otto became embroiled in the affairs of Italy. This first venture into the south on his part proved something of a fiasco. The north Italian 'kingdom of the Lombards', centred on Pavia, had passed into the hands of the Margraves of Spoleto after the deposition of the emperor Charles the Fat in 887. Their line had been short-lived and the kingdom had been fought over by various contestants until acquired by Hugh of Arles, formerly count of Provence in 926.[33] His son and successor, Lothar, died suddenly in 950, and the kingship was assumed by the *marchio* or margrave Berengar of Ivrea, the relative of an earlier king, who had been the power behind the throne since 945.[34] When, to strengthen his position, Berengar tried to force Lothar's widow, Adelheid, to marry his son, she refused, and then, escaping from detention in Como, she offered her hand to Otto I if he would come to her aid. As an heiress of the kingdom of Burgundy and with a claim to that of Italy, she was a desirable match for the recently widowed Otto, whose first wife, Edith (died 947), had been a daughter of king Edward the Elder of Wessex (899–925).

Otto formed his intention of intervening in Italy while celebrating Easter at Aachen in 951, and it may be that the precedent of Charlemagne influenced his decision.[35] Following his great predecessor, he marched on Pavia, took it quickly and had himself crowned king of the Lombards. However, here the resemblance to Charles ended. Otto's venture into the south and his ensuing marriage to Adelheid gave so many opportunities for rebellion in the East Frankish kingdom, and aroused so much family mistrust, that a major rising against him took place in Germany, and he was forced to make a hasty retreat northwards to face a revolt, which involved all the duchies. Otto's return to Italy was to be delayed for a decade, and was the result of an appeal from a pope rather than from a royal widow.[36]

The papacy at this time was in the midst of a period in its history apparently so divorced from the high ideals of its earlier history as to prompt the original *Cambridge Medieval History* to label it 'the Pornocracy'.[37] Titillating as many of the tales of murder, lust and intrigue at the papal court in the tenth century may be, we need to exercise the utmost care in assessing their veracity. The principal source for most of these stories is the truncated work by bishop Liudprand of Cremona, known as the *De Ottone Rege* ('On King Otto'), written about 965, together with his earlier *Antapodosis* or 'Retribution'.[38] Liudprand (d. 972) had been a member of Otto I's court since 950, and was a learned and well-read man.[39] Though his works have normally been characterised by modern commentators as idiosyncratic and scandal-mongering, this is to miss their continuities with some of the literary traditions of late antiquity.[40]

Ever since the period of the early Roman Empire, accusations of sexual impropriety had been used as a weapon not only in the literary denigration of an opponent but also politically. This tradition continued to resurface at various points in the history of the papacy. Accusations of 'adultery' were used against, for example, pope Symmachus (498–514) by supporters of his rival Laurentius, and against Leo III (795–816) by his enemies in 799.[41] So it was not necessarily his personal salaciousness that made Liudprand employ similar charges against a pope who had opposed Otto I.

While we should not place too much trust in the details of Liudprand's stories, what he describes in general confirms the tendency, first apparent in the late eighth century, for the papal office to be an object of competition between rival aristocratic factions in the city of Rome.[42] By the early 900s this often expressed itself violently. Thus, Leo V was deposed after a thirty-day pontificate in September 903 by Christopher, who was in turn overthrown in January 904 by Sergius III (897 and 904–11), with the military backing of duke Alberic of Spoleto. Sergius III is then said to have had both Leo V and Christopher strangled in prison 'so as not to prolong their sufferings'. He is also accused of having a son by the fifteen-year-old daughter of Theophylact, 'consul' and commander of the Roman militia.[43] Again, the source for this and many similar stories is Liudprand of Cremona, in his earlier *Antapodosis* or *Book of Revenge* of *c.* 958. His hostility to the family who came to dominate the city of Rome between 904 and 963 was the product both of their opposition to his new master, Otto I, and of earlier Italian political conflicts in which he himself had played a minor role.[44]

After the pontificate of Sergius III, power in Rome passed into the hands of the 'consul' Theophylact (d. 920), who was also papal treasurer, and then to his son-in-law, Alberic I, duke of Spoleto (d. 925). Pope John X (914–28), formerly patriarch of Ravenna, who is accused by Liudprand of a liaison with Theophylact's other daughter, Theodora, was brought to Rome, despite the canon (that is, ecclesiastical) law ban on a bishop moving from one see to another because of his proven ability as a soldier rather than as a pastor, and he personally took a role in raising the forces against and defeating the Arab marauders established on the mouth of the River Garigliano.[45] His legates were active in both East and West Francia, in Dalmatia, and in Constantinople. But his growing independence of the new political masters of Rome after 925, Theophylact's daughter Marozia and her second husband Guido,

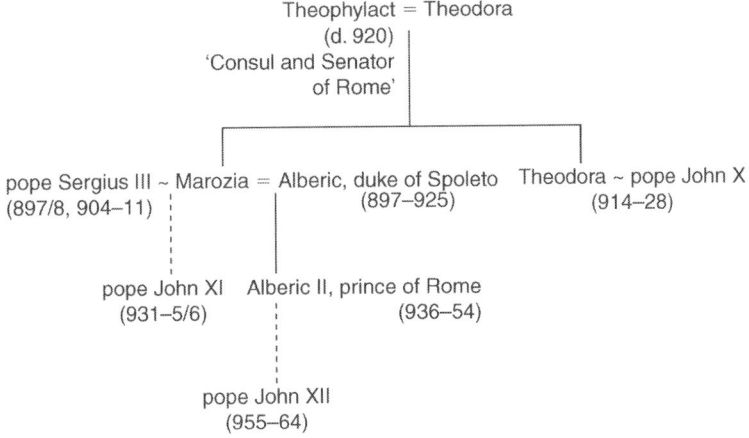

The house of Theophylact and its allies, 904–64

the marquis of Tuscany, led to his fall. He was deposed by them in 928, imprisoned and murdered the following year.[46] After two short interim pontificates, Marozia installed her son by Sergius III as pope John XI (931–5/6).

The power of the house of Theophylact, now led by Marozia, should have expanded further when the once-more widowed 'Senatrix' married Hugh of Arles, the king of the Lombards, in 932. However, there was an intense local patriotism in Rome ready to be manipulated, and Marozia's son by her first husband, Alberic II, was able to organise a coup against the foreign king and his new wife soon after their marriage. Hugh escaped, but Marozia and John XI became Alberic's prisoners.[47] Under the title of 'Senator' (932) and then 'prince of the Romans' (936) he ruled the city until his death in 954. He could do so, like his mother and grandfather before him, only with the support of the majority of the other leading families of the city, who expected to share in any rewards that were available. These included lucrative posts in the papal bureaucracy, and favourable leases of Church and monastic lands. While this sounds like a ruthless exploitation of secular power in the papal territories at the expense of the Church, it must be noted that Alberic and other members of his family were committed patrons of monasticism in Rome and beyond.[48]

On his deathbed, Alberic II is said by Liudprand of Cremona to have asked the leading Roman clergy and nobles to swear that they would appoint his illegitimate son, Octavian, as the next pope. He succeeded to his father's temporal authority in 954 and was elected pope as John XII in 955 at the age of about eighteen.[49] Such a move was hardly unprecedented in Europe at this period. Many major ecclesiastical offices were given to young men not yet old enough to meet the minimum age requirements laid down for ordination in canon law, and in some cases even to children. Not surprisingly, such practices were much criticised in the reform movement that swept through most of the Western Church in the eleventh century.[50] However, whatever the complaints of later generations of reformers, in this period the close local identification of secular and ecclesiastical power could benefit the Church. Many of the 'princely' (that is, the de facto independent comital or ducal) dynasties of Western Europe defended their territories against external enemies and patronised the monasteries and other churches within them, at a time when monarchs were too weak and too impoverished to fill these roles. To strengthen these alliances by giving local ecclesiastical offices to junior members of these noble families made sense in the local context. Nor should we assume that such dynasties would naturally be opposed to reform or to the improvement of the Church in their lands. For example, relatives of the counts of Barcelona held several of the abbatial and episcopal offices within the Catalan counties during much of the tenth and early eleventh centuries, but they also made substantial gifts to the Church and were the leading promoters of reform in monastic life and ecclesiastical discipline in the region.[51]

For all of his later reputation, largely a product of Liudprand's skilful pen, John XII was an active supporter of the reformed monasticism that was making itself felt in a number of houses in central Italy, western Francia and England from the mid-tenth century onwards.[52] This was also the period in which the reform of monastic life and the adoption of the *Rule of Benedict* was accepted by many of the monasteries of Rome.[53] Materially, however, John XII's pontificate saw the decline of the territorial power of the papacy in central Italy, as a result of the aggression of the restored king of the Lombards, Berengar II (950–1, 951–63), who conquered John XII's family duchy of Spoleto in 959. Faced with this menace, the pope appealed to Otto I for help, offering as an inducement the imperial title that had been refused him in 951.[54]

Germany, Rome and Constantinople, 962–83

Otto's rapid conquest of Berengar's kingdom was followed by his imperial coronation in Rome on 2 February 962. In return, the new emperor gave the papacy the privilege known as the 'Ottonianum', confirming earlier gifts of lands supposedly made by the Carolingian rulers Pippin III, Charlemagne and Louis.[55] These territories were extended considerably by new concessions, but the pope was obliged in return to recognise the emperor as his secular overlord in all his lands. This was to prove a contentious legacy, especially in the period of reform and the development of new papal ideology in the eleventh and twelfth centuries. In many respects, the new 'Roman Empire' the popes had created and tried to mould for their own purposes was then to prove something of a Frankenstein's monster.

From the point of view of the new emperor, who proposed to take a more active and personal interest in Italy than had been the case with his great exemplar, Charlemagne, the papal invitation had been irresistibly attractive. For one thing, the role of the German kings was, as has been seen in the case of Otto's predecessors, a very difficult one. Their family origins did not distinguish them from the other ducal houses of eastern Francia, and they lacked hereditary rights inherited from the Carolingians. Despite attempts to enhance their status by increased formality in both court and liturgical ritual – far in excess of anything that had been practised by the Carolingians – their power still depended on a mixture of military success and political consensus.[56] The prospect of the imperial title, and with it an enhancement in status and a more clearly articulated claim to the Carolingian legacy, was attractive.

They would also inherit, by at the same time acquiring the kingdom of the Lombards, a better-governed state. In addition, the economic resources of the Italian monarchy were more immediately accessible than those of Germany, where the regional power and independence of the duchies' offices were greater, and the administrative structures of the monarchy far less developed. Even when members of Otto's family or other close allies could be installed as dukes, none could be fully trusted, and they had no interest in allowing the kings, whose principal land holdings were still those of their family duchy of Saxony, any control over the economic resources of the great regional principalities.

In Italy, on the other hand, the much smaller scale of the original Lombard duchies in the north and their gradual elimination under Carolingian rule, left the king of the Lombards less challenged by such territorial equals as the German dukes, and with greater resources of property and patronage at his disposal. Educational traditions and the apparatus of government in Italy were more developed than those to be found further north. The greater sophistication of such Pavia-trained courtiers as Liudprand, a former supporter of king Hugh of Arles, who had fled to join Otto in 950, must have been apparent. Liudprand and other exiles in Otto's entourage, such as bishop Rather of Verona, with experience of Italy, helped to keep the German ruler's interest in it alive in the period 951–61.

The case of Rather highlights some of the dangers of this involvement that Otto might not have appreciated. A native of Liège in Lotharingia, Rather had been appointed to the bishopric of Verona in 931 by Hugh of Arles, to whose court he had been attracted. However, in his diocese, local anti-alien sentiment led to his twice being ejected from the city, and to his supporting the failed bid of duke Arnulf the Bad of Bavaria to conquer the Lombard kingdom in 934. This resulted in Rather going into exile in Germany, where from 948 he served as tutor to Otto's brother, Bruno (d. 965), later royal chancellor and archbishop of Cologne, and also became an occasional visitor to the royal court. After Otto's conquest of the kingdom of the Lombards in 961 he was able to regain his see of Verona, but his experiences prefigured the problems that were to affect alien clergy inserted into the Italian Church. They could maintain themselves locally only so long as the monarch was able to protect them with the threat of military force.[57]

Italian lack of enthusiasm for foreign rule soon showed itself in imperial–papal relations. By 962, John XII had begun scheming with Berengar II's son Adalbert against Otto, and is even accused by Liudprand of having entered into communication with the Magyars.[58] In consequence, Otto had him deposed at a synod in Rome in 963, but once the emperor had left the city, his own nominee Leo VIII (963–5) lacked local backing to resist John XII's supporters and was forced in turn to flee. Only the death of John in 964 – of a stroke, while in bed with a married woman, according to Liudprand – regularised the situation.[59]

Imperial nominees to the papacy, as well as to local bishoprics, were disliked by the local Italian populace, who became increasingly xenophobic, and anti-German in particular, and they could only maintain themselves with the emperor's backing. In practice, this required his presence in Italy, but imperial power fluctuated. On Otto I's death in 973, his heir Otto II (973–83) had to establish himself in Germany before he could become involved in Italy, and at his own early death the long minority of his three-year-old heir, Otto III (983–1002), initiated a sustained period of imperial weakness in the peninsula. In such periods, imperially sponsored popes came to unfortunate ends, as happened to Benedict VI (973–4) and John XIV (983–4), both of whom were deposed and murdered following a change of emperor.[60]

Behind both of their deaths was pope Boniface VII (974, 984–5) who was later categorised as an anti-pope. He was the candidate for the papal office of a new aristocratic faction in the city of Rome, that of the Crescentii, but in flight in 974 and in his brief restoration ten years later he was also supported by the Byzantine emperors, who were keen to discomfit the Ottonians, whom they regarded as Frankish usurpers.[61]

The Byzantine empire had enjoyed a considerable revival in the tenth century under the direction of a succession of competent emperors, who in many cases were former generals, and who made themselves the legitimate successors of Basil I. The Bulgar dominance in the eastern Balkans had fluctuated during this period, and came to an end in the reign of the emperor Basil II (976–1025) – later and not entirely appropriately to be known as 'the Bulgar-slayer'. The eastern frontier in Asia Minor had also been expanded successfully, and the emperor Nicephorus Phocas (963–9) regained Antioch in 969, lost by Heraclius over three centuries before. The same emperor also recovered Cyprus from the Arabs in 965.[62] In southern Italy in this period, however, the main threat in Byzantine eyes changed from that posed by the Arabs to that of the rising power of the Ottonian empire.

The Aghlabid amirate in Tunisia that had carried out the conquest of Sicily was overthrown in 909 by a religious rising in favour of the Fatimids, a Shi'ite Muslim dynasty, which claimed descent from the Prophet's daughter, Fatima, the wife of 'Ali. They also took over the Aghlabid conquests in Sicily, but their attention was primarily directed eastwards, and in 969 their capital was moved from Kairouan in *Ifriqiya* to Fustat (Cairo) in recently-conquered Egypt.[63] There they became involved in expanding into Palestine and Syria, and this contributed to putting an end to Byzantine expansion into Syria from Asia Minor. But even after this significant shift in the power and focus of the Muslim states in the central Mediterranean, Arab raids from strongholds in Calabria continued to make conditions in southern Italy unstable.

After 964, when the grip of the new emperor, Otto I, on the north and centre of the peninsula seemed secure, he became drawn into the complex problems of the south, not least to secure his hold over Rome. This was assisted by a temporarily more favourable situation in southern Italy. Duke Pandolf I 'Ironhead' (961–80) of Capua-Benevento wanted Ottonian help in making himself dominant in the region, both over his neighbours in Salerno and Naples as well as in expanding his territory at the expense of the Byzantines.[64] At the same time, Calabria was under threat from the Fatimid rulers of Sicily and Tunisia, and an attempt to relieve this by a Byzantine expedition to Sicily in 964 resulted in a military and naval disaster. In 967, Nicephorus II Phocas (963–9), ruling in tandem with two child emperors of the Macedonian dynasty, was forced to make a treaty with the Fatimids, agreeing to the payment of an annual tribute. Taking advantage of these circumstances, Otto I led an army into Apulia in 968, to try to wrest Bari from the Byzantines. This failed, but caused some damage. Otto made more headway over the winter of 968/9 with further campaigning in Byzantine Calabria. He also hoped to capitalise on the military threat he was posing by sending a mission to Constantinople in 968 to demand Byzantine recognition of the new western imperial dynasty, something he hoped would be cemented by a marriage alliance.[65]

On his return in 969, Otto's envoy to Constantinople, bishop Liudprand of Cremona, wrote a very bitter account of his mission and of the court he had visited. In it he likened the emperor Nicephorus to an Ethiopian pygmy – 'one whom it would not be pleasant to meet in the middle of the night' – and claimed that he 'lives on garlic, onions and leeks, and drinks bath water'.[66] Above all, Liudprand indicated that the Byzantine emperor, who was genuinely furious at the westerners' unprovoked attacks on imperial territory, was unwilling to negotiate with Otto as an equal. The Byzantine court refused to acknowledge the latter's imperial title, and insisted on referring to him as *Rex* or king.[67]

Liudprand was equally concerned to suggest that the Roman Church had been insulted by the Byzantines. This resulted from the arrival of messengers sent by pope John XIII (965–72), who referred to Nicephorus as emperor of the Greeks and to Otto as emperor of the Romans. The Byzantine patrician Christophorus expressed to Liudprand an eastern version of the consequences of supposedly crucial transfer of Constantine I's seat of government from Rome to Constantinople: 'The stupid silly pope does not know that the holy Constantine transferred hither [Constantinople] the imperial sceptre, the senate and all the Roman knighthood, and left in Rome nothing but vile minions – fishers, namely, peddlers, bird catchers, bastards, plebeians, slaves.'[68]

By the time that Liudprand was writing, the situation in southern Italy had changed, which may explain his undiplomatic tone. Otto had been forced to return north, leaving Pandolf Ironhead to pursue the siege of Bari, but the Beneventan duke had been captured and sent as a prisoner to Constantinople.[69] However, when all his hopes might have seemed to have been frustrated, Otto I was able to achieve some of his diplomatic intentions, following the murder of the emperor Nicephorus II in December 969. This was carried out by one of his generals, who succeeded him as John I Tzimisces (969–76). The new emperor released duke Pandolf, and agreed to the marriage of his own niece, Theophanu, to Otto's son (Otto II) in 972. It is notable, though, that the chosen bride was not a member of the senior ruling house, the Macedonian dynasty, nor was she 'born in the purple'; that is, the offspring of a reigning emperor. Such imperial princesses were never to be sent to 'barbarian' husbands.[70] Theophanu's dowry was supposed to include the increasingly beleaguered Byzantine imperial possessions in Italy, but during the long period extending from 973 to 980 while Otto II was forced to fight wars in Germany against his relative, the duke of Bavaria, against the Danish king Harald Bluetooth, against the Slav dukes of the Poles and of the Bohemians, and against the West Frankish king Lothar (954–86), who sacked Aachen in 978, Ottonian control over southern Italy was largely lost.[71]

When Otto II finally felt able to turn his attention to Italy, he faced a complex situation in the south. His father-in-law, John Tzimisces, had died, and his hopes of peacefully gaining the Byzantine lands in southern Italy were thus lost. War was the only way to make his claim a reality. Otto succeeded in expelling the Byzantine forces from Taranto, but on 13 July 982 he suffered a major defeat at the hands of the Arabs at Stilo in Calabria, only narrowly avoiding capture, and was then forced to make a hasty withdrawal to the north, where other military problems were also reappearing.[72] To deal with the threat of renewed war on several fronts, Otto held a conference with the principal German dukes in Verona, where, among other things, it was agreed that his infant son and heir, also named Otto, should be formally elected and then crowned as king at Aachen later that year. This was to ensure a smooth future succession, and mirrored the early election and coronation of Otto II himself in 967. It did not indicate any expectation of the imminent end of the emperor's reign. However, while still developing his plans for future action against the Danes and the Slavs, Otto's health suddenly declined, and he died in Rome in December 983, aged only twenty-eight, leaving his three-year-old son a host of problems.

The eastwards expansion of Europe

The reign of Otto III, which lasted from 983 to 1002, has long intrigued historians, though more for what it appeared to promise than for what it actually achieved.[73] The son of a Byzantine princess, he was taught and advised from 997 by Gerbert, who as abbot of Bobbio (982–83), archbishop of Rheims (991–97), archbishop of Ravenna (998–999) and then pope as Sylvester II (999–1003), was an experienced ecclesiastical politician and probably the foremost scholar of the period. Others of Otto III's tutors included the Greek-speaking John Philagathos from Calabria, abbot of Nonantula, who was briefly pope as John XVI (997–8). From his antecedents and training, Otto III gave the impression that he might have developed into a sophisticated ruler, who could have combined elements of the old and the new and from East and West into a new synthesis. It was not to be. He died aged only twenty-two, and with some of what he had hoped to achieve already in ruins.

The reign of Otto III falls into two parts: first, the regencies of his mother, the Byzantine princess Theophanu (d. 991) and of his grandmother, Otto I's widow, Adelheid (d. 999); and, second, the few years in which he was able to direct the empire in person, from 994 onwards. The earlier and longer period has left relatively limited records of itself as, after an initial contested succession in Germany, this was a time of governmental inactivity caused by the length of the regency and the political caution with which the two regents had to proceed. Attention has been given recently to some of the cultural achievements of Theophanu's rule, as well as to possible Byzantine influences she brought to the court and its art.[74]

The standing of the imperial office remained ambiguous at this time. Otto was accepted as king prior to his father's death by the magnates assembled in Verona in 983, and this was confirmed after duke Henry, later known as 'the Wrangler' or 'the Quarrelsome' of Bavaria (d. 994), gave up a brief bid for the kingship in 984, but he was not crowned as emperor until May 996. This occurred in Rome at the hands of Gregory V (996–9), who was also his cousin and a recent appointee to the papal office.[75] On the other hand, Otto's mother Theophanu had been crowned empress alongside her husband in 973, and she made use of the imperial title up to her death, sometimes employing her own regnal years in the dating of charters.[76]

For evidence on his reign, beyond the testimony of a small number of monastic annals, the formal charters of his court and the artistic legacy of some impressive illuminated manuscripts, there is one dominant, if idiosyncratic, source, the chronicle written by Thietmar, bishop of Merseburg (1009–18). Thietmar was the son of a Saxon count from Walbeck on the Aller, who began his chronicle in 1012, intending it to be a history of his see, which had only been founded in 968.[77] His work rapidly developed into something much more than that. Beginning with borrowings from the *Res Gestae Saxonicae* ('Deeds of the Saxons') of the earlier Saxon historian Widukind of Corvey, which had ended with the death of Otto I in 973, Thietmar made his chronicle into a detailed and very personal view of the history of the later Ottonian monarchs and their realm.

While loyal to the Saxon ruling dynasty, he could be critical of it when royal actions seemed to threaten the well-being of the see of Merseburg. This was notably the case with Otto II, who had secured papal support for the suppression of the diocese in 981, to provide a legal justification for its then bishop Giselher (971–81) being transferred to the archbishopric of Magdeburg, as translations from one see to another were still prohibited by canon law.[78] The diocese of Merseburg was only revived on archbishop Giselher's death in 1004, when it was given to Wigbert (1004–9), Thietmar's predecessor.

He was still working on his chronicle at the time of his death in 1018, and it is, not surprisingly, at its most detailed in treating the years during which it was being composed. Even so, its fourth book provides the fullest narrative of the reign of Otto III, which is accompanied at the end by a series of vignettes on the lives of some of the leading secular and ecclesiastical personages of the period. This culminates in a remarkably candid self-portrait of Thietmar himself: 'Know, O reader, that you would see in me a tiny little man. My lower jaw and the side of my face are deformed, because here there once erupted a now permanently swollen fistula. A nose broken in childhood makes me appear ridiculous.'[79] While honest, this description should be seen in the light of the intense focus of this period on the preservation of 'face' – both in the metaphorical sense of honour and literally in the avoidance of blemishes and mutilation. Less than perfect features were regarded as signs of dishonour, and an elaborate code of conduct meant that actions causing someone to 'lose face' – for example, the king refusing a nobleman's publicly stated request for an office to which he felt he had a right – would in itself be a cause of feud, and could produce serious political consequences. Thus many of the participants in the frequent revolts that mark the Ottonian period were motivated by anger at some intended or accidental 'loss of face', rather than by careful political calculation.[80]

Thietmar's idiosyncratic but highly perceptive views on this period can usefully be complemented by the more restrained and official notices of the major annals, notably those of the convent of Quedlinburg, upon which he had himself occasionally drawn. This great monastic house to the north of Merseburg was founded in 936 as her retreat by Matilda, widow of Henry I, in the immediate aftermath of her husband's death. It was visited frequently by the royal court, notably for the celebration of Easter, and its abbesses, like those of Essen, Gandersheim and Gernrode, were ladies of the royal house or those of the greater aristocracy. Its royal founder was quickly revered as a saint, and became the subject of two works of hagiography.[81] The first of these was written for her grandson, Otto II, and the second dedicated to a great-grandson, Henry II (1002–24). She was succeeded as abbess by her granddaughter Matilda, daughter of Otto I, who held the office from 966 to 999. The abbey then passed directly to Adelheid, daughter of Otto II and sister of Otto III, who held it until her death in 1045. She also acquired the abbacies of Gernrode and Vreden in 1014, and in 1039 succeeded her younger sister Sophia as abbess of Gandersheim.

The Quedlinburg annals come as close as anything to presenting the Ottonian dynasty's image of itself. They also convey a very Saxon, and more specifically eastern Saxon, perspective on the activities and concerns of the royal government in this period. That virtually all the major works of Ottonian historiography were written by Saxons in Saxony, and are unmatched by comparable bodies of literary evidence from other eastern Frankish regions is bound to have a distorting effect, both on the historical record and on modern interpretations of it. Relatively little sympathy is thus aroused by the activities and aspirations of the contemporary Bavarian dukes, who in later tradition came to be known by such epithets as 'the Bad' and 'the Quarrelsome', and whose actions have often in consequence been seen by modern historians as weakening the attempts of the Ottonians to create a strong, centralised monarchy. That the latter was the most desirable political development in medieval Germany is not necessarily as self-evident as it has often been assumed.

It was inevitable that the various components of the eastern Frankish kingdom should have different concerns and priorities in this period. Lotharingia, for example, was bound to be more affected by developments in western Francia than was Bavaria, which on the other hand was in much closer touch with what was happening in Italy and out on the plains of the Danube. In the same way, Saxony was predominantly concerned with what was happening beyond its expanding eastern frontiers, above all the lands of the Slavs located between the Elbe and the Baltic. Numerous relatively small and often mutually antagonistic Slav tribes lived here, of whom the best known are the Abodrites, the Wends and the Wiltzi or Liutzi.

The western fringes of this region beyond the Elbe had been in the hands of the Saxons up to the time of Charlemagne, who had deported those of them who lived east of the river in 804, and given their lands to his Slav allies, principally the Abodrites. The rivalries between the different Slav groups that succeeded the Saxons here prevented a large-scale threat from building up on this frontier, even during some of the most difficult times for the East Frankish Carolingians. Under Louis the German (840–76), marcher counties were established and attempts were made, as in the time of Charlemagne, to ensure that the Slav rulers close to the frontiers became Frankish clients.[82] While efforts were made, particularly by bishop Anskar under Louis the Pious, to launch missionary ventures among the Danes and Swedes, few attempts were made by the Franks to convert the Slavs.[83]

The emergence of the Ottonians led to more sustained efforts being made, both at conversion and at the imposition of eastern Frankish rule or hegemony over some of the Slav peoples living closest to the frontiers. In particular, this affected those living in the region known as 'Nordalbingia', the territory lying in the angle between the River Elbe and the Baltic. This developed from the way various noble families who lived on the Frankish side of the frontiers succeeded in building up their wealth and the numbers of their followers – and therefore also their wider political influence in Saxony – through successful raids on their Slav neighbours, resulting in looting, slave-taking and some expansion of territory, as well as the imposing of annual tribute payments The greatest of these local dynasties in eastern Saxony was that of the Liudolfings or Ottonians themselves. The first Liudolf had been given responsibility for the control of the eastern Saxon march, together with a ducal title, by his brother-in-law, king Louis the Younger (876–82). His descendents, kings from 919 onwards, remained personally very interested in this region, from which most of their family wealth stemmed.

Henry I, when temporarily freed from the Magyar threat, conquered much of what would become the march of Brandenburg, and established a new marcher lordship based at Meissen on the Elbe. Otto I added two further marches to the east of the Elbe and the Saale, thus creating a layered structure of four parallel marches extending southwards from the Baltic coast to the northern edge of the lands of the Bohemians. Both Henry and Otto created new fortified settlements or burgs for German settlers in the conquered territories, and destroyed equivalent Slav ones when faced with resistance. These were all mainly small-scale affairs, defended initially with earth and timber ramparts. Larger ones also served as the military, administrative and ecclesiastical centres for the new marches. Otto I also instituted an aggressive programme of conversion among the Slavs who had been brought under his rule. One consequence of this was fierce Slav resistance that prevented the Saxon contingents from joining the rest of the royal army for the campaign that put an end to the Magyar threat at the battle of the Lech in 955.

After the initial phases of open conflict, the political and cultural integration of the temporarily pacified southern Baltic Slavs into the Ottonian Empire required an extension of the ecclesiastical administration in northern Germany. This still organised around the two great Rhineland archbishoprics of Mainz and Cologne, of which the former held a primacy of honour but no superior authority. To these two archdioceses a third had been added in 834, with its centres at Hamburg and Bremen, on the northern fringes of East Francia, whose main purpose was to concern itself with the Scandinavian missions.

The eastward expansion of Ottonian territory and the need for a dedicated centre for the ecclesiastical organisation of the lands east of the Elbe and for the missions to the Slavs made the creation of a new archdiocese for this extensive region desirable, as it was far removed from the older centres in the Rhineland. Otto I planned to create such a new metropolitan see at Magdeburg, where he had founded a monastery dedicated to the soldier martyr St Maurice in 937. As previously mentioned, his mother had established her own convent of Quedlinburg only a little to the south of this in the previous year, and other important monastic centres in the region included Gernrode, founded around 960 by count Gero, who from 937 to 965 served as warden of the East Saxon March under both Otto I and Otto II.[84]

As the presence of these religious houses indicates, an ecclesiastical administrative organisation had already had to come into existence in eastern Saxony, with new bishoprics being created and monasteries built, but this continued to depend on institutional links to the distant archbishoprics of Mainz and of Hamburg-Bremen. These were not, on the other hand, easily persuaded to forgo what they saw as their rights over the new churches in the east; at least not without compensation.

So, while Otto's foundation of his monastery in Magdeburg in 937 has been seen as the first step in his plan to create the new archdiocese, it was to prove a slow and laborious process. New bishoprics were founded in 947/8 at Aarhus, Ribe and Schleswig to serve the needs of the emerging church in southern Denmark, and these were put under the authority of the archdiocese of Hamburg-Bremen; so too was a new bishopric that was established more gradually at Oldenburg in northern Brandenburg in the course of the years 968–72. The archbishopric of Mainz, by far the largest of the German metropolitan sees, saw its authority extended through the creation of new bishoprics at Brandenburg and Havelburg. When a new bishopric was established in 973 or 976 to serve the needs of the recently converted Bohemians, it too was placed under the authority of Mainz.

Despite such concessions, there was continued opposition from vested ecclesiastical interests, not least from the bishop of Halberstadt, whose see, located immediately to the west of Magdeburg, would have to be suppressed to endow the proposed new archbishopric. Only in 968, following the deaths of the main ecclesiastical opponents of the scheme in Germany and when Otto I, now emperor, had also secured the support of a temporarily compliant papacy, was it possible for the new archdiocese to be established. This was accompanied by the setting up of new suffragan bishoprics at Merseburg, Meissen and Zeitz. At the same time the dioceses of Brandenburg and Havelburg, created in the 940s, were transferred from the authority of the archbishop of Mainz to that of his new colleague in Magdeburg.

As in the case of the Saxons in the time of Charlemagne, Christianisation of the northern Slavs was a dimension of a predatory lordship, which involved the establishment of the small fortified centres or burgs from which the conquerors could impose their rule on and take their profits from the surrounding territory. The churches built inside these fortresses also extracted tithes from the Slav population. So there may have been little affection felt for either Ottonian rule or the new religion to which it was allied among the Slavs upon whom both were being imposed. Opportunities for revolt were eagerly awaited, and a major Slav rising took place in 983, following closely on from Otto II's disastrous defeat at the hands of the Arabs in southern Italy the previous year. The timing can hardly have been coincidental.

The outcome was a disaster for the Saxons, from which it took them more than a generation to recover. The fortresses of Brandenburg and Havelburg, both of which were the centres of new dioceses, were destroyed by the Liutzi. At the same time, Hamburg was sacked by the Abodrites. Only the intervention in August of 983 of a Saxon army led by archbishop Giselher of Magdeburg (981–1004) prevented further losses, but Saxon rule, and with it the hold of Christianity over the area between the Elbe and the Baltic, was temporarily at an end.

More constructive developments were taking place at this time among other Slav peoples further south and east, who were not under Saxon rule or the threat of it. While the Saxons had kept the Elbe Slavs generally disunited and divided, as well as oppressed, other, larger Slavic population groupings had formed beyond this region. Some were relatively long-established, while others may have still been in the process of formation and growth.

In part, the emergence of larger-scale Slav ethnic and political groups was a response to the eastward expansion of Carolingian and then Ottonian power from the late eighth century onwards. The Bohemians, who are first recorded in Frankish annals at the very beginning of the ninth century, were probably united under a single ruler called Lecho (k. 805) in reaction to Charlemagne's conquests of Saxony and Bavaria.[85] For reasons that are not made clear in the annals, they themselves became the target of Carolingian attacks in 805/6, and seem to have lost their political unity then or soon after.

Certainly they were in no position to resist the rapid subsequent rise of the Moravian kingdom. By the mid-ninth century the Moravians, the much debated centre of whose state lay somewhere to the south-east, had made themselves into a greater threat to the Bohemians than the Franks had previously been. In consequence, the Bohemians began to regard entry into the Frankish cultural orbit with more enthusiasm. In 845, fourteen unnamed leaders of the Bohemians came to the eastern Frankish king Louis the German to ask for baptism, which he provided for them.[86] Despite this, the Bohemians soon seem to have fallen under Moravian control and took an active part in raids made on east Frankish and Bavarian frontier regions. Their subjection to the Moravian ruler, Sventopulk I (*c.* 869–93) – also known by the Germanic version of his name as Zwentibald – was confirmed in a treaty made by the East Frankish king Arnulf in 890.[87]

Only after the collapse of the Moravian realm at the very end of the century did the Bohemians regain their independence under a single ruling house of their own, known as the Przemyslids. Once again this involved closer political and cultural contacts with the eastern Franks, not least as the new Magyar threat grew in intensity. In 895, two leaders of the Bohemians, Spitignevo and Witizla, submitted to Arnulf at Regensburg. In later tradition if not contemporary record, they are held to be brothers and to have built churches in Bohemia after their return, including the first one to be erected in Prague.

Another church was built in Prague early in the tenth century and dedicated to St Vitus, whose cult was actively promoted by the Saxon monastery of Corvey, on the River Weser. This choice of dedication and source of relics indicates the influence of the Saxon church on the newly developing Christianity of Bohemia at this time. The founder of this church of St Vitus was a young prince of the name of Vaclav (Wenceslas), who around 935 was murdered by his brother Boleslav. A cult of the young prince, venerated as a Christian martyr, developed rapidly, without apparently weakening the secular power of his murderer. In this and other ways the cult of St Wenceslas parallels the slightly later ones of St Edward the Martyr, king of Wessex (975–8), and St Magnus, earl of Orkney (*c.* 1105–15).[88]

A further cultural dimension to this fratricidal conflict has been detected. From around 930 Bohemia was increasingly dominated by the duchy of Bavaria under its duke Arnulf 'the Bad', and the Bavarian church had long-established interests in extending its missionary activities in this north-easterly direction. So it has been argued that the rivalry between Vaclav and Boleslav reflected a wider struggle between two factions in the Bohemian aristocracy that supported Saxon and Bavarian political and cultural hegemony, respectively. Though enticing, this argument cannot be substantiated, because of the limited nature of the evidence. German chroniclers make few references to Bohemia, and an indigenous historiographical tradition would only start with the writing of the *Chronica Bohemorum* of Cosmas of Prague (d. 1125).

Boleslav I (*c.* 935–67) proved to be a highly successful ruler, who, as duke of the Bohemians, seems to have established a relatively stable and secure realm for his people within the political and cultural orbit of the Ottonian empire. His successor, Boleslav II (*c.* 967–1004) became a significant figure in the troubled internal politics of the empire, supporting Henry the Quarrelsome of Bavaria against Otto II in 974 and again in his short-lived bid for the crown against the infant Otto III in 984. The conversion of the Bohemians advanced steadily during the reigns of both these dukes, but not in spectacular fashion. The first bishop of Prague was only consecrated in 973 or 976, and he and his successors have been called 'little more than the chaplains of the Przemyslid dukes', who showed no interest at this time in promoting an independent Bohemian church with its own archbishopric.[89]

Bohemian influence may, however, have been behind the extension of Christianity into a neighbouring region at this time. To the north-east of the lands of the Bohemians and east of 'Nordalbingia', another large Slav ethnic group seems to have been forming under the leadership of what the Ottonians recognised as its own ducal dynasty, the Piasts. It has been argued that this family was of Viking origin, but it ruled over the Slav population that came to be known as the Poles, of whose earlier history hardly any trace remains. It may well be that it was the military conquests of this dynasty that welded together previously disparate elements of population and thus forged the new Polish ethnic identity.

The Piast duke Mieszko, who is the first to emerge clearly into historiographical light, married a daughter of Boleslav I of Bohemia in 964. As Thietmar reports, she quickly converted her pagan husband to Christianity. However, it is likely that Mieszko's interest in a marriage tie with the Przemyslids indicates a predisposition in favour of the wider cultural links that they represented, not least with the Ottonian empire and therefore the acceptance of Christianity. This was reconfirmed by his second marriage in 978, this time to the daughter of Thietrich (Theoderic), warden of the Saxon North March (965–85).[90]

Mieszko was baptised in 966, and established a church dedicated to St George in his court centre at Gniezno. A bishopric (which became an archbishopric in 1000) was founded there in 968, and from Gniezno a new missionary centre and a second diocese was developed at Poznan. Other sees were created as the frontiers of Piast rule rapidly expanded in succeeding decades. To avoid the claims to authority over it of the German archbishoprics, in particular that of Magdeburg, the Polish duke placed the church in his territories under direct papal patronage in 990. This should not necessarily be seen as a threat to his political loyalty to the Ottonians, but it marks a clear distancing of his duchy from too close a dependence on the personnel and institutions of the German Church.[91]

Mieszko (d. 992) expanded his power from this central area around Gniezno and Poznan southwards into Silesia, which led to territorial disputes with the Bohemian dukes, and into the area around Cracow, where another bishopric was soon founded. Towards the end of his reign he also extended his conquests into Pomerania and the Baltic coast. He, like Boleslav II of Bohemia, accepted the claims made by Henry the Quarrelsome of Bavaria, and initially recognised him as king in 984. A realignment to accept the authority of Otto III did neither of these dukes any harm, especially as the ensuing regime of the two regents was largely passive as far as the eastern lands were concerned. Mieszko's son, Boleslav I Chobry or 'the Mighty' (992–1025), took an even more independent line than his father in relation to the Ottonian empire, overrunning the March of Meissen in the aftermath of the death of Otto III in 1002.

This, and his attacks on the Bohemians, suggest that Boleslav had little long-term interest in preserving the concord between the various Slav rulers and their imperial overlord, which Otto III seems to have wanted to foster. This had been symbolised by Otto's investing of Boleslav Chobry with the title *Frater et Cooperator Imperii* ('Brother and Partner') during the emperor's ground-breaking visit to the shrine of St Adalbert at Gniezno in the year 1000.

St Adalbert, whose original name was Vojteck, was a Bohemian noble whose family, the Slavnikids, had long been hostile to the Przemyslid dukes (and were massacred by them in 995). After training at Magdeburg under its archbishop Adalbert, whose name he subsequently took, he had been made bishop of Prague in 983 as a result of the patronage of the emperor Otto II. He had been forced to abandon his see in 988 after frustrated attempts at imposing reforms, and quarrels with duke Boleslav II. Following a period of exile in at the monastery of Sts Boniface and Alessio in Rome, where he met the empress Theophanu, he was obliged to resume his episcopal duties in Prague in 992, under pressure from his ecclesiastical superior, the archbishop of Mainz. This proved no more successful than the previous incumbency, and he returned to Rome in 994, where he impressed the young Otto III when he came to the city for his imperial coronation. In 996, he was sent by pope Gregory V to assist the evangelisation of the Polish frontiers. Heading into the lands of the still pagan Liutzi, he was killed by them on 23 April 997.[92] A *Life of Adalbert* was written in Rome in 999. This was followed in 1004 by a second one, written by Bruno of Querfurt, a cousin of Thietmar of Merseburg, who later became both a missionary bishop and then a martyr in Hungary.

Otto III's visit to the tomb of Adalbert at Gniezno three years after Adalbert's death has been seen both as an act of personal piety towards a man whom he knew and admired, and as a public demonstration of the new eastward extension of the authority of his imperial office. His journey, which needs to be seen as a whole, began in Rome and ended at Aachen, where he had the grave of Charlemagne opened so that he could inspect his bones and the regalia that had been buried with him. In between these two points Otto's route took him to Regensburg, Meissen and Magdeburg, as well as Gniezno, where he came as the first German ruler to honour the shrine of a Slav saint in Slav lands. He approached Gniezno, the location of Adalbert's relics, 'barefoot, as a suppliant' and entering the church he appealed for the martyr's intercession. He then proclaimed the see of Gniezno to be an archbishopric. In his report of this, Thietmar of Merseburg felt impelled to add the rather sardonic wish: 'legitimately, I hope', as prior papal approval had not been obtained. The dioceses of Poznan, Cracow, Wroclaw and Kolberg were then made into the suffragan sees of the new metropolitanate.[93]

The emperor's actions in Gniezno, seen as part of his great journey linking the former imperial capitals of Rome and Aachen, are bound to appear highly charged with symbolism. One aspect of this was Otto's transportation of some of the relics of St Adalbert from Gniezno to Aachen, for reburial alongside Charlemagne, thus explicitly linking the new saint and the Polish duchy with the imperial founder. The young emperor was taking new initiatives here in more ways than one. As Thietmar's remark implies, the authority by which Otto intervened in the highly contentious field of ecclesiastical organisation and hierarchy to create a new archbishopric might not seem to be above challenge. From Thietmar's account it was clearly not papal authority but imperial decree that was employed to elevate the Polish see to an archbishopric. In contrast, Otto I had taken perhaps as much as thirty years to achieve the comparable enhancement of the status of Magdeburg and had secured it in the end by diplomacy, consensus and papal authorisation. The pope in the year 1000 was Otto's former tutor, Gerbert, who took the very symbolic name of Sylvester II when elected – by imperial command – the previous year. In Roman tradition, though not reality, Sylvester I had been the pope who baptised Constantine, the first Christian emperor, and had been the recipient of the 'donation', upon which later papal claims to territorial authority and powers of crowning emperors rested.

Emperor and pope

The short-lived period of very close links between pope and emperor under Sylvester II and Otto III was further emphasised in the joint conferral of a crown and royal title on the first king of the Magyars in 1001. The Magyars had developed a more stable and settled form of society in the aftermath of their final defeat by the Ottonians at the battle of the Lech in 955, and had become more open to the cultural influences to which they were subjected from both Byzantium and the Ottonian empire. Around 980, a Magyar ruler called Geza (d. 997) became a nominal Christian, but his son Waik seems to have been a more wholehearted convert. He adopted the baptismal name of Stephen, by which he is better known. In his reign as the first king of Hungary (1001–38) the formal conversion of the Magyars was achieved and an ecclesiastical organisation was developed for the church in the new kingdom.

The value accorded their old Magyar foes by the Ottonian rulers can be deduced from the marriage that was arranged in the mid-990s between Waik/Stephen and Gisela, the sister of duke Henry of Bavaria. The latter, son of the infamous Henry the Quarrelsome (d. 995), would succeed his cousin Otto III as king and emperor in 1002, though this was hardly to be foreseen at the time. Even so, in comparison with the rewards offered to the Polish and Bohemian ruling houses, Stephen of Hungary's marriage into the Ottonian dynasty and his subsequent investment with a royal rather than a ducal title indicates how great a weight was placed by Otto III on securing the loyalty of the Magyar ruler.

The question remains as to whether Otto III, advised by Sylvester II, saw these involvements with the Slavs and the Magyars around the turn of the millennium primarily as a dimension of his imperial duty to promote the spread of the Christian faith, or whether he was interested more in the role they could play in developing the earthly power and prestige of his office. The depiction of Otto in the illuminated Gospel book prepared for him *c.* 998–1001 shows the emperor enthroned and being approached by gift-bearing female figures representing 'Sclavinia', 'Germania', 'Gallia' and 'Roma' (in place of 'Italia' in comparable earlier versions of similar scenes).[94] The presence for the first time of the personification of the Slav lands testifies to the importance currently being accorded at the imperial court to the eastward extension of imperial hegemony.

Otto himself might not have made too much of a distinction between the extension of the bounds of his imperial authority and those of the Church. Certainly the precedents from the reign of Charlemagne, with whom he was also interesting himself at this time, would have led him to look for opportunities to further the expansion of his rule eastwards as well as in Italy, and into expressing an overwhelming sense of responsibility for the spiritual well-being of his subjects. Too much of a contrast should thus not be made between the emperor's southern and eastern concerns, even though in practice the separate demands they made on him were hard to reconcile.

In Rome, where the imperial court was located for most of the relatively short time in which Otto conducted his own affairs, the missionary ventures in the east became as much a major concern as they were for the churches in Saxony and Bavaria. The monastery of St Alessio, where Adalbert stayed during his self-imposed exile from Prague, was a major centre of inspiration for missionary ventures. Both of the *Lives* of Adalbert were written by monks of this community, which was home to members of several leading German aristocratic families, such as Bruno of Querfurt.[95] Other monks from this house accompanied Adalbert on his return to Prague in 992 and were encouraged by him to found a monastery near the Bohemian capital. The first archbishop of Gniezno, following its elevation by Otto III in 1000 was Gaudentius, brother of Adalbert and another former monk of San Alessio.

Ultimately, it is hard to decide the precise nature of Otto III's imperial aspirations. His actual reign, following the long regencies, was too brief, and his views may have still been in process of formation at the time of his death. Undoubtedly, there are Byzantine influences to be detected in the style of his court in Rome. Here, for example, his count of the palace employed the Byzantine title of Protospatharios, and other officials signed imperial charters using Greek letters, albeit for clearly German names.[96] The emperor himself adopted the practice of dining publicly but alone, which was found mildly shocking by those accustomed to the more egalitarian or convivial style of other and earlier western courts.[97] While such features may be symptomatic of new ideas and experiments in protocol and imperial ideology that were being developed, at least in Italy, at this time, they proved in practice to be short-lived.

Similarly, the rhetoric of a *Renovatio Imperii Romanorum* or 'Renewal of the Empire of the Romans', which appears in a small number of works written by authors linked to Otto's court, may not have been anchored on a fully developed plan of action by the time of the emperor's premature death. Its meaning, according to Thietmar, was certainly not understood or approved by all.[98] The phrase itself, which was used on Otto's imperial seal from 998 onwards, had previously been employed for the first imperial seal of Charlemagne. So it did not imply a revival of a Roman as opposed to a Carolingian ideology of empire. However, the first Carolingian emperor changed both his title and his seal within little more than a year of his coronation in 800, to escape from some of the implications of too close an association between his office and the city and see of Rome. This would not have been acceptable to the Franks, any more than it would have been two centuries latter to the Germans. Otto III, with a pope of his own choosing in the person of his former tutor Gerbert, and perhaps bemused by the antiquarian splendours of the city, may have thought that he could avoid some of the problems that worried his great predecessor. If so, he was probably mistaken.

Like his father and grandfather before him, Otto III was caught in the dilemma of the weakness of the royal position in Germany if the king was not present to impose his authority on the dukes and to lead his forces in person against the Slavs, Danes, Magyars or western Franks. He also needed to be equally attentive to Italian affairs if the kingship of the Lombards, and above all the imperial title, were to be maintained. As for the popes, they too were prisoners of a similar dilemma. They needed a powerful secular protector against the many external enemies and internal rivals they faced. Yet they did not want that protector to be too dominant or permanently resident in the city of Rome, as this could inhibit their exercise of power within the territorial state they had built up in central Italy. At the same time, too long an absence from Italy on the part of their imperial master could expose them to personal danger. Thus after Otto III returned to Germany in the autumn of 996 the Romans expelled his German pope, Gregory V. Worse was to follow, in that while Otto III returned and re-established Gregory in 997, and later appointed his own former tutor Gerbert to succeed him as Sylvester II (999–1003), a revolt in Rome in 1001 forced both the emperor and his pope to flee the city. In the aftermath of this, Otto caught malaria and died in January 1002.[99]

Otto III had high expectations of his imperial office, blending traditions deriving from his Carolingian predecessor Charlemagne with others inherited from his Byzantine mother. He had restored Aachen, looted by the western Franks in 978, and had had the body of Charlemagne dug up for his inspection and then given a more grandiose reburial. Rome, even more than Aachen, became the idealised centre of his empire, and he used the title *Imperator Augustus Romanorum* with relish. In January 1001 in a charter he rightly dismissed the concept 'donation of Constantine' as a forgery – it would take nearly 500 years before anyone else would do the same – and made it clear that papal authority was to be subordinate to imperial.[100] It is perhaps not likely that he, any more than a line of distinguished predecessors extending back to Louis the Pious, would have been able to turn all these theoretical aspirations into reality. It was his particular misfortune that the Rome he idealised for its past had become no more than another large Italian town, prey to parochial aristocratic factionalism. Otto's imperial dreams ended with an ignominious flight into the malarial marshes.

The death of this young emperor, who may have hoped to revive some of the cultural, if not the military, greatness of the Roman Empire, provides a usefully symbolic point at which to end this book. However, most historians would agree that Otto III's ambitions, whatever they may have been, were unlikely to have led to significant long-term results. They would point instead to another, far less precisely dated feature of this period as being of much greater importance, and representing major social and economic change affecting most parts of Europe. This is what has been called 'the Feudal Revolution'.[101] By this is meant the disappearance of the social, ideological and administrative structures that distinguish the existence of a state, and their replacement by others primarily dependent upon personal ties of loyalty and service. While the term 'state' can be used rather generally to refer to any large scale, independent political entity, it really applies more precisely to ones with defined frontiers and a centralised government; with the latter reliant upon trained professional classes (a bureaucracy) for its ability to levy tax, distribute its proceeds and provide a functioning system of justice for the punishment of crime and the resolution of civil disputes.

Simply put, this was the kind of socio-political organisation that had been represented by the Roman Empire and survived to some degree in its 'Byzantine' successor in the eastern Balkans and Asia Minor, but the description would be less and less appropriate for Rome's more numerous western heirs, including the Carolingian Empire.[102] Instead of citizens theoretically equal under the law, and with the government controlling its own military forces, we have seen how western kings and emperors, less and less able to exercise tax raising powers and lacking the educated professionals needed to run a more sophisticated administrative and judicial system, became increasingly reliant upon the leaders of local society, the territorial aristocracies whose power and wealth rested upon landownership and the service they could demand from their own dependents, to provide them with military power. Rather than civic obligation, the ties that bound together the upper echelons of these societies became ones of personal dependence, expressed formally though acts of homage or vassalage. The administration of justice was decentralised to the territorial magnates, as the rulers lost the ability to impose it themselves. Financially, they also had to rely largely upon their own landed resources, and could call on few other sources of revenue. The social and political effects of this so-called 'Feudal Revolution' are generally agreed to have fully developed in the eleventh century, but argument exists as to how far back their roots should be traced. Some answers have been suggested in earlier chapters of this book. But it is with the prospect of this very different kind of society from that of the former Roman Empire coming into maturity in the years around 1000 that it makes sense to end this book, and to leave it to others to provide guidance on what lay ahead.

Abbreviations

AB   *Annales Bertiniani* or Annals of Saint-Bertin
ARF   *Annales Regni Francorum* (see Bibliography);
          ARF Rev refers to the revised version of *c.* 814
ASC   Anglo-Saxon Chronicle
CC   *Corpus Christianorum, series latina*
CFHB   *Corpus Fontium Historiae Byzantinae*
CHFM   *Les Classiques de l'Histoire de France au Moyen Age*
CLA   *Codices Latini Antiquiores*, ed. E. A. Lowe, 11 vols plus a
          Supplement (Oxford, 1934–71)
CSEL   *Corpus Scriptorum Ecclesiasticorum Latinorum*
CSHB   *Corpus Scriptorum Historiae Byzantinae*
FC   Fathers of the Church
FEHL   *Colección Fuentes y Estudios de Historia Leonesa*
Fontes   *Fontes ad Historiam Regni Francorum Aevi Karolini*
          Illustrandam, ed. R. Rau (3 vols, Darmstadt, 1955–60)
MGH   *Monumenta Germaniae Historica*, subdivided by series:

	AA	*Auctores Antiquissimi*
	Capit	*Capitularia*
	Epp	*Epistulae*
	LL	*Leges*
	SS	*Scriptores*
	SRG	*Scriptores Rerum Germanicarum*
	SRM	*Scriptores Rerum Merovingicarum*

MIöG   *Mitteilungen des Instituts für österreichische*
          Geschichtsforschung
PG   *Patrologia Graeca*, ed. J. P. Migne
PL   *Patrologia Latina*, ed. J, P. Migne
PLRE   *Prosopography of the Later Roman Empire*,
          ed. J. R. Martindale *et al.*, 3 vols:
          Vol. I: AD 260–395 (Cambridge, 1971)
          Vol. II: AD 395–527 (Cambridge, 1980)
          Vol. III: AD 527–641 (Cambridge, 1992)
RIC   *Roman Imperial Coinage*
SC   *Sources Chrétiennes*
SHA   *Scriptores Historiae Augustae*
SHF   *Société de l'Histoire de France*
SLH   *Scriptores Latini Hiberniae*

Notes

1 CRISIS AND CHANGE IN THE ROMAN EMPIRE, 235–305

1. Ammianus Marcellinus, XXIII. v. 17; F. Millar, *The Roman Empire and its Neighbours* (London and New York, 1967), pp. 238–48.
2. A. A. Barrett, *Caligula: The Corruption of Power* (London, 1990), pp. xix, 1–41, 172–80.
3. Herodian, VI. viii. i and VII. i. 1–2.
4. *Scriptores Historiae Augustae: Maximini Duo*, I. 5–7, and II. 5; see also the discussion in R. Syme, 'The Emperor Maximinus', in his *Emperors and Biography* (Oxford, 1971), pp. 179–93. For the imperial portraiture of Maximin, see S. Wood, *Roman Portrait Sculpture, 217–260 A.D.* (Leiden, 1986), pp. 33–5, 66–8, 126–7.
5. Herodian, VIII. v. 8–9 and vi. 2.
6. F. Millar, *The Emperor in the Roman World* (London, 1977), pp. 122–31.
7. Sextus Aurelius Victor, *Liber de Caesaribus*, 28, anon. *Epitome de Caesaribus*, 28; Zosimus, *Historias Neas*, I. 18–23.
8. Sextus Aurelius Victor 29; Epitome 29; Zosimus I. 21–5. See also Wood, *Roman Portrait Sculpture*, pp. 42–5, 77–9.
9. Sextus Aurelius Victor 30–2; Epitome 30–2; Zosimus I. 24–30, 36; *Scriptores Historiae Augustae: Valeriani Duo*. See Wood, *Roman Portrait Sculpture*, pp. 43–8, 109–11.
10. The capture of Valerian is represented graphically both on the Sasanian cameo of Shapur I in the Bibliothèque Nationale in Paris, and in the monumental rock carving of Naqsh-i-Rustam; see R. Ghirshman, *Iran: Parthians and Sassanians* (London, 1962), plates 195–7.
11. On the Gallic empire, see J. Drinkwater, *The Gallic Empire* (Stuttgart, 1987).
12. RIC, vol. 5(1), ed. H. Mattingly and E. A. Sydenham, pp. 248–62.
13. C. Lepelley, 'The Survival and Fall of the Classical City in Late Roman Africa', in J. Rich (ed.), *The City in Late Antiquity* (London, 1992), pp. 50–76.
14. L. de Blois, *The Policy of the Emperor Gallienus* (Leiden, 1976), pp. 29–30.
15. R. Syme, 'The Emperor Claudius Tacitus', in his *Emperors and Biography* (Oxford, 1971), pp. 237–47, shows that Tacitus belongs to this military group, and that the presentation of him in the *SHA* as a senator is a deliberate distortion.
16. Sextus Aurelius Victor 38.3, Epitome 38.3.
17. Epitome 34.5 (Quintillus); Sextus Aurelius Victor 36, Zosimus I.63–4 (Florian).
18. Sextus Aurelius Victor 37.4; Zosimus I. 71. *Scriptores Historiae Augustae: Probus*, xx is completely unreliable.
19. Sextus Aurelius Victor 39.1–16, Zosimus I. 73.

20. Sextus Aurelius Victor 39.17–19; Eutropius, *Breviarium*, xxii; S. Williams, *Diocletian and the Roman Recovery* (London, 1985), pp. 43–8.

21. Williams, *Diocletian*, pp. 61–70; W. Seston, *Dioclétien et la Tétrarchie* (Paris, 1946), pp. 231–57. T. D. Barnes, *Constantine and Eusebius* (Cambridge, Mass., 1981), pp. 8–10.

22. P. Salway, *Roman Britain* (Oxford, 1981), pp. 288–314.

23. Seston, *Dioclétien*, pp. 137–54.

24. See RIC, vol. VI, ed. C. H. V. Sutherland and R. A. G. Carson, for the coins of the tetrarchy.

25. R. Bianchi Bandinelli, *Rome: the Late Empire* (London, 1971), plate 256; H. P. L'Orange, *Art Forms and Civic Life in the Later Roman Empire* (Princeton, NJ, 1965), pp. 37–68.

26. XII *Panegyrici Latini*, XI. xi. 4, ed. R. Mynors (Oxford, 1964), p. 265.

27. Barnes, *Constantine and Eusebius*, pp. 7–8.

28. A. H. M. Jones, *The Later Roman Empire, 284–602* (3 vols) (Oxford, 1964), Vol. 1, pp. 42–52.

29. Ibid., pp. 52–60; E. N. Luttwak, *The Grand Strategy of the Roman Empire* (Baltimore, Md. and London, 1976), pp. 127–90.

30. T. Frank, *Economic Survey of Ancient Rome* (Baltimore, Md., 1940), Vol. 5, pp. 310–421.

31. Jones, *Later Roman Empire*, Vol. 1, pp. 68–70.

32. Suetonius, *Vita Neronis*, xvi.

33. Eusebius of Caesarea, *Ecclesiastical History*, VI. xxxix. I–VI. xlv. 5.

34. Cyprian, bishop of Carthage, *Epistolae*, lxxx.

35. Translated by H. Bettensen, *Documents of the Christian Church* (2nd edn) (Oxford, 1963), III g, pp. 13–14.

36. For some arguments about the causes of the persecutions, see G. E. M. de Ste Croix, 'Why Were the Early Christians Persecuted?', together with a reply by A. N. Sherwin-White and de Ste Croix's riposte, all to be found conveniently in M. I. Finley (ed.), *Studies in Ancient Society* (London, 1974), pp. 210–62.

37. RIC, vol. 4 (3), eds H. Mattingly, E. A. Sydenham and C. H. V. Sutherland, pp. 117–18 and 130–3; these coins were all struck in Milan.

38. On Christians in the Roman army, see A. D. Nock, 'The Roman Army and the Roman Religious Year', *Harvard Theological Review*, 45 (1952), 186–252, esp. section III. iv.

39. Eusebius of Caesarea, *Ecclesiastical History*, VI, xli. 1–xlii. 4.

40. Eusebius, *Ecclesiastical History*, VII. x. 3–9.

41. Lactantius, *De Mortibus Persecutorum*, X. 6, XI. 1–4; Barnes, *Constantine and Eusebius*, pp. 15–27.

42. Barnes, ibid., pp. 149–62.

2   THE AGE OF CONSTANTINE, 305–50

1. Lactantius, *De Mortibus Persecutorum*, 19; Eutropius, *Breviarium*, IX. xxvi–xxviii.

2. Eutropius, X. i–ii. Zosimus, *Historias Neas*, II. viii.

3. Eutropius, X. ii. 2. T. D. Barnes, *Constantine and Eusebius* (Cambridge, 1981), pp. 28–9.

4. Lactantius, *De Mortibus Persecutorum*, 29.

5. Barnes, *Constantine and Eusebius*, pp. 32–3 and nn. 36 and 38, indicates that in practice neither Constantine nor Maximin used the title of *Filius Augusti* within their own territories.

6. Lactantius, *De Mortibus Persecutorum*, 35.

7. Zosimus, II. xv–xvi; Lactantius, *De Mortibus Persecutorum*, 44.

8. H. A. Drake, *Constantine and the Bishops* (Baltimore, Md., 2000), pp. 154–91.

9. Older arguments are dealt with in N. H. Baynes, *Constantine the Great and the Christian Church* (2nd edn, with preface by H. Chadwick) (Oxford, 1972).

10. From an original papyrus letter of the emperor addressed to the inhabitants of the Province of Palestine; see E. Hartley, J. Hawkes and M. Henig (eds), *Constantine the Great: York's Roman Emperor* (York, 2006), p. 120, and p. 15 for the translation. For Eusebius's presentation of the ideology of the Christian Empire, see G. F. Chesnut, *The First Christian Histories* (Paris, 1977), pp. 61–166.

11. J. Toynbee and J. Ward Perkins, *The Shrine of St. Peter and the Vatican Excavations* (London, 1956), plate 32 and pp. 72–4.

12. P. Bruun, 'The Disappearance of Sol from the Coins of Constantine', *Arctos*, ns 2 (1958), 15–37.

13. A. D. Nock, 'The Emperor's Divine *Comes*', *Journal of Roman Studies*, 37 (1947), 102–16. See also S. G. MacCormack, 'Rome, Constantinopolis, the Emperor, and His Genius', *Classical Quarterly*, 25 (1975), 131–50.

14. *Liber Pontificalis*, trans. Davis, Vol. 1, pp. 14–26.

15. Toynbee and Ward Perkins, *Shrine of St. Peter*, pp. 195–239; H. P. L'Orange, *Art Forms and Civic Life in the Later Roman Empire* (Princeton, NJ, 1965), pp. 79–85; R. Krautheimer, *Early Christian and Byzantine Architecture* (Harmondsworth, 1965), pp. 17–44; idem, *Rome: Profile of a City, 312–1308* (Princeton, 1980), pp. 3–31 and 42–5. Krautheimer, *Rome*, pp. 7–8.

16. S. G. MacCormack, *Art and Ceremony in Late Antiquity* (Berkeley and Los Angeles, 1981).

17. Krautheimer, *Rome*, pp. 54–8; idem, *Early Christian and Byzantine Architecture*, pp. 25–6.

18. R. R. Holloway, *Constantine and Rome* (New Haven, Conn. and London, 2004), pp. 57–117.

19. See R. Collins, *Keepers of the Keys of Heaven: A History of the Papacy* (London and New York, 2009), ch. 3.

20. Letter of Constantine I to Anullinus, Proconsul of Africa, in Eusebius, *Ecclesiastical History*, X. v. 15–17. On Anullinus, see PLRE, I, pp. 78–9 (Anullinus 2).

21. Eusebius, *Ecclesiastical History*, IX. ii. 1–iv. 4, for petitions sent to Maximin II against the Christians in Egypt.

22. Lactantius, *De Mortibus Persecutorum*, 48; Eusebius, *Ecclesiastical History*, X. v. 1–14.

23. Eusebius, *Ecclesiastical History*, X. viii. 8–19.
24. P. Brown, *The World of Late Antiquity* (London, 1971), pp. 34–40.
25. Barnes, *Constantine and Eusebius*, pp. 62–4.
26. Ibid., pp. 64–77.
27. PLRE, vol. I, pp. 563 (Martinianus 2), and 931 (Valens 13). PLRE is wrong, however, in giving Martinianus only the title of Caesar. That he, like Valens, was an Augustus, is proved by his coinage: RIC, vol. 7, ed. P. Bruun, pp. 608 and 645.
28. Lactantius, *De Mortibus Persecutorum*, 50.
29. Barnes, *Constantine and Eusebius*, pp. 34–6 on this episode and the sources for it.
30. PLRE, vol. I, p. 233 (Crispus 4); PLRE, vol. I, pp. 325–6 (Fausta).
31. L'Orange, *Art Forms and Civic Life*, pp. 121–5.
32. G. Dagron, *Naissance d'une capitale: Constantinople et ses institutions de 330 à 451* (Paris, 1974), pp. 13–47.
33. Tacitus, *Annales*, XV. 40; *Scriptores Historiae Augustae: Commodus Antoninus*, VIII. 6–9 (attributed to Aelius Lampridius).
34. PLRE, vol. I, pp. 223 (Constantinus 3), 233 (Crispus), 509–10 (Licinius 4). The proclamation of the new Caesars took place on 1 March 317.
35. *Codex Theodosianus*, IV. vi. 2–3 (2 laws of 336); ed. T. Mommsen (4th printing, Dublin and Zurich, 1971), Vol. 1, ii, pp. 175–6. He therefore already was, or was made, a eunuch.
36. PLRE, vol. I, pp. 241 (Dalmatius 7), 407 (Hannibalianus 2).
37. Zosimus II, 39–40.
38. Zosimus II. 41 is confusing. See Eutropius, *Breviarium*, X. 9.
39. Julian, *Oration II: On the Heroic Deeds of Constantius*, 94, ed. W. C. Wright, *The Works of the Emperor Julian* (3 vols, Loeb Library), Vol. 1, pp. 248, 250.
40. Barnes, *Constantine and Eusebius*, pp. 17–19.
41. E. Stein, *Histoire du Bas-Empire* (2 vols) (Paris and Bruges, 1959), Vol. 1, pp. 137–8, with references.
42. See the introduction, pp. vii–liii, of P. Dufraigne's edition of (Sextus) Aurelius Victor (Paris, 1975); also H. W. Bird, *Sextus Aurelius Victor: A Historiographical Study* (Liverpool, 1984).
43. P. Salway, *Roman Britain* (Oxford, 1981), pp. 348–53; S. Johnson, *Late Roman Fortifications* (London, 1983), pp. 204–6.
44. Zosimus II. 42. On Centcelles, see R. Collins, *Oxford Archaeological Guide to Spain* (Oxford, 1998), pp. 110–13.

3   PROTECTING THE EMPIRE, 350–95

1. On Ammianus, see J. F. Matthews, *The Roman Empire of Ammianus* (London, 1989).
2. PLRE, vol. I, p. 624 (Nepotianus 5).
3. PLRE, vol. I, p. 924 (Vetranio 1).
4. Zosimus, II. 43–54 provides the most substantial account of these years. On him, see W. Goffart, 'Zosimus, the First Historian of Rome's Fall', *American Historical Review*, 76 (1971), 412–41; and

A. Cameron, 'The Date of Zosimus's New History', *Philologus*, 113 (1969), 106–10.

5. Ammianus Marcellinus, XVII. 9–10.
6. Ammianus, XVI. xii. 5.
7. Ammianus, XVI. i. 1–xi. 25.
8. Ammianus, XV. v. 1–v. 34.
9. Ammianus, XV. viii. 19, XVI. iii. 1–2.
10. Ammianus, XV. viii. 1–17.
11. Ammianus, XVI. ii. 1–13. For the war with the Alamans in 356–361 see J. Drinkwater, *The Alamanni and Rome, 213–496* (Oxford, 2007), pp. 217–265.
12. Ammianus, XVI. iii. 1–3.
13. Ammianus, XVI. iv. 1–5.
14. Ammianus, XVI. xii. 1–63.
15. Ammianus, XVII. 1. 12–13.
16. Ammianus, XVII. ii. 1–4, viii. 1–3.
17. Ammianus, XVII. ix. 1, XVIII. ii. 5–6.
18. Ammianus, XVIII. iii. 1–5.
19. Ammianus, XIX. i. 1–ix. 2.
20. Ammianus, XX. iv. 1–v. 10.
21. Ammianus, XXI. xii. 3, XXII. i. 2–ii. 1.
22. Ammianus, XIV. v. 6–9, XXII. iii. 11. For Arianism, see Chapter 5 below.
23. Ammianus, XXII. iv. 1–10, vii. 1–10, XXV. iv. 7–9, 19–21.
24. Ammianus, XXII. v. 1–5.
25. Ammianus, XXII. x. 7, XXV. iv. 20.
26. P. Athanassiadi, *Julian: An Intellectual Biography* (London, 1992), pp. 161–92; G. W. Bowersock, *Hellenism in Late Antiquity* (Cambridge, 1990), pp. 1–13.
27. G. W. Bowersock, *Julian the Apostate* (London, 1978), pp. 79–93. Julian's writings are edited in three volumes by W. C. Wright in the Loeb Classical Library. See vols 2 and 3 in particular.
28. Ammianus, XXII. iv. 1–2.
29. Ammianus, XXII. xiv. 1–3. The work is edited by Wright, Vol. 2, pp. 420–510.
30. Eunapius, *Lives of the Philosophers:* see the accounts of Maximus of Ephesus and of Chrysanthius of Sardis; also Ammianus, XXV. iv. 17.
31. For the Persian campaign, see Ammianus, XXIII. ii. 1–XXV. vii. 14. A penetrating analysis of the weaknesses of Julian's strategy can be found in A. Ferrill, *The Fall of the Roman Empire: The Military Explanation* (London, 1986), pp. 52–6.
32. Ammianus, XXV. iii. 1–24.
33. Libanius, Oration XXIV: 'On Avenging Julian', vi. In earlier works, Orations XVII and XVIII, Libanius accepts the view that a Persian had been responsible.
34. Ammianus, XXV. v. 1–x. 17.
35. Ammianus, XXVII. xii. 1–18.
36. Ammianus, XXXI. xiv. 1–8.
37. Stein, *Histoire du Bas-Empire*, Vol. 1, p. 175 and references.

38. Ammianus, XXVI. v. 8–ix. 11. PLRE, vol. I, pp. 742–3 (Procopius 4).
39. Ammianus, XXVII. v. 1–10.
40. Ammianus, XXIX. i. 1–ii. 28.
41. Ammianus, XXVIII. viii. 1–57; A. Alföldi, *A Conflict of Ideas in the Late Roman Empire* (Oxford, 1952), esp. pp. 48–95.
42. Ammianus, XXX. vi. 1–6.
43. Ammianus, XXX. x. 1–6.
44. J. F. Matthews, *Western Aristocracies and Imperial Court A.D. 364–425* (Oxford, 1975), pp. 51–5, 69–76. For relations with the Alamans, see Drinkwater, *The Alamanni and Rome*, pp. 266–319.
45. Ammianus, XXXI. x. 1–22.
46. Zosimus, IV. 35.
47. PLRE, vol. I, pp. 598–9 (Merobaudes 2).
48. Matthews, *Western Aristocracies*, pp. 176–7.
49. Zosimus, IV. 42–3.
50. Zosimus, IV. 46.
51. Zosimus, IV. 53–4.
52. On this episode, see H. Bloch, 'The Pagan Revival in the West at the End of the Fourth Century', in A. Momigliano (ed.), *The Conflict between Paganism and Christianity in the Fourth Century* (Oxford, 1963), pp. 193–218; and idem, 'A New Document of the Last Pagan Revival in the West', *Harvard Theological Review*, 38 (1945), 199–244.
53. For an account and analysis of the battle, see Ferrill, *Fall of the Roman Empire*, pp. 71–5.
54. Zosimus, IV. 59. *Epitome de Caesaribus* xlviii. 19–20.

4   FROM THE BATTLE OF ADRIANOPLE TO THE SACK OF ROME, 378–410

1. J. Vogt, *Kulturwelt und Barbaren – Zum Menschheitsbild der spätantiken Gesellschaft* (Mainz, 1967).
2. Priscus of Panium, fragments, ed. and trans. R. C. Blockley, *The Fragmentary Classicising Historians of the Later Roman Empire*, Vol. II (Liverpool, 1983), pp. 222–377.
3. See the arguments over the ethnic attributes of such major finds as the Pietroasa and Nagyszentmiklós Treasures; for example in G. Lázló and I. Rácz, *The Treasure of Nagyszentmiklós* (English trans., Budapest, 1984). See also the example given in nt 2 of Chapter 7 below, and some discussion of methodological problems in E. James, 'Burial and Status in the Early Medieval West', *Transactions of the Royal Historical Society*, 5th series, 39 (1989), 23–40; and G. Halsall, *Settlement and Social Organisation. The Merovingian Region of Metz* (Cambridge, 1995).
4. Ammianus Marcellinus, *Res Gestae*, XXXI, ii. 1–12; Jordanes, *Getica*, xlviii.
5. Ammianus, XXXI. iii. I–iv. 13.
6. C. J. Wickham, 'Pastoralism and Underdevelopment in the Early Middle Ages', *Settimane di studio sull' Alto Medioevo*, 31 (1985), 401–51; see also O. Lattimore, *Inner Asian Frontiers of China* (Boston, Mass., 1951), pp. 58–80.

7. The best treatment of the Huns is to be found in the, regrettably incomplete, work of O. Maenchen-Helfen, *The World of the Huns* (Berkeley, Calif., 1973), but see also C. Kelly, *Attila the Hun* (London, 2008), pp.7–54 for an up-to-date survey.

8. M. Kazanski, *Les Goths* (Paris, 1991), pp. 9–59; P. Heather, *The Goths* (Oxford, 1996), pp. 51–93.

9. On whom, see A. A. Vasiliev, *The Goths in the Crimea* (Cambridge, Mass., 1936).

10. Recent work on these cultures is usefully summarised in P. Heather and J. Matthews, *The Goths in the Fourth Century* (Liverpool, 1991), pp. 51–101; and Heather, *The Goths*, pp. 11–50.

11. P. Heather, *Goths and Romans, 332–489* (Oxford, 1991), pp. 84–121.

12. As suggested by the freezing of the Sea of Azov (on which, see Vasiliev, *The Goths in the Crimea* (Cambridge, Mass., 1936), pp. 31–2).

13. See E. A. Thompson, *The Historical Work of Ammianus Marcellinus* (London, 1947), pp. 87–133 for discussion of the final parts of the work and for other reasons why Ammianus should have wished to terminate it in 378.

14. Ammianus, XXXI. iv. 1–8.

15. Ammianus, XXXI. v. 1–9; vi. 1–8.

16. Ammianus, XXXI. v. I–xii. 17.

17. Ammianus, XXXI. xiii. 1–19.

18. H. Wolfram, *History of the Goths* (English trans.) (Berkeley, Calif., etc., 1988), pp. 131–9.

19. Zosimus, IV. xxiii. 4–5 (also Ammianus, XXXI. xi. 1–4) provides one example of a defeat that the Romans were able to inflict on the Goths in 378, when the latter were scattered around the countryside foraging. No great reliance should be placed on modern estimates of the size of 'barbarian' populations; not only because no real evidence of a statistical kind exists, but also because all models are conditioned by preconceived ideas of the nature of these confederacies.

20. Zosimus, IV. xxxi. 5.

21. Wolfram, *History of the Goths*, pp. 133–4, who compares and contrasts this treaty with that made in 376.

22. For criticism of Theodosius I's use of the Visigoths as allies, see A. Ferrill, *The Fall of the Roman Empire: The Military Explanation* (London, 1986), pp. 75–85.

23. Wolfram, *History of the Goths*, pp. 136–7.

24. Zosimus, V. xi. 1–2; *Codex Theodosianus*, IX. xlii. 22 (22 November 408).

25. PLRE, vol. I, pp. 853–88 for the career of Stilicho.

26. For a damning critique of Stilicho, see J. B. Bury, *A History of the Later Roman Empire from the Death of Theodosius to the Death of Justinian* (reprint, 2 vols) (New York, 1958), pp. 172–3. A. Cameron, *Claudian: Poetry and Propaganda at the Court of Honorius* (Oxford, 1970), pp. 187–8 is more impressed by him.

27. Jordanes, *Getica*, xxix/146; see Wolfram, *History of the Goths*, pp. 32–4,143–6; P. Heather, *The Goths* (Oxford, 1996), pp. 113–17 and 166–78 is rightly sceptical of the supposed antiquity of the Amals.

28. These are (here all too briefly expressed) the arguments of W. Goffart, *Barbarians and Romans, A.D. 418–584: The Techniques of Accommodation* (Princeton, NJ, 1980). See also W. Goffart, *Barbarian Tides* (Philadelphia, 2006), pp. 119–186 , and J. Durliat, 'Le salaire de la paix sociale dans le royaumes barbares (Ve–VIe siècles)', in H. Wolfram and A. Schwarcz (eds), *Anerkennung und Integration* (Vienna, 1988), pp. 21–72.

29. H. Wolfram, 'Athanaric the Visigoth: Monarchy or Judgeship? A Study in Comparative History', *Journal of Medieval History*, I (1975), 259–78.

30. D. Claude, *Adel, Kirche und Königtum im Westgotenreich* (Sigmaringen, 1971), pp. 21–9.

31. E. Demougeot, *De l'unité à la division de l'empire romain* (Paris, 1951), pp. 267–81; Cameron, *Claudian*, pp. 180–7.

32. Cameron, *Claudian*, pp. 30–62.

33. Zosimus, V. xxix. 5–9; Olympiodorus fragment 5.

34. For Gainas, see PLRE, vol. I, pp. 379–80. For the eastern court and politics in Constantinople at this time, see A. Cameron and J. Long, *Barbarians and Politics at the Court of Arcadius* (Berkeley, Calif., 1993), pp. 199–252; and J. H. W. G. Liebeschuetz, *Barbarians and Bishops* (Oxford, 1990), pp. 89–145.

35. *Codex Theodosianus*, XIV. x. 4 (12 December 416).

36. Zosimus, V. xxxiv. 1–7.

37. Zosimus, V. xxxviii. 1–xlii. Cameron, *Claudian*, pp. 371–7 on Stilicho's use of barbarians in the Roman army – hence possibly inhibiting his use of that army against other barbarians.

38. For an analysis of Honorius's reign, see B. Bleckmann, 'Honorius und das Ende der römischen Herrschaft in Westeuropa', *Historische Zeitschrift*, 265 (1997), 561–95. The most detailed presentation of the complicated pattern of events is Demougeot, *De l'unité à la division de l'empire romain*, pp. 376–494.

39. Zosimus, V. xli. 1–2; cf. Jerome *ep*. 123. xvi.

40. Zosimus, VI. vii. I–viii.; PLRE, vol. II, pp. 180–1 (Priscus Attalus 2).

41. Zosimus, VI. xii.

42. Olympiodorus fragment 3; on whom, see J. F. Matthews, 'Olympiodorus of Thebes and the History of the West (A.D. 407–425)', *Journal of Roman Studies*, 60 (1970), 79–97; and E. A. Thompson, 'Olympiodorus of Thebes', *Classical Quarterly*, 38 (1944), 43–52. PLRE, vol. II, pp. 798–9 (Olympiodorus 1).

43. Olympiodorus fragment 10.

44. Zosimus, VI. ii; C. E. Stevens, 'Marcus, Gratian, Constantine', *Athenaeum*, 35 (1957), 316–47.

45. On the Alans, see V. Kouznetsov and I. Lebedynsky, *Les Alains* (Paris, 1997).

46. For a discussion of the dating, see Demougeot, *De l'unité à la division de l'empire romain*, pp. 381–2, nt 155, which provides a full listing of the relevant sources. The belief that the Rhine froze in 406 and this allowed the Vandals and the others to cross it has no foundation: see M. Kulikowski, 'Barbarians in Gaul, usurpers in Britain', *Britannia* 31 (2000), pp. 325–45 at pp. 328–9.

47. Hydatius, *Cronica,* 42 (=AD 409).
48. PLRE, vol. II, pp. 316–17 (Constantinus 21).
49. Olympiodorus fragment 16; Zosimus, VI. v.
50. Zosimus, VI. v. For some controversial interpretations of the chroniclers' words see: E. A. Thompson, 'Britain A.D. 406–410', *Britannia,* 7 (1977), 303–18. More orthodox is P. Salway, *Roman Britain* (Oxford, 1981), pp. 426–45.

5   A DIVIDED CITY: THE CHRISTIAN CHURCH, 300–460

1. Jerome, *ep.* cxxvii. 12, citing Psalm 79. vv 1–3 and Virgil, *Aeneid II.* 361–5 and 369. On Jerome, see J. N. D. Kelly, *Jerome: his Life, Writings and Controversies* (London, 1975).
2. Jerome, *ep.* cxxvii. 3.
3. Zosimus, V. xii. 2.
4. For anti-pagan legislation of the time of Theodosius I, see P.-P. Joannou, *La législation impériale et la christianisation de l'empire romain (311–476)* (Rome, 1972), pp. 46–8, and the laws from the Theodosian Code listed on pp. 79–89; for the context, see J. F. Matthews, 'A Pious Supporter of Theodosius I: Maternus Cynegius and his Family', *Journal of Theological Studies,* ns 18 (1967), 438–46; and idem, *Western Aristocracies and Imperial Court A.D. 364–425* (Oxford, 1975), pp. 101–45; also M. R. Salzman, *The Making of a Christian Aristocracy* (Cambridge, Mass., 2002).
5. Edited by C. Zangemeister, *Historiarum adversum pagans libri VII,* CSEL, Vol. V (reprinted Hildesheim, 1967); see also B. Lachoix, *Orose et ses idées* (Montreal, 1965).
6. E. T. Mommsen, 'Orosius and Augustine', reprinted in his *Medieval and Renaissance Studies* (New York, 1959), pp. 325–48. It is worth noting that Orosius was unwilling or unable to minimise the horrors of events occurring in his native Spain in the years 409–17.
7. See Zangemeister's edition, pp. vii–xxxv.
8. For the analysis of Augustine's views, see R. A. Marcus, *Saeculum: History and Society in the Theology of St Augustine* (Cambridge, 1970), esp. chs 1–4.
9. P. R. L. Brown, *Augustine of Hippo* (new edn) (London, 2000), pp. 340–407.
10. See the articles of N. H. Baynes on 'The Thought-World of East Rome', 'The Byzantine State' and 'Eusebius and the Christian Empire' in his *Byzantine Studies and Other Essays* (London, 1955), pp. 24–46, 47–66 and 168–72.
11. For the history of the Arian controversy in the time of Constantine I, see T. D. Barnes, *Constantine and Eusebius* (Cambridge, Mass., 1981), pp. 202–44. On fourth-century Arianism, see R. Williams, *Arius: A Heresy and Tradition* (London, 1987); and M. R. Barnes and D. H. Williams (eds), *Arianism after Arius* (Edinburgh, 1993).
12. E. A. Thompson, 'The *Passio S. Sabae* and Early Visigothic Society', *Historia,* 4 (1955), 331–8; and idem, *The Visigoths in the Time of Ulfila* (Oxford, 1966), pp. 64–132.

13. A. C. Vega (ed.), *Opuscula omnia Potamii Olisiponensis* (El Escorial, 1934); M. Méslin, *Les Ariens d'Occident, 335–430* (Paris, 1967).

14. For aspects of Greek Christian thought in the later fourth century, see R. R. Ruether, *Gregory of Nazianzas: Rhetor and Philosopher* (Oxford, 1969).

15. Kelly, *Jerome*, pp. 141–67, 283–95, but rather brief on the exegesis.

16. Kelly, *Jerome*, pp. 227–40.

17. For Ambrose's earlier career, see N. B. McLynn, *Ambrose of Milan: Church and Court in a Christian Capital* (Berkeley, Calif., 1994), pp. 1–52; and J. Moorhead, *Ambrose* (London, 1999), pp.15–39.

18. J. Gaudemet, *L'Eglise dans l'empire romain (IVe–Ve siècles)* (Paris, 1958), pp. 330–40.

19. Ambrose, *ep*. 20, for the fullest account.

20. McLynn, *Ambrose of Milan*, pp. 158–219; D. H. Williams, *Ambrose of Milan and the End of the Arian–Nicene Conflicts* (Oxford, 1995), pp. 185–229; Moorhead, *Ambrose*, 129–156.

21. Ambrose, *epp*. xvii and xviii; Symmachus, *Relatio* iii, ed. R. H. Barrow, *Prefect and Emperor: The Relationes of Symmachus A.D. 384* (Oxford, 1973), pp. 32–47.

22. Ambrose, *epp*. 40 and 41.

23. Ambrose, *ep*. 51.

24. Ambrose, *ep*. 57.

25. T. D. Barnes, *Tertullian: A Historical and Literary Study* (Oxford, 1971); M. M. Sage, *Cyprian* (Cambridge, Mass., 1975).

26. On the conversion of the aristocracy of the city of Rome, see P. R. L. Brown, 'Aspects of the Christianization of the Roman Aristocracy', *Journal of Roman Studies*, 51 (1961), 1–11; and Salzman, *The Making of a Christian Aristocracy*, pp. 69–177.

27. M. Wojtowytsch, *Papsttum und Konzile von den Anfängen bis zu Leo I* (Stuttgart, 1981), pp. 205–83. R. Collins, *Keepers of the Keys of Heaven: A History of the Papacy* (London and New York, 2009), chs 3–5.

28. See O. Wermelinger, *Rom und Pelagius* (Stuttgart, 1975), pp. 88–133, 146–65.

29. C. Pietri, *Roma Christian, Recherches sur l'Eglise de Rome, son organisation, sa politique, son idéologie de Miltiade à Sixte III 311–440* (2 vols) (Paris, 1976), pp. 98–156, 461–724, 1537–96 for the administrative, liturgical and pastoral developments up to the death of Sixtus III in 440.

30. Pietri, *Roma Christiana*, pp. 431–60, 1628–51.

31. A. Dufourcq, *Etude sur les Gesta Martyrum romaine* (Paris, 1900), esp. Vol. I, pt iii, pp. 265–383; Pietri, *Roma Christiana*, pp. 98–156, 461–724; and see the articles by K. Sessa, H. Jones and C. Leyser in K. Cooper and J. Hillner (eds), *Religion, Dynasty and Patronage in Early Christian Rome, 300–900* (Cambridge, 2007), pp. 77–161.

32. Pope Gelasius I's attempt to suppress the Lupercalia is the best known example: *Gélase la Lettre contre les Lupercales*, ed. G. Pomarès (SC 65), with a valuable introductory study of the role of liturgy in this conflict; see also A. W. J. Holleman, *Pope Gelasius I and the Lupercalia* (Amsterdam, 1974).

33. W. Ullmann, 'Leo I and the Theme of Papal Primacy', *Journal of Theological Studies*, ns 11 (1960), 25–51; and idem, *Gelasius I* (492–496) (Stuttgart, 1981), pp. 61–87. For the development of the Petrine ideology prior to the pontificate of Leo, see Pietri, *Roma Christiana*, pp. 272–401, 1413–1524, 1596–1628; also Collins, *Keepers of the Keys*, chs 1–4.

34. For the conflict between the two Churches, see N. H. Baynes, 'Alexandria and Constantinople: A Study in Ecclesiastical Diplomacy', in his *Byzantine Studies*, pp. 97–115.

35. On the Origenist controversy, see J. Binns, *Ascetics and Ambassadors of Christ* (Oxford, 1994), pp. 201–17; also P. de Labriolle, 'Saint Jerome et l'Origenisme', in A. Fliche and V. Martin (eds), *Histoire de l'Eglise*, Vol. IV (Paris, 1945), pp. 31–46; and Kelly, *Jerome*, pp. 196–209.

36. The most substantial study of Chrysostom remains that of C. Bauer, *Die heilige Johannes Chrysostomos und seine Zeit* (2 vols) (Munich, 1929/1930); English trans. *John Chrysostom and his Time*, (2 vols) (London, 1959), but see now also J. N. D. Kelly, *Golden Mouth: The Story of John Chrysostom, Ascetic, Preacher, Bishop* (London, 1995). For his fall, see J. H. W. G. Liebeschuetz, *Barbarians and Bishops: Army, Church and State in the Age of Arcadius and Chrysostom* (Oxford, 1990), pp. 157–227.

37. E. Amann, 'L'affaire de Nestorius vue de Rome', *Revue des Sciences Réligieuses*, 23 (1949), 5–37, 207–44; and 24 (1950), 28–52, 235–65; also Pietri, *Roma Christiana*, pp. 1347–74 ('Rome, Alexandrie et Nestorius').

38. For the Council of Ephesus, see Caspar, *Geschicte des Papsttums*, Vol. I, pp. 389–422; and Pietri, *Roma Christiana*, pp. 1375–1405. For the Nestorian Christians beyond the Roman frontiers, see C. Baumer, *The Church of the East* (English trans.) (London, 2006); also ch. 25, 'Christians in Iran', of *Cambridge History of Iran*, ed. E. Yarshater (2 vols) (Cambridge, 1983), pp. 924–48 (by J. P. Asmussen).

39. W. H. C. Frend, *The Rise of the Monophysite Movement* (Cambridge, 1972), pp. 1–49: 'The Road to Chalcedon, 428–51'. Wojtowytsch, *Papsttum und Konzile*, pp. 318–29; P. Batiffol, *Le Siège Apostolique* (2nd edn) (Paris, 1924), pp. 493–527; Caspar, *Geschichte des Papsttums*, Vol. I, pp. 462–503.

40. R. V. Sellers, *The Council of Chalcedon: A Historical and Doctrinal Survey* (London, 1961); Caspar, *Geschichte des Papsttums*, pp. 506–27.

41. Leo the Great, *ep.* 28, originally sent to Bishop Flavian of Constantinople, 13 June 449; Wojtowytsch, *Papsttum und Konzile*, pp. 429–50.

42. Leo the Great, *ep.* 104 to the Emperor Marcian (22 May 452); Ullmann, *Gelasius 1*, pp. 88–107; Batiffol, *Siège Apostolique*, pp. 562–89.

43. That this was already an issue by the time of the patriarchate of Acacius and the pontificate of Gelasius I was suggested by Caspar, *Geschichte des Papsttums*, Vol. II, pp. 747–8.

44. Frend, *Rise of the Monophysite Movement*, pp. 143–359 for the later history of the Monophysites, up to the Arab conquests.

45. PG 26, cols 835–976. See D. Brakke, *Athanasius and the Politics of Asceticism* (Oxford, 1995), and T. D. Barnes, *Athanasius and Constantius:*

Theology and Politics in the Constantinian Empire (Cambridge, Mass., 1993).

46. P. Brown, 'The Rise and Function of the Holy Man in Late Antiquity', *Journal of Roman Studies*, 61 (1971), 80–101 is fundamental to the understanding of these processes. See also P. Rousseau, *Ascetics, Authority and the Church in the Age of Jerome and Cassian* (Oxford, 1978), pp. 9–76; D. Chitty, *The Desert a City* (Oxford, 1966), esp. chs 1 and 2; and C. Rapp, *Holy Bishops in Late Antiquity* (Berkeley, Calif., 2005), pp. 100–152.

47. P. Brown, *The Making of Late Antiquity* (Cambridge, Mass., 1978), pp. 81–101; P. Rousseau, *Pachomius: The Making of a Community in Fourth Century Egypt* (Berkeley, Calif., 1985). For the *Lives* of Pachomius, see F. Halkin (ed.), *Sancti Pachomii Vitae Graecae* (Brussels, 1932).

48. Brown, 'Rise and Function of the Holy Man', p. 83; C. C. Walters, *Monastic Archaeology in Egypt* (Warminster, 1974), pp. 7–18, with references, for evidence of the earliest communities.

49. Chitty, *The Desert a City*, pp. 2, II, 22, 41 n. 71, 44 n. 130.

50. See Binns, *Ascetics and Ambassadors of Christ*, esp. pp. 80–147; also A. Vööbus, *A History of Asceticism in the Syrian Orient*, Vol. II: *Early Monasticism in Mesopotamia and Syria* (Louvain, 1960).

51. For the Syrian setting, see G. Tchalenko, *Villages antiques de la Syrie du nord* (3 vols) (Paris, 1953); also Brown, 'Rise and Function'; for Simeon, see A. J. Festugère, *Antioche païenne et chrétienne: Libanius, Chrysostome et les moines de Syrie* (Paris, 1959), pp. 347–401; H. Klengel, *Syrien zwischen Alexander und Mohammed* (Darmstadt, 1987), esp. p. 54 for the reconstruction of a stylite's pillar-top living area. See also E. K. Fowden, *The Barbarian Plain: St. Sergius between Rome and Iran* (Berkeley, Calif., 1999).

52. For the text of the *Life* of Daniel, see H. Delehaye, *Les Saints stylites* (Brussels, 1923), pp. 1–94; there is an English translation in E. Dawes and N. H. Baynes, *Three Byzantine Saints* (London, 1948).

53. Chitty, *The Desert a City*, pp. 82–167.

54. Rousseau, *Ascetics, Authority and the Church*, pp. 99–139; Kelly, *Jerome*, pp. 116–40.

55. See the study of this subject by E. D. Hunt, *Holy Land Pilgrimage in the Later Roman Empire, AD 312–460* (Oxford, 1982), esp. pp. 155–80.

56. Rousseau, *Ascetics, Authority and the Church*, pp. 169–234; idem, 'Cassian, Contemplation and the Coenobitic Life', *Journal of Ecclesiastical History*, 26 (1975), 113–26; O. Chadwick, *John Cassian* (2nd edn) (Cambridge, 1968), esp. pp. 1–81.

57. PLRE, vol. II, pp. 575–6 (Hypatia 1); Sozomen, *Ecclesiastical History*, VII. xv for the destruction of the Serapeum. On Hypatia, see M. Dzielska, *Hypatia of Alexandria* (Cambridge, Mass., 1995).

58. P. R. L. Brown, 'Saint Augustine's Attitude to Religious Coercion', *Journal of Roman Studies*, 54 (1964), 107–16; and for the context, Wermelinger, *Rom und Pelagius* (n. 28 above), and Pietri, *Roma Christiana*, pp. 1177–1265.

59. Brown, *Augustine of Hippo*, pp. 427–33.

6 THE WARLORDS

1. For example, G. Webster, *The Roman Imperial Army* (2nd edn) (London, 1979), but for this period, see now P. Southern and K. R. Dixon, *The Late Roman Army* (London, 1996), and H. Elton, *Warfare in Roman Europe A.D. 350–425* (Oxford, 1996).
2. Olympiodorus fragment 12, followed by Zosimus, VI. ii.
3. Orosius, *Historiarum adversus paganos libri VII*, VII. xliii; R. Collins, *Early Medieval Spain, Unity in Diversity, 400–1000* (2nd edn) (London, 1995), pp. 15–19.
4. PLRE, vol. II, pp. 237–40 (Bonifatius 3).
5. Hydatius, *Chronicon*, 69, dates this to 418; Prosper, *Epitoma Chronicon*, 1271, locates it with the events of 419. This difference has never been resolved, but it has become conventional to use the 418 date.
6. Prosper, 1298.
7. Olympiodorus fragments 17 and 19; cf. Hydatius 51 and 54, who makes no reference to the Visigoths; Prosper 1251 is very brief. PLRE, vol. II, pp. 621–2 (Jovinus 2), 983 (Sebastianus 2).
8. Prosper, 1335; for his career and death, see PLRE, vol. II, pp. 684–5 (Litorius).
9. Prosper, 1322, 1324, 1326; *Chronica Gallica A CCCCLII*, 112, 117–19, 127 (use of Alans). See C. Kelly, *Attila the Hun* (London, 2008), pp. 83–87; for the Alans, see V. Kouznetsov and I. Lebedynsky, *Les Alains* (Paris, 1997), pp. 11–55.
10. *Chronica Gallica A CCCCLII*, 128.
11. For Prosper and Hydatius, and for the brief 'Gallic Chronicle of 452', see the excellent study by S. Muhlberger, *Fifth Century Chronicles* (Liverpool, 1990).
12. I. Wood, 'The End of Roman Britain: Continental Evidence and Parallels', in M. Lapidge and D. Dumville (eds), *Gildas: New Approaches* (Woodbridge, 1984), p. 19; for the career of Aetius, see PLRE, vol. II, pp. 21–9 (Aetius 7).
13. PLRE, vol. II, pp. 493–4 (Gaudentius 5).
14. For Johannes (423–25) see PLRE, vol. II, pp. 594–5 (Joannes 6); it is worth suggesting that he is identical to the Iohannes 2 of PLRE, vol. I, p. 459. Both men held office as Primicerius Notariorum, and the exercise of the office of Praetorian Prefect of Italy (412–13, 422?) by 'Johannes 2' might help to explain the choice of 'Ioannes 6' to succeed the childless Honorius as emperor.
15. Prosper, 1303; for Felix see PLRE, vol. II, pp. 461–2 (Felix 14; A portrait of him exists on his consular diptych (of 428): R. Delbrueck, *Die Consulardiptychen und verwandte Denkmäler* (Leipzig and Berlin, 1929), no. 3, pp. 93–5.
16. Prosper, 1310; *Cronica Gallica A CCCLII*, III; Hydatius 99.
17. For Sebastian, see PLRE, vol. II, pp. 983–4 (Sebastianus 3).
18. Gildas, *De Excidio Britonum*, XX. 1.
19. Hydatius, 96, 98.
20. C. Courtois, *Les Vandales et l'Afrique* (Paris, 1955), pp. 155–74 for the conquest and the treaty.

21. S. I. Oost, *Galla Placidia Augusta* (Chicago, 1968), esp. pp. 189–90, 228–43 for relations between the empress and Aetius.
22. B. L. Twyman, 'Aetius and the Aristocracy', *Historia*, 19 (1970), 480–503; the best narrative of Aetius's ascendancy is still that of E. Stein, *Histoire du Bas-Empire* (2 vols) (Paris and Bruges, 1959), Vol. 1, pp. 317–50.
23. O. Maenchen-Helfen, *The World of the Huns* (Berkeley, Calif., 1973), pp. 59–125.
24. Thompson, *History of Attila and the Huns*, pp. 73–124; J. B. Bury, *History of the Later Roman Empire from the Death of Theodosius I to the Death of Justinian* (2 vols) (London, 1923), Vol. I, pp. 271–88, which includes a translation of Priscus's account of his embassy to Attila; also in Blockley's edition of Priscus (see Bibliography), pp. 246–95.
25. Hydatius, 150; Priscus, fragment 15. In fragment 16 Priscus also indicates that a cause of friction may have been a disputed succession among the (Ripuarian) Franks, with one contender seeking Attila's support while his brother appealed to Aetius.
26. This story comes from the *Vita Aniani Aurelianensis Episcopi*, chs vii–ix, *MGH SRM*, Vol. III, pp. 104–17, and is likely to be no more than a mistaken elaboration of the account, found in Jordanes (*Getica*, 194–5), that the Alan garrison of Orléans was preparing to surrender the city to the Huns, but was frustrated by the rapid arrival of Visigothic and Roman forces.
27. Jordanes 197–215; Jordanes was writing almost exactly a century after the event, and it is possible to place too much reliance on the detail given in his narrative. See Kelly, *Attila the Hun*, 194–199. The location of the battlefield has remained uncertain, but somewhere in the region of Champagne is likely. See Bury, *Later Roman Empire*, Vol. I, pp. 293, n. 1.
28. Jordanes, 215–16.
29. Prosper, 1367; Jordanes (in part following Priscus) 221–4; Hydatius 154 refers to famine and disease among the Huns.
30. Jordanes (following Priscus), 254–64; Prosper 1370; Hydatius 154.
31. Prosper, 1373; Hydatius 160. For this Boethius, see PLRE, vol. II, p. 231 (Boethius 1).
32. Prosper, 1375; Hydatius 162.
33. *Marcellini Comitis Chronicon*, s.c. Aetii et Studii, 2, ed. Mommsen, MGH *AA*, vol. XI, p. 86. Marcellinus also refers to the deposition of Romulus in 476 (p. 91) as marking the end of the western Empire. Could he not make up his mind, or is the text corrupted? On this chronicler, see B. Croke, *Count Marcellinus and his Chronicle* (Oxford, 2001). For Aetius as 'the last of the Romans', see Bury, *Later Roman Empire*, Vol. I, p. 300 with references.
34. PLRE, vol. I, pp. 372–3 (Flavius Fravitta), and pp. 379–80 (Gainas); Zosimus, V. xiii–xxii. See J. H. W. G. Liebeschuetz, *Barbarians and Bishops* (Oxford, 1990), pp. 89–125.
35. PLRE, vol. II, pp. 164–9 (Aspar).
36. Candidus fragment 1, preserved in the *Biblioteca* of Photius 79; for Candidus himself, see PLRE, vol. II, p. 258 (Candidus 1).

37. PLRE, vol. II, pp. 749–51 (Maximus 22); Prosper 1375; Hydatius 162; John of Antioch fragment 201, for the brick.
38. PLRE, vol. II, pp. 196–8 (Avitus 5); as Master of the Soldiers to Petronius Maximus, see Sidonius Apollinaris, Panegyric on Avitus (*Carmen* vii), lines 377–8, 392–4, 399–402, 464–8.
39. Hydatius, 173–8. Collins, *Early Medieval Spain,* pp. 19–24.
40. Hydatius, 183; *Victori Tonnennensis Episcopi Chronica,* 16, ed. C. Cardelle de Hartmann in CCSL vol. CLXXIIIA, p. 8; and the continuation of Prosper's chronicle in the *Codex Havniensis:* ed. Mommsen, MGH *AA,* vol. IX, p. 304.
41. PLRE, vol. II, pp. 702–3 (Maiorianus); Stein, *Histoire du Bas-Empire,* Vol. 1, pp. 371–80.
42. Hydatius, 200; for the visit to Zaragoza, see the *Consularia Caesaraugustana,* 23a, ed. C. Cardelle de Hartmann, CCSL vol. CLXXIIIA, p. 10, and note in the 'Historical Commentary' by R. Collins, pp. 96–7. For *Adventus,* see S. G. MacCormack, *Art and Ceremony in Late Antiquity* (Berkeley, Calif., 1981), pp. 17–89.
43. Hydatius, 209 (peace with Gaiseric), 210 (killed by Ricimer); John of Antioch fragment 203; Marcellinus s.c. Dagalaifus and Severinus 2 (ed. Mommsen, p. 88), who has him killed at Dertona.
44. Victor Tonnonnensis, s.c. Vivianus (ed. Mommsen, p. 187); PLRE, vol. II, pp. 1004–5 (Severus 18), and pp. 11–12 (Aegidius).
45. Hydatius, 228 for the death by poison or in an ambush of Aegidius, and 231 for the death of Severus. The claim that Severus was poisoned by Ricimer appears in Cassiodorus, *Chronica,* 1280. PLRE, vol. II, p. 1005 is wrong to give this reference 's.a. 464'.
46. PLRE, vol. II, pp. 96–8 (Anthemius 3).
47. Candidus fragment 2, preserved in the *Suda* or Suidas, X. 245; Procopius, *History of the Wars,* III. vi. 2–26; Courtois, *Les Vandales,* pp. 201–5.
48. Cassiodorus, 1293; Procopius, *History of the Wars,* III. vii. 1. For doubts on Anthemius being a pagan, see P. Chuvin, *Chronique des derniers païens* (Paris, 1990), pp. 124–6.
49. PLRE, vol. II, pp. 796–8 (Olybrius 6).
50. *Chronica Gallica A DXI,* 651, 652, ed. Mommsen, *MGH AA,* IX, pp. 664–5.
51. PLRE, vol. II, p. 514 (Glycerius); John of Antioch fragment 209. For Gundobad and his return to Gaul, see PLRE, vol. II, p. 524.
52. PLRE, vol. II, pp. 777–8 (Nepos 3).
53. PLRE, vol. II, pp. 811–12 (Orestes 2), and pp. 949–50 (Romulus 4).
54. For Glycerius's possible involvement see the résumé of the lost work of Malchus in Photius, *Biblioteca,* 78.
55. Malchus fragment 10.
56. *Notitia Dignitatum,* ed. O. Seeck (Berlin, 1876; reprinted Frankfurt, 1962); see also A. H. M. Jones, *The Later Roman Empire 284–602* (3 vols) (Oxford, 1964), Vol. III, pp. 347–80.
57. See H. Elton, *Warfare in Roman Europe AD 350–425* (Oxford, 1996).
58. Vegetius, *De Re Militari,* I. xx; see Ferrill, *Fall of the Roman Empire,* pp. 127–32. For a convincing redating of Vegetius to the fifth

century, see W. Goffart, 'The Date and Purpose of Vegetius's *De Re Militari*', *Traditio*, 33 (1977), pp. 65–100, reprinted in his *Rome's Fall and After* (London, 1989), pp. 45–80, with additional comments on p. 355.

59. B. Ward-Perkins, *The Fall of Rome and the End of Civilization* (Oxford, 2005); and P. Heather, *The Fall of the Roman Empire: A New History* (London, 2005).

60. Ward-Perkins, *Fall of Rome*, p. 183.

61. J. Smith, *Europe after Rome: A New Cultural History 500–1000* (Oxford, 2005), pp. 29–30; on this tendency, see R. Collins, 'Making Sense of the Early Middle Ages', *English Historical Review*, vol. 124 (2009), pp. 641–65.

62. E. Gibbon, *The Decline and Fall of the Roman Empire*, ed. J. B. Bury, Vol. IV (London, 1901), pp. 160–3; see P. Brown, 'Gibbon's Views on Culture and Society in the Fifth and Sixth Centuries', *Daedalus*, 105 (1976), 73–88; on the development of Christian teachings on virginity, see idem, *The Body and Society: Men, Women and Sexual Renunciation in Early Christianity* (New York, 1988).

63. P. Fouracre (ed.) *New Cambridge Medieval History Vol. 1, c.500–c.700* (Cambridge, 2005), p. 8.

63. P. Sarris, *Economy and Society in the Age of Justinian* (Cambridge, 2006), pp. 131–48 for the historiography, and more generally for the argument in favour of the predominance of such great estates; Jones, *Later Roman Empire*, Vol. II, p. 1066.

64. C. Wickham, *Framing the Middle Ages: Europe and the Mediterranean, 400–800* (Oxford, 2005), p. 161.

65. M. I. Rostovtzeff, *Social and Economic History of the Roman Empire* (2nd edn) (Oxford, 1957).

7   THE NEW KINGDOMS

1. For reconstructions derived from archaeology, see R. Christlein, *Die Alamannen: Archäologie eines lebendigen Volkes* (Stuttgart, 1978); for Alamannic society, see K. Krapp, *Die Alamannen. Krieger, Siedler, frühe Christen* (Stuttgart, 2007), pp. 45–141; and J. Drinkwater, *The Alamanni and Rome, 213–496* (Oxford, 2007), pp. 117–44.

2. For example, an identical type of buckle and pin can be found around the lower Loire (D. Costa, *Art mérovingien de la Musée Th. Dobrée, Nantes* (Paris, 1964), nos 268, 271, 280, 281), in the area of Paris (P. Perrin, *Collections mérovingiennes de la Musée Carnavalet* (Paris, 1985), nos 565–8, 571), but also in the centre of Spain (G. Ripoll, *La necropolis visigoda de El Carpio de Tajo (Toledo)* (Madrid, 1985), pp. 163–73 and illustrations on pp. 213 and 219. It also turns up in southern England: for example, F. R. Aldsworth, 'Droxford Anglo-Saxon Cemetery, Soberton, Hampshire', *Proceedings of the Hampshire Field Club and Archaeological Society*, 35 (1979), fig. 32, nos 9 and 10. All have been dated (independently!) to the mid-sixth century.

3. *Codex Theodosianus*, XIV. x. 2, 3 and 4.

4. *Codex Theodosianus*, XIV. x. 1.
5. For the Missorium, see J. R. Melida, *El Disco de Teodosio* (Madrid, 1930); J. Beckwith, *The Art of Constantinople* (2nd edn) (London, 1968), plates 14 and 22, and pp. 15–22.
6. PLRE, vol. I, pp. 163 (Bonitus 1 and 2), and pp. 840–1 (Silvanus 2); Ammianus Marcellinus, *Res Gestae*, XV. v. 16.
7. PLRE, vol. I, pp. 765–6 (Richomeres).
8. PLRE, vol. I, pp. 95–7 (Arbogastes).
9. PLRE, vol. II, pp. 128–9 (Arbogastes).
10. Sidonius Apollinaris, *epistulae*, bk IV, letter 17.
11. PLRE, vol. I, pp. 159–60 (Bauto); for his daughter the Empress Eudoxia see PLRE, vol. II, p. 410 (Eudoxia 1).
12. PLRE, vol. I, pp. 94–5 (Arbitio 2).
13. PLRE, vol. I, p. 539 (Mallobaudes).
14. Priscus fragments 7 and 8.
15. Jordanes, *Getica*, 277.
16. Gregory of Tours, *Historiarum Libri Decem*, II. 18. It would be interesting to know more about the source for this brief chapter.
17. For Odovacer's career, see PLRE, vol. II, pp. 791–3.
18. PLRE, vol. II, p. 806 (Onoulphus).
19. See the stimulating conference paper of W. Goffart, 'The Theme of the Barbarian Invasions in Late Antique and Modern Historiography', reprinted in his *Rome's Fall and After* (London, 1989), pp. 111–32.
20. Heruli: Procopius, *History of the Wars*, IV. iv. 30, VI. xiv. 1–xv. 4; Hydatius, *Chronica*, 171, 194. Suevi: Procopius, op. cit., V. xv. 26, xvi. 9 and 12, Isidore of Seville, *Historia Sueborum, passim*.
21. E. F. Gauthier, *Genseric, Roi des Vandales* (Paris, 1951) embraces the conspiracy theory, which makes the Vandal king the prime mover in virtually all the major events of the fifth century. See Jordanes 184 for Gaiseric inciting Attila to invade the West in 451.
22. Ammianus, XXVII. v. 6; XXXI. iii. 1. For a view that stresses continuities, see H. Wolfram, *History of the Goths* (English trans.) (Berkeley, Calif., 1988) pp. 248–58.
23. On Jordanes, see W. Goffart, 'Jordanes and his Three Histories', in his *The Narrators of Barbarian History* (Princeton, NJ, 1988), pp. 20–111; Arne Søby Christensen, *Cassiodorus, Jordanes and the History of the Goths* (Copenhagen, 2002); also J. J. O'Donnell, *Cassiodorus* (Berkeley, Calif., 1979), pp. 43–54.
24. Cassiodorus, *Variae*, IX, letter 25.
25. Jordanes, *Getica*, 79–81.
26. D. Dumville, 'Kingship, Genealogies and Regnal Lists', in P. Sawyer and I. N. Woods (eds), *Early Medieval Kingship* (Leeds, 1977), pp. 72–104; also K. Sisam, 'Anglo-Saxon Royal Genealogies', *Proceedings of the British Academy*, 39 (1953), 287–348. While both of these deal with Anglo-Saxon and Celtic materials exclusively, their methodology and conclusions are equally significant for continental regnal lists and genealogies.
27. PLRE, vol. II, pp. 1073–7 (Theoderic 5).

28. PLRE, vol. II, pp. 151 (Arnegisclus) and 75–6 (Anagastes).
29. PLRE, vol. II, p. 936 (Recitach); John of Antioch fragment 214 (3) for the murder.
30. See A. H. M. Jones, 'The Constitutional Position of Odoacer and Theoderic', *Journal of Roman Studies*, 52 (1962), 126–30.
31. John of Antioch fragment 214a for the most vivid account.
32. For the careers of the elder Cassiodorus and Liberius, see PLRE, vol. II, pp. 264–5 (Cassiodorus 3) and 677–81 (Liberius 3). Also J. Sundwall, *Abhandlungen zur Geschichte des ausgehenden Römertums* (Helsinki, 1919) pp. 106–7, 133–6.
33. PLRE, vol. II, p. 597 (Ioannes 13).
34. PLRE, vol. II, pp. 265–9 (Cassiodorus 4). See also O'Donnell, *Cassiodorus*; and R. Macpherson, *Rome in Involution: Cassiodorus'* Variae *in their Literary and Historical Setting* (Poznan, 1989), esp. pp. 79–118.
35. Tacitus, *Germania*, vii. 1.
36. Jordanes, 271, 281.
37. A. Chastagnol, *Le Sénat romain sous le regne d'Odoacre: Recherches sur l'épigraphie du Colisée au Ve siècle* (Bonn, 1966).
38. *Anonymi Valesiani Pars Posterior*, 70–1; see also B. Ward-Perkins, *From Classical Antiquity to the Middle Ages: Urban Public Building in Northern and Central Italy, A.D. 300–850* (Oxford, 1984), pp. 128–9, 158–66, 192–3; and M. J. Johnson, 'Toward a History of Theoderic's Building Program', *Dumbarton Oaks Papers*, 42 (1988), 73–96.
39. Anonymous Valesianus 60. J. Moorhead, *Theoderic in Italy* (Oxford, 1992), pp. 60–3.
40. Anonymous Valesianus 65. W. Ensslin, *Theoderich der Große* (Munich, 1947), pp. 111–17, and plate 5.
41. Anonymous Valesianus 48; Eugippius, *Commemoratorium Vitae Sancti Severini*, xliii. 3–5. See E. A. Thompson, 'The End of Noricum', in his *Romans and Barbarians* (Wisconsin, 1982), esp. pp. 124–8.
42. Jordanes, 300–2; Moorhead, *Theoderic in Italy*, pp. 173–211; T. Burns, *A History of the Ostrogoths* (Bloomington, 1984), pp. 190–5; E. A. Thompson, *The Goths in Spain* (Oxford, 1969), pp. 7–9.
43. PLRE, vol. II, pp. 63 (Amalaberga), 63–4 (Amalafrida), 1068 (Theodegotha).
44. Gregory of Tours, *Historiae*, II. 27.
45. On the *Variae* of Cassiodorus, see O'Donnell, *Cassiodorus*, pp. 55–102, and Macpherson, *Rome in Involution*, pp. 79–119, 151–203. On Ennodius, see S. A. H. Kennell, *Magnus Felix Ennodius: A Gentleman of the Church* (Ann Arbor, Mich., 2000).
45. On the arguments about two phases of composition, see, decisively, W. Goffart, 'From *Historiae* to *Historia Francorum* and Back Again: Aspects of the Textual History of Gregory of Tours', in T. F. X. Noble and J. J. Contreni (eds), *Religion, Culture and Society in the Early Middle Ages* (Kalamazoo, Mich., 1987), pp. 55–76; reprinted in his *Rome's Fall and After*, pp. 255–74.
46. L. Halphen, 'Grégoire de Tours, historien de Clovis', in *Mélanges d'histoire du moyen âge offerts à M. Ferdinand Lot par ses amis et ses éleves*

(Paris, 1925); and M. Heinzelmann, *Gregory of Tours* (English trans.) (Cambridge, 2001).

47. A. Van der Vyver, 'La victoire contre les Alamans et la conversion de Clovis', *Revue belge de philologie et d'histoire*, 15 (1936), 859–914, and 16 (1937), 35–94; idem, 'L'unique victoire contre les Alamans et la conversion de Clovis en 506', ibid., 17 (1938), 793–813.

48. I. N. Wood, 'Gregory of Tours and Clovis', *Revue belge de philologie et d'histoire*, 63 (1985), 249–72; Wood does not, however, suggest that Clovis himself had been an Arian.

49. Avitus of Vienne, *ep*. 46, ed. R. Peiper, *MGH AA*, vol. VI. 2, pp. 75–6; *Epistolae Austrasicae*, nos 1 and 2; Avitus of Vienne, *ep*. 46; letter of Clovis to the bishops of Aquitaine, ed. A. Boretius, MGH *Capit.*, vol. I, pp. 1–2.

50. For Childeric's burial, see P. Périn and M. Kazanski, 'Das Grab Childerichs I', in A. Wieczorek (ed.), *Die Franken. Wegbereiter Europas* (Mainz, 1996), Vol. I, pp. 173–182, and Vol. II, pp. 879–83 for its contents; see also R. Bruce-Mitford, 'A Comparison between the Sutton Hoo Burial Deposit and Childeric's Treasure', in *Acts du Colloque internationale d'archéologie, Rouen 3–5 Juillet 1975* (Rouen, 1978), pp. 365–71. For Alaric's burial, see Jordanes 158.

51. *Epistolae Austrasicae*, no. 2.

52. PLRE, vol. II, pp. 115–18 (Apollinaris 6).

53. PLRE, vol. II, pp. 285–6 (Childericus I); E. James, *The Franks* (Oxford, 1988), pp. 64–77.

54. PLRE, vol. II, p. 945 (Riotamus); L. Fleuriot, *Les origines de la Bretagne* (Paris, 1980), pp. 163–78 wishes to make him identical to the Romano-British leader Aurelius Ambrosius!

55. V. I. Evison, *The Fifth-Century Invasions South of the Thames* (London, 1965); see also I. N. Wood, *The Merovingian North Sea* (Alingsås, 1983), pp. 12–14.

56. Gregory of Tours, *Historiae*, II. 12.

57. Gregory of Tours, *Historiae*, II. 19.

58. Gregory of Tours, *Historiae*, II. 27.

59. Gregory of Tours, *Historiae*, II. 27 and 30; see the articles by Van der Vyver cited in nt 47 above.

60. James, *The Franks*, pp. 73–5, 85.

61. Gregory of Tours, *Historiae*, II. 37.

62. Gregory of Tours, *Historiae*, II. 32–3; Marius of Avenches, *Chronica*, s.a. 500 (NB this dating is not intrinsic to the text), ed. Mommsen, MGH *AA*, vol. XI, p. 234.

63. On the Visigothic kingdom before 507, see A. M. Jiménez Garnica, *Orígenes y desarrollo del Reino Visigodo de Tolosa* (Valladolid, 1983).

64. Gregory of Tours, *Historiae*, II. 37.

65. Gregory of Tours, *Historiae*, II. 40–2.

66. *Liber Pontificalis*, Vol. I, pp. 269–74. This pontificate began in 513, but among the gifts recorded as having been received by the papacy at this time was *corona aurea cum gemmis pretiosis a rege Francorum Cloduveum* (ed. Mommsen, MGH *GPR*, vol. I, p. 130.)

8   THE TWILIGHT OF THE WEST, 518–68

1. Gregory of Tours, *Libri Decem Historiarum*, II. 38.
2. For his reign, see F. K. Haarer, *Anastasius I: Politics and Empire in the Late Roman World* (Leeds, 2006); also PLRE, vol. II, pp. 78–80 (Anastasius 4); and P. T. R. Gray, *The Defense of Chalcedon in the East (451–553)* (Leiden, 1979), pp. 34–44.
3. See H. Chadwick, *Boethius: The Consolations of Music, Logic, Theology and Philosophy* (Oxford, 1981), pp. 174–222.
4. PLRE, vol. II, pp. 1200–2 (Zenon 7).
5. A. H. M. Jones, *The Later Roman Empire, 284–602* (3 vols) (Oxford, 1964), Vol. I, pp. 230–1. See also PLRE, vol. II, pp. 689–90 (Longinus 6).
6. Procopius, *History of the Wars*, I. vii. 3–ix. 20; *Chronicle of Joshua the Stylite*, xlviii–lxxxi.
7. *Marcellini Comitis Chronicon*, s.c. Celer and Venantius, ed. Mommsen, MGH *AA*, vol. XI, p. 97 for the naval raid of 508.
8. For Justin I's seizure of power, see A. A. Vasiliev, *Justin the First* (Cambridge, Mass., 1950), pp. 68–82.
9. PLRE, vol. II, p. 438 (Eutharicus); *Cassiodori Senatoris Chronica*, 1364, ed. Mommsen, MGH *AA*, vol. XI, p. 161.
10. Vasiliev, *Justin*, pp. 160–90.
11. PLRE, vol. II, pp. 1044–6 (Symmachus 9); for possible influence of his lost work, see M. A. Wes, *Das Ende des Kaisertums im Westen des römischen Reichs* ('s-Gravenhage, 1967), but also the comments of B. Croke, 'A.D. 476: The Manufacture of a Turning Point', *Chiron*, 13 (1983), 81–119.
12. PLRE, vol. II, pp. 491 (Galla 5), 907 (Probe 1); Fulgentius of Ruspe, *epp.* 2, 3, 4.
13. PLRE, vol. II, pp. 233–7.
14. See J. Matthews, 'Anicius Manlius Severinus Boethius', in M. Gibson (ed.), *Boethius: his Life, Thought and Influence* (Oxford, 1981), pp. 37–8. Wolfram, *History of the Goths* (English trans.) (Berkeley, 1988), pp. 331–2, is almost apocalyptic on the supposed consequences.
15. See esp. Chadwick, *Boethius: the Consolations of Music, Logic, Theology, and Philosophy*.
16. Procopius, *History of the Wars*, V. i. 32–9. Gregory the Great, *Dialogorum Libri IV*, IV. 31. See, in general, P. Courcelle, *La consolation de philosophie dans la tradition littéraire: antecedents et posterité de Boece* (Paris, 1967) for the growth of the 'cult' of Boethius.
17. PLRE, vol. II, p. 267. For his work at this time, see *Variae* bk V.
18. C. H. Coster, 'The *Iudicium Quinquevirale* in Constantinople', and 'The *Iudicium Quinquevirale* Reconsidered', in his *Late Roman Studies* (Cambridge, Mass., 1968), pp. 1–45 for the judicial process; see also P. Rousseau, 'The Death of Boethius: The Charge of Maleficium', *Studi Medievali*, 3rd ser. 20 (1979), 871–89.
19. Boethius, *De Consolatione Philosophiae*, I. iv. 13–17. See the comments of T. Burns, *A History of the Ostrogoths* (Bloomington, Ind., 1984), pp. 103–5.

20. PLRE, vol. II, pp. 215 (Basilius 9), 904 (Praetextatus 4).
21. PLRE, vol. II, p. 231 (Boethius 1).
22. Chadwick, *Boethius*, pp. 26–9, 179–81. The identification of the Deacon John with the later pope is very probable, if not definite.
23. Chadwick, *Boethius*, pp. 60–4.
24. *Liber Pontificalis*, lvi: Felix IV, ed. Mommsen, p. 138: *ordinatus est ex iusso Theoderici regis*.
25. The subtitle of Vasiliev's book, *Justin the First*, is *An Introduction to the Epoch of Justinian the Great*, and he wrote in the preface that Justinian's 'rule, behind the throne, of course, started, in my opinion, from the moment of Justin's elevation' (p. v). See now W. Treadgold, *A History of the Byzantine State and Society* (Stanford, Calif., 1997), pp. 174–78.
26. Corippus, *In Laudem Iustini Augusti Minoris libri IV*, bk I, lines 130–45, makes the Senators tell Justin II that the people knew it was his advice and actions that had maintained the empire during the reign of his uncle Justinian, and that 'he achieved nothing without you'. In lines 179–80 they are made to state that Justinian himself had nominated Justin as his successor.
27. PLRE, vol. II, pp. 505–7 (Germanus 4).
28. PLRE, vol. II, pp. 645–8 (Iustinianus 7); for his appointment as Magister Militum, see *Victoris Tonnennensis Episcopi Chronica*, s.c. Rusticio, 2, ed. Mommsen, MGH *AA*, vol. XI, p. 196.
29. PLRE, vol. III, pp. 750–54 (Justinus 4). He was exiled and murdered in 566. For the emperor Justin II, see PLRE vol. III, pp. 754–56 (Justinus 5).
30. *Codex Theodosianus*, XV. xii. 1: gladiatorial games were abolished by Constantine I on 1 October 325, but a law of April 397 (XV. xii 3) refers to the continued existence of gladiatorial schools. Wild beast shows were abolished by Anastasius I in 499 – with an equal lack of success. See *Chronicle of Joshua the Stylite*, xxxiv.
31. J. H. W. G. Liebeschutz, *Antioch: City and Imperial Administration in the Later Roman Empire* (Oxford, 1972), pp. 208–19; for the imperial context, see A. Cameron, *Circus Factions: Blues and Greens at Rome and Byzantium* (Oxford, 1976), pp. 157–92; for claques, see ibid., pp. 237–49.
32. The *Relationes* are edited by R. H. Barrow in his *Prefect and Emperor* (Oxford, 1973). For riots in Rome, see A. H. M. Jones, *The Later Roman Empire, 284–602* (3 vols) (Oxford, 1964), Vol. II, p. 693 and references.
33. Corippus, *In Laudem Iustini*, bk II, lines 278–430 provides an elaborate if formal account of the encounter of the new emperor and the populace in the hippodrome. In general, see O. Treitinger, *Die öströmische Kaiser und Reichsidee vom öströmischen Staats- und Reichsgedanken* (2nd edn) (Darmstadt, 1956).
34. Cameron, *Circus Factions*, pp. 271–96.
35. Procopius, *History of the Wars*, I. xxiv. 1–58.
36. For the change in the nature of Justinian's regime in the years 532–5, see the evocative (if evidentially impressionistic) pp. 152–4 of P. Brown, *The World of Late Antiquity* (London, 1971).

37. Procopius, *History of the Wars*, I. xxii. 16, I. xxiv. 40, III. ix. 25–6.

38. Courtois, *Les Vandales et l'Afrique* (Paris, 1955), pp. 173, 201–4 for the fifth-century expeditions; also Procopius, *History of the Wars*, III. iii. 14–viii. 29. Malchus fragment 2 records Theoderic Strabo's agreement to fight for the emperor Zeno against all enemies other than the Vandals.

39. H. Pirenne, *Mahomet et Charlemagne* (Brussels, 1937); for the emphasis on Vandal 'piracy', see N. H. Baynes, 'M. Pirenne and the Unity of the Mediterranean World', in his *Byzantine Studies and Other Essays* (London, 1955), pp. 309–16. See also the assessment of Pirenne's book by P. Brown in *Daedalus*, 102 (1973), 25–33, and Courtois, *Vandales*, pp. 205–14 for African shipping, trade and raiding.

40. J. W. Hayes, *Late Roman Pottery* (London, 1972), pp. 128–50; see also S. Tortorella, 'Produzione e circolazione della ceramica africana di Cartagine (V–VII sec.)', *Opus*, 2 (1983), 15–30.

41. Procopius, *History of the Wars*, III. x. 26–7, xi. 22–3, xxiv. 1–3, xxv. 10–26.

42. Ibid., III. xii. I–IV. viii. 1 for the narrative of the war.

43. Ibid., III. x. 1–21 for opposition to the plan, and for the Syrian bishop. Isidore of Seville, *Historia Vandalorum*, lxxxiii states that Justinian was inspired by a vision of the martyred African bishop Laetus.

44. A documented case is that of the family of Fulgentius of Ruspe: *Vita Fulgentii*, I; see also Courtois, *Les Vandales*, pp. 275–89.

45. Courtois, *Les Vandales*, pp. 289–310.

46. Conveniently available in R. B. Eno (trans.), *Fulgentius: Selected Works* (Fathers of the Church, Vol. 95) (Washington, DC, 1997).

47. C. Courtois, *Victor de Vita et son oeuvre* (Algiers, 1954).

48. *Victoris Tonnennensis Episcopi Chronica*, s.c. Maximus, 2, ed. Mommsen, MGH *AA*, vol. XI, p. 197; Courtois, *Les Vandales*, pp. 304–10.

49. Procopius, *History of the Wars*, III. vii. 29–viii. 6.

50. Ibid., III. ix. 1. PLRE, vol. II, pp. 564–5 (Hildericus).

51. Procopius, *History of the Wars*, III. ix. 3–5; Victor of Tunnunna, s.c. Maximus, 1, ed. Mommsen, pp. 196–7.

52. Cassiodorus, *Variae*, V. 16 for the creation of a fleet. Procopius, *History of the Wars*, III. ix. 6–9 for the overthrow of Hilderic. For the name Geilamir rather than Gelimer, as used by Procopius, see the king's coinage: P. Grierson and M. Blackburn, *Medieval European Coinage I: The Early Middle Ages* (Cambridge, 1986), p. 420; and his silver *missorium*, now in the Bibliothèque Nationale, Paris.

53. Procopius, *History of the Wars*, III. xvii. 11–12.

54. Ibid., III. ix. 10–13.

55. Ibid., III. xvii. 13; IV. ii. 8 and 32; IV. iii. 22–5.

56. Edited in C. Courtois, L. Leschi, C. Perrat and C. Saumagne, *Les Tablettes Albertini* (Paris, 1952).

57. PLRE, vol. II, pp. 748–9 (Maximus 20).

58. Procopius, *History of the Wars*, V. iv. 4–11.

59. Jordanes, *Getica*, 306; the interpretation is that of A. Momigliano, 'Cassiodorus and the Italian Culture of his Time', *Proceedings of*

the British Academy, 41 (1955), pp. 207–45. See A. S. Christensen, *Cassiodorus, Jordanes and the History of the Goths* (Copenhagen, 2002); and P. Heather, *Goths and Romans 332–489* (Oxford, 1991), pp. 34–67.

60. Procopius, *History of the Wars*, V. iv. 25–7.
61. Ibid., V. vi. 1–13; PLRE, vol. II, pp. 1067–8 (Theodahadus).
62. Procopius, *History of the Wars*, V. vii. 1–5.
63. Ibid., V. v. I–VIII. xxxv. 38; and Agathias, preface and bk I provide the narrative account of the war of 535–53.
64. Procopius, *History of the Wars*, V. v. 2–4.
65. Ibid., V. viii. I–x. 48 (Naples), xiv. 1–14 (Rome).
66. Ibid., V. xi. 1–9.
67. Ibid., V. v. 1–xxviii. 35.
68. Ibid., VI. xxix. 1–2.
69. Ibid., VI. xxix. 3–31.
70. Ibid., VI. xxx. 4–VII. ii. 18.
71. Ibid., II. ii. 1–12.
72. Ibid., VI. xxx. 17–VII. i. 49.
73. Ibid., VIII. xxix. 1–xxxii. 36, xxxiii. 6–xxxv. 29.
74. R. Collins, 'Theodebert I: *Rex Magnus Francorum*', in P. Wormald, D. Bullough and R. Collins (eds), *Ideal and Reality in Frankish and Anglo-Saxon Society* (Oxford, 1983), pp. 7–33.
75. For the Lombard invasion of Italy, see M. Todd, *The Early Germans* (Oxford, 1992), pp. 239–52; also Chapter 12, first section, below.
76. E. A. Thompson, *The Goths in Spain* (Oxford, 1969), pp. 320–34; see also P. Goubert, 'Byzance et l'Espagne wisigothique', *Revue des études byzantines*, 2 (1944), 5–78.
77. Procopius, *History of the Wars*, V. xxv. 13–14.
78. Ibid., V. xxvi. 1–2.
79. Ibid., VIII. xxxiv. 6, after the battle of Busta Gallorum in 552 the Byzantine forces massacred those Goths who surrendered to them: VIII. xxxii. 20.
80. C. Wickham, 'Historical and Topographical Notes on Early Medieval South Etruria', *Papers of the British School at Rome*, 46 (1978), 132–79.

9 CONSTANTINOPLE, PERSIA AND THE ARABS

1. For a general history of the Sasanian Empire, see A. Christensen, *L'Iran sous les Sassanides* (2nd edn) (Copenhagen, 1944), but the best treatment of its final phase is P. Pourshariati, *Decline and Fall of the Sasanian Empire* (London, 2008).
2. S. Der Nersessian, *Armenia and the Byzantine Empire* (Cambridge, Mass., 1947); P. Charanis, *The Armenians in the Byzantine Empire* (Lisbon, 1964). For Byzantine–Persian relations in the fifth to seventh centuries, see the chapter by N. Garsoïan in *Cambridge History of Iran*, Vol. III (2 vols) (Cambridge, 1983), pp. 568–92.
3. Theophylact Simocatta, *Histories*, IV. xi. 2; Malalas 449. 19–20, and Peter the Patrician, fragment 13. Note the very different usage in Ammianus, *Res Gestae*, XVII. v. 10. See also the vivid evocation

of late Sasanian Persia in P. Brown, *The World of Late Antiquity* (London, 1971), pp. 160–70.

4. Menander Protector, fragment 6.2.

5. *Chronicle of Joshua the Stylite*, 10. On this chronicle, see F. Hasse, 'Die Chronik des Josua Stylites', *Oriens Christianus*, ns 9 (1920), 62–73.

6. On the Hephthalites, see R. Ghirshman, *Les Chionites–Hephthalites* (Cairo, 1948), esp. pp. 115–34.

7. Procopius, *History of the Wars*, I. iv. 34–5, vi. 10–17; *Chronicle of Joshua the Stylite*, 19 and 24.

8. *Chronicle of Zachariah of Mitylene*, VII. iii.

9. *Chronicle of Joshua the Stylite*, 24.

10. Procopius, *History of the Wars*, I. xi. 28–9, xii. 1–19, II. xv. 1–35, II. xvii. 1–28, II. xxviii. 3–xxx. 48; Agathias, *Histories* II. xviii. 1–8 (7 reveals the strategic importance of Lazica to the Empire), II. xxi, xxvii, III, i–v, xi–xvi, xviii, xxiii, IV. i–iii, v–vii, ix–xiii, xv, xvii, xx–xxiii, xxx *passim;* Menander Protector, fragments 2, 6.1, and 9.1.

11. Procopius, *History of the Wars*, V. i. 1 is an oblique reference to Mazdakite influence on Kavad. See A. Christensen, *Le regne du roi Kawadh I et le communisme mazdakite* (Copenhagen, 1925), and ch. 27 (b) of *Cambridge History of Iran*, Vol. III, pp. 991–1024 (Mazdakism'), by E. Yarshater.

12. *Cambridge History of Iran*, Vol. III, p. 154.

13. Ibid., p. 155; Procopius, *History of the Wars*, II. xiv. 1–4. Z. Rubin, 'The Reforms of Khusrow Anushirwan' in A. Cameron and L. I. Conrad (eds), *The Byzantine and Early Islamic Near East III: States, Resources and Armies* (Princeton, NJ, 1995), pp. 227–97.

14. G. Widengren, 'Xosrau Anosurvan, les Hephthalites et les peuples turcs', *Orientalia Suecana*, I (1952), pp. 69–94.

15. Menander Protector, fragments 2, 4.2, 10.1–10.5, 19.1; see D. Obolensky, *The Byzantine Commonwealth: Eastern Europe, 500–1453* (London, 1971), pp. 164–70.

16. Procopius, *History of the Wars*, VIII. xvii. 1–8.

17. J. Ryckmans, *La Persecution des Chrétiens Himyarites au sixième siècle* (Istanbul, 1956); A. Moberg, *The Book of the Himyarites* (Lund, 1924); J. S. Trimingham, *Christianity among the Arabs in Pre-Islamic Times* (London and Beirut, 1979), pp. 287–307. See also I. Shahid, 'Byzantium in South Arabia', *Dumbarton Oaks Papers*, 33 (1979), pp. 23–94.

18. Procopius, *History of the Wars*, I. xix. I–xx. 13; A. Kammerer, *Essai sur l'histoire antique d'Abyssinie* (Paris, 1926), pp. 107–17. Trimingham, *Christianity among the Arabs*, pp. 273–6.

19. Trimingham, *Christianity among the Arabs*, pp. 154–8, 178–99; G. Rothstein, *Die dynastic der Lahmiden in al-Hira* (Berlin, 1899).

20. P. Goubert, *Byzance avant l'Islam*, Vol. I: *Byzance et l'Orient* (Paris, 1951), pp. 249–72.

21. Ibid., pp. 121–90; M. Whitby, *The Emperor Maurice and his Historian* (Oxford, 1988), pp. 197–221, 292–304.

22. *The Chronicle of Theophanes* a.m. 6095–101; A. N. Stratos, *Byzantium in the Seventh Century*, Vol. I: 602–34 (Amsterdam, 1968), pp. 57–65 provides a narrative of events, if rather uncritically.

23. Ibid., pp. 103–17; the main texts for the events of 602–616 are conveniently translated with commentary in G. Greatrex and S. N. C. Lieu, *The Roman Eastern Frontier and the Persian Wars, Part II AD 363–630* (London and New York, 2002), pp. 182–97, and to which can be added F. C. Conybeare, 'Antiochus Strategos' Account of the Sack of Jerusalem in A.D. 614', *English Historical Review*, 25 (1910), 502–17.

24. This is the thesis of J. Jarry, *Hérésies et factions dans l'empire byzantin du ive au vile siècle* (Cairo, 1968), esp. pp. 422–529; it is disputed by A. Cameron in *Circus Factions* (Oxford, 1976), pp. 126–53. See also nt 27 below.

25. *The Chronicle of Theophanes*, a.m. 6098, 6101; Jarry, *Hérésies et factions*, pp. 474–505.

26. Goubert, *Byzance avant l'Islam*, pp. 211–14 for Maurice's anti-Monophysite policy in Armenia; and W. H. C. Frend, *The Rise of the Monophysite Movement* (Cambridge, 1972), pp. 329–36.

27. A. H. M. Jones, 'Were Ancient Heresies National or Social Movements in Disguise?', *Journal of Theological Studies*, ns 10 (1959), 280–98 – with an answer in the negative. On the Monophysites in this period, see Frend, *Rise of the Monophysite Movement*, pp. 296–353.

28. Procopius, *History of the Wars*, VII. xxxviii. 1–23, xl. 1–45, VIII. xxv. 1–10; Whitby, *The Emperor Maurice*, pp. 55–91; J. J. Wilkes, *Dalamatia* (London, 1969), pp. 435–7; and in general, Obolensky, *Byzantine Commonwealth*, pp. 42–68.

29. Stratos, *Byzantium in the Seventh Century*, Vol. 1, pp. 173–96; F. Barisic, 'Le Siège de Constantinople par les Avares et les Slaves en 626', *Byzantion*, 24 (1956), 371–95. See, in general, W. Pohl, 'Ergebnisse und Probleme der Awarenforschung', *MIöG*, 96 (1988), 247–74, and idem, *Die Awaren: Ein Steppenvolk im Mitteleuropa, 567–822* (Munich, 1988).

30. *Poemi*, ed. A. Pertusi (Ettal, 1960). For a translation of the *Paschal Chronicle*, see M. Whitby and M. Whitby, *Chronicon Paschale, 284–628 A.D.* (Liverpool, 1989), and for other sources Greatrex and Lieu, *The Roman Eastern Frontier*, pp. 198–209.

31. *Paschal Chronicle*, Olympiad 350–2, trans. Whitby, pp. 164–88, and Greatrex and Lieu, *The Roman Eastern Frontier*, pp. 209–228; see also Christensen, *L'Iran sous les Sassanides*, pp. 492–4.

32. Pourshariati, *Decline and Fall*, pp. 161–219; Christensen, *L'Iran sous les Sassanides*, pp. 494–509.

33. Sebeos, ch. xxix; *The Chronicle of Theophanes* a.m. 6120; N. H. Baynes, 'The Restoration of the Cross at Jerusalem', *English Historical Review*, 27 (1912), 287–99. See, in general, A. Frolow, *La relique de la Vrai Croix* (Paris, 1961). This event may have marked the terminal point of the now truncated *Paschal Chronicle*: see Whitby and Whitby, *Chronicon Paschale*, pp. x–xii.

34. Elishe, *History of Vardan and the Armenian War.*

35. P. Peeters, 'Les ex-voto de Khosrau Aparwez à Sergiopolis', *Analecta Bollandiana*, 65 (1947), 5–56; J. Neusner, *A History of the Jews in Babylonia*, Vol. V (Leiden, 1970), pp. 119–21.
36. D. M. Dunlop, *The History of the Jewish Khazars* (Princeton, NJ, 1954).
37. For the more orthodox presentation of the life of Muhammad and the origins of Islam, see W. M. Watt, *Muhammad at Mecca* (Oxford, 1953), and *Muhammad at Medina* (Oxford, 1956). For a provocative alternative view, see P. Crone and M. Cook, *Hagarism: The Making of the Islamic World* (Cambridge, 1977).
38. See D. M. Dunlop, *Arab Civilization to A.D. 1500* (London and Beirut, 1971), pp. 70–88, and esp. 72–3.
39. *Bell's Introduction to the Qur'an*, ed. W. M. Watt (Edinburgh, 1970), esp. pp. 40–56; J. Wansborough, *Quranic Studies* (Oxford, 1977), esp. pp. 1–52.
40. W. M. Watt, *Companion to the Qur'an* (London, 1967), pp. 73–9.
41. Introduction to R. H. Charles' translation (see Bibliography), pp. iv–ix.
42. A useful short account of the life and work of Muhammad will be found in M. Cook, *Muhammad* (1983).
43. Cook, *Muhammad*, pp. 42–50; T. Andrae, *Mohammed: The Man and his Faith* (revd English edn) (New York, 1955), pp. 53–93.
44. Watt, *Muhammad at Mecca*, pp. 1–16. See also M. J. Kister, 'Mecca and Tamim (Aspects of their Relations)', *Journal of the Economic and Social History of the Orient*, 8 (1965), 113–63.
45. Ibn Hisham's revision of Ibn Ishaq, 314–39 (pp. 212–30).
46. Ibid., 808–1013 (pp. 544–683) for the return to Mecca and the last two years.
47. Watt, *Muhammad at Medina*, pp. 121–3.
48. P. Crone, *Meccan Trade and the Rise of Islam* (Oxford, 1987).
49. S. H. M. Jafri, *The Origins and Early Development of Shi'a Islam* (London and Beirut, 1979), pp. 1–57.
50. A. N. Stratos, *Byzantium in the Seventh Century*, Vol. II: *634–41* (Amsterdam, 1972), pp. 40–73.
51. This episode is interpreted as being deliberately messianic by Crone and Cook, *Hagarism*, p. 5.
52. Pourshariati, *Decline and Fall*, pp. 219–281; Christensen, *L'Iran sous les Sassanides*, pp. 501–9.
53. See the monumental study by A. J. Butler, *The Arab Conquest of Egypt and the Last Thirty Years of the Roman Dominion* (2nd edn) (Oxford, 1978).
54. For an account of the events, see Stratos, *Byzantium*, Vol. II, pp. 134–52, 175–205.
55. For the conquests, see F. M. Donner, *The Early Islamic Conquests* (Princeton, NJ, 1981).
56. Ibn Abd al-Hakam, *Futah Misr wa'l-Maghrib*, bk iv.
57. Ibn Abd al-Hakam, bk v.
58. B. J. Bamberger, 'A Messianic Document of the Seventh Century', *Hebrew Union College Annual*, 15 (1940), 425–31; I. Lévi, 'L'Apocalypse

de Zorobabel et le roi de Perse Siroes', *Revue des Etudes Juives*, 68 (1914), 129–60; cf. also *Doctrina Iacobi nuper baptizati*, ed. N. Bonwetsch (Göttingen, 1910).

59. Procopius, *The Buildings*, II. i. I–xi. 8; V. viii. 9 for the fort built at the foot of Mt Sinai, the only one intended for defence against Arab raids.

60. D. R. Hill, *The Termination of Hostilities in the Early Arab Conquests A.D. 634–656* (London, 1971); for some examples from the conquest of Spain, see R. Collins, *The Arab Conquest of Spain, 710–797* (Oxford, 1989), pp. 38–44, but this trusts them too easily.

61. *The Chronicle of Theophanes* a.m. 6164; R. J. H. Jenkins, *Byzantium: The Imperial Centuries, A.D. 610–1071* (London, 1966), pp. 43–4.

10 DECADENT AND DO-NOTHING KINGS, 511–711

1. For example, C. Wickham, *Framing the Early Middle Ages* (Oxford, 2005), pp. 656–665.

2. R. Collins, *Early Medieval Spain: Unity in Diversity, 400–1000* (2nd edn) (London, 1995), pp. 88–145, and Collins, *The Arab Conquest of Spain, 710–797* (Oxford, 1989), pp. 6–22 for a positive presentation of this society. For bibliography on most aspects of it, consult A. Ferreiro, *The Visigoths in Gaul and Spain A.D. 418–711: A Bibliography* (Leiden, 1988), and *A Supplemental Bibliography, 1984–2003* (Leiden, 2004) and *A Supplemental Bibliography, 2004–2006* (Leiden, 2008).

3. *Chronicle of John of Biclar*, 91, ed. C. Cardelle de Hartmann, Corpus Christianorum Series Latina pp. 81–82.

4. R. Collins, 'Mérida and Toledo, 550–585', in E. James (ed.), *Visigothic Spain: New Approaches* (Oxford, 1980), pp. 189–219; L. A. García Moreno, *Historia de España visigoda* (Madrid, 1989), pp. 113–31.

5. E. A. Thompson, *The Goths in Spain* (Oxford, 1969), pp. 320–34.

6. R. Collins, *The Basques* (Oxford, 1986), pp. 82–98.

7. On the Suevic kingdom, see W. Reinhart, *Historia general del rein hispánico de los Suevos* (Madrid, 1952), and the four articles of E. A. Thompson on the Sueves, reprinted in his *Romans and Barbarians* (Madison, Wisc., 1982), pp. 137–229.

8. For this argument, see Collins, 'Mérida and Toledo', pp. 215–18, and 'King Leovigild and the Conversion of the Goths', in idem, *Law, Culture and Regionalism in Early Medieval Spain* (Aldershot, 1992), item II; for the context of the conversion. Isidore of Seville, *De Viris Illustribus*, xxviii; U. Dominguez del Val, *Leandro de Sevilla y la lucha contra el arianismo* (Madrid, 1981).

9. See J. Orlandis and D. Ramos Lissón, *Die Synoden auf der iberischen Halbisel bis zum Einbruch des Islam (711)* (Paderborn, 1981).

10. R. Collins, 'Julian of Toledo and the Education of Kings in Late Seventh-Century Spain', in idem, *Law, Culture and Regionalism*, item III, for the role of Toledo.

11. G. Martínez Díez, *La colección canónica Hispana*, Vol. I (Madrid, 1966); the collection itself is to be found published in the subsequent volumes, though not yet complete.

12. P. Cazier, *Isidore de Séville et la naissance de l'Espagne catholique* (Paris, 1994), pp. 13–48; and J. Fontaine, *Isidore de Séville. Genèse et originalité de la culture hispanique au temps des Wisigoths* (Paris, 2000).

13. M. Reydellet, 'Les intentions idéologiques et politiques dans la Chronique de Isidore de Séville', *Mélanges de l'Ecole française de Rome*, 82 (1970), 363–400; idem, *La royauté dans la littérature latine de Sidoine Apollinaire à Isidore de Séville* (Rome, 1981), pp. 505–97.

14. XII Toledo (681), canon vi.

15. L. A. García Moreno, *Prosopografía del reino visigodo de Toledo* (Salamanca, 1974), no. 253, p. 122.

16. P. D. King, *Law and Society in the Visigothic Kingdom* (Cambridge, 1971) for an analysis of the legal evidence.

17. Translated in J. Martínez Pizarro, *The Story of Wamba: Julian of Toledo's 'Historia Wambae regis'* (Washington, DC, 2005).

18. A. Canellas López, *Diplomática hispano-visigoda* (Zaragoza, 1979), nos. 119, 178, 192, 209, 229.

19. L. Caballero Zoreda, *La iglesia y el monasterio visigodo de Santa Maria de Melque (Toledo), San Pedro de la Mata (Toledo) y Santa Comba de Bande (Orense)* (Madrid, 1980).

20. S. Garren, 'Santa María de Melque and Church Construction under Muslim Rule', *Journal of the Society of Architectural Historians*, Vol. 51 (1992), pp. 288–305. For further bibliography and discussion, see R. Collins, *Visigothic Spain, 409–711* (Malden, Mass. and Oxford, 2004), pp. 186–196. See also nt 23 below.

21. *Vita Sancti Aemiliani* 9–34; Latxaga, *Arkaitzetako Bisigotiko Baselizak Araban/Iglesias rupestres visigóticas en Alava* (Bilbao, 1976); and L. A. Monreal Jimeno, *Eremitorios rupestres altomedievales (el Alto Valle del Ebro)* (Bilbao, 1989).

22. Many of these texts were originally published in M. Gomez-Moreno, *Documentación goda en pizarra* (Madrid, 1966), but reference should be made now to I. Velazquez Soriano, *El Latin de las pizarras visigóticas* (Murcia, 1989), and her even fuller edition: *Documentos de época visigoda escritos en pizarra (siglos VI–VIII)* (2 vols) (Turnhout, Belgium, 2001).

23. L. Caballero, P. Mateos and M. A. Utrero (eds), *El siglo VII frente al siglo VII. Arquitectura*, in *Anejos del Anuario Española de Arqueología* (Madrid, 2009) for the most recent work on these and several other sites.

24. For a synoptic account and bibliography, see R. Collins, *Visigothic Spain, 409–711* (Malden, Mass. and Oxford, 2004), pp. 205–212; more such sites are being discovered.

25. C. Wickham, *Framing the Early Middle Ages: Europe and the Mediterranean, 400–800* (Oxford, 2005), pp. 442–518.

26. P. de Palol i Salellas, *El Bovalar (Serós: Segria): Conjunt d'época paleo-cristiana i visigótica* (Lleida, 1989); idem, 'Las excavaciones del conjunto de "El Bovalar"', in *Los Visigodos*, ed. González Blanco, pp. 513–23. The full publication of the site, said to be imminent in 1991, is still awaited (in 2010).

27. *Chronicle of 754*, 54–55; Collins, *Arab Conquest*, pp. 30–44.

28. Collins, *Arab Conquest*, pp. 32–6, 144–9; for views that take some of this material more seriously, see M. Coll i Alentorn, *Els successors de Vititza en la zona nord-est del domini visigotic* (Barcelona, 1971).

29. Collins, *Visigothic Spain, 409–711*, pp. 81–116 for royal relations with the court nobility and these events.

30. *Chronicle of 754*, 59–74; Collins, *Arab Conquest*, pp. 36–51.

31. W. Goffart, 'From *Historiae* to *Historia Francorum* and Back Again: Aspects of the Textual History of Gregory of Tours', in T. F. X. Noble and J. J. Contreni (eds), *Religion, Culture and Society in the Early Middle Ages* (Kalamazoo, Mich., 1987), pp. 55–76; also M. Heinzelmann, *Gregory of Tours* (English trans.) (Cambridge, 2001).

32. These are edited by B. Krusch in MGH *SRM*, vol. I, pt ii; see P. R. L. Brown, *Relics and Social Status in the Age of Gregory of Tours* (Reading, 1977).

33. See above, p. 162 and nts 47–8 of Chapter 7.

34. I. N. Wood, 'Gregory of Tours and Clovis', *Revue belge de philologie et d'histoire*, 63 (1985), esp. pp. 259–61.

35. For example, Gregory of Tours, *Libri Decem Historiarum* III. 32. In general, he has very little of any independent value to say about Italian affairs, other than for the account of the consecration of pope Gregory I in 590 (X. 1), at which a deacon of the Church of Tours was present.

36. Ibid., V. 18, V. 44, VI. 46.

37. On the original seventh-century chronicle attributed to 'Fredegar', see R. Collins, *Die Fredegar-Chroniken*, Vol. 44 of MGH *Texte und Schriften* (Hanover, 2008), pp. 8–81.

38. Ed. T. Mommsen, MGH *AA*, vol. VI, pp. 227–39.

39. For a useful survey of Frankish archaeology, see the contributions to A. Wieczorek (ed.), *Die Franken. Wegbereiter Europas* (2 vols) (Mainz, 1996).

40. Gregory of Tours, *Historiae*, V. 34; see also W. Goffart, 'Old and New in Merovingian Taxation', *Past and Present*, 96 (1982), 3–21.

41. *De Fisco Barcinonensi;* see Thompson, *Goths in Spain*, pp. 99–100.

42. Wallace-Hadrill, *The Long-Haired Kings*, pp. 231–48. See T. Kölzer, 'Die letzen Merowinger: rois fainéants?', in M. Becher and J. Jarnut (eds), *Der Dynastiewechsel von 751* (Münster, 2004), pp. 33–60.

43. For an overview of this period, see K. F. Werner, *Les origines*, Vol. I of J. Favier (ed.), *Histoire de France* (Paris, 1984), pp. 207–497.

44. I. Wood, *The Merovingian Kingdoms, 450–751* (London, 1994), pp. 55–70 for the ideas behind, and the practice and effects of, succession in the sixth-century Merovingian realms.

45. E. Ewig, *Die fränkischen Teilungen und Teilreiche (511–613)* (Wiesbaden, 1953), pp. 651–67.

46. Gregory of Tours, *Historiae*, III. 11; Procopius, *History of the Wars* V. xiii. 26–8. On Gregory's account of the Burgundian war, see I. N. Wood, 'Clermont and Burgundy: 511–534', in *Nottingham Medieval Studies*, 32 (1988), 119–25.

47. Gregory of Tours, *Historiae*, III. 6 and 18.

48. R. Collins, 'Theodebert I: *Rex Magnus Francorum*', in P. Wormald, D. Bullough and R. Collins (eds), *Ideal and Reality in Frankish and Anglo-Saxon Society* (Oxford, 1983), pp. 7–33.

49. *Epistulae Austrasicae*, nos 18–20; Collins, 'Theodebert', pp. 28–33.

50. M. Prou, *Catalogue des monnaies françaises de la Bibliothèque Nationale: les monnaies mérovingiennes* (Paris, 1928), pp. xxix–xxxv and 9–16. For an illustration of two unique pieces, see *Ideal and Reality*, plate 1.

51. Gregory of Tours, *Historiae*, IV. 9 and 14.

52. Ibid., IV. 51.

53. Wood, *Merovingian Kingdoms*, pp. 88–101.

54. See nt 39 above.

55. These will be discussed in greater detail in Chapter 15 below.

56. *Vita Arnulf*, 11, 12, 17.

57. H. E. Bonnell, *Die Anfänge des karolingischen Hauses* (Munich, 1866), pp. 157–81; I. Haselbach, 'Aufstieg und Herrschaft der Karolinger in der Darstellung der sogennanten Annalen Mettenses Priores', *Historische Studien*, 406 (1970), 1–208.

58. *Annales Mettenses Priores*, pp. 1–15.

59. Photographic facsimiles of the extant original Merovingian charters will be found in H. Atsma and J. Vezin (eds), *Chartae latinae antiquiores*, Vols 13–15 (Zurich, 1981–4), but for the full corpus, recourse still has to be made to J. M. Pardessus, *Diplomata, Chartae, Epistolae, Leges ad Res Gallo-Francicas spectantia* (2 vols) (Paris, 1843).

60. *Chronicle of Fredegar;* S. McK. Crosby, *The Royal Abbey of Saint-Denis* (New Haven, Conn., 1987), pp. 29–50 for excavation of what is probably Dagobert's church.

61. For the study of charters and their particular problems, see H. Bresslau, rev. H. W. Klewitz, *Handbuch der Urkundenlehre* (4th edn) (Berlin, 1968/9).

62. H. Ebling, *Prosopographie der Amsträger des Merowingerreiches von Chlotar II (613) bis Karl Martel* (Munich, 1974) provides a valuable collection of the evidence relating to all known individuals of importance in this period. See also P. Geary, *Aristocracy in Provence* (Stuttgart and Philadelphia, 1985), pp. 126–52.

63. For example, H. St. L. B. Moss, *The Birth of the Middle Ages* (Oxford, 1935), p. 198: 'Meroving princes are born and die, short-lived phantoms, worn out by premature debauchery, *rois fainéants*, exhibiting at best a weak piety or a pliant amiability.'

64. *Chronicle of Fredegar*, IV. 35, 56, continuations 1.

65. Wallace-Hadrill, *Long-Haired Kings*, pp. 206–48 for the kings from Chlotar II to 751.

66. *Chronicle of Fredegar*, IV. 79–80, continuations (*recte* the *Historia vel Gesta Francorum*, 1–2. For this distinction, see Collins, *Fredegar-Chroniken*, pp. 1–7.

67. J. Nelson, 'Queens as Jezebels: The Careers of Brunhild and Baldhild in Merovingian History', in D. Baker (ed.), *Medieval Women* (Oxford, 1978), pp. 31–77; for the suggestion based on the *Vita Eligii* that Baldechildis's retirement to Chelles was forced, see

pp. 51–2, but if Chlotar III had attained his majority at this point, such a move was perhaps less surprising.

68. *Chronicle of Fredegar,* continuations 2; *Liber Historiae Francorum* 45.

69. For Ebroin, see P. Fouracre, 'Merovingians, Mayors of the Palace and the Notion of a "Low-born" Ebroin', *Bulletin of the Institute of Historical Research,* 57 (1984), 1–14; and Gerberding, *Rise of the Carolingians,* pp. 67–88.

70. *Chronicle of Fredegar,* continuations 2; *Liber Historiae Francorum* 45.

71. For example, Pardessus, vol. II, nos. 400, 402, 410 (*vestra industria*) etc.

72. For towns and administration, see E. James, *The Origins of France, from Clovis to the Capetians, 500–1000* (London, 1982), pp. 43–63, and the various contributions in A. Wieczorek (ed.), *Die Franken,* Vol. I, pp. 121–70.

73. For an example of such an assembly, see the preface to the *Edictus Domni Chilperici Regis pro Tenore Pacis,* ed. K. A. Eckhardt in MGH *Leges,* vol. IV (i), p. 261, and the records of the legal ordinances agreed on at a sequence of 'Marchfield' assemblies in the reign of Childebert II (ibid., pp. 267–9).

74. The earliest MS of *Lex Salica* (Wolfenbüttel, Weissenburg 97) is Eckhardt's A2, dated on the advice of B. Bischoff to *c.* 770 in R. McKitterick, *The Carolingians and the Written Word* (Cambridge, 1989), pp. 44 and 48. For the Edict of Chilperic, see note 75 above.

75. Ed. Eckhardt, MGH *Leges,* vol. IV (i), pp. 269–73.

76. This first appears in the 'Epilogue' attached to some of the MSS of the 'A' class, and which cannot be dated with certainty to anything earlier than the year 715. See Eckhardt's edition, pp. 253–4.

77. For the Frankish aristocracy, see F. Irsigler, *Untersuchungen zur Geschichte des frühfränkischen Adels* (2nd edn) (Bonn, 1981); H. Grahn-Hoek, *Die fränkische Oberschicht im 6. Jahrhundert* (Sigmaringen, 1976); and R. Sprandel, *Der merovingische Adel und die Gebiete östlich des Rheins* (Freiburg, 1957).

11 FROM BRITAIN TO THE KINGDOMS OF THE ANGLES, 410–874

1. On this period, see P. Salway, *Roman Britain* (Oxford, 1981).

2. D. Dumville, 'Sub-Roman Britain: History and Legend', *History,* 62 (1977), 173–92 for the revisionist approach to post-Roman British history.

3. On 'Nennius', see the preface in J. Morris's edition of the *Historia Brittonum,* and the editor's Introduction for a somewhat optimistic view of its worth.

4. An edition of the work in which each separate manuscript will receive its own volume is currently being produced under the direction of D. Dumville: Vol. 3: *The Historia Brittonum – the 'Vatican' Recension* (Cambridge, 1985). Twenty-four years later this remains the only volume published.

5. Section 56 in the Harleian recension; see Morris's edition, p. 76.

6. The literature on Arthur is vast, and mostly silly. For a sensible approach, see L. Alcock *Arthur's Britain* (Harmondsworth, 1971).

7. D. N. Dumville, '"Nennius" and the *Historia Brittonum*', *Studia Celtica*, 10/11 (1975/6), 78–95.

8. Section 66 in the Harleian version; see Morris's edition, p. 80.

9. A. O. H. Jarman (ed. and trans.) *Aneirin, Y Gododdin* (Llandysul, 1988); see also I. Williams, 'The Gododdin Poems', in his *The Beginnings of Welsh Poetry*, ed. R. Bromwich (2nd edn) (Cardiff, 1980), pp. 50–69.

10. J. Gwenogvryn Evans (ed. and trans.) *The Book of Aneirin* (Llanbedrog, 1922).

11. See the introduction to Jarman (ed.), *Y Gododdin*, pp. xiii–lxxv.

12. See, in general, the studies in M. Lapidge and D. N. Dumville (eds) *Gildas: New Approaches* (Woodbridge, 1984); for a suggested locating of Gildas in the north rather than the west, see E. A. Thompson, 'Gildas and the History of Britain', *Britannia*, 10 (1979), 203–26.

13. For these lives, see the edition in *Cymrodorion Record Series*, Vol. 3, pt II (1901), pp. 317–413.

14. Ed. L. Bieler, *Irish Penitentials*, SLH vol. V, pp. 60–5.

15. *De Excidio* 14–26. D. N. Dumville, 'The Chronology of *De Excidio Britanniae*, Book I', in Lapidge and Dumville (eds), *Gildas: New Approaches*, pp. 61–84 treats the text as being chronologically sequential.

16. The anonymous author of the *Chronica Gallica A* CCCCLII, 126, ed. T. Mommsen, MGH *AA*, vol. IX, p. 660, records for this year that Britain came under the authority of the Saxons. Such a rare continental notice of Britain and the phraseology used would make sense if some form of imperial treaty had been made, along the lines of that concluded with the Vandals in the same year.

17. Gildas, *De Excidio*, 26. 1.

18. Ibid., 28–33.

19. D. N. Dumville, 'Gildas and Maelgwn: Problems of Dating', in *Gildas: New Approaches*, pp. 51–9.

20. For these, see P. C. Bartrum (ed.) *Early Welsh Genealogical Tracts* (Cardiff, 1966).

21. This is too optimistic: *The Times Atlas of Medieval Civilisations*, pt 1, 22 September 1990, p. 6, still states that the Britons were pushed into Wales by the Anglo-Saxons! See A. S. Esmonde Cleary, *The Ending of Roman Britain* (London, 1989), esp. pp. 162–205 on discontinuity in Britain after Roman rule; and K. R. Dark, *Civitas to Kingdom: British Political Continuity, 300–800* (Leicester, 1994) for a contrary emphasis on continuities, at least in the areas under Romano-British rulers.

22. The best example of this is the 'first dynasty' of the kings of Wessex; all of this family, from Cerdic to Cynewulf (d. 786), had either pure or hybrid Celtic names.

23. *Anglo-Saxon Chronicle* ('Laud' or 'E' version), s.a. 519, 560, 597.

24. *Anglo-Saxon Chronicle*, s.a. 556, 560, 568, 571, 577, 584, 593; see also J. N. L. Myres, *The English Settlements* (Oxford, 1986), pp. 162–73

for the traditional approach, including belief (unsound) in a 'Ceawlin Saga'.

25. *Anglo-Saxon Chronicle* (ASC), s.a. 495, 508.
26. He is stated to be the son of Cynric in the genealogy placed at the head of the 'A' version of ASC; on the lack of trust to be placed in such West Saxon genealogies, see D. N. Dumville, 'Kingship, Genealogies and Regnal Lists', in P. H. Sawyer and I. N. Wood (eds), *Early Medieval Kingship* (Leeds, 1977), pp. 72–104.
27. ASC, s.a. 568, 571, 577; 'E' version s.a. 571; Myres, *English Settlements*, p. 169 identifies Cutha with Cuthwine.
28. J. S. Wacher, *Cirencester Roman Amphitheatre* (HMSO, 1981).
29. C. Heighway, *Anglo-Saxon Gloucestershire* (Gloucester, 1987), pp. 1–40.
30. ASC, s.a. 597, 607.
31. D. Dumville, 'The Origins of Northumbria: Some Aspects of the British Background', in S. Bassett (ed.), *The Origins of Anglo-Saxon Kingdoms* (Leicester, 1989), pp. 213–22; cf. P. Hunter Blair, *The Origins of Northumbria* (Newcastle upon Tyne, 1947).
32. See, in general, C. Thomas, *Christianity in Roman Britain to A.D. 500* (London, 1981).
33. Thomas, *Christianity*, pp. 275–94; Bede, *Historia Ecclesiastica* (HE) III. iv.
34. C. Thomas, *Whithorn's Christian Beginnings* (Whithorn Lecture, 1992); P. Hill, *Whithorn and St. Ninian: The Excavation of a Monastic Town 1984–91* (Stroud, 1997), pp. 1–40, 67–133.
35. On the Picts, see F. T. Wainwright (ed.), *The Problem of the Picts* (London, 1955; reissued Perth, 1980), I. Henderson, *The Picts* (London, 1967); and S. M. Foster, *Picts, Gaels and Scots* (London, 1996), among many others. For the stones, see G. and I. Henderson, *The Art of the Picts* (London, 2004); and I. Fraser and J. Borland, *The Pictish Symbol Stones of Scotland* (Edinburgh, 2008).
36. Bede, HE III. iv; cf. *Vita Columbae* 102b.
37. See J. E. Fraser, *The Pictish Conquest* (Stroud, 2006), pp. 31–3.
38. Bede, HE I. xxv.
39. The point is made about Nynia in E. A. Thompson, 'The Origins of Christianity in Scotland', *Scottish Historical Review*, 37 (1958), 17–22, but applies equally to Liudhard.
40. Bede, HE I. xxvi.
41. Ibid., II. v–vi, III. viii.
42. Bede, HE II. 9 and 20; see also H. M. R. E. Mayr-Harting, 'Paulinus of York', *Studies in Church History*, 4 (1967), 15–21.
43. Bede, HE III, i, iii.
44. Ibid., I. xxix.
45. Ibid., I. xxv.
46. See index to Colgrave and Mynors's edition of Bede for references. For Wroxeter, see P. A. Barker, 'The Latest Occupation of the Baths Basilica at Wroxeter', in P. J. Casey (ed.), *The End of Roman Britain* (Oxford, 1979), pp. 175–81; on Carlisle, see M. R. McCarthy, *A Roman, Anglian and Medieval Site at Blackfriars Street, Carlisle; Excavations 1977–79* (Kendal, 1990), though

relatively little has emerged here from the early Anglo-Saxon period.

47. B. Hope-Taylor, *Yeavering* (London, 1977).

48. On these, see Bede's *Historia Abbatum*, first edited by the Irish scholar Sir James Ware in 1666; the best edition is that of C. Plummer, *Venerabilis Baedae Opera Historica* (Oxford 1896), pp. 364–87. See also E. Fletcher, *Benedict Biscop* (Jarrow Lecture 1981), and R. Cramp, *Wearmouth and Jarrow Monastic Sites* (2 vols) (London, 2005–6).

49. On the Synod of Whitby, see Bede, HE III. xxv; see also H. M. R. E. Mayr-Harting, *The Coming of Christianity to Anglo-Saxon England* (London, 1972), pp. 103–13.

50. *The Earliest Life of Gregory the Great*, ed. B. Colgrave (Laurence, Kan., 1968).

51. Bede, HE IV. xviii; *Historia Abbatum*, pp. 365–7.

52. R. Bruce-Mitford, *The Art of the Codex Amiatinus* (Jarrow Lecture for 1967, publ. 1969).

53. See G. Henderson, *From Durrow to Kells: The Insular Gospel Books, 650–800* (London, 1987).

54. *The Corpus of Anglo-Saxon Stone Sculpture*, vols. I–III, ed. R. Cramp, R. Bailey and J. T. Lang (Oxford, 1984–91) for the northern counties. Vol. IV (1996) deals with the south-east.

55. Bede, HE II. 20; ASC ('Parker' or 'A' version) s.a. 626; W. Davies, 'Annals and the Origin of Mercia', in A. Dornier (ed.), *Mercian Studies* (Leicester, 1977), pp. 17–29; and N. Brooks, 'The Formation of the Mercian Kingdom', in Bassett, *Origins of Anglo-Saxon Kingdoms*, pp. 159–70.

56. W. Davies and H. Vierck, 'The Context of the *Tribal Hideage*: Social Aggregates and Settlement Patterns', *Frühmittelalterliche Studien*, 8 (1974), 223–93.

57. Bede, HE I. xv, III. xxi, xxiv.

58. Ibid., II. xx.

59. Ibid., III. i.

60. Ibid., III. ii.

61. Ibid., III. xviii, xxiv; ASC s.a. 644.

62. Bede, HE III. xxiv.

63. Ibid., III. xxx, IV. iii.

64. Ibid., IV. xii cf. xxi–xxii for a Mercian defeat of Northumbria in 679.

65. Ibid., IV. 26; Smyth, *Warlords*, pp. 64–6.

66. F. M. Stenton, 'The Ascendancy of the Mercian Kings', *English Historical Review*, 33 (1918), 433–52, a classic paper in many ways, does less than justice to the late-seventh-century kings, largely because of the obsessive hold of Bede's list of seven kings who 'exercised a supremacy over all of the provinces which lay to the south of the Humber' (p. 433). See below and nt 73 for this.

67. Bede, HE III. xxi, xxiv, IV. iii.

68. Ibid., IV. iii, vi.

69. On this, see C. Stancliffe, 'Kings Who Opted Out', in P. Wormald, D. Bullough and R. Collins (eds), *Ideal and Reality in Frankish and Anglo-Saxon Society* (Oxford, 1983), pp. 154–76.

70. Bede, HE V. xix; *Liber Pontificalis*, Constantine, Vol. I, p. 393.

71. ASC, s.a. 688.

72. ASC, s.a. 715.

73. Bede, HE V. xxiii.

74. Ibid., II. v.

75. On this question of the 'Bretwaldaship', see P. Wormald, 'Bede, the *Bretwaldas* and the Origins of the *Gens Anglorum*', in Wormald *et al.* (eds), *Ideal and Reality*, pp. 99–129; and S. Keynes, 'Rædwald the Bretwalda', in C. B. Kendall and P. S. Wells (eds), *Voyage to the Other World: the Legacy of Sutton Hoo* (Minneapolis, Minn., 1992), pp. 103–23.

76. B. Yorke, *Kings and Kingdoms of Early Anglo-Saxon England* (London, 1990), p. 31, with references.

77. Bede, HE III. vii.

78. On Offa, see J. M. Wallace-Hadrill, *Early Germanic Kingship in England and on the Continent* (Oxford, 1971), pp. 110–23.

79. See nt 74 above.

80. P. H. Sawyer, *Anglo-Saxon Charters: An Annotated List* (London, 1968), nos 104–47, with comments on authenticity.

81. *Asser's Life of King Alfred*, 14, ed. W. H. Stevenson (Oxford, 1904), p. 12. The argument over the authenticity of this work has been re-opened in A. P. Smyth, *King Alfred the Great* (Oxford, 1995), pp. 149–367. Reactions have generally not been favourable to this attempt to make the *Life* a product of the late-tenth-century monk, Byrhtferth of Ramsey.

82. For the classic boundary marker interpretation, see C. Fox, *Offa's Dyke* (London, 1955); for some alternative interpretations, see D. Hill, 'Offa's and Wat's Dykes: Some Aspects of Recent Work', *Transactions of the Lancashire and Cheshire Antiquarian Society*, 79 (1977), 21–33.

83. Alcuin, *Epistolae*, nos 7, 64, 100, 101, ed. E. Dümmler, MGH *Epp IV.*

84. On this episode, see N. P. Brooks, *The Early History of the Church of Canterbury* (Leicester, 1984), pp. 111–27.

85. For Breedon, see A. Dornier, 'The Anglo-Saxon Monastery at Breedon-on-the-Hill, Leicestershire', and R. Cramp, 'School of Mercian Sculpture', both in Dornier, *Mercian Studies*, pp. 155–68 and 191–234; for Offa's Dyke, see nt 78 above, and D. Hill, 'The Construction of Offa's Dyke', *The Antiquaries Journal*, 65 (1985), 140–2.

86. For the reference to the (lost?) laws of Offa, see the Preface to the *Code of Alfred*. The most convenient edition is that of F. Attenborough, *The Laws of the Earliest English Kings* (Cambridge, 1922), p. 62. For a possible identification of the text with the acts of the legatine synod of 786, see P. Wormald, 'In Search of Offa's "law-code"', in I. Wood and N. Lund (eds), *People and Places in Northern Europe 500–1600* (Woodbridge, 1991), pp. 25–45.

87. On this period, see Stenton, *Anglo-Saxon England*, pp. 94–5, 223–36; also N. P. Brooks, 'England in the Ninth Century: The Crucible of Defeat', *Transactions of the Royal Historical Society*, 5th series, 29 (1979), 1–20.

88. ASC, s.a. 805, 823 (*recte* 807, 825).
89. ASC, s.a. 823, 825 (*recte* 825, 827); Florence of Worcester s.a. 825 is the source for Ludeca's death in East Anglia.
90. *Series Regum Northymbrensium*, ed. T. Arnold, Rolls Series, Vol. 75, pt ii, p. 391. Also *Historia Dunelmensis Ecclesiae*, ibid., pt i, pp. 52–4.
91. ASC, s.a. 821, 823, 825, 827, 828. See S. Keynes, 'King Alfred and the Mercians', in M. A. S. Blackburn and D. N. Dumville (eds), *Kings, Currency and Alliances* (Leicester, 1998), pp. 1–45, and idem, 'Mercia and Wessex in the Ninth Century', in M. P. Brown and C. A. Farr (eds), *Mercia: An Anglo-Saxon Kingdom in Europe* (London, 2001), pp. 310–28.
92. Genealogy at the head of the 'A' version of ASC; for Eahlmund, see Sawyer, *Anglo-Saxon Charters*, no. 38.
93. ASC, s.a. 784 (*recte* 786); for the Mercian line, see Chapter 18 below.
94. ASC, s.a. 827, 828 (*recte* 829, 830).
95. See Chapter 18 below.
96. ASC, s.a. 853. See T. M. Charles-Edwards, 'Wales and Mercia, 613–918', in Brown and Farr (eds), *Mercia*, pp. 89–105.

12   THE LOMBARDS IN ITALY, *c.* 540–712

1. *De Origine et Situ Germanorum*, 40. 1; admittedly, there could not have been many such readers, judging from the fact that, fragments of one tenth-century MS apart, no pre-Renaissance copies of it are known.
2. See the map opposite p. 230 of J. G. C. Anderson's edition of the *Germania* (Oxford, 1938). For a discussion of early Lombard history, see J. Jarnut, 'Zur Frühgeschichte der Langobarden', *Studi Medievali*, 24 (1983), 1–16; and N. Christie, *The Lombards* (Oxford, 1995), pp. 1–30.
3. On Paul's Beneventan interests and the probable intended dedicatee, see K. H. Kruger, 'Zur "beneventanishen" Konzeption der Langobardengeschichte des Paulus Diaconus', *Frühmittelalterliche Studien*, 15 (1981), 18–35.
4. See the valuable discussion of some of these in W. Goffart, *The Narrators of Barbarian History* (Princeton, NJ, 1988), pp. 329–33.
5. Paul, *History*, I. 18; *Origo*, II; Mommsen, MGH *AA*, vol. IX, p. 499.
6. The fifth of the kings, Gudeoc, is a contemporary of Odovacer (476–93) in Paul, *History* I. 19. For a reconstruction of Lombard history in the pre-Italian phase, see J. Jarnut, *Geschichte der Langobarden* (Stuttgart, 1982), pp. 17–32; and Christie, *Lombards*, pp. 31–68.
7. See the arguments of P. Amory, *People and Identity in Ostrogothic Italy, 489–554* (Cambridge, 1997), pp. 13–42.
8. Procopius, *History of the Wars*, VI. xiv. I–xv. 36.
9. For Lombards and Heruls fighting in imperial armies on the Persian frontier, see Agathias, *Histories*, III. xx. 10.
10. Procopius, *Histories* VII. xxxiv. 1–45; F. E. Wozniak, 'Byzantine Diplomacy and the Lombard–Gepid Wars', *Balkan Studies*, 20 (1979), 139–58.

11. Theophylact, *Chronicle*, VI. x. 9–12; Menander Protector, frs 12.1 and 2.

12. For the archaeological evidence relating to Gepid settlement north of the Danube, see I. Bona, *The Dawn of the Dark Ages: The Gepids and the Lombards in the Carpathian Basin* (Budapest, 1976), pp. 14–19, 28–39, 83–7.

13. Menander Protector, fragments 12.3–8.

14. Theophylact Simocatta, *History*, I. iii. 3.

15. Bona, *Dawn of the Dark Ages*, pp. 93–105.

16. Paul the Deacon, *History of the Lombards*, II. 7.

17. Marius of Avenches, *Chronica*, s.a. (in Mommsen's ed.) 569, p. 238.

18. Isidore, *Chronica*, 402, ed. Mommsen, MGH *AA* vol. XI, p. 476; Fredegar, *Chronicle*, III. 65; Paul the Deacon, *History*, II. 5.

19. For use of Lombards in the war against Baduila, see Procopius, *Histories*, VIII. xxv. 15, xxxiii. 2–3.

20. For Paul's references to Secundus, see his *History*, III. 29, IV. 27, and 40. He calls him *servos Christi*, and this probably justifies our seeing him as a bishop rather than an abbot or ascetic; as does the fact that he was chosen to be godfather to King Agilulf's son Adaloald (IV. 27).

21. Paul the Deacon, *History* II. 14, 25–7.

22. G. P. Bognetti, 'Teodorico di Verona e Verona longobarda, capitale di regno', in *Scritti giuridici in onore di Mario Cavalieri* (Padua, 1959), pp. 3–39.

23. Paul the Deacon, *History*, II. 28–30; Fredegar, III. 65–6.

24. Marius of Avenches, *Chronica*, s.a. 572, ed. Mommsen, p. 238.

25. To take just one example: 'they are the anarchists of the *Völkerwanderung*, whose delight is only in destruction, and who seem incapable of culture': T. Hodgkin, *Italy and Her Invaders*, Vol. V (Oxford, 1895), p. 156.

26. Fredegar, *Chronicle*, III. 65; *Epistolae Austrasicae*, 8 (letter of bishop Nicetius of Trier to Chlotsuintha *c.* 565).

27. Paul the Deacon, *History*, III. 5–7, here largely relying on Gregory of Tours, *Histories*, V. 15.

28. G. P. Bognetti, 'La rivalitá tra Austrasia e Burgundia' in his *L'Eta longobarda*, Vol. IV (Milan, 1968), pp. 559–82; C. Wickham, *Early Medieval Italy: Central Power and Local Society, 400–1000* (London, 1981), pp. 30–1 is sceptical.

29. *Epistolae Austrasicae*, 40, 41, 46; Paul the Deacon, *History*, III. 17; see W. Goffart, 'Byzantine Policy in the West under Tiberius II and Maurice', *Traditio*, 13 (1957), pp. 73–118.

30. Paul the Deacon, *History*, III. 29, 31 and 34.

31. Procopius, *Histories*, VII. xxxiv. 24.

32. Gregory I, *Libri IV Dialogorum*, III. 27–8, IV. 37; Paul the Deacon, *History*, IV. 16.

33. This is more probable than the idea that the conversion was a cynical bid initiated around 565 to make the Lombards seem sympathetic to the remnants of the Ostrogothic population in Italy: Wickham, *Early Medieval Italy*, p. 30, summarising Bognetti.

34. Bona, *Dawn of the Dark Ages*, pp. 35–43, 73–82; J. Werner, *Die Langobarden im Pannonien* (Munich, 1962).
35. Paul the Deacon, *History*, II. 32; cf. Fredegar, III. 68.
36. *Edictus Rothari*, cc. 6, and 20–5.
37. Wickham, *Early Medieval Italy*, pp. 41–2; as with all late and post-Roman administrative structures, anomalies abounded.
38. G. P. Bognetti, 'Tradizione Longobarda e politica bizantina nelle origini del ducato di Spoleto', in his *L'Eta longobarda*, Vol. III, pp. 441–75.
39. Paul the Deacon, *History*, III. 18–19.
40. Ibid., III. 13.
41. Ibid., III. 33 (Duke Zotto of Benevento); 32 (Authari in the South). On Zotto, see S. Gasparri, *I Duchi Longobardi* (Rome, 1978), p. 86.
42. Ibid., II. 31; Marius of Avenches, s.a. 573, ed. Mommsen, p. 238.
43. Marius of Avenches, s.a. 574, ed. Mommsen, p. 238. The meaning of *puer* is unclear here, but seems to imply a youth in the royal entourage.
44. Paul the Deacon, *History*, II. 32.
45. For a discussion, see Wickham, *Early Medieval Italy*, pp. 31–2; also H. Fröhlich, *Studien zur langobardischen Thronfolge von de Anfängen bis zur Eroberung des italienischen Reiches durch Karl den Grossen* (Dissertation, University of Tübingen, 1971), Vol. I, pp. 105–16.
46. G. P. Bognetti, 'L'influsso delle istituzioni militari romane sulle istituzioni longobarde del secolo VI e la nature della "fara"', in his *L'Eta longobarda*, Vol. III (Milan, 1967), pp. 3–46, esp. pp. 9–11.
47. R. Schneider, *Königswahl und Königserhebung im Frühmittelalter* (Stuttgart, 1972), p. 24 (and nt 112 for other references).
48. S. Barnish, 'Taxation, Land and Barbarian Settlement in the Western Empire', *Papers of the British School at Rome*, 54 (1986), 170–95.
49. W. Goffart, *Barbarians and Romans A.D. 418–584: The Techniques of Accommodation* (Princeton, NJ, 1980), pp. 176–89.
50. Is it actually 'out of the question to suppose that Roman officials ... presided over a peaceful and harmonious accommodation between barbarians and provincials', or entirely accurate to say that 'the Lombards imposed themselves by force, in considerable confusion, and with brutality'? Ibid., p. 176.
51. II. 32, quoting from W. D. Foulke's translation (Philadelphia, Pa., 1907), pp. 89–91. See nt 1, pp. 91–3 for older arguments concerning this passage.
52. Goffart, *Barbarians and Romans*, pp. 180–1 and nt 14 discusses the historiography: his own views (pp. 181–5) are judicious.
53. J. Niermeyer, *Mediae Latinitis Lexicon Minus* (Leiden, 1976), p. 1043, following usages in Gregory of Tours, *Lex Salica* and so on.
54. See, for example, Authari's adoption of the title of Flavius; on this, see H. Wolfram, *Intitulatio I. Lateinishe Königs- und Fürstentitel bis zum Ende des 8 Jh.* (Vienna, 1967), pp. 56–76.
55. III. 16: *Populi tamen adgravati per Langobardos hospites partiuntur.* W. D. Foulke, pp. 114–16, nt 2 for the arguments in the older historiography.

56. See Goffart, *Barbarians and Romans*, pp. 185–9. His argument that the *populi adgravati* were the 'settled, hereditarily burdened slaves and *coloni* of the late Roman world' (p. 187) is hard to accept.

57. Niermeyer, *Lexicon*, p. 30.

58. A modification (and over-simplication) of the basic arguments of Goffart, *Barbarians and Romans*.

59. Paul, *History*, III. 16; Goffart, *Barbarians and Romans*, p. 185 for a more sensible understanding of *substantiae* than that of Bognetti, *L'Eta longobarda*, pp. 651–2, but still not going far enough. It must be admitted that C. Brühl, 'Zentral- und Finanzverwaltung im Franken- und im Langobardenreich', *Settimane di studio del Centro italiano di studi sell' alto medioevo*, 20 (1973), pp. 61–94 is far more pessimistic about the survival of land tax in Lombard Italy. See also the discussion in ibid., pp. 169–85.

60. Obviously, in practice, the Frankish and Visigothic kings faced similar problems with locally entrenched aristocracies, but none of these commanded *de jure* anything like the resources available to the Lombard dukes.

61. John of Biclar, *Chronica*, s.a. IV Mauricii, s.a. V Mauricii; ed. Mommsen, pp. 217–18.

62. Gregory of Tours, *Histories*, VIII. 18 (585), IX. 25 (588). On the latter, see also Paul the Deacon, *History*, III. 23 (585), III. 29 (588).

63. Gregory X. 3 (590); Paul III. 31 and 34.

64. J. Jarnut, *Agilolfingerstudien* (Stuttgart, 1986), pp. 44–61.

65. For discussions of Bavarian ethnogenesis see, among many others, H. Wolfram and A. Schwarcz (eds), *Die Bayern und ihre Nachbarn*, Vol. I (Vienna, 1985) and H. Friesinger and F. Daim (eds), idem, Vol. II (Vienna, 1985); also H. Dannheimer, *Auf den Spuren der Baiuwaren* (Munich, 1987) for a survey of recent archaeology.

66. Paul the Deacon, *History*, III. 35; *Origo*, 6 suggests that Agilulf carried out a *coup d'état*, then legitimised it by the marriage. See Fröhlich, *Studien*, Vol. 1, pp. 124–38; Schneider, *Königswahl*, pp. 28–32.

67. Paul, *History*, IV. 3 and 13 (four dukes executed). For Agilulf's reign, see Jarnut, *Geschichte der Langobarden*, pp. 43–6.

68. Paul the Deacon, *History*, IV. 12, 20 and 24.

69. Gregory I, *Epistolae*, bk II, no. 45. For Gregory and the Lombards, see R. Markus, *Gregory the Great and His World* (London, 1997), pp. 99–107.

70. *Gens nefandissima Langobardorum: Epistolae Austrasicae*, 40; also Gregory I, *Epistolae*, bk VII, letter 26.

71. G. P. Bognetti, 'Santa Maria foris portas di Castelseprio e la storia religiosa dei Longobardi', in his *L'Eta longobarda*, Vol. II (Milan, 1966), pp. 11–673 is the most forceful attempt to make sense of it, but is rather too prone to politicise religious affiliation.

72. Gregory I, *Epistolae* bk. 1, no. 17.

73. R. Collins, 'King Leovigild and the Conversion of the Visigoths', in idem, *Law, Culture and Regionalism in Early Medieval Spain* (Aldershot, 1992), item II.

74. Wickham, *Early Medieval Italy*, pp. 34–6 discusses Bognetti's arguments and proposes that the issue is really one of 'the near-total irrelevance of personal religious alignment inside a resolutely secular political system', (p. 36) – wishful thinking?

75. For example, Gregory I, *Libri quattuor Dialogorum*, III. 29, referring to an Arian Lombard bishop in Spoleto (580s), and III. 30 for an Arian church in Rome (of Ostrogothic foundation or earlier?).

76. Paul the Deacon, *History*, IV. 42.

77. On the 'Three Chapters' and the Istrian schism, see L. Duchesne, *L'Eglise au VIe siècle* (Paris, 1925), pp. 156–255; and Markus, *Gregory the Great*, pp. 127–33.

78. See S. C. Fanning, 'Lombard Arianism Reconsidered', *Speculum*, 56 (1981), 241–58.

79. See the useful comments of G. Tabacco, *Egemonie sociali e strutture del potere nel medioevo italiano* (Turin, 1979), pp. 119–20, 125–9.

80. For Agilulf's crown, of which only the central pendant cross survives, see M. Brozzi *et al.*, *Longobardi* (Milan, 1980), p. 110. For Bobbio, see Jonas, *Vita Columbani*, I. 30; C. Brühl, *Studien zu den langobardischen Königsurkunden* (Tübingen, 1970), pp. 19–48; idem, (ed.) *Codice diplomatico longobardo*, III, 1 (Rome, 1973), pp. 3–7. Bobbio also benefited from the Arian kings Rothari and Rodoald: ibid., pp. 18–21.

81. Paul the Deacon, *History*, IV. 41.

82. Ibid., IV. 42 and 45; for the Code, see the Bibliography.

83. Ibid., IV. 42; *Edictus Rothari*, 386.

84. *Codex Theodosianus: Gesta Senatus Urbis Romae*, 4; Justinian, *Institutionum libri quattuor*, Preface; *Codex Iustinianus, lex in conf.: Edictum Theodorici Regis*, Preface. This edict contained 154 chapters, compared to 388 in Rothari's.

85. *Edictus Rothari*, 243; on the Lombard charters, see C. Brühl, *Studien zu den langobardischen Königsurkunden* (Tübingen, 1970).

86. *Edictus Rothari*, 386 and 367.

87. Hodgkin, *Italy and her Invaders*, Vol. VI (Oxford, 1895), p. 238.

88. *Edictus Rothari*, 376 – because Christians should not believe that a woman could eat a living man from inside him.

89. B. Ward-Perkins, *From Classical Antiquity to the Middle Ages: Urban Public Building in Northern and Central Italy AD 300–850* (Oxford, 1984), pp. 173–4; J. Jarnut, 'La funzione centrale della città nel regno longobardo', *Società e storia*, 46 (1989), 967–71. *Edictus Rothari*, 244 is also significant here.

90. Ward-Perkins, *From Classical Antiquity*, pp. 196–9, with references. For Pavia in particular in the Lombard period, see D. Bullough, 'Urban Change in Early Medieval Italy: The Example of Pavia', *Papers of the British School at Rome*, 34 (1966), 82–130.

91. C. La Rocca, 'Public Buildings and Urban Change in Northern Italy in the Early Medieval Period', in J. Rich (ed.), *The City in Late Antiquity* (London, 1992), pp. 161–80.

92. Paul the Deacon, *History*, IV. 30, V. 36; M. McCormick, *Eternal Victor: Triumphal Rulership in Late Antiquity, Byzantium and the Early Medieval West* (Cambridge, 1986), pp. 287–9, 294.

93. Paul the Deacon, *History*, V. 5–12, 19–21.
94. Wickham, *Early Medieval Italy*, pp. 37–8 argues cogently that competition for the royal office is an indicator of 'the substantial cohesion of the political system'.
95. Paul the Deacon, *History*, V. 32–3. Perctarit's inclusion in the Durham monastic 'Book of Life' (*Liber Vitae Ecclesiae Dunelmensis* (London: Surtees Society, 1841), p. 1: 'Berctred') and *Vita Wilfridi*, ch. 28 indicate continuing contacts with Northumbria.
96. Paul the Deacon, *History*, V. 36–41; on Alahis, see J. Jarnut, 'Des Herzogtum Trient in langobardischer Zeit', *Atti dell'Accadamia Roveretana degli Agiati*, 235 (1985), pp. 167–78.
97. Paul the Deacon, *History*, VI. 35. For the events of this period, see Jarnut, *Geschichte der Langobarden*, pp. 61–6; and for the royal successions, Schneider, *Königswahl*, pp. 50–4 and Fröhlich, *Studien*, pp. 166–73. On Duke Theotpert, see Jarnut, *Agilolfingerstudien*, p. 8.
98. For aspects of the Lombard kingdom in the eighth century, see Chapters 13 and 16 below.

13 THE PARTING OF EAST AND WEST

1. *Sancti Fulgentii Episcopi Ruspensis Opera*, ed. J. Fraipont, CC vols XCI and XCIA; R. Collins, 'Fulgentius von Ruspe', *Theologische Realenzyklopädie*, Vol. XI 4/5, pp. 723–7.
2. J. Durliat, *Les dédicaces d'ouvrages de défence dans l'Afrique byzantine* (Rome, 1981).
3. On the 'Three Chapters' dispute, see C. Chazelle and C. Cubitt (eds.), *The Crisis of the Oikumene: The Three Chapters and the Failed Search for Unity in the Sixth-Century Mediterranean* (Turnhout, Belgium, 2007); also P. T. R. Gray, *The Defense of Chalcedon in the East (451–553)* (Leiden, 1979), pp. 61–8; and for its Italian dimension, R. A. Markus, *Gregory the Great and his World* (Cambridge, 1997), pp. 125–42.
4. J. Fontaine, *Isidore de Séville et la culture classique dans l'Espagne wisigothique* (3 vols) (Paris, 1959–83), Vol. II, pp. 854–9.
5. The possibility that the addressee of a lost grammatical treatise of Julian of Toledo was the African abbot Hadrian of Canterbury was raised by B. Bischoff in the discussion following the lecture by T. J. Brown, 'An Historical Introduction to the Use of Classical Latin Authors in the British Isles from the Fifth to the Eleventh Centuries', *Settimane di studio del Centro italiano di studi sull' alto medioevo*, Vol. XXII (1975), p. 299.
6. *Vita Fructuosi*, 17; E. A. Thompson, 'Two Notes on St. Fructuosus of Braga', *Hermathena*, 90 (1957), 54–63; for the significance of Eugenius's work, see R. Collins, *The Arab Conquest of Spain, 710–797* (Oxford, 1989), p. 15.
7. Adamnán, *De locis sanctis*, Preface, and the introduction to Meehan's edition (see Bibliography), pp. 6–14.
8. Monotheletism remains little studied, but more attention has been paid recently to one of its principal opponents, Maximus the

Confessor: A. Louth, *Maximus the Confessor* (London, 1996); and P. Allen and B. Neil (eds, with intro. and trans.), *Maximus the Confessor and His Companions* (Oxford, 2002).

9. Bede, *Historia Ecclesiastica Gentis Anglorum*, IV. 17 (by the numeration of the Colgrave and Mynors edn).

10. F. X. Murphy, 'Julian of Toledo and the Condemnation of Monotheletism in Spain', in *Mélanges J. de Ghellinck* (Gembloux, 1951), pp. 361–73.

11. For the use of papyrus by the notaries of Ravenna, see J.-O. Tjäder (ed.), *Die nichtliterarischen Papyri Italiens aus der Zeit 445–700* (3 vols) (Lund and Stockholm, 1955–82); see also H. Pirenne, 'Le commerce de papyrus dans la Gaule mérovingienne', *Comptes rendus des séances de l'Academie des Inscriptions et Belles-Lettres* (1928), 178–91, and M. McCormick, *Origins of the European Economy: Communications and Commerce AD 300–900* (Cambridge, 2001), pp. 65 and 704–8.

12. On Tintagel, see now R. C. Barrowman, C. E. Batey and C. D. Morris (eds), *Excavations at Tintagel Castle, Cornwall, 1990–1999* (London, 2007).

13. P. Courcelle, *Late Latin Writers and their Greek Sources* (Cambridge, Mass., 1969), pp. 149–223. For Isidore, see Fontaine, *Isidore de Séville*, Vol. II, pp. 849–54. On Gregory I, see G. J. M. Bartelink, 'Pope Gregory the Great's Knowledge of Greek', in J. C. Cavadini (ed.), *Gregory the Great: A Symposium* (Notre Dame, Indiana, 1995), pp. 117–36.

14. For the process of compilation, see A. M. Honore, *Justinian's Digest: Work in Progress* (Oxford, 1971); and idem, *Tribonian* (London, 1978), pp. 139–222.

15. For a useful overview, see W. Berschin, *Greek Letters and the Latin Middle Ages, from Jerome to Nicholas of Cusa* (revd edn) (Washington, DC, 1988).

16. Y. Duval, 'La discussion entre l'apocrisiaire Grégoire et le patriarche Eutychios au sujet de la résurrection de la chair', in J. Fontaine *et al.* (eds), *Grégoire le Grand* (Paris, 1986), pp. 347–66.

17. C. Courtois, 'Grégoire VII et l'Afrique du Nord', *Revue Historique*, 195 (1945), 97–122, 193–226; C.-E. Dufourcq, 'La coexistence des chrétiens et des musulmans dans *Al-Andalus* et dans le Maghrib aux Xe siècle', in *Occident et Orient au Xe Siècle* (Paris, 1979), pp. 209–34.

18. These is not well studied, but for useful parallels, see T. Canaan, *Mohammedan Saints and Sanctuaries in Palestine* (Jerusalem, 1927).

19. For the continuing intellectual vitality and leading role of Toledo in the eighth century, see Collins, *Arab Conquest of Spain*, pp. 52–80 and 217–30; for Adoptionism, see, above all, J. C. Cavadini, *The Last Christology of the West: Adoptionism in Spain and Gaul, 785–820* (Philadelphia, Pa., 1993).

20. For the reign of Justinian II, see C. F. Head, *Justinian II of Byzantium* (Madison, Wisc., 1972); and A. N. Stratos, *Byzantium in the Seventh Century*, Vol. V (Antwerp, 1980). Shorter but sounder is Herrin, *Formation of Christendom*, pp. 280–90.

21. See E. W. Brooks, 'The Arabs in Asia Minor (641–750), from Arabic Sources', *Journal of Hellenic Studies*, 18 (1898), 182–208; *Chronicle of Theophanes*, a.m. 6218–a.m. 6233.

22. For example, R. J. H. Jenkins, *Byzantium: The Imperial Centuries* (London, 1966), pp. 58–89, but see now M. Whittow, *The Making of Orthodox Byzantium, 600–1025* (London, 1996), pp. 143–9, and W. Treadgold, *A History of the Byzantine State and Society* (Stanford, Calif., 1997), pp. 346–70.

23. *Chronicle of Theophanes*, a.m. 6211.

24. *Chronicle of Theophanes*, a.m. 6217 and 6218. See M. V. Anastos, 'Leo III's Edict Against the Images in the Year 726–27 and Italo-Byzantine Relations between 726 and 730', *Byzantinische Forschungen*, 3 (1968), 5–41.

25. *Chronicle of Theophanes*, a.m. 6218.

26. For the Iconoclast conflict, see Herrin, *Formation of Christendom*, pp. 307–43, and E. Kitzinger, 'The Cult of Images in the Age before Iconoclasm', *Dumbarton Oaks Papers*, 8 (1954), 83–150; also Whittow, *Making of Orthodox Byzantium*, pp. 139–64. For detailed discussion of the evidence, see A. Grabar, *L'Iconoclasme byzantin* (2nd edn) (Paris, 1984), pp. 17–132.

27. *Chronicle of Theophanes*, a.m. 6215. See A. Grabar, *L'Iconoclasme*, pp. 128–9 for other evidence relating to the edict of Yazid.

28. R. Cormack, *Writing in Gold: Byzantine Society and its Icons* (London, 1985), pp. 95–140; Grabar, *L'Iconoclasme*, pp. 135–210.

29. *Chronicle of Theophanes*, a.m. 6232.

30. Herrin, *Formation of Christendom*, pp. 337–40.

31. *Chronicle of Theophanes*, a.m. 6233–a.m. 6235.

32. W. Treadgold, *Byzantium and its Army, 284–1081* (Stanford, Calif., 1995), for a substantial discussion.

33. W. Goffart, *Barbarians and Romans, A.D. 418–584: The Techniques of Accommodation* (Princeton, NJ, 1980); and the contributions, esp. that of J. Durliat, to H. Wolfram and A. Schwarcz (eds), *Anerkennung und Integration* (Vienna, 1988).

34. Equally thought-provoking should be the conclusions of the study of some late Roman administrative papyri from Egypt: J. Gascou, 'L'institution des bucellaires', *Bulletin de l'Institution française d'Archéologie orientale*, 76 (1976), 143–56. See, in general, on these records, P. Sarris, *Economy and Society in the Age of Justinian* (Cambridge, 2006), pp. 29–70.

35. Treadgold, *Byzantium and Its Army*, pp. 21–27; Whittow, *Making of Orthodox Byzantium*, pp. 120–21.

36. A. N. Stratos, *Byzantium in the Seventh Century*, Vol. IV: *668–85* (Amsterdam, 1978), pp. 93–113; R. Browning, *Byzantium and Bulgaria* (London, 1975), pp. 45–9.

37. *Chronicle of Theophanes*, a.m. 6257–a.m. 6259.

38. PG, 10, cols 1013–92; see, on this work, G. Huxley, 'On the *Vita* of Saint Stephen the Younger', *Greek, Roman and Byzantine Studies*, 18 (1977), 97–108, and the use made of it in P. Brown, 'A Dark Age Crisis: Aspects of the Iconoclastic Controversy', *English Historical Review*, 88 (1973), 1–34.

39. Herrin, *Formation of Christendom*, pp. 277–80 on the Sixth Ecumenical Council; and pp. 284–9 on the Quinisext.
40. For Martin I, see *Liber Pontificalis*, Vol. I, pp. 336–40; E. Caspar, *Geschichte des Papstums* (2 vols) (Tübingen, 1930–3), Vol. II, pp. 553–78. See also Herrin, *Formation of Christendom*, pp. 253–9 and P. Llewellyn, *Rome in the Dark Ages* (London, 1971), pp. 150–6.
41. *Liber Pontificalis*, Vol. I, p. 373. See A. Guillou, *Régionalisme et independence dans l'empire byzantin au vii siècle* (Rome, 1969), pp. 209–11.
42. *Liber Pontificalis*, Vol. I, pp. 385–7; P. J. Nordhagen, *The Frescoes of John VII in S. Maria Antiqua* (Rome, 1968), but cf. E. Kitzinger, *Byzantine Art in the Making* (London, 1977), pp. 113–22 and references; see also J. Breckenridge, 'Evidence for the Nature of Relations between Pope John VII and the Byzantine Emperor Justinian II', *Byzantinische Zeitschrift*, 65 (1972), 364–74.
43. Caspar, *Geschichte des Papstums*, Vol. II, pp. 639–40.
44. *Chronicle of Theophanes*, a.m. 6204.
45. *Chronicle of Theophanes*, a.m. 6217; see E. Caspar, 'Papst Gregor II und der Bilderstreit', *Zeitschrift für Kirchengeschichte*, 52 (1933), 29–70.
46. *Liber Pontificalis*, Vol. I, pp. 403–4 for Gregory II's involvement in the revolt over taxes, but cf. p. 408 – Gregory II's opposition to the setting up of a rebel emperor Tiberius in south Etruria. See also Caspar, *Geschichte des Papstums*, Vol. II, pp. 643–64 and Llewellyn, *Rome in the Dark Ages*, pp. 166–8. T. F. X. Noble, *The Republic of St. Peter: The Birth of the Papal State, 680–825* (Philadelphia, Pa., 1984), pp. 28–40 argues, on the other hand, that 'a papal Republic' came into existence between 729 and 733. See R. Collins, *Keepers of the Keys of Heaven: A History of the Papacy* (London and New York, 2009), ch. 7.
47. *Chronicle of Theophanes*, a.m. 6224.
48. R. A. Markus, *Gregory the Great and his World* (Cambridge, 1997), pp. 97–107.
49. J. T. Hallenbeck, *Pavia and Rome: The Lombard Monarchy and the Papacy in the Eighth Century* (Philadelphia, Pa., 1982), pp. 39–44.
50. R. Krautheimer, *Rome, Profile of a City, 312–1308* (Princeton, NJ, 1980), p. 107.
51. Caspar, *Geschichte des Papstums*, Vol. II, pp. 737–7; Hallenbeck, *Pavia and Rome*, pp. 45–52.
52. Hallenbeck, *Pavia and Rome*, pp. 52–3.
53. As argued by Hallenbeck, *Pavia and Rome*, pp. 21–9 (for Liutprand) and 55–61 (for Aistulf in the years 749–52), but seeing a deliberate intent on Aistulf's part to try to take Rome in 753 (pp. 64–9).
54. *Liber Pontificalis*, Vol. I, p. 441.
55. *Chronicle of Theophanes*, a.m. 6243.

14   MONKS AND MISSIONARIES

1. D. Obolensky, *The Byzantine Commonwealth* (London, 1971), esp. chs 1–5.
2. R. Fletcher, *The Conversion of Europe* (London, 1997), pp. 327–68.
3. W. Ullmann, *The Growth of Papal Government* (2nd edn) (London, 1962), pp. 36–7, and idem, *A Short History of the Papacy in the Middle*

Ages (corrected reprint, London, 1974), pp. 51–70; his thesis that Gregory launched the mission to extend papal authority into areas beyond the emperor's control is firmly put to rest in R. Markus, 'Gregory the Great's Europe', *Transactions of the Royal Historical Society*, 5th series, 31 (1981), 21–36.

4. R. R. Ruether, *Gregory of Nazianzus: Rhetor and Philosopher* (Oxford, 1969), pp. 18–33, 136–55.

5. *Vita Martini*, VIII. 1–3; X. 1–9. On the early medieval remains at Ligugé, see J. Coquet, *L'intérêt des fouilles de Ligugé* (2nd edn) (Ligugé, 1978).

6. For Honoratus, see the text of and introduction to M.-D. Valentin's edition of Hilary's *Vita Honorati* (Bibliography).

7. R. Collins, 'Faustus von Reji', *Theologische Realenzyklopädie*, Vol. XI, pp. 63–7.

8. For the suggestion that the Rule for Nuns is Caesarius's *only* authentic rule, see R. Collins, 'Caesarius von Arles', ibid., Vol. VII, pp. 531–6; in general on Caesarius, see W. E. Klingshirn, *Caesarius of Arles: The Making of a Community in Late Antique Gaul* (Cambridge, 1994).

9. *Cassiodori Senatoris Institute*, ed. R. Mynors (Oxford, 1947); J. J. O'Donnell, *Cassiodorus* (Berkeley, Calif., 1979), pp. 177–222.

10. For editions of the *Rule of the Master* and of the *Rule of Benedict*, see Bibliography; on the priority of the former, against older arguments, see D. Knowles, 'The *Regula Magistri* and the *Rule* of St Benedict' in his *Great Historical Enterprises* (London, 1962), pp. 135–95; and the introduction to de Vogüé's edition (SC 181–6), Vol. 1, pp. 245–314. An attempt to reverse this verdict is made and refuted in *English Historical Review*, 105 (1990), 567–94 and 107 (1992), 95–111.

11. Book II of the *Dialogues* (Grégoire le Grand, *Dialogues*, ed. A. de Vogüé (SC vols. 251, 260, 265), bk II, Vol. 2, pp. 126–249) is the main source for the life of Benedict.

12. J. M. Wallace-Hadrill, *The Barbarian West* (revised edn) (Oxford, 1985), pp. 47–9.

13. *Regula Benedicti*, vii.

14. MGH *Epp.*, vols I and II; D. Norberg, *Critical and Exegetical Notes on the Letters of St. Gregory the Great* (Stockholm, 1982); and idem, 'Qui a composé les lettres de Grégoire le Grand?', *Studi Medievali*, 21 (1980), 1–17.

15. J. McClure, *Gregory the Great: Exegesis and Audience* (DPhil thesis, University of Oxford, 1979); and C. Straw, *Gregory the Great: Perfection in Imperfection* (Berkeley, Calif., 1988).

16. R. A. Markus, *Gregory the Great and his World* (Cambridge, 1997), pp. 17–33 and 68–82.

17. L. Bieler, *Ireland: Harbinger of the Middle Ages* (London, 1963), pp. 85–93: 'The Franks were ... nominal Christians ... a decadent nobility, and a worldly clergy'! (p. 85); C. Dawson, *The Making of Europe, 400–1000 AD* (London, 1939), pp. 196–213.

18. For example, D. A. Binchy, 'Irish History and Irish Law', *Studia Hibernica*, 15 (1975), 7–36, and 16 (1976), pp. 7–45.

19. Ibid., and Binchy, 'The Linguistic and Historical Value of the Irish Law Tracts', *Proceedings of the British Academy*, 29 (1943), 3–35.

20. J. F. Kenney, *The Sources for the Early History of Ireland (Ecclesiastical)*, revd by L. Bieler (Dublin, 1979), provides a comprehensive treatment of individual works; valuable generic accounts will be found in K. Hughes, *Early Christian Ireland: Introduction to the Sources* (London, 1972).

21. See items in nts 8 and 9 above; also D. O. Corráin, L. Breatnach and A. Breen, 'The Laws of the Irish', *Peritia*, 3 (1984), 382–438 (with bibliography cited there).

22. A. P. Smyth, 'The Earliest Irish Annals: Their First Contemporary Entries and the Earliest Centres of Recording', *Proceedings of the Royal Irish Academy*, 72C, no. 1 (1972), 1–48 argues that some entries from the mid-sixth century onwards are contemporary; Hughes, *Sources*, pp. 99–162 is more cautious.

23. For such largely fictional works, once much relied on, as *Cogadh Gaedhel re Gallaibh*, see Hughes, *Sources*, pp. 284–301; also in this category belong some (but not all) of *Fragmentary Annals of Ireland*, ed. J. Radnor (Dublin, 1978). On the early Irish annals in general, see T. Charles-Edwards (trans.), *The Chronicle of Ireland* (3 vols) (Liverpool, 2006), Vol. 1, pp. 1–24.

24. Hughes, *Sources*, pp. 217–47.

25. The literature on Patrick is enormous; see, for some of the arguments, R. P. C. Hanson, *Saint Patrick: His Origins and Career* (Oxford, 1968) (early dating); J. Carney, *The Problem of St. Patrick* (Dublin, 1973) (late dating); E. A. Thompson, *Who Was St. Patrick?* (Woodbridge, 1985) (either, neither or both); and, for a real counsel of despair: T. F. O'Rahilly, *The Two Patricks* (Dublin, reprinted 1981). See also D. Dumville *et al.*, *Saint Patrick, A.D. 493–1993* (Woodbridge, 1993).

26. Kenney, *The Sources*, nos 127 and 128, pp. 329–35.

27. Ibid., no. 135, pp. 342–5. See R. Sharpe, 'St. Patrick and the See of Armagh', *Cambridge Medieval Celtic Studies*, 4 (1982), 33–59 for some doubts on Armagh's claims.

28. E. A. Thompson, 'St. Patrick and Coroticus', *Journal of Theological Studies*, n.s. 31 (1980), 12–27, and idem, *Who Was St. Patrick?*, pp. 125–43 offer a new approach to the identity of this man; it is certainly a corrective to the older, poorly grounded, certainties.

29. *Confessio*, 1–23.

30. Thompson, 'St. Patrick and Coroticus', pp. 12–27.

31. D. N. Dumville, 'Some British Aspects of the Earliest Irish Christianity', in P. Ní Chatháin and M. Richter (eds), *Irland und Europa* (Stuttgart, 1984), pp. 16–24 extends the logic of Thompson's argument (see n. 28) to include Palladius.

32. L. Laing, The Romanization of Ireland in the Fifth Century', *Peritia*, 4 (1985), 261–78 for the material culture. Some discussion of possible earlier Roman influences has been generated recently by the discovery of what might be a Roman fort, or more likely a trading station, near Dublin.

33. Prosper, *Chronica*, 1307, ed. Mommsen, p. 473.

34. Muirchú, *Vita Patricii*, 8–9.

35. C. Thomas, *Christianity in Roman Britain to AD 500* (London, 1981), esp. pp. 275–94 and 347–55; for his views on Patrick, see pp. 307–46.

36. F. Henry, 'Early Irish Monasteries, Beehive Huts and Dry-Stone Houses in the Neighbourhood of Caherciveen and Waterville', *Proceedings of the Royal Irish Academy*, 58C (1957), 45–166; T. Fanning, 'Excavation of the Early Christian Cemetery and Settlement at Reask, County Kerry', ibid., 81C (1981), 67–172; *Royal Commission on the Ancient and Historical Monuments of Scotland: Argyll*, Vol. IV: *Iona* (Edinburgh, 1982), pp. 31–48 for excavations of early Irish monastic foundations. See now A. Ritchie, *Iona* (London, 1997), pp. 31–46.

37. K. Hughes, *The Church in Early Irish Society* (London, 1966), pp. 65–78. The existence of Irish monasteries in the mid-sixth century rests largely on the identification of a certain *Vennianus*, who was a correspondent of Gildas (*c.* 540), with the author of the *Penitentialis Vinniani*. See P. ó Riain 'Finnio and Winniau: A Return to the Subject', in J. Carey, J. T. Koch and P.-Y. Lambert (eds), *Ildánach Ildírech: A Festschrift for Proinsias Mac Canna* (Andover and Aberystwyth, 1999), pp. 187–202.

38. Much of value can still be found in the introduction and notes to W. Reeves' edition of Adamnán's *Life of Columba*, as well as in the introduction to the more recent edition by the Andersons (for these, see Bibliography); see also A. D. S. Macdonald, 'Aspects of the Monastery and Monastic Life in Adamnán's Life of Columba', *Peritia*, 3 (1984), 271–302.

39. Hughes, *The Church in Early Irish Society*, pp. 79–90 for a statement of the orthodox view. See also J. Ryan, *Irish Monasticism* (Dublin, 1931), pp. 167–90.

40. R. Sharpe, 'Some Problems Concerning the Organization of the Church in Early Medieval Ireland', *Peritia*, 3 (1984), 230–70 is superbly and rightly iconoclastic.

41. For Ireland in the sixth century, see D. Ó. Crónín, *Early Medieval Ireland, 400–1200* (London, 1995), and chs. 4–7 of T. Charles-Edwards, *Early Christian Ireland* (Cambridge, 2000).

42. E. Mac Neill, *Celtic Ireland* (Dublin, 1921), pp. 96–113, and F. J. Byrne, *Irish Kings and High Kings* (London, 1973), pp. 28–47 give detailed and learned presentations of the traditional view.

43. Hughes, *Church in Early Irish Society*, pp. 65–78.

44. J. E. C. Williams, 'The Court Poet in Medieval Ireland', *Proceedings of the British Academy*, 57 (1971), 1–51; R. Flower, *The Irish Tradition* (Oxford, 1947) make useful starting points for the immense literature on the Bards.

45. J. Stevenson, 'The Beginnings of Literacy in Ireland', *Proceedings of the Royal Irish Academy*, 89C (1989), 127–65; and idem, 'Literacy in Ireland: The Evidence of the Patrick Dossier in the Book of Armagh', in R. McKitterick (ed.), *The Uses of Literacy in Early Medieval Europe* (Cambridge, 1990), pp. 11–35.

46. For aspects of the Irish role in the transmission of such learning, see V. Law, *The Insular Latin Grammarians* (Woodbridge, 1982), but see also the doubts expressed in L. Holtz, 'Les grammairiens hibernolatins étaient-ils des Anglo-Saxons?', *Peritia*, 2 (1983), 169–84.

47. T. M. Charles-Edwards, 'The Social Background to Irish *Peregrinatio*' *Celtica*, II (1976), 43–59. Irish texts relating to *Peregrinatio* may be rationalising and systematising a practice recently developed within the Irish Church under external influence, rather than it being an inherent feature that caused the Irish monks to have a decisive and unique impact on the Continent.

48. Adamanán, *Vita Columbae*, I. 14, 38–40, 42, 49–50, 11. 2, 36.

49. See the *Life of Columbanus* (Bibliography); and for various studies, see H. B. Clarke and M. Brennan (eds), *Columbanus and Merovingian Monasticism* (Oxford, 1981), and M. Lapidge (ed.), *Columbanus: Studies on the Latin Writings* (Woodbridge, 1997).

50. For discussion of the identity of 'Vinnian', see D. N. Dumville (ed.), 'Gildas and Uinniau', in *Gildas: New Approaches* (Woodbridge, 1984), pp. 207–14; and see nt 37 above; for the penitential, see L. Bieler (ed.), *The Irish Penitentials* (Dublin, 1963), pp. 74–95.

51. Columbanus, *Epistulae*, 1–3, ed. Walker, pp. 2–25.

52. *Vita Columbani*, I. 18–29; see also *Codice diplomatico del monasterio di S. Colombano di Bobbio*, ed. C. Cipolla, Vol. I (Rome 1918), docs I–V, and M. Richter, *Bobbio in the Early Middle Ages* (Dublin, 2008), pp. 13–48.

53. Direct, unmediated links between southern Spain and Ireland have not been established. See the three papers on the subject collected in J. N. Hillgarth, *Visigothic Spain, Byzantium and the Irish* (London, 1985), items VI–VIII; and E. James, 'Ireland and Western Gaul in the Merovingian Period', in D. Whitelock, R. McKitterick and D. Dumville (eds), *Ireland in Early Medieval Europe* (Cambridge, 1982), pp. 362–86.

54. Bertulf, the second abbot, was a Frankish noble and relative of bishop Arnulf of Metz, the progenitor of the Arnulfing line: *Vita Columbani*, II. 23.

55. F. Prinz, *Frühes Mönchtum im Frankenreich* (2nd edn) (Darmstadt, 1988), pp. 121–51.

56. Prinz, *Frühes Mönchtum*, pp. 131–3; *Vita (prima) Sancti Wandregisili*, ed. B. Krusch, MGH *SRM*, vol. V, pp. 1–24.

57. Prinz, *Frühes Mönchtum*, map VIIA, p. 674.

58. For example, M. de Paor and L. de Paor, *Early Christian Ireland* (London, 1958), pp. 48, 64–8.

59. C. Stancliffe, 'Early "Irish" Biblical Exegesis', *Studia Patristica*, XII (Berlin, 1975), 361–70; W. Stevens, 'Scientific Instruction in Early Insular Schools', in M. W. Herren (ed.), *Insular Latin Studies* (Toronto, 1981), pp. 83–111; and see also note 36 above.

60. Prinz, *Frühes Mönchtum*, pp. 263–92.

61. Bede, *Historia Ecclesiastica*, III. vii. See the Commentary by J. M. Wallace-Hadrill, p. 99.

62. See P. Rousseau, 'The Spiritual Authority of the "Monk-bishop"', *Journal of Theological Studies*, n.s. 22 (1971), 380–419.

63. H. I. Marrou, *A History of Education in Antiquity* (English trans.) (New York, 1956), pp. 419–51.

64. For example, IV Toledo (633), c. lii, ed. Vives, p. 209; Conc. Parisiense (614), xiv, ed. de Clercq, p. 279, etc.

65. C. Stancliffe, *St. Martin and his Biographer* (Oxford, 1983) is an excellent study of Sulpicius and his Martinian writings; see, in particular, pp. 328–40 for 'Martin's Campaign against Paganism'.

66. Gregory of Tours, *De Virtutibus Sancti Martini*, I. xi; idem, *Libri Decem Historiarum*, V. xxxvii.

67. Bede, *Historia Ecclesiastica, III.* iv; see also the Commentary by J. M. Wallace-Hadrill, p. 92.

68. Bede, ibid., I. xxiv; Commentary p. 32; further letters will be found in Gregory, *Epistolae*, bk XI, nos 55–62.

69. Bede, *Historia Ecclesiastica*, III. vii; IV. xii; II. xv; Commentary pp. 99, 148, 77–8.

70. For the arguments against this supposed Frankish hegemony, see R. Collins and J. McClure, 'Rome, Canterbury, Wearmouth-Jarrow: Three Viewpoints on Augustine's Mission' in S. Barton and P. Linehan (eds), *Cross, Crescent and Conversion. Studies in Memory of Richard Fletcher* (Leiden: Brill, 2008), pp. 17–42.

71. C. A. Bernoulli, *Die Heiligen der Merowinger* (Tübingen, 1900), pp. 73–149; see also F. Graus, *Volk, Herrscher und Heiliger im Reich der Merowinger. Studien zur Hagiographie der Merowingerzeit* (Prague, 1965).

72. For discussions of datings, see Krusch's introductions to the items in MGH *SRM*, vols 3–7; for modern revisions, see I. N. Wood, 'Forgery in Merovingian Hagiography', in *Fälschungen im Mittlealter*, Vol. V (*Schriften* of the MGH, Hanover, 1988), pp. 369–84.

73. *Vita Amandi*, 14; also 24.

74. See the introduction to Krusch's edition of the *Vita* for a late dating; cf. Wood 'Forgery', pp. 371–2, and R. Collins, 'The *Vaccaei*, the *Vaceti* and the Rise of *Vasconia*', in idem, *Law, Culture and Regionalism in Early Medieval Spain* (Aldershot, 1992), item XI, esp. p. 212 for a mid-eighth century date. Some (for example, Dierkens in nt 85 below) believe it to be genuinely late-seventh-century.

75. *Vita Amandi*, 4; Prinz, *Frühes Mönchtum*, pp. 19–46 for the cult.

76. *Vita Amandi*, 6–7; C. Straw, *Gregory the Great*, pp. 194–212.

77. *Liber Pontificalis*, Vol. I, pp. 323–7; J. N. D. Kelly, *Dictionary of Popes* (Oxford, 1986), pp. 70–1.

78. For the royal land grant, see Amandus's instruction for the disposition of his body: MGH *SRM*, vol. V, pp. 483–4. Acharius had been a monk at Luxeuil, and so his role in all this is seen (unnecessarily) as representing 'Irish influence'.

79. *Vita Amandi*, 16; the combination of Slavs and 'across the Danube' might locate this venture in Samo's kingdom (?), another area of special interest to Dagobert I: Fredegar, *Chronica*, IV. 48, 68, 75.

80. *Vita Amandi*, 17.

81. Fredegar, *Chronica*, IV. 59, 75.

82. *Vita Amandi*, 20–1; R. Collins, *The Basques* (2nd edn) (Oxford, 1990), pp. 102–4.

83. M. Werner, *Der Lütticher Raum im frühkarolingischer Zeit* (Göttingen, 1980), pp. 235–56.

84. It is preserved in a text known as the *Suppletio Milonis*: edited by Krusch, MGH *SRM*, vol. V, pp. 452–6 for the letter.

85. I am convinced by the reconstruction of these events offered by A. Dierkens, 'Saint Amand et la fondation de l'abbaye de Nivelles', *Revue du Nord*, 69 (1986), 325–32.

86. A. Dierkens, *Abbayes et chapitres entre Sambre et Meuse (VII–XI siècles)* (Paris, 1985), pp. 65–76.

87. *Vita Amandi*, 23.

88. Bede, *Historia Ecclesiastica*, III. xix; Commentary pp. 114–15.

89. *Liber Historiae Francorum*, 43; for an analysis of these events, see R. A. Gerberding, *The Rise of the Carolingians and the Liber Historiae Francorum* (Oxford, 1987), pp. 47–66.

90. The best study of the Frisians, though primarily concerned with them as traders and navigators, is S. Lebecq, *Marchands et navigateurs frisons du haut moyen âge* (2 vols) (Lille, 1983); for their history in the seventh century, see esp. pp. 106–10.

91. (Eddius) Stephanus, *Vita Wilfridi*, xxvi. The identification of the author of this work, Stephanus, with the cantor Aedde derives from Bede, *Historia Ecclesiastica*, IV. ii, but is not strong.

92. *Vita Wilfridi*, xxviii and xxxiii.

93. *Vita Wilfridi*, xxiv. See also W. Goffart, 'Bede and the Ghost of Bishop Wilfrid', in his *Narrators of Barbarian History* (Princeton, NJ, 1988), pp. 235–328.

94. D. O'Cróinin, 'Rash Melsigi, Willibrord, and the Earliest Echternach Manuscripts', *Peritia*, 3 (1984), 17–42.

95. Alcuin, *Vita Willibrordi Archepiscopi Traiectensis*, 3 and 4.

96. Bede, *Historia Ecclesiastica*, V. xi; Commentary, pp. 183–5.

97. Alcuin, *Vita Willibrordi*, 6–8.

98. J. M. Wallace-Hadrill, *The Frankish Church* (Oxford, 1983), pp. 144–7; W. Levison, *England and the Continent in the Eighth Century* (Oxford, 1946), pp. 45–69.

99. Pardessus, vol. II, nos 449, 458, 459, 461, 467, 474, 476, 481, 483, 485, 490, 500, 502, 503, 519–21, 537–40.

100. No all-embracing modern study of Aldhelm exists, but see M. Winterbottom, Aldhelm's Prose Style and Its Origins', *Anglo-Saxon England*, 6 (1977), 39–76, which stresses his continental as opposed to Irish intellectual and stylistic debts; also A. Orchard, *The Poetic Art of Aldhelm* (Cambridge, 1994).

101. For Boniface's career, see Levison, *England and the Continent*, pp. 70–94; Wallace-Hadrill, *Frankish Church*, pp. 150–61; and idem, 'A Background to St. Boniface's Mission', in P. Clemoes and K. Hughes (eds), *England before the Conquest* (Cambridge, 1971), pp. 35–48, reprinted in his *Early Medieval History* (Oxford, 1975), pp. 138–54; but above all, T. Schieffer, *Winfrid-Bonifatius und die christliche Grundlegung Europas* (Freiburg, 1954).

102. CLA 1197; see also M. B. Parkes, 'The Handwriting of St. Boniface: A Reassessment of the Problems', in *Beiträge zur Geschichte der deutschen Sprache und Literatur,* 98 (2) (1976), 161–79.

103. On the Rhineland aristocracy, see R. Sprandel, *Der merovingische Adel und die Gebiete östlich des Rheins* (Freiburg, 1957); see Wallace-Hadrill, 'Background', pp. 141–50, and Boniface, *epp.* 50, 51, 57, 60. See also Wallace-Hadrill, *Frankish Church,* pp. 132–42 for the Church in Francia under Charles Martel.

104. Boniface, *ep.* 12. See also A. Angenendt, 'Bonifatius und die Sacramentum initiationis', *Römische Quartalschaft,* 72 (1977), 133–83.

105. H. Löwe, 'Bonifatius und die bayerisch-fränkische Spannung', *Jahrbuch für fränkische Landesforschung,* 15 (1955), 85–127.

106. For the Bavarian ducal house, see J. Jarnut, *Agilolfingerstudien* (Stuttgart, 1986); see also H.-D. Kahl, 'Die Baiern und ihre Nachbarn bis zum Tode des Herzogs Theodo (717/18)', in H. Wolfram and A. Schwarcz (eds), *Die Bayern und ihre Nachbarn,* I (Vienna, 1985), pp. 160–225, and J. Jahn, *Ducatus Baiuvariorum. Das bairische Herzogtum der Agilolfinger* (Stuttgart, 1991).

107. Boniface, *ep.* 80; on *Virgil, see* Schieffer, *Winfrid-Bonifatius,* pp. 246–9. See also H. Löwe, 'Salzburg als Zentrum literarischen Schaffens im 8. Jahrhundert', *Mitteilungen der Gesellschaft für Salzburger Landeskunde,* 115 (1975), 99–143.

108. Boniface, *epp.* 40, 41, 89.

109. Schieffer, *Winfrid-Bonifatius,* pp. 199–256.

110. J. Jarnut, 'Wer hat Pippin 751 zum König gesalbt?', *Frühmittlealterliche Studien,* 16 (1982), 45–57; for the origins of the ceremony, see R. Schneider, *Königswahl und Königserhebung im Frühmittelalter* (Stuttgart, 1972); see also A. Angenendt, 'Rex et Sacerdos. Zur Genese der Königsalbung', in N. Kamp and J. Wollasch (eds), *Tradition als historische Kraft* (Berlin and New York, 1982), pp. 100–18.

111. Arbeo of Freising, *Vita vel Passio Sancti Haimhramni Martyris,* ed. B. Bischoff (Munich, 1953).

112. *Conversio Bagoariorum et Carantanorum,* ed. H. Wolfram (Vienna, 1979), pp. 34–8, and 60–70 for comment.

113. See for Emmeram, Rupert and Corbinian, H. Wolfram, *Die Geburt Mitteleuropas* (Berlin, 1987), pp. 109–26.

15 FRANCIA REVIVED, 714–68

1. *Chronicle of Fredegar,* continuations, 34. (I continue to use the older form of reference as no proper edition of the *Historia vel Gesta Francorum* – the late-eighth-century work that re-uses and extends the seventh-century original Fredegar – yet exists.)

2. *Annales Mosellani,* s.a. 708, ed. G. Pertz, MGH *SS,* vol. XVI, p. 494; *Annales Sancti Amandi,* s.a. 708, MGH *SS,* vol. I, p. 6, etc. For some discussion of these annals, see R. Collins, 'The *Vaccaei,* the *Vaceti* and the Rise of *Vasconia*', in idem, *Law, Culture and Regionalism in Early Medieval Spain* (Aldershot, 1992), item XI, esp. pp. 216–19.

3. R. A. Gerberding, *The Rise of the Carolingians and the 'Liber Historiae Francorum'* (Oxford, 1987), pp. 150–9.
4. *Liber Historiae Francorum*, 50; Fredegar continuations, 7.
5. Fredegar, continuations, 8–9.
6. *Liber Historiae Francorum*, 51; Fredegar continuations, 8.
7. *Liber Historiae Francorum*, 52; Fredegar continuations, 9.
8. *Liber Historiae Francorum*, 53; Fredegar continuations, 10. For the period 714–18 in the *LHF*, *see* Gerberding, *Rise of the Carolingians*, pp. 116–45.
9. Fredegar continuations, 10; see, for the history of Aquitaine at this time, M. Rouche, *L'Aquitaine des Wisigoths aux Arabes, 418–751: Naissance d'une région* (Paris, 1979), pp. 98–111. For the use of Basque mercenaries by the dukes of Aquitaine, see R. Collins, *The Basques* (2nd edn) (Oxford, 1990), pp. 106–12.
10. Fredegar continuations, 11–13 cover the years 719–33.
11. Fredegar, continuations, 5.
12. *Annales Mettenses Priores*, s.a. 687; *Gesta Abbatum Fontanellensis*, IV. 1. For Audramnus as count of the palace, see Pardessus, vol. II no. 431.
13. Gerberding, *Rise of the Carolingians*, pp. 109–15.
14. Pardessus, vol. II, nos 440, 477–8.
15. Gerberding, *Rise of the Carolingians*, p. 104; see also in general, P. Fouracre, *Placita* and the Settlement of Disputes in Later Merovingian Francia', in W. Davies and P. Fouracre (eds), *The Settlement of Disputes in Early Medieval Europe* (Cambridge, 1986), pp. 23–43.
16. *Gesta Abbatum Fontanellensis*, IV. 1.
17. Gerberding, *Rise of the Carolingians*, pp. 138–9.
18. I am convinced by the analysis offered in ibid., pp. 116–24.
19. Ibid., p. 130; see also M. Werner, *Der Lütticher Raum im frühkarolingischer Zeit* (Göttingen, 1980), pp. 126–39.
20. *Chronicle of Fredegar*, IV. 74.
21. Fredegar continuations, 11 and 19; *Annales Sancti Amandi* s.a. 718 and 720.
22. Fredegar continuations, 12.
23. For the background to the Battle of Poitiers, and for some arguments on its dating, see R. Collins, *The Arab Conquest of Spain, 710–797* (Oxford, 1989), pp. 24–5, 89–92.
24. Fredegar continuations, 15; Rouche, *L'Aquitaine*, pp. 115–16.
25. Fredegar continuations, 14 and 18.
26. Fredegar continuations, 20. For Maurontus and his supporters, see P. J. Geary, *Aristocracy in Provence: The Rhône Basin at the Dawn of the Carolingian Age* (Stuttgart, 1985), pp. 123–7, 138–43.
27. R. Collins, 'Deception and Misrepresentation in Early Eighth Century Frankish Historiography: Two Case Studies', in J. Jarnut, U. Nonn and M. Richter (eds), *Karl Martell in seiner Zeit* (Sigmaringen, Germany, 1994), pp. 227–47.
28. Fredegar continuations, 20.
29. Fredegar continuations, 21.

30. J. M. Wallace-Hadrill, *The Frankish Church* (Oxford, 1983), pp. 123–42, 270–1 is judicious on this; see also R. Collins, 'Pippin I and the Kingdom of Aquitaine', in P. Godman and R. Collins (eds), *Charlemagne's Heir: New Perspectives on the Reign of Louis the Pious* (Oxford, 1990), esp. pp. 370–2.

31. Fredegar continuations, 35 (and implied in 32); *Annales Regni Francorum* (ARF), s.a. 741, 747, 748, 753. Revised Version of ARF (ARF Rev), s.a. 747.

32. Fredegar continuations, 25 and ARF, s.a. 742.

33. Fredegar continuations, 28; on the terminology, see Collins, '*Vaccaei*, the *Vaceti*, and the Rise of *Vasconia*', pp. 211–23.

34. Fredegar continuations, 25, 27, 29; ARF, s.a. 742 (only). See J. Jarnut, 'Alemannien zur zeit der Doppelherrschaft der Hausmeier Karlmann und Pippin', in R. Schieffer (ed.), *Beiträge zur Geschichte des Regnum Francorum* (Sigmaringen, Germany, 1990), pp. 57–66.

35. Fredegar continuations, 25, 26, 32; ARF, s.a. 743, 748.

36. ARF, 745 and 746; ARF Rev, 746, and Fredegar continuations, 30 (the implied 747 of the Fredegar continuator is to be preferred to the 746 of ARF); on the ideological background, see C. Stancliffe, 'Kings Who Opted Out', in P. Wormald, D. Bullough and R. Collins (eds), *Ideal and Reality in Frankish and Anglo-Saxon Society* (Oxford, 1983), pp. 154–76; and K. H. Kruger, 'Königskonversionen im 8. Jahrhundert', *Frühmittelalterliche Studien*, 7 (1973), 169–222. For the political context, see M. J. Enright, *Iona, Tara and Soissons* (Berlin and New York, 1985), pp. 110–14 with references.

37. Boniface, *ep.* 79 as evidence for the brief tenure of authority on the part of Drogo. See M. Becher, 'Drogo und die Königserhebung Pippins', *Frühmittelalterliche Studien*, 23 (1989), 131–53.

38. P. Fouracre, 'Observations on the Outgrowth of Pippinid Influence in the "Regnum Francorum" after the Battle of Tertry (687–715)', *Medieval Prosopography*, 5 (1984), 1–31. See also O. P. Clavadetscher, 'Zur Verfassungsgeschichte des merowingischen Rätien', *Frühmittelalterliche Studien*, 8 (1974), 60–70.

39. Doubts on Aquitaine: see Collins, 'The *Vaccaei*, the *Vaceti* and the Rise of *Vasconia*', and 'Pippin I and the Kingdom of Aquitaine', esp. pp. 387–9; for Burgundy, see I. Wood, 'Ethnicity and the Ethnogenesis of the Burgundians', in H. Wolfram and W. Pohl (eds), *Typen der Ethnogenese unter besonderer Berücksichtigung der Bayern*, Vol. I (Vienna, 1990), pp. 53–69.

40. Geary, *Aristocracy in Provence*, pp. 101–43.

41. Fredegar, IV. 48, 68, 72, 74–5, 77, 87.

42. J. Jarnut, *Agilolfingerstudien* (Stuttgart, 1986), pp. 44–90.

43. Rouche, *L'Aquitaine*, pp. 98–109 prefers to see Aquitaine as an independent kingdom under Eudo.

44. Gregory of Tours, *Libri Historiarum*, IV. 49–50; Fredegar, *Chronica* IV. 38.

45. B. L. Bachrach, 'Was the Marchfield Part of the Frankish Constitution?', in his *Armies and Politics in the Early Medieval West* (Aldershot, 1993), item IX.

46. Childeric III receives no mention in narrative sources, but appears in a small number of charters. The problems of the dating of his reign and its end are discussed by B. Krusch in MGH *SRM*, vol. VII, pp. 508–10.
47. ARF, s.a. 749; see R. McKitterick, *History and Memory in the Carolingian World* (Cambridge, 2004), pp. 101–119, and 141–142.
48. Fredegar continuations, 33.
49. J. Semmler, *Der Dynastiewechsel von 751 und die fränkische Königssalbung* (Düsseldorf, 2003), esp. pp. 1–57.
50. ARF, s.a. 754; the contemporary continuator of Fredegar makes no reference to this event at all.
51. For the argument involving an Irish origin, see Enright, *Iona, Tara, Soissons*, but the views of A. Angenendt, 'Rex et Sacerdos. Zur Genese der Königsalbung', in N. Kamp and E. Wollasch (eds), *Tradition als historische Kraft* (Berlin, 1982), pp. 100–18 are to be preferred.
52. J. T. Hallenbeck, *Pavia and Rome: The Lombard Monarchy and the Papacy in the Eighth Century* (Philadelphia, Pa., 1982), pp. 69–78.
53. Ibid., pp. 78–80; Fredegar continuations, 36 and 37. See D. H. Miller, 'The Motivation of Pepin's Italian Policy, 754–768', *Studies in Medieval Culture*, 4 (1973), 44–54.
54. *Liber Pontificalis*, Vol. I, pp. 444–50.
55. Fredegar continuations, 38 and 39; Hallenbeck, *Pavia and Rome*, pp. 81–5.
56. ARF, s.a. 758; not mentioned by the continuator of Fredegar.
57. ARF, s.a. 760–8; Fredegar continuations, 41–52; Rouche, *L'Aquitaine*, pp. 122–32.

16 CHARLEMAGNE, 768–814

1. Fredegar continuations, 53 is by far the most reliable account. ARF gives no details and ARF Rev claims, tendentiously, that all of Aquitaine was allotted to Charles. For the division in Neustria, see Map I (d) on p. 438 of P. Perrin and L.-C. Feffer (eds), *La Neustria: les pays au nord de la Loire de Dagobert à Charles le Chauve* (Rouen, 1985).
2. M. Lintzel, 'Karl der Grosse und Karlaman', *Historische Zeitschrift*, 140 (1929), 1–22; P. D. King, *Charlemagne* (London, 1986), pp. 6–8.
3. ARF, s.a. 771.
4. It has been suggested that the intention to convert was inherent in Charlemagne's Saxon wars from the start. This is based on the very generalised presentation in Eigil, *Vita Sancti Sturmi*, 22 (ed. G. Pertz, MGH *SS*, vol. II, pp. 375–6. The probable date of composition of this work (*c.* 814–20) gives it no independent value. It is better to see Charles' first campaigns as aiming at containment, like those of Charles Martel and Pippin III, and to see a change to a planned conquest and integration (via conversion) occurring in 775.
5. ARF, s.a. 772.
6. ARF, s.a. 774 and 775.

7. ARF, Rev makes significant additions for 775, including a near-disaster for the Franks.

8. ARF, s.a. 776 and 777.

9. T. Capelle, *Die Sachsen der frühen Mittelalters* (Stuttgart, 1998); W. Winkelmann, 'Fine westfalische Siedlung des 8. Jahrhundert bei Warendorft, Kr. Warendorf' and 'Die Ausgrabung in der frühmittelalterlichen Siedlung bei Warendorf', in his *Beiträge* zur *Frühgeschichte Westfalens* (Münster, 1984), pp. 30–42 and 43–54, and plates 21–39.

10. *Liber Pontificalis*: Vita Hadriani, 9, Vol. I, p. 488.

11. ARF and ARF Rev, s.a. 773 and 774.

12. H. Wolfram, *Intitulatio*, I (Vienna, 1967), p. 222 discusses the title only in relation to Charles' son Pippin, and (pp. 185–94) the use of it prior to 774.

13. See O. Bertolini, 'Carlomagno e Benevento', in W. Braunfels (ed.), *Karl der Grosse. Lebenswerk und Nachleben*, Vol. I (Dusseldorf, 1967), pp. 609–71.

14. ARF, s.a. 775–6.

15. ARF and ARF Rev, s.a. 777.

16. The deliberate omissions and distortions of ARF 778 are exposed by comparison with ARF Rev, 778 and Einhard, *Vita Karoli*, 9; for the actual context of this campaign – as opposed to Frankish perceptions of it, see Collins, *Arab Conquest of Spain*, pp. 168–82.

17. ARF and ARF Rev, s.a. 778–80.

18. For the royal investitures of 781, see P. Classen, 'Karl der Grosse und die Thronfolge im Frankenreich', in *Festschrift für Hermann Heimpel* (2 vols) (Göttingen, 1972), Vol. II, pp. 109–34.

19. ARF and ARF Rev, s.a. 782.

20. ARF, s.a. 785.

21. Bertolini, 'Carlomagno e Benevento'; ARF Rev, s.a. 786 and 787.

22. *Chronicle of Theophanes*, a.m. 6241.

23. *Chronicle of Theophanes*, a.m. 6277–80.

24. ARF, s.a. 787 and 788. Here the ARF is an almost exactly contemporary source. Cf. ARF Rev, s.a. 787 and 788. The best treatment of the misrepresentation of this affair in the Frankish sources is that of M. Becher, *Eid und Herrschaft* (Sigmaringen, Germany, 1993), pp. 25–77.

25. *Council of Frankfurt*, canon 3, ed. A. Boretius, MGH *Capit.*, vol. I, no. 28.

26. ARF, s.a. 788.

27. ARF, s.a. 791, 795–7, 799; ARF Rev, s.a. 790–3, 795–7, 799; see W. Pohl, *Die Awarenkriege Karts des Grossen*, 788–803 (Vienna, 1988); also H. Wolfram, *Die Geburt Mitteleuropas* (Berlin, 1987), pp. 251–67.

28. W. Kaemmerer, 'Die Aachener Pfalz Karls des Grossen', in Braunfels (ed.), *Karl der Grosse*, Vol. I, pp. 322–48; also R. McKitterick, *Charlemagne: The Formation of a European Identity* (Cambridge, 2008), pp. 157–71 on not over-emphasising the role of Aachen.

29. A. Freeman, 'Theodulf of Orléans and the *Libri Carolini*', *Speculum*, 32 (1957), 663–705; idem, 'Further Studies in the *Libri Carolini*',

ibid., 40 (1965), 203–89; idem, 'Further Studies in the *Libri Carolini III*', ibid., 46 (1971), 597–612; and P. Meyvaert, 'The Authorship of the "Libri Carolini": Observations Prompted by a Recent Book', *Revue Bénédictine*, 89 (1979), 29–57.

30. ARF Rev, s.a. 788; cf. *Chronicle of Theophanes*, a.m. 6281.
31. *Chronicle of Theophanes*, a.m. 6282–4.
32. *Chronicle of Theophanes*, a.m. 6289.
33. *Annales Laureshamenses*, s.a. 801, ed. Pertz, MGH *SS*, vol. I, p. 38.
34. P. Llewellyn, *Rome in the Dark Ages* (London, 1971), pp. 221–51 on the city and the papacy in the reign of Charles; also T. F. X. Noble, *The Republic of St. Peter: The Birth of the Papal State, 680–825* (Philadelphia, Pa., 1984), pp. 122–255.
35. ARF and ARF Rev, s.a. 796.
36. *Liber Pontificalis*: Leo III, 11–16, vol. II, pp. 4–6; ARF and ARF Rev, s.a. 799 (with some differences in their accounts).
37. *Liber Pontificalis*: Leo III, 14–15, vol. II, p. 5; Alcuin, *epp.* 177–8.
38. That the accusations against Leo had reached the ears of some of the clergy in Francia by at least 798 is clear from Alcuin, *epp.*, 159 and 184. For an introduction to Alcuin, see D. Bullough, 'Charlemagne's "men of God": Alcuin, Hildebald, Arn', in J. Story (ed.), *Charlemagne: Empire and Society* (Manchester, 2005), pp. 136–150.
39. Alcuin, *ep.* 179, drawing on doctrines developed in a set of forged documents supposedly dating to the time of Constantine, but in fact produced in the course of the Laurentian schism in the papacy, around the year 500.
40. ARF and ARF Rev, s.a. 800 and 801; *Annales Laureshamenses*, s.a. 800. For the circumstances, see R. Collins, 'Charlemagne's Imperial Coronation and the Annals of Lorsch', in Story (ed.), *Charlemagne*, pp. 52–70.
41. For imperial ideas in the circle of Charlemagne's advisers in the late 790s, see Folz, *Coronation of Charlemagne*, pp. 118–31; and Alcuin, *epp.*, 174, 177, and 178, all from 799.
42. R. Collins, *Charlemagne* (London, 1998), pp. 141–59.
43. For the ceremonial, see ARF, s.a. 800–1. For an analysis, see R. Folz, *The Coronation of Charlemagne* (English trans.) (London, 1974), pp. 144–8 and 231–3.
44. Einhard, *Vita Karoli*, 28. For arguments in favour of an earlier date, see McKitterick, *Charlemagne*, pp. 7–20. See also D. Ganz, 'Einhard's Charlemagne: The Characterisation of Greatness', in Story (ed.), *Charlemagne*, pp. 38–51.
45. *Annales Laureshamenses*, s.a. 800 indicate that the question was discussed at the council held in Rome early in December 800, but it is reasonable to suspect an earlier phase of discussion during Leo III's stay in Paderborn in the winter of 799. Folz, *Coronation*, pp. 139–43.
46. On the usage in Bede, see J. McClure, 'Bede's Old Testament Kings', in P. Wormald, D. Bullough and R. Collins (eds), *Ideal and Reality in Frankish and Anglo-Saxon Society* (Oxford, 1983), esp. pp. 96–8.
47. Folz, *Coronation*, pp. 118–31. For litanies and fasts prior to the Avar campaign of 791, see Charles' letter to his wife Fastrada: MGH

Epp., vol. IV, p. 528–9; for the changed view on the 778 campaign, see *Annales Mettenses Priores*, s.a. 778.

48. See J. Deer, 'Zum Patricius Romanorum Titel Karl des Grossen', *Archivum Historiae Pontificiae*, 3 (1965), 32–86; see also D. H. Miller, 'The Roman Revolution of the Eighth Century: A Study of the Ideological Background of the Papal Separation from Byzantium and Alliance with the Franks', *Medieval Studies*, 36 (1974), 79–133, but with reservations.

49. *Chronicle of Theophanes*, a.m. 6303–4; for a gentlemanly defence of Irene, see S. Runciman, 'The Empress Irene the Athenian', in D. Baker (ed.), *Medieval Women* (Oxford, 1978), pp. 101–18; on her reign, see W. Treadgold, *The Byzantine Revival 780–842* (Stanford, Calif., 1988), pp. 60–126.

50. P. Classen, 'Romanum gubernans Imperium', *Deutsches Archiv*, 9 (1951), 103–21; F. L. Ganshof, 'The Imperial Coronation of Charlemagne: Theories and Facts', in his *The Carolingians and the Frankish Monarchy* (trans. J. Sondheimer) (London, 1971), pp. 41–54.

51. *Vita Karoli*, 29.

52. Procopius, *History of the Wars*, VI. vi. 17. For the power of the emperor, see W. W. Buckland, *A Text Book of Roman Law from Augustus to Justinian* (3rd edn, corrected reprint) (Cambridge, 1975), pp. 7–20.

53. This is the 'K' or Karolina redaction in Eckhardt's edition (see Bibliography).

54. For a brief statement of the conservative Germanic tradition on the origin and nature of the supposedly customary codes, see W. Ullmann, *Law and Politics in the Middle Ages* (London, 1975), pp. 193–8; on the codes of 802/3, see R. Büchner, *Die Rechtsquellen*, a 'Beiheft' of Wattenbach-Levison, *Deutschlands Geschichtsquellen im Mittlelater* (Weimar, 1953), pp. 39–44.

55. *Leges Saxonum*, cc. xxi, xxiii, xxiv.

56. This argument is developed in R. Collins, 'The *Vaccaei*, the *Vaceti* and the Rise of *Vasconia*', in idem, *Law, Culture and Regionalism in Early Medieval Spain* (Aldershot, 1992), item XI.

57. The contrary view of an overriding and long-lasting Aquitanian identity is presented in M. Rouche, *L'Aquitaine des Wisigoths aux Arabes, 418–781* (Paris, 1979).

58. R. Collins, 'Pippin I and the Kingdom of Aquitaine', in P. Godman and R. Collins (eds), *Charlemagne's Heir: New Perspectives on the Reign of Louis the Pious* (Oxford, 1990), esp. pp. 386–9.

59. I. N. Wood, 'Ethnicity and the Ethnogenesis of the Burgundians', in H. Wolfram and W. Pohl (eds), *Typen der Ethnogenese*, Vol. I (Vienna, 1990), pp. 53–69.

60. See J. M. Wallace-Hadrill, 'The *Via Regia* of the Carolingian Age', reprinted in his *Early Medieval History* (Oxford, 1975), p. 195.

61. See Büchner, *Rechtsquellen*, p. 5.

62. As argued by R. Collins, *Early Medieval Spain: Unity in Diversity, 400–1000* (2nd edn) (London, 1995), pp. 24–30.

63. A. N. Sherwin White, *The Roman Citizenship* (2nd edn) (Oxford, 1973).

64. On Arab clientage, see P. Crone, *Slaves on Horses: The Evolution of the Islamic Polity* (Cambridge, 1980), pp. 37–57.

65. It could be speculated that such feelings influenced Frankish hostility to the restoration of icon veneration in Byzantium, as evidenced by *c.* 2 of the Council of Frankfurt of 794.

17 THE CAROLINGIAN REGIME

1. J. Smith, *Europe after Rome: A New Cultural History 500–1000* (Oxford, 2005), pp. 3–4.

2. S. MacLean, *Kingship and Politics in the Late Ninth Century* (Cambridge, 2003), pp. 1–22; and H. J. Hummer, *Politics and Power in Early Medieval Europe* (Cambridge, 2005), for an excellent regional study.

3. For the imperial administration, see John Lydus, *De Magistratibus*, ed. I Bekker, CSHB (Bonn, 1837), pp. 119–272 (Greek text/Latin trans.). For an overview of the government and politics of the Byzantine empire in the time of Charlemagne, see W. Treadgold, *A History of the Byzantine State and Society* (Stanford, Calif., 1997), pp. 417–29.

4. See, for example, I. Wood, 'Disputes in Late Fifth- and Sixth-century Gaul: Some Problems', in W. Davies and P. Fouracre (eds), *The Settlement of Disputes in Early Medieval Europe* (Cambridge, 1986), esp. pp. 12–14 on the survival of *Gesta Municipalia*; for Aquitanian towns, see Rouche, *L'Aquitaine*, pp. 261–300.

5. The best introduction is the two contributions of F. L. Ganshof to Braunfels (ed.), *Karl der Grosse*, on institutions under Charlemagne and on the administration of justice; conveniently, these are both translated by B. Lyon and M. Lyon in F. L. Ganshof, *Frankish Institutions under Charlemagne* (New York, 1968), pp. 3–55 and 71–97 (plus notes). See also M. Innes, 'Charlemagne's government', in J. Story (ed.), *Charlemagne: Empire and Society* (Manchester, 2005), pp. 71–89; and R. McKitterick, *Charlemagne* (Cambridge, 2008), pp. 214–291.

6. T. Reuter, 'Plunder and Tribute in the Carolingian Empire', *Transactions of the Royal Historical Society*, 5th series, 35 (1985), 75–94.

7. T. Reuter, 'The End of Carolingian Military Expansion', in Godman and Collins, *Charlemagne's Heir*, pp. 391–405.

8. F. L. Ganshof, 'Charlemagne et l'usage de l'écrit en matière administrative', *Le Moyen Age*, 57 (1951), 1–25; English trans. in idem, *Carolingians and Frankish Monarchy*, pp. 125–42. R. McKitterick, *The Carolingians and the Written Word* (Cambridge, 1989), pp. 25–7 wishes to be more optimistic. See also J. L. Nelson, 'Literacy in Carolingian Government', in R. McKitterick (ed.), *The Uses of Literacy in Early Medieval Europe* (Cambridge, 1990), pp. 258–96.

9. Ganshof, 'Charlemagne et l'usage de l'écrit'; McKitterick, *Carolingians and the Written Word*, pp. 26, 28–9, and idem, *Charlemagne: The Making of a European Identity* (Cambridge, 2008), pp. 233–63.

10. F. L. Ganshof, 'Charlemagne's Programme of Imperial Government' (English trans. of a conference paper published in Faenza in 1963), in his *Carolingians and the Frankish Monarchy*, pp. 55–85.

11. *Vita Karoli*, 25.

12. G. Brown, 'The Carolingian Renaissance', in R. McKitterick (ed.), *Carolingian Culture: Emulation and Innovation* (Cambridge, 1994), pp. 1–51; McKitterick, *Charlemagne*, pp. 292–380.

13. Well discussed in L. Nees, *A Tainted Mantle: Hercules and the Classical Tradition at the Carolingian Court* (Philadelphia, Pa., 1991), pp. 3–17.

14. V. Law, 'The Study of Grammar', in McKitterick (ed.), *Carolingian Culture* , pp. 88–110.

15. See D. Bullough, '*Aula Renovata*: The Carolingian Court before the Aachen Palace', *Proceedings of the British Academy*, 71(1985), 267–301.

16. Einhard, *Vita Karoli*, 25.

17. W. Goffart, 'Paul the Deacon and Lombard History', in his *The Narrators of Barbarian History* (Princeton, NJ, 1988), pp. 329–431; also D. Bullough, 'Ethnic History and the Carolingians: An Alternative Reading of Paul the Deacon's *Historia*', in C. Holdsworth and T. P. Wiseman (eds), *The Inheritance of Historiography, 350–900* (Exeter, 1986), pp. 85–105. For the possible dedication of the *Historia*, *see* K. H. Kruger, 'Zur beneventanischen Konzeption der Langobardengeschichte des Paulus Diaconus', *Frühmittelalterliche Studien*, 15 (1981), 18–35; but for the view that the intended readership was primarily Frankish, see R. McKitterick, *History and Memory in the Carolingian World* (Cambridge, 2004), pp. 60–83.

18. J. M. Wallace-Hadrill, *The Frankish Church* (Oxford, 1983), pp. 217–25. For a suggestion on Theodulf's origins, see R. Collins, 'Poetry in Ninth-Century Spain', *Papers of the Liverpool Latin Seminar*, Vol. 4 (Liverpool, 1983), 181–95.

19. See nt 86 of Chapter 15 above.

20. For a general account of Alcuin recourse, there is still C. J. B. Gaskoin, *Alcuin: His Life and Work* (Cambridge, 1904), but for the years up to 796 see the magisterial D. A. Bullough, *Alcuin: Achievement and Reputation* (Leiden, 2004), and the same author's articles, usefully collected in his *Carolingian Renewal* (Manchester, 1991).

21. For Alcuin and Adoptionism, see the introduction to G. Blumenshine (ed.), *Liber Alcuin contra haeresem Felicis* (Vatican, 1980), pp. 9–41, and D. Bullough, 'Alcuin and the Kingdom of Heaven', in U.-R. Blumenthl (ed.), *Carolingian Essays* (Washington, DC, 1983), pp. 1–69.

22. For example, Alcuin, *epp.* 61, 64, 100, 101. See also J. M. Wallace-Hadrill, *Early Germanic Kingship in England and on the Continent* (Oxford, 1971), pp. 114–20.

23. R. Wright, *Late Latin and Early Romance in Spain and Carolingian France* (Liverpool, 1982), pp. 108–22. Even if the idea is accepted, it is hard to see how such a project was put into practice.

24. For the Mass Book, see H. Lietzmann (ed.), *Das Sacramentarium Gregorianum nach dem Aachener Urexemplar* (Münster, 1921). For the formal reception of the Dionyiso-Hadriana, see *Annales Laureshamenses*,

s.a. 802. It was, however, already the basis for most of the regulations of the *Admonitio Generalis* of 789. As a warning against overestimating the importance of Charles' 'Roman books', see R. Schieffer, *'Redeamus ad fontem*: Rom as Hort authentischer Überlieferung im frühen Mittelalter', in *Roma – Caput et Fons* (Opladen, 1989), pp. 45–70.

25. P. Godman, *Poets and Emperors* (Oxford, 1987), pp. 38–92; and idem (ed.), *Poetry of the Carolingian Renaissance* (London, 1985), pp. 9–33.

26. Wallace-Hadrill, *Frankish Church*, p. 195.

27. Ibid., pp. 195–204; to these, Fardulf should almost certainly be added. On him, see ARF Rev, s.a. 792.

28. On the nature and purposes of capitularies, see F. L. Ganshof, *Recherches sur les Capitulaires* (French trans. of Flemish original) (Paris, 1958). See also H. Mordek, 'Karolingische Kapitularien', in idem (ed.), *Uberlieferung und Geltung normativer Texte des frühen und hohen Mittelalters* (Sigmaringen, Germany, 1986), pp. 25–50; and McKitterick, *Charlemagne*, pp. 233–66.

29. K. F. Werner, 'Gouvener l'empire chrétien', in Godman and Collins, *Charlemagne's Heir*, esp. pp. 83–8.

30. A. H. M. Jones, *The Later Roman Empire* (3 vols) (Oxford, 1964), Vol. I, pp. 470–9.

31. MGH *Capit.*, vol. I, ed. A. Boretius, nos 22 and 23, items 1–16.

32. Ibid., no. 22, *praef.* The translation is that of P. D. King, *Charlemagne: Translated Sources* (Kendal, 1987), p. 209.

33. ARF Rev, s.a. 792; the by this time probably contemporary ARF deliberately omit to mention this episode. W. Goffart, 'Paul the Deacon's "Gesta Episcopum Mettensium" and the Early Design of Charlemagne's Succession', *Traditio*, 42 (1986), 59–93 argues that Pippin the Hunchback had been excluded from the succession to the component parts of the Frankish empire in 781.

34. MGH *Capit.*, vol. I, nos 24 and 25. See F. L. Ganshof, 'Charlemagne et le serment', in *Mélanges Louis Halphen* (Paris, 1951), pp. 259–70, and English trans. in his *Carolingians*, pp. 111–24; also M. Becher, *Eid und Herrschaft* (Sigmaringen, Germany, 1993), pp. 78–87.

35. *Annales Laureshamenses*, s.a. 792.

36. MGH *Capit.*, vol. I, no. 21.

37. Ibid., no. 33, items 1–9.

38. Ibid., no. 44, item 9.

39. Ibid., no. 33, item 3; trans. King, p. 234.

40. Ibid., no. 33, items 4 and 8; trans. King, pp. 234–5.

41. Ibid., no. 33, item 9; trans. King, p. 235.

42. Ibid., no. 29; trans. King, pp. 232–3.

43. Council of Frankfurt, canon 1: MGH *Capit.*, vol. I, no. 28; on the Frankish response to Adoptionism, see J. C. Cavadini, *The Last Christology of the West: Adoptionism in Spain and Gaul, 785–820* (Philadelphia, Pa., 1993), pp. 71–102.

44. For the *Annales Bertiniani* (AB), see J. L. Nelson, 'The *Annals of St Bertin*', in M. T. Gibson and J. L. Nelson (eds), *Charles the Bald: Court and Kingdom* (2nd edn) (Aldershot, 1990), pp. 23–40.

45. Ibid.; also J. M. Wallace-Hadrill, 'History in the Mind of Archbishop Hincmar', in R. H. C. Davis and J. M. Wallace-Hadrill (eds), *The Writing of History in the Middle Ages* (Oxford, 1981), pp. 43–70.

46. See the introduction to T. Reuter (trans.), *The Annals of Fulda* (Manchester, 1992), pp. 1–14.

47. H. Löwe, 'Studien zu den Annales Xantenses', *Deutsches Archiv*, 8 (1950), 59–99.

48. On this author, writing *c.* 908, see H. Löwe, 'Regino von Prüm und das historische Weltbild der Karolingerzeit', in W. Lammers (ed.), *Geschichtsdenken und Geschichtsbild im Mittelalter* (Darmstadt, 1961), pp. 91–134.

49. *Annales Xantenses*, s.a. 869; Louis the German is *sapientior et iustior caeteris*, whereas Charles in his dealings with the Vikings *semper [que] eis censum opponens et numquam in bello victor existens*.

50. F. L. Ganshof, 'Notes critiques sur Eginhard, biographe de Charlemagne', *Revue belge de philologie et d'histoire*, 3 (1924), 725–58; and idem, 'Eginhard, biographe de Charlemagne', *Bibliothèque d'humanisme et renaissance*, 13 (1951), 217–30, with good discussion of the previous literature; the latter is available in English in idem, *The Carolingians and the Frankish Monarchy*, trans. J. Sondheimer (London, 1971), pp. 1–16. M. S. Kempshall, 'Some Ciceronian Models for Einhard's Life of Charlemagne', *Viator*, 26 (1995), 11–37 uncovers his other literary debts. See also McKitterick, *Charlemagne*, pp. 7–20.

51. On the two *Lives*, see E. Tremp, 'Thegan und Astronomus, die beiden Geschichtsschreiber Ludwigs des Frommen', in P. Godman and R. Collins (eds), *Charlemagne's Heir: New Perspectives on the Reign of Louis the Pious* (Oxford, 1990), pp. 691–700; and idem, *Die Überlieferung der Vita Hludowici imperatoris des Astronomus* (Hanover, 1991), as well as his edition of both works in MGH *SRG*, vol. 64 (1995); now also M. de Jong, *The Penitential State: Authority and Atonement in the Age of Louis the Pious* (Cambridge, 2009), pp. 72–89.

18 'THE DISSENSION OF KINGS', 814–911

1. F. L. Ganshof, 'La fin du règne de Charlemagne. Une décomposition', *Zeitschrift für Schweizerische Geschichte*, 28 (1948), 533–52; English trans. in idem, *The Carolingians and the Frankish Monarchy*, trans. J. Sondheimer (London, 1971), pp. 240–55, which is challenged by the optimism of P. D. King, *Charlemagne* (London, 1986), pp. 45–7.

2. P. Classen, 'Karl der Grosse und die Thronfolge im Frankenreich', *Festschrift für Hermann Heimpel* (Göttingen, 1972), Vol. 2, pp. 109–34, who sees the 781 coronations as the first step towards the *Divisio* of 806. However, the eldest son, Charles, received no royal title or realm at any stage prior to the *Divisio*.

3. MGH *Capit.*, vol. I, ed. A. Boretius, no. 45. L. Halphen, *Charlemagne et l'empire carolingien* (reprint) (Paris, 1968), pp. 124–6.

4. R. Folz, *The Coronation of Charlemagne* (English trans.) (London, 1974), pp. 167–71.

5. ARF, s.a. 810, 811, 813.

6. Thegan, *Vita Hludovici imperatoris*, 6.

7. R. Schieffer, 'Ludwig "der Fromme". Zur Entstehung eines karolingischen Herrscherbeinamens', *Frühmittelalterliche Studien*, 16 (1982), 58–73.

8. ARF, s.a. 816; T. F. X. Noble, *The Republic of St. Peter: The Birth of the Papal State, 680–825* (Philadelphia, Pa., 1984), pp. 202–3, 298–308.

9. MGH *Capit.*, vol. I, no. 136; see F. L. Ganshof, 'Oservations sur *l'Ordinatio Imperii* de 817', in *Festschrift für Guido Kisch* (Stuttgart, 1955), pp. 15–31 for an alternative view.

10. J. Fridh, 'Ludwig der Fromme, das Papsttum und die fränkische Kirche', in Godman and Collins, *Charlemagne's Heir*, pp. 231–73; Noble, *Republic of St. Peter*, pp. 256–324, who prefers to see it as 'an alliance'.

11. ARF, s.a. 823 and 824; see the discussion of this episode in Noble, *Republic of St. Peter*, pp. 308–12.

12. ARF, s.a. 827.

13. ARF, s.a. 817: a covered arcade leading from the palace chapel collapsed on the emperor and his suite on Maundy Thursday.

14. See, in general, H. Wolfram, 'Lateinische Herrschertitel im neunten und zehnten Jahrhundert', in idem (ed.), *Intitulatio*, II (Vienna, 1973), pp. 19–178 (MIöG, vol. XXIV).

15. E. Boshof, 'Einheitsidee und Teilungsprinzip in der Regierungszeit Ludwigs des Frommen', in Godman and Collins (eds), *Charlemagne's Heir*, pp. 161–89.

16. ARF, s.a. 818 and 819. Thegan, *Vita Hludovici*, 25 and 26.

17. ARF, s.a. 817.

18. For a view of Theodulf as being driven into conspiring with Bernard by the provisions of the *Ordinatio*, see T. F. X. Noble, 'The Revolt of King Bernard of Italy in 817: Its Causes and Consequences', *Studi Medievali*, 15 (1974), 315–26, but cf. the argument of P. Godman, 'Louis "the Pious" and his poets', *Frühmittelalterliche Studien*, 19 (1985), esp. pp. 245–8.

19. ARF, s.a. 817. Thegan, *Vita Hludovici*, 22–3.

20. J. Jarnut, 'Ludwig der Fromme, Lothar I und das Regnum Italiae', in Godman and Collins, *Charlemagne's Heir*, pp. 349–62.

21. Halphen, *Charlemagne et l'empire carolingien*, pp. 199–201.

22. Almost all the novel or positive elements that Ganshof detected in his 'Louis the Pious Reconsidered' relate to the period of the ascendancy of Benedict of Aniane. See also F. L. Ganshof, 'A propos de la politique de Louis le Pieux avant la crise de 830', *Revue belge d'archéologie et d'histoire de l'art*, 37 (1968), 37–48; and J. Semmler, '*Renovatio Regni Francorum*: Die Herrschaft Ludwigs des Frommen im Frankenreich 814–829/30', in Godman and Collins, *Charlemagne's Heir*, pp. 125–46.

23. ARF, s.a. 821; L. Weinrich, *Wala, Mönch, Graf und Rebel: Die Biographie eines Karolingers* (Lübeck, 1963), pp. 33–43; on Adalhard,

see B. Kasten, *Adalhard von Korbie. Die Biographie eines karolingischen Politikers und Klostervorstehers* (Dusseldorf, 1985).

24. ARF, s.a. 822 and 823.
25. See M. de Jong, 'Power and Humility in Carolingian Society: The Public Penance of Louis the Pious', *Early Medieval Europe*, 1 (1992), pp. 29–52.
26. Anonymous, *Vita Hludovici*, 35 for the comparison with Theodosius I. See also ARF, s.a. 822.
27. J. Jarnut, 'Ludwig der Fromme, Lothar I. und das Regnum Italiae', in Godman and Collins, *Charlemagne's Heir*, pp. 349–62.
28. T. Reuter, 'The End of Carolingian Military Expansion', in ibid., pp. 391–405.
29. T. F. X. Noble, 'Louis the Pious and the Frontiers of the Frankish Realm', in ibid., pp. 333–48.
30. ARF, s.a. 814–29.
31. For the developments in Spain and these interpretations, see R. Collins, *The Arab Conquest of Spain, 710–797* (Oxford, 1989), pp. 113–40, 168–216.
32. J. M. Salrach, *El proces de formació national de Catalunya (segles VIII–IX)* (2nd edn; 2 vols) (Barcelona, 1981), Vol. I, pp. 27–50.
33. ARF, s.a. 826 and 827; Anonymous, *Vita Hludovici*, 40–1. Salrach, *El proces*, Vol. I, pp. 73–90.
34. ARF, s.a. 828 and 829. For the suggestion that the fall of Hugh and Matfried was deliberately planned, see R. Collins, 'Pippin I and the Kingdom of Aquitaine', in Godman and Collins (eds), *Charlemagne's Heir*, esp. pp. 377–81.
35. Anonymous, *Vita Hludovici*, 43–5; Thegan, *Vita Hludovici*, 36; *Annales Bertiniani*, s.a. 830; for the best recent interpretation of these years, see M. de Jong, *The Penitential State: Authority and Atonement in the Age of Louis the Pious* (Cambridge, 2009), pp. 148–213.
36. Nithard, *Historiae*, I. 3.
37. *Annales Bertiniani*, s.a. 830; Anonymous, *Vita Hludovici*, 45.
38. Thegan, *Vita Hludovici*, 36; also Paschasius Radbertus, *Epitaphium Arsenii;* translated in A. Cabaniss, *Charlemagne's Cousins* (Syracuse, NY, 1967), pp. 83–204. See D. Ganz, 'The *Epitaphium Arsenii* and Opposition to Louis the Pious', in Godman and Collins (eds), *Charlemagne's Heir*, pp. 537–50.
39. *Annales Bertiniani*, s.a. 831–3; Anonymous, *Vita Hludovici*, 46–9; Collins, 'Pippin I and the Kingdom of Aquitaine', in Godman and Collins (eds), *Charlemagne's Heir*, esp. pp. 383–6; see now de Jong, *The Penitential State*, pp. 214–28.
40. Anonymous, *Vita Hludovici*, 49–52; *Annales Bertiniani*, s.a. 833–4.
41. Anonymous, *Vita Hludovici*, 52–3.
42. An optimistic view of this period is taken by J. Nelson, 'The Last Years of Louis the Pious', in Godman and Collins (eds), *Charlemagne's Heir*, pp. 147–60.
43. Collins, 'Pippin I and the Kingdom of Aquitaine', ibid., pp. 386–9. See also J. Martindale, 'Charles the Bald and the Government of the Kingdom of Aquitaine', in Gibson and Nelson, *Charles the Bald*,

pp. 115–38. See Chapter 18 below for some of the later adventures of Pippin II.

44. *Annales Bertiniani*, s.a. 839; Nithard, *Historiae*, I. 7. For the role of Louis the German, see E. J. Goldberg, *Struggle for Empire: Kingship and Conflict under Louis the German, 817–876* (Ithaca, NY and London, 2006), pp. 86–94.

45. *Annales Bertiniani*, s.a. 840; Anonymous, *Vita Hludovici*, 62–4. For a more enthusiastic view of the reign than that offered here, see T. Schieffer, 'Die Krise des karolingischen Imperiums', in *Aus Mittelalter und Neuzeit* (Bonn, 1957), pp. 1–15 (no notes); and by F. L. Ganshof, 'Louis the Pious Reconsidered', *History*, 42 (1957), 171–80; Ganshof himself became less enthusiastic about Louis personally in his subsequent publications.

46. E. Boshof, 'Einheitsidee und Teilungsprinzip in der Regierungzeit Ludwigs des Frommen', in Godman and Collins (eds), *Charlemagne's Heir*, pp. 161–89; idem, *Erzbischof Agobard von Lyon: Leben uncle Werk* (Cologne, 1969).

47. T. Reuter, 'The End of Carolingian Military Expansion', in P. Godman and R. Collins (ed.), *Charlemagne's Heir: New Perspectives on the Reigh of Louis the Pious* (Oxford, 1990), pp. 391–405.

48. E.J. Goldberg, *Struggle for Empire: Kingship and Conflict under Louis the German, 817–876* (Ithaca and London, 2006), pp. 86–116.

49. Nithard, *Historiae*, II. 1–4; *Annales Bertiniani*, s.a. 840–1.

50. Nithard, *Historiae*, II. 9–10.

51. Nithard, *Historiae*, III. 5.

52. F. L. Ganshof, 'Zur Entstehungsgeschichte und Bedeutung des Vertrages von Verdun (843)', *Deutsches Archiv*, 12 (1956), 313–30, English trans. The Genesis and Significance of the Treaty of Verdun', in idem, *The Carolingians and the Frankish Monarchy* (London, 1971), pp. 289–302.

53. J. L. Nelson, 'Public *Histories* and Private History in the Work of Nithard', *Speculum*, 60 (1985), 251–93.

54. For discussion of the dating, see Nelson, 'Public *Histories*', app. 2.

55. Martindale, 'Charles the Bald and the Government of the Kingdom of Aquitaine', in Gibson and Nelson, *Charles the Bald*, pp. 135–8 tabulates documentary references to the presence of the Carolingian kings in Aquitaine up to 854.

56. *Annales Bertiniani*, s.a. 853; *Annales Fuldenses*, s.a. 853; for this part of his reign, see J. L. Nelson, *Charles the Bald* (London, 1992), pp. 160–89. On Louis's western ambitions, see E. Goldberg, *Struggle for Empire: Kingship and Conflict under Louis the German, 817–876* (Ithaca, NY and London, 2006), pp. 233–62.

57. *Annales Bertiniani*, s.a. 854; see Chapter 18 below for Pippin's dealings with the Vikings.

58. *Annales Bertiniani*, s.a. 856 and 858; *Annales Fuldenses*, s.a. 858.

59. J. Devisse, *Hincmar, Archevêque de Reims 845–882* (3 vols) (Geneva, 1975) Vol. I, pp. 281–366; C. Brühl, 'Hinkmariana', *Deutsches Archiv*, 20 (1964) 55–77.

60. *Annales Fuldenses*, s.a. 870.

61. K. F. Werner, '*Misses-Marchio-Comes*. Entre l'administration centrale et l'administration locale de l'empire carolingien', in W. Paravicini and K. F. Werner (eds), *Histoire comparée de l'administration* (Frankfurt, 1980), pp. 193–239.

62. *Annales Bertiniani*, s.a. 858; see Nelson, *Charles the Bald*, pp. 183–7 and 194–7.

63. *Annales Bertiniani*, s.a. 844 (a papal anointing as king) and 850.

64. *Annales Bertiniani*, s.a. 875–6. For Louis the German's Italian interests in the 870s, see Goldberg, *Struggle for Empire*, pp. 304–34.

65. *Annales Bertiniani*, s.a. 876–7; *Annales Fuldenses*, s.a. 876–7 for an eastern Frankish account of these events.

66. John VIII, *epp.* 1, 8, 22, 23, 27, 32, 56, 63. On Charles the Fat, the best study is S. MacLean, *Kingship and Politics in the Late Ninth Century: Charles the Fat and the End of the Carolingian Empire* (Cambridge, 2003).

67. Halphen, *Charlemagne et l'empire carolingien*, pp. 379–83. See John VIII, *epp.* 193, 205, 220, 221, 224, 225, 251, 257 for appeals to sundry Carolingians, and eventual concentration on Charles the Fat.

68. *Annales Vedastini*, s.a. 882, 884, 893.

69. Halphen, *Charlemagne et l'empire carolingien*, pp. 327–42; see also Devisse, *Hincmar*, Vol. I, pp. 369–459.

70. *Annales Bertiniani*, s.a. 882; *Annales Vedastini*, s.a. 880 and 882, *Annales Fuldenses*, s.a. 880 and 882. On the historical writing of this period, see H. Löwe, 'Geschichtschreibung der ausgehenden Karolingerzeit', *Deutsches Archiv*, 23 (1967), 1–30.

71. Regino of Prüm, *Chronica*, s.a. 881; Halphen, *Charlemagne et l'empire carolingien*, pp. 383–9.

72. Notker Balbulus, *Gesta Karoli Magni*, 11 and 14. See Maclean, *Kingship and Politics*, 199–229 for a rather different interpretation.

73. The epic poem *Bella Parisiacae urbis*, written by the monk Abbo of Saint-Germain-des Prés before 897, provides the fullest account of the Siege (see Bibliography.) For the background, see Chapter 18 below.

74. *Annales Fuldenses*, s.a. 887; Halphen, *Charlemagne et l'empire carolingien*, pp. 398–400.

75. On these two, see J. Fleckenstein, *Die Hofkapelle der deutschen Könige* (Stuttgart, 1959), Vol. 1, pp. 185–200, and MacLean, *Kingship and Politics*, pp. 169–191.

76. Reuter, *Germany in the Early Middle Ages*, pp. 119–20.

77. *Annales Fuldenses*, s.a 887.

78. *Annales Fuldenses*, s.a. 888.

79. *Annales Vedastini*, s.a. 887. cf. Regino of Prüm, *Chronica*, s.a. 887 and 888; *Annales Fuldenses*, s.a. 887. On the causes of the fall of Charles the Fat, see H. Keller, 'Zum Sturz Karls III', *Deutsches Archiv*, 22 (1966), 333–84; and E. Hlawitschka, 'Die lotharische Blutslinie und der Sturz Karls III', reprinted in idem (ed.), *Königswahl und Thronfolge in fränkisch-karolingischer Zeit* (Darmstadt, 1975), pp. 495–547.

80. *Annales Fuldenses*, s.a. 887.

81. Regino of Prüm, *Chronica*, s.a. 888.

82. On Lothar's divorce, see P. R. McKeon, *Hincmar of Laon and Carolingian Politics* (Urbana, Ill., 1978), pp. 39–56.

83. C. Wickham, *Early Medieval Italy: Central Power and Local Society, 400–1000* (London, 1981), pp. 169–74.

84. *Annales Fuldenses*, s.a. 893, 895, 896; Regino of Prüm, *Chronica*, s.a. 896; see G. Arnaldi, 'Papa Formoso e gli imperatori della case di Spoleto', *Annali della Facolta di Lettere di Napoli*, 1 (1951), 84–104.

85. J. Duhr, 'Le concile de Ravenne en 898: la rehabilitation du pape Formose', *Recherches de science réligieuse*, 22 (1932), 541–79.

86. E. Hlawitschka, *Vom Frankenreich zur Formierung der europäischen Staatenund Völkergemeinschaft, 840–1046* (Darmstadt, 1986), pp. 76–96.

87. For Charles the Simple, see A. Eckel, *Charles le Simple* (Paris 1899), and J. Dunbabin, *France in the Making, 843–1180* (Oxford, 1985), pp. 30–6.

88. MacLean, *Kingship and Politics*, pp. 191–8.

89. Hlawitschka, *Vom Frankenreich*, pp. 264–6 for a bibliography of works relating to this subject.

90. E. Bourgeois, *Le Capitulaire de Kiersy-sur-Oise (877)* (Paris, 1885), esp. pp. 127–54, argued that this capitulary institutionalised hereditary office holding, but see Halphen, *Charlemagne et l'empire carolingien*, pp. 371–4, 411–21.

91. *Annales Bertiniani*, s.a. 879, 880, 881; for his death in 887, see *Annales Fuldenses*, s.a. 887.

92. J. Dhondt, *Etudes sur la naissance des principautés térritoriales en France (IXe – Xe siècles)* (Bruges, 1948); Dunbabin, *France in the Making*, pp. 44–100.

93. See P. Hill, *The Age of Athelstan* (Stroud, 2004).

19 'THE DESOLATION OF THE PAGANS'

1. *Anglo-Saxon Chronicle*, s.a. 793 ('E' or Laud version); Symeon of Durham ii. 5, ed. and trans. D. Rollason (Oxford, 2000), pp. 88–91.

2. For the alternative view of the Vikings, see J. M. Wallace-Hadrill, *The Vikings in Francia* (Reading, 1974), reprinted in his *Early Medieval History* (Oxford, 1975), pp. 217–36. See, in general, A. Forte, R. Oram and F. Pedersen, *Viking Empires* (Cambridge, 2005).

3. For recent historiography and controversies, see E. Christiansen, *The Norsemen in the Viking Age* (Oxford and Malden, Mass., 2002), pp. 301–24.

4. P. H. Sawyer, *Kings and Vikings: Scandinavia and Europe, 700–1100* (London, 1982), pp. 8–38.

5. For these, see in general R. W. V. Elliott, *Runes* (Manchester, 1959), and S. B. F. Jansson, *Runes in Sweden* (English trans.) (Värnamo, 1997).

6. L. Hedeager, 'Scandinavia', in P. Fouracre (ed.), *The New Cambridge Medieval History vol. 1 c.500–c.700* (Cambridge, 2005), pp. 496–523.

7. D. Ó Corráin, *Ireland before the Normans* (Dublin, 1972), pp. 80–1 is categoric on the role of overpopulation, but greater caution is indicated: Sawyer, *Kings and Vikings*, pp. 67–9.

8. S. Lebecq, *Marchands et navigateurs frisons du haut moyen âge* (2 vols) (Lille, 1983), Vol. I, pp. 165–224 for eighth-century shipping and navigation.

9. For some discussion of Viking motivation, see G. Jones, *A History of the Vikings* (Oxford, 1968), pp. 182–203.

10. Except in Ireland, where inter-kingdom warfare, including the destruction of churches, was almost unending: Ó Corráin, *Ireland before the Normans*, pp. 85–8.

11. *Anglo-Saxon Chronicle*, s.a. 787 (*recte* 789) – only in the 'A' or Parker version.

12. Alcuin, *Epistolae*, 20. trans. H. R. Loyn and J. Percival, *The Reign of Charlemagne* (London, 1975) p. 110.

13. See J. Hines, *The Scandinavian Character of Anglian England in the pre-Viking Period* (Oxford, 1984); and idem, 'The Scandinavian Character of Anglian England: An Update', in M. Carver (ed.), *The Age of Sutton Hoo* (Woodbridge, 1992), pp. 315–29.

14. Sawyer, *Kings and Vikings*, pp. 65–8.

15. R. Bruce-Mitford, 'The Sutton Hoo Ship-Burial: Comments on General Interpretation' (1949), reprinted in his *Aspects of Anglo-Saxon Archaeology* (London, 1974), discusses the Swedish connections on pp. 47–60. For still pertinent doubts as to the royal status of the burial, see J. M. Wallace-Hadrill, 'The Graves of Kings: An Historical Note on some Archaeological Evidence', reprinted in his *Early Medieval History* (Oxford, 1975), pp. 39–59; and see J. Campbell, 'The Impact of the Sutton Hoo Discovery on the Study of Anglo-Saxon History', in C. B. Kendall and P. S. Wells (eds), *Voyage to the Other World: the Legacy of Sutton Hoo* (Minneapolis, Minn., 1992), pp. 79–101.

16. For Dorestad, see W. A. Van Es and W. J. H. Verwers, *Excavations at Dorestad*, Vol. I (Amersfoort, 1980); also S. Lebecq, *Marchands et navigateurs frisons du haut moyen âge* (2 vols, Lille, 1983), Vol. I, pp. 139–63.

17. R. Hodges and D. Whitehouse, *Mohammed, Charlemagne and the Origins of Europe* (London, 1983), pp. 93–101; R. Hodges, *The Anglo-Saxon Achievement* (London, 1989), pp. 69–114.

18. D. M. Wilson, *Civil and Military Engineering in Viking Age Scandinavia* (Basildon, 1978), pp. 3–6.

19. ARF, s.a. 808.

20. Ibid.

21. ARF and *Annales Bertiniani* under these years.

22. Attempts have been made to locate some of these men in their Scandinavian contexts, but as this largely depends on the use of later saga or legendary-historical materials, they have rarely convinced: see A. P. Smyth, *Scandinavian Kings in the British Isles, 850–880* (Oxford, 1977), pp. 17–100.

23. Jones, *History of the Vikings*, pp. 86–9, and nt 1 on p. 89.

24. Sawyer, *Kings and Vikings*, pp. 46–56.

25. For the eastward expansion of the Vikings, see T. S. Noonan, 'Scandinavians in European Russia', in P. Sawyer (ed.), *The Oxford Illustrated History of the Vikings* (Oxford, 1997), pp. 134–55.

26. Sawyer, *Kings and Vikings,* pp. 39–42 for slaves and freedmen.
27. Good examples to be found in *Orkneyinga Saga:* 105–6, trans. H. Pálsson and P. Edwards (Harmondsworth, 1981), pp. 214–15.
28. For example, *Annals of Ulster,* ed. S. MacAirt and G. MacNiocaill (Dublin, 1983), s.a. 780, 783, 784, 788, 789, 790, and so on.
29. Ibid., s.a. 802, 806 (68 killed), 807; see also *Argyll: An Inventory of the Monuments,* Vol. 4, *Iona* (Edinburgh, 1982), pp. 47–8.
30. R. Ernst, *Die Nordwestslaven und das frankische Reich* (Berlin, 1976), pp. 110–87.
31. ARF, s.a. 802, 804.
32. Ibid., s.a. 809, 810.
33. Ermoldus Nigellus, *In Honorem Hludovici Augusti,* II. 2167–513; on the significance of the emperor as godfather, see A. Angenendt, *Kaiserherrschaft und Königstaufe. Kaiser, Könige und Papste als geistliche Patröne in der abendlandischen Missionsgeschichte* (Berlin, 1984).
34. *Annales Bertiniani,* s.a. 834, 835, 836.
35. Sawyer, *Kings and Vikings,* pp. 82–3; ASB, s.a. 837.
36. *Annales Bertiniani,* s.a. 841, 842.
37. Ibid., s.a. 844–8; for the Spanish raid, see W. E. D. Allen, *The Poet and the Spae-Wife* (Dublin, 1960), pp. 1–13; and E. Lévi-Provençal, *Histoire de l'Espagne musulmane* (Leiden, 1950), Vol. I, pp. 218–25.
38. *Annales Bertiniani,* s.a. 845.
39. Ibid., s.a. 847, 848.
40. Ibid., s.a. 852–8.
41. For Viking use of islands, see *Anglo-Saxon Chronicle,* s.a. 832, 855 (Sheppey), s.a. 853, 865 (Thanet), AB s.a. 847, 850, 859 (Batavia) cf. s.a. 859 Vikings in the Rhône: 'in insula quae Camarias dicitur sedes ponunt'.
42. *Annales Bertiniani,* s.a. 858.
43. On the slave trade in this period, see C. Verlinden, *L'ésclavage dans l'Europe médiévale,* Vol. I (Brugge, 1955), pp. 181–247.
44. *Annals of Ulster,* s.a. 845; for other examples of prominent captives, see s.a. 831, 832, 840 and so on.
45. Ó Corráin, *Ireland before the Normans,* pp. 89–93.
46. For some of the consequences of all this, see D. A. Binchy, 'The Passing of the Old Order', in B. Ó Cuív (ed.), *The Impact of the Scandinavian Invasions on the Celtic-speaking Peoples c. 800–1100 A.D.* (Dublin, 1975), pp. 119–32.
47. This is largely a question of what weight to put on negative evidence. It has been suggested that Bordeaux was abandoned by the late ninth century, but is this a fair deduction from what is no more than an absence of evidence to show that it did still function? Archaeology cannot always help: there are still no certain traces of pre-Norman Dublin, but plenty of documentary references to its existence.
48. See A. P. Smyth, *Scandinavian York and Dublin,* Vol. I (Dublin, 1975).
49. MGH *Capit.,* vol. II, no. 280, p. 354.
50. *Annales Vedastini,* s.a. 879.
51. AB, s.a. 880, 881, 882; *Annales Vedastini,* s.a. 879–82.

52. For other inconsequential victories over Vikings, see *Annales Vedastini*, s.a. 882, 888, 891.

53. *Annales Vedastini*, s.a. 893–8. A. Eckel, *Charles le Simple* (Paris, 1899), pp. 1–29.

54. *Annales Vedastini*, s.a. 897, 898.

55. R. H. Bautier, 'L'historiographie en France aux X et XI siècles', in *Settimane di studi sull' Alto Medioevo*, 17 (Spoleto, 1970), 793–850.

56. On the agreement of 911, see A. Eckel, *Charles le Simple* (Paris, 1899), pp. 64–90. On Richer and his work, see J. Glenn, *Politics and History in the Tenth Century: The World and Work of Richer of Reims* (Cambridge, 2004).

57. Richer, *Historia*, I. 28–33; Flodoard, *Annales,* s.a. 921.

58. D. Bates, *Normandy before 1066* (London, 1982), pp. 2–43 for the tenth century. Rollo and his successors are attributed with a variety of titles in the sources: normally that of count, occasionally that of *princeps* or prince, and sometimes that of duke.

59. Anonymous, *Vita Hludovici imperatoris*, 40; *Annales Bertiniani*, s.a. 852.

60. *Annales Vedastini*, s.a. 882. On this episode, and comparisons with Charlemagne, see S. MacLean, *Kingship and Politics in the Late Ninth Century* (Cambridge, 2003), p. 213–15.

61. ASC – 'A' or Parker version – s.a. 832, 839. The chronology of the ASC is normally three years out in its dating of the events of this period.

62. Ibid., s.a. 835; the chronicler calls them 'Danes', but all Vikings were Danes to the scribes of Alfred's time.

63. ASC (Parker version), s.a. 837, 845, 851 (*recte* 840, 848, 850).

64. Ibid., s.a. 833, 837, 838, 839, 840 (*recte* 836, 840, 841, 842, 843).

65. N. Brooks, *The Early History of the Church of Canterbury* (Leicester, 1984), pp. 30–1, 49, 150–2.

66. *Annales Bertiniani*, s.a. 865.

67. ASC, s.a. 867; *Historia Regum*, p. 106.

68. ASC, s.a. 868, 869, 870 (*recte* 867, 868, 869); for a controversial discussion of the killing of King (St) Edmund, see Smyth, *Scandinavian Kings*, pp. 201–13; for pertinent methodological criticisms, see R. Frank, 'Viking Atrocity and Skaldic Verse: The Rite of the Blood-Eagle', *English Historical Review*, 99 (1984), 332–43.

69. ASC, s.a. 871, 872 (*recte* 870, 871). For Alfred's wars in the early 870s, see A. P. Smyth, *King Alfred the Great* (Oxford, 1995), pp. 51–66.

70. ASC, s.a. 874.

71. ASC, s.a. 875, 876 (*recte* 874–6); see Smyth, *Scandinavian Kings*, pp. 255–66 (with reservations as to the use of late sources).

72. ASC, s.a. 877.

73. ASC, s.a. 877.

74. ASC, s.a. 878; D. Whitelock, *The Importance of the Battle of Edington A.D. 878* (Westbury, 1977); Smyth, *Alfred the Great*, pp. 66–98.

75. P. Stafford, *The East Midlands in the Early Middle Ages* (Leicester, 1985); and J. Graham-Campbell, R. Hall, J. Jesch and D. N. Parsons (eds),

Vikings and the Danelaw (Oxford, 2001) for discussion of Viking settlement in that region.

76. G. Fellows Jensen, *Scandinavian Settlement Names in Yorkshire* (Copenhagen, 1972), and idem, 'The Vikings in England: A Review', *Anglo-Saxon England*, 4 (1975), 181–206. See also F. M. Stenton, 'The Danes in England', *Proceedings of the British Academy*, 13 (1927), 203–46; and A. L. Binns, *The Viking Century in East Yorkshire* (Beverley, 1963), pp. 35–52.

77. ASC, MS 'D' (B. L. Cotton Tiberius B iv), s.a. 901 (*recte* 899).

78. For the Viking kingdom in the north, from 867 to 954, see Smyth, *Scandinavian York and Dublin*, Vols I and II (Dublin, 1975–9).

79. F. L. Attenborough, *The Laws of the Earliest English Kings* (Cambridge, 1922), pp. 98–101; for the frontier, see R. H. C. Davis, 'Alfred and Guthrum's Frontier', *English Historical Review*, 97 (1982), 803–10.

80. Usefully described in S. Keynes and M. Lapidge, *Alfred the Great* (Harmondsworth, 1983), pp. 23–41.

81. ASC, s.a. 879, 880. For the view of the army in the Thames as recently arrived see Asser, *Vita Alfredi*, 58.

82. *Annales Vedastini*, s.a. 892.

83. Regino of Prüm, *Chronica*, s.a. 867, 874; see F. Amory, 'The Viking Hastings in Franco-Scandinavian Legend', in M. H. King and W. M. Stevens (eds), *Saints, Scholars and Heroes*, Vol. II (Collegeville, Minn., 1979), pp. 265–86.

84. ASC, s.a. 893–7 (*recte* 892–6); on this war, see Smyth, *Alfred the Great*, pp. 117–46.

85. P. Stafford, *Unification and Conquest* (London, 1989), pp. 25–9 for a discussion of the evidence.

86. For the Vikings in Ireland in this period, see Ó Corráin, *Ireland before the Normans*, pp. 80–110, and H. B. Clarke, M. ní Mhaonaigh and R. ó Floinn (eds), *Ireland and Scandinavia in the Early Viking Age* (Dublin, 1998).

87. MGH *Epp.* VI, no. 16, p. 163.

88. For an assessment (perhaps overly critical?) of this work, see I. Wood, 'Christians and Pagans in Ninth-Century Scandinavia', in B. Sawyer *et al.* (eds), *The Christianization of Scandinavia* (Alingsås, Sweden, 1987), pp. 36–67. This also provides a useful discussion of the relationship between mission and politics in this period.

89. P. Sawyer, 'The Process of Scandinavian Christianization in the Tenth and Eleventh Centuries', in ibid., pp. 68–87.

90. Ibid., pp. 70–3 on this and other indications of Christian influence in Norway in the mid-tenth century.

91. ASC, s.a. 905 (*recte* 904).

92. ASC, 'D' version, s.a. 948. See D. Whitelock, 'The Dealings of the Kings of England with Northumbria in the Tenth and Eleventh Centuries', in P. A. M. Clemoes (ed.), *The Anglo-Saxons* (London, 1959), pp. 70–88.

93. The Emperor Theophilus sent a group of captured *Rhos* to the Frankish ruler Louis the Pious: *Annales Bertiniani*, s.a. 839; see

J. Shephard, 'The Rhos Guests of Louis the Pious: Whence and Wherefore?', *Early Medieval Europe*, 4 (1995), 41–60.

94. Continuator of the *Chronicle of Theophanes*, 196; on the eastern movement of the Vikings and their relations with Byzantium, see H. R. Ellis Davidson, *The Viking Road to Byzantium* (London, 1976).

95. On whom, see D. M. Dunlop, *A History of the Jewish Khazars* (Princeton, NJ, 1954). In general, for the history of early Russia, see S. Franklin and J. Shephard, *The Emergence of Rus 750–1200* (London, 1996), esp. ch. 1–4.

96. Franklin and Shephard, *Emergence of Rus*, pp. 112–38.

97. D. Obolensky, *The Byzantine Commonwealth* (London, 1971), pp. 183–5; see also nt 98 below.

98. J. Fennell, *A History of the Russian Church to 1448* (London, 1995), pp. 20–44. The principal source, *The Russian Primary Chronicle* (trans. S. H. Cross and O. P. Sherbowitz-Wetzor) (Cambridge, Mass., 1973), is both relatively late in date and prone to fictional elaboration of events. It was first compiled in the late eleventh century, and exists now in two slightly later redactions.

99. Adalbert's continuation of the *Chronicle of Regino of Prüm*, s.a. 959.

100. Widukind, *Res gestae Saxonicae*, III. 65; for Olga, see Franklin and Shephard, *Emergence of Rus*, pp. 133–9 and 300–3.

20 THE WESTERN FRONTIERS OF CHRISTENDOM: SPAIN, 711–1037

1. D. Pérez Sánchez, *El ejército en la sociedad visigoda* (Salamanca, 1989), pp. 129–88.

2. R. Collins, 'Julian of Toledo and the Education of Kings in Late-Seventh-Century Spain', in idem, *Law, Culture and Regionalism in Early Medieval Spain* (Aldershot, 1992), item III.

3. A. A. Duri, *The Rise of Historical Writing among the Arabs*, trans. F. M. Donner, (Princeton, NJ, 1983), pp. 136–51.

4. A. Noth, *The Early Arabic Historical Tradition. A Source-Critical Study* (Darwin, 1994); R. Brunschvig, 'Ibn 'Abdalhakam et la conquête de l'Afrique du Nord par les Arabes; étude critique', *Annales de l'Institut des études orientales*, 6 (1942–7), 110–55.

5. R. Collins, *The Arab Conquest of Spain, 710–797* (Oxford, 1989), pp. 23–65.

6. Ibid., pp. 39–42; cf. D. R. Hill, *The Termination of Hostilities in the Early Arab Conquests, 634–656* (London, 1971).

7. M. Brett, 'The Arab Conquest and the Rise of Islam in North Africa', in J. D. Fage (ed.), *The Cambridge History of Africa*, Vol. 2 (Cambridge, 1978), pp. 490–555.

8. M. A. Shaban, *The 'Abassid Revolt* (Cambridge, 1970); P. Crone, *Slaves on Horses: the Evolution of the Islamic Polity* (Cambridge, 1980), pp. 37–57.

9. Collins, *Arab Conquest*, pp. 168–82.

10. R. Bulliett, *Conversion to Islam in the Medieval Period* (Cambridge, Mass., 1979), pp. 114–27.

11. M. J. Romani Suay (trans.), *Ibn Hawkal, Configuración del mundo* (Valencia, 1971), p. 63.

12. J. Vernet, 'Los médicos andaluces en el "Libro de las Generaciones de Médicos" de Ibn Yulyul', *Anuario de Estudios Medievales*, 5 (1968), 445–62.

13. D. Millet-Gérard, *Chrétiens mozarabes et culture islamique* (Paris, 1984); also C. M. Sage, *Paul Albar of Córdoba: Studies on his Life and Writings* (Washington, 1943), and K. B. Wolf, *Christian Martyrs in Muslim Spain* (Cambridge, 1988), pp. 51–74.

14. J. A. Coope, *The Martyrs of Córdoba* (Lincoln, 1995); Collins, *Early Medieval Spain*, pp. 210–17.

15. Alvar, *Indiculus Luminosus*, xxxv; D. Wasserstein, 'The Language Situation in Al-Andalus', in A. Jones and R. Hitchcock (eds), *Studies on the Muwassah and the Kharja* (Oxford, 1991), p. 5; R. Wright, 'La muerte del ladino escrito en Al-Andalus', *Euphrosyne*, 22 (1994), 255–68.

16. R. Collins, 'Poetry in Ninth-Century Spain', *Papers of the Liverpool Latin Seminar*, 4, (1984), 181–95.

17. Not all of these inscriptions have been published. Those that have will be found in A. Hübner, *Inscriptiones Hispaniae Christianae* (Berlin, 1900), pp. 69–75 and 99–105.

18. M. C. Hernandez, *El Islam de al-Andalus. Historia y estructura de su realidad social* (Madrid, 1992), pp. 172–3; R. Fletcher, *Moorish Spain* (London, 1992), pp. 112–13.

19. Brett, 'The Arab Conquest and the Rise of Islam in North Africa', p. 546.

20. L. A. Gomez-Moreno, *Iglesias mozarabes* (2 vols) (Madrid, 1919); M. Mentré, *La peinture mozarabe* (Paris, 1984).

21. R. Hitchcock, 'El supuesto mozarabismo andaluz', *Actas del I Congreso de Historia de Andalucia*, 1 (Córdoba, 1978), 149–51.

22. An underlying theme in much of the medieval Spanish historiography of the early and middle decades of the twentieth century; for example, J. Pérez de Urbel, *Historia del condado de Castilla* (3 vols) (Madrid, 1945).

23. J. I. Ruiz de la Peña, 'Estudio preliminar', in J. Gil Fernández, J. L. Moralejo and J. I. Ruiz de la Peña, *Crónicas asturianas* (Oviedo, 1985), pp. 13–42.

24. J. Gil, 'Introducción', in ibid. pp. 45–105.

25. *Chronicle of Alfonso III* (both versions) ch. 9, pp. 124–27. See J. Montenegro and A. del Castillo, 'Don Pelayo y los orígenes de la Reconquista', *Hispania*, 52 (1992), 5–32.

26. Ibid., ch. 8, pp. 122–24; *Chronicle of Albelda*, XV. 1, p. 173.

27. C. Sánchez-Albornoz, 'Data de la batalla de Covadonga', in idem, *Orígenes de la nación española*, Vol. 2 (Oviedo, 1974), pp. 97–135.

28. S. Barton, *The Aristocracy in Twelfth-Century León and Castile* (Cambridge, 1997), pp. 28–9; M. Carlé, 'Gran propriedad y grandes proprietarios', *Cuadernos de Historia de España*, 57/8 (1973), 1–224.

29. C. Baliñas Pérez, *Do Mito â Realidade: a definición social e territorial de Galicia na Alta Idade Media (Séculos VIII e IX)* (Santiago de Compostela, 1992), pp. 59–86.

30. *Chronicle of Alfonso III* (both versions – with differences), ch. 14, pp. 132–33.

31. S. de Moxó, *Repoblación y sociedad en la España cristiana medieval* (Madrid, 1979); C. Sánchez-Albornoz, 'Repoblación del Reino asturleonés', in idem, *Viejos y nuevos estudios sobre las instituciones medievales españolas*, Vol. 2 (Madrid, 1976), pp. 581–790; anon. (ed.), *Despoblación y colonización del valle del Duero (siglos VIII–XX)* (Avila, 1995).

32. P. Barraca de Ramos, 'La ciudad de Avila entre los siglos V al X', *IV Congreso de Arqueología Medieval Española*, Vol. 2 (Alicante, 1994), pp. 39–46.

33. C. Sánchez–Albornoz, 'Los siervos en el noroeste hispano hace un milenio', in idem, *Viejos y nuevos estudios*, 3 (Madrid, 1979), 1525–1611.

34. E. Sáez (ed.), *Colección documental del Archivo de la Catedral de León (775–1230)*, Vol. I, doc. 1 (León, 1987), pp. 3–5.

35. A. C. Floriano, *Diplomática española del periodo astur*, Vol. 1 (Oviedo, 1949).

36. Collins, *Arab Conquest*, pp. 201–7.

37. *Chronicle of Albelda*, XV. 9, p. 174.

38. C. García de Castro Valdés, *Arqueología cristiana de la Alta Edad Media en Asturias* (Oviedo, 1995).

39. J. Pérez de Urbel and R. del Arco y Garay, *España cristiana: comienzo de la Reconquista (711–1038)*, Vol. VI of R. Menéndez Pidal (ed.), *Historia de España* (Madrid, 1956), pp. 47–51; C. Sánchez-Albornoz, 'La restauración del orden gótico en el palacio y en la iglesia', in his *Orígenes de la nation española*, Vol. 2 (Oviedo, 1974), pp. 623–39.

40. Einhard, *Vita Karoli*, xvi.

41. *Chronicle of Albelda*, XV. 9, p. 174; no mention is made of this in the *Chronicle of Alfonso III*.

42. R. Collins, *The Basques* (2nd edn) (Oxford, 1990), pp. 134–71.

43. C. Sánchez-Albornoz, 'Problemas de la Historia Navarra del siglo IX', *Cuadernos de Historia de España*, 25/6 (1957), 5–82.

44. A. Canada Juste, 'Los Banu Qasi (714–924)', *Principe de Viana*, 41 (1980), 5–95.

45. P. Stafford, *Unification and Conquest: A Political and Social History of England in the Tenth and Eleventh Centuries* (London, 1989), pp. 24–44.

46. *Chronicle of Alfonso III*, ch. 23, pp. 142–43; J. E. Casariego, 'Una revolution asturiana en el siglo IX: el interregno del conde Nepociano', *Boletín del Instituto de Estudios Asturianos*, 68 (1969), 4–29, who, unlike the medieval compilers of the Asturian regnal lists, does not recognise Nepotian as a legitimate, if short-reigned, king.

47. For recent excavations on Monte Naranco, see A. Arbeiter and S. Noack-Haley, *Asturische Königsbauten des 9. Jahrhunderts* (Mainz, 1994).

48. H. Kennedy, *Muslim Spain and Portugal* (London, 1996), pp. 63–81.
49. C. Sánchez-Albornoz, 'El tercer rey de España', *Cuadernos de Historia de España*, 49/50 (1969), 5–49.
50. J. Valdeón Baruque, 'Evolution histórica del reinado de Alfonso III', in F. J. Fernández Conde (ed.), *La época de Alfonso III y San Salvador de Valdedíos* (Oviedo, 1994), pp. 19–26.
51. J. Pérez de Urbel, *Sampiro, su crónica y la monarquía leonesa en el siglo X* (Madrid, 1957), pp. 437–84 for documents relating to various bishops and notaries called Sampiro.
52. P. Linehan, *History and the Historians of Medieval Spain* (Oxford, 1993), pp. 125–31.
53. R. Collins, *Sicut lex Gothorum continet:* Law and Charters in Ninth- and Tenth-Century León and Catalonia', *English Historical Review*, 100 (1985), 489–512.
54. On the city of León in the tenth century, see C. Sánchez-Albornoz, *Una ciudad de la España cristiana pace mil años* (Madrid, 1976).
55. C. Baliñas, *Defensores e traditores: un modelo de relation entre poder monárquico e oligarquía na Galicia altomedieval (718–1037)* (Santiago de Compostela, 1988), pp. 57–84; A. Isla Frez, *La sociedad gallega en la Alta Edad Media* (Madrid, 1992), pp. 129–202.
56. A. Herrero Alonso, *Voces de origen vasco en la geografía castellana* (Bilbao, 1977).
57. A process described in detail in J. Pérez de Urbel, *Historia del Condado de Castilla* (Madrid, 1945), Vol. 1, and documented in Vol. 3.
58. Ibid., Vol. 2.
59. See Vol. 3 of the 1945 edition of Pérez de Urbel, *Condado de Castilla* (n. 57 above); these texts are not included in the 1969 reprint.
60. Kennedy, *Muslim Spain*, pp. 82–97.
61. J. Rodríguez, *Ramiro II Rey de León* (Madrid, 1972), pp. 339–90.
62. G. Martínez Díez, 'Los fueros leoneses: 1017–1336', in J. M. Fernández Catón (ed.), *El Reino de León en la Alta Edad Media*, Vol. 1: *Cortes, concilios y fueros* (León, 1988), pp. 285–352.
63. G. Martínez Díez, *Fueros locales en el territorio de la Provincia de Burgos* (Burgos, 1982), pp. 11–116.
64. R. Collins, 'Visigothic Law and Regional Custom in Disputes in Early Medieval Spain', in W. Davies and P. Fouracre (eds), *The Settlement of Disputes in Early Medieval Europe* (Cambridge, 1986), pp. 85–104.
65. V. Aguliar and F. R. Mediano, 'Antroponomía de origen árabe en la documentación leonesa, siglos VIII–XIII', *El Reino de León en la alta Edad Media*, Vol. 6 (1994), pp. 499–633.
66. Rodríguez, *Ramiro II*, pp. 391–507.
67. J. Rodríguez Fernández, *Reyes de León: García I, Ordoño II, Fruela II, Alfonso IV* (Burgos, 1997), pp. 137–88 for the reign of Fruela II.
68. Sampiro, *Chronica*, 20, ed. Pérez de Urbel, pp. 318–9.
69. Ibn Hayyan, *al-Muqtabis*, V. 233, trans. M. J. Viguera and F. Corriente, *Crónica del Califa'Abdarrahman III an-Nasir entre los años 912 y 942* (Zaragoza, 1981), pp. 258–60.

70. Rodríguez, *Ramiro II*, pp. 74–76 and 105–32; idem, *Reyes de León*, pp. 210–23.
71. Rodríguez, *Ramiro II*, pp. 405–17; idem, *Ordoño III* (León, 1982), pp. 59–64.
72. J. Rodríguez Fernández, *Sancho I y Ordoño IV, Reyes de León* (León, 1987), pp. 137–57.
73. Rodríguez, *Sancho I y Ordoño IV,* pp. 170–85.
74. R. Collins 'Queens-Dowager and Queens-Regent in Tenth-Century León and Navarre', in J. C. Parsons (ed.), *Medieval Queenship* (New York, 1993), pp. 79–92.
75. Ibid. pp. 87–91.
76. Sampiro, *Chronica,* 27, ed. Pérez de Urbel, pp. 338–9.
77. Ibid. 29, pp. 342–3.
78. On the reign of Alfonso V, see J. M. Fernández del Pozo, 'Alfonso V, Rey de León', in J. M. Fernández Catón (ed.), *León y su Historia,* Vol. 5 (León, 1984), pp. 11–262.

21 THE EMPIRE REVIVED, 875–1002

1. ARF, s.a. 798, 799.
2. AB, s.a. 840, 850, 869.
3. G. Marçais, 'Aghlabids', in *Encyclopaedia of Islam* (2nd edn) (Leiden and London, 1960), Vol. I, pp. 247–9.
4. *Liber Pontificalis,* vol. II, pp. 81–2; S. Gibson and B. Ward-Perkins, 'The Surviving Remains of the Leonine Wall', pt I: *Papers of the British School at Rome,* 47 (1979), pp. 30–57; pt II: ibid., 51 (1983), pp. 222–39.
5. F. E. Endgreen, 'Pope John VIII and the Arabs', *Speculum,* 20 (1945), 318–30.
6. R. Jenkins, *Byzantium: The Imperial Centuries AD 610 to 1071* (London, 1966), pp. 185–90.
7. *Constitutum Constantini,* 18: Constantine transferring his *imperium* and his *regni potestas* to the East; 11: *potestas, dignitas, honorificentia imperialis* given to the see of Peter, together with the gift of Constantine's own imperial diadem and robes. On this text, see J. Fried, *Donation of Constantine and 'Constitutum Constantini'* (Berlin and New York, 2007).
8. Translated Jenkins, *Byzantium: The Imperial Centuries,* p. 190.
9. C. Wickham, *Early Medieval Italy: Central Power and Local Society, 400–1000* (London, 1981), pp. 60–3, with references.
10. John VIII, *ep.* 207.
11. On the conflict between the Churches of Rome and Constantinople in this period, see F. Dvornik, *The Photian Schism* (Paris, 1950); see also idem, *Byzantium and the Roman Primacy* (2nd edn) (New York, 1979), pp. 101–23, which is rather too inclined to play down conflict in the interests of a modern ecumenical ideal.
12. Anastasius Bibliotecarius, *ep.* 5. Cf. the traditional Roman view of the order of precedence in *Constitutum Constantini,* 12.
13. Dvornik, *Photian Schism,* pp. 172–225.

14. A. Toynbee, *Constantine Porphyrogenitus and his World* (Oxford, 1973), pp. 267–8 and nt 4 on p. 268.

15. A. Eckel, *Charles le Simple* (Paris, 1899), pp. 91–101.

16. T. Reuter, *Germany in the Early Middle Ages, 800–1056* (London, 1991), p. 130.

17. Widukind of Corvey, *Res Gestae Saxonicae* I. 32; Thietmar of Merseburg, *Chronica* I. 9,

18. *Vita antiquior Mathildis regime,* 1, ed. B. Schütte, MGH *SRG,* vol. 66 (1994), pp. 113–4.

19. Discussed in D. C. Jackman, *The Konradiner. A Study in Genealogical Methodology* (Frankfurt am Main, 1990), pp. 78–80.

20. For a bibliography on Conrad, see E. Hlawitschka, *Vom Frankenreich zur Formierung der europaischen Staaten- und Völkergemeinschaft 840–1046* (Darmstadt, 1986), pp. 278–9.

21. C. R. Bowlus, *Franks, Moravians and Magyars. The Struggle for the Middle Danube, 788–907* (Philadelphia, Pa., 1995) for a Moravia centred around the lower Sava; and Martin Eggers, *Das 'Großmährische Reich'. Realität oder Fiktion?* (Stuttgart, 1995) for the Hungarian alternative.

22. Regino of Prüm, *Chronica,* s.a. 889.

23. *Annales Fuldenses,* s.a. 892.

24. *Annales Fuldenses,* s.a. 900–2; Adalbert's continuation of Regino of Prüm, s.a. 907–10 (whose dates in general are one year behind the real ones); on which, see K. Hauck, 'Erzbishof Adalbert von Magdeburg als Geschichtsschreiber', in H. Beumann (ed.), *Festshrift für Walter Schlesinger* (Cologne, 1974), Vol. II, pp. 298–305; Widukind of Corvey, *Res Gestae Saxonicae,* I. xx.

25. Adalbert's continuation of Regino, s.a. 913.

26. Adalbert's continuation of Regino, s.a. 919; Thietmar of Merseburg, *Chronica,* I. 8. See W. Giese, *Heinrich I* (Darmstadt, 2008), pp. 58–61; and in general, K. J. Leyser, 'Henry I and the Beginnings of the Saxon Empire', *English Historical Review,* 83 (1968), 1–32.

27. Adalbert's continuation of Regino, s.a. 924; Widukind *Res Gestae Saxonicae,* I. xxxii. On Widukind, see H. Beumann 'Historiographische Konzeption und politische Ziele Widukinds von Corvey', *Settimane di studio sull'alto medioevo,* 17 (Spoleto, 1970), pp. 857–94.

28. Widukind, I. xxxviii.

29. G. Ostrogorsky, *History of the Byzantine Empire* (English trans. of 3rd edn) (Oxford, 1968), p. 282; see also M. Whittow, *The Making of Orthodox Byzantium, 600–1025* (London, 1996), pp. 235–40 for Byzantium and the Magyars in the ninth century.

30. Adalbert's continuation of Regino, s.a. 938 and 944; Widukind, *Res Gestae Saxonicae,* II xiv, III. xxx, and III. xliv. See K. J. Leyser, 'The Battle at the Lech, 955', *History,* 50 (1965), 1–25.

31. Adalbert's continuation of Regino, s.a. 938, 939; see also K. J. Leyser, 'Otto I and his Saxon Enemies', in his *Rule and Conflict in an Early Medieval Society* (London, 1979), pp. 9–42.

32. Widukind, *Res Gestae Saxonicae,* II. xxiv–xxvi and xxxvi. Adalbert's continuation of Regino, s.a. 947, 950 (for Liudolf).

33. Wickham, *Early Medieval Italy*, pp. 177–83.
34. Liudprand of Cremona, *Antapodosis*, V. xxvii–VI. ii.
35. Adalbert's continuation of Regino, s.a. (correctly) 951.
36. Ibid., s.a. 952, 953; Thietmar of Merseburg, *Chronica*, II. 6–8.
37. *Cambridge Medieval History*, Vol. III (Cambridge, 1922), p. 151.
38. P. Squatriti (trans.), *The Complete Works of Liudprand of Cremona* (Washington, DC, 2007); for the Latin texts, see now P. Chiesa (ed.), *Liudprandi Cremonensis Opera Omnia* (Turnhout, Belgium, 1998).
39. For aspects of Liudprand's reading, see the notes to Bauer and Rau's edition (see Bibliography), and K. Leyser, 'Liudprand of Cremona, Preacher and Homilist', in K. Walsh and D. Wood (eds), *The Bible in the Medieval World* (Oxford, 1985), pp. 43–60; in general, the bibliography concerning Lintprand is smaller than it ought to be.
40. See the introduction to P. Chiesa's edition, nt 38 above.
41. For the Laurentian schism, see J. Moorhead, *Theoderic in Italy* (Oxford, 1992), pp. 114–39, and R. Collins *Keepers of the Keys of Heaven: A History of the Papacy* (New York and London, 2009), pp. 77–82.
42. P. Llewellyn, *Rome in the Dark Ages* (London, 1971), pp. 286–315; a substantial modern study of the tenth-century papacy is still much to be desired.
43. Liudprand, *Antapodosis*, II. 48. L. Duchesne, 'Serge III et Jean XI', *Mélanges d'archéologie et d'histoire*, 33 (1913), 25–55.
44. See the Introduction to Bauer and Rau's edition, pp. 235–6.
45. Liudprand, *Antapodosis*, II. 48.
46. The fullest account of this pontificate will be found in T. Venni, 'Giovanni X', *Archivio della Deputazione Romana di Storia Patria*, 59 (1936), 1–136.
47. Liudprand, *Antapodosis*, III. 43–6.
48. P. Toubert, *Les structures du Latium médiéval* (Rome, 1973), pp. 974–98 gives an admirable assessment of Alberic's aims and the limitations on his personal power in Rome. See also R. Collins, *Keepers of the Keys of Heaven: A History of the Papacy* (London and New York, 2009), ch. 10.
49. Toubert, *Structures*, pp. 997–8.
50. For the reform movement in the Church in the eleventh century and its attack on such practices, see G. Tellenbach, *Church, State and Christian Society at the Time of the Investiture Contest* (Oxford, 1940).
51. This still awaits a full study, but some impressions can be formed from the career of the count-abbot-bishop Oliba: see R. d'Abadal i de Vinyals, *L'abat Oliba i la seva epocà* (Barcelona, 1948) and A. M. Albareda, *L'abat Oliba* (new edn) (Montserrat, 1972).
52. P. Jaffe, *Regesta Pontificum Romanorum* (2 vols) (Leipzig, 1885), nos 3675–6, 3678–80, 3684, 3688, 3689, 3692, 3694, 3696.
53. B. Hamilton, 'Monastic Revival in Tenth-Century Rome', *Studia Monastica*, 4 (1962), pp. 35–68.
54. Liudprand, *Liber de Ottone rege*, i–iii; Adalbert s.a. 961.

55. MGH *Constitutions*, vol. I, pp. 23–7; see also W. Ullmann, 'The Origins of the Ottonianum', *Cambridge Historical Journal*, II (1953), 114–28.
56. K. Leyser, 'Sacral Kingship', in his *Rule and Conflict*, pp. 75–107.
57. See the Introduction to P. L. D. Reid's edition of Rather, CC, *cont. med.*, vol. 46, for an outline of his life and works.
58. Liudprand, *de Ottone rege*, vi.
59. Liudprand, *de Ottone rege*, xx.
60. *Liber Pontificalis*, vol. II, pp. 255–7 (Benedict VI), 259 (John XIV).
61. H. Zimmermann, *Papstabsetzungen des Mittelalters* (Graz, 1968), pp. 99–103.
62. W. Treadgold, *A History of the Byzantine State and Society* (Stanford, Calif., 1997), pp. 446–579 for an outline history of Byzantium between 842 and 1025.
63. H. Kennedy, *The Prophet and the Age of the Caliphates* (London, 1986), pp. 309–45.
64. B. M. Kreutz, *Before the Normans. Southern Italy in the Ninth and Tenth Centuries* (Philadelphia, Pa., 1991), pp. 102–6.
65. See, not least, K. Leyser, 'The Tenth Century in Byzantine–Western Relations', in D. Baker (ed.), *The Relations between East and West in the Middle Ages* (Edinburgh, 1973), pp. 29–63.
66. Liudprand of Cremona, *Legatio ad Imperatorem Constantinopolitanum Nicephorum Phocam*, iii, and xl; the translation is that of L. H. Nelson and M. V. Shirk, *Liudprand of Cremona, Mission to Constantinople (968 AD)* (Lawrence, Kansas, 1972), pp. 3, 32.
67. Liudprand, *Legatio*, ii, trans. Nelson, p. 2.
68. Ibid., li, trans. Nelson, p. 40.
69. The principal source for these events in southern Italy is the *Chronicon Salernitanum*, ed. U. Westerbergh (Stockholm, 1956); on which, see Kreutz, *Before the Normans*, pp. 94–5.
70. K. Leyser, '*Theophanu Divina Gratia Imperatrix Augusta*: Western and Eastern Emperorship in the Later Tenth Century', in idem, *Communications and Power in Medieval Europe: The Carolingian and Ottonian Centuries* (London, 1994), pp. 143–64.
71. For Otto II's reign, see K. Uhlirz, *Jahrbücher des Deutschen Reiches unter Otto II und Otto III*, Vol. I: *Otto II. 973–83* (Berlin, 1902).
72. Thietmar of Merseburg, *Chronica*, III. 20–5.
73. For Otto III's reign, see Uhlirz, *Jahrbücher*, Vol. II: *Otto III. 983–1002* (Berlin 1954).
74. For example, A. von Euw and G. Sporbeck, *Abenländische Buchkunst zur Zeit der Kaiserin Theophanu* (Cologne, 1991); R. McKitterick, 'Ottonian Intellectual Culture in the Tenth Century and the Role of Theophanu', *Early Medieval Europe*, Vol. 2 (1993), 53–74.
75. Thietmar, IV. 27.
76. Leyser, '*Theophanu Divina Gratia Imperatrix Augusta*', p. 164.
77. K. Leyser, 'Three Historians: c) Thietmar of Merseburg', in his *Carolingian and Ottonian Centuries*, pp. 27–8.
78. T. Reuter, *Germany in the Early Middle Ages, 800–1056* (London, 1991), pp. 163–5.
79. Thietmar, IV. 75.

80. D. A. Warner, 'Ideals and Action in the Reign of Otto III', *Journal of Medieval History*, Vol. 25 (1999), pp. 1–18.

81. Bernd Schütte (ed.), *Die Lebensbeschreibungen der Königin Mathilde*, MGH *SRG*, vol. 66 (1994).

82. For relations with the Slavs in the time of Louis the German, see Reuter, *Germany in the Early Middle Ages*, pp. 77–84.

83. On the conversion of Scandinavia, see R. Fletcher, *The Conversion of Europe* (London, 1997), pp. 369–417.

84. L. Grote, *Die Stiftskirche in Gernrode* (Burg bei Magdeburg, 1932).

85. *Annales Regni Francorum*, s.a. 805 and 806.

86. *Annales Fuldenses*, s.a 845; trans. T. Reuter, *The Annals of Fulda* (Manchester, 1992), p. 24.

87. Regino of Prüm, s.a. 890.

88. R. Folz, *Les saints rois du Moyen Age en Occident (vie–xiiie siècles)* (Brussels, 1984), pp. 31–6.

89. Reuter, *Germany in the Early Middle Ages*, p. 262.

90. Thietmar of Merseburg, IV. 55–7.

91. On the history of Poland in this period, see H. Ludat, 'The Medieval Empire and the Early Piast State', *Historical Studies*, 6 (1968), 1–21, and various sections of G. Barraclough (ed.), *Eastern and Western Europe in the Middle Ages* (London, 1970).

92. Fletcher, *Conversion of Europe*, pp. 427–9.

93. Thietmar, IV. 45.

94. On this manuscript and its art, see H. Mayr-Harting, *Ottoman Book Illumination: an Historical Study*, Vol. 1: *Themes* (London, 1991), pp. 157–78.

95. Bernard Hamilton, 'The monastery of San Alessio and the religious and intellectual renaissance in tenth-century Rome' in *idem*, *Monastic Reform, Catharism and the Crusades, 900–1300* (London, 1979), item III.

96. *MGH Diplomata*, vol. II, pt. 2, pp. 844–46: judgement in favour of the monastery of St. Felix, Pavia, dated 14th October 1001.

97. Thietmar, IV. 47; see Karl Leyser, 'Ritual, Ceremony and Gesture: Ottonian Germany', in his *Communications and Power in Medieval Europe: The Carolingian and Ottonian Centuries* (London, 1994), pp. 189–213, esp. p. 202.

98. Thietmar, IV. 47.

99. Thietmar, IV. 47–9.

100. MGH *Diplomata*, vol. II. ii, pp. 818–20; a deed of gift to the church of St Peter.

101. For an introduction, see T. N. Bisson, 'The "Feudal Revolution"', *Past & Present*, 142 (1994), pp. 6–42, and several subsequent contributions to 'The Debate: the "Feudal Revolution", including those by T. Reuter in *Past & Present*, 155 (1997), pp. 177–195, and D. Barthelemy, *ibid.* 152 (1996), pp. 197–205.

102. The late Anglo-Saxon kingdom, created by the rulers of Wessex in the tenth century, has been seen as something of an exception: see J. Campbell, 'The Late Anglo-Saxon State: A Maximum View', in idem, *The Anglo-Saxon State* (London, 2000), pp 1–30.

Bibliography

A: Primary sources

Suggested editions and, where possible, English translations are here given for many of the sources that are referred to in the notes to the chapters of this book. For texts that are used sparingly, references are given in the notes.

Abbo, *Bella Parisiacae Urbis,* ed. H. Waquet, CHFM, 1964.

Adalbert of Trier, continuation of the *Chronicle* of Regino of Prüm, ed. A. Bauer and R. Rau (2nd edn) (Darmstadt, 1977), pp. 190–231.

Adamnán, *De Locis Sanctis,* ed. D. Meehan, SLH, vol. III (1958); see also *Vita Columbae.*

Agathias, *Histories,* ed. R. Keydell, trans. J. D. Frendo, CFHB, vols II and IIA.

Alcuin, *Epistolae,* ed. E. Dümmler, MGH *Epp.,* vol. IV.

Alvar of Córdoba, *Indiculus Luminosus,* ed. J. Gil, *Corpus Scriptorum Muzarabicorum* (2 vols) (Madrid, 1973), Vol. 1, pp. 270–315.

Ambrose, *Epistolae,* in PL, vol. XVI, *cc.* 913–1342; tr. M. M. Beyenka, FC vol. 26 (revd edn, 1967).

Ammianus Marcellinus, *Res Gestae,* ed. and trans. J. C. Rolfe (Loeb Library, 3 vols) or ed. A. Loren (3 vols) (Paris, 1960); abridged trans. W. Hamilton (Penguin Classics, 1986).

Anglo-Saxon Chronicle, ed. C. Plummer, *Two Saxon Chronicles in Parallel* (2 vols) (Oxford, 1892); trans. G. N. Garmonsway (revd edn) (London, 1960).

Annales Bertiniani, ed. F. Grat, J. Vielliard, S. Clémencet, SHF, 1964; also ed. R. Rau, *Fontes,* Vol. II, pp. 12–287; trans. J. L. Nelson, *The Annals of St-Bertin* (Manchester, 1991).

Annales Fuldenses, ed. R. Rau, *Fontes,* Vol. II, pp. 20–177; trans. T. Reuter, *The Annals of Fulda* (Manchester, 1992).

Annales Laureshamenses, ed. G. Pertz, MGH *SS,* vol. I, pp. 22–39; partial trans. P. D. King, *Charlemagne: Translated Sources* (Lancaster, 1987), pp. 137–45.

Annales Mettenses Priores, ed. B. de Simson, MGH *SRG*; partial trans. P. Fouracre and R. A. Gerberding, *Late Merovingian France. History and Hagiography 640–720* (Manchester, 1996), pp. 330–70.

Annales Mosellani, ed. G. Pertz, MGH *SS,* vol. XVI, pp. 494–9.

Annales Regni Francorum, ed. F. Kurze, MGH *SRG*.

ARF Revised Version – same edition on opposite pages. The sections of both versions relating to Charlemagne's reign, trans. P. D. King, *Charlemagne: Translated Sources* (Lancaster, 1987), pp. 74–131.

Annales Sancti Amandi, ed. G. Pertz, MGH *SS,* vol. I, pp. 6–14.

Annals of Ulster, ed. and trans. S. Mac Airt and G. MacNiocaill (Dublin, 1983).

Annales Vedastini, ed. R. Rau, *Fontes*, Vol. II, pp. 291–337.

Annales Xantenses, ed. R. Rau, *Fontes*, Vol. II, pp. 340–71.

Anonymus Valesianus (part II), ed. J. Moreau, *Excerpta Valesiana* (Leipzig, 1968); trans. in Vol. 3 of Rolfe's edn of Ammianus Marcellinus – see above.

Avitus of Vienne, *Letters and Selected Prose*, trans. D. Schanzer and I. Wood (Liverpool, 2002).

Bede, *Historia Ecclesiastica Gentis Anglorum*, ed. B. Colgrave and R. A. B. Mynors (Oxford, 1969). Commentary: the companion volume of commentary by J. M. Wallace-Hadrill (Oxford, 1988), updated by the notes in J. McClure and R. Collins, *Bede: Ecclesiastical History of the English People* (Oxford, 1994), which also trans. part of Bede's *Greater Chronicle*.

Boethius, *De Consolatione Philosophiae*, ed. L. Bieler, CC vol. XCIV; also ed. and trans. H. F. Stewart, E. K. Rand and S. J. Tester (Loeb Library, revd edn, 1973).

Boniface, *Epistolae*, ed. M. Tangl, MGH *Epistolae Selectae*, vol. I; trans. E. Emerton, *The Letters of Saint Boniface* (New York, 1940).

Candidus, fragments, ed. and trans. R. Blockley, *Fragmentary Classicising Historians*, Vol. II (Liverpool, 1983).

Cassiodorus, *Chronica*, ed. T. Mommsen, MGH *AA*, vol. XI, pp. 111–61; *Variae*, ed. T. Mommsen, MGH *AA*, vol. XII.

Cassiodorus, *Variae*, trans. S. J. B. Barnish (Liverpool, 1992).

Chronica Gallica A CCCCLII, ed. T. Mommsen, MGH *AA*, vol. IX, pp. 615–62.

Chronicle of Albelda, ed. J. Gil Fernández, J. L. Moralejo and J. I. Ruiz de la Peña, *Crónicas asturianas* (Oviedo, 1985), pp. 153–88.

Chronicle of Alfonso III (both versions): ibid., pp. 114–49; Roda version translated in K. B. Wolf, *Conquerors and Chroniclers of Early Medieval Spain* (Liverpool, 1990), pp. 159–77.

Chronicle of John of Nikiu, ed. and trans. R. H. Charles (London, 1916).

Chronicle of Joshua the Stylite, ed. and trans. W. Wright (Cambridge, 1882); trans. F. R. Trombley and J. W. Watt, *The Chronicle of Pseudo-Joshua the Stylite* (Liverpool, 2000).

Chronicle of Zachariah of Mitylene, trans. F. J. Hamilton and E. W. Brooks (London, 1899).

Chronicle of 754 or *Mozarabic Chronicle*, ed. J. E. López Pereira, *Crónica mozárabe de 754* (Zaragoza, 1980); trans. K. B. Wolf, *Conquerors and Chroniclers of Early Medieval Spain* (Liverpool, 1990), pp. 111–58.

Codex Carolinus, ed. W. Gundlach, MGH *Epp*, vol. III, pp. 476–653; partial trans. P. D. King, *Charlemagne: Translated Sources* (Lancaster, 1987), pp. 269–307.

Codex Iustinianus, ed. P. Krueger, Vol. II of *Corpus Iuris civilis* (Berlin, 1900).

Codex Theodosianus, ed. T. Mommsen (3 vols, 4th edn) (Dublin and Zurich, 1971); trans. C. Pharr, *Theodosian Code* (repr. New York, 1969).

Columbanus, *Epistolae*, ed. and trans. G. S. M. Walker, SLH vol. II; *Penitential*, ed. and trans. L. Bieler, SLH vol. V, pp. 96–107.

Corippus, *In laudem Iustini Augusti Minoris*, ed. and trans. A. Cameron (London, 1976).

Councils of Toledo: ed. J. Vives, *Concilios visigóticas e hispano-romanos* (Barcelona and Madrid, 1963).

Edictus Rothari, ed. F. Bluhme, MGH *Fontes Iuris Germanici Antiqui*; tr. K. F. Drew, *The Lombard Laws* (Philadelphia, Pa., 1973).

Einhard, *Vita Karoli Magni*, ed. O. Holder-Egger, MGH *SRM;* trans. P. E. Dutton, *Carolingian Civilization: A Reader* (Peterborough, Ontario, 1993), pp. 24–42.

Elishé, *History of Vardan and the Armenian War,* trans. R. W. Thomson (Cambridge, Mass., 1982).

Epistolae Austrasicae, ed. W. Gundlach, MGH *Epp.*, vol. III, pp. 110–53.

Epitome de Caesaribus, ed. F. Pichlmayr (Leipzig, 1970).

Ermoldus Nigellus, ed. E. Faral, CHFM (1964).

Eugippius, *Vita Severini,* ed. R. Noll (Berlin, 1963; Passau, 1981); trans. L. Bieler, FC, vol. 55 (1965).

Eunapius, *Lives of the Philosophers,* ed. and trans. W. C. Wright (Loeb Library).

Eusebius of Caesarea, *Historia Ecclesiastica,* ed. and trans. H. J. Lawlor and J. E. L. Oulton (2 vols) (London, 1954).

Eusebius, *Life of Constantine,* trans. A. Cameron and S. G. Hall (Oxford, 1999)

Eutropius, *Breviarium,* ed. F. Ruehl (Leipzig, 1909); trans. H. W. Bird (Liverpool, 1993).

Fragmentary Annals of Ireland, trans. J. Radnor (Dublin, 1978).

Fredegar, Chronicle of – book IV and the Continuations – ed. and trans. J. M. Wallace-Hadrill (London, 1960).

Gesta Abbatum Fontanellensis, ed. F. Lohier and J. Laporte (Rouen, 1936).

Gildas, *De Excidio Britonum,* ed. and trans. M. Winterbottom (London, 1978).

Gregory the Great, Pope, *Dialogorum Libri IV,* ed. with French trans. A. de Vogüé, SC, vols 254, 260, 265.

Gregory of Tours, *Libri Decem Historiarum,* ed. B. Krusch and W. Levison, MGH *SRM,* vol. I (revd edn, 1951); trans. O. M. Dalton, *The History of the Franks by Gregory of Tours* (2 vols) (Oxford, 1927).

Herodian, ed. and trans. C. R. Whittaker (2 vols, Loeb Library).

Historia Dunelmensis Ecclesiae, ed. T. Arnold, Rolls Series, vol. 75. 1.

Hydatius, *Chronica,* ed. and trans. R. W. Burges, *The Chronicle of Hydatius and the Consularia Constantinopolitana* (Oxford, 1993), pp. 69–123.

Ibn Abd al-Hakam, *Futah Misr,* trans. J. H. Jones (Göttingen, 1858).

Ibn Ishaq, *Sirat Rasul Allah,* trans. A. Guillaume, *The Life of Muhammad* (Lahore, 1955).

Isidore of Seville, *Chronicon,* ed. J. C. Martín, CC, vol. CXII (2003).

Isidore of Seville, *Historia Gothorum, Vandalorum et Sueborum,* ed. C. Rodríguez Alonso, FEHL, vol. 13 (León, 1975); trans. K. B. Wolf, *Conquerors and Chroniclers of Early Medieval Spain* (Liverpool, 1990), pp. 81–110.

Isidore, *De Viris Illustribus,* ed. C. Codoñer Merino (Salamanca, 1964).

Jerome, *Epistolae,* ed. Hilberg, CSEL, vols LIV, LV and LVI.

John of Antioch, fragments, ed. and trans. R. Blockley – *see under* Candidus.

John of Biclar, *Chronica*, ed. C. Cardelle de Hartmann, CC, vol. CLXXIIIA (2001); trans. K. B. Wolf, *Conquerors and Chroniclers of Early Medieval Spain* (Liverpool, 1990), pp. 61–80.

John VIII, Pope, *Epistolae*, ed. E. Caspar, MGH *Epp*, vol. VII, pp. 1–333.

Jordanes, *Getica*, ed. T. Mommsen, MGH *AA*, vol. V; trans. C. C. Mierow, *The Gothic History of Jordanes* (Princeton, NJ, 1915).

Julian, the Emperor, *Works*, ed. and trans. W. C. Wright (3 vols, Loeb Library).

Lactantius, *De Mortibus Persecutorum*, ed. J. Creed (revd reprint) (Oxford, 1989).

Leo the Great, Pope, *Epistolae*, ed. C. Silva-Tarouca (3 vols) (Rome, 1932–5); trans. E. Hunt, FC, vol. 34 (1957).

Lex Salica, ed. A. Eckhardt, MGH *LL*, vol. IV. 1; trans. T. J. Rivers, *Laws of the Salian and Ripuarian Franks* (New York, 1986), pp. 39–152.

Lex Saxonum, ed. C. von Schwerin, MGH *Fontes Iuris Germanici Antiqui*.

Lex Visigothorum (or *Forum Iudicum*), ed. K. Zeumer, MGH *LL*, vol. I.

Libanius, *Orations*, selection ed. and trans. A. F. Norman (2 vols, Loeb Library).

Liber Historiae Francorum, ed. B. Krusch, MGH *SRM*, vol. II, pp. 215–328.

Liber Pontificalis, ed. L. Duchesne (3 vols) (reprinted Paris, 1955–7); also ed. by T. Mommsen for MGH (but only Vol. 1 appeared, ending in 715); the whole trans. R. Davis (3 vols) (Liverpool, 1989, 1992, 1995).

Life of St. John the Almsgiver, of Leontius, trans. E. Dawes and N. H. Baynes, *Three Byzantine Saints* (London, 1948), pp. 199–262.

Liudprand of Cremona, *Antapodosis, De Ottone Rege, Legatio*, ed. J. Becker, MGH *SRG*; trans. F. A. Wright, *Liudprand of Cremona: The Embassy to Constantinople and Other Writings* (London, 1930; reprinted 1993), pp. 1–156; P. Squatriti, *The Complete Works of Liudprand of Cremona* (Washington, DC, 2008).

Marcellinus Comes, *Chronica*, ed. T. Mommsen, MGH *AA*, vol. XI, pp. 60–108; trans. B. Croke, *The Chronicle of Marcellinus* (Sydney, 1995).

Marius of Avenches, *Chronica*, ed. T. Mommsen, MGH *AA*, vol. XI, pp. 232–9.

Menander Protector, fragments, ed. and trans. R. Blockley, *The History of Menander the Guardsman* (Liverpool, 1985).

Muirchú, *Vita Patricii*, ed. and trans. A. B. E. Hood – *see under* Patrick.

'Nennius' or the *Historia Brittonum*, ed. and trans. J. Morris (London, 1978); a 'volume per manuscript' edition is currently being published under the editorship of D. Dumville (Cambridge, 1985–?).

Nithard, *Historiae*, ed. with French trans. P. Lauer, CHFM (1964).

Notker Balbulus, *Gesta Karoli Magni*, ed. R. Rau, *Fontes*, Vol. III, pp. 320–427.

Olympiodorus of Thebes, fragments of, ed. and trans. R. Blockley – *see under* Candidus.

Paschal Chronicle, trans. M. Whitby and M. Whitby (Liverpool, 1989).

Patrick, *Epistolae*, ed. and trans. A. B. E. Hood (London, 1978).

Paul the Deacon, *Historia Gentis Langobardorum*, ed. G. Waitz, MGH *SRG*; trans. W. D. Foulke, *History of the Lombards* (Philadelphia, Pa., 1907; reprinted 1974).

Photius, *Biblioteca*, ed. and French trans. R. Henry (8 vols) (Paris, 1959–77).

Priscus of Panium, fragments of, ed. and trans. R. Blockley – *see under* Candidus.

Procopius, *History of the Wars*, and *The Buildings*, ed. and trans. H. B. Dewing (6 vols, Loeb Library).

Prosper, *Chronica*, ed. T. Mommsen, MGH *AA*, vol. IX, pp. 342–499.

Regino of Prüm, *Chronica*, ed. R. Rau, *Fontes*, Vol. III, pp. 180–319.

Regula Magistri, ed. and French trans. A. de Vogüé, SC, 105–7.

Regula Sancti Benedicti, ed. and French trans. A. de Vogüé, SC, vols 181–6.

Richer, *Historia*, ed. and French trans. R. Latouche, CHFM (2 vols, 1967).

Sampiro, *Chronica*, ed. J. Pérez de Urbel, *Sampiro, su crónica y la monarquía leonesa en el siglo X* (Madrid, 1952).

Scriptores Historiae Augustae, ed. and trans. D. Magie (3 vols, Loeb Library).

Sebeos, *History of Heraclius*, French trans. F. Macler (Paris, 1904).

Sextus Aurelius Victor, *De Caesaribus*, ed. P. Dufraigne (Paris, 1975); English trans. H. W. Bird (Liverpool, 1994).

Sidonius Apollinaris, *Epistolae*, ed. and trans. W. B. Anderson (2 vols, Loeb Library).

Symeon of Durham, *Libellus de Exordio atque Procursu istius hoc est Dunhelmensis Ecclesie*, ed. and trans. D. Rollason (Oxford, 2000).

Suetonius, *De Caesaribus*, ed. and trans. J. C. Rolfe (2 vols, Loeb Library).

Tacitus, *Germania*, ed. J. G. C. Anderson (Oxford, 1938); trans. H. Mattingly (revd edn, Penguin Classics, 1970).

Thegan, *Vita Hludovici Imperatoris*, ed. R. Rau, *Fontes*, Vol. I, pp. 216–53; trans. P. E. Dutton, *Carolingian Civilization: A Reader* (Peterborough, Ontario, 1993), pp. 141–55.

Theophanes, *Chronicle*, ed. C. de Boor (2 vols) (Leipzig, 1883–5); trans. H. Turtledove (Philadelphia, Pa., 1982) and C. Mango (Oxford, 1997).

Theophylact Simocatta, *Histories*, trans. M. Whitby and M. Whitby (Oxford, 1986).

Thietmar of Merseburg, *Chronica*, ed. R. Holtzman and W. Trillmich (Darmstadt, 1957); trans. David A. Warner, *Ottonian Germany: The Chronicon of Thietmar of Merseburg* (Manchester, 2001).

Vegetius, *De Re Militari*, ed. C. Lang (Stuttgart, 1967); trans. N. P. Milner, *Vegetius: Epitome of Military Science* (Liverpool, 1993).

Victor Tonnennensis, *Chronicon*, ed. C. Cardelle de Hartmann, CC, vol. CLXXIIIA (2001).

Victor Vitensis, *Historia persecutionis Africanae provinciae*, ed. S. Lancel, *Victor de Vita* (Paris, 2002); trans. J. Moorhead, *Victor of Vita: History of the Vandal Persecution* (Liverpool, 1992).

Vita Aemiliani, of Braulio, ed. L. Vazquez de Parga (Madrid, 1943); trans.
A. T. Fear, *Lives of the Visigothic Fathers* (Liverpool, 1997), pp. 15–43.
Vita Amandi, anon., ed. B. Krusch, MGH *SRM*, vol. V, pp. 395–485; trans.
J. N. Hillgarth, *Christianity and Paganism, 350–750* (Philadelphia, Pa.,
1986), pp. 139–49.
Vita Arnulfi., anon., ed. B. Krusch, MGH *SRM*, vol. II, pp. 426–46.
Vita Columbae, of Adamnán, ed. W. Reeves (Dublin, 1857), and ed. and
trans. A. O. Anderson and M. O. Anderson (London, 1961).
Vita Columbani, of Jonas, ed. B. Krusch, MGH *SRM*, vol. IV, pp. 1–61.
Vita Fructuosi, anon., ed. M. C. Díaz y Díaz (Braga, 1974); trans.
A. T. Fear, *Lives of the Visigothic Fathers* (Liverpool, 1997), pp. 123–44.
Vita Fulgentii, of Ferrandus, ed. G.-G. Lapèyre (Paris, 1929).
Vita Hludovici Imperatoris, of 'the Astronomer'/anon., ed. R. Rau,
Fontes, Vol. I, pp. 258–381; trans. A. Cabaniss, *Son of Charlemagne:
A Contemporary Life of Louis the Pious* (Syracuse, NY, 1961).
Vita Honorati, of Hilary, ed. and French trans. M.-D. Valentin, SC, vol. 235.
Vita Martini, of Sulpicius Severus, ed. and French trans. J. Fontaine,
SC, vol. 133.
Vita Wilfridi, of Stephanus, ed. and trans. B. Colgrave (Cambridge, 1927).
Vita Wilibrordi, of Alcuin, ed. H. J. Reischmann, *Willibrord. Apostel der
Friesen* (Darmstadt, 1989), pp. 44–89.
Widukind of Corvey, *Res Gestae Saxonicae*, ed. A. Bauer and R. Rau
(Darmstadt, 1977).
Zosimus, *Historias Neas*, ed. F. Paschoud (5 vols.) (Paris, 1971–86); trans.
J. J. Buchanan and H. T. Davis, *Zosimus: Historia Nova* (San Antonio,
1967).

B: Selected secondary reading

Only a limited number of the most pertinent books and articles
are listed here. More detailed suggestions can be gained from the
references in the notes to each chapter.

GENERAL

J.-J. Aillagon and U. Roberto, *Rome and the Barbarians: The Birth of a
New World* (Venice, 2008).
P. Brown, *The Rise of Western Christendom* (2nd edn) (Malden, Mass. and
Oxford, 2003).
J.-C. Cheynet (ed.), *Le monde byzantin*: Vol. 2, *L'Empire byzantin 641–1204*
(Paris, 2006).
F. Curta, *Southeastern Europe in the Middle Ages, 500–1250* (Cambridge,
2006).
G. Halsall, *Warfare and Society in the Barbarian West, 450–900* (London,
2003).
A. H. M. Jones, *The Later Roman Empire, 284–602* (3 vols) (Oxford,
1964).
S. Mitchell, *A History of the Later Roman Empire AD 284–641* (Malden,
Mass. and Oxford, 2007).

C. Morrisson (ed.), *Le Monde byzantin:* Vol. I, *L'Empire romain d'Orient 330–641* (Paris, 2004).

New Cambridge Medieval History: Vol. 1 (*c*.500–*c*.700), ed. P. Fouracre (Cambridge, 2007); Vol. 2 (*c*.700–*c*.900), ed. R. McKitterick (Cambridge, 1995); Vol. 3 (*c*.900–*c*.1024), ed. T. Reuter (Cambridge, 1999).

J. M. H. Smith, *Europe after Rome* (Oxford, 2005).

C. Wickham, *Framing the Early Middle Ages: Europe and the Mediterranean, 400–800* (Oxford, 2005).

1   CRISIS AND CHANGE IN THE ROMAN EMPIRE, 235–305

T. D. Barnes, *The New Empire of Diocletian and Constantine* (Cambridge, Mass., 1982).

P. Brown, *The World of Late Antiquity* (London, 1971).

S. Corcoran, *The Empire of the Tetrarchs* (Oxford, 2000).

E. R. Dodds, *Pagan and Christian in an Age of Anxiety* (Cambridge, 1965).

L. Grig, *Making Martyrs in Late Antiquity* (London, 2004).

M. Kulikowski, *Rome's Gothic Wars* (Cambridge, 2007).

H. P. L'Orange, *Art Forms and Civic Life in the Late Roman Empire* (Princeton, NJ, 1965).

E. N. Luttwak, *The Grand Strategy of the Roman Empire* (Baltimore, Md., 1976).

F. Millar, *The Roman Empire and Its Neighbours* (London, 1967).

F. Millar, *The Emperor in the Roman World (31 BC–337 AD)* (London, 1977).

A. Watson, *Aurelian and the Third Century* (London, 1999).

S. Williams, *Diocletian and the Roman Recovery* (London, 1985).

S. Wood, *Roman Portrait Sculpture 217–260 AD* (Leiden, 1986).

2   THE AGE OF CONSTANTINE, 305–50

A. Alföldi, *The Conversion of Constantine and Pagan Rome* (2nd edn) (Oxford, 1969).

T. D. Barnes, *Constantine and Eusebius* (Cambridge, Mass., 1981).

N. H. Baynes, *Constantine the Great and the Christian Church* (2nd edn) (Oxford, 1972).

G. Dagron, *Naissance d'une capitale: Constantinople et ses institutions de 330 à 451* (Paris, 1974).

A. Demandt and J. Engemann (ed.), *Imperator Caesar Flavius Constantinus: Constantin der Grosse* (Mainz, 2007).

H. A. Drake, *Constantine and the Bishops* (Baltimore, Md. and London, 2000).

R. R. Holloway, *Constantine and Rome* (New Haven, Conn. and London, 2004).

H. Leppin and H. Ziemssen, *Maxentius. Der letze Kaiser in Rom* (Mainz, 2007).

R. MacMullen, *Christianizing the Roman Empire A.D. 100–400* (New Haven, Conn., 1984).

A. Momigliano (ed.), *The Conflict between Paganism and Christianity in the Fourth Century* (Oxford, 1963).

J. Straub, *Regeneratio Imperii* (Darmstadt, 1972) – selected studies.

3   PROTECTING THE EMPIRE, 350–95

A. Alföldi, *A Conflict of Ideas in the Late Roman Empire* (Oxford, 1952).

P. Athanassiadi, *Julian: An Intellectual Biography* (London, 1992).

T. D. Barnes, *Athanasius and Constantius* (Cambridge, Mass., 1993).

G. W. Bowersock, *Julian the Apostate* (London, 1978).

G. W. Bowersock, *Hellenism in Late Antiquity* (Cambridge, 1990).

P. Chuvin, *Chronique des derniers païens* (Paris, 1990).

J. Drinkwater, *The Alamanni and Rome, 213–496 (Caracalla to Clovis)* (Oxford, 2007).

A. Ferrill, *The Fall of the Roman Empire: The Military Explanation* (London, 1986), chs 1–4.

K. Krapp, *Die Alamanen. Krieger, Siedler, frühe Christen* (Stuttgart, 2007).

N. Lenski, *The Failure of Empire: Valens and the Roman State in the Fourth Century A.D.* (Berkeley, Calif., 2002).

S. N. C. Lieu and D. Montserrat, *From Constantine to Julian: Pagan and Christian Views, a Source History* (London and New York, 1996).

A. Lippold, *Theodosius der grosse und seine Zeit* (Stuttgart, 1968).

J. Matthews, *Western Aristocracies and Imperial Court A.D. 364–425* (Oxford, 1975).

J. Matthews, *The Roman Empire of Ammianus Marcellinus* (London, 1989).

S. Williams and G. Friell, *Theodosius: The Empire at Bay* (London, 1994).

4   FROM THE BATTLE OF ADRIANOPLE TO THE SACK OF ROME, 378–410

A. Cameron, *Claudian: Poetry and Propaganda at the Court of Honorius* (Oxford, 1970).

P. Courcelle, *Histoire littéraire des grands invasions germaniques* (3rd edn) (Paris, 1964), pp. 31–77.

E. Demougeot, *De l'unité à la division de l'empire romain 395–410* (Paris, 1951).

H. Elton, *Warfare in Roman Europe AD 350–425* (Oxford, 1996).

W. Goffart, *Barbarian Tides: The Migration Age and the Later Roman Empire* (Philadelphia, Pa., 2006)

G. Halsall, *Barbarian Migrations and the Roman West, 376–568* (Cambridge, 2007).

C. Kelly, *Attila the Hun: Barbarian Terror and the Fall of the Roman Empire* (London, 2008).

O. Maenchen-Helfen, *The World of the Huns* (Berkeley, Calif., etc., 1973).

E. A. Thompson, *A History of Attila and the Huns* (Oxford, 1948).

E. A. Thompson, *The Visigoths in the Time of Ulfila* (Oxford, 1966).

M. Todd, *The Barbarians: Goths, Franks and Vandals* (London, 1972).

B. Ward-Perkins, *The Fall of Rome and the End of Civilization* (Oxford, 2005).

H. Wolfram, *History of the Goths* (English edn) (Berkeley, Calif., etc., 1988), pp. 1–171.

5   A DIVIDED CITY: THE CHRISTIAN CHURCH, 300–460

J. Binns, *Ascetics and Ambassadors of Christ* (Oxford, 1994).

D. Brakke, *Athanasius and the Politics of Asceticism* (Oxford, 1995).

P. Brown, *Augustine of Hippo* (London, 1967).

P. Brown, *The Making of Late Antiquity* (Cambridge, Mass., 1978).

P. Brown, *Society and the Holy in Late Antiquity* (London, 1982) – selected studies.

P. Brown, *The Body and Society* (London, 1989), esp. pts 2 and 3.

H. Chadwick, *The Church in Ancient Society, from Galilee to Gregory the Great* (Oxford, 2001).

S. Elm, *Virgins of God: The Making of Asceticism in Late Antiquity* (Oxford, 1994).

A. J. Festugière, *Antioch païenne et chrétienne* (Paris, 1959).

E. D. Hunt, *Holy Land Pilgrimage in the Later Roman Empire AD 312–400* (Oxford, 1982).

J. N. D. Kelly, *Jerome* (London, 1975).

N. B. McLynn, *Ambrose of Milan: Church and Court in a Christian Capital* (Berkeley, Calif., 1994).

F. Millar, *A Greek Roman Empire: Power and Belief under Theodosius II* (Berkeley, Calif., 2006).

J. Moorhead, *Ambrose: Church and Society in the Roman World* (London, 1999).

P. Rousseau, *Basil of Caesarea* (Berkeley, Calif., 1994).

C. Rapp, *Holy Bishops in Late Antiquity* (Berkeley, Calif. and London, 2005).

M. R. Salzman, *The Making of a Christian Aristocracy: Social and Religious Change in the Western Roman Empire* (Cambridge, Mass., 2002).

C. Stancliffe, *St. Martin and his Hagiographer* (Oxford, 1983).

D. H. Williams, *Ambrose of Milan and the End of the Arian–Nicene Conflicts* (Oxford, 1995).

6   THE WARLORDS

A. Cameron and J. Long, *Barbarians and Politics at the Court of Arcadius* (Berkeley, Calif., 1993).

A. S. Christensen, *Cassiodorus, Jordanes and the History of the Goths* (Copenhagen, 2002).

P. Courcelle, *Histoire littéraire des grandes invasions germaniques* (3rd edn) (Paris, 1964).

B. Croke, *Count Marcellinus and his Chronicle* (Oxford, 2001).

E. Demougeot, *L'Empire romain et les barbares d'occident* (IVe – VIIe siècles – scripta varia) (Paris, 1988).

S. Johnson, *Late Roman Fortifications* (London, 1983).

W. E. Kaegi, Jnr, *Byzantium and the Decline of Rome* (Princeton, NJ, 1968).

J. H. W. G. Liebeschuetz, *Barbarians and Bishops* (Oxford, 1990).

P. Southern and K. R. Dixon, *The Late Roman Army* (London, 1996).

E. A. Thompson, *Romans and Barbarians: The Decline of the Western Empire* (Madison, Wisc., 1982) – selected studies.

R. Van Dam, *Leadership and Community in Late Antique Gaul* (Berkeley, Calif., 1985).

7 THE NEW KINGDOMS

P. Amory, *People and Identity in Ostrogothic Italy, 489–554* (Cambridge, 1997).

Anon. (ed.), *Die Alamannen* (Stuttgart, 1997).

P. S. Barnwell, *Emperor, Prefects and Kings: The Roman West, 395–565* (London, 1992).

T. S. Burns, *The Ostrogoths: Kingship and Society* (Wiesbaden, 1980).

T. S. Burns, *A History of the Ostrogoths* (Bloomington, Ind., 1984).

R. Christlein, *Die Alamannen: Archäologie eines lebendigen Volkes* (Stuttgart, 1978).

J. Harries, *Sidonius Apollinaris and the Fall of Rome* (Oxford, 1995).

P. Heather, *The Goths* (Oxford, 1996).

S. A. H. Kennell, *Magnus Felix Ennodius: A Gentleman of the Church* (Ann Arbor, Mich., 2000).

E. James, *The Franks* (Oxford, 1988).

J. Moorhead, *Theoderic in Italy* (Oxford, 1992).

J. J. O'Donnell, *Cassiodorus* (Berkeley, Calif., 1979).

J. M. Wallace-Hadrill, *The Barbarian West 400–1000* (revd edn) (Oxford, 1985).

H. Wolfram, *History of the Goths* (trans. T. Dunlap) (Berkeley, Calif., 1988).

H. Wolfram, *The Roman Empire and Its Germanic Peoples* (trans. T. Dunlap, Berkeley, Calif., 1997).

8 THE TWILIGHT OF THE WEST, 518–68?

A. Cameron, *Agathias* (Oxford, 1970).

A. Cameron, *Continuity and Change in Sixth-Century Byzantium* (London, 1981) – selected studies.

A. Cameron, *Procopius* (London, 1985).

C. Courtois, *Les Vandales et l'Afrique* (Paris, 1955).

F. K. Haarer, *Anastasius I: Politics and Empire in the Late Roman World* (Leeds, 2006).

A. Honore, *Tribonian* (London, 1978).

C. Kelly, *Ruling the Later Roman Empire* (Cambridge, Mass., 2004).

M. Maas, *John Lydus and the Roman Past* (London, 1992).

M. Maas (ed.), *The Cambridge Companion to the Age of Justinian* (Cambridge, 2005).

A. H. Merrills (ed.), *Vandals, Romans and Berbers* (Aldershot, 2004).

J. Moorhead, *Justinian* (London, 1994).
A. A. Vasiliev, *Justin I* (Cambridge, Mass., 1950).
O. G. von Simson, *Sacred Fortress* (Chicago, 1948).

9   CONSTANTINOPLE, PERSIA AND THE ARABS

A. J. Butler, *The Arab Conquest of Egypt* (2nd edn) (Oxford, 1978).
A. Cameron, *Circus Factions* (Oxford, 1976).
P. Crone, *Meccan Trade and the Rise of Islam* (Oxford, 1987).
B. Dignas and E. Winter, *Rome and Persia in Late Antiquity* (Cambridge, 2007).
P. Goubert, *Byzance avant l'Islam*, Vol. I (Paris, 1951).
J. Howard-Johnston, *Sasanian Persia and the End of Antiquity: Historiographical and Historical Studies* (Aldershot, 2006).
J. Jarry, *Hérésies et factions dans l'empire byzantin du IVe au VII siècles* (Cairo, 1968).
W. E. Kaegi, *Byzantium and the Early Islamic Conquests* (Cambridge, 1995).
W. E. Kaegi, *Heraclius, Emperor of Byzantium* (Cambridge, 2003).
H. Kennedy, *The Prophet and the Age of the Caliphates* (London, 1986).
D. W. Phillipson, *Ancient Ethiopia* (London, 1998).
P. Pourshariati, *Decline and Fall of the Sasanian Empire* (London, 2008).
C. F. Robinson, *Empire and Elites after the Muslim Conquest* (Cambridge, 2000).
C. F. Robinson, *'Abd al-Malik* (Oxford, 2005).
I. Shahid, *Byzantium and the Arabs in the Sixth Century* (2 vols) (Washington, DC, 1995).
W. M. Watt, *Muhammad at Mecca* (Oxford, 1953).
W. M. Watt, *Muhammad at Medina* (Oxford, 1956).
M. Whitby, *The Emperor Maurice and His Historian* (Oxford, 1988).

10   DECADENT AND DO-NOTHING KINGS

Spain (507–711)

R. Collins, *Early Medieval Spain: Unity in Diversity, 400–1000* (2nd edn) (London, 1995).
R. Collins, *Visigothic Spain, 409–711* (Malden Mass. and Oxford, 2004).
B. Dumézil, *La reine Brunehaut* (Paris, 2008)
J. Fontaine, *Isidore de Seville et la culture classique dans l'Espagne wisigothique* (3 vols) (Paris, 1959–83).
L. A. García Moreno, *Historia de España visigoda* (Madrid, 1989).
J. N. Hillgarth, *Visigothic Spain, Byzantium and the Irish* (collected studies) (London, 1985).
P. D. King, *Law and Society in the Visigothic Kingdom* (Cambridge, 1972).
M. Kulikoski, *Late Roman Spain and Its Cities* (Baltimore, Md., and London, 2004).
J. Orlandis, *Historia del reino español visigodo* (Madrid, 1988).
E. A. Thompson, *The Goths in Spain* (Oxford, 1969).

Francia (511–687)

E. Ewig, *Die Merowinger und das Frankenreich* (2nd edn) (Stuttgart, 1993).

L. C. Feffer and P. Perrin, *Les Francs*, Vol. 2 (Paris, 1987).

M. Heinzelmann, *Gregory of Tours* (English trans.) (Cambridge, 2001).

F. Irsigler, *Untersuchungen zur Geschichte des frühfränkischen Adels* (Bonn, 1981).

E. James, *The Franks* (Oxford, 1988).

K. Mitchell and I. Wood (eds), *The World of Gregory of Tours* (Leiden, 2002).

O. Pontal, *Histoire des conciles mérovingiens* (Paris, 1989).

J. M. Wallace-Hadrill, *The Long-haired Kings* (London, 1962).

J. M. Wallace-Hadrill, *The Frankish Church* (Oxford, 1983).

A. Wieczorek (ed.), *Die Franken. Wegbereiter Europas* (2 vols) (Mainz, 1996).

I. Wood, *The Merovingian Kingdoms, 450–751* (London, 1994).

11 FROM BRITAIN TO THE KINGDOMS OF THE ANGLES, 410–874

S. Bassett (ed.), *The Origins of Anglo-Saxon Kingdoms* (Leicester, 1989).

M. A. S. Blackburn and D. N. Dumville (eds), *Kings, Currency and Alliances: History and Coinage of Southern England in the Ninth Century* (Leicester, 1998).

M. P. Brown and C. A. Farr (eds.), *Mercia: An Anglo-Saxon Kingdom in Europe* (London, 2001).

J. Campbell (ed.), *The Anglo-Saxons* (Oxford, 1982).

J. Campbell, *Essays in Anglo-Saxon History* (London and Ronceverte, 1986).

J. Campbell, *The Anglo-Saxon State* (London, 2000).

C. Cubitt, *Anglo-Saxon Church Councils c. 650–c. 850* (Leicester, 1995).

A. S. Esmonde Cleary, *The Ending of Roman Britain* (London, 1989).

J. E. Fraser, *The Pictish Conquest: The Battle of Dunnichen 685 and the Birth of Scotland* (Stroud, 2006).

R. Gameson (ed.), *St. Augustine and the Conversion of England* (Stroud, 1999).

D. Hill, *An Atlas of Anglo-Saxon England* (Oxford, 1981).

E. John, *Reassessing Anglo-Saxon England* (Manchester, 1996).

M. E. Jones, *The End of Roman Britain* (Ithaca, NY, 1996).

D. P. Kirby, *The Earliest English Kings* (London, 1991).

H. M. R. E. Mayr-Harting, *The Coming of Christianity to Anglo-Saxon England* (2nd edn) (London, 1972; revd edn, 1991).

P. Salway, *Roman Britain* (Oxford, 1981).

C. A. Snyder, *An Age of Tyrants: Britain and the Britons, A.D. 400–600* (Stroud, 1998).

I. W. Walker, *Mercia and the Origins of England* (Stroud, 2000).

A. Woolf, *From Pictland to Alba, 789–1070* (Edinburgh, 2007).

P. Wormald, *The Making of English Law* (Oxford and Malden, Mass., 1999), chs. 1 and 2.

B. Yorke, *Kings and Kingdoms of Early Anglo-Saxon England* (London, 1990).

12   THE LOMBARDS IN ITALY, *c.* 540–712

G. P. Bognetti, *L'eta longobarda* (4 vols of collected studies) (Milan, 1966–8).

T. S. Brown, *Gentlemen and Officers: Imperial Administration and Aristocratic Power in Byzantine Italy A.D. 554–800* (Rome, 1984).

C. Brühl, *Studien zu den langobardischen Königsurkunden* (Tübingen, 1970).

N. Christie, *The Lombards* (Oxford, 1995).

N. Everett, *Literacy in Lombard Italy, c. 568–774* (Cambridge, 2003).

S. Gasparri, *I duchi longobardi* (Rome, 1978).

M. Hegewisch (ed.), *Die Langobarden. Das Ende der Völkerwanderung* (Darmstadt, 2008).

J. Jarnut, *Geschichte der Langobarden* (Stuttgart, 1982).

W. Menghin, *Die Langobarden* (Stuttgart, 1985).

G. Tabacco, *The Struggle for Power in Medieval Italy* (English trans.) (Cambridge, 1989).

E. Zanini, *Le Italie bizantine* (Bari, 1998).

13   THE PARTING OF EAST AND WEST

N. H. Baynes, *Byzantine Studies and Other Essays* (London, 1960).

R. Cormack, *Writing in Gold* (London, 1985), chs 1–3.

P. Courcelle, *Late Latin Writers and their Greek Sources* (English trans.) (Cambridge, Mass., 1969).

A. Grabar, *L'Iconoclasme byzantin* (2nd edn) (Paris, 1984).

J. T. Hallenbeck, *Pavia and Rome: The Lombard Monarchy and the Papacy in the Eighth Century* (Philadelphia, Pa., 1982).

J. Herrin, *The Formation of Christendom* (Oxford, 1987).

P. Llewellyn, *Rome in the Dark Ages* (London, 1971).

R. Macmullen, *Christianity and Paganism in the Fourth to Eighth Centuries* (New Haven, Conn., 1997).

T. F. X. Noble, *The Republic of St. Peter: The Birth of the Papal State 680–825* (Philadelphia, Pa., 1984).

J. Richards, *The Popes and the Papacy in the Early Middle Ages 476–752* (London, 1979).

14   MONKS AND MISSIONARIES

F. J. Byrne, *Irish Kings and High Kings* (London, 1973).

T. Charles-Edwards, *Early Christian Ireland* (Cambridge, 2000).

B. Dumézil, *Les racines chrétiennes de l'Europe* (Paris, 2005).

K. Hughes, *The Church in Early Irish Society* (London, 1966).

K. Hughes, *Early Christian Ireland: An Introduction to the Sources* (London, 1972).

R. A. Markus, *Gregory the Great and His World* (Cambridge, 1997).

D. Ó Cróinín, *Early Medieval Ireland, 400–1200* (London, 1995).

T. Schieffer, *Winfrid-Bonifatius und die christliche Grundlegung Europas* (Freiburg, 1954).

A. de Vogüé, *Regards sur le monachisme des premiers siècles* (Rome, 2000).

J. M. Wallace-Hadrill, 'A Background to St. Boniface's Mission', in his *Early Medieval History* (Oxford, 1975), pp. 138–54.

H. Wolfram, *Die Geburt Mitteleuropas* (Berlin, 1987).

I. Wood, *The Missionary Life* (London, 2001)

15 FRANCIA REVIVED, 714–68

M. Becher and J. Jarnut (eds), *Der Dynastiewechsel von 751* (Münster, 2002).

R. Collins, *The Arab Conquest of Spain, 710–797* (Oxford, 1989).

R. Collins, *Die Fredegar Chroniken* (Hanover, 2008).

M. Costambeys, *Power and Patronage in Early Medieval Italy* (Cambridge, 2007).

P. Fouracre, *The Age of Charles Martel* (London, 2000).

P. J. Geary, *Aristocracy in Provence. The Rhône Basin at the Dawn of the Carolingian Age* (Stuttgart, 1985).

R. A. Gerberding, *The Rise of the Carolingians and the 'Liber Historiae Francorum'* (Oxford, 1987).

C. Landes (ed.), *Les derniers romaine en Septimanie, IV–VIII siècles* (Lattes, 1988).

M. Rouche, *L'Aquitaine des Wisigoths aux Arabes, 418–781* (Paris, 1979).

J. Semmler, *Die Dynastiewechsel von 751* (Düsseldorf, 2003).

J. M. Wallace-Hadrill, *The Frankish Church* (Oxford, 1983).

16 AND 17 CHARLEMAGNE, 768–814 AND THE CAROLINGIAN REGIME

M. Becher, *Eid und Herrschaft. Untersuchungen zum Herrscherethos Karls des Grossen* (Sigmaringen, Germany, 1993).

M. Becher, *Charlemagne* (English trans.) (New Haven, Conn. and London, 2003).

B. Bischoff (trans. M. M. Gorman), *Manuscripts and Libraries in the Age of Charlemagne* (Cambridge, 1994).

D. A. Bullough, *Alcuin: Achievement and Reputation* (Leiden, 2004).

R. Collins, *Charlemagne* (London, 1998).

J. Favier, *Charlemagne* (Paris, 1999).

H. Fichtenau, *The Carolingian Empire* (English trans.) (Oxford, 1968).

R. Folz, *The Coronation of Charlemagne* (English trans.) (London, 1974).

F. L. Ganshof, *Recherches sur les capitulaires* (Paris, 1958).

F. L. Ganshof, *Frankish Institutions under Charlemagne* (New York, 1968).

F. L. Ganshof, *The Carolingians and the Frankish Monarchy* (English trans. of selected studies) (London, 1971).

R. Hodges, *Towns and Trade in the Age of Charlemagne* (London, 2000).

R. McKitterick, *History and Memory in the Carolingian World* (Cambridge, 2004).

R. McKitterick, *Charlemagne: The Formation of a European Identity* (Cambridge, 2008).

J. L. Nelson, *The Frankish World, 750–900* (London, 1996) – selected studies.

C. Stiegemann and M. Wemhoff (eds), *799: Karl der Grosse und Papst Leo III in Paderborn* (3 vols) (Mainz, 1999).

J. Story (ed.), *Charlemagne: Empire and Society* (Manchester, 2005).

W. Ullmann, *The Carolingian Renaissance and the Idea of Kingship* (Cambridge, 1969).

18 'THE DISSENSION OF KINGS', 814–911

E. Boshof, *Ludwig der Fromme* (Darmstadt, 1996).

J. Devisse, *Hincmar, Archevêque de Reims* (3 vols) (Geneva, 1975).

F. L. Ganshof, 'L'Historiographie dans la monarchic franque sous les Mérovingiens et les Carolingiens', *Settimane di studio del Centro italiano di studi sull' alto medioevo*, 17 (1970), 631–750.

M. T. Gibson and J. Nelson (eds), *Charles the Bald: Court and Kingdom* (2nd edn) (Aldershot, 1990).

P. Godman, *Poets and Emperors: Frankish Politics and Carolingian Poetry* (Oxford, 1987).

P. Godman and R. Collins (eds), *Charlemagne's Heir: New Aspects of the Reign of Louis the Pious* (Oxford, 1990).

E. J. Goldberg, *Struggle for Empire: Kingship and Conflict under Louis the German, 817–876* (Ithaca, NY and London, 2006).

W. Hartmann, *Ludwig der Deutsche* (Darmstadt, 2002).

H. J. Hummer, *Politics and Power in the Early Middle Ages: Alsace and the Frankish Realm, 600–900* (Cambridge, 2005).

M. de Jong, *The Penitential State: Authority and Atonement in the Age of Louis the Pious, 814–840* (Cambridge, 2009).

R. McKitterick, *The Carolingians and the Written Word* (Cambridge, 1989).

R. McKitterick (ed.), *Carolingian Culture: Emulation and Innovation* (Cambridge, 1994).

J. L. Nelson, *Charles the Bald* (London, 1992).

J. M. Wallace-Hadrill, *Early Germanic Kingship in England and on the Continent* (Oxford, 1971).

J. M. Wallace-Hadrill, 'A Carolingian Renaissance Prince', *Proceedings of the British Academy*, 64 (1978), 155–84.

J. M. Wallace-Hadrill, 'History in the Mind of Archbishop Hincmar', in R. H. C. Davis and J. M. Wallace-Hadrill (eds), *The Writing of History in the Middle Ages* (Oxford, 1981), pp. 43–70.

K. F. Werner, *Naissance de la noblesse* (Paris, 1998).

19 'THE DESOLATION OF THE PAGANS'

E. Christiansen, *The Norsemen in the Viking Age* (Oxford and Malden, Mass., 2002)

H. R. Ellis Davidson, *The Viking Road to Byzantium* (London, 1976).

A. Forte, R. Oram and F. Pedersen (eds), *Viking Empires* (Cambridge, 2005).

J. Graham-Campbell, R. Hall, J. Jesch and D. N. Parsons (eds), *Vikings and the Danelaw* (Oxford, 2001).

G. Jones, *A History of the Vikings* (Oxford, 1968).

S. Maclean, *Kingship and Politics in the Late Ninth Century: Charles the Fat and the End of the Carolingian Empire* (Cambridge, 2003).

P. H. Sawyer, *The Age of the Vikings* (London, 1962).

P. H. Sawyer, *Kings and Vikings* (London, 1982).

P. H. Sawyer (ed.), *The Oxford History of the Vikings* (Oxford, 1997).

A. P. Smyth, *Alfred the Great* (Oxford, 1997).

A. Willemsen, *Wikinger am Rhein, 800–1000* (Utrecht, 2004).

A. Williams, *Aethelred the Unready: The Ill-counselled King* (London, 2003).

20 THE WESTERN FRONTIERS OF CHRISTENDOM: SPAIN, 711–1037

A. Christys, *Christians in al-Andalus 711–1100* (Richmond, UK, 2002).

R. Collins, *The Arab Conquest of Spain, 710–797* (Oxford, 1989).

R. Collins, 'Spain: The Northern Kingdoms and the Basques, 711–910', in R. McKitterick (ed.), *New Cambridge Medieval History*, Vol. II: *c. 700–c. 900* (Cambridge, 1995), pp. 272–89.

J. Coope, *The Martyrs of Córdoba* (Lincoln, Neb., 1995).

P. García Toraño, *Historia de el Reino de Asturias* (Oviedo, 1986).

T. F. Glick, *Islamic and Christian Spain in the Early Middle Ages* (Princeton, NJ, 1979).

P. Linehan, *History and the Historians of Medieval Spain* (Oxford, 1993).

J. Pérez de Urbel, *Historia del Condado de Castilla* (3 vols) (Madrid, 1945).

J. Rodríguez, *Ramiro II, Rey de León* (Madrid, 1972).

C. Sánchez-Albornoz, *Orígenes de la Reconquista: el Reino de Asturias* (3 vols) (Oviedo, 1972–5).

K. B. Wolf, *Christian Martyrs in Muslim Spain* (Cambridge, 1988).

21 THE EMPIRE REVIVED, 875–1002

G. Althoff, *Otto III* (Darmstadt, 1996); English trans. P. G. Jestice (Pennsylvania, Pa., 2003).

C.-R. Brühl, *Naissance de deux peuples: Français et Allemands (IX–XIe siècles)* (Paris, 1994).

A. Davids (ed.), *The Empress Theophano: Byzantium and the West at the Turn of the First Millennium* (Cambridge, 2002).

A. von Euw and P. Schreiner (eds.), *Kaiserin Theophanu* (2 vols) (Cologne, 1991).

W. Giese, *Heinrich I* (Darmstadt, 2008).

C. Goehrke, *Frühzeit des Ostslaventums* (Darmstadt, 1992).

K. Görich, *Otto III. Romanus Saxonicus et Italicus. Kaiserliche Rompolitik und sächsische Historiographie* (Sigmaringen, Germany, 1993).

B. Hamilton, *Monastic Reform, Catharism and the Crusades* (London, 1979), items I to V.

B. M. Kreutz, *Before the Normans: Southern Italy in the Ninth and Tenth Centuries* (Philadelphia, Pa., 1991).

J. Laudage, *Otto der Grosse. Eine Biographie* (Regensburg, 2001).

K. J. Leyser, *Rule and Conflict in an Early Medieval Society* (London, 1979).

K. J. Leyser, *Medieval Germany and Her Neighbours, 900–1250* (London, 1982) – selected studies.

K. J. Leyser, *Communications and Power in Medieval Europe: The Carolingian and Ottonian Centuries* (London, 1994) – selected studies.

T. Reuter, *Germany in the Early Middle Ages, 800–1056* (London, 1991).

A. Róna-Tas, *Hungarians and Europe in the Early Middle Ages* (English trans.) (Budapest, 1999).

F. J. Ronig (ed.), *Egbert Erzbischoff von Trier, 977–993* (2 vols) (Trier, 1993).

B. Schneidmüller and S. Weinfurter (ed.), *Ottonische Neuanfänge* (Mainz, 2001).

Index

Made in the USA
Middletown, DE
14 March 2021